# The World's
# GREAT
# FIGHTER
# AIRCRAFT
### The inside story of 100 classics in the evolution of fighter aircraft

The World's
# GREAT
# FIGHTER
# AIRCRAFT

**The inside story of 100 classics in the evolution of fighter aircraft**

**Compiled by William Green and Gordon Swanborough**

Published by
**CRESCENT BOOKS**
New York

# A Salamander Book

Contents: © Pilot Press Ltd. 1981
Presentation: © Salamander
Books Ltd. 1981

hgfedcba

Printed in Belgium.

ISBN: 0-517-358255

All correspondence concerning this volume
should be addressed to Salamander Books Ltd.,
Salamander House, 27 Old Gloucester Street,
London WC1N 3AF, United Kingdom.

# Credits

**Editor:** Philip de Ste. Croix
**Designers:** Lloyd Cowman-Martin and Barry Savage
**Line artwork:** © Pilot Press Ltd.
Cutaway drawings by John Weal and
M.A. Badrocke
General arrangement drawings by
Dennis I. Punnett
**Diagrams:** Alan Hollingbery © Salamander Books Ltd.
**Filmset:** Modern Text Typesetting Ltd., England.
**Reproduction:** Color and monochrome,
Bantam Litho Ltd., England.
**Printed:** In Belgium by Henri Proost et Cie.

# The Compilers

**William Green**
William Green entered aviation journalism early in World
War II with the *Air Training Corps Gazette* (now *Air
Pictorial*) and has gained an international reputation for
his many works of aviation reference, covering both
aeronautical history and the current aviation scene.
Following RAF service, he was European correspondent
to US, Canadian and South African aeronautical journals
and British correspondent to several European
publications. He was Technical Director to the RAF
*Flying Review*, then Editorial Director when it became
*Flying Review International*. In 1971 he and Gordon
Swanborough jointly created the monthly *Air
International* now one of Europe's foremost aviation
journals, and they have also produced a number of books
under joint authorship.

**Gordon Swanborough**
Gordon Swanborough has spent his working life as an
aviation journalist and author, with the exception of a
year-long appointment in 1964 as a Sales Publicity
Officer with the British Aircraft Corporation. From 1943
until 1963 he was a member of the editorial staff of the
weekly magazine *The Aeroplane*, specializing for much
of that time in air transport affairs. In 1965 he became
editor of *Flying Review International*, and in 1971 joined
forces with William Green to create *Air International*. As
a team, these two authors are also responsible for the
production of the thrice-yearly *Air Enthusiast*, devoted
exclusively to aviation history, and the annual RAF
*Yearbook* as well as a series of authoritative works on
both current aircraft and various aspects of aeronautical
history.

# Preface

Since the first aircraft intended for aerial combat *per se* climbed into
European skies almost seventy years ago and the term *scout* took on the
connotation of *fighter*, the speeds attainable by such warplanes have
increased from less than 100 to more than 1,500 miles per hour; their
ability to climb from sea level has risen from less than 1,000 to more than
60,000 feet per minute; fuel capacities have grown from less than a
dozen to several thousand gallons, and maximum take-off weights have
soared from fewer than 1,000 to as much as 100,000 pounds. The
purpose of this book is to portray this dramatic evolutionary process
by means of detailed cutaway drawings illustrating the structures,
systems and equipment of the most important fighter aircraft to have
achieved service since the birth of the genus.

Such has been the prolificity of succeeding generations of fighter
designers in their attempts to achieve an advance in the state of the art
that our selection of aircraft types to portray fighter evolution has been
perforce arbitrary. Some of the aircraft illustrated on the pages that
follow may assuredly be described as classics in that they established
new standards that others endeavoured to emulate; some were
outstandingly successful without being classics, and yet others,
perhaps as a result of short-sightedness on the part of their designers,
ineptness on the part of those responsible for framing the requirements
for which they were conceived, or inadequacies in the engines available
to power them or weaponry available to arm them, were somewhat less
than successful. Each had its own significance, nationally or
internationally, however, and played its role in the development of the
fighter category.

Space considerations have, at times, dictated selection of but one
from a group of equally deserving warplanes to portray a particular
aspect of the evolutionary process. A case in point is provided by
inclusion of the Reggiane Re 2001 to represent an entire generation of
Italian fighters when such as the Macchi C.205 and Fiat G.55 were
equally efficacious. Thus, this book is a synopsis of the history of
fighter development rather than an attempt to chronicle the evolution of
the species in depth. An attempt has been made to place each type in its
context—the aberrations from the mainstream of fighter evolution, such
as the rocket-driven Me 163, are few—and the aircraft appear in
chronological sequence of their début in prototype form, their
backgrounds and histories being briefly related and specifications being
provided for comparison purposes.

The definition of *fighter* has undergone metamorphosis over the
years, a process that has accelerated in the past two decades. Whereas
a fighter was once defined as an aircraft primarily designed to intercept
and destroy other aircraft, such tasks as ground attack being purely
fortuitous and very secondary to its primary air-air role, WWII saw
examples of a secondary role taking precedence, although air-air
capability was retained, the Typhoon providing an outstanding
example. This development became ever more pronounced in the
post-WWII years, with the use of the term *fighter* becoming increasingly
generic until it embraced a wide variety of loosely related aircraft types,
varying tremendously in primary role, performance capability and size.

The adoption of the wider definition of the fighter classification is
reflected in this book by the inclusion of such aircraft as the Harrier and
F-111, which cannot be considered as fighters in the traditional sense.
Today, a fighter may be categorised as multi-role, its mission spectrum
ranging from air superiority and interception to deep penetration strike
and counterair activities. Alternatively, it may be optimised for specific
tasks such as ground attack, its air-air capability being confined
to—what is in some cases a rather dubious—self-defence potential, and
its likely use against other aircraft in the *traditional* fighter sense is
remote. All the aircraft appearing on the following pages are *categorised*
as fighters, but the reader may well find himself asking "When is a
fighter a fighter?"

WG and FGS

# Contents

# The History of the Fighter

by **Roy Braybrook,** one of Britain's leading freelance writers and consultants on military aviation. His previous appointments include Senior Project Engineer with Hawker Aircraft, and Technical Marketing Advisor to the Kingston-Brough Division of British Aerospace.

Under an agreement reached at the Hague Conference of 1899 (only to be rescinded at a similar conference in 1907), the discharging of projectiles or explosives from any aerial machine was banned, just as more recently the nations of the world have agreed not to place nuclear weapons in space vehicles.

At the time that they made their first powered flights in December 1903, the Wright brothers, far from regarding the aeroplane (or "Flyer", as they called it) as a potential weapon of war, dreamed that they were introducing an invention that would make further wars practically impossible. There was no way they could then foresee that aircraft would play a major role in future wars, or that fighters (ie, aircraft dedicated specifically to aerial combat) would lead to the growth of powerful manufacturing companies, with production lines many times the length of their Flyer's initial hops into the air.

Nor could Orville Wright, in discussing the aerial warfare being waged over France in World War I, have foreseen how military aviation technology would develop. Today, supersonic interceptors powered by gas turbine engines and flown largely by black boxes can engage multiple targets beyond visual range by launching miniature, unmanned, rocket-powered aircraft, guided by inertial systems, radar, or infra-red homing. Such weapon systems are the products of many advanced technologies, all undreamed of in 1917 when Orville wrote: "What a dream it was; what a nightmare it has become".

After all this progress, fighter development continues, although (as in the Wright brothers' day) the pace of advance is restricted by the funds available, which, in turn, are a function of political priorities.

We can, however, look ahead a little way. We can anticipate a generation that will combine supersonics with V/STOL capability, and fighters that will cruise supersonically for extended periods, rather than making a brief dash before the fuel runs out. The hypersonic interceptor is technically feasible, although currently its military priority is low. The "Stealth Fighter" is sure to come, its reduced radar- and IR-signatures making it the modern equivalent of a WWI experiment in which one manufacturer tried to produce an invisible aircraft by giving it a covering of cellulose rather than fabric.

In terms of fighter armament, we know that "death rays" in the form of directed energy weapons (high energy lasers and particle beam devices) are only waiting on the development of lightweight "guns". Armament that today is aimed by a crude gunsight or head-up display (HUD) will soon be directed at offset targets by helmet-mounted sights, or possibly by movement of the pilot's eyes, and fired by voice command. Missiles are already under development to enable conventional supersonic fighters to engage satellites in orbit. Tomorrow, star wars?

## Early beginnings

Following on from earlier military use of the balloon and dirigibles (observation balloons were first used in the Battle of Fleurus in 1794, and subsequently in the American Civil War, the Franco-Prussian War and the Boer War), the aircraft was initially seen by army staffs purely in a reconnaissance context. It was on this basis that in 1908, the US Army purchased for $25,000 a two-seat Wright biplane, which crashed in the course of demonstrations. However, its replacement was officially designated: "Aeroplane No 1, Heavier-Than-Air Division, United States Aerial Fleet".

The US Army also took the lead in experiments with various types of armament on aircraft, although France and Germany were soon to replace America in the military application of aviation. The first firearm to be fired from an

aircraft in flight was a rifle discharged by Lt Fickel of the US Army, flying in a Curtiss biplane near New York in August 1910. Also during that year, the German engineer Euler took out a patent on a machine gun installation for an aircraft, the Voisin company exhibited a two-seat pusher biplane armed with a *mitrailleuse* at the Paris Salon, and radio signals were transmitted from a Farman aircraft during British Army manoeuvres.

The year 1910 also witnessed the first take-off from a ship, when, on 14 November, Eugene Ely flew a Curtiss biplane from a platform on the forward deck of the cruiser USS *Birmingham*. However, it was not until the following 18 January that the first landing on a ship took place, Ely putting the Curtiss down on a platform over the stern of the USS *Pennsylvania*, to be brought to a stop by three arrester hooks on the landing gear engaging with ropes attached to sandbags. That same month saw the first bomb dropped, in a trial near San Francisco using a Wright biplane.

That year of 1911 was to be an important one for military aviation, since aircraft were used in war for the first time. Visual reconnaissance, aerial photography and bombing (strictly speaking, grenade-dropping) missions were flown by Italian aircraft near Tripoli in North Africa, the first operational sortie of this Italo-Turkish War taking place on 23 October 1911. Also during that year, a machine gun was fitted experimentally to a Nieuport two-seater in France and to a Bleriot monoplane in England. Equally significant, 1911 signalled the appearance of the Gnome rotary, often regarded as the first true aero-engine.

The first firing of an automatic weapon from an aircraft in flight occurred on 2 June 1912, when a Lewis gun was fired from a US Army two-seat Wright B biplane flying over Maryland. However, the US Army decided against adoption of the weapon, so Col Isaac Newton Lewis formed a company in Liege, Belgium, to manufacture it. The Lewis gun became the standard light machine gun of the Belgian and British armies, and was to be used extensively as an aircraft armament, even by the US Army Air Service. For aircraft use, it had the advantage of being moderately light and reliable, and of being fed from drum-type magazines (initially housing 47 rounds and later 94), which made it more suitable for flexible mountings than belt-fed guns.

The Sopwith Camel (**opposite top**) was one of the most manoeuvrable fighters of WWI, but, as related on page 42, it was an unforgiving aeroplane. Its primary significance lay in the fact that it was the first British service fighter with twin synchronised guns. The intended successor of the Camel, the Snipe (**opposite bottom**) began to appear in service in the summer of 1918, its first patrol being performed (with No 43 Sqdn) on 23 September of that year. Retaining much of the capriciousness of its predecessor, the Snipe was not considered to possess wholly satisfactory control response when it arrived in France, but it nevertheless remained the RAF's standard single-seat fighter well into the 'twenties, being finally withdrawn in 1927. Contemporaneous with the Morane "Bullet" (see page 34) and thus one of the first of the fighter genus, the Fokker monoplane had a dramatic effect on the air war over the Western Front in 1915. The Fokker E II (**above**) represented an attempt to optimise the basic monoplane design for the offensive role. Armament comprised a single synchronised rifle-calibre machine gun. As the popularity of the monoplane configuration waned, Fokker concentrated on the biplane for his next series of fighters, the D II (**right**), seen in German Navy service, being built in both single- and two-bay forms. The D II failed to emulate the success that had been enjoyed by the Fokker monoplanes when it arrived at the Front in July—August 1916.

The S.E.5a (**above**) introduced to British fighter design increased emphasis on tractability at some expense to agility. Outstandingly robust, it provided the mount for most of the Royal Flying Corps' top-scoring fighter pilots once it had overcome its initial problems (referred to on pages 40-41). The Hanriot HD.1 (**left**) was an extremely compact and agile fighter which appeared in 1916. Although not accepted by France's Aviation militaire, it was adopted by Belgium and licence-manufactured in Italy, the air arms of both countries using it with some success and retaining it in service well into the post-WWI years. The Bristol F.2B two-seat fighter (**opposite top**) was one of the true immortals of WWI. Entering service with the RFC from April 1917, it proved extraordinarily successful and production was to continue until September 1919, by which time a total of 4,747 had been built. The F.2B was widely exported in various modified versions which served well into the 'thirties, one such in Spanish service being illustrated (**far right**). Somewhat less successful was the Airco D.H.5 (**right**), unusual for its pronounced negative wing stagger, which entered service from May 1917, some 550 being built. The operational career of the D.H.5. was noteworthy for its brevity; it had been withdrawn by February 1918.

During 1912, the Lewis gun was demonstrated on a Henri Farman biplane over Laffan's Plain near Farnborough, but at that stage there was no interest on the part of Britain's War Office. The same year saw the first take-off from a moving ship, when, in January, the Royal Navy's famous pioneer pilot, Lt C.R. Samson, flew a Short S.27 biplane from a platform on the battleship HMS *Hibernia* while the vessel was steaming at 10½ knots (19,5 km/hr).

Prior to this time, many small aircraft had been monoplanes. For example, the French military aircraft competition (*Concours Militaire*) of 1911 had been won by a Nieuport monoplane, carrying a 660-lb (300-kg) load over a 187·5-mile (300-km) course at an average speed of 73·1 mph (117 km/hr). However, following a series of fatal accidents (on the British side, six pilots of the newly-formed Royal Flying Corps were killed in the course of a few weeks in Nieuport, Deperdussin and Bristol monoplanes), in May 1912 the British and French military authorities announced a ban on monoplanes; a ban that was to stay in force almost until the outbreak of WWI.

Aside from the dictates of the authorities, one of the principal factors affecting the configuration of an armed aircraft was the need to separate the propeller disc and the machine gun's field of fire. Just prior to the war, patents were applied for by various inventors to enable an automatic weapon to fire through the propeller disc, but little had been done to put these "interruptor gears" into practice.

Designers in the period immediately before WWI thus concentrated on pusher layouts, such as those of Henri and Maurice Farman, and the Vickers EFB.1 which led to the FB.5 Gunbus of 1914. However, the armed services of the Great Powers still regarded the aircraft primarily as a means of extending their field of view, and hence purchased them simply as two-seat reconnaissance platforms. In the UK, Vickers was left to build 50 Gunbuses as a private venture, anticipating that a demand for armed aircraft would arise on the outbreak of the war that many considered inevitable.

## World War One

During the early weeks of the war, there was no real aerial combat, partly because the aircraft available were not equipped for it. On ferrying their aircraft to France, the

pilots of the four RFC squadrons were told that, in the event of meeting a Zeppelin, they should ram it! Aside from lack of armament, there was also a feeling that aviation was somehow divorced from actual combat; pilots on both sides sharing the comradeship of the air rather than being divided by the conflict between nations. However, such feelings changed with the German victory at Mons on 24 August 1914. Before the end of the month, the first airman (a pilot of No 5 Sqn, RFC) had fired his revolver at an enemy aircraft. Aerial combat had begun.

Although the role of the scouts was still to watch and photograph enemy movements and to direct artillery fire, they thus began to be armed with rifles, with which the observers would engage enemy aircraft. At this stage most scouts were not powerful enough to mount a machine gun and still retain a reasonable performance. However, fitted with a 150 hp engine, Germany's Albatros C I managed to combine firepower and performance, and set the pattern for two-seat scouting aircraft for the remainder of the biplane era. Whereas previously the observer had been placed ahead of the pilot for forward view and to minimise the

required CG range, the Albatros C I had the observer in the rear cockpit to provide the best possible field of fire. He was armed with a 7,92-mm Parabellum LMG 14 (*Luftgekühlt Maschinengewehr*, or air-cooled machine gun) on a Schneider ring-mount, and later in the war the series was fitted with a synchronised, forward-firing Spandau LMG 08/15 of the same calibre.

The appearance of the Albatros C I in early 1915 thus represented the solution of the armament problem for the two-seater, but for the single-seater the basic incompatibility of the propeller and the machine gun remained. Typical of the early experiments, several aircraft (including the Bristol Scout C) were fitted with a Lewis gun angled off to the side, to fire outside the propeller disc. However, this called for beam attacks with the aircraft flying on parallel courses, and was virtually useless against anything but a completely docile target.

A more practical scheme was tried in the case of France's Morane-Saulnier L, a parasol-wing aircraft that had entered service in 1913. A machine gun was mounted above the wing, firing elevated above the line of flight to miss the

propeller. This gave the pilot more opportunity to approach his quarry unseen (ie, from below the tail, or what would now be termed the low six o'clock position). However, for a manoeuvring target, there was no substitute for a gun firing along the line of flight. Since a pusher arrangement (as in the Vickers Gunbus) led to a loss of propeller efficiency, and consequently an unacceptably low performance, the development of an effective single-seat "fighting scout" depended on the development of a reliable interruptor gear. A means had to be found by which the action of a forward-firing, engine-mounted machine gun could be synchronised with the movement of the propeller.

Just before the war, Raymond Saulnier of the Morane-Saulnier company had been experimenting with a system to synchronise the rotation of the propeller with the firing of a *militrailleuse*, using both a Hotchkiss and Saint-Etienne types. However, the system did not work very well, and the 8-mm *cartouches* tended to hang-fire, so Saulnier fitted steel deflector plates to the blades. This clearly did nothing to improve their efficiency, but eliminated the possibility of damage from the soft (copper-jacketed) bullets.

Compromise between biplane and monoplane, the Nieuport sesquiplane established a configuration to be widely copied. The first service version, the Nie 11, became affectionately known as the *Bébé*. this subsequently being used generically and also being applied to the larger Nie 17 (**left**) which entered service from May 1916. One of the earliest operational uses of rockets as air-to-air weapons was made by the Nie 17 (**immediately above**), Le Prieur rockets being attached to the interplane struts. By the summer of 1917, the day of the Nie 17 was over. The Spad 7 (**head of page**), too, had lost its edge with the appearance of faster, more heavily armed adversaries, although the balance was restored to some measure by the introduction of a more powerful engine. This was fortunate in that, owing to delays in deliveries of the larger and sturdier Spad 13 (**right**), the earlier fighter was forced to carry much of the burden of the air war over the western front into the summer of 1918.

With the urgent practical demands of war, the Saulnier system of synchronisation was abandoned, but the steel deflector plates were fitted to the blades of a Morane L monoplane. Operational evaluation of the scheme was carried out by the company pilot Roland Garros, who succeeded in shooting down five enemy aircraft in April 1915, before being forced to land behind the German lines.

Although this "secret weapon" had been lost to the enemy, it was of no direct use to the Germans, since the deflector plates were incapable of protecting propeller blades against steel-jacketed Parabellum ammunition. Tasked with developing an alternative system, the Dutch designer Anthony Fokker (then working in Germany) took as his team's basis a concept patented by Franz Schneider in 1913. This had already been fitted experimentally to a two-seat LVG (made by the company for which Schneider worked), but the aircraft had crashed while being delivered for operational trials. Fokker fitted an interruptor gear to his M 5K *Eindecker* (monoplane), and demonstrated it to the German authorities, firing a Parabellum LMG through the propeller. The aircraft was put into production as the Fokker E I, in which Max

Immelmann made his first "kill" with a synchronised weapon on 15 July 1915. Others who won fame in the days of the "Fokker Scourge" were Oswald Boelcke and Ernst Udet.

Although undoubtedly one of the most important fighters historically, the Fokker E-series were not outstanding as flying machines. Even the E III was inferior to the Morane-Saulnier N in every respect. In addition, the interruptor gear was far from perfect, sometimes shooting off the propeller. Nonetheless, the Fokker monoplane gave Germany air superiority until August 1916, when a new generation of British and French aircraft arrived at the front, some equipped with synchronised forward-firing guns.

As the single-seat fighting scout became a practical proposition, the various air arms began to develop tactics and formations that would minimise their losses and simultaneously maximise their kills. The Allies took the lead in the use of defensive formations of two-seaters, providing mutually-protective fire. However, the accuracy of the observer's gun was inevitably less than that of the fighter, firing along its line of flight.

Formations were arranged to be close enough for hand-

The fighter progeny of the Fokker company were of considerable importance in WWI, and the Dr I triplane (**right**) attained considerable réclame, but, as noted on pages 48-49, was an aberration from the mainstream of fighter development and a failure. The D VII biplane (**above left**) and the D VIII monoplane (**left**), conversely, enjoyed considerable success, the latter after overcoming initial structural failures. Only 288 of the monoplanes were delivered but more than 1,700 of the biplanes were produced.

signalling and to reduce the need for large throttle movements to hold station, yet spaced sufficiently to avoid collisions. They had to provide security for all the aircraft and allow safe turning. Since a dive out of the sun into the six o'clock position was the best form of attack (combining a high overtaking speed with reduced chance of detection), a defensive formation would be stepped up down-sun, to give each aircraft a clear view of the probable direction of attack. This also ensured that the up-sun aircraft was protected by aircraft with more height, which could be converted into speed in coming to its aid. In the course of formation development, the leader (who was also respons-ible for navigation) came to fly on the up-sun side, since this was where most attention was concentrated, and hence his signals (by hand, or wing-waggling) could readily be seen.

In the development of offensive formations, Boelcke is said to have pioneered the idea of operating aircraft as a pair (*Rotte*), patrolling roughly in line abreast, either pilot scanning a hemisphere of sky centred on the other aircraft. On entering combat the No 2 would swing behind the leader, who would do the fighting, while the No 2 guarded his tail. A section (*Schwarm*) of four aircraft gave an even higher probability of sighting the enemy, and conveniently broke down into two fighting elements in combat. By the summer of 1916, several squadrons (*Jagdgeschwader*) were flying together. Such formations were too large to be flown line abreast, hence multiple-vee formations and diamonds came into use.

While the dogfights raged over the Continent, another important aspect of fighter operations had its beginnings in the air defence of Great Britain. Blériot's cross-Channel flight of 25 July 1909 had given rise to fears that in the next war Britain might be vanquished by aerial invasion, but fortunately this threat did not materialise. Instead, Britain was subjected to bombing raids by Zeppelin rigid airships and (later) winged aircraft, and this led to an air defence system that could operate both by day and night.

The first rigid airship with an engine had been produced by Paul Haenlein in 1875, but it was not until 2 July 1900 that the first of Count Ferdinand von Zeppelin's series, the LZ 1 (*Luftschiff Zeppelin*) left its mooring for its maiden flight, at which point in time the Count was already 72 years of age.

In the following years, his products were purchased by the Imperial German Army and Navy (he was not permitted to export), and the air transport company DELAG (*Deutsche Luftschiffahrt AG*), which operated with an extremely good safety record prior to the outbreak of war.

In 1914, Zeppelins were used to raid Antwerp in Belgium, and on 19 January 1915 they made the first of a series of attacks on the East coast of England. Neither the RFC nor the RNAS (Royal Naval Air Service) was equipped to defend the UK, their aircraft having neither the climb performance nor the armament for the job. Nor did they have radios, blind-flying instruments, or even cockpit lighting. Nonetheless, during the night of 7 June 1915, a Morane L of the RNAS succeeded in destroying LZ 37 by dropping 20-lb (9-kg) incendiary bombs on it while it was in flight over Ghent in Belgium.

Although the Kaiser had initially insisted that attacks should be restricted to military targets, following French raids on Karlsruhe and Baden in June 1915, the Zeppelins were cleared to attack London, the first bombing taking place on 17 August. The raids were discontinued during the

winter because of bad weather, and by the summer of 1916, the RFC had flarepaths, and aircraft equipped with luminous instruments, synchronised machine guns and effective ammunition (Pomeroy and Brook explosive bullets and Buckingham incendiaries). In August and September, the Zeppelins experienced heavy losses resulting from both ground fire and interception by aircraft, and the raids petered out.

Zeppelins remained a threat to shipping in the North Sea, although, since early 1915, Sopwith Pups had been able to take-off from 200-ft (60-m) decks on the early "carriers" HMS *Campania* and *Manxman*, recovering by ditching alongside so that the pilot could be rescued. A 20-ft (6-m) take-off platform was also installed on the cruiser HMS *Yarmouth*, and on 21 August 1917, a Pup operating from this ship destroyed the LZ 23, which had been shadowing British vessels in this area.

As the Zeppelins withdrew from raids on the UK, large aircraft took over. Gothas carried out many daylight strikes between May and August 1917, after which they switched to night raids until May 1918. The principal RFC types used for

air defence were the Sopwith Camel, the SE 5a and the Bristol Fighter. On the night 28/29 January 1918, two Sopwith Camels achieved the first nocturnal "kill" of an aircraft, shooting down a Gotha in flames. The Gothas were supplemented in 1918 by multi-engined "Giants" (*Riesenflugzeuge*), which made eleven raids without loss.

Meanwhile, in the dogfights over the trenches, superiority had swung back and forth as new types of fighting scout were introduced in quick succession. The tide began to turn against the "Fokker Scourge" in the spring of 1916 with the arrival of large numbers of the single-seat D.H.2 and the two-seat FE 2b. Although both were crude pushers, they out-performed the even cruder Fokker E-series. Allied superiority was then ensured by the 1½-Strutter—the first British fighter to enter service with an interruptor gear—the lightweight Pup and the fast-climbing, RNAS-operated Triplane, all from the Sopwith stable. These aircraft all had rotary engines, as did France's Nieuport 17, but the Spad 7 that entered service in September 1916 had a liquid-cooled Hispano-Suiza engine, pointing the way to the course of probable future powerplant development.

Representative of the first post-WWI generation of fighters were the Fairey Flycatcher (**above left**), the first postwar shipboard fighter to achieve service, and the Boeing P-12, which entered US Army service (in P-12B form) early in 1930, and is represented (**opposite**) by a Model 100 (one of four similar aircraft built for civil use) repainted in authentic P-12 finish. The era of the fighter monoplane was ushered in for the US Army by the Boeing P-26 (**right**), the P-26A illustrated belonging to the 94th Pursuit Sqdn. The Curtiss Hawk III (**below**) was an export contemporary photographed in China.

Germany regained the advantage late in 1916 by replacing the Fokker E-series monoplane and Halberstadt biplane single-seaters with the Albatros D-series biplanes. These were the first single-seaters with paired synchronised guns and were powered by liquid-cooled Benz or Mercedes engines. They were followed in the summer of 1917 by the rotary-engined Fokker Dr I (*Dreidecker*, or triplane), in which type Werner Voss and Manfred von Richthofen achieved many "kills", and by the less successful Pfalz D III biplane powered by a liquid-cooled Mercedes engine.

However, that summer saw superiority regained by the Allies, with the twin-gun Sopwith Camel, which was difficult to fly yet achieved more "kills" than any other type, the Rolls-Royce engined Bristol Fighter, probably the finest general-purpose combat aircraft of the war, and the Hispano-engined Spad 13, arguably the best French fighter to appear during the conflict.

Germany won back control of the sky in April 1918 with the outstanding Fokker D VII, powered by a liquid-cooled Mercedes or BMW engine. France's last shot of the war was the Nieuport 28, which entered service just before the Armistice and was widely used by the Americans. Britain's Sopwith Snipe also served briefly, its 230 hp Bentley making it the ultimate in rotary-engined fighters. Its excellent manoeuvrability compensated to some extent for the slight speed advantage of the D VII, but the Snipe suffered its share of control problems and the Martinsyde F.4 Buzzard (which narrowly missed active service) was certainly technically more advanced.

To summarise fighter performance developments during the four years of war, rotary engines had increased from around 80 hp to the 230 hp of the Snipe, while liquid-cooled engines had gone to 180 hp in the D VII, 275 hp in the Bristol Fighter and 300 hp in the Buzzard. Level speeds had correspondingly risen from 70 mph (112 km/hr) for the Gunbus to 122 mph (195 km/hr) for the Nieuport 28, and 144 mph (230 km/hr) for the Buzzard. Service ceilings had gone up from around 13,000 ft (3,960 m) to 21,800 ft (6,650 m) for the Spad 13 and 23,950 ft (7,300 m) for the Buzzard.

At the end of the war, most aircraft still had wooden structures with fabric covering, although the Albatros, Roland and Pfalz series had wooden monocoque fuselages.

The principal antagonists of the epic aerial conflict of all time, the 'Battle of Britain', were the Luftwaffe's Messerschmitt Bf 109 and Bf 110 and the RAF's Hurricane and Spitfire. Opposite are illustrated (**inset**) Bf 109E-7/Trop fighters flying over the Western Desert, and a Hurricane I flying in formation with two Spitfire Vs, with (**head of page**) two Bf 110Ds of ZG 26 in the Mediterranean Theatre. (**Immediately above**) An early production Curtiss P-40 under test from Wright Field in 1940. Lacking self-sealing fuel tanks, protective armour and adequate firepower, this initial model was short on practical capability by contemporary European standards, and the introduction of these items was to have a deleterious effect on performance. The Grumman F4F Wildcat (**right**), on the other hand, was unquestionably the best shipboard fighter of its day, and no fewer than 7,815 aircraft of this type were to be built. The Royal Navy, by which it was originally known as the Martlet, received no fewer than 920 Wildcats.

The shortage of good quality spruce had raised interest in the use of metal structures, especially in Germany, where Junkers flew the J 1, the world's first all-metal, fully cantilevered monoplane, in 1915. Junkers continued with the concept of a corrugated steel skin on top of a welded-steel, load-carrying framework until the J 7 of 1917 finally succeeded in winning a production order. Fitted with two forward-firing Spandau machine guns, it was known as the D I, but only 41 had been delivered at the end of the war. The Rohrbach company also tried metal construction, using smooth skins, which gave less drag but lacked stiffness.

The standard air-air armament was still a lightweight version of an army machine gun, although other types of weapon were used experimentally. The Le Prieur rocket was tested on various aircraft (eg, Sopwith Pup) as a means to attack balloons and Zeppelins, but had a range of only 300 ft (90 m). A 37-mm Hotchkiss cannon was fitted between the cylinder blocks of the Spad 12 Ca 1, and the Vickers one-pounder pom-pom naval gun was used on the FE 2b to attack trains, but the slow fire rate of heavy-calibre guns was generally felt to offset the benefit of the larger projectile.

Several types of aircraft were fitted with armour plate (eg, Sopwith Salamander), as fighters were used later in the war for trench-strafing.

Other aircraft features that became important later in the story of fighter development had their origins in this period. The S.E.4 experimental biplane of 1914 had camber-changing flaps and a celluloid cockpit canopy; the Sopwith 1½-Strutter of 1916 had airbrakes and a variable-incidence tailplane. The same year saw a supercharger tested in an aircraft and 1918 witnessed the use of a two-pitch propeller. A crude form of semi-retractable undercarriage had appeared even before the war, on the German Eugen Wiencziers' monoplane of 1911.

Radios were used on some two-seaters, which trailed a 120-ft (37-m) length of copper wire with a weighted end. They communicated by wireless telegraphy (ie, Morse code) over a range of 10 miles (16 km). Oxygen equipment and electrically-heated clothing were developed to facilitate high-altitude flying, but were not used operationally.

The parachute is said to date back to 1797, but the first human demonstration is reported to have occurred in 1908,

when US showman Leo Stevens jumped from a balloon. In October 1912, a man jumped from a Wright biplane using a Stevens' "Life Pack". By 1918, parachutes made by Paulus and Heinecke were in limited use in German aircraft, and the Calthrop "Guardian Angel" was available on the British side (and selected for the Snipe), but not used.

## Between Wars

With the Armistice of November 1918, Germany was temporarily out of the running, and the US was intent on never again becoming involved in war, hence the lead in fighter development was left to Britain and France. Italy had been successful with bombers, but it was to be some years before she was to produce a really competitive fighter.

Britain's Royal Air Force (formed on 1 April 1918 by merging the RFC and the RNAS) was initially restricted in improving its equipment by a rolling "Ten-Year Rule", which foresaw no threat in that period and hence recognised no call to spend money on new equipment. The Snipe (rather than the Buzzard) was chosen to be the RAF's standard

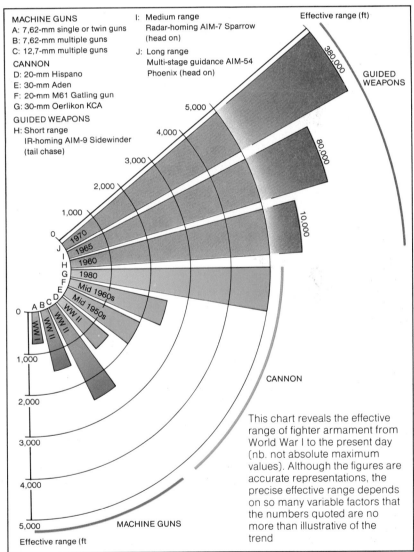

MACHINE GUNS
A: 7,62-mm single or twin guns
B: 7,62-mm multiple guns
C: 12,7-mm multiple guns
CANNON
D: 20-mm Hispano
E: 30-mm Aden
F: 20-mm M61 Gatling gun
G: 30-mm Oerlikon KCA
GUIDED WEAPONS
H: Short range
    IR-homing AIM-9 Sidewinder
    (tail chase)
I: Medium range
    Radar-homing AIM-7 Sparrow
    (head on)
J: Long range
    Multi-stage guidance AIM-54
    Phoenix (head on)

Effective range (ft)

GUIDED WEAPONS

CANNON

MACHINE GUNS

Effective range (ft

This chart reveals the effective range of fighter armament from World War I to the present day (nb. not absolute maximum values). Although the figures are accurate representations, the precise effective range depends on so many variable factors that the numbers quoted are no more than illustrative of the trend

Conceptual obsolescence notwithstanding, both the Fiat CR.42 (**top p20**) and the Polikarpov I-153 (**middle p20**), seen respectively in Swedish and Chinese markings, were to see considerable operational use in WWII. The Macchi C 205 Veltro (**bottom p20**) was representative of the final WWII generation of Italian fighters but appeared too late to have major impact. The P-40E-1 (**top left**) was the

first of the Hawk 87A series fighters procured in quantity for the USAAF, its performance being decidedly pedestrian, but the Vought Corsair, illustrated in its F4U-7 variant (**middle left**), represented a quantum advance in shipboard fighter capability. The Kawanishi N1K2-J (**bottom left**) was the most efficaceous of WWII Japanese Navy fighters and comparable with the best fighters fielded by the Allies.

fighter, and as such it remained in service until 1926. The 1920s produced a rash of new British biplane fighters, all fitted with (fixed) radial engines: the 325 hp Armstrong Whitworth Siskin III, the 400 hp Gloster Grebe, and 425 hp Gloster Gamecock and Siskin IIIA, and the 490 hp Bristol Bulldog. For its generation the Bulldog was a fine aircraft, with a maximum speed of 174 mph (278 km/hr) and a ceiling of 27,000 ft (8,230 m). It entered service in 1929, and was the RAF's most widely-used fighter until 1936. The most significant aircraft on the naval side was the 400 hp Fairey Flycatcher, which served with the Fleet Air Arm from all the RN carriers in the period 1923-34.

France's equivalent of the Snipe was the much faster Nieuport 29 biplane, but thereafter her fighters lost ground to the British, the all-metal Wibault 72 and the Loire-Gourdou-Leseurre 32 (both parasol-wing aircraft) and the Nieuport-Delage 62/622/629 sesquiplane series being notably slower than their RAF contemporaries. Dewoitine had meanwhile been developing a line of parasol-wing fighters of metal construction, but with fabric-covered wings. These aircraft did not initially win French orders, but they were used abroad, notably in Switzerland and Italy. The series culminated in the Swiss-built D 27 of 1930 and the French-built D 371 of 1934.

The 1920s had not been an outstanding decade in terms of operational fighters, but significant developments had been initiated. In 1920, Short Bros exhibited the Silver Streak biplane with a monocoque duralumin fuselage. The same year saw the first fully-retractable main undercarriage members fitted to the Dayton-Wright high-wing racer, the mainwheels being housed by the fuselage. In 1922, the Verville-Sperry racer had the main gear retracting into the wings. Two years later, in 1924, the British Air Ministry declared that all primary structure in its future aircraft would be metal, but did not rule against fabric covering. Significantly, in 1925, the Schneider Trophy race was won for the last time by a biplane, the Curtiss R3C-2 averaging 232.5 mph (372 km/hr). In 1928-29, the first rocket-powered-glider flights were made in Germany.

During the 1930s, biplanes gave way to monoplanes, and stressed skin structures came into general use, as did enclosed cockpits, radio telephony (ie, voice transmissions),

The P-38 Lightning (**above**) was the only twin-engined single-seat fighter to see large-scale service in WWII, and the de Havilland Mosquito (**left**), although conceived primarily as a bomber, found its true métier as a two-seat fighter, a class in which it was to become one of the most versatile. The Thunderbolt, illustrated in its initial P-47B form (**top right**), was by far the largest and heaviest single-engined fighter ever built when it first entered USAAF service, dwarfing the North American Mustang, a P-51D version of which is illustrated beneath. Conceived originally to meet an RAF requirement, the Mustang emerged as arguably the best all-round single-seat fighter fielded by any of WWII's combatants. In its initial Allison-engined P-51A form it lacked the necessary altitude capability for the air-air role, but once mated with the Merlin engine it was transformed and its range capability for escort missions was second to none. The Northrop Black Widow, seen in its initial P-61A production form (**right**), was the first fighter designed primarily for the nocturnal intercept role from the outset.

retractable undercarriages, high octane fuels, and variable-pitch propellers. Research into gas turbines for jet propulsion was pursued actively in Germany, Britain and elsewhere.

It was at this time that the United States was first to take the lead in fighter development, albeit only briefly. The Curtiss series of liquid-cooled engines developed for racers in the 1920s had led to a series of biplane fighters, but none of these had been produced in large numbers. Curtiss had begun the Hawk biplane series with the P-1 pursuit aircraft for the USAAC and the F6C for the USN, completing it with the P-6E, the Army's last biplane fighter, which entered service in 1932. Boeing used the Curtiss engines in the Army's PW-9 and the Navy's FB-1 series, but switched to the P&W Wasp radial for the Army P-12 and Navy F4B. The US Navy persisted longer with biplanes than the Army, ordering in the mid-1930s, the Grumman F2F series, with mainwheels retracting into the fuselage. However, the aircraft that put the US briefly in the vanguard of fighter development was the Boeing P-26 all-metal monoplane. When it entered service with the Army at the end of 1933, it was arguably

the most advanced fighter in the world, despite such anachronistic features as bracing wires and fixed, spatted undercarriage (see photograph on page 17).

In Britain, some highly streamlined biplanes were built around liquid-cooled Rolls-Royce engines, notably the Hawker Fury and the same company's Demon turret fighter. However, for the RAF's final biplanes, radial engines were to be used. The Gloster Gauntlet of 1935 was used in the first radar-directed interception two years later, and its descendant, the Gladiator of 1937, made some concessions to modernity in having an enclosed cockpit, a reflector gunsight, and a quartet of Colt-Browning machine guns, which had replaced the unreliable Vickers in aircraft use. The Gladiator had a maximum speed of 253 mph (405 km/hr), which was marginally better than the 240 mph (384 km/hr) of the Curtiss Hawk III, but not as good as the 264 mph (422 km/hr) of the Grumman F3F-3, the US Navy's last biplane fighter.

The rebirth of the German Air Force was revealed officially in March 1935, but deliveries of the Heinkel He 51 biplane fighter had started late in 1933. Although historically important as the first of Germany's new single-seat fighters, which saw service in the Spanish Civil War from November 1936, its performance was unremarkable. Some of the finest biplane fighters were by now produced in Italy, notably the Fiat CR.32 (which was also used in Spain) and, from the same stable, the CR.42 Falco, the last and the fastest of the series, with a maximum speed of 267 mph (427 km/hr) equalling the contemporary Polikarpov I-153 which featured undercarriage retraction. However, the biplane fighter is held by some experts to have reached its peak with Czechoslovakia's Avia B.534, which came second to the Messerschmitt Bf 109 in the Zurich Air Meeting of 1937.

The Boeing P-26, which had first flown on 30 March 1932 and had entered service late in 1933, was soon to be overtaken by other fixed-gear monoplanes from Europe and Japan. Poland's high-wing PZL P.11 had flown in 1931 and was marginally faster, but only entered service in 1934. It still formed the backbone of Poland's air force when war broke out in September 1939, by which time it was completely outclassed by Germany's fighters. In France, Dewoitine finally abandoned the parasol wing in favour of a

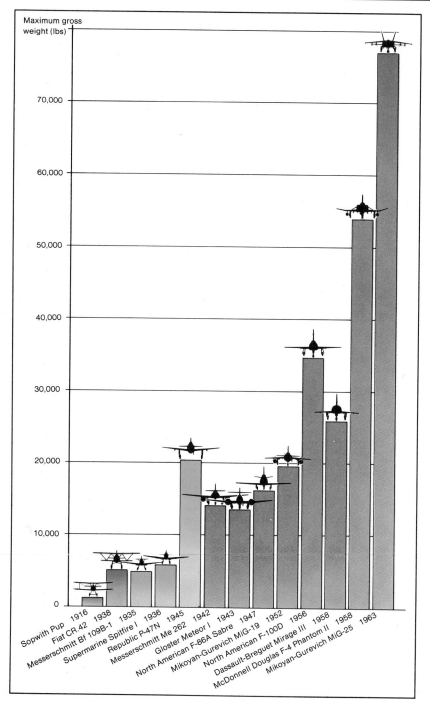

The Messerschmitt Me 262A (**above top**) was one of the few truly epoch-making fighters; it launched a new era in aerial warfare and was one of the most formidable warplanes of World War II.

The diagram (**left**) illustrates the maximum gross weight of succeeding generations of fighters, beginning with the piston-engined biplanes and monoplanes of the early years and concluding with contemporary jet-powered aircraft. The MiG-25 set new payload-to-height standards.

low setting for the wing of the D.500 series, which had a maiden flight on 19 June 1932 and entered service late in 1934. The D.501 differed in having a *moteur canon* mounted between the cylinder blocks and firing through the propeller boss, and the 860 hp D.510 reached 250 mph (400 km/hr). However, an even faster fixed-gear aircraft was the Japanese Imperial Navy's Mitsubishi A5M, which was employed against China in 1937, but had been virtually withdrawn from the first-line inventory by the time of the Pacific War, which started with the attack on Pearl Harbor. Its Army contemporary was the Nakajima Ki.27, which *did* see quite extensive wartime use and which had a maximum speed of 286 mph (458 km/hr), making it joint leader in this class with the Fokker D XXI.

The aircraft which opposed the A5M over China in 1937 was conceptually more advanced, but an older aircraft of inferior performance. This was the Soviet Union's Polikarpov I-16, which had first flown at the end of 1933, and was the world's first single-seat, low-wing monoplane fighter with a retractable undercarriage to enter service. Later models did reasonably well against the Bf 109B in Spain, and in its

ultimate form it reached a speed of 326 mph (522 km/hr).

Other retractable-gear monoplane fighters followed the I-16 in rapid succession. The year 1935 saw the first flight of the Curtiss P-36, Messerschmitt Bf 109, Morane-Saulnier MS 406, Seversky P-35 and the Hawker Hurricane, to be followed in 1936 by the Supermarine Spitfire, Messerschmitt Bf 110 and the Junkers 88, the last-mentioned being destined to become one of WWII's finest multi-role combat aircraft. In 1937, more single-seaters appeared in the form of the Fiat G.50, Bloch 150, Grumman F4F Wildcat (the first American naval fighter able to compete with its Japanese contemporaries on reasonably even terms) and the Macchi C.200. These were followed, in 1938, by the Curtiss P-40 prototype (the basis for the Tomahawk and Kittyhawk alias Warhawk) and the Dewoitine D.520, the most advanced French fighter of the period. Finally, in the last few months before the war, appearances were made by the Lockheed P-38 Lightning twin-boom fighter, the Japanese Army's Nakajima Ki.43 and its Navy rival, the Mitsubishi A6M Zero, Germany's outstanding Focke-Wulf Fw 190 and Britain's Bristol Beaufighter. All were to prove important fighters in the conflict

Contemporary of the Messerschmitt Me 262, the Gloster Meteor (**immediately above**) saw only limited World War II service, the F Mk 4 version illustrated entering RAF service from 1948.

The diagram (**right**) is indicative of the increase in horse power (piston engines-front projection) and thrust (jets-back projection) that has occurred over the past 65 years. The MiG-19 and F-100 were the principal fighters that introduced afterburners.

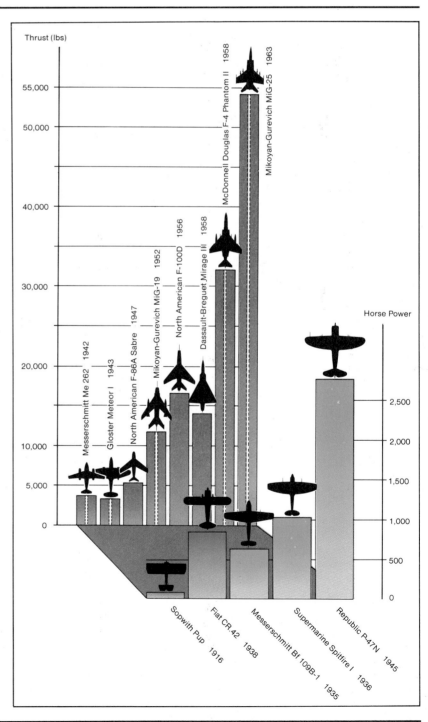

that began in September, but from a technology viewpoint perhaps the most important event of 1939 was the first flight of the turbojet-propelled Heinkel He 178 on 27 August. Crude as it was, the He 178 served notice that the piston-engined fighter would not survive another decade.

## World War Two

The second four decades of aviation development will naturally be better known to the average reader, and this later period is therefore summarised only briefly below.

France's M.S.406 was numerically the country's most important fighter, but was completely outclassed by the Bf 109. The Dewoitine D.520 was more comparable to the German aircraft, but was not available in sufficient numbers to affect the outcome of the battle over France. Italy had emphasised biplanes, rather than monoplanes, and lacked sufficiently powerful engines to exploit its designers' talents. The Fiat G.50 and Macchi C.200 were inferior in performance as distinct from agility to their British contemporaries, and were relegated to escort and fighter-bomber roles.

Later, the availability of the Daimler-Benz DB 601 engine enabled Italian fighters to take a major step forward, with the Macchi C.202 and Reggiane Re.2001, which were reasonably successful. The even more powerful DB 605 powered the Fiat G.55, the Macchi C.205V and the Reggiane Re.2005 which were equal to any other fighters of the period, but arrived too late to play really significant roles.

The "Battle of Britain" was won by sheer numbers of Hurricanes, the dogfight qualities of the Spitfire and the force-multiplier effect of ground-controlled interceptions, making the first significant use of radar. It can be argued that the results would have been even more dramatic if the British 0.303-inch (7,7-mm) machine gun had been replaced by that of 0.50-inch (12,7-mm) used by the Americans, Russians and Germans. However, Britain instead made the leap to the 20-mm Hispano cannon, which became the RAF's standard fighter armament until the 30-mm Aden was introduced by the Hunter in the mid-1950s.

The Spitfire was superseded by the Hawker Typhoon and Tempest at low levels, but remained supreme at high altitudes throughout the war, production finally terminating in

The supremely graceful Hawker Sea Hawk (**above**), seen in German Marineflieger markings (Mk 100), entered Royal Navy service in the early 'fifties and was still serving with the Indian Navy at the end of 1981. The North American Sabre, the F-86F version being illustrated (**left**), represented an outstanding technological milestone in fighter performance and was the first service combat aircraft to utilise sweepback to delay compressibility. Its opponent over Korea, the MiG-15, was somewhat less sophisticated, but the Soviet fighter's shortcomings were largely overcome by the progressive development of the basic design, the MiG-17 (**top right**). Seen in its initial Fresco-A version in Cuban service, the Soviet MiG-17 fighter was a thoroughgoing redesign of the MiG-15, although the entire fuselage of the earlier fighter forward of the engine plenum chamber rear frame was retained. The only fighter of Canadian design to achieve quantity production, the Avro Canada CF-100 Canuck (**middle right**) all-weather fighter, was optimised for the rigorous Canadian operating conditions. The Hawker Hunter (**right**) was considered by many the classic fighter of the 'fifties and remains in service with several air forces to this day.

1947. The Hurricane was quickly relegated to ground attack, convoy protection and service in secondary theatres. The Typhoon excelled mainly in ground attack, but the Tempest could match the best of German piston-engined fighters at low and medium levels.

The radar-equipped Beaufighter played an important part in stemming the night-time *Blitz*, and the aircraft was later used as a long-range fighter, especially in anti-shipping strikes. However, it was the de Havilland Mosquito that became Britain's most outstanding multi-role fighter, despite what many viewed as the retrogressive use of a wooden structure. In naval operations, British fighters failed to excel, although the two-seat Fairey Firefly did play a useful role later in the war and in the Korean conflict.

The first British turbojet-powered aircraft—the Gloster E.28/39— made its maiden flight on 15 May 1941. It led to the Gloster Meteor, early versions of which were much slower than the contemporary Messerschmitt Me 262, but were nonetheless effective in intercepting V-1s, the forerunners of the cruise missile. The de Havilland Vampire missed the war completely.

Germany's Messerschmitt Bf 109 was produced in greater numbers than any other fighter, but reached its peak of development early in the war with the Bf 109F, after which it became overloaded and lost its manoeuvrability. The Bf 110 failed as an escort fighter, but performed usefully later as a radar-equipped night fighter, alongside the multi-role Ju 88. The Fw 190 and its Ta 152 descendant represented the peaks of German piston-engined fighter evolution.

Germany was the only country to make significant use of jet fighters during the war, with the turbojet-powered Me 262 and rocket-powered Me 163, both swept-wing aircraft, although, in the case of the former, sweepback had been adopted purely for CG reasons. The Germans also led in the development of air-air guided weapons, and ended the war with a 30-mm cannon that formed the basis for the post-WW II Aden and DEFA. Insofar as larger calibres were concerned, the ground-attack Henschel Hs 129 was fitted with a 75-mm cannon, and (experimentally) with a six-barrel 77-mm rocket mortar for use against tanks.

The Soviet Union entered the war in June 1941, and later produced some excellent fighters, of which the Yakovlev series is generally agreed to have been the best, if rudimentarily equipped by Western standards of the day. Of this family, the Yak-9 and the lightweight Yak-3 were outstanding. The radial-engined Lavochkin La-5 and La-7 were able to compete successfully with their German contemporaries, and the Mikoyan-Gurevich MiG-3 achieved some measure of distinction during the early part of the war for its speed and altitude capabilities. Soviet wartime fighters introduced cannon of 23-mm and 37-mm calibres. The former calibre proved exceptionally successful and is still in use today, whereas Soviet 37-mm aerial cannon were too slow-firing and did not survive the early jet fighters.

Japan and the United States entered the war on 7 December 1941 with the former's attack on Pearl Harbor. The Japanese Navy's Mitsubishi A5M had already been largely superseded by the retractable-gear A6M Zero-Sen, which was built in far greater numbers than any other Japanese fighter and excelled in range and manoeuvrability. Mitsubishi's ultimate Navy (albeit shore-based) single-seat fighter was the J2M, which proved to be Japan's best high-altitude interceptor, outranking even the Kawasaki Ki-61, the nation's

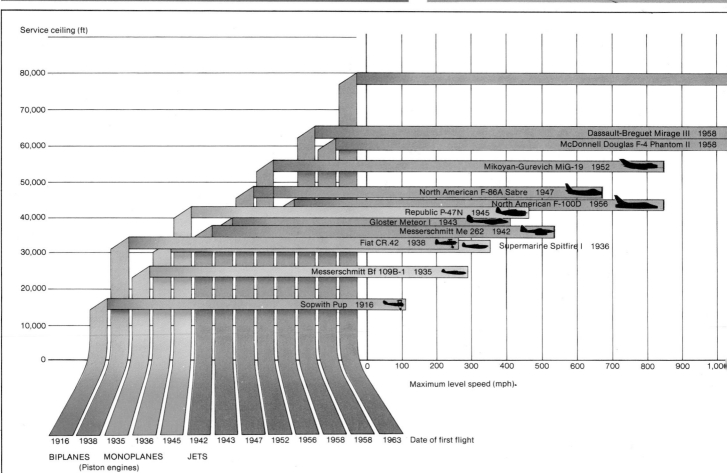

only fighter with an in-line engine (a licensed DB 601).

Early in the war, the Army's Nakajima Ki-27 began to give place to the Ki-43, the service's most widely-used fighter. The same company developed the Ki-44 for home defence. Japan's most advanced fighters, which could hold their own with the best American types, were arguably the Army's Nakajima Ki-84 and the Navy's Kawanishi *Shiden*.

The United States' earlier fighters of WWII were somewhat pedestrian in capability, although some performed usefully, eg, the Curtiss P-40 as a sturdy fighter-bomber and the Bell P-39 Airacobra as a Lease-Lend aircraft for the Soviet Union. Of later types, the Northrop P-61 Black Widow was an effective night fighter and the Lockheed P-38 excelled in the long-range operations of the Pacific theatre once tactics had been developed enabling it to mix it with the more manoeuvrable Japanese fighters.

The finest American fighter of the war was probably the North American P-51 Mustang, combining a Rolls-Royce Merlin with the low drag of a laminar-flow wing to produce the ultimate long-range air superiority fighter of that era. The Republic P-47 Thunderbolt was not as good a dogfight aircraft, but its greater weight provided operational flexibility and the radial engine with which it was equipped reduced vulnerability to enemy fire.

In naval operations, the Grumman F6F Hellcat was virtually the equivalent of the P-51, but it was surpassed in certain performance aspects by the Vought F4U Corsair, which, if leaving much to be desired in respect of deck characteristics, continued in service through the Korean War. The USA made a slow start in gas turbine engine development, but both the Bell P-59 Airacomet and Lockheed P-80 Shooting Star flew in limited numbers prior to the end of the war in August 1945, although neither saw operational service in that conflict.

## Post-War Years

The early post-war period saw the entry into service of the last of the great piston-engined naval fighters, namely the Hawker Sea Fury and the Grumman F8F Bearcat, and the first important straight-wing jets, as instanced by the Republic F-84 Thunderjet and the Hawker Sea Hawk. These

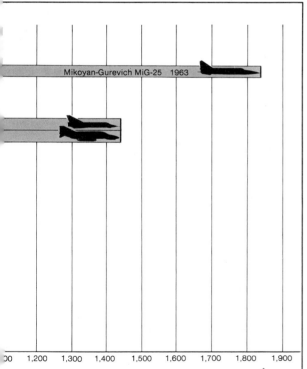

The Republic F84F Thunderstreak (**far left**), derived from the straight-wing F-84G Thunderjet, was optimised for the fighter-bomber mission and served with several NATO air forces until the early 'seventies. The Dassault Super Mystère B2 (**middle left**) was the first West European fighter capable of supersonic speeds in level flight, but, eclipsed by the Mirage tailless delta fighter, it was built in only limited numbers. The first fighter capable of level-flight supersonic performance was the North American Super Sabre, the F-100D version being illustrated (**left**) which remained in service with the Turkish Air Force at the end of 1981. The Lockheed F-104G Starfighter (**below**) is a multi-role derivative of the original F-104A interceptor, one of the first generation of bisonic fighters and was destined to become one of the most controversial of warplanes.

Mikoyan-Gurevich MiG-25  1963

1,200  1,300  1,400  1,500  1,600  1,700  1,800  1,900

The graph (**left**) illustrates the clear progression of attainable maximum speed and service ceiling in fighter evolution. The Mikoyan-Gurevich MiG-25 is unique in that it is the world's only interceptor capable of approaching speeds near Mach 3. The Mirage III and F-4 Phantom are representatives of the upper speed limit for aluminium structures. It should be noted that an aircraft does not necessarily achieve its maximum speed and maximum altitude at the same time.

years also saw the advent of a new generation of swept-wing jet fighters.

The North American F-86 Sabre, which first flew on 1 October 1947, was one of the truly great fighters, combining a major advance in performance with good handling qualities and successful operation in combat. Its development also marked the somewhat late transition of the USAF from the 0.50-inch (12,7-mm) machine gun to the 20-mm cannon, introduced on the F-86H, which also had a nuclear delivery capability. The F-86D limited all-weather fighter had nose radar, an afterburning engine and a retractable pack of 2.75-inch (70-mm) unguided rockets. Later Sabres could use the AIM-9 Sidewinder air-air missile, but it is the six-gun F-86A, E and F variants that fought over Korea for which the type will best be remembered.

The MiG-15, which first flew on 30 December 1947, was an equally bold design, but was noteworthy mainly for squeezing a high-subsonic performance from a centrifugal-flow engine, a pirated copy of the Rolls-Royce Nene foolishly sold to the Soviet Union by Britain's government of the day. The aircraft had a very good ceiling, but was inferior to the

F-86 in a number of respects, having been evolved primarily as an anti-bomber weapon rather than for fighter-versus-fighter combat, and it was soon superseded by the MiG-17, a large-scale rehash, some variants of which had an afterburner. The MiG-17 was a major improvement and remains in service in the early 'eighties with some smaller air forces as a light fighter-bomber, roughly equivalent to Britain's Hawker Hunter. It is noteworthy that the first European swept-wing fighter was the Saab J 29, which first flew on 1 September 1948.

Some aircraft capable of level supersonic flight were already under development during the Korean War. These included the North American F-100 Super Sabre, which became an outstanding fighter-bomber, and the MiG-19, which is still widely used, and has been developed in China as a tactical strike aircraft. However, Korea gave rise to a demand for low-cost air superiority aircraft with genuine Mach 2 performance, which in turn resulted in three outstanding fighters: the MiG-21, the Lockheed F-104 and the Dassault Mirage III. The Saab J35 Draken was in the same class, but failed to achieve fame due to Swedish export restrictions. Another important dogfight aircraft was the Vought F-8 Crusader, which proved its value in Vietnam.

In the field of interceptors, the Convair F-102 and F-106 were early examples of Area Ruled fuselages and internal weapon bays, while the BAC Lightning was more of a technical curiosity, with its high wing sweep and vertically-stacked engines. The massive Tupolev Tu-28P illustrated the size of aircraft required to provide area defence over the Soviet Union. However, the most important interceptor to originate in the 1950s was the McDonnell Douglas F-4 Phantom II, with an armament of four AIM-9 Sidewinder and four AIM-7 Sparrow missiles. Designed as a US Navy interceptor, this incredibly flexible aircraft was used later in Vietnam and the Middle East both as a fighter-bomber and an air superiority fighter.

The outstanding strike fighter of the period was the Republic F-105 Thunderchief, with an internal bay for nuclear weapons and highly sophisticated intakes. It performed well in Vietnam and continues in service today. At the opposite end of the weight spectrum, the lightweight Northrop F-5 combined the aerodynamic advantages of Area

The remarkable variety of configuration adopted during the late 'fifties through the 'sixties for supersonic fighters is graphically illustrated on these pages. The Republic F-105 Thunderchief (**top p30**) was designed from the outset for the fighter-bomber role and featured a wing swept 45 deg at quarter-chord and mated with an inordinately long fuselage. The Saab 35 Draken (**middle p30**) intended primarily for the intercept mission, introduced a double-delta wing platform that has remained unique to this day. The Mikoyan-Gurevich MiG-21 (**bottom p30**), originally conceived as a lightweight diurnal air superiority fighter and progressively developed as a limited all-weather dual-role fighter, adopted the tailed-delta arrangement which endowed it with certain advantages over its Western contemporaries, whereas the Dassault Mirage III (**above left**) opted for the tailless delta arrangement, with its attendant approach speed and landing performance penalties. The BAC Lightning (**above top**) employed the maximum feasible sweepback of 60 deg, a wing that was referred to as a "notched delta" and mated with a deep fuselage in which two turbojets were vertically staggered, and the McDonnell Douglas F-4 Phantom (**above**) the most significant and successful jet fighter of the 'sixties, adopted a more moderate 45 deg quarter-chord sweepback, enhancing directional stability with upward-canted outer panels. The Northrop F-5E Tiger II (**left**), designed primarily as a low-cost air-to-air fighter and widely exported in the 'seventies, reverted to an unswept wing configuration, while the Saab Viggen, the JA 37 version of which is illustrated (**below left**), is a unique close-coupled canard delta, the foreplane contributing a substantial proportion of lift. The configuration adopted for the Viggen was being utilised by several fighter projects being offered in the early 'eighties.

Rule with the weight saving of small afterburning engines and highly accurate IR-homing missiles. It became a supersonic fighter that even small nations could afford and provided a sound basis for a long line of developments which are likely to reach their apex with the F-5G of 1982.

The 1960s were characterised by an explosion in fighter development costs in the West, hence only the most dramatic advances were funded. The start of the decade saw the first hovers and transitions by the Hawker P.1127, the world's first practical high-performance V/STOL aircraft. The P.1154 proposed as a supersonic development was cancelled in 1965, but the subsonic Harrier entered service with the RAF in 1969 and with the US Marine Corps as the AV-8A in 1971, progressive development continuing with the AV-8B for both the USMC and RAF in the mid 'eighties. The radar-equipped Sea Harrier was issued to the RN in 1979, three years after the Soviet VTOL Yak-36 was first seen.

The other dramatic development of the early 1960s was the Lockheed YF-12A, the first interceptor capable of Mach 3. This was abandoned, but the series continued in the form of the SR-71 reconnaissance aircraft. The Soviet Union

adopted a brute-force approach to the same problem, producing the aerodynamically less refined MiG-25, which is used both as an interceptor and for reconnaissance.

The Lockheed approach of optimising the airframe for supersonic cruise had virtually ignored airfield performance. The variable-sweep wing concept was developed in the 1960s to make a good supersonic shape compatible with normal airfields. The first practical application was the General Dynamics F-111 strike fighter, but a similar wing geometry was later used in the MiG-23 and the more recent Su-24, which is directly comparable to the F-111, while a form of semi-variable-geometry has been utilized by the Su-17 series which saw birth in a form of an incremental design development exercise based on the fixed-wing Su-7.

In pure fighter terms, the most remarkable application of variable geometry is perhaps the Grumman F-14 Tomcat naval interceptor, with long-range AIM-54 Phoenix missiles and AWG-9 radar, making possible simultaneous engagements of multiple targets at over 100 miles (160 km) radius. One of the most recent VG fighters is the Panavia Tornado, effectively a miniature F-111 with more advanced systems

and multi-role capability. Sweden's equivalent of Tornado is the Saab Viggen, which used instead a canard configuration.

One outcome of the Vietnam War has been a demand for long-range, highly manoeuvrable air superiority fighters, based on a new generation of engines and new armament and control concepts. The first result of this demand was the McDonnell Douglas F-15 Eagle, using two P&W F100 engines. Requirements for a lightweight, low-cost complement for the F-15 led to the General Dynamics F-16 Fighting Falcon, with a single F100 engine, and featuring a sidestick controller, relaxed static stability and fly-by-wire controls.

Its naval equivalent is the McDonnell Douglas/Northrop F-18 Hornet, with two GE F404 engines and a unique capability to operate to high angles of attack and sideslip. These three US fighters represent tremendous advances in manoeuvrability, acceleration, and climb rate, but they are still armed with the 20-mm six-barrel Gatling gun, and AIM-7 and AIM-9 missiles that originated in the 1950s. France's competitor in this class is the Mirage 2000, potentially another outstanding aircraft, but currently not as well powered as its American rivals.

Variable wing geometry, while introducing a measure of complexity, offers certain advantages over a fixed-geometry wing when particularly exacting low-speed and endurance requirements are coupled with demands for high speed capability. Two examples of production fighters utilising the VG wing are provided by the shipboard Grumman F-14 Tomcat (**above left**) and the multi-national Panavia Tornado (**inset**). The McDonnell Douglas F-15 Eagle (**left**) employs an essentially simple and comparatively lightly loaded wing in order to achieve outstanding agility, and the comparable Dassault-Breguet Super Mirage 4000 (**right**) reverts to the tailless delta configuration but overcomes the principal shortcomings previously inherent in such by means of advanced control technology. The McDonnell Douglas AV-8B (**below**) STOVL aircraft is a progressive development of the BAe Harrier being developed for the RAF and the USMC and is expected to enter service with both forces in the latter half of the decade.

# Morane-Saulnier Type N (May 1914)

Comparatively few of aviation's early practitioners foresaw a *combat* role for single-seat aircraft while accepting their potential value as 'scouts' for the Army. The concept of the *fighter* intended primarily for aerial combat was, in the event, to evolve during the first year of World War I; the first dedicated single-seat fighters were to result from fortuity rather than original intent. Among what were effectively the earliest single-seat fighters were the Morane-Saulnier Type N and its German contemporary, the Fokker E I, neither conceived with a military application in mind and both to prove significant for their contributions to the evolution of practical fighter armament.

Both French and German types were flown in May 1914, the former being demonstrated in the following month at Aspern, Vienna. The Type N followed a series of aerodynamically clean monoplanes created by Léon Morane and Raymond Saulnier, emulating its predecessors in the use of wing warping for lateral control but offering a noteworthy advance in refinement. Its fabric-skinned fuselage was faired out fully to a circular cross section, the aerodynamic entry to which was afforded by an enormous

aluminium propeller spinner (much in evidence in the cutaway drawing below; see key number 8).

The performance of the Type N, which was to be referred to widely, albeit inaccurately, as the Morane Monocoque, aroused some interest on the part of the *Aviation militaire*, and a military production version was defined in June 1915. At this time, the Type N was fitted with a propeller equipped with heavy steel deflector plates intended to deflect bullets striking the propeller from the forward-firing machine gun. This rudimentary and somewhat alarming means of firing through the propeller arc was adopted for the score or so Type N monoplanes accepted by the *Aviation militaire*, and the 24 similar aircraft that were to be delivered to the Royal Flying Corps from March 1916.

Some of the RFC Type N monoplanes—which were to become unofficially known as Bullets—were equipped with a wing of modified section which produced a modest performance improvement but did little to alleviate the execrable handling characteristics. The Type N was unusually difficult to fly owing to the uneasy combination of heavy lateral control dubiously provided by wing warping

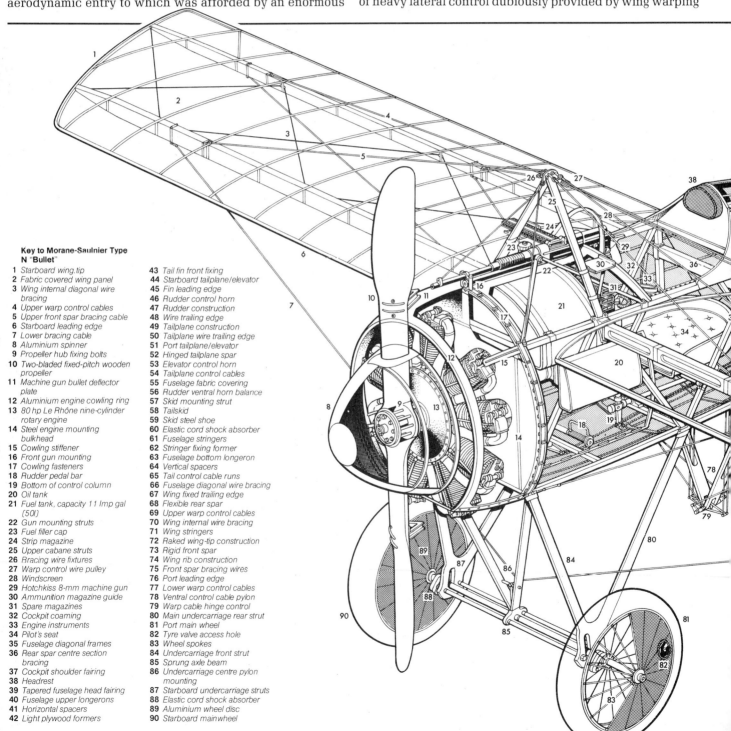

**Key to Morane-Saulnier Type N "Bullet"**

1 Starboard wing, tip
2 Fabric covered wing panel
3 Wing internal diagonal wire bracing
4 Upper warp control cables
5 Upper front spar bracing cable
6 Starboard leading edge
7 Lower bracing cable
8 Aluminium spinner
9 Propeller hub fixing bolts
10 Two-bladed fixed-pitch wooden propeller
11 Machine gun bullet deflector plate
12 Aluminium engine cowling ring
13 80 hp Le Rhône nine-cylinder rotary engine
14 Steel engine mounting bulkhead
15 Cowling stiffener
16 Front gun mounting
17 Cowling fasteners
18 Rudder pedal bar
19 Bottom of control column
20 Oil tank
21 Fuel tank, capacity 11 Imp gal (50l)
22 Gun mounting struts
23 Fuel filler cap
24 Strip magazine
25 Upper cabane struts
26 Bracing wire fixtures
27 Warp control wire pulley
28 Windscreen
29 Hotchkiss 8-mm machine gun
30 Ammunition magazine guide
31 Spare magazines
32 Cockpit coaming
33 Engine instruments
34 Pilot's seat
35 Fuselage diagonal frames
36 Rear spar centre section bracing
37 Cockpit shoulder fairing
38 Headrest
39 Tapered fuselage head fairing
40 Fuselage upper longerons
41 Horizontal spacers
42 Light plywood formers
43 Tail fin front fixing
44 Starboard tailplane/elevator
45 Fin leading edge
46 Rudder control horn
47 Rudder construction
48 Wire trailing edge
49 Tailplane construction
50 Tailplane wire trailing edge
51 Port tailplane/elevator
52 Hinged tailplane spar
53 Elevator control horn
54 Tailplane control cables
55 Fuselage fabric covering
56 Rudder ventral horn balance
57 Skid mounting strut
58 Tailskid
59 Skid steel shoe
60 Elastic cord shock absorber
61 Fuselage stringers
62 Stringer fixing former
63 Fuselage bottom longeron
64 Vertical spacers
65 Tail control cable runs
66 Fuselage diagonal wire bracing
67 Wing fixed trailing edge
68 Flexible rear spar
69 Upper warp control cables
70 Wing internal wire bracing
71 Wing stringers
72 Raked wing-tip construction
73 Rigid front spar
74 Wing rib construction
75 Front spar bracing wires
76 Port leading edge
77 Lower warp control cables
78 Ventral control cable pylon
79 Warp cable hinge control
80 Main undercarriage rear strut
81 Port main wheel
82 Tyre valve access hole
83 Wheel spokes
84 Undercarriage front strut
85 Sprung axle beam
86 Undercarriage centre pylon mounting
87 Starboard undercarriage struts
88 Elastic cord shock absorber
89 Aluminium wheel disc
90 Starboard mainwheel

and extreme sensitivity of the balanced elevators. With-drawn from French operational service before the end of 1915, the Type N remained with the RFC throughout 1916, seeing much action in the grim summer of that year.

## SPECIFICATION: Type N

**Power Plant:** One Le Rhône 9C nine-cylinder rotary air-cooled engine rated at 80 hp at 1,200 rpm for take-off. Two-bladed wooden fixed-pitch propeller. Internal fuel capacity, 11 Imp gal (50 l).

**Performance:** Max speed (original wing), 90 mph (144 km/h) at sea level, (revised wing), 94·5 mph (152 km/h) at sea level; time to 3,280 ft (1000 m), 4·0 min, to 6,560 ft (2 000 m), 10·0 min; endurance, 1·5 hrs.

**Weights:** Loaded, 976 lb (443 kg).

**Dimensions:** Span, 26 ft 8⅝ in (8,15 m); length, 19 ft 1½ in (5,83 m); height, 7 ft 4½ in (2,25 m); wing area, 118·4 sq ft (11,00 m²).

**Armament:** One 8-mm Hotchkiss machine gun or one 0·303-in (7,7-mm) Vickers machine gun with seven 47-round ammunition drums.

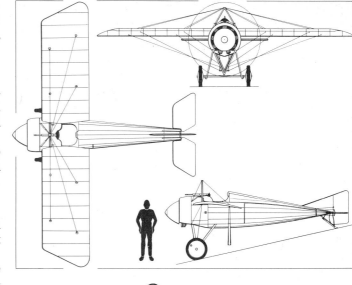

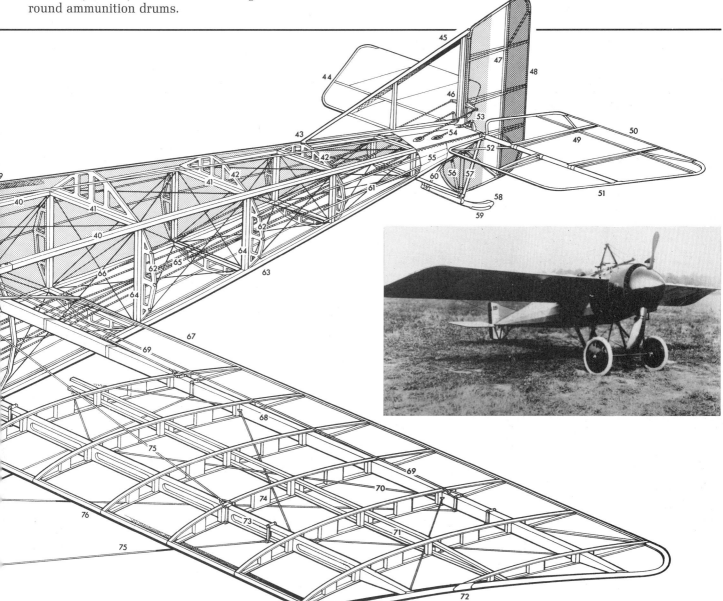

**Above:** A standard production Type N of France's Aviation militaire. The Hotchkiss machine gun can clearly be seen protruding from between the upper cabane struts as can the deflector propeller. It is doubtful if any other fighter of WWI rendered its pilot's task so difficult. Its efficiency reduced progressively with height and at about 10,000 ft (3 050 m) a steep banking turn could not be effected without stalling. Pilots likened the gliding angle of the Type N to that of a brick!

# Sopwith Scout (February 1916)

The first single-seat military aircraft were described as 'scouts' and were intended for use precisely in that capacity, as high-speed reconnaissance aircraft. As the air war evolved, the term single-seat scout took on the connotation of *fighter,* however, and the first British single-seat aircraft designed from the outset to bring a synchronised gun to bear as a fighter was to carry the official appellation of Sopwith Scout. In the event, this mundane designation was to give place unofficially but universally to the frivolous but affectionately bestowed sobriquet of Pup.

Owing much to a small single-seat aircraft built for the personal use of Harry G. Hawker and embodying all the essential elements that were to be incorporated in the Pup, the prototype fighter was flown for the first time in February 1916, and was classic in its simplicity, both aerodynamic and structural. Of wooden construction, with two-spar mainplanes forming a single-bay wing cellule and a wire-braced box girder fuselage typical of the period, the Pup was much more robust than its lightweight structure and delicacy of line suggested. Its most significant feature was its centrally-mounted machine gun synchronised to fire through the propeller disc by means of a Sopwith-Kauper interrupter system.

Immediately recognised as a brilliant success, the Pup was ordered by both the RFC and RNAS (the former officially naming it Scout on 31 July 1916), and arrived in France at the end of 1916. Offering impeccable handling and being almost viceless, with harmonious and effective controls, the Pup immediately endeared itself to the pilots. Its performance was surprisingly good in view of the low power of its engine and fully adequate for the combat demands of early 1917. It was more than a match for the contemporary Albatros D I and D II, offering a much smaller turning circle and the invaluable ability to maintain height in turns, even at considerable altitudes. It was this outstanding quality that enabled the Pup to survive in France until the end of 1917, although such was the tempo of fighter development that, by mid-year, it had already been outclassed in all respects other than manoeuvrability. Nevertheless, despite withdrawal from the Western Front, the Pup remained in production until the Armistice in November 1918, albeit for use only by training units, the total quantity

## Key to Sopwith Pup

1 Fabric covered port elevator
2 Fabric covered rudder
3 Light tubular steel fin and rudder construction
4 Rudder post
5 Rudder operating crank
6 Tailskid elastic cord shock absorber
7 Wooden tailskid
8 Tailskid hinge mounting
9 Steel tailskid shoe
10 Starboard elevator
11 Elevator hinge bar
12 Elevator operating crank
13 Tailplane rib construction
14 Tailplane bracing wires
15 Elevator cables
16 Fabric covered rear fuselage top decking
17 Elevator cable guide panel
18 Top longeron
19 Vertical spacers
20 Rudder cables
21 Bottom longeron
22 Fuselage cross bracing
23 Entry step, port
24 Plywood top decking
25 Port lower mainplane fabric
26 Port lower aileron
27 Aileron connection cable
28 Interplane struts
29 Diagonal wire bracing
30 Light steel tube trailing edge
31 Rear spar
32 Wing ribs
33 Diagonal bracing wires
34 Spar bracing strut
35 Port upper aileron
36 Aileron operating crank
37 Wingtip diagonal bracing frame
38 Front spar
39 Leading edge construction
40 Port upper wing spar joints
41 Wing centre section struts
42 Trailing edge cut out
43 Fixed synchronised 0·303-in (7·7-mm) Vickers machine gun
44 Gun synchronising drive
45 Padded pilot's face guard
46 Gun cocking lever
47 Padded cockpit coaming
48 Instrument panel
49 Control column
50 Pilot's seat
51 Cartridge ejector chute
52 Rudder bar
53 Ammunition tank
54 Ammunition feed chute
55 Petrol tank
56 Engine bearer frame
57 Engine bulkhead
58 80-hp Le Rhône rotary engine
59 Aluminium engine cowling
60 Propeller hub
61 Two-bladed wooden propeller
62 Starboard upper wing ribs
63 Leading edge stiffeners
64 Front spar
65 Spar bracing strut
66 Wing internal wire bracing
67 Wingtip diagonal bracing frame
68 Aileron balance cable
69 Aileron operating crank
70 Starboard upper aileron
71 Interplane bracing wires
72 Light steel tube trailing edge
73 Engine cooling air duct
74 Fabric covered fuselage framework
75 Footboards
76 Lower wing/fuselage attachment rib
77 Port mainwheel
78 Undercarriage vee strut
79 Axle beam
80 Half axle pivot fixing
81 Undercarriage bracing wires
82 Starboard mainwheel
83 Axle hub
84 Wing internal bracing wires
85 Interplane struts
86 Diagonal bracing wires
87 Spar bracing strut
88 Lower wing ribs
89 Aileron connecting cable
90 Starboard lower aileron
91 Aileron operating crank
92 Wingtip diagonal bracing frame
93 Light steel tube wingtip

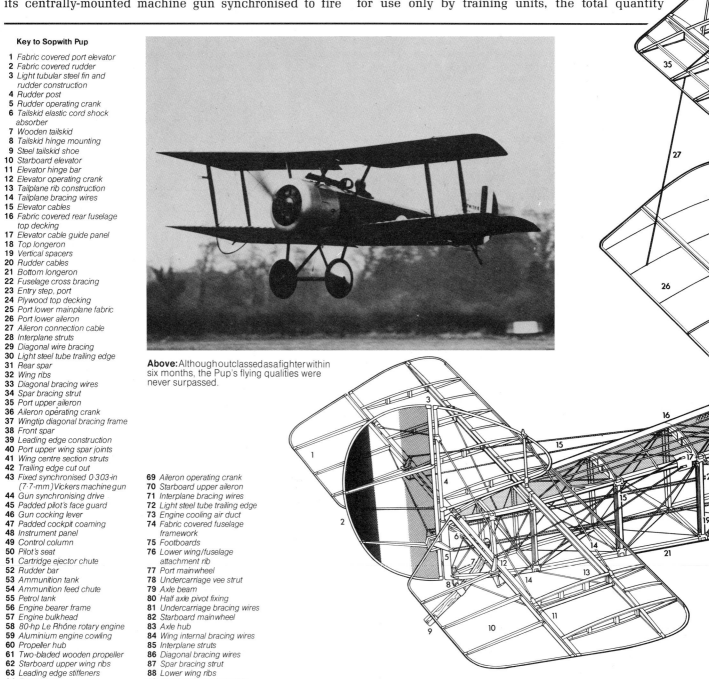

**Above:** Although outclassed as a fighter within six months, the Pup's flying qualities were never surpassed.

delivered (although the figure cannot now be stated with exactitude) being around 1,770 aircraft.

and (some) provision for eight Le Prieur rocket missiles (usually as alternative to machine gun).

## SPECIFICATION: Sopwith Scout (Pup)

**Power Plant:** One Le Rhône 9C nine-cylinder rotary air-cooled engine rated at 80 hp at 1,200 rpm for take-off. Two-bladed Lang fixed-pitch wooden propeller. Internal fuel capacity, 18·5 Imp gal (84 l).

**Performance:** Max speed, 111·5 mph (179 km/h) at sea level, 106·5 mph (171 km/h) at 6,500 ft (1 980 m), 104·5 mph (168 km/h) at 10,000 ft (3 050 m), 94 mph (151 km/h) at 15,000 ft (4 570 m); time to 5,000 ft (1 525 m), 5·16 min, to 10,000 ft (3 050 m), 13·16 min; service ceiling, 17,500 ft (5 335 m); endurance, 4 hrs.

**Weights:** Empty, 787 lb (357 kg); loaded, 1,099 lb (498 kg).

**Dimensions:** Span, 26 ft 6 in (8,08 m); length, 19 ft 3¾ in (5,89 m); height, 9 ft 5 in (2,87 m); wing area, 254 sq ft (23,59 m²).

**Armament:** One 0·303-in (7,7-mm) Vickers machine gun with 500 rounds.(RNAS version) One 0·303-in (7,7-mm) Lewis machine gun firing upwards with 291 rounds

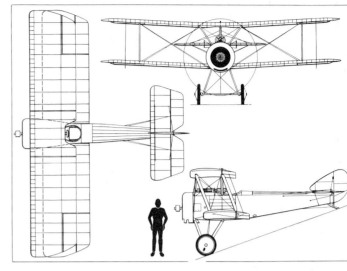

**Right:** An RNAS Pup photographed during its second landing aboard HMS *Furious* on 7 August 1917 during shipboard trials. Note Lewis gun of the RNAS Pup.

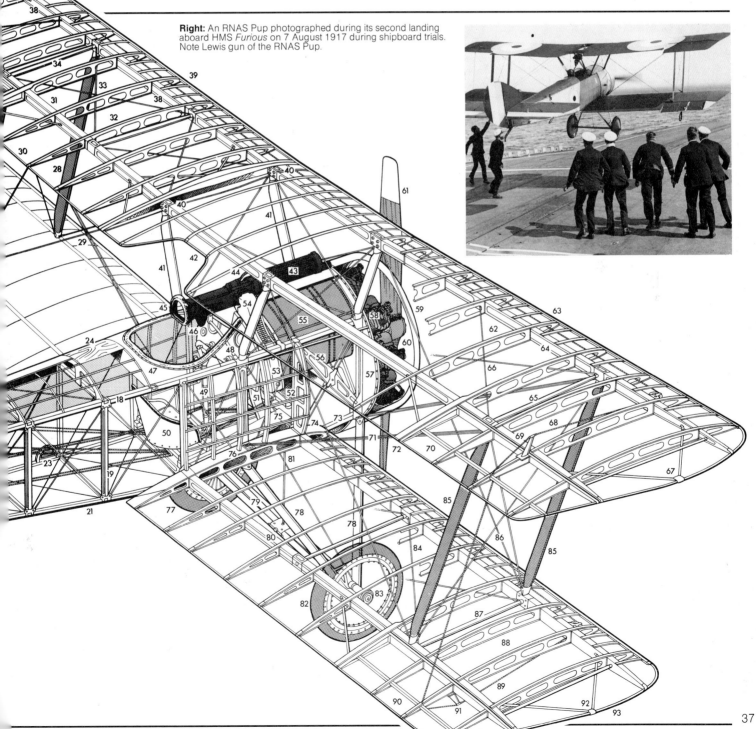

# Nieuport 17 (February 1916)

Within two years of the fighter's debut as a distinct aircraft species, a multiplicity of possible configurations had been examined, including triplanes, quadruplanes and even quintuplanes. Most were to be discarded, the monoplane and the biplane emerging predominant and their respective merits becoming a subject for much controversy. There was one promising alternative, however, and this was the sesquiplane; a biplane in which the lower wing possessed less than half the area of the upper. The leading exponent of this compromise configuration was Gustave Delage who established the distinctive unequal-chord sesquiplane arrangement with V-form interplane strutting and single-spar lower wing, a basic pattern that was to endure through successive Nieuport types.

The first single-seat fighter adhering to this configuration was the 80 hp Le Rhône-engined Nie.11 of 1915. The lower wing was little more than a faired spar, providing girder bracing to the upper mainplane but extended outboard beyond the V-strut attachment points to provide additional lifting surface. The Nie.11 quickly acquired the affectionate sobriquet of Bébé, although this was subsequently to be applied to all Nieuport sesquiplane single-seaters.

Derived from the Nie.11 by way of the unsuccessful Nie.16 with the 110 hp Le Rhône was the similarly powered Nie.17, which, flown in February 1916, possessed greater wing area and embodied various structural refinements. Entering service in the following May, it proved an outstanding success, despite a propensity towards wing shedding, and equipped every French escadrille de chasse at some time during 1916. Many early Nie.17s featured a so-called cône de pénétration, a hemispherical fixed fairing mounted on an extension of the stationary crankshaft, and the Nieuport fighter was considered to establish new standards of efficiency in its class.

By late July 1917, the day of the Nie.17 over the Western Front was past. Rather than design an entirely new replacement, however, Delage obsessively persisted with the refinement of what was by now a manifestly outmoded basic design. The Nie.17bis with a 130 hp Clerget 9B engine and fully faired fuselage sides; the Nie.23 scarcely distinguishable from the Nie.17, and the Nie.24; none could match contemporary Spads. Thus, the Nieuport sesquiplanes were

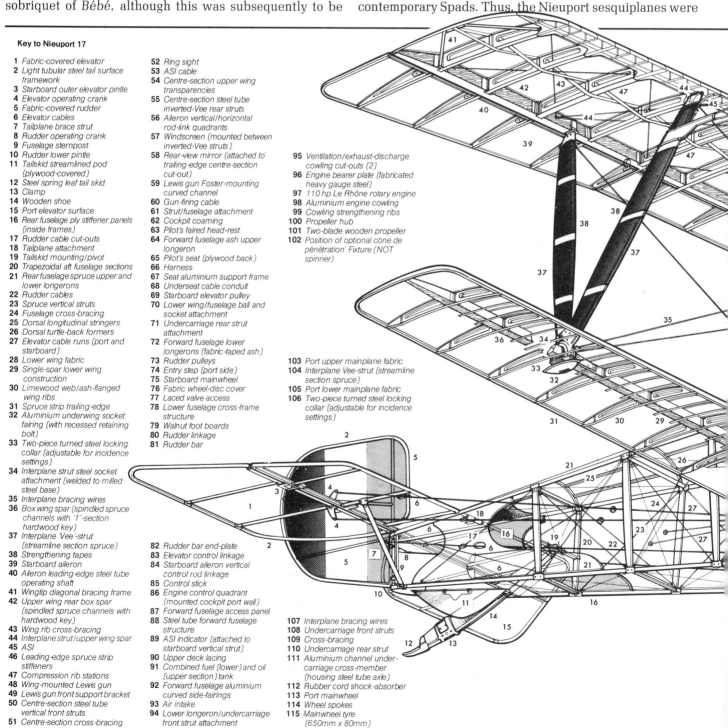

**Key to Nieuport 17**

1 Fabric-covered elevator
2 Light tubular steel tail surface framework
3 Starboard outer elevator pintle
4 Elevator operating crank
5 Fabric-covered rudder
6 Elevator cables
7 Tailplane brace strut
8 Rudder operating crank
9 Fuselage sternpost
10 Rudder lower pintle
11 Tailskid streamlined pod (plywood-covered)
12 Steel spring leaf tail skid
13 Clamp
14 Wooden shoe
15 Port elevator surface
16 Rear fuselage ply stiffener panels (inside frames)
17 Rudder cable cut-outs
18 Tailplane attachment
19 Tailskid mounting/pivot
20 Trapezoidal aft fuselage sections
21 Rear fuselage spruce upper and lower longerons
22 Rudder cables
23 Spruce vertical struts
24 Fuselage cross-bracing
25 Dorsal longitudinal stringers
26 Dorsal turtle-back formers
27 Elevator cable runs (port and starboard)
28 Lower wing fabric
29 Single-spar lower wing construction
30 Limewood web/ash-flanged wing ribs
31 Spruce strip trailing-edge
32 Aluminium underwing socket fairing (with recessed retaining bolt)
33 Two-piece turned steel locking collar (adjustable for incidence settings)
34 Interplane strut steel socket attachment (welded to milled steel base)
35 Interplane bracing wires
36 Box wing spar (spindled spruce channels with 'I'-section hardwood key)
37 Interplane 'Vee'-strut (streamline section spruce)
38 Strengthening tapes
39 Starboard aileron
40 Aileron leading-edge steel tube operating shaft
41 Wingtip diagonal bracing frame
42 Upper wing rear box spar (spindled spruce channels with hardwood key)
43 Wing rib cross-bracing
44 Interplane strut/upper wing spar
45 ASI
46 Leading-edge spruce strip stiffeners
47 Compression rib stations
48 Wing-mounted Lewis gun
49 Lewis gun front support bracket
50 Centre-section steel tube vertical front struts
51 Centre-section cross-bracing

52 Ring sight
53 ASI cable
54 Centre-section upper wing transparencies
55 Centre-section steel tube inverted-Vee rear struts
56 Aileron vertical/horizontal rod-link quadrants
57 Windscreen (mounted between inverted-Vee struts)
58 Rear-view mirror (attached to trailing-edge centre-section cut-out)
59 Lewis gun Foster-mounting curved channel
60 Gun-firing cable
61 Strut/fuselage attachment
62 Cockpit coaming
63 Pilot's faired head-rest
64 Forward fuselage ash upper longeron
65 Pilot's seat (plywood back)
66 Harness
67 Seat aluminium support frame
68 Underseat cable conduit
69 Starboard elevator pulley
70 Lower wing/fuselage ball and socket attachment
71 Undercarriage rear strut attachment
72 Forward fuselage lower longerons (fabric-taped ash)
73 Rudder pulleys
74 Entry step (port side)
75 Starboard mainwheel
76 Fabric wheel-disc cover
77 Laced valve access
78 Lower fuselage cross-frame structure
79 Walnut foot boards
80 Rudder linkage
81 Rudder bar

82 Rudder bar end-plate
83 Elevator control linkage
84 Starboard aileron vertical control rod linkage
85 Control stick
86 Engine control quadrant (mounted cockpit port wall)
87 Forward fuselage access panel
88 Steel tube forward fuselage structure
89 ASI indicator (attached to starboard vertical strut)
90 Upper deck lacing
91 Combined fuel (lower) and oil (upper section) tank
92 Forward fuselage aluminium curved side-fairings
93 Air intake
94 Lower longeron/undercarriage front strut attachment

95 Ventilation/exhaust-discharge cowling cut-outs (2)
96 Engine bearer plate (fabricated heavy gauge steel)
97 110 hp Le Rhône rotary engine
98 Aluminium engine cowling
99 Cowling strengthening ribs
100 Propeller hub
101 Two-blade wooden propeller
102 Position of optional cône de pénétration' fixture (NOT spinner)

103 Port upper mainplane fabric
104 Interplane Vee-strut (streamline section spruce)
105 Port lower mainplane fabric
106 Two-piece turned steel locking collar (adjustable for incidence settings)

107 Interplane bracing wires
108 Undercarriage front struts
109 Cross-bracing
110 Undercarriage rear strut
111 Aluminium channel under-carriage cross-member (housing steel axle)
112 Rubber cord shock-absorber
113 Port mainwheel
114 Wheel spokes
115 Mainwheel tyre (650mm x 80mm)

to remain more or less in eclipse until the end of WWI. Total production of *all* Le Rhône-engined Nieuports reached approximately 7,200 aircraft.

**SPECIFICATION: Nieuport 17 C.1**

**Power Plant:** One Le Rhône 9Ja nine-cylinder air-cooled rotary engine rated at 113 hp at 1,200 rpm for take-off. Two-bladed fixed-pitch wooden propeller. Internal fuel capacity, 17·6 Imp gal (80 l).

**Performance:** Max speed, 103 mph (165 km/h) at sea level, 99 mph (160 km/h) at 6,560 ft (2 000 m), 96 mph (154 km/h) at 9,840 ft (3 000 m); time to 6,560 ft (2 000 m), 6·83 min, to 9,840 ft (3 000 m), 11·5 min; service ceiling, 17,390 ft (5 300 m); endurance, 1·75 hrs.

**Weights:** Empty, 825 lb (375 kg); loaded 1,232 lb (560 kg).

**Dimensions:** Span, 26 ft 9 in (8,16 m); length, 19 ft 0¼ in (5,80 m); height, 7 ft 10 in (2,40 m); wing area, 158·8 sq ft (14,75 m²).

**Armament:** One 7,7-mm Vickers synchronised machine gun or one 7,7-mm Lewis machine gun with three 97-round ammunition drums.

**Above right, top:** A Nieuport 17 serving with No 111 Sqdn. RFC, at Deir-el-Belah Palestine, early in 1918, before this squadron re-equipped with the S.E.5a.

**Above right:** A Nieuport 17 of the Red Air Force during the post-revolutionary fighting of 1918-20.

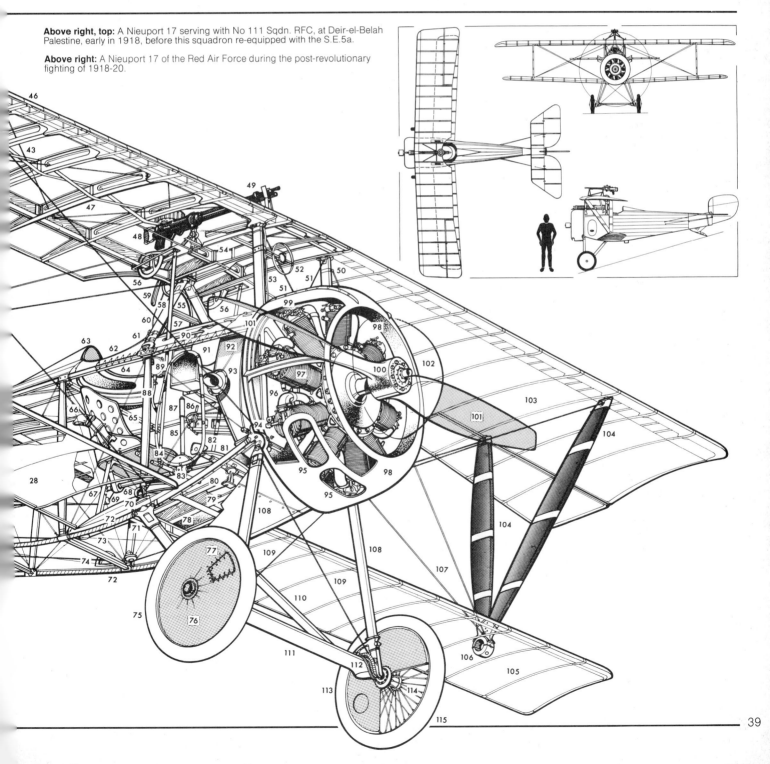

# RAF S.E. 5 (November 1916)

Functional optimization from mid-1916 hastened the emergence of the fighter from a truncated infancy; its translation from scout with combat capability to fully-fledged fighting machine. In Britain, the struggle to exceed or at least match the performance capability of the newer enemy fighters being fielded resulted in two new types, the Camel and the S.E.5, which, evolved in parallel, flew as prototypes within five weeks of each other.

These fighters reflected philosophies as different as their appearances. The Camel, characterised by squatness of form and lightness of weight, was to place emphasis on agility at some expense to handling. The S.E.5, on the other hand, was rakish, angular and heavy by standards of the day; it was to have none of its contemporary's waspish sensitivity, its emphasis being on tractability. Indeed, the S.E.5 was a compromise *between* agility and tractability, handling characteristics being, from certain aspects, the antithesis of those of the Camel.

The aim of H.P. Folland and the Royal Aircraft Factory team was to design around the brilliant new Hispano-Suiza V-8 engine a robust fighter capable of being flown with a reasonable degree of safety by pilots of limited experience. Although intended for the 200 hp geared Hispano-Suiza 8B engine, the prototype, flown on 22 November 1916, and a comparatively small initial production batch (S.E.5s) had

S.E.5a

**Key to S.E.5a**

1 Laminated wooden propeller
2 Propeller attaching plate
3 Attaching bolts
4 Radiator
5 Radiator shutter plates
6 Filler cap
7 Radiator mounting strut
8 Bottom fitting
9 200 hp Wolseley Viper engine
10 Engine mounting structure
11 Top cowling
12 Hinged bottom cowling
13 Oil tank
14 Oil filler cap
15 Engine cooling air duct
16 Main fuel tank
17 Fuel tank fixing
18 Centre section forward strut

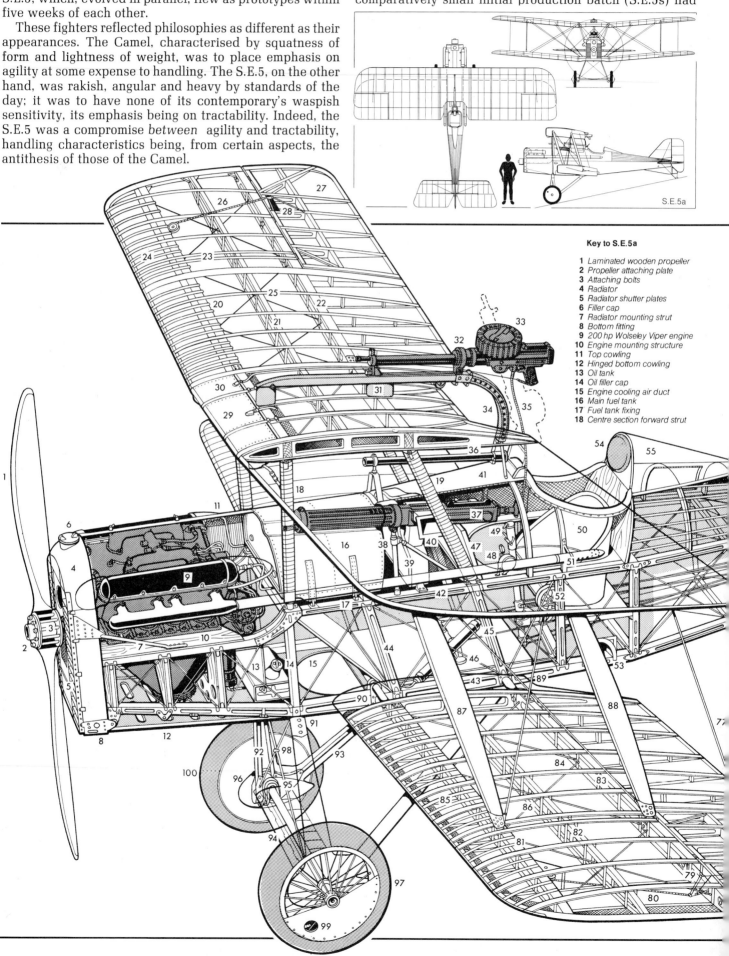

the 150 hp direct-drive Hispano-Suiza 8A. Subsequent aircraft (S.E.5a's) were mostly fitted with either the intended Hispano-Suiza or the similarly-rated direct-drive Wolseley Viper. At a time when an armament of twin belt-fed synchronised guns was becoming vogue, the S.E.5 opted for one synchronised gun and another on a Foster mounting firing over the wing.

Fundamentally sturdy, the new fighter's early service was nevertheless marred by failures of the upper mainplane centre section, a problem exacerbated by engine reduction gear and gun synchronisation difficulties. But once these tribulations were overcome, the S.E.5 was to prove one of WWI's most competent fighters, and 5,205 S.E.5s and 5a's were to be manufactured.

Unlike the Camel, the S.E.5 proved a forgiving aeroplane, tolerant of inexperienced pilots. Control forces about all three axes were light; there was some adverse aileron yaw, but stalling characteristics were totally innocuous. It was usefully manoeuvrable yet stable enough to facilitate accurate shooting, and if it lacked anything in agility it more than compensated in the liberties that it permitted without risk of structural failure. It was more than coincidence that most of the RFC's top-scoring pilots flew the S.E.5a.

## SPECIFICATION: S.E.5a

**Power Plant:** One Wolseley W.4a Viper eight-cylinder water-cooled vee engine rated at 215 hp at 2,100 rpm for take-off. Two-bladed fixed-pitch wooden propeller. Internal fuel capacity, 35 Imp gal (159 l).

**Performance:** Max speed, 138 mph (222 km/h) at sea level, 126 mph (203 km/h) at 10,000 ft (3 050 m), 123 mph (198 km/h) at 15,000 ft (4 570 m); time to 5,000 ft (1 525 m), 4·92 min, to 10,000 ft (3 050 m), 11·0 min, to 15,000 ft (4 570 m), 19·92 min; service ceiling, 19,500 ft (5 945 m), endurance, 3·0 hrs.

**Weights:** 1,459 lb (662 kg); loaded, 1,976 lb (896 kg).

**Dimensions:** Span, 26 ft 7½ in (8,11 m); length, 20 ft 11 in (6,37 m); height, 9 ft 6 in (2,89 m); wing area, 245·8 sq ft (22,83 m²).

**Armament:** One fixed 0·303-in (7,7-mm) Vickers MG with 400 rounds and one 0·303-in Lewis MG with 4 x 97-round drums.

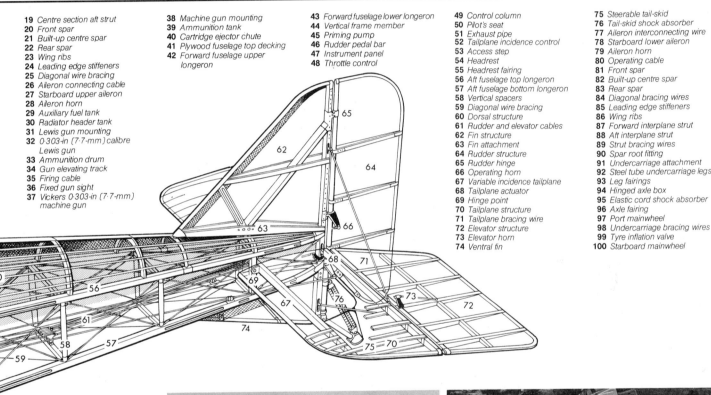

19 Centre section aft strut
20 Front spar
21 Built-up centre spar
22 Rear spar
23 Wing ribs
24 Leading edge stiffeners
25 Diagonal wire bracing
26 Aileron connecting cable
27 Starboard upper aileron
28 Aileron horn
29 Auxiliary fuel tank
30 Radiator header tank
31 Lewis gun mounting
32 0·303-in (7·7-mm) calibre Lewis gun
33 Ammunition drum
34 Gun elevating track
35 Firing cable
36 Fixed gun sight
37 Vickers 0·303-in (7·7-mm) machine gun
38 Machine gun mounting
39 Ammunition tank
40 Cartridge ejector chute
41 Plywood fuselage top decking
42 Forward fuselage upper longeron
43 Forward fuselage lower longeron
44 Vertical frame member
45 Priming pump
46 Rudder pedal bar
47 Instrument panel
48 Throttle control
49 Control column
50 Pilot's seat
51 Exhaust pipe
52 Tailplane incidence control
53 Access step
54 Headrest
55 Headrest fairing
56 Aft fuselage top longeron
57 Aft fuselage bottom longeron
58 Vertical spacers
59 Diagonal wire bracing
60 Dorsal structure
61 Rudder and elevator cables
62 Fin structure
63 Fin attachment
64 Rudder structure
65 Rudder hinge
66 Operating horn
67 Variable incidence tailplane
68 Tailplane actuator
69 Hinge point
70 Tailplane structure
71 Tailplane bracing wire
72 Elevator structure
73 Elevator horn
74 Ventral fin
75 Steerable tail-skid
76 Tail-skid shock absorber
77 Aileron interconnecting wire
78 Starboard lower aileron
79 Aileron horn
80 Operating cable
81 Front spar
82 Built-up centre spar
83 Rear spar
84 Diagonal bracing wires
85 Leading edge stiffeners
86 Wing ribs
87 Forward interplane strut
88 Aft interplane strut
89 Strut bracing wires
90 Spar root fitting
91 Undercarriage attachment
92 Steel tube undercarriage legs
93 Leg fairings
94 Hinged axle box
95 Elastic cord shock absorber
96 Axle fairing
97 Port mainwheel
98 Undercarriage bracing wires
99 Tyre inflation valve
100 Starboard mainwheel

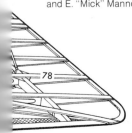

**Immediately right:** S.E. 5a's of No 111 Sqdn at Ramleh, Palestine, in 1918, and (below right) an S.E.5a operated by the US Army Air Service in the immediate post-WWI years.

**Far right:** S.E.5a's of No 85 Sqdn at St Omer on 21 May 1918. Formed nine months earlier, No 85 Sqdn was successively commanded by Majors W.A. "Billy" Bishop and E. "Mick" Mannock.

# Sopwith Camel (December 1916)

Since the birth of the fighter genus there have always been members of the class that have aroused intense controversy among their pilots; aircraft seen as anathema by some and sheer ambrosia by others. The Camel assuredly came within this category. There were pilots who acclaimed it as the best single-seat fighter to emerge from WWI; others called it a vicious killer, as equally prepared to destroy its own pilot as his adversary.

The Camel *was* a mercilessly unforgiving aeroplane, it is true, but to those pilots who mastered its potent peculiarities it was a dogfighter *par excellence,* and it was to claim the distinction of being WWI's most destructive fighter, accounting for more 'kills' (2,790) than any other single fighter type of any nation! The Camel's lack of stability and extreme sensitivity were assets in the hands of a competent pilot and potentially fatal to the novice. It offered turning capabilities unmatched by any fighter, although if the turn was tightened too much the Camel would spin; this was an inevitable result of coarse handling.

The Camel was markedly tail heavy at full throttle and tiring to fly. It afforded its pilot poor upward vision and it lacked the speed and climb rate of its later-generation German opponents. But it offered an instantaneous response to the slightest touch on the controls; it could be looped under perfect control from a low airspeed and flick-rolled without any loss of altitude. Its manoeuvrability was phenomenal and this was primarily due to the concept of concentrating all the principal weight masses—engine, guns, pilot and fuel—within an extraordinarily small section of fuselage.

The first prototype was to fly as the F.1 at the end of December 1916, with the first production deliveries commencing in the following May. A snub-nosed hump-backed little aeroplane devoid of elegance, it was structurally orthodox, with single-bay fabric-covered wooden wings and a wire-braced wooden box-girder fuselage, but its significance lay in its armament. For the first time, a British fighter emulated the recently-established German practice of mounting a pair of synchronised rifle-calibre machine guns to fire through the propeller disc.

The somewhat humped profile engendered the epithet Camel, which was unofficial but became so popular that

## Key to Sopwith F.1 Camel

1 Two-blade wooden propeller
2 Propeller attachment plate
3 Attaching bolts
4 Engine cowling
5 130 hp Clerget seven-cylinder rotary engine
6 Engine mounting bulkhead
7 Engine bearing member
8 Gravity oil tank
9 Oil tank mounting
10 Fuselage cross member
11 Fuselage frame
12 Twin synchronised 0·303-in (7,7-mm) Vickers machine guns
13 Ammunition tank
14 Ammunition feed chute
15 Cartridge ejector chute
16 Gun cocking lever
17 Gunsight
18 Hinged windscreen
19 Carburettor intake
20 Centre section front strut
21 Centre section bracing wires
22 Centre section rear strut
23 Wind driven fuel pressurising pump
24 Hand operated fuel pressurising pump
25 Front spar
26 Leading edge stiffeners

27 Spar connecting strut
28 Rear spar
29 Inner/outer wing spar joint
30 Wing ribs
31 Port aileron
32 Aileron operating horn
33 Diagonal cross bracing
34 Interplane strut
35 Strut bracing wires
36 Interplane bracing wires
37 Padded cockpit coaming
38 Pilot's basket-work seat
39 Seat mounting frame
40 Main fuel tank
41 Secondary fuel tank
42 Fuel filler cap
43 Control cables beneath seat
44 Fuselage top longeron
45 Fuselage bottom longeron
46 Vertical spacers
47 Cross members (frames)
48 Diagonal wire bracing
49 Dorsal frame
50 Dorsal stringers

51 Rudder cables
52 Elevator up cable
53 Elevator down cable
54 Port tailplane structure
55 Tailplane stay (upper)

56 Port elevator
57 Elevator operating horn
58 Elevator hinge
59 Fixed fin structure
60 Rudder
61 Rudder hinge
62 Rudder operating horn
63 Starboard elevator
64 Starboard tailplane structure

65 Tailskid
66 Tailskid pivot mounting
67 Elastic cord shock absorber
68 Starboard aileron (top)
69 Aileron interplane cable
70 Starboard aileron (bottom)
71 Aileron operating cable
72 Aft interplane strut
73 Forward interplane strut

74 Strut bracing wires
75 Rear spar
76 Spar connecting strut
77 Front spar
78 Wing ribs
79 Diagonal wire bracing
80 Leading edge stiffeners
81 Rear spar/fuselage attachment
82 Front spar/fuselage fitting

**Above:** An F.1 Camel of No 46 Sqdn, RFC, fitted with four 25-lb Cooper bombs on a rack beneath the fuselage for ground attack tasks, in which casualties were high.

it was ultimately accepted. It first entered service with the RNAS and immediately afterward with the RFC, and a total of 5,597 F.1 Camels was ordered of which apparently 5,490 were delivered with the remainder being cancelled at the war's end.

## SPECIFICATION: F.1 Camel

**Power Plant:** One Clerget 9B nine-cylinder rotary air-cooled engine rated at 130 hp at 1,250 rpm for take-off. Two-bladed fixed-pitch wooden propeller. Internal fuel capacity, 37 Imp gal (168 l).

**Performance:** Max speed, 115 mph (185 km/h) at 6,500 ft (1 980 m), 113 mph (182 km/h) at 10,000 ft (3 050 m), 106·5 mph (171 km/h) at 15,000 ft (4 570 m); time to 6,500 ft (1 980 m)), 6·0 min, to 10,000 ft (3 050 m), 10·58 min, to 15,000 ft (4 570 m), 21·83 min; service ceiling, 19,000 ft (5 790 m); endurance, 2·5 hrs.

**Weights:** Empty 929 lb (421 kg); loaded, 1,453 lb (659 kg).

**Dimensions:** Span, 28 ft 0 in (8,53 m); length, 18 ft 9 in (5,71 m); height, 8 ft 6 in (2,59 m); wing area, 231 sq ft (21,46 m²).

**Armament:** Two 0·303-in (7,7-mm) Vickers machine guns with 250 rpg. Four 25-lb (11,3-kg) bombs could be carried on external racks.

83 *Undercarriage leg mounting*
84 *Undercarriage leg*
85 *Undercarriage bracing wires*
86 *Axle fairing*
87 *Starboard mainwheel*
88 *Pivoted half-axle*
89 *Elastic cord shock absorber*
90 *Port mainwheel*
91 *Tyre inflation valve*

**Above:** The F.1 Camel had few pretensions to elegance, its snub-nosed, hump-backed appearance being clearly portrayed by these photographs.

# Albatros D V (March 1917)

As the tempo of aviation development accelerated under the pressures of war, closer attention had begun to be paid to the effects of airframe drag on fighter performance and the results were particularly apparent in the single-seat progeny of the Albatros company. Designed by Robert Thelen, these fighters established new standards in elegance, mating neatly-cowled engines with carefully streamlined semi-monocoque wooden fuselages.

The first of the genus, the D I and D II, had had an immediate impact on the air war upon arrival at the Front almost simultaneously in September 1916, being the first fighters produced in quantity to mount twin synchronised guns and the first to employ the excellent Mercedes D III engine. Their successor, the D III, had discarded their robust parallel-strutted single-bay wing cellule in favour of the lighter, lower-drag Nieuport-style sesquiplane cellule, appearing at the Front in December 1916. Representing an attempt to achieve higher performance with the same engine and without sacrificing manoeuvrability, the D V,

flown as a prototype in March 1917, was essentially a refinement of this basic design.

Utilising a lighter, less sturdy structure, the D V supplanted the near-rectangular fuselage cross section of its predecessors with a new elliptical section, and arguably carried WWI fighter aerodynamic refinement to its ultimate. Reaching the *Jagdstaffeln* in May 1917, the D V proved structurally unsound, despite which fact 900 were built while a thorough structural reappraisal was undertaken. The end product of this reappraisal was the D Va, with stronger spars, heavier ribs and additional fuselage members, which entered service in October 1917.

The heavier weight of the D Va without commensurate power increase resulted in some performance degradation, but it was still a formidable opponent when flown by a skilled pilot, and 1,612 were to be built. On 30 April 1918, 928 D Va fighters were at the Front, representing 47·6 per cent of available fighter strength, and these assumed a primary role in the German spring offensive of 1918. A modest performance gain accompanied installation of the higher-compression D IIIa engine from March 1918, but

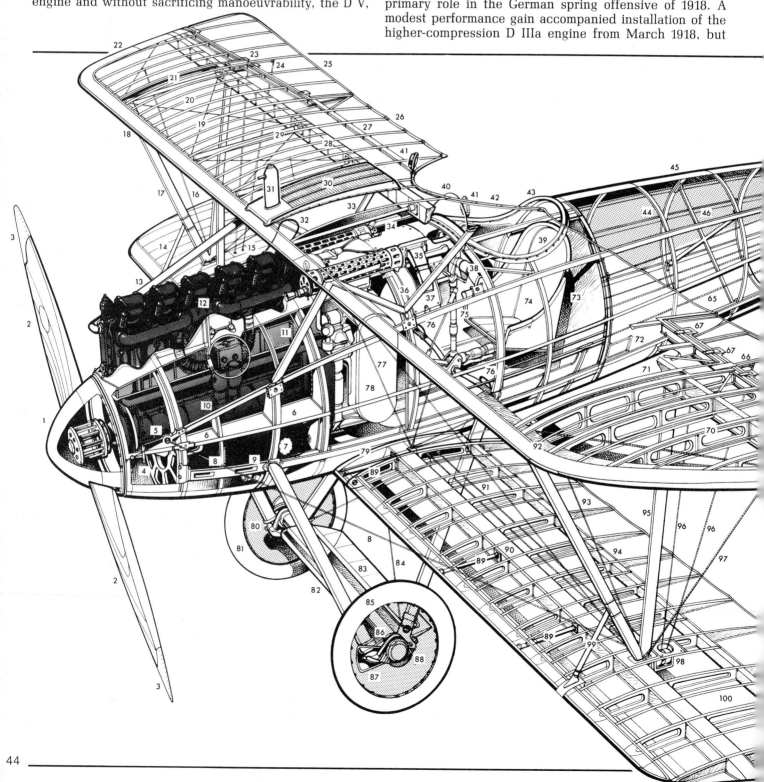

the D Va faded away rapidly with availability of the Fokker D VII from the following month.

## SPECIFICATION: Albatros D Va

**Power Plant:** One Mercedes D IIIa six-cylinder inline water-cooled engine rated at 160 hp at 1,250 rpm for take-off and 180 hp at 3,280 ft (1 000 m). Two-bladed fixed-pitch wooden propeller. Internal fuel capacity, 22 Imp gal (100 l).

**Performance:** Max speed, 116 mph (187 km/h) at sea level, 117 mph (188 km/h) at 3,280 ft (1 000 m), 102 mph (165 km/h) at 9,840 ft (3 000 m); time to 3,280 ft (1 000 m), 4·0 min, to 9,840 ft (3 000 m), 17·15 min; service ceiling, 20,500 ft (6 250 m); max range, 217 mls (350 km).

**Weights:** Empty, 1,580 lb (717 kg); loaded, 2,018 lb (915 kg).

**Dimensions:** Span, 29 ft 8$^1$/$_3$ in (9,05 m); length 24 ft 0$^5$/$_8$ in (7,33 m); height 8 ft 10¼ in (2,70 m); wing area, 220·67 sq ft (20,50 m$^2$).

**Armament:** Two 7,92-mm Maxim LMG 08/15 with 500 rpg.

**Above top:** The Albatros D V prototype in the newly-developed hexagonal camouflage, and (immediately above) a D V of the final production batch with tail raised on trestle for gun sighting. Note propeller made of laminations of walnut and maple, the large copper exhaust pipe and the water pipe to the radiator.

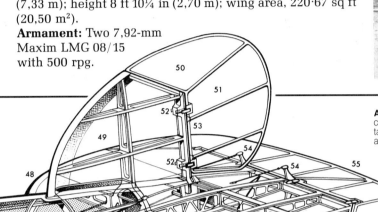

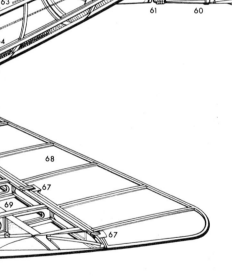

**Key to Albatros DVa**

1 Propeller boss
2 Laminated wooden propeller
3 Metal tips
4 Front fuselage frame
5 Bracing wire anchor point
6 Engine mounting structure
7 Access panel
8 Bracing wire
9 Lower longeron
10 Upper longeron
11 Centre-section 'N'-strut
12 Mercedes D.IIIa engine
13 Water pipe to radiator
14 Auxiliary bracing strut (modification)
15 Aileron control cables
16 Starboard wingtip bracing wire
17 Interplane struts
18 Composite leading edge member
19 Drift wires
20 Wing rib stations
21 Steel compression tube (strut anchorage)
22 Leading edge carry-round
23 Aileron crank
24 Aileron actuating cables
25 Welded steel aileron frame
26 Steel wire trailing edge
27 Auxiliary spar
28 Rear spar
29 Steel compression tube
30 Teeves und Braun radiator
31 Radiator header tank
32 Copper exhaust pipe (starboard side)
33 Steel-tube centre-section strut
34 Twin Maxim machine guns in fuselage decking
35 Spent cartridge chute
36 Support frame
37 Ammunition box
38 Gun support bar
39 Open cockpit
40 Windshield
41 Rear-view mirror (sometimes mounted on cockpit coaming)
42 Trailing-edge cut-out
43 Padded cockpit coaming
44 Fuselage frames (plywood former)
45 Fuselage skin
46 'X'-tube bracing strut
47 Upper longeron (spruce)
48 Starboard tailplane
49 Fin structure
50 Rudder balance
51 Rudder frame (metal)
52 Rudder hinges
53 Rudder post
54 Elevator control horns
55 Elevator frame (metal)
56 Elevator balance
57 Tailplane structure (wooden framed)
58 Under-fin
59 Steel shoe
60 Ash tail-skid
61 Elastic cord shock-absorber
62 Tailplane stub attachment
63 Control cables (rudder)
64 Lower longeron (spruce)
65 Control cables (elevator)
66 Aileron crank
67 Wooden hinge blocks
68 Welded steel aileron frame
69 Rear spar
70 Plywood wing ribs
71 Strut anchorage
72 Entry step
73 Plywood bulkhead
74 Pilot's seat
75 Control column
76 Rudder pedals
77 Interplane bracing wires
78 Fuel tank
79 Wing stub
80 Starboard wheel
81 700 mm × 100 mm tyre
82 Axle
83 Compression strut
84 Undercarriage bracing
85 Port tyre
86 Metal retaining strap
87 Access panel
88 Elastic cord shock-absorber
89 Forward section compression struts (3)
90 Wing spar
91 Aileron cables
92 Upper mainplane front spar
93 Interplane bracing wire
94 False rear spar (not anchored)
95 Aileron control cables
96 Aileron control cables
97 Port wingtip bracing wire
98 Aileron control cables
99 Auxiliary bracing strut (modification)
100 Lower wing structure

# Spad 13 (March 1917)

A trend towards heavier, more powerful and, in consequence, less agile, more stable single-seat fighters had begun to make itself apparent with the service début in the autumn of 1916 of the first of the acronymically dubbed Spads powered by the superb, albeit somewhat refractory, Hispano-Suiza V-8 engine. Designed by Louis Béchereau of the Société anonyme pour l'Aviation et ses Dérivés, the 150 hp Spad 7 had flown in April 1916, reflecting the demand for increased emphasis on level speed and dive capabilities at some expense to manoeuvrability resulting from combat experience over the Western Front.

The Spad 7 had made a noteworthy impact on the air war, but by the beginning of 1917 had lost its edge with the appearance of faster, more heavily armed adversaries in the see-saw battle for aerial superiority. Thus, another turn in the upward weight and power spiral was taken by its successor, the Spad 13 with twin-gun armament and a geared 200 hp Hispano-Suiza engine flown late in March 1917. The new fighter bore a close family resemblance to its predecessor, retaining many characteristic features, such as the oval car-type frontal radiator with its vertical venetian-blind shutters for temperature control, but it was, in fact, a larger, sturdier and structurally very different aeroplane.

Despite the urgency attached to replacing the out-classed Nieuport sesquiplanes and Spad 7s, the Spad 13 was somewhat slow in reaching the *Aviation militaire*, only 25 having been delivered by August 1917, and no more than 372 being on strength eight months later. This delay was, in part, due to the ailments suffered by its geared engine; defects which did not initially permit the full exploitation of the Spad 13's performance potential. At first, the Spad 13 failed to obtain universal approbation. Cockpit vision was poor, it was difficult to handle at low airspeeds, it

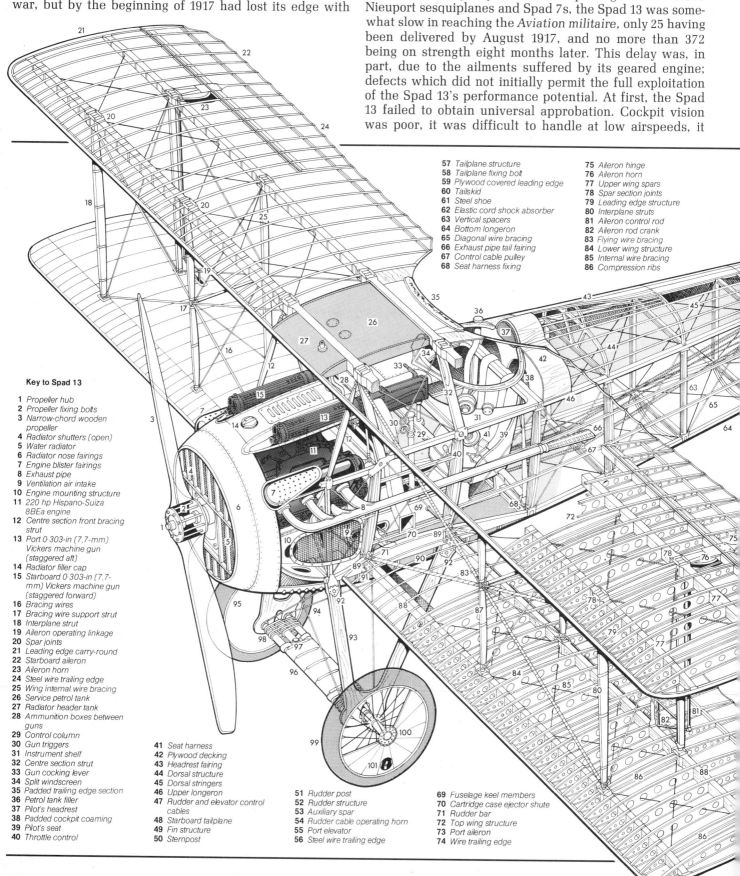

**Key to Spad 13**

1 Propeller hub
2 Propeller fixing bolts
3 Narrow-chord wooden propeller
4 Radiator shutters (open)
5 Water radiator
6 Radiator nose fairings
7 Engine blister fairings
8 Exhaust pipe
9 Ventilation air intake
10 Engine mounting structure
11 220 hp Hispano-Suiza 8BEa engine
12 Centre section front bracing strut
13 Port 0·303-in (7,7-mm) Vickers machine gun (staggered aft)
14 Radiator filler cap
15 Starboard 0·303-in (7,7-mm) Vickers machine gun (staggered forward)
16 Bracing wires
17 Bracing wire support strut
18 Interplane strut
19 Aileron operating linkage
20 Spar joints
21 Leading edge carry-round
22 Starboard aileron
23 Aileron horn
24 Steel wire trailing edge
25 Wing internal wire bracing
26 Service petrol tank
27 Radiator header tank
28 Ammunition boxes between guns
29 Control column
30 Gun triggers
31 Instrument shelf
32 Centre section strut
33 Gun cocking lever
34 Split windscreen
35 Padded trailing edge section
36 Petrol tank filler
37 Pilot's headrest
38 Padded cockpit coaming
39 Pilot's seat
40 Throttle control

41 Seat harness
42 Plywood decking
43 Headrest fairing
44 Dorsal structure
45 Dorsal stringers
46 Upper longeron
47 Rudder and elevator control cables
48 Starboard tailplane
49 Fin structure
50 Sternpost

51 Rudder post
52 Rudder structure
53 Auxiliary spar
54 Rudder cable operating horn
55 Port elevator
56 Steel wire trailing edge

57 Tailplane structure
58 Tailplane fixing bolt
59 Plywood covered leading edge
60 Tailskid
61 Steel shoe
62 Elastic cord shock absorber
63 Vertical spacers
64 Bottom longeron
65 Diagonal wire bracing
66 Exhaust pipe tail fairing
67 Control cable pulley
68 Seat harness fixing

69 Fuselage keel members
70 Cartridge case ejector shute
71 Rudder bar
72 Top wing structure
73 Port aileron
74 Wire trailing edge

75 Aileron hinge
76 Aileron horn
77 Upper wing spars
78 Spar section joints
79 Leading edge structure
80 Interplane struts
81 Aileron control rod
82 Aileron rod crank
83 Flying wire bracing
84 Lower wing structure
85 Internal wire bracing
86 Compression ribs

possessed a dauntingly high glide angle, it had to be literally flown onto the ground and it was prone to ground looping. Its manoeuvrability, too, was somewhat deficient, but it was one of the fastest fighters of its day; it could out-dive most, if not all, its contemporaries and it was perhaps the sturdiest fighter of WWI.

The Spad 13 came into its own as the air war reached its zenith. It could not compete effectively in a turning battle with such adversaries as the Fokker D VII, but then it was not conceived for the classic dogfighting mode of combat. Once its pilots had learned to take full advantage of its high level speed and dive capabilities, accustoming themselves to its tail heaviness, tendency to hunt in a turn and stiffness of control response, the Spad 13 was to establish an enviable combat record.

No fewer than 8,472 Spad 13s were ordered from the French aircraft industry, but only some 7,300 had been completed when production terminated in 1919.

**SPECIFICATION: Spad 13 C1**

**Power Plant:** One Hispano-Suiza 8BEa eight-cylinder water-cooled vee engine rated at 220 hp at 2,100 rpm for take-off. Two-bladed Chauvière 222H wooden fixed-pitch propeller. Internal fuel capacity, 30 Imp gal (136 l).

**Performance:** Max speed, 132·5 mph (213 km/h) at 6,560 ft (2 000 m), 131 mph (211 km/h) at 9,840 ft (3 000 m), 127 mph (205 km/h) at 13,125 ft (4 000 m); time to 3,280 ft (1 000 m), 2·5 min, to 6,560 ft (2 000 m), 5·17 min, to 9,840 ft (3 000 m), 8·33 min; service ceiling, 22,310 ft (6,800 m); endurance, 1·85 hrs.

**Weights:** Empty, 1,326 lb (601 kg); loaded, 1,888 lb (856 kg).

**Dimensions:** Span, 26 ft 6 in (8,08 m); length, 20 ft 6 in (6,25 m); height 8 ft 6½ in (2,60 m); wing area, 217·43 sq ft (20,20 m²).

**Armament:** Two 7,7-mm Vickers MGs with 400 rpg.

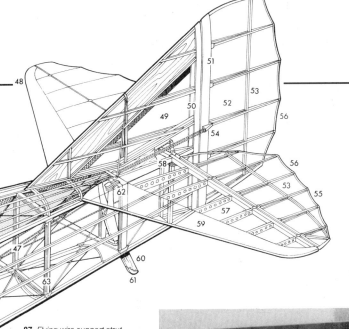

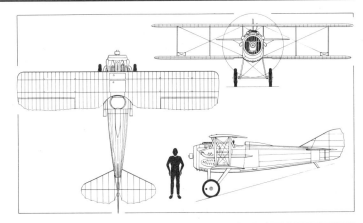

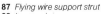

87 *Flying wire support strut*
88 *Lower wing spars*
89 *Spar root fitting*
90 *Main petrol tank*
91 *Oil tank*
92 *Undercarriage leg top fitting*
93 *Laminated wooden undercarriage legs*
94 *Undercarriage bracing wires*
95 *Starboard mainwheel*
96 *Faired axle beam*
97 *Swing axle fitting*
98 *Elastic cord shock absorber*
99 *Port mainwheel*
100 *Hub fixing*
101 *Tyre inflation valve*

**Right:** Late production examples of the Spad 13 as indicated by chute for spent cartridge cases in the fuselage flank below the mid-point of the exhaust pipe.

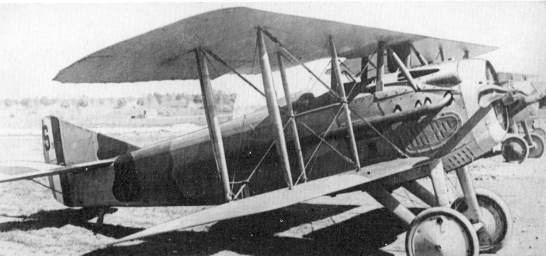

# Fokker Dr I (June 1917)

**Above:** One of the Dr I prototypes (F I 103/17) being taxied by Werner Voss at the Jasta 10 airfield near Marckebeeke from where he was evaluating the fighter when shot down by No 56 Sqdn, RAF.

Seen in its fighter context as a formula for combining good climbing qualities with extreme lateral manoeuvrability made possible by an exceedingly small overall wing span, the triplane was an aberration from the mainstream of fighter development. It was to enjoy a brief heyday in 1917 and be obsolescing before that year's end. Indeed, of many fighter triplanes developed, but two were to see combat.

Triplane investigation in Germany dated from aviation's early pioneering days, but the catalyst in its further development for the fighter role was provided by the February 1917 operational debut of the Royal Naval Air Service's Sopwith Triplane. The *Fliegertruppen* were startled by the remarkable manoeuvrability and climb rate demonstrated by the Sopwith, Germany being panicked into launching a massive single-seat fighter triplane development effort, which, with the sole exception of one type, the Fokker Dr I, was to prove an abysmal failure. The Dr I was thus conceptually unoriginal in being engendered by the Sopwith, but it nevertheless embodied some highly innovatory features.

Designed by Reinhold Platz, the prototype—at that time

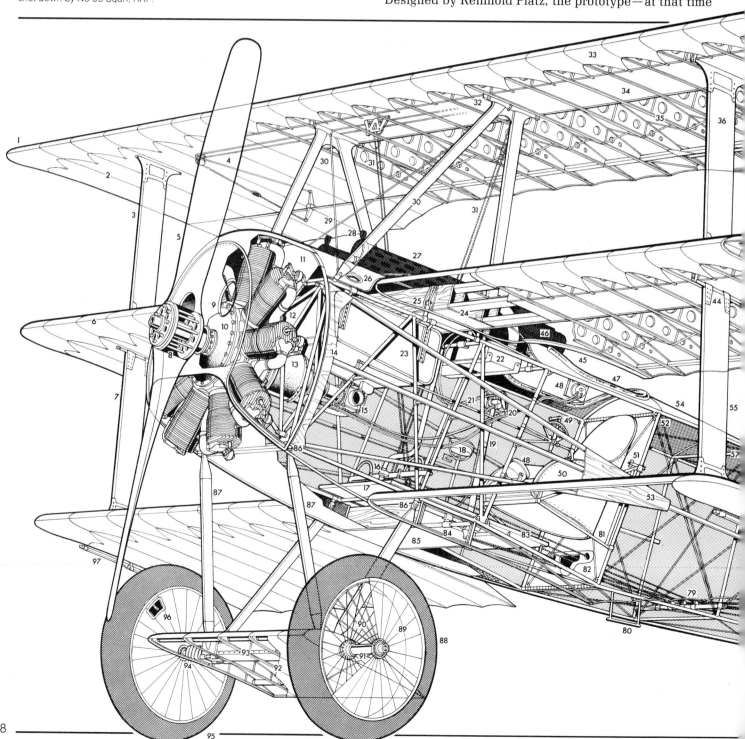

known as the D VI, Fokker having still to adopt V-series designations for experimental aircraft—was an outstandingly compact triplane with *verspannungslos* (literally "without bracing"), or cantilever, wings dispensing with flying, landing and incidence wires, the necessary strength being imparted by an original single-spar arrangement, which was actually two boxspars joined vertically. The fuselage was of welded steel tubing with transverse bracing to form a rigid box-girder structure. Wing oscillation in certain flight regimes dictated introduction of thin, non-structural spruce I-type interplane struts to provide the desired rigidity.

Enjoying the patronage of no less a personality than Manfred *Freiherr* von Richthofen, the triplane was ordered into production on 14 July 1917, two prototypes being tested at the Front in the following month by von Richthofen and Werner Voss. Production Dr Is reached the Front from October proving very sensitive about all axes and most taxing to fly. The Dr I, nevertheless, possessed superlative aerobatic qualities, and if a slow, low-altitude performer, it made a dangerous adversary with a skilled pilot at its controls. Its manoeuvrability was arguably second to no other fighter. In developing the Dr I, however, the *Fliegertruppe* had not comprehended the inherent limitations of the triplane configuration and its early demise was inevitable, only 320 fighters of this type being built.

**SPECIFICATION: Fokker Dr I**

**Power Plant:** One Oberursel Ur II nine-cylinder rotary air-cooled engine rated at 110 hp at 1,200 rpm for take-off. Two-bladed fixed-pitch wooden propeller. Internal fuel capacity, 20 Imp gal (91 l).

**Performance:** Max speed, 115 mph (185 km/h) at sea level, 102·5 mph (165 km/h) at 13,125 ft (4 000 m); initial climb, 1,800 ft/min (9,15 m/sec); time to 3,280 ft (1 000 m), 2·9 min, to 9,840 ft (3 000 m), 10·1 min, to 16,405 ft (5 000 m), 23·85 min; range, 185 mls (300 km).

**Weights:** Empty, 894 lb (406 kg); loaded, 1,291 lb (586 kg).

**Dimensions:** Span, 23 ft 7 in (7,19 m); length, 18 ft 11 in (5,77 m); height, 9 ft 8 in (2,95 m); wing area, 200·86 sq ft.

**Armament:** Two 7,92-mm Maxim LMG 08/15 with 500 rpg.

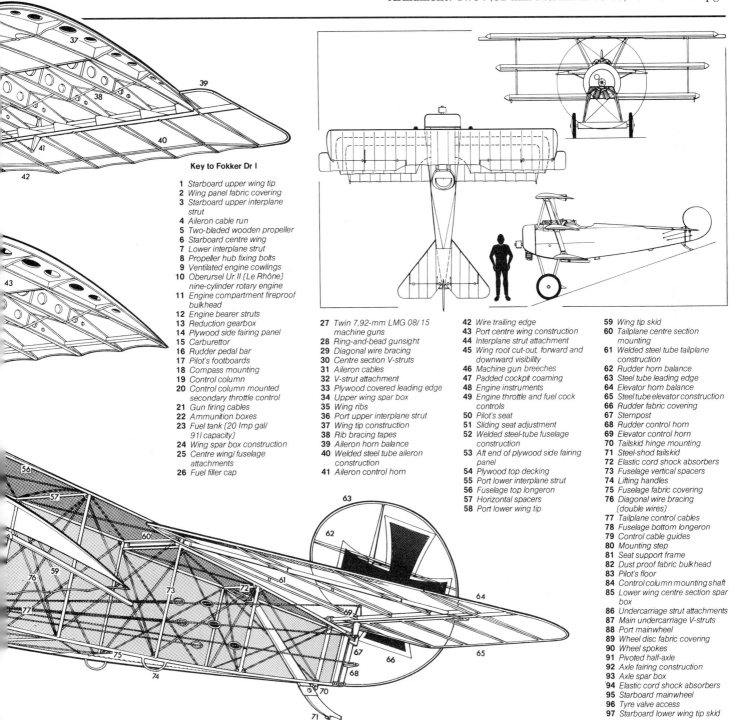

**Key to Fokker Dr I**

1 Starboard upper wing tip
2 Wing panel fabric covering
3 Starboard upper interplane strut
4 Aileron cable run
5 Two-bladed wooden propeller
6 Starboard centre wing
7 Lower interplane strut
8 Propeller hub fixing bolts
9 Ventilated engine cowlings
10 Oberursel Ur.II (Le Rhône) nine-cylinder rotary engine
11 Engine compartment fireproof bulkhead
12 Engine bearer struts
13 Reduction gearbox
14 Plywood side fairing panel
15 Carburettor
16 Rudder pedal bar
17 Pilot's footboards
18 Compass mounting
19 Control column
20 Control column mounted secondary throttle control
21 Gun firing cables
22 Ammunition boxes
23 Fuel tank (20 Imp gal/ 91l capacity)
24 Wing spar box construction
25 Centre wing/fuselage attachments
26 Fuel filler cap

27 Twin 7,92-mm LMG 08/15 machine guns
28 Ring-and-bead gunsight
29 Diagonal wire bracing
30 Centre section V-struts
31 Aileron cables
32 V-strut attachment
33 Plywood covered leading edge
34 Upper wing spar box
35 Wing ribs
36 Port upper interplane strut
37 Wing tip construction
38 Rib bracing tapes
39 Aileron horn balance
40 Welded steel tube aileron construction
41 Aileron control horn

42 Wire trailing edge
43 Port centre wing construction
44 Interplane strut attachment
45 Wing root cut-out, forward and downward visibility
46 Machine gun breeches
47 Padded cockpit coaming
48 Engine instruments
49 Engine throttle and fuel cock controls
50 Pilot's seat
51 Sliding seat adjustment
52 Welded steel-tube fuselage construction
53 Aft end of plywood side fairing panel
54 Plywood top decking
55 Port lower interplane strut
56 Fuselage top longeron
57 Horizontal spacers
58 Port lower wing tip

59 Wing tip skid
60 Tailplane centre section mounting
61 Welded steel tube tailplane construction
62 Rudder horn balance
63 Steel tube leading edge
64 Elevator horn balance
65 Steel tube elevator construction
66 Rudder fabric covering
67 Sternpost
68 Rudder control horn
69 Elevator control horn
70 Tailskid hinge mounting
71 Steel-shod tailskid
72 Elastic cord shock absorbers
73 Fuselage vertical spacers
74 Lifting handles
75 Fuselage fabric covering
76 Diagonal wire bracing (double wires)
77 Tailplane control cables
78 Fuselage bottom longeron
79 Control cable guides
80 Mounting step
81 Seat support frame
82 Dust proof fabric bulkhead
83 Pilot's floor
84 Control column mounting shaft
85 Lower wing centre section spar box
86 Undercarriage strut attachments
87 Main undercarriage V-struts
88 Port mainwheel
89 Wheel disc fabric covering
90 Wheel spokes
91 Pivoted half-axle
92 Axle fairing construction
93 Axle spar box
94 Elastic cord shock absorbers
95 Starboard mainwheel
96 Tyre valve access
97 Starboard lower wing tip skid

# Fokker D VII (December 1917)

The close-in high-g manoeuvring style of fighter-versus-fighter conflict, which had become known as dogfighting, had been brought to a fine art as the aerial warfare of WWI developed. Pursuit of the agility and control finesse necessary to excel in this mode of combat was inevitably compromised, however, by demands for higher level speeds and climb rates, the fulfilment of which was possible only at some expense to manoeuvrability. Thus, fighter designers constantly sought the ideal compromise between these conflicting requirements, and perhaps the supreme example of success in such was the Fokker D VII.

When committed to the Front in April 1918, with the tide of aerial warfare running strongly against Germany, the D VII revealed standards of controllability that were to

become legendary; standards against which new fighters were to be adjudged for a decade or more. It was not the fastest fighter at the Front during the summer and autumn of 1918, nor was it the most manoeuvrable, but it was certainly the most effective.

Inheriting some of the innovatory structural features first used by Reinhold Platz for the Dr I (see pages 48-49), the D VII had thick-section high-lift wings each built up on two wooden boxspars and dispensing with flying, landing and incidence wires, the fuselage retaining the typical Fokker wire-braced steel-tube primary structure. The first of two (V XI) prototypes was flown in December 1917, winning the D-Type contest at Adlershof in the following month. Large-scale production was immediately initiated by Fokker and by Albatros as licensee, the standard D VII with the Mercedes D IIIa engine and the D VIIF following shortly afterwards with the marginally more powerful BMW IIIa.

It was to be said of the D VII that it could translate the mediocre into the good pilot and the good pilot into an 'ace'. If this was perhaps an exaggeration, the D VII was certainly an outstandingly easy aeroplane to fly. It was forgiving yet

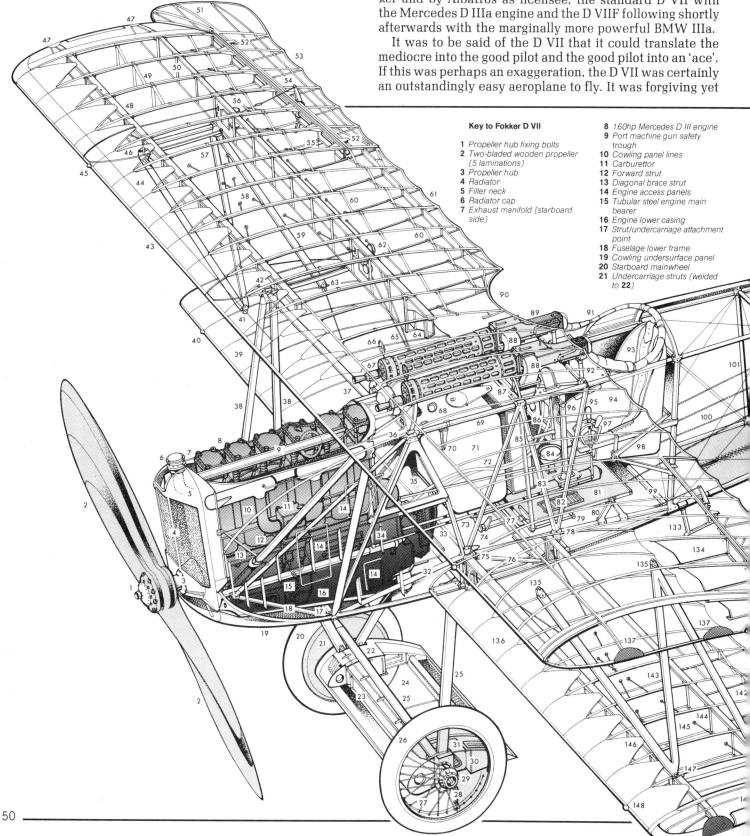

**Key to Fokker D VII**

1. Propeller hub fixing bolts
2. Two-bladed wooden propeller (5 laminations)
3. Propeller hub
4. Radiator
5. Filler neck
6. Radiator cap
7. Exhaust manifold (starboard side)
8. 160hp Mercedes D III engine
9. Port machine gun safety trough
10. Cowling panel lines
11. Carburettor
12. Forward strut
13. Diagonal brace strut
14. Engine access panels
15. Tubular steel engine main bearer
16. Engine lower casing
17. Strut/undercarriage attachment point
18. Fuselage lower frame
19. Cowling undersurface panel
20. Starboard mainwheel
21. Undercarriage struts (welded to **22**)

extraordinarily responsive; its stall was straightforward and it spun reluctantly. It remained under full control when its adversaries stalled and spun, and it could "hang on its propeller" at angles up to 45 degrees and remain a stable gun platform! Fokker produced 861 D VIIs and Albatros built at least that many again.

### SPECIFICATION: Fokker D VII

**Power Plant:** One Mercedes D IIIa six-cylinder inline water-cooled engine rated at 160 hp at 1,250 rpm for take-off and 180 hp at 3,280 ft (1 000 m). Two-bladed fixed-pitch propeller. Internal fuel, 21 Imp gal (95 l).
**Performance:** Max speed, 115 mph (185 km/h) at sea level, 116 mph (187 km/h) at 3,280 ft (1 000 m), 114 mph (183 km/h) at 6,560 ft (2 000 m); time to 3,280 ft (1 000 m), 3·8 min, to 13,125 ft (4 000 m), 18·5 min.
**Weights:** Empty, 1,508 lb (684 kg); loaded, 2006 lb (910 kg).
**Dimensions:** Span, 29 ft 2$^1$/$_3$ in (8,90 m); length, 22 ft 9$^2$/$_3$ in (6,95 m); ht, 9 ft (2,75 m); wing area, 217·44 sq ft.
**Armament:** Two 7,92-mm Maxim LMG 08/15 with 500 rpg.

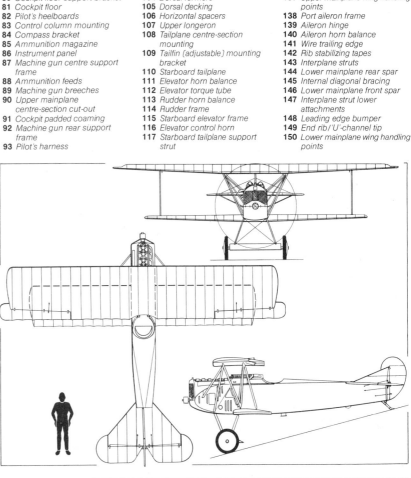

**Above:** The Fokker D VII was to soldier on in the inventories of a number of the world's air forces, some not being finally withdrawn until the mid 'thirties.

22 Sheet steel axle end box
23 Aluminium axle box spar
24 Axle fairing structure
25 Undercarriage port struts
26 Port mainwheel
27 Wheel spokes
28 Tyre valve
29 Axle hub
30 Wheel disc fabric covering
31 Elastic cord shock absorbers
32 Fuselage lower frame

33 Engine accessories
34 Engine controls linkage
35 Strengthened angle frame
36 Centre-section strut attachment
37 Machine gun muzzles
38 Starboard struts
39 Starboard lower mainplane
40 Leading edge bumper
41 Interplane strut lower mainplane attachment

42 Forward strut/mainplane spar attachment
43 Plywood leading edge
44 Interplane strut upper mainplane attachment
45 Leading edge bumper
46 Reinforced rib
47 Wing handling points
48 Front spar
49 Rib stabilizing tapes
50 Rear spar
51 Aileron horn balance
52 Aileron hinge points
53 Starboard aileron
54 Aileron control horn
55 Torque tube
56 Aileron outer pulleys
57 Interplane centre strut
58 Internal diagonal bracing
59 Interplane aft strut
60 Rib stabilizing tapes
61 Wire trailing edge
62 Wing aileron inner pulleys
63 Interplane strut lower mainplane attachment
64 Box spar structure
65 Aileron control cables
66 Ring-and-bead gunsight
67 Twin 7,92-mm Maxim LMG 08/15 machine guns
68 Fuel filler point
69 Fuselage upper longeron
70 Tank support welded bracket
71 Fuel (and oil) tank
72 Gun-firing cables
73 Engine control rods
74 Aileron control linkage
75 Lower front spar/fuselage attachment
76 Diagonal strut
77 Rudder pedal bar
78 Lower rear spar/fuselage attachment
79 Lower frame member

80 Cockpit floor support bracket
81 Cockpit floor
82 Pilot's heelboards
83 Control column mounting
84 Compass bracket
85 Ammunition magazine
86 Instrument panel
87 Machine gun centre support frame
88 Ammunition feeds
89 Machine gun breeches
90 Upper mainplane centre-section cut-out
91 Cockpit padded coaming
92 Machine gun rear support frame
93 Pilot's harness

94 Pilot's seat
95 Throttle lever
96 Control column/trigger mounting
97 Fuel control lever
98 Seat support frame
99 Fuselage cross brace

100 Elevator control cables
101 Fuselage frame
102 Rudder control cables
103 Wire bracing
104 Dorsal formers
105 Dorsal decking
106 Horizontal spacers
107 Upper longeron
108 Tailplane centre-section mounting
109 Tailfin (adjustable) mounting bracket
110 Starboard tailplane
111 Elevator horn balance
112 Elevator torque tube
113 Rudder horn balance
114 Rudder frame
115 Starboard elevator frame
116 Elevator control horn
117 Starboard tailplane support strut

118 Tailskid upper attachment
119 Control cable leather grommets
120 Tailskid snubbing springs
121 Rudder post
122 Elevator control horn
123 Tailplane bracing wire
124 Elevator frame
125 Elevator horn balance
126 Elevator torque tube
127 Rudder control horns
128 Tailskid metal shoe
129 Aft fuselage strengthening brace
130 Handhold/lifting point (port and starboard)
131 Lower longeron
132 Fuselage ventral centre-line lacing
133 Fixed entry step
134 Solid ribs
135 Interplane strut upper attachments
136 Plywood leading edge
137 Upper mainplane wing handling points
138 Port aileron frame
139 Aileron hinge
140 Aileron horn balance
141 Wire trailing edge
142 Rib stabilizing tapes
143 Interplane struts
144 Lower mainplane rear spar
145 Internal diagonal bracing
146 Lower mainplane front spar
147 Interplane strut lower attachments
148 Leading edge bumper
149 End rib/'U'-channel tip
150 Lower mainplane wing handling points

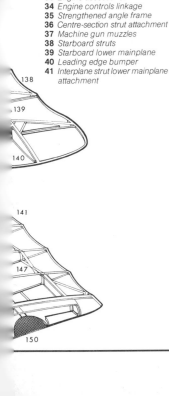

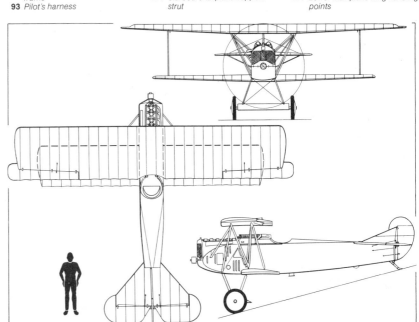

# Fairey Flycatcher (November 1922)

The first single-seat shipboard fighter of post-WWI concept to achieve service status and the intended successor of the Nieuport Nightjar and the Parnell Panther, both of which had their origins in that conflict, the Flycatcher was aesthetically a singularly unattractive aeroplane. Its strongly individual, rather ungainly appearance, belied its true character, however, for it was a superbly aerobatic fighter, with remarkably well co-ordinated controls and beautiful handling characteristics—it was to be described as having the stable docility of the Sopwith Pup mated with the response of the Sopwith Camel. To these qualities it added excellent robustness; it was the first warplane to be required by the Air Ministry to be capable of diving vertically at full power until it reached terminal velocity.

When the first Flycatcher prototype flew on 28 November 1922, shipboard aviation was in its infancy; the Royal Navy possessed only one true aircraft carrier, HMS *Argus*. Mainly of wooden construction with fabric skinning, the Flycatcher incorporated the Fairey-patented camber-changing mechanism for the wings, which, comprising wide-chord flaps which ran along the entire trailing edges of both wings (the

outer sections also serving as ailerons), shortened take-off and landing runs, and steepened the glide path.

Ordered into production in 1923, the Flycatcher entered service with the Fleet Air Arm's No 402 Flight the same year, successive orders maintaining production until the 192nd and last (excluding three prototypes) was flown to Gosport on 20 June 1930. Until 1932, when it began to give place to Nimrods and Ospreys, being entirely superseded by 1934, the Flycatcher was the Fleet Air Arm's standard—and only—single-seat fighter, and it served on all the Royal Navy's carriers of the day, was used both as a landplane and floatplane from shore bases, and was, in fact, to be the last type capable of taking-off without catapult aid from platforms on the turrets of capital ships. It was also the last fighter capable of being utilised for so-called "slip flights" from carriers, taking-off from a 60 ft (18,25 m) tapered runway, straight from the hangar and over the bows while other aircraft were being flown from the main deck above. Among other things, it was to be remembered for the "blue note" that it emitted in a full-power dive as a result of propeller shock wave and tip flutter.

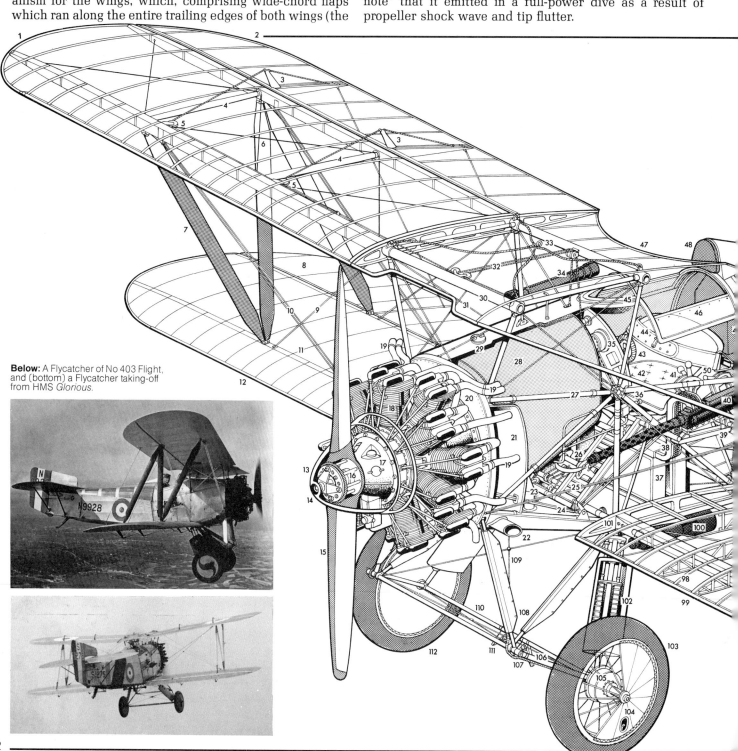

**Below:** A Flycatcher of No 403 Flight, and (bottom) a Flycatcher taking-off from HMS *Glorious*.

## SPECIFICATION: Flycatcher I

**Power Plant:** One Armstrong Siddeley Jaguar IV 14-cylinder two-row radial air-cooled engine rated at 410 hp at 1,700 rpm for take-off. Two-bladed fixed-pitch wooden propeller. Internal fuel capacity, 50 Imp gal (227 l).

**Performance:** Max speed, 134 mph (216 km/h) at sea level, 133 mph (214 km/h) at 5,000 ft (1 525 m), 130 mph (209 km/h) at 10,000 ft (3 050 m), 117 mph (188 km/h) at 15,000 ft (4 570 m); range at 10,000 ft (3 050 m), 311 mls (500 km) at 110 mph (177 km/h), 263 mls (423 km) at 130 mph (209 km/h); initial climb, 1,090 ft/min (5,54 m/sec); time to 5,000 ft (1 525 m), 5·92 min, to 10,000 ft (3 050 m), 9·5 min; service ceiling, 19,000 ft (5 790 m).

**Weights:** Empty, 2,038 lb (924 kg); normal loaded, 3,028 lb (1 373 kg).

**Dimensions:** Span, 29 ft 0 in (8,84 m); length, 22 ft 10 in (6,96 m); height, 10 ft 0 in (3,05 m); wing area, 288 sq ft (26,76 metres$^2$).

**Armament:** Two 0·303-in (7,7 mm) Vickers Mk I machine guns and provision for four 20-lb (9,07-kg) bombs beneath centre section of fuselage.

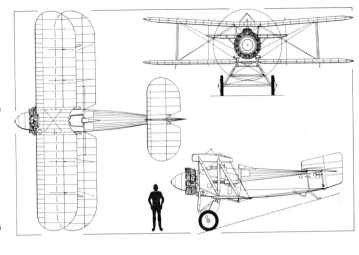

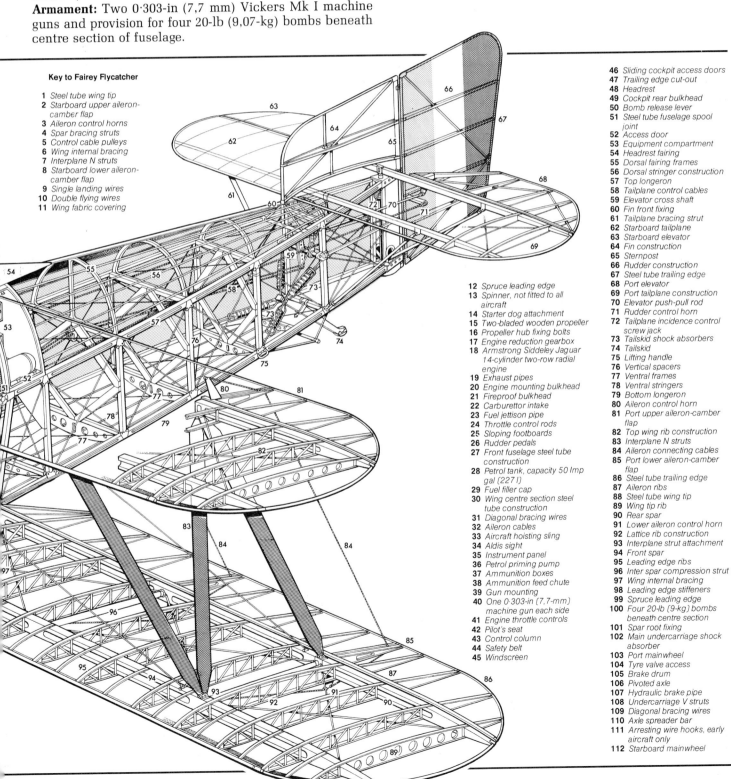

**Key to Fairey Flycatcher**

1 Steel tube wing tip
2 Starboard upper aileron-camber flap
3 Aileron control horns
4 Spar bracing struts
5 Control cable pulleys
6 Wing internal bracing
7 Interplane N struts
8 Starboard lower aileron-camber flap
9 Single landing wires
10 Double flying wires
11 Wing fabric covering
12 Spruce leading edge
13 Spinner, not fitted to all aircraft
14 Starter dog attachment
15 Two-bladed wooden propeller
16 Propeller hub fixing bolts
17 Engine reduction gearbox
18 Armstrong Siddeley Jaguar 14-cylinder two-row radial engine
19 Exhaust pipes
20 Engine mounting bulkhead
21 Fireproof bulkhead
22 Carburettor intake
23 Fuel jettison pipe
24 Throttle control rods
25 Sloping footboards
26 Rudder pedals
27 Front fuselage steel tube construction
28 Petrol tank, capacity 50 Imp gal (227 l)
29 Fuel filler cap
30 Wing centre section steel tube construction
31 Diagonal bracing wires
32 Aileron cables
33 Aircraft hoisting sling
34 Aldis sight
35 Instrument panel
36 Petrol priming pump
37 Ammunition boxes
38 Ammunition feed chute
39 Gun mounting
40 One 0·303-in (7,7-mm) machine gun each side
41 Engine throttle controls
42 Pilot's seat
43 Control column
44 Safety belt
45 Windscreen
46 Sliding cockpit access doors
47 Trailing edge cut-out
48 Headrest
49 Cockpit rear bulkhead
50 Bomb release lever
51 Steel tube fuselage spool joint
52 Access door
53 Equipment compartment
54 Headrest fairing
55 Dorsal fairing frames
56 Dorsal stringer construction
57 Top longeron
58 Tailplane control cables
59 Elevator cross shaft
60 Fin front fixing
61 Tailplane bracing strut
62 Starboard tailplane
63 Starboard elevator
64 Fin construction
65 Sternpost
66 Rudder construction
67 Steel tube trailing edge
68 Port elevator
69 Port tailplane construction
70 Elevator push-pull rod
71 Rudder control horn
72 Tailplane incidence control screw jack
73 Tailskid shock absorbers
74 Tailskid
75 Lifting handle
76 Vertical spacers
77 Ventral frames
78 Ventral stringers
79 Bottom longeron
80 Aileron control horn
81 Port upper aileron-camber flap
82 Top wing rib construction
83 Interplane N struts
84 Aileron connecting cables
85 Port lower aileron-camber flap
86 Steel tube trailing edge
87 Aileron ribs
88 Steel tube wing tip
89 Wing tip rib
90 Rear spar
91 Lower aileron control horn
92 Lattice rib construction
93 Interplane strut attachment
94 Front spar
95 Leading edge ribs
96 Inter spar compression strut
97 Wing internal bracing
98 Leading edge stiffeners
99 Spruce leading edge
100 Four 20-lb (9-kg) bombs beneath centre section
101 Spar root fixing
102 Main undercarriage shock absorber
103 Port mainwheel
104 Tyre valve access
105 Brake drum
106 Pivoted axle
107 Hydraulic brake pipe
108 Undercarriage V struts
109 Diagonal bracing wires
110 Axle spreader bar
111 Arresting wire hooks, early aircraft only
112 Starboard mainwheel

# Bristol Bulldog (May 1927)

**Above:** A Bulldog II of No 3 Sqdn, RAF, with which this fighter first entered service in June 1929 at Upavon, Wiltshire, as a replacement for the Gamecock. No 3 Sqdn took its Bulldogs to the Sudan during the Abyssinian crisis.

Successor in RAF fighter squadrons of the Siskin and Gamecock, both of which had been progressive developments of designs with origins in World War I, the Bulldog reflected a changing British attitude towards the operational use of fighters. From the early 'twenties, there were signs of some re-assessment of fighter requirements; a trend of thought away from the concept of standing patrols of fighters of modest performance towards the high-performance fast-climbing interceptor. The catalyst was provided by the emergence of two-seat day bombers (eg, the Fairey Fox) capable of outpacing contemporary single-seat fighters, and the Bulldog was closely, albeit somewhat circumstantially, related to the mutating British views on this category of warplane.

Designed by Capt Frank Barnwell and of high-tensile steel strip construction, the Bulldog evolved as a private venture via proposals tendered to meet a succession of official specifications, and despite thus being something of an interloper, emerged as the winning contender in the RAF's most hotly-contested inter-war re-equipment programme (F.9/26). Flown as a prototype on 17 May 1927, the

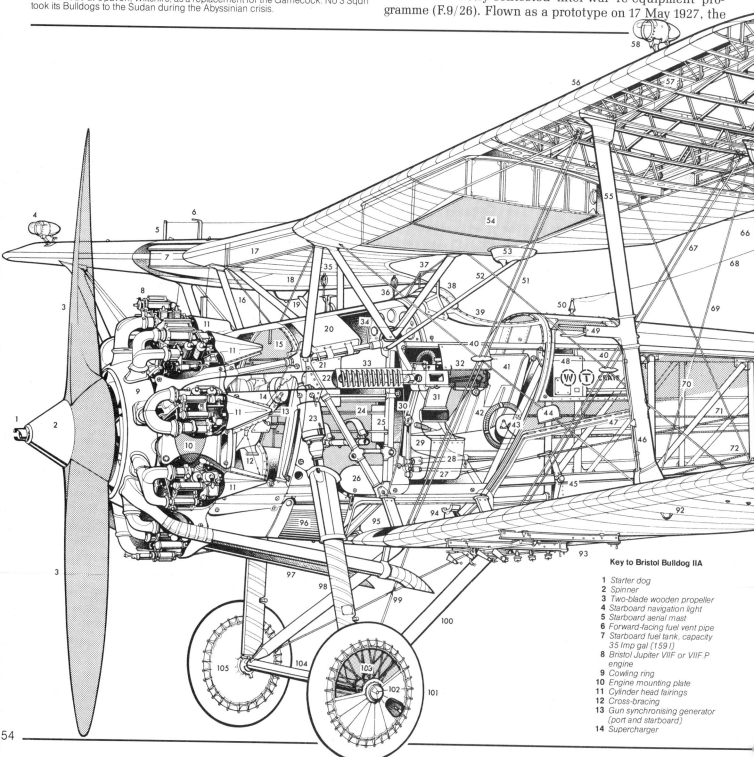

**Key to Bristol Bulldog IIA**

1. Starter dog
2. Spinner
3. Two-blade wooden propeller
4. Starboard navigation light
5. Starboard aerial mast
6. Forward-facing fuel vent pipe
7. Starboard fuel tank, capacity 35 Imp gal (159 l)
8. Bristol Jupiter VIIF or VIIF.P engine
9. Cowling ring
10. Engine mounting plate
11. Cylinder head fairings
12. Cross-bracing
13. Gun synchronising generator (port and starboard)
14. Supercharger

Bulldog proved to possess excellent manoeuvrability and well-harmonised controls, a second prototype being ordered by the Air Ministry with a lengthened fuselage to improve spin recovery, this being ordered into production in August 1928 as the Bulldog II. RAF deliveries commenced in May of the following year, 312 being delivered to the service, the 49th and subsequent aircraft being Bulldog IIAs embodying some structural strengthening, revised oil system and a modified undercarriage.

The dominant RAF fighter of the early 'thirties, the Bulldog equipped nine squadrons, finally giving place to the Gladiator (see pages 76-77) in 1937. The Bulldog was supplied to Australia (8), Estonia (12), Siam (2), Sweden (3) and the US Navy (2), and an extensively revised development, the Bulldog IVA, intended to compete with its ultimate successor, the Gladiator, was ordered by Finland (17) in April 1934, remaining in first-line Finnish service until the spring of 1940, and thus serving during the Soviet-Finnish "Winter War" of November 1939 to March 1940.

## SPECIFICATION: Bulldog IIA

**Power Plant:** One Bristol Jupiter VIIF radial air-cooled engine rated at 440 hp at 1,950 rpm and 520 hp at 10,000 ft (3 050 m). Two-bladed fixed-pitch wooden propeller. Internal fuel capacity, 70 Imp gal (318 l).

**Performance:** Max speed, 178 mph (286 km/h) at 10,000 ft (3 050 m), 162 mph (260 km/h) at 20,000 ft (6 100 m); range, 350 mls (563 km) at 15,000 ft (4 570 m); time to 20,000 ft (6 100 m), 14·5 minutes; service ceiling, 29,300 ft (8 930 m).

**Weights:** Empty, 2,412 lb (1 094 kg); max loaded, 3,530 lb (1 601 kg), later increased to 3,660 lb (1 660 kg).

**Dimensions:** Span, 33 ft 10 in (10,31 m); length, 25 ft 0 in (7,62 m); height, 9 ft 10 in (2,99 m); wing area, 306·5 sq ft (28,50 m²).

**Armament:** Two 0·303-in (7,7-mm) Vickers Mk II or Mk IIIN machine guns with 600 rounds for each gun, and with provision for four 20-lb (9,07-kg) Mk I HE bombs carried on wing racks.

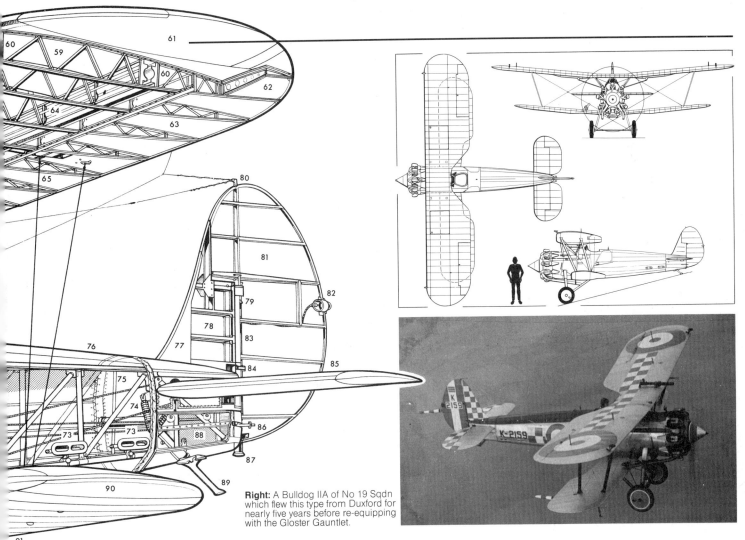

**Right:** A Bulldog IIA of No 19 Sqdn which flew this type from Duxford for nearly five years before re-equipping with the Gloster Gauntlet.

| | | | |
|---|---|---|---|
| 15 Firewall | 32 Port Vickers 0·303-in (7,7-mm) Mk II or Mk IIIN gun | 49 ASI horn | 68 Aerials |
| 16 Centre-section support struts | 33 Gun cooling louvres | 50 Aerial mast | 69 Strut cross-bracing |
| 17 Wing centre-section | 34 Instrument panel | 51 Interplane bracing | 70 Fuselage tubular framework |
| 18 Bracing wire | 35 Ring sight (combined with Aldis tube front mounting) | 52 Port fuel pipe | 71 Rudder/tailplane controls |
| 19 Starboard fuel pipe | 36 Bead sight | 53 Fuel lead fairing | 72 Elevator controls |
| 20 Oil tank, capacity 7·5 Imp gal (34,1 l) | 37 Windscreen | 54 Port fuel tank, capacity 35 Imp gal (159 l) | 73 Handholds with lifting-bars behind |
| 21 Forward fuselage framework | 38 Padded coaming | 55 Front interplane strut | 74 Tailskid spring |
| 22 Gun trough | 39 Cockpit | 56 Upper mainplane leading edge ribbing | 75 Rear fuselage lacing |
| 23 Oleo leg attachment | 40 Fibre acorns | 57 Front spar | 76 Fuselage decking |
| 24 Rudder pedals | 41 Pilot's adjustable seat | 58 Port navigation light | 77 Fin solid section |
| 25 Accumulator (lighting system) | 42 Tailplane adjusting wheel | 59 Wing rib | 78 Fin frame structure |
| 26 Air bottle (high-pressure cylinder) | 43 Chain and sprocket | 60 Spar strip steel sections | 79 Upper rudder hinge |
| 27 Elevator link tube | 44 Handhold/step | 61 Upper mainplane tip | 80 Aerial anchor point |
| 28 Aileron rockshaft | 45 Elevator cable arm | 62 Aileron balance | 81 Rudder frame |
| 29 Ammunition box, capacity 600 rounds (one each gun) | 46 ASI cable on strut leading edge | 63 Aileron construction | 82 Rear navigation light |
| 30 Control column | 47 Fuselage lacing | 64 Rear spar | 83 Rudder post |
| 31 Empty case chute | 48 Wireless compartment and crate | 65 Aileron cable | 84 Centre rudder hinge |
| | | 66 Rear interplane strut | 85 Port tailplane |
| | | 67 Interplane bracing | 86 Lower rudder hinge |
| | | | 87 Support pad with trolley- |

| |
|---|
| fitting track rail |
| 88 Stern frame construction |
| 89 Tailskid |
| 90 Lower mainplane tip |
| 91 Port lower mainplane |
| 92 Tie-down lug |
| 93 Light bomb racks |
| 94 Air-driven generator mounting cradle |
| 95 Centre-section lower frames |
| 96 Oil cooler |
| 97 Exhaust pipes |
| 98 V-strut undercarriage |
| 99 Cross-bracing wires |
| 100 Fixed-length radius rod |
| 101 700 × 100 Palmer Cord Aero Tyre |
| 102 Tyre valve |
| 103 Wheel spokes |
| 104 Axle strut |
| 105 Wheel cover |

# Hawker Fury (March 1929)

Singularly few among combat aircraft are those that can be pronounced without equivocation as epoch-marking paragons, but one such is assuredly the Fury, which carried warplane performance beyond 200 mph (322 km/h) for the first time. Representing a further stage in the trend in British fighter evolution towards the fast-climbing high-performance interceptor begun with the Bulldog (see pages 54-55), the Fury established a level of design elegance entirely new to combat aircraft and fresh standards in control sensitivity for fighters of its generation.

The Fury's handling characteristics were as near perfect by the standards of the day as could be, with light and positive aileron and rudder, and only slightly heavier elevator; it could glide and be flown straight and level hands-off; its stall was gentle and readily recoverable, and a spin could be terminated at will. These it combined with high speed and good climb-and-dive performance, while its delicacy of line belied its innate sturdiness.

Entering RAF service in May 1931, two years after the Bulldog, the Fury prototype was first flown in March 1929 as the private-venture Hornet, being re-named when pur-

chased by the Air Ministry in the following September. Production was initiated in August 1930, the first series aircraft flying on 21 March 1931, and the first export order (for six) meanwhile having been obtained from Yugoslavia as the forerunner of purchases by Iran (24), Norway (1), Portugal (3), South Africa (7) and Spain (3). Purchases of the initial model for the RAF totalled 118 aircraft, these becoming Fury Is retrospectively with the debut of the Fury II, and being used as frontline fighters by three squadrons. The Fury II, which first flew on 3 December 1936 and entered service early in the following year, differed essentially in having a 640 hp Kestrel VI and augmented fuel tankage, 112 being built to complete RAF Fury procurement.

The Fury had virtually disappeared from the RAF inventory by the beginning of WWII, but the South African Furies, supplemented by 24 ex-RAF aircraft, saw some action in East Africa. Yugoslavia, too, flew Furies operationally, having procured an additional 10 aircraft from the parent company and licence-built a further 40. Although its operational achievements were destined to be few, the Fury was an elegant expression of the genius of Sydney Camm,

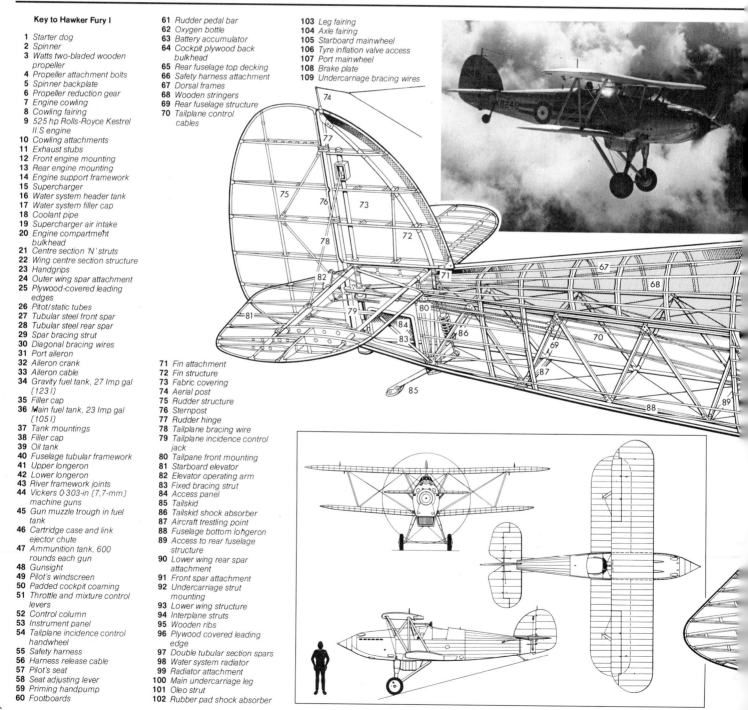

**Key to Hawker Fury I**

1 Starter dog
2 Spinner
3 Watts two-bladed wooden propeller
4 Propeller attachment bolts
5 Spinner backplate
6 Propeller reduction gear
7 Engine cowling
8 Cowling fairing
9 525 hp Rolls-Royce Kestrel II.S engine
10 Cowling attachments
11 Exhaust stubs
12 Front engine mounting
13 Rear engine mounting
14 Engine support framework
15 Supercharger
16 Water system header tank
17 Water system filler cap
18 Coolant pipe
19 Supercharger air intake
20 Engine compartment bulkhead
21 Centre section 'N' struts
22 Wing centre section structure
23 Handgrips
24 Outer wing spar attachment
25 Plywood-covered leading edges
26 Pitot/static tubes
27 Tubular steel front spar
28 Tubular steel rear spar
29 Spar bracing strut
30 Diagonal bracing wires
31 Port aileron
32 Aileron crank
33 Aileron cable
34 Gravity fuel tank, 27 Imp gal (123 l)
35 Filler cap
36 Main fuel tank, 23 Imp gal (105 l)
37 Tank mountings
38 Filler cap
39 Oil tank
40 Fuselage tubular framework
41 Upper longeron
42 Lower longeron
43 River framework joints
44 Vickers 0·303-in (7,7-mm) machine guns
45 Gun muzzle trough in fuel tank
46 Cartridge case and link ejector chute
47 Ammunition tank, 600 rounds each gun
48 Gunsight
49 Pilot's windscreen
50 Padded cockpit coaming
51 Throttle and mixture control levers
52 Control column
53 Instrument panel
54 Tailplane incidence control handwheel
55 Safety harness
56 Harness release cable
57 Pilot's seat
58 Seat adjusting lever
59 Priming handpump
60 Footboards
61 Rudder pedal bar
62 Oxygen bottle
63 Battery accumulator
64 Cockpit plywood back bulkhead
65 Rear fuselage top decking
66 Safety harness attachment
67 Dorsal frames
68 Wooden stringers
69 Rear fuselage structure
70 Tailplane control cables
71 Fin attachment
72 Fin structure
73 Fabric covering
74 Aerial post
75 Rudder structure
76 Sternpost
77 Rudder hinge
78 Tailplane bracing wire
79 Tailplane incidence control jack
80 Tailpane front mounting
81 Starboard elevator
82 Elevator operating arm
83 Fixed bracing strut
84 Access panel
85 Tailskid
86 Tailskid shock absorber
87 Aircraft trestling point
88 Fuselage bottom longeron
89 Access to rear fuselage structure
90 Lower wing rear spar attachment
91 Front spar attachment
92 Undercarriage strut mounting
93 Lower wing structure
94 Interplane struts
95 Wooden ribs
96 Plywood covered leading edge
97 Double tubular section spars
98 Water system radiator
99 Radiator attachment
100 Main undercarriage leg
101 Oleo strut
102 Rubber pad shock absorber
103 Leg fairing
104 Axle fairing
105 Starboard mainwheel
106 Tyre inflation valve access
107 Port mainwheel
108 Brake plate
109 Undercarriage bracing wires

one of the most notable British fighter designers of the period and the creator of the Hurricane (see pages 92-93).

**SPECIFICATION: Fury I**

**Power Plant:** One Rolls-Royce Kestrel II.S 12-cylinder vee liquid-cooled engine rated at 485 hp at 2,100 rpm for take-off and 575 hp at 13,000 ft (3 965 m). Two-bladed Watts B.274 wooden fixed-pitch propeller. Internal fuel capacity, 50 Imp gal (227 l).

**Performance:** Max speed, 192 mph (309 km/h) at 5,000 ft (1 525 m), 207 mph (333 km/h) at 14,000 ft (4 270 m); range, 305 mls (491 km) at 160 mph (257 km/h); initial climb, 2,380 ft/min (12,09 m/sec); time to 10,000 ft (3 050 m), 4·42 min, to 20,000 ft (6 100 m), 8·6 min; ceiling, 28,000 ft (8 450 m).

**Weights:** Empty equipped, 2,623 lb (1 190 kg); normal loaded, 3,490 lb (1 583 kg).

**Dimensions:** Span, 30 ft 0 in (9,15 m); length, 26 ft 3¾ in (8,00 m); height, 9 ft 6 in (2,89 m); wing area, 251·8 sq ft 23,40 m²).

**Armament:** Two 0·303-in (7,7-mm) Vickers Mk II (star) or Mk IIID machine guns with 600 rpg.

**Above:** One of the three Furies of the Portuguese Arma da Aeronautica, which, supplied in 1934, remained in service until 1939. They were similar to the RAF's Fury Is apart from fuel tankage.

**Left:** A Fury II serving with No 87 Sqdn, RAF, which was reformed on this type at Tangmere in March 1937, moving to Debden to convert to Gladiators three months later. Most Fury IIs were built by General Aircraft.

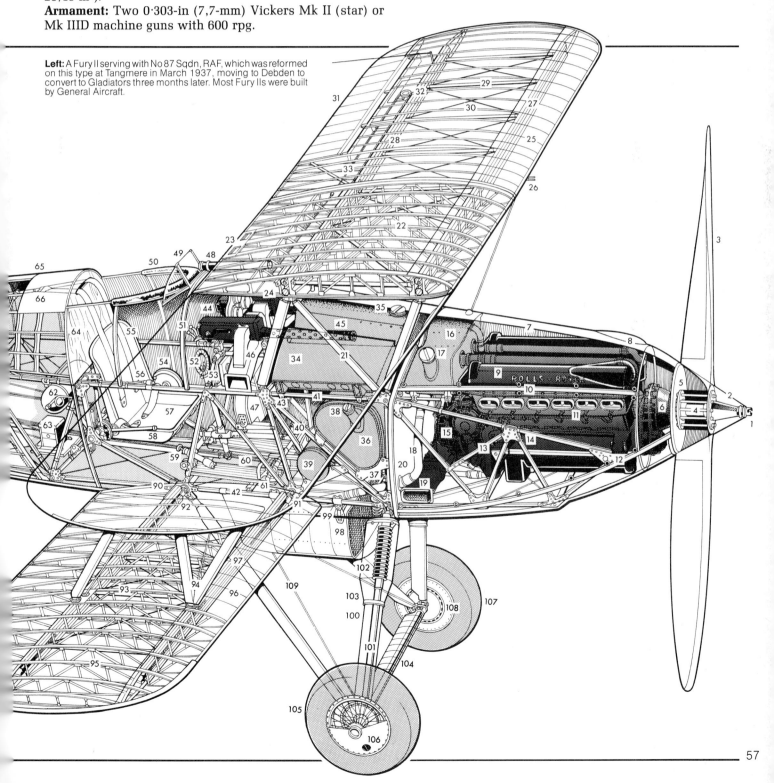

# Curtiss P-6E (mid 1931)

In constant pursuit of increased performance, the Curtiss company subjected one basic fighter design, sporting the company-assigned epithet of Hawk, to a continuous process of evolutionary development throughout the second half of the 'twenties. Designed by William E. Gilmore and George Page, the Hawk remained fundamentally unchanged from the début of the XPW-8B in December 1924—this, as prototype of the P-1, being effectively first of the genus—to December 1931, and commencement of deliveries of the P-6E which was to bring the era of the Hawk biplane in US Army service to its close.

During the intervening seven years, this evolutionary process in fact increased Hawk speed by a mere 30 mph (48 km/h), or 18·4 per cent, which was to seem decidedly unspectacular by comparison with the quantum performance advances to follow over the next seven years. The same time-span saw installed power increase 20 per cent, power loading decrease by 12 per cent and wing loading increase by 14 per cent.

The P-6E, an amalgam of the experimental YP-20 and XP-22, both P-6 airframe adaptations, was arguably an example of overdevelopment of a basic design; a process of continuous refinement having carried it beyond its apex. Excelling in aesthetic appeal, it was nevertheless a mediocrity as a fighter. Overly stable, the P-6E was a good precision aerobatic aircraft, but it offered slower control response than European contemporaries such as the Hawker Fury, a total of only 45 being built and deliveries coming to an end in March 1932.

## SPECIFICATION: P-6E

**Power Plant:** One Curtiss V-1570-23 Conqueror 12-cylinder vee liquid-cooled engine rated at 625 hp at 2,400 rpm for take-off and 600 hp at 5,000 ft (1 525 m). Three-bladed

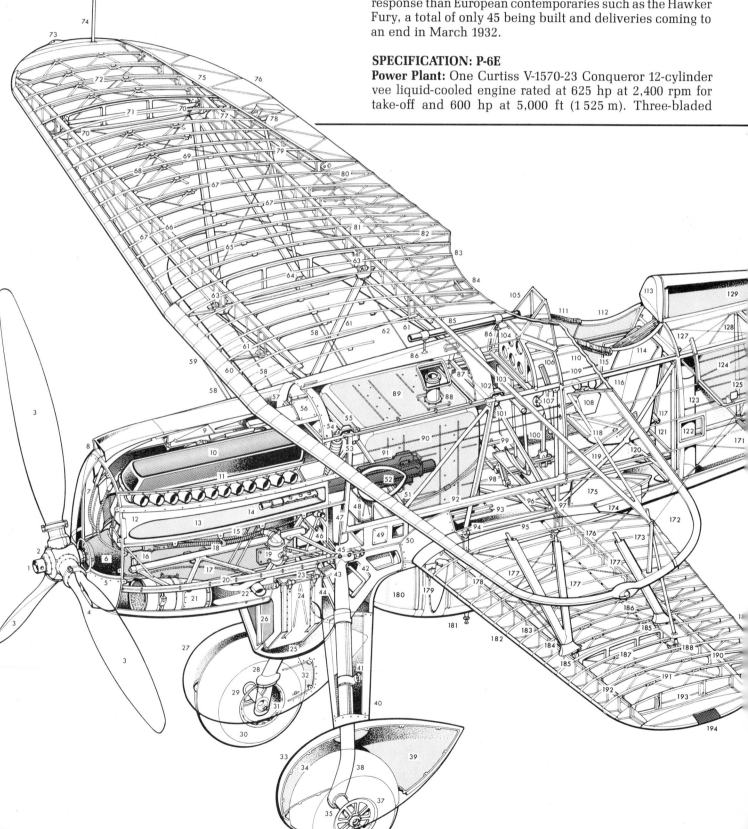

Hamilton Standard ground-adjustable metal propeller. Internal fuel capacity, 41·6 Imp gal (189 l), with provision for 41·6 Imp gal (189 l) auxiliary tank.

**Performance:** Max speed, 193 mph (310 km/h) at sea level, 191 mph (307 km/h) at 5,000 ft (1 525 m), 188 mph (302 km/h) at 10,000 ft (3 050 m); econ cruise, 167 mph (269 km/h); range (internal fuel), 285 mls (459 km), (with auxiliary tank), 572 mls (920 km); initial climb, 2,460 ft/min (12,5 m/sec); time to 5,000 ft (1 525 m), 2·3 min, to 10,000 ft (3 050 m), 5·2 min; service ceiling, 23,900 ft (7 285 m).

**Weights:** Empty, 2,743 lb (1 244 kg); normal loaded, 3,436 lb (1 559 kg); max, 3,750 lb (1 701 kg).

**Dimensions:** Span, 31 ft 6 in (9,60 m); length, 23 ft 2 in (7,06 m); height, 8 ft 11 in (2,72m); wing area, 252 sq ft (23,41 m²).

**Armament:** Two 0·30-in (7,62-mm) machine guns with 600 rpg or one 0·30-in (7,62-mm) machine gun and one 0·50-in (12,7-mm) machine gun with 600 and 200 rounds respectively.

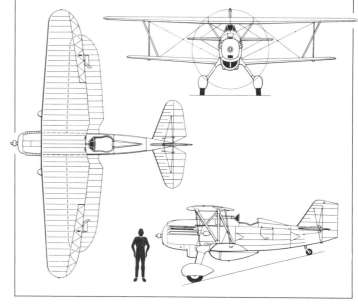

**Above:** A P-6E of the 17th Pursuit Sqdn, 1st Pursuit Group, at Selfridge Field, Mich, early 'thirties. Note unit "Snow Owl" insignia.

**Key to Curtiss P-6E Hawk**

1 Starter dog
2 Propeller hub
3 Three-blade Hamilton Standard metal propeller
4 Oil cooler chin intake
5 Nose cowling front panel line
6 Gear housing
7 Front curved panel
8 Carburettor air intake
9 Intake trunk
10 Curtiss V-1570-C Conqueror engine
11 Exhaust stubs (2 per cylinder)
12 Stainless steel trough surround
13 Gun trough
14 Machine gun muzzle
15 Cowling access panel line
16 Diagonal brace
17 Struts
18 Main engine support bearer
19 Filter
20 Lower panel lines
21 Oil cooler assembly
22 Telescopic access/servicing step
23 Radiator attachment mounts
24 Prestone radiator
25 Radiator fairing
26 Intake
27 Starboard mainwheel spat
28 Starboard undercarriage strut
29 Axle
30 Starboard low-pressure mainwheel tyre
31 Anchor point
32 Inboard access panel (brake servicing)
33 Port mainwheel spat
34 Flathead screw panel line
35 Port axle assembly
36 Port low-pressure mainwheel tyre
37 Hub assembly forging
38 Angled undercarriage strut
39 Removable spat half-section
40 Undercarriage leg fairing
41 Strut/fairing attachment
42 Strut support forged frame member
43 Strut pivot
44 Hinged cover plate
45 Front wires fuselage attachment
46 Engine accessories
47 Fuselage forward frame
48 Port ammunition magazine (600 rounds per gun)
49 Deflector panel
50 Cartridge chute
51 Gun support strut
52 Ammunition feed fairing
53 Oleo shock strut/rebound spring
54 Upper pivot point
55 Cabane forward attachment
56 Oil access point
57 Bulkhead panel
58 Starboard wires
59 Aluminium leading-edge panels
60 Upper wing centre-section
61 Cabane struts
62 Cabane wires
63 Cabane upper wing attachment points
64 Reinforced strut
65 Starboard lower wing plan
66 Front spar
67 Interplane 'N'-struts
68 Upper wing ribs
69 Internal bracing wires
70 Interplane strut upper attachment points
71 Reinforced rib
72 Outer rib assemblies
73 Starboard navigation light
74 Aerial mast
75 Aileron/rear spar join
76 Welded steel aileron (fabric-covered)
77 Aileron hinge link
78 Metal plate
79 Aileron interplane actuating link
80 Aileron profile
81 Rear spar
82 Trailing-edge rib assembly
83 Centre-section cut-out
84 Handhold
85 Telescopic gunsight
86 Gunsight supports
87 Hinged fuel access panel
88 Filler neck
89 Fuselage main fuel tank (50 US gals/189 l)
90 Engine controls
91 Port 0·30-in (7,62-mm) Browning machine gun
92 Lower longeron
93 Fuel tank bearer
94 Lower wing front spar attachment
95 Wingroot walkway
96 Diagonal strut frame
97 Lower wing rear spar attachment
98 Aileron control linkage
99 Hanging rudder pedal assembly
100 Control column
101 Fuselage frame
102 Cabane rear attachment
103 Instrument centre panel
104 Main instrument panel
105 Windscreen
106 Control grip
107 Side switch panel
108 Engine control quadrant
109 Throttle lever
110 Upper wing trailing-edge
111 Padded forward coaming
112 Cockpit cut-out
113 Headrest/turnover frame
114 Bad-weather cover (snap-on rubber tarpaulin)
115 Oxygen access panel (starboard)
116 Pilot's seat
117 Seat support frame
118 Inspection 'Vee' panel
119 Cockpit floor
120 Fuselage diagonal side frames
121 Oxygen cylinder (starboard)
122 Metal door flap
123 Parachute flare stowage (port)
124 Baggage compartment hinged side door
125 Hasp and lock
126 Baggage compartment hinged upper panel
127 Snap fasteners
128 Fuselage top frames
129 All-metal dorsal decking
130 Diagonal brace wires
131 Elevator control cables
132 Rudder control cables
133 Fuselage structure
134 Pulleys
135 Cross-member
136 Dorsal cross-section transition (round/point)
137 Tailplane front beam attachment
138 Bearer frame
139 Tailfin front beam attachment
140 Tailfin leading-edge
141 Starboard tailplane
142 Aerials
143 Tailfin structure
144 Tailplane brace wires
145 Rudder balance
146 Aerial post
147 Tail navigation light recess
148 Rudder upper hinge
149 Rudder frame
150 Spacers
151 Rudder post
152 Elevator control horns
153 Tailfin rear beam attachment
154 Elevator control cable
155 Rudder control horns
156 Port elevator frame
157 Brace wire attachment
158 Port (adjustable) tailplane
159 Tailplane front beam
160 Tail dolly lug
161 Swivel/steerable tailwheel
162 Axle fork
163 Metal grommet collar
164 Fuselage strut
165 Tailwheel shock-strut leg
166 Leather grommets (elevator control cables)
167 Tailwheel leg upper attachment
168 Access 'Vee' panel
169 Diagonal brace wires
170 Lower longeron
171 Ventral skinning
172 Port aileron
173 Aerial mast
174 Lower wingroot cut-out
175 Ventral tank aft fairing
176 Rear spar
177 Interplane 'N'-struts
178 Upper wing leading-edge
179 Drop tank filler cap
180 Drop tank (41.6 Imp gal/189 l)
181 Vent
182 Lower wing aluminium leading-edge panels
183 Nose ribs
184 Wire turnbuckle clamp
185 'N'-strut lower attachments
186 Port navigation light
187 Reinforced rib
188 Aileron actuating linkage
189 Lower wing trailing-edge
190 Rear spar
191 Outer rib assemblies
192 Front spar
193 Wingtip structure
194 Handling point

# P.Z.L. P.11c (September 1931)

The annals of fighter development are punctuated by examples of aircraft that, at the time of their débuts, signified major advances in the state of the art. One such was without doubt the P.1, which, designed by Zygmunt Pulawski and built by the Polish State Aircraft Factory in Warsaw, was flown in September 1929. Of all-metal construction with finely corrugated Wibault duralumin skinning, the P.1 established new standards in aerodynamic cleanliness, its most innovative feature being its wing. Pulawski had eliminated the cabane normally featured by high-wing monoplanes, reducing the thickness of the wing centre section and "gulling" this into the fuselage, simultaneously gaining a substantial reduction in drag and a virtually unobstructed forward field of vision. The wing incorporated slotted ailerons, which also served as landing flaps and was braced at one-third span by pairs of aerofoil-section struts.

Progressive development of the basic design resulted within two years in the P.11, which, evolved by way of the configurationally similar but lower-powered P.7, commenced

flight testing September 1931, six months after Pulawski's death, and entered production in 1933 as the P.11a, 30 being manufactured for the Polish air arm and these, in fact, being preceded by 50 examples of an export equivalent, the P.11b, for Rumania. Meanwhile, major redesign of the fighter was being undertaken by Wsieviod Jakimiuk. The engine thrust line was lowered, the pilot's seat was raised and moved aft, the wing centre section dihedral was increased, the tail assembly was redesigned and armament was doubled. Designated P.11c, this extensively modified fighter entered production in 1934—licence manufacture was also undertaken in Rumania as the P.11f— and 175 were built for Polish service, deliveries being completed in 1937.

Although barely eight years had elapsed between the début of the P.1 and completion of deliveries of its P.11c derivative, such was the tempo of international fighter development at this time that the Pulawski configuration had already been overtaken, rendering the P.11c obsolescent. When the Wehrmacht assault on Poland began on 1 September 1939, 128 P.11c fighters were included in the Polish Order of Battle, equipping 12 of the 15 squadrons

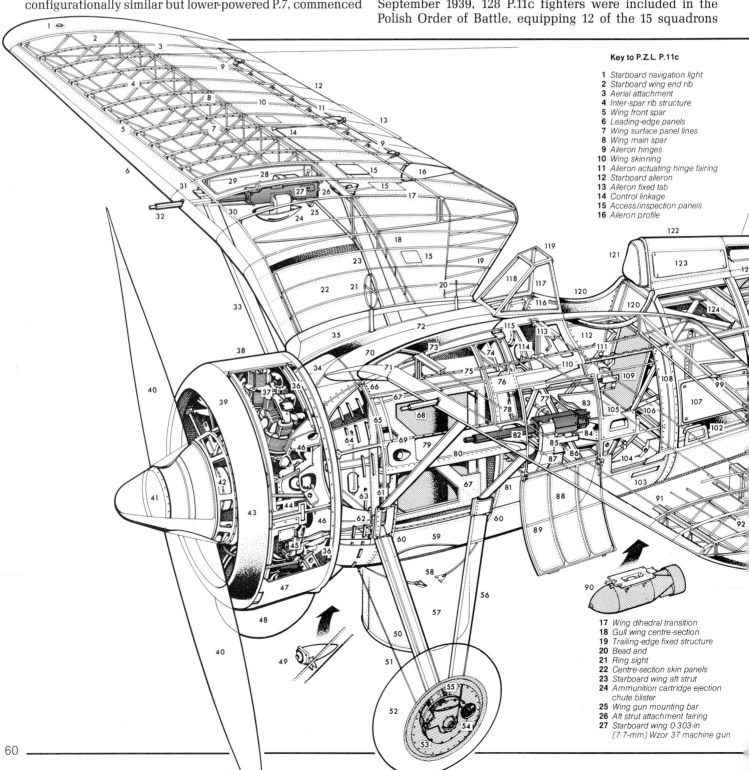

**Key to P.Z.L. P.11c**

1 Starboard navigation light
2 Starboard wing end rib
3 Aerial attachment
4 Inter-spar rib structure
5 Wing front spar
6 Leading-edge panels
7 Wing surface panel lines
8 Wing main spar
9 Aileron hinges
10 Wing skinning
11 Aileron actuating hinge fairing
12 Starboard aileron
13 Aileron fixed tab
14 Control linkage
15 Access/inspection panels
16 Aileron profile

17 Wing dihedral transition
18 Gull wing centre-section
19 Trailing-edge fixed structure
20 Bead and
21 Ring sight
22 Centre-section skin panels
23 Starboard wing aft strut
24 Ammunition cartridge ejection chute blister
25 Wing gun mounting bar
26 Aft strut attachment fairing
27 Starboard wing 0·303-in (7·7-mm) Wzor 37 machine gun

forming the fighter force. Despite the sturdiness and manoeuvrability of the Polish fighter, and the skill and determination of its pilots, its performance was inadequate for the effective interception of most Luftwaffe bombers and it was totally outclassed by opposing fighters.

### SPECIFICATION: P.11c

**Power Plant:** One Skoda-built Bristol Mercury VI S2 nine-cylinder radial air-cooled engine rated at 620 hp at 2,400 rpm for take-off, 605 hp at 12,500 ft (3 810 m) and 645 hp at 15,500 ft (4 725 m). Two-bladed fixed-pitch wooden Szomański propeller. Fuel capacity, 71 Imp gal (323 l).

**Performance:** Max speed, 186 mph (300 km/h) at sea level, 242 mph (390 km/h) at 18,045 ft (5,500 m); range at econ cruise, 435 mls (700 km); time to 16,405 ft (5 000 m), 6·0 min, to 22,965 ft (7 000 m), 13·0 min; service ceiling, 26,245 ft (8 000 m).

**Weights:** Empty equipped, 2,529 lb (1 147 kg); normal loaded, 3,593 lb (1 630 kg).

**Dimensions:** Span, 35 ft 2 in (10,72 m); length, 24 ft 9¼ in (7,55 m); height, 9 ft 4¼ in (2,85 m); wing area, 192·7 sq ft.

**Armament:** Two 7,7-mm KM Wz 33 machine guns with 500 rpg and (some aircraft) two wing-mounted Wz 33 machine guns with 300 rpg.

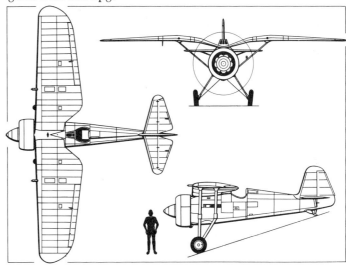

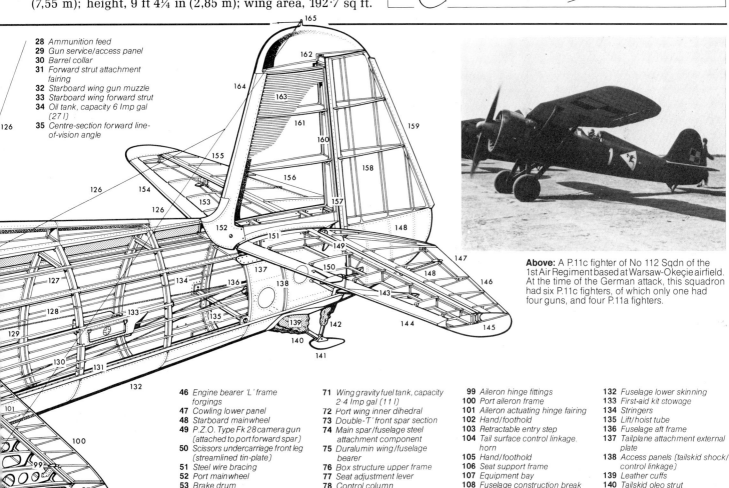

**Above:** A P.11c fighter of No 112 Sqdn of the 1st Air Regiment based at Warsaw-Okęcie airfield. At the time of the German attack, this squadron had six P.11c fighters, of which only one had four guns, and four P.11a fighters.

28 Ammunition feed
29 Gun service/access panel
30 Barrel collar
31 Forward strut attachment fairing
32 Starboard wing gun muzzle
33 Starboard wing forward strut
34 Oil tank, capacity 6 Imp gal (27 l)
35 Centre-section forward line-of-vision angle

36 Cowling aft ring
37 560 hp Bristol (Skoda-P.Z.L.-built) Mercury VI S2 radial engine
38 Engine cowling
39 Collector ring
40 Two-blade Szomanski wooden propeller
41 Spinner
42 Propeller hub shaft
43 Townend ring
44 Cowling fasteners
45 External engine data plate

46 Engine bearer 'L' frame forgings
47 Cowling lower panel
48 Starboard mainwheel
49 P.Z.O. Type Fk 28 camera gun (attached to port forward spar)
50 Scissors undercarriage front leg (streamlined tin-plate)
51 Steel wire bracing
52 Port mainwheel
53 Brake drum
54 Hub
55 Axle/leg fairing
56 Undercarriage rear leg
57 Jettisonable fuselage main fuel tank, capacity 47 Imp gal (213 l)
58 Main tank restraining/release strap and buckle
59 Cylindrical main tank ventral cut-out
60 Undercarriage leg attachment fairings
61 Avia-type oleo shock absorber
62 Engine/firewall lower attachment
63 Filter assembly
64 Cooling louvres
65 Firewall/forward frame
66 Engine bearer/firewall upper attachment
67 Forward fuselage main duralumin box structure
68 Port wing machine gun muzzle
69 Outlet
70 Gull-wing port section

71 Wing gravity fuel tank, capacity 2·4 Imp gal (11 l)
72 Port wing inner dihedral
73 Double-'T' front spar section
74 Main spar/fuselage steel attachment component
75 Duralumin wing/fuselage bearer
76 Box structure upper frame
77 Seat adjustment lever
78 Control column
79 Port wing forward strut
80 Fuselage machine gun trough
81 Port wing aft strut
82 Machine gun barrel collar
83 Fuselage port 0·303-in (7,7-mm) Wzor 37 machine gun
84 Gun support frame
85 Ammunition feed
86 Pilot's heel boards
87 Ammunition magazine
88 Fuselage gun (hinged) access panel
89 Fuselage ventral skinning
90 Underwing (optional) bomb shackles (one or two 27·5-lb [12·5-kg] bombs)
91 Port wing front spar
92 Inter-spar rib structure
93 Port navigation light
94 Port wingtip
95 Port wing main spar
96 End rib assembly
97 Aileron profile
98 Aerial attachment

99 Aileron hinge fittings
100 Port aileron frame
101 Aileron actuating hinge fairing
102 Hand/foothold
103 Retractable entry step
104 Tail surface control linkage, horn
105 Hand/foothold
106 Seat support frame
107 Equipment bay
108 Fuselage construction break
109 Pilot's seat
110 Box frame/dorsal decking attachment
111 Throttle quadrant
112 Cockpit hinged entry flap
113 External handgrip
114 Instrument panel
115 Compass (Zuru-Kolberg)
116 Radio R/T control panel
117 Quarterlights
118 Plexiglas windscreen
119 Windscreen frame
120 Cockpit padded coaming
121 Pilot's headrest
122 Dorsal decking
123 Upper spine equipment bay
124 Radio support tray (Type N2L/M R/T optional)
125 Aerial lead-in
126 Aerial array
127 Fuselage frame
128 Upper longeron
129 Rudder control cables
130 Elevator control cables
131 Lower longeron

132 Fuselage lower skinning
133 First-aid kit stowage
134 Stringers
135 Lift/hoist tube
136 Fuselage aft frame
137 Tailplane attachment external plate
138 Access panels (tailskid shock/control linkage)
139 Leather cuffs
140 Tailskid oleo strut
141 Tailskid
142 Tailskid attachment strut
143 Port tailplane brace strut
144 Port tailplane structure
145 End rib
146 Port elevator
147 Elevator tab
148 Tab hinge linkage
149 Elevator control linkage
150 Rudder actuating hinge fairing
151 Tailplane attachments
152 Tailplane root fairing
153 Starboard tailplane brace strut
154 Starboard tailplane
155 Starboard elevator
156 Elevator tab
157 Rudder centre hinge
158 Rudder
159 Rudder fixed tab
160 Rudder post
161 Tailfin
162 Rudder upper hinge
163 Tailfin corrugated skin
164 Tailfin leading-edge panels
165 Aerial attachment stub

# Boeing P-26 (March 1932)

**Above:** A P-26A of the 19th Pursuit Sqdn, 18th Pursuit Group, US Army Air Corps, photographed over Oahu on 6 March 1939. This Hawaii-based Group operated from Wheeler Field, retiring its P-26s in 1941.

At the beginning of the 'thirties, the biplane had been firmly entrenched as principal among fighter configurations since WWI, and the advent of the all-metal semi-monocoque low-wing monoplane was seen as little more than an aberration from the mainstream of fighter development. The Boeing fighter, flown on 20 March 1932 and designed under the leadership of C.N.Monteith, was one such.

When adopted by the US Army it was acclaimed as radical; barely three years later it was viewed as obsolescent. With anachronistic multiplicity of bracing wires, open cockpit and fixed undercarriage adopted to render palatable to the traditionalists the more advanced aspects of the fighter, the Boeing fighter was to be seen to represent no more than a brief inter-war transitional stage.

A private venture of which the three company-funded prototypes were eventually procured by the US Army as XP-26s (later Y1P-26s) on 15 June 1932, the Boeing fighter was ordered into production as the P-26A, entering service in 1934. The US Army procured 136, two of which were completed with fuel-injection engines as P-26Bs and 23 with provision for such engines as P-26Cs. Unofficially dubbed

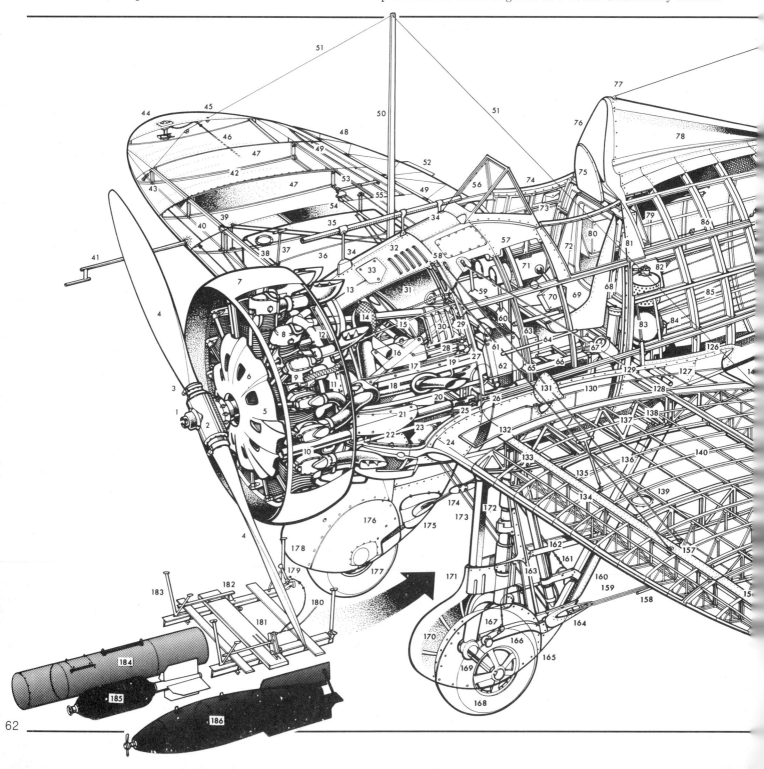

*Peashooter*, it was sturdy, responsive and manoeuvrable; less attractive foibles were an overly abrupt stall and a side-to-side rocking motion at speed on the ground.

## SPECIFICATION: P-26A

**Power Plant:** One Pratt & Whitney R-1340-27 Wasp nine-cylinder radial air-cooled engine rated at 600 hp at 2,200 rpm for take-off and 570 hp at 7,500 ft (2 285 m). Hamilton Standard ground-adjustable metal two-bladed propeller. Internal fuel capacity, 89 Imp gal (405 l), including 43 Imp gal (195 l) in two auxiliary wing tanks.

**Performance:** Max speed, 211 mph (339 km/h) at sea level, 226 mph (364 km/h) at 15,000 ft (4 570 m); max continuous cruise, 199 mph (320 km/h) at 7,500 ft (2 285 m); range (max internal fuel), 570 mls (917 km) at max cruise; initial climb, 2,360 ft/min (11,99 m/sec); time to 7,500 ft (2 285 m), 3·65 min, to 15,000 ft (4 570 m), 8·0 min; service ceiling, 27,400 ft (8 350 m).

**Weights:** Empty, 2,271 lb (1 030 kg); normal loaded, 3,012 lb (1 366 kg); max, 3,360 lb (1 524 kg).

**Dimensions:** Span, 27 ft 11⅝ in (8,52 m); length, 23 ft 7¼ in (7,19 m); height (tail down), 10 ft 5 in (3,17 m); wing area, 149·5 sq ft (13,88 m²).

**Armament:** Two 0·30-in (7,62-mm) Browning M-2 machine guns with 500 rpg (optional starboard alternative of 0·50-in/12, 7-mm M-1921 machine gun with 200 rounds).

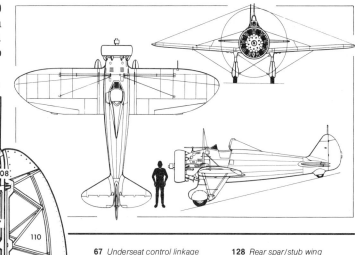

**Key to Boeing P-26A**

1 Starter dog
2 Propeller hub sleeve
3 Sleeve attachment
4 Two-blade propeller
5 Engine face plate
6 Cooling inlets
7 Engine cowling ring
8 Pratt & Whitney R-1340-27 Wasp engine
9 Cylinder heads
10 Gun barrel blast tube extension
11 Exhaust pipes
12 Engine bearer ring
13 Louvred exhaust stacks
14 Carburettor cold air intake
15 Engine bearer upper support struts
16 Starter primer access
17 Cowling panel fasteners
18 Hot air intake
19 Cockpit heater
20 Exhaust stub
21 Gun blast tube
22 Oil cooler
23 Lower panel access
24 Wingroot stub
25 Port gun barrel
26 Bulkhead/lower longeron attachment
27 Fuselage forward frame
28 Air intake/starter controls
29 Support strut attachment
30 Cooling louvres
31 Oil tank, capacity 8 US gal (30 l)
32 Upper louvres
33 Oil filler access
34 Gunsight tube supports
35 Tubular gunsight
36 Starboard wing fuel tank
37 Starboard landing wires support strut and brace
38 Fuel filler cap
39 Landing wires outboard attachment
40 Front spar
41 Pitot tube
42 Wing panelling
43 Aerial spring brace attachment
44 Starboard navigation lights (upper and lower surfaces)
45 Aerial lead-in
46 Electrical leads
47 Wing main rib stations
48 Starboard aileron
49 Aileron hinge points
50 Transmitter aerial mast
51 Aerials
52 Aileron tab
53 Aileron control linkage
54 Control rods
55 Rear landing wire
56 Windscreen panel
57 Main instrument panel
58 Landing wires/fuselage attachment points
59 Fuselage upper longeron
60 Lower instrument panel (fuel cocks and light switches)
61 Rudder pedal assembly
62 Ammunition loading access (magazines in cockpit floor)
63 Transmitter
64 Landing wires spacer
65 Ammunition feed
66 Port 0·30-in (7,62-mm) machine gun
67 Underseat control linkage
68 Seat support frame
69 Pilot's seat
70 Throttle quadrant
71 Maps and document holder
72 Hinged entry flap
73 Equipment pouch
74 Cockpit coaming
75 Pilot's headrest
76 Headrest fairing
77 Receiver aerial brace
78 Turnover structure
79 Wireless receiver
80 Bulkhead hatch (rear fuselage access)
81 Fuselage main frame
82 Access panel
83 Liquid oxygen vapouriser
84 Holding tray
85 Tail surface control cables
86 Receiver lead-in insulator
87 Abbreviated upper longeron
88 Fuselage frames
89 Rudder control cables
90 Elevator control cables
91 Elevator tab controls
92 Abbreviated lower longeron
93 Tailwheel control cables
94 Turnbuckles
95 Rear fuselage structure
96 Tailwheel control linkage
97 Elevator control runners
98 Fuselage aft main frame/tailplane support
99 Fin root fillet
100 Starboard elevator linkage
101 Starboard tailplane
102 Tailplane spar
103 Elevator outer hinge
104 Starboard elevator
105 Fin front spar
106 Tail identification light
107 Fin structure
108 Rudder upper hinge
109 Receiver aerial mast
110 Rudder inner frame
111 Rudder hinge
112 Elevator torque tube
113 Rudder post
114 Rudder control horns
115 Elevator tab
116 Port elevator
117 Elevator hinge
118 Tailplane structure
119 Elevator tab control linkage
120 Tailplane front spar/fuselage attachment
121 Tailwheel leg fairing
122 Tailwheel
123 Tailwheel leg
124 Tailwheel control runs
125 Fuselage skinnig
126 Wingroot fillet
127 Aileron control rod assembly
128 Rear spar/stub wing attachment
129 Fuselage angled main frame attachment
130 Fuselage main fuel tank
131 Fuel filler access
132 Front spar/stub wing attachment
133 Mainwheel leg attachment
134 Front spar
135 Landing wires support strut and brace
136 Undercarriage "V"-strut rear member
137 Stub wing structure
138 "V"-strut/rear spar attachment
139 Fuel filler cap
140 Port wing fuel tank
141 Rear spar
142 Transmitter aerial
143 Trailing edge ribs
144 Port aileron
145 Aileron tab
146 Aileron hinges
147 Aileron control linkages
148 Rear landing wire anchor point
149 Aileron control rods
150 Wing main rib stations
151 Outboard rib stations
152 Transmitter aerial lead-in
153 Port wingtip
154 Port navigation lights (upper and lower surfaces)
155 Wing structure
156 Front spar section
157 Landing wires anchor points
158 Flying wires brace
159 Outboard flying wires
160 Undercarriage trouser fairing
161 Brake cable assembly
162 Cross-brace member
163 "V"-strut front member
164 Flying wires attachment fairing
165 Wheel spat
166 Treadle
167 Brake arm
168 Port mainwheel
169 Axle
170 Spat inner frame
171 Spat/leg join
172 Mainwheel oleo leg
173 Inboard flying wires
174 Centre-line spacer
175 Starboard wheel fairing attachment
176 Spat panel
177 Starboard mainwheel
178 Under-fuselage bomb-rack installation, inc (items 179-183):
179 Arming handle
180 Bomb release wire (to cockpit)
181 Bomb-rack main member
182 Support frame
183 Forward sway braces
184 Possible loads inc (items 184-186):
185 30-lb (13,6 kg) practice bombs (five) or
186 100-lb (45-kg) bombs (two)

# Dewoitine D 500-510 (June 1932)

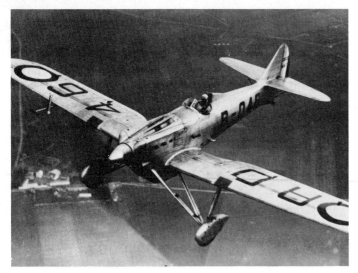

**Above:** The first production D 500 fighter which was flown for the first time at Francazal on 29 November 1934 — in fact, the second production airframe had flown 15 weeks earlier. It shed an aileron as a result of aileron flutter after delivery to Villacoublay, resulting in standardisation of mass balances.

Technical innovations initiated spontaneously and independently in two or more countries simultaneously are by no means unknown in aviation history, and the all-metal semi-monocoque low-wing fighter monoplane provides but one example. Such warplanes were evolving over a broadly parallel timescale in both France and the USA, but that conceived in the former country by Emile Dewoitine as the D 500 was, from certain aspects, the more advanced and was to place the French aircraft industry temporarily in the vanguard of international fighter development.

The American fighter, the P-26 (see page 62-63), was conceptually similar to the D 500 but antithetic in detail — the one portly and curvaceous and the other angularly rakish — and more conservative. Dewoitine was uncompromising in his effort to achieve the greatest practicable advance in the state of the art, whereas the Boeing team made concessions to the traditionalists. Both fighters employed flush-riveted metal-skinned semi-monocoque structures, but whereas the two-spar wing of the P-26 was braced by lift and drag wires, the single-spar wing of the D 500 was cantilevered and this feature represented a more

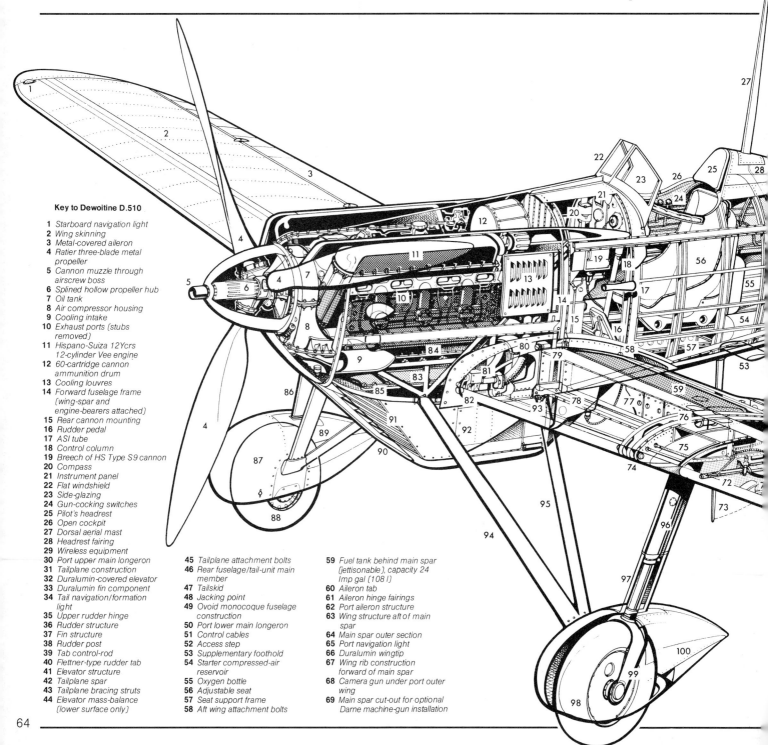

**Key to Dewoitine D.510**

1 Starboard navigation light
2 Wing skinning
3 Metal-covered aileron
4 Ratier three-blade metal propeller
5 Cannon muzzle through airscrew boss
6 Splined hollow propeller hub
7 Oil tank
8 Air compressor housing
9 Cooling intake
10 Exhaust ports (stubs removed)
11 Hispano-Suiza 12Ycrs 12-cylinder Vee engine
12 60-cartridge cannon ammunition drum
13 Cooling louvres
14 Forward fuselage frame (wing-spar and engine-bearers attached)
15 Rear cannon mounting
16 Rudder pedal
17 ASI tube
18 Control column
19 Breech of HS Type S9 cannon
20 Compass
21 Instrument panel
22 Flat windshield
23 Side-glazing
24 Gun-cocking switches
25 Pilot's headrest
26 Open cockpit
27 Dorsal aerial mast
28 Headrest fairing
29 Wireless equipment
30 Port upper main longeron
31 Tailplane construction
32 Duralumin-covered elevator
33 Duralumin fin component
34 Tail navigation/formation light
35 Upper rudder hinge
36 Rudder structure
37 Fin structure
38 Rudder post
39 Tab control-rod
40 Flettner-type rudder tab
41 Elevator structure
42 Tailplane spar
43 Tailplane bracing struts
44 Elevator mass-balance (lower surface only)

45 Tailplane attachment bolts
46 Rear fuselage/tail-unit main member
47 Tailskid
48 Jacking point
49 Ovoid monocoque fuselage construction
50 Port lower main longeron
51 Control cables
52 Access step
53 Supplementary foothold
54 Starter compressed-air reservoir
55 Oxygen bottle
56 Adjustable seat
57 Seat support frame
58 Aft wing attachment bolts

59 Fuel tank behind main spar (jettisonable), capacity 24 Imp gal (108 l)
60 Aileron tab
61 Aileron hinge fairings
62 Port aileron structure
63 Wing structure aft of main spar
64 Main spar outer section
65 Port navigation light
66 Duralumin wingtip
67 Wing rib construction forward of main spar
68 Camera gun under port outer wing
69 Main spar cut-out for optional Darne machine-gun installation

radical step forward in the evolution of fighter design.

Although conceived a year earlier than the Boeing fighter, the D 500 did not fly until three months later, on 18 June 1932. More stable than the fighters then serving the Armée de l'Air, it was, nevertheless, very manoeuvrable and well behaved under most circumstances. Like its Boeing contemporary it was to be criticised on the score of its high approach and landing speeds; it was also demanding in stick force for recovery from a spin due to a tendency towards control reversal resulting from elevator upfloat after spin entry.

The D 500 was committed to production on 23 November 1933, 100 being supplied to the Armée de l'Air, which also received 133 cannon-armed D 501s. Availability of the more powerful HS 12 Ycrs prompted replacement of the 690 hp HS 12 Xbrs in a D 500 airframe, this combination flying in August 1934 as the prototype D 510. Essentially similar to the D 501, apart from increased fuel capacity and modified undercarriage, the D 510 entered service with the Armée de l'Air mid-1935, the service receiving 88 of the 118 D 510s subsequently built.

## SPECIFICATION: D 510

**Power Plant:** One Hispano-Suiza 12 Ycrs 12-cylinder liquid-cooled vee engine rated at 760 hp at 2,400 rpm for take-off and 860 hp at 10,830 ft (3 300 m). Ratier 1239 ground-adjustable metal three-bladed propeller. Internal fuel capacity, 76 Imp gal (345 l).

**Performance:** Max speed, 205 mph (330 km/h) at sea level, 212 mph (341 km/h) at 3,280 ft (1 000 m), 230 mph (369 km/h) at 9,840 ft (3 000 m), 250 mph (402 km/h) at 16,405 ft (5 000 m) econ cruise, 199 mph (320 km/h) at 13,125 ft (4 000 m); range 435 mls (700 km) climb to 3,280 ft (1 000 m), 1·32 min, to 9,840 ft (3 000 m), 3·6 min, to 16,405 ft (5 000 m), 5·95 min; service ceiling, 34,450 ft (10 500 m).

**Weights:** Empty equipped, 3,142 lb (1 425 kg); normal loaded, 4,253 lb (1 929 kg).

**Dimensions:** Span, 39 ft 8 in (12,09 m); length, 26 ft 0⅔ in (7,94 m); height, 7 ft 11¼ in (2,42 m); wing area, 177·6 sq ft (16,50 m²).

**Armament:** One 20-mm Hispano-Suiza S9 (Oerlikon) cannon with 60 rounds and two 7,5-mm MAC modèle 34 machine guns with 300 rpg.

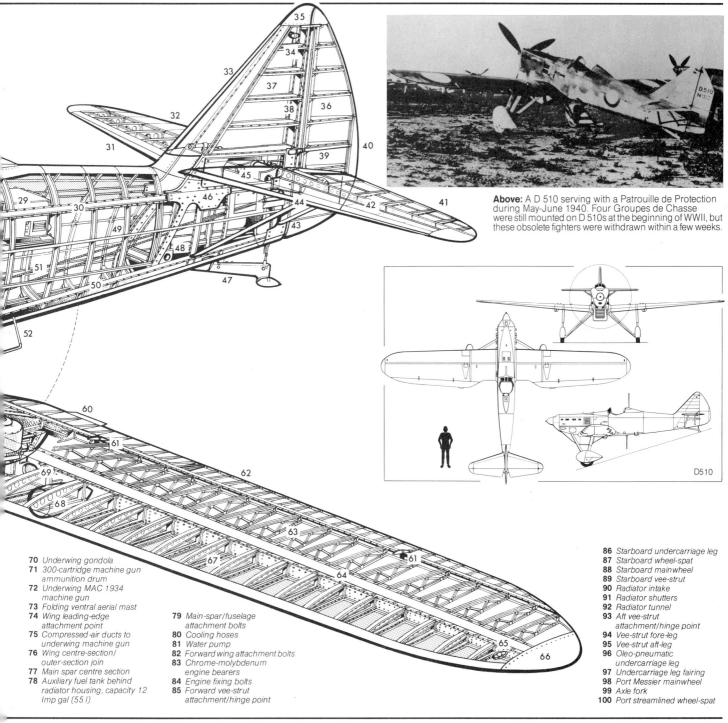

**Above:** A D 510 serving with a Patrouille de Protection during May-June 1940. Four Groupes de Chasse were still mounted on D 510s at the beginning of WWII, but these obsolete fighters were withdrawn within a few weeks.

D510

70 Underwing gondola
71 300-cartridge machine gun ammunition drum
72 Underwing MAC 1934 machine gun
73 Folding ventral aerial mast
74 Wing leading-edge attachment point
75 Compressed-air ducts to underwing machine gun
76 Wing centre-section/ outer-section join
77 Main spar centre section
78 Auxiliary fuel tank behind radiator housing, capacity 12 Imp gal (55 l)

79 Main-spar/fuselage attachment bolts
80 Cooling hoses
81 Water pump
82 Forward wing attachment bolts
83 Chrome-molybdenum engine bearers
84 Engine fixing bolts
85 Forward vee-strut attachment/hinge point

86 Starboard undercarriage leg
87 Starboard wheel-spat
88 Starboard mainwheel
89 Starboard vee-strut
90 Radiator intake
91 Radiator shutters
92 Radiator tunnel
93 Aft vee-strut attachment/hinge point
94 Vee-strut fore-leg
95 Vee-strut aft-leg
96 Oleo-pneumatic undercarriage leg
97 Undercarriage leg fairing
98 Port Messier mainwheel
99 Axle fork
100 Port streamlined wheel-spat

# Fiat CR.32 (April 1933)

**Above:** CR.32s of the XXIII Gruppo "Asso di Bastoni" during Spanish conflict.

The synthesis of a decade of continuous fighter evolution, its genus dating to 1923 and the debut of the CR.1, the CR.32 was a thoroughbred with a distinguished pedigree. Indisputably one of the truly outstanding fighters of the mid 'thirties, its success was in no small part responsible for the reluctance of the Regia Aeronautica to relinquish the biplane configuration for fighters and persistence in development of such long after they had become outmoded.

Of fabric-covered light alloy and steel construction and utilising the distinctive rigid interplane strutting arranged in the form of Warren trusses and inherited from the S.V.A. fighter of 1917, the Fiat CR.32 offered superlative manoeuvrability and extremely good diving characteristics. It excelled in the close-in, tight-manoeuvring, high-g style of combat, being a dogfighter *par excellence,* and when opposed by fighters armed with rifle-calibre machine guns, the longer-ranging 12,7-mm weapons of the CR.32 endowed the Italian warplane with an advantage. Perhaps its most outstanding virtue was its remarkable robustness, enabling it to withstand the roughest usage and absorb a high degree of battle damage yet remain airborne.

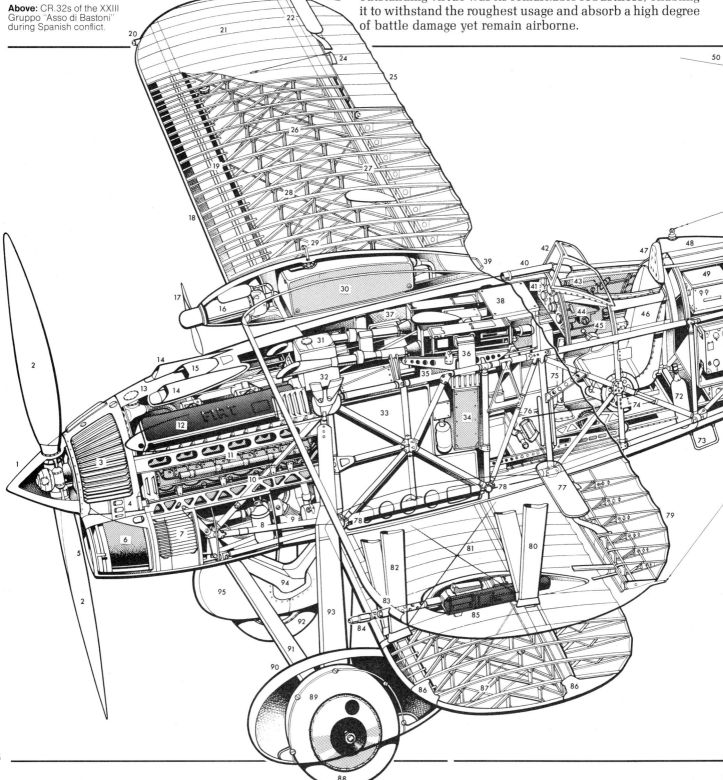

The CR.32 was first flown on 28 April 1933, and the initial batch (of 24) was exported to China where it made its combat debut, production of 282 of the initial model following between March 1934 and February 1936 for the Regia Aeronautica. A further 283 with two- replaced by four-gun armament were built as the CR.32bis for the Italian service, similar fighters being exported to Austria (45) and Hungary (52). The CR.32ter, of which 150 were built, reverted to twin-gun armament, but the fighter was badly afflicted with obsolescence by January 1938, when the definitive version, the CR.32quater entered production. Nevertheless, 337 were built for the Regia Aeronautica, plus five for Paraguay and nine for Venezuela, before production ended in May 1939, a total of 1,211 having been built, to which were to be added 100 licence-built (1940-43) in Spain.

The CR.32 was a thoroughly proven warplane when committed to combat over Spain from August 1936 as the vanguard of the Italian Aviación de el Tercio, 375 being sent of which 127 were flown by Spanish Nationalists and participated in every campaign of the conflict.

## SPECIFICATION: CR.32bis

**Power Plant:** One Fiat RA.30 R.A.bis 12-cylinder vee liquid-cooled engine rated at 800 hp at 2,900 rpm for take-off (for three minutes) and 600 hp at 9,840 ft (3 000 m). Two-bladed Fiat ground-adjustable metal propeller. Internal fuel capacity, 77 Imp gal (350 l), including 5·5 Imp gal (25 l) supplementary upper wing tank.

**Performance:** Max speed, 205 mph (330 km/h) at sea level, 217 mph (350 km/h) at 9,840 ft (3 000 m), 204 mph (329 km/h) at 16,405 ft (5 000 m); range, 485 mls (780 km) at 195 mph (314 km/h) at 15,750 ft (4 800 m); time to 3,280 ft (1 000 m), 1·46 min, to 9,840 ft (3 000 m), 5·5 min, to 16,405 ft (5 000 m), 11·43 min; service ceiling, 26,245 ft (8 000 m).

**Weights:** Empty equipped, 3,086 lb (1 400 kg); normal loaded, 4,343 lb (1 970 kg).

**Dimensions:** Span, 31 ft 1⅞ in (9,50 m); length, 24 ft 5⅓ in (7,45 m); height, 8 ft 7½ in (2,63 m); wing area, 237·89 sq ft (22,10 m²).

**Armament:** Two 12,7-mm Breda SAFAT machine guns with 350 rounds for each gun and two 7,7-mm Breda SAFAT machine guns.

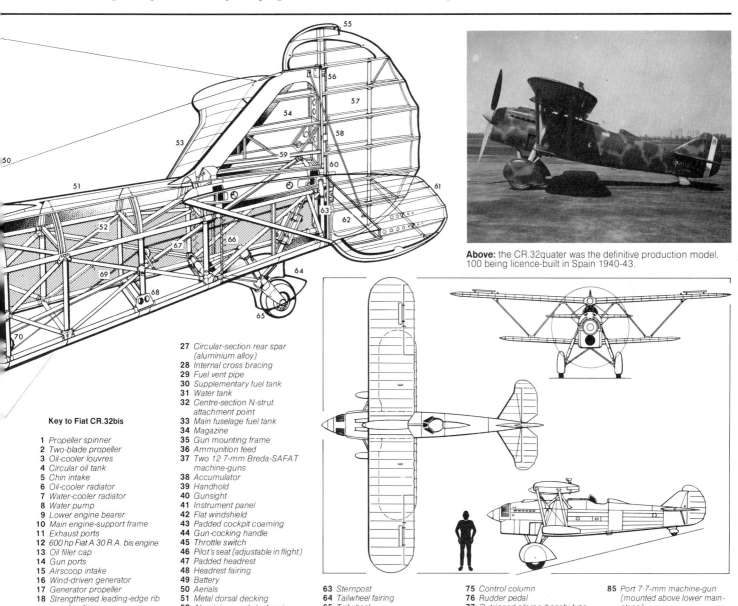

**Above:** the CR.32quater was the definitive production model, 100 being licence-built in Spain 1940-43.

**Key to Fiat CR.32bis**

1 Propeller spinner
2 Two-blade propeller
3 Oil-cooler louvres
4 Circular oil tank
5 Chin intake
6 Oil-cooler radiator
7 Water-cooler radiator
8 Water pump
9 Lower engine bearer
10 Main engine-support frame
11 Exhaust ports
12 600 hp Fiat A 30 R.A. bis engine
13 Oil filler cap
14 Gun ports
15 Airscoop intake
16 Wind-driven generator
17 Generator propeller
18 Strengthened leading-edge rib construction
19 Circular-section front spar (aluminium alloy)
20 Starboard navigation light
21 Wing skinning
22 Outrigged aileron 'Bench'-type balance
23 Aerial anchor point
24 Aileron control hinge
25 Starboard aileron
26 Aluminium square tube wing ribs
27 Circular-section rear spar (aluminium alloy)
28 Internal cross bracing
29 Fuel vent pipe
30 Supplementary fuel tank
31 Water tank
32 Centre-section N-strut attachment point
33 Main fuselage fuel tank
34 Magazine
35 Gun mounting frame
36 Ammunition feed
37 Two 12·7-mm Breda-SAFAT machine-guns
38 Accumulator
39 Handhold
40 Gunsight
41 Instrument panel
42 Flat windshield
43 Padded cockpit coaming
44 Gun-cocking handle
45 Throttle switch
46 Pilot's seat (adjustable in flight)
47 Padded headrest
48 Headrest fairing
49 Battery
50 Aerials
51 Metal dorsal decking
52 Aluminium and steel main fuselage framework
53 Starboard tailplane
54 Tailfin construction
55 Rear navigation light
56 Upper rudder hinge
57 Rudder construction
58 Tailplane bracing wire
59 Tailplane control linkage
60 Rudder post
61 Port elevator
62 Port tailplane
63 Sternpost
64 Tailwheel fairing
65 Tailwheel
66 Tailwheel spring
67 Tailplane control shroud
68 Lifting/jacking point
69 Rudder cable
70 Cable linkage
71 Radio equipment bay (or camera bay for photo-recce version)
72 Oxygen bottle
73 Fixed entry step
74 Tail-surface control wheel
75 Control column
76 Rudder pedal
77 Outrigged aileron 'bench'-type balance
78 Fuselage/lower mainplane attachment points
79 Aileron construction
80 Rear Warren-type interplane struts (cutaway)
81 Interplane strut cross-bracing
82 Forward Warren-type interplane struts (cutaway)
83 Port navigation light
84 Gun muzzle
85 Port 7·7-mm machine-gun (mounted above lower main-plane)
86 Wingtip strengthening plates
87 Lower mainplane construction (square-tube ribs)
88 Port mainwheel
89 Removable spat section
90 Large wheel spat
91 Mainwheel leg
92 Starboard mainwheel
93 Hydraulic shock-absorber strut
94 Mainwheel leg/spat attachment
95 Starboard spat

# Curtiss Model 68 Hawk III (May 1933)

By the mid 'thirties, the world's major air forces had, with but two or three noteworthy exceptions, accepted as inevitable the imminent demise of the biplane as a standard fighter configuration. Smaller air arms, conversely, were reluctant to embrace the less tractable and forgiving fighter monoplane, with the demands that it imposed in exchange for advanced speed and climb capabilities. An export market thus remained for high-performance fighter biplanes and pre-eminent in this field was the Hawk III, the synthesis of a decade of Hawk evolution with retractable main undercarriage members as a concession to modernity.

The appellation of Hawk had become effectively a generic name for the many single-seat fighting biplanes evolved from the basic design by William E. Gilmore and George Page, and what was to be considered a second generation in the Hawk series stemmed from the Hawk II demonstrator, which, flown early in 1932, had been purchased by the US Navy as the XF11C-2. Twenty-eight production examples had been ordered as F11C-2s, the fourth being completed with manually-retractable main undercarriage members and flown in May 1933 as the XF11C-3. Meanwhile, a second

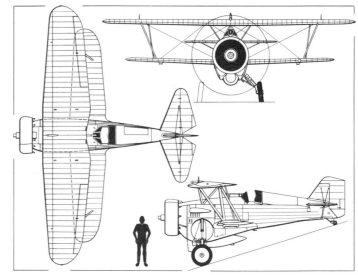

**Above:** Hawk IIIs of the Air Force of the Chinese Central Government. These provided the backbone of the Chinese fighter force opposing the Japanese during 1937-38.

### Key to Curtiss Hawk III

1 Starboard navigation light
2 Duralumin-framed aileron
3 Aileron push-pull actuating rod
4 Space for emergency flotation bag (optional)
5 Interplane strut attachment points
6 Built-up wood-truss wing ribs
7 Hollow-box section rear spar
8 Hollow-box section forward spar
9 Carry-over strut attachment points
10 Strengthened wing centre section
11 Aluminium alloy wire and strut attachments
12 Port interplane strut
13 Three-bladed Hamilton Standard controllable-pitch airscrew
14 Gun ports
15 Wright SR-1820-F53 Cyclone

nine-cylinder radial air-cooled engine
16 Machine gun barrel shroud
17 Exhaust stubs
18 Engine bearer ring
19 Welded tubular engine mounting frame
20 Forward fuselage frame
21 Cooling louvres
22 Cylindrical oil tank (7·5 Imp gal/34 l capacity)
23 Undercarriage retraction screw
24 Starboard synchronised 7,62-mm Colt-Browning machine gun
25 Forward lower fuel tank (46 Imp gal/209 l capacity)
26 Aft upper fuel tank (46 Imp gal/209 l capacity)
27 Undercarriage counter-balance
28 Fuel filler cap
29 Centre-section bracing struts
30 Telescopic sight

31 Flat windscreen
32 Shock-protected instrument panel
33 Starboard gun charger
34 Central console (static, radio battery and aircraft battery gauges)
35 Radio dial
36 Undercarriage retraction chain
37 Bracing-wire anchor points
38 Lower mainplane/fuselage attachment bolt
39 Rudder pedal
40 Auxiliary tank release lever
41 Bomb release lever
42 Fire extinguisher
43 Pilot's seat and safety straps
44 Undercarriage retraction crank
45 Wire brace
46 Leather-padded headrest
47 Interplane bracing struts
48 Corrugated aluminium sheet turtledeck
49 Canopy track (canopy optional)
50 "U" cross-section members

51 Seat brace
52 Rudder control chain
53 elevator truss tube
54 Welded tubular fuselage framework
55 Warning beacon
56 Tailfin bracing wire
57 Interplane 'N' struts
58 Aileron push-rod
59 Metal-frame tailfin structure
60 Metal rudder post
61 Rudder construction (metal framed)
62 Flettner trim tab
63 Metal-framed tailplane
64 Elevator control
65 Metal-framed elevator
66 Lower wingtip hand-holds
67 Tailwheel steel-spring shock-absorbers
68 Bell-crank fairing
69 Fully-swivelling solid-rubber tailwheel
70 Underwing bomb shackles
71 M3 100-lb (45,3-kg)

demolition bombs
72 Auxiliary fuel tank connection
73 Inspection covers
74 Auxiliary tank (41·6 Imp gal/189 l capacity) not carried with bombs
75 Mainwheel rail
76 Undercarriage retraction leg
77 Mainwheel shock-absorber strut
78 Removable wheel cover
79 Low-pressure mainwheel tyre
80 Undercarriage flap
81 Retracting 'Y'-member
82 Undercarriage-extension fairing frame
83 Ventral tunnel (bomb/tank attachment point)
84 Port undercarriage door
85 Auxiliary tank wind cowl
86 Brake cord
87 Brake arm
88 Port mainwheel
89 Mainwheel/leg pivot
90 Oil cooler intake

prototype in which metal supplanted the traditional Hawk wooden wing structure had been ordered as the XF11C-1.

The undercarriage system of the XF11C-3 and the metal wing of the XF11C-1 had then been combined with a raised aft turtle deck and a partial cockpit canopy to produce the BF2C-1. The delivery of 27 examples to the US Navy had begun on 7 October 1934, but it had soon been discovered that, at cruising rpm, the Cyclone engine set up a potentially disastrous sympathetic vibration with the metal wing structure, the problem proving insoluble and the BF2C-1s being hurriedly withdrawn from service.

Curtiss, reluctant to write off the development and anxious to offer an improved Hawk on the export market in which the Hawk II, equivalent of the F11C-2, had enjoyed much success, reverted to the wooden wing structure of the XF11C-3 and offered the retractable-gear fighter as the Hawk III. During 1935-38, 138 Hawk IIIs were exported, 102 of these to China (where 90 were assembled from kits), and with delivery of the last in June 1938, production of a truly classic fighter series came to an end.

## SPECIFICATION: Hawk III

**Power Plant:** One Wright SR-1820-F53 Cyclone nine-cylinder radial air-cooled engine rated at 785 hp at 2,200 rpm for take-off and 745 hp at 9,600 ft (2 925 m). Three-bladed ground-adjustable Hamilton Standard metal propeller. Internal fuel capacity, 92 Imp gal (418 l) with provision for 41·6 Imp gal (209 l) auxiliary tank.

**Performance:** Max speed, 202 mph (325 km/h) at sea level, 240 mph (387 km/h) at 11,500 ft (3 505 m); normal cruise, 204 mph (328 km/h) at 11,500 ft (3 505 m); range (internal fuel), 575 mls (925 km), (with auxiliary tank), 790 mls (1 270 km); initial climb, 2,200 ft/min (11,18 m/sec); time to 5,000 ft (1 525 m), 2·4 min; service ceiling, 25,800 ft (7 865 m).

**Weights:** Empty equipped, 3,213 lb (1 457 kg); normal loaded, 4,317 lb (1 958 kg); max, 4,645 lb (2 107 kg).

**Dimensions:** Span, 31 ft 5 in (9,58 m); length, 23 ft 5 in (7,14 m); height, 9 ft 9½ in (2,98 m); wing area, 262 sq ft (24,33 m²).

**Armament:** Two 0·30-in (7,62-mm) Colt-Browning machine guns with 600 rpg.

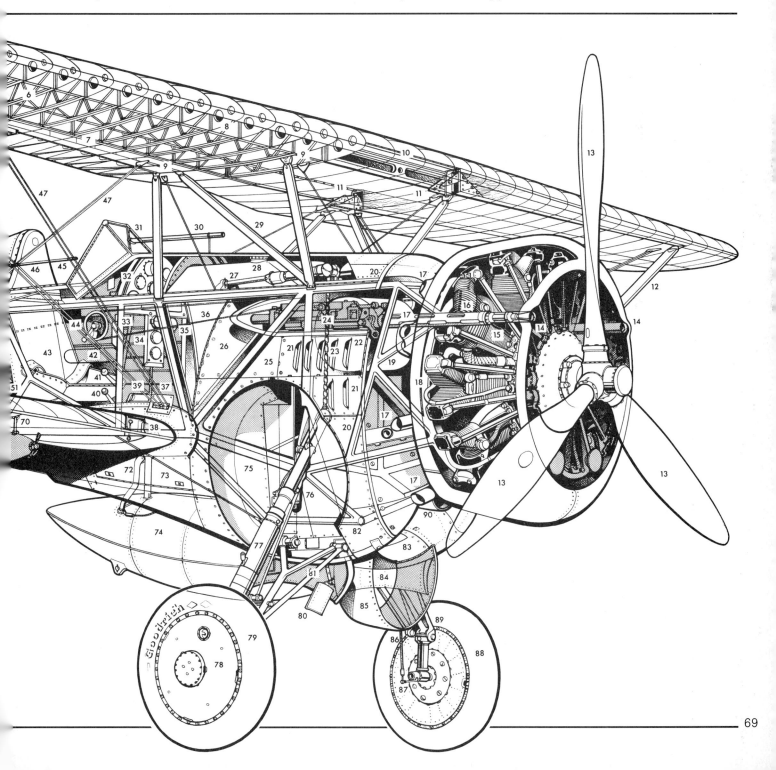

# Heinkel He 51 (Summer 1933)

Noteworthy in that it symbolised the renaissance of German military aviation rather than for any originality of concept or intrinsic capability, the He 51 was the warplane on which the Luftwaffe fighter element metaphorically cut its teeth. The first German aircraft to fire its guns in anger since WWI, the He 51 was a sturdy, thoroughly orthodox fighter displaying something of the elegance of line that the Günter brothers, Walter and Siegfried, were to make the indelible hallmark of mid to late 'thirties Heinkel aircraft. The He 51 was mettlesome and did not suffer fools gladly. Forward visibility in the three-point attitude was totally obscured and comparatively high training attrition resulted from an incipient bounce on landing.

A progressive development of the experimental He 49, the He 51 was the first post-WWI German fighter to be built in large numbers. An initial series of 150 was divided between Heinkel and Arado, with the first production He 51A-1 leaving the former's line in April 1935. Production switched to the minimally-modified He 51B-1 with twin-wire undercarriage bracing and shackles for an auxiliary tank, contracts being placed for a further 150 from Arado and 200 from Erla, with, as a direct result of the Spanish Civil War, yet 200 more being ordered from Fieseler.

The He 51 first saw combat over Spain in the late summer of 1936, flown by the so-called Jagdstaffel Eberhard which was to provide the nucleus of the Legion Condor. By late 1936, it was tacitly admitted that the He 51 was inferior in all respects to the opposing I-15 in the classic close-in high-g manoeuvring style of combat. It thus relinquished the air-air role from the late spring of 1937, those He 51s retained by the Legion being assigned the close air support mission, but most being transferred to the Spanish Nationalists for similar tasks. The final 100 Fieseler-built aircraft were intended primarily for Spanish close air support units, or Grupos de Cadena, and were fitted from the outset with racks for six 22-lb (10-kg) bombs as He 51Cs. Production was completed mid-1937, and a total of 135 He 51s was shipped to Spain. Forty-six completed as He 51B-2 twin-float fighters, but, as a type, the Heinkel biplane enjoyed a comparatively short first-line operational life, being relegated to the Jagdfliegerschulen in 1938.

**Left:** He 51B-1s of 3. Staffel of Jagdgeschwader 134 "Horst Wessel" at Werl, near Dortmund, in the summer of 1936, shortly before this JG converted to the Ar 68F. JG 134 was the first to receive the improved B-model.

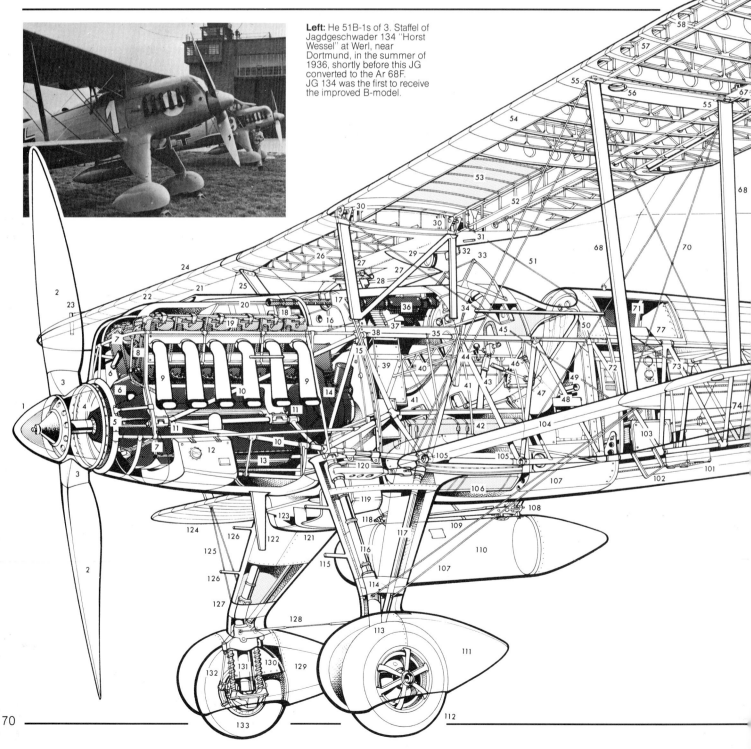

## SPECIFICATION: He 51B-1

**Power Plant:** One BMW VI 7,3Z 12-cylinder vee liquid-cooled engine rated at 750 hp at 1,700 rpm for take-off and having a normal rating of 550 hp at 1,530 rpm. Fixed-pitch two-bladed Schwarz wooden propeller. Internal fuel capacity, 46 Imp gal (210 l).

**Performance:** Max speed, 205 mph (330 km/h) at sea level, 193 mph (310 km/h) at 13,125 ft (4 000 m); range (85% max continuous power), 242 mls (390 km) at 174 mph (280 km/h) at sea level, 345 mls (570 km) at 162 mph (260 km/h) at 13,125 ft (4 000 m), 435 mls (700 km) at 137 mph (220 km/h) at 19,685 ft (6 000 m); time to 3,280 ft (1 000 m), 1·4 min, to 6,560 ft (2 000 m), 3·1 min; service ceiling, 25,260 ft (7 700 m).

**Weights:** Empty, 3,247 lb (1 473 kg); normal loaded, 4,189 lb (1 900 kg).

**Dimensions:** Span, 36 ft 1 in (11,00 m); length, 27 ft 6¾ in (8,40 m); height, 10 ft 6 in (3,20 m); wing area, 292·78 sq ft (27,20 m²).

**Armament:** Two synchronised 7,9-mm MG 17 machine guns in forward fuselage with 500 rpg.

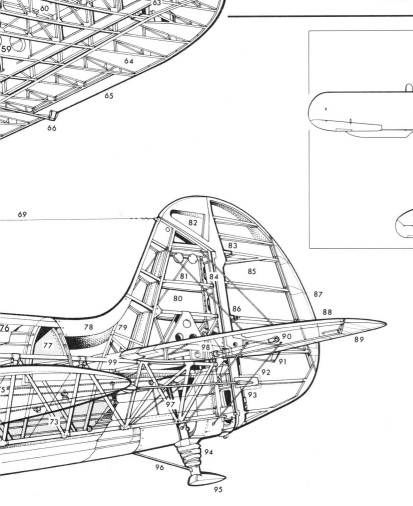

51 Interplane cross-bracing
52 Upper wing rear spar
53 Upper wing plywood decking
54 Plywood leading edge skin
55 Interplane strut upper attachment points
56 Adjustment access
57 Leading edge members
58 Upper wing front spar
59 Solid wing ribs (intermediate)
60 Lattice ribs
61 Port aerial mast
62 Rounded wingtip
63 Aileron outer hinge
64 Aileron structure
65 Flettner-type tab
66 Tab hinge
67 Tab control linkage
68 Interplane struts
69 Wireless aerial
70 Interplane strut bracing
71 Baggage compartment
72 Radio equipment
73 Welded steel-tube fuselage framework
74 Rudder control line
75 Elevator control lines
76 Fabric dorsal decking
77 Dural/wood dorsal frames
78 Fuselage/tailfin bracing
79 Tailfin leading edge frame
80 Tailfin structure
81 Tailplane bracing wires (upper)
82 Rudder balance
83 Rudder upper hinge
84 Rudder post
85 Rudder structure
86 Rudder centre hinge
87 Rudder tab
88 Port tailplane
89 Elevator balance
90 Elevator hinge rod
91 Elevator tab hinge
92 Tailplane bracing wires (lower)
93 Rudder hinge actuator
94 Leather cuff
95 Tailskid
96 Tailskid supporting strut

97 Tailskid shock absorber leg
98 Elevator control horns
99 One-piece carry-through tailplane
100 Fabric ventral covering
101 Battery
102 Entry step
103 Radio equipment
104 Port lower wing leading edge
105 Lower wing/fuselage attachment points
106 Fuel tank access cover plate (removed)
107 Lower bracing wires
108 Auxiliary tank rear shackles
109 Fuel line
110 Jettisonable auxiliary tank (37.4 Imp gal/170l capacity)
111 Port mainwheel fairing
112 Port mainwheel
113 Vertical leg section
114 Chrome-molybdenum cranked 'knee' section
115 Inspection/maintenance footholds
116 Mainwheel leg
117 Leg support strut
118 Auxiliary tank forward shackles
119 Radiator
120 Undercarriage fairing/ fuselage attachment plate
121 Ventral radiator bath
122 Airflow vane
123 Controllable shutter
124 Starboard lower wing skinning
125 Lower bracing wires
126 Inspection/maintenance footholds
127 Faired undercarriage legs
128 Twin-wire undercarriage bracing
129 Starboard mainwheel fairing
130 Springs
131 Hydraulic shock absorber dampers
132 Lubricant lead
133 Starboard mainwheel

**Key to Heinkel He 51B-1**

1 Propeller boss
2 Two-blade fixed-pitch wooden propeller
3 Propeller cuff fittings
4 Propeller shaft
5 Forward ring frame
6 Cowling face auxiliary intakes
7 Cowling framework
8 Fuel overflow pipe
9 S-section exhaust pipes
10 Engine bearers
11 Bearer attachment points
12 Oil tank
13 Coolant pump
14 Engine accessories
15 Bearer/bulkhead attachment
16 Fireproof bulkhead
17 Bulkhead cut-out for machine gun (port and starboard)

18 Protruding gun muzzle
19 BMW VI 7,3Z 12-cylinder liquid-cooled engine
20 Auxiliary starter tank
21 Upper intake
22 Front-hinged cowling decking
23 Starboard aerial mast
24 Starboard upper leading edge
25 Starboard centre-section N-struts
26 Centre section structure
27 Port centre section N-struts
28 Aileron control conduit and linkage (starboard side only)
29 Compass fairing
30 N-strut attachment points
31 Handholds
32 Rearview mirror
33 Three-piece windscreen

34 Padded cockpit coaming
35 Instrument panel (T-shaped)
36 Twin 7,9-mm MG 17 machine guns
37 Oxygen bottles (between machine guns)
38 Ammunition feed
39 Ammunition boxes (500 rpg)
40 Cross-section framework
41 Rudder pedals
42 Underfloor main fuel tank (46 Imp gal/210 l)
43 Control column
44 Elevator trim lever
45 Control yoke
46 Throttle lever
47 Pilot's seat
48 Recessed entry step/ handhold
49 Seat support bar
50 Hinged cockpit side flap

# Avia B.534 (August 1933)

When, in the second half of 1935, the B.534 began to enter the active inventory of the Czechoslovak air arm, it was widely acclaimed the finest fighting biplane in Continental Europe. Aerodynamically refined, with well-balanced contours and a finely-cowled engine, it established new standards in performance. Yet, within two years, it was to provide the unwitting means of demonstrating that the fighter biplane was manifestly *passé*. The venue for the demonstration was the 4th International Flying Meeting held at Zürich-Dübendorf between 23 July and 1 August 1937, where the B.534, the most-favoured contender, only achieved the placing of runner-up to the Bf 109 *monoplane* in all the important events!

Created by Ing František Novotný, the B.534 was, without doubt, a classic design and arguably carried the fighter biplane to its mid 'thirties zenith. Its genesis lay in the B.34, a fabric-covered all-metal biplane flown during the summer of 1932. While retaining the fundamental structure, the B.534, which flew as a prototype in August 1933, possessed little external resemblance to its progenitor, a second, even more refined prototype improving on an already advanced performance to establish a Czechoslovakian national speed record in April 1934.

Ordered into production on 17 July 1934, the B.534 was to be built in five series, each introducing equipment or aerodynamic refinements, to a total of 466 aircraft, including six for Greece and 14 for Yugoslavia, the definitive models being the Bk.534 (in which it was *intended* to displace two of the four 7,92-mm guns in favour of an engine-mounted 20-mm Oerlikon cannon—hence the prefix "k" for *kanón* —which proved unavailable) and B.534.IV (ie, *IV série*) with aft-sliding cockpit canopy and raised aft fuselage decking.

**Above:** A B.534.IV of the Slovakian Air Force on skis operating from Nitra in the winter of 1941. Three B.534-equipped Slovakian squadrons operated briefly on the Russian Front.

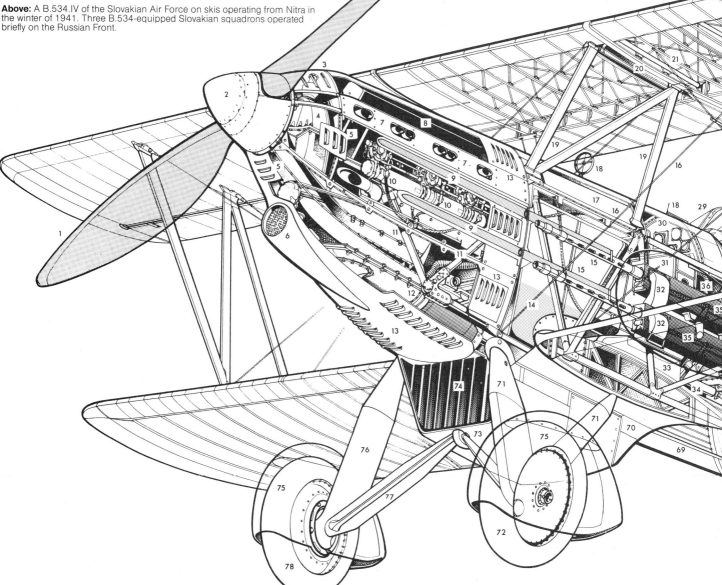

On 1 September 1938, a total of 272 Bk.534 and B.534 fighters were included in the Order of Battle, and when, six months later, the Czechoslovak Republic was dissolved, some 65 were taken by the new Slovak Air Force, 72 sold to Bulgaria and the remainder taken by the Luftwaffe.

## SPECIFICATION: B.534.IV
**Power Plant:** One Avia-built Hispano-Suiza 12Ydrs 12-cylinder vee liquid-cooled engine rated at 750 hp (for two min) at 2,400 rpm for take-off and 850 hp at 10,170 ft (3 100 m). Two-bladed fixed-pitch metal propeller. Internal fuel capacity, 76·3 Imp gal (347 l).
**Performance:** Max speed, 232 mph (375 km/h) at sea level, 245 mph (394 km/h) at 14,435 ft (4 400 m); max continuous cruise, 214 mph (345 km/h) at 14,435 ft (4 400 m); max range, 360 mls (580 km); initial climb, 2,953 ft/min (15,0 m/sec); time to 16,405 ft (5 000 m), 4·47 min; service ceiling, 34,775 ft (10 600 m).
**Weights:** Empty equipped, 3,219 lb (1 460 kg); normal loaded, 4,376 lb (1 985 kg); max, 4,674 lb (2 120 kg).
**Dimensions:** Span, 30 ft 10 in (9,40 m); length, 26 ft 10⅞ in (8,20 m); height, 10 ft 2 in (3,10 m); wing area, 253·6 sq ft (23,56 m²).
**Armament:** Four 7,92-mm Model 30 machine guns with 300 rpg and provision for six 44-lb (20-kg) bombs on wing racks.

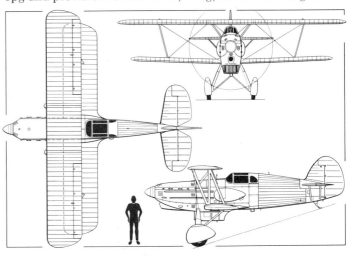

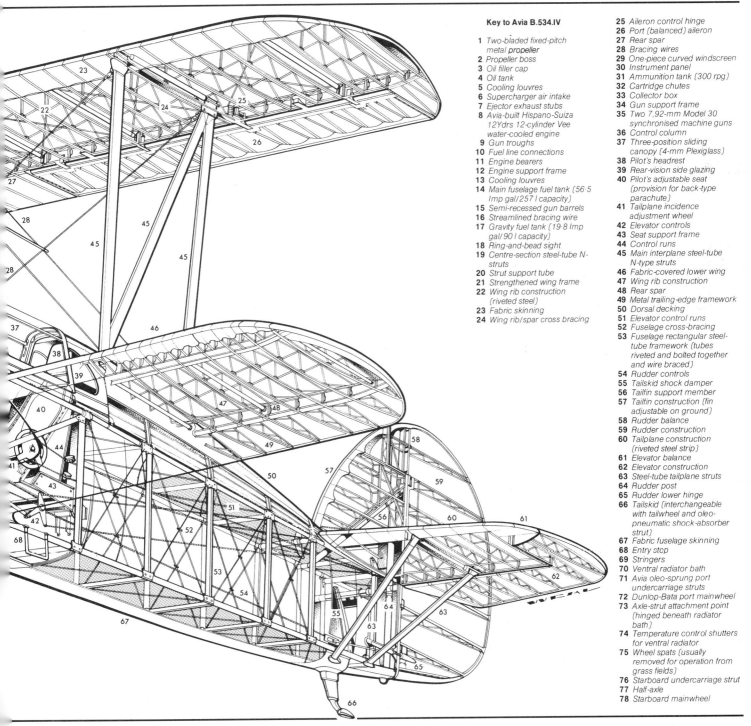

**Key to Avia B.534.IV**

1 Two-bladed fixed-pitch metal propeller
2 Propeller boss
3 Oil filler cap
4 Oil tank
5 Cooling louvres
6 Supercharger air intake
7 Ejector exhaust stubs
8 Avia-built Hispano-Suiza 12Ydrs 12-cylinder Vee water-cooled engine
9 Gun troughs
10 Fuel line connections
11 Engine bearers
12 Engine support frame
13 Cooling louvres
14 Main fuselage fuel tank (56·5 Imp gal/257 l capacity)
15 Semi-recessed gun barrels
16 Streamlined bracing wire
17 Gravity fuel tank (19·8 Imp gal/90 l capacity)
18 Ring-and-bead sight
19 Centre-section steel-tube N-struts
20 Strut support tube
21 Strengthened wing frame
22 Wing rib construction (riveted steel)
23 Fabric skinning
24 Wing rib/spar cross bracing
25 Aileron control hinge
26 Port (balanced) aileron
27 Rear spar
28 Bracing wires
29 One-piece curved windscreen
30 Instrument panel
31 Ammunition tank (300 rpg)
32 Cartridge chutes
33 Collector box
34 Gun support frame
35 Two 7,92-mm Model 30 synchronised machine guns
36 Control column
37 Three-position sliding canopy (4-mm Plexiglass)
38 Pilot's headrest
39 Rear-vision side glazing
40 Pilot's adjustable seat (provision for back-type parachute)
41 Tailplane incidence adjustment wheel
42 Elevator controls
43 Seat support frame
44 Control runs
45 Main interplane steel-tube N-type struts
46 Fabric-covered lower wing
47 Wing rib construction
48 Rear spar
49 Metal trailing-edge framework
50 Dorsal decking
51 Elevator control runs
52 Fuselage cross-bracing
53 Fuselage rectangular steel-tube framework (tubes riveted and bolted together and wire braced)
54 Rudder controls
55 Tailskid shock damper
56 Tailfin support member
57 Tailfin construction (fin adjustable on ground)
58 Rudder balance
59 Rudder construction
60 Tailplane construction (riveted steel strip)
61 Elevator balance
62 Elevator construction
63 Steel-tube tailplane struts
64 Rudder post
65 Rudder lower hinge
66 Tailskid (interchangeable with tailwheel and oleo-pneumatic shock-absorber strut)
67 Fabric fuselage skinning
68 Entry step
69 Stringers
70 Ventral radiator bath
71 Avia oleo-sprung port undercarriage struts
72 Dunlop-Bata port mainwheel
73 Axle-strut attachment point (hinged beneath radiator bath)
74 Temperature control shutters for ventral radiator
75 Wheel spats (usually removed for operation from grass fields)
76 Starboard undercarriage strut
77 Half-axle
78 Starboard mainwheel

# Polikarpov I-16 (December 1933)

Precursor of a new vogue in single-seat fighters in being the first cantilever monoplane with a retractable undercarriage to enter service, the I-16 briefly carried Soviet fighter development *ahead* of international standards. Its appearance was bizarre—its truncated fuselage, with ponderous, abbreviated nose seemed better suited for a biplane—but aspect notwithstanding, the I-16 represented a very real advance in the state of the fighter art.

Designed by Nikolai N. Polikarpov, the I-16 employed a primarily fabric-covered two-spar metal wing mated with a wooden monocoque fuselage. Split-type ailerons also fulfilled the function of landing flaps, the mainwheels were retracted by handcrank and the initial series featured a forward-sliding cockpit canopy, an item soon discarded. The first prototype (TsKB-12) was flown on 31 December 1933, and, as the I-16 Type 5, the fighter began to enter service early in 1935, making its combat debut over Spain in support of the Republican Government in November 1936.

If less suited than contemporary biplanes for close-in high-g manoeuvring combat, the I-16 was very manoeuvrable by the standards later established by

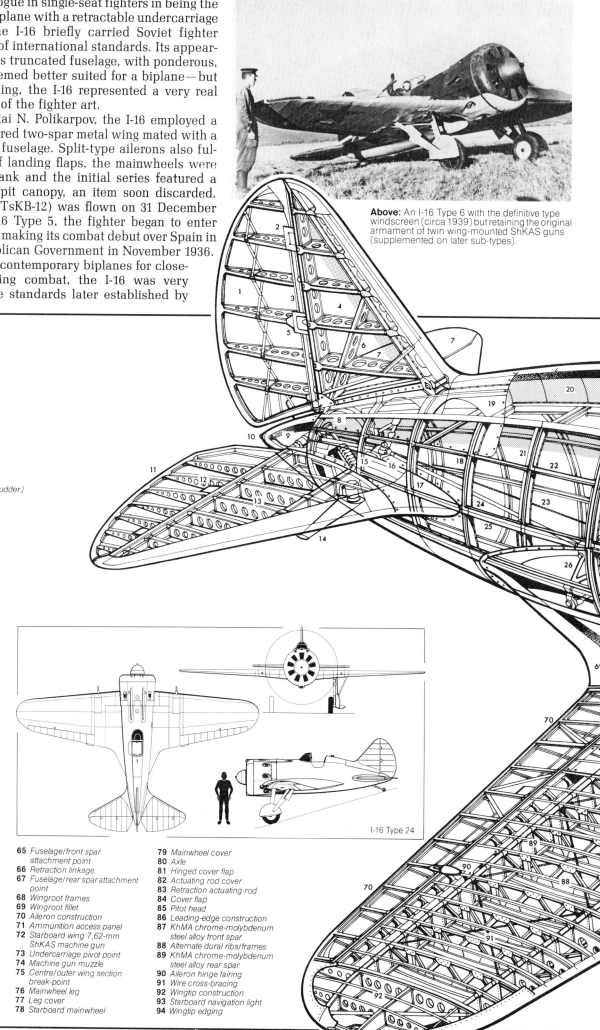

**Above:** An I-16 Type 6 with the definitive type windscreen (circa 1939) but retaining the original armament of twin wing-mounted ShKAS guns (supplemented on later sub-types).

I-16 Type 24

### Key to Polikarpov I-16 Type 10

1 Rudder construction
2 Rudder upper hinge
3 Rudder post
4 Fin construction
5 Rudder lower hinge
6 Fin auxiliary spar
7 Port tailplane
8 Rudder actuating mechanism
9 Tail cone
10 Rear navigation light
11 Elevator construction
12 Elevator hinge
13 Tailplane construction
14 Tailskid
15 Tailskid damper
16 Control linkage (elevator and rudder)
17 Tailplane fillet
18 Fuselage half frames
19 Fin root fairing
20 Dorsal decking
21 Fuselage monocoque construction
22 Main upper longeron
23 Rudder control cable
24 Elevator control rigid rod
25 Main lower longeron
26 Control linkage crank
27 Seat support frame
28 Pilot's seat
29 Headrest
30 Cockpit entry flap (port)
31 Open cockpit
32 Rear-view mirror (optional)
33 Curved one-piece windshield
34 Tubular gunsight (PBP-1 reflector sight optional)
35 Instrument panel
36 Undercarriage retraction handcrank
37 Control column
38 Rudder pedal
39 Fuselage fuel tank, capacity 56 Imp gal (255 l)
40 Fuel filler caps
41 Ammunition magazines
42 Machine-gun fairing
43 Split-type aileron (landing flap)
44 Aileron hinge fairing
45 Fabric wing covering
46 Port navigation light
47 Aluminium alloy leading-edge skin
48 Two-blade propeller
49 Conical spinner
50 Hucks-type starter dog
51 Hinged mainwheel cover
52 Port mainwheel
53 Lip intake
54 Adjustable (shuttered) cooling apertures
55 Propeller shaft support frame
56 Machine gun muzzles
57 750 hp M-25V radial engine
58 Oil tank
59 Starboard synchronized 7,62-mm ShKAS machine gun
60 Exhaust exit ports
61 Engine bearers
62 Firewall/bulkhead
63 Centre-section trussed-type spar carry-through
64 Wheel well

65 Fuselage/front spar attachment point
66 Retraction linkage
67 Fuselage/rear spar attachment point
68 Wingroot frames
69 Wingroot fillet
70 Aileron construction
71 Ammunition access panel
72 Starboard wing 7,62-mm ShKAS machine gun
73 Undercarriage pivot point
74 Machine gun muzzle
75 Centre/outer wing section break-point
76 Mainwheel leg
77 Leg cover
78 Starboard mainwheel

79 Mainwheel cover
80 Axle
81 Hinged cover flap
82 Actuating rod cover
83 Retraction actuating rod
84 Cover flap
85 Pitot head
86 Leading-edge construction
87 KhMA chrome-molybdenum steel alloy front spar
88 Alternate dural ribs/frames
89 KhMA chrome-molybdenum steel alloy rear spar
90 Aileron hinge fairing
91 Wire cross-bracing
92 Wingtip construction
93 Starboard navigation light
94 Wingtip edging

## SPECIFICATION: Gladiator II

**Power Plant:** One Bristol Mercury VIIIA or VIIIAS nine-cylinder radial air-cooled engine rated at 725 hp at 2,750 rpm for take-off and 830 hp at 14,500 ft (4 420 m). Fairey Reed three-blade fixed-pitch metal propeller. Internal fuel capacity, 84 Imp gal (382 l).

**Performance:** Max speed, 215 mph (346 km/h) at sea level, 226 mph (364 km/h) at 5,000 ft (1 525 m), 249 mph (400 km/h) at 10,000 ft (3 050 m), 257 mph (413 km/h) at 14,600 ft (4 450 m); range, 444 mls (714 km) at 225 mph (362 km/h) at 14,600 ft (4 450 m); initial climb, 2,430 ft/min (12,34 m/sec); time to 4,000 ft (1 220 m), 1·42 min, to 8,000 ft (2 440 m), 2·9 min, to 15,000 ft (4 570 m), 5·66 min.

**Weights:** Empty equipped, 3,847 lb (1 745 kg); normal loaded, 4,864 lb (2 206 kg).

**Dimensions:** Span, 32 ft 3 in (9,83 m); length, 27 ft 5 in (8,36 m); height (tail down and over propeller disc), 10 ft 7 in (3,22 m); wing area, 323 sq ft (30,01 m²).

**Armament:** Four 0·303-in (7,7-mm) BSA (Colt) Browning machine guns, with 600 rpg for fuselage-mounted pair and 400 rpg for wing-mounted pair.

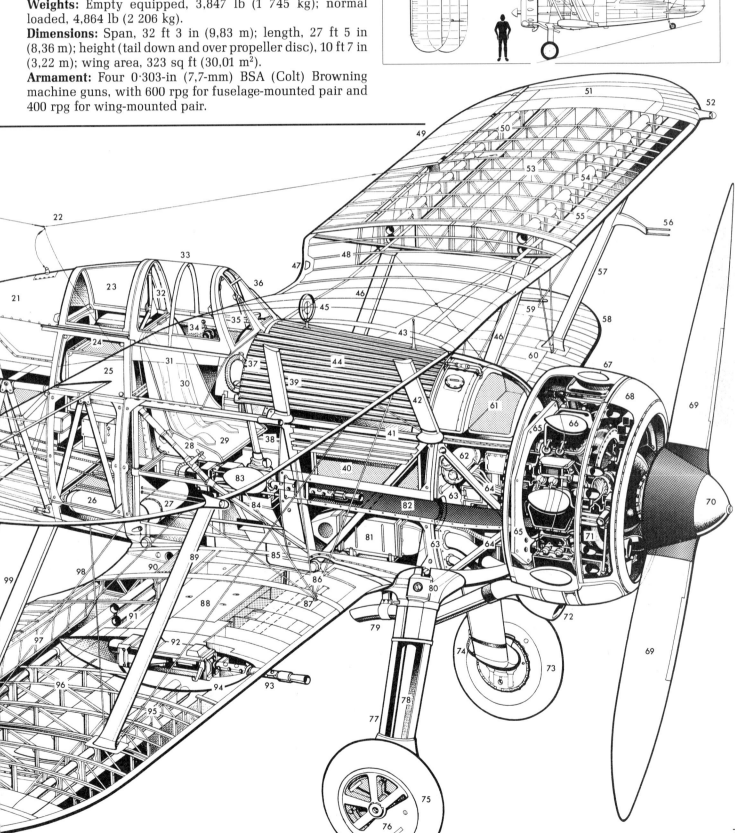

# Mitsubishi A5M (February 1935)

**Above:** An A5M2b of the Imperial Navy's 12th Kokutai flying in the vincinity of Hankow, China, in 1938. The A5M2 was first deployed operationally over China in September of the previous year and rapidly established aerial ascendancy.

Claiming the distinction of being the world's first service shipboard single-seat cantilever monoplane fighter, the A5M (or Type 96) did more than any aircraft to raise Japanese aeronautical design and manufacture to world standard. An attempt to translate the qualities of the biplane into terms of the monoplane, close-in dogfighting prowess still taking precedence in Japan over all other qualities, the A5M was radical insofar as was concerned carrier aviation and was arguably the most agile fighter monoplane ever built.

Designed by Jiro Horikoshi to the imaginative and singularly demanding requirements of a 9-Shi (1934) specification calling for a quantum performance advance, the A5M was aerodynamically very clean, had a comparatively light all-metal flush-riveted stressed-skin structure and was equipped with landing flaps. The first prototype (Ka-14) flew on 4 February 1935, production being initiated as the A5M1 in the following year on the basis of a revised second prototype, service debut taking place early 1937.

The A5M2a with uprated engine was the first model employed operationally, appearing over China in September 1937, and giving place to the A5M2b with three-bladed

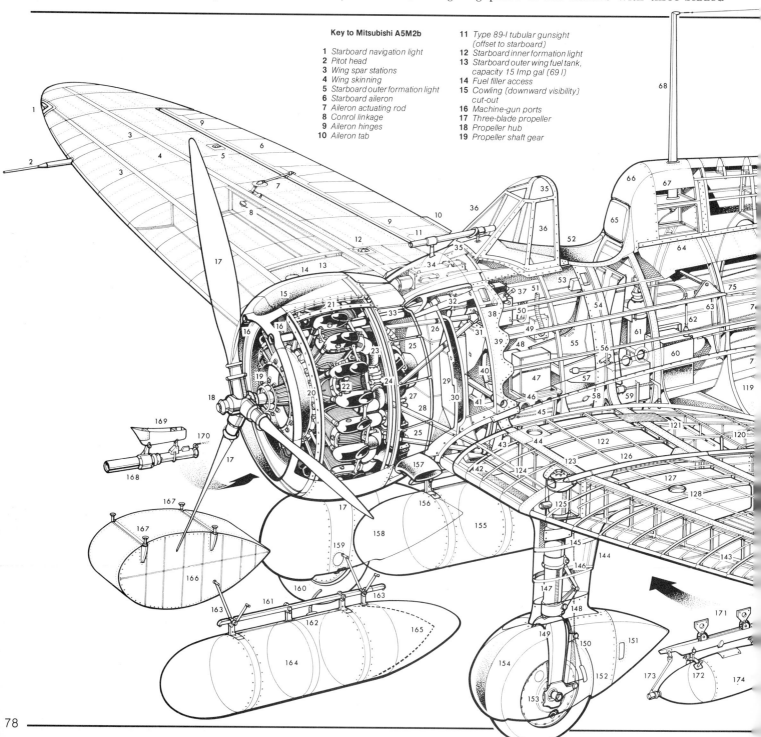

**Key to Mitsubishi A5M2b**

1 Starboard navigation light
2 Pitot head
3 Wing spar stations
4 Wing skinning
5 Starboard outer formation light
6 Starboard aileron
7 Aileron actuating rod
8 Conrol linkage
9 Aileron hinges
10 Aileron tab
11 Type 89-I tubular gunsight (offset to starboard)
12 Starboard inner formation light
13 Starboard outer wing fuel tank, capacity 15 Imp gal (69 l)
14 Fuel filler access
15 Cowling (downward visibility) cut-out
16 Machine-gun ports
17 Three-blade propeller
18 Propeller hub
19 Propeller shaft gear

propeller and (quickly discarded) cockpit canopy. The definitive version with further engine uprating, the A5M4, appeared in 1938, production continuing into 1941 to bring the total of single-seat models (excluding prototypes) to 982.

## SPECIFICATION: A5M4

**Power Plant:** One Nakajima Kotobuki 41 nine-cylinder radial air-cooled engine rated at 710 hp at 2,600 rpm for take-off and 785 hp at 9,845 ft (3 000 m). Three-blade SS-22 two-pitch (ground adjustable) metal propeller. Internal fuel capacity, 76 Imp gal (346 l), with provision for 35 Imp gal (160 l) or 46 Imp gal (210 l) auxiliary tank.

**Performance:** Max speed, 236 mph (380 km/h) at sea level, 248 mph (398 km/h) at 3,280 ft (1 000 m), 270 mph (434 km/h) at 9,845 ft (3 000 m); range (internal fuel), 500 mls (805 km) at 250 mph (402 km/h) at 9,845 ft (3 000 m), (with 35 Imp gal/160 l auxiliary tank), 746 mls (1 200 km); time to 9,845 ft (3 000 m), 3·58 minutes; service ceiling, 32,150 feet (9 800 metres).

**Weights:** Empty equipped, 2,681 lb (1 216 kg); normal loaded, 3,684 lb (1 671 kg); max, 3,763 lb (1 707 kg).

**Dimensions:** Span, 36 ft 1⅛ in (11,00 m); length 24 ft 9⅞ in (7,56 m); height, 10 ft 8¾ in (3,27 m); wing area, 191·6 sq ft (17,80 m²).

**Armament:** Two 7,7-mm Type 89 machine guns with 500 rpg and provision for two 66-lb (30-kg) bombs.

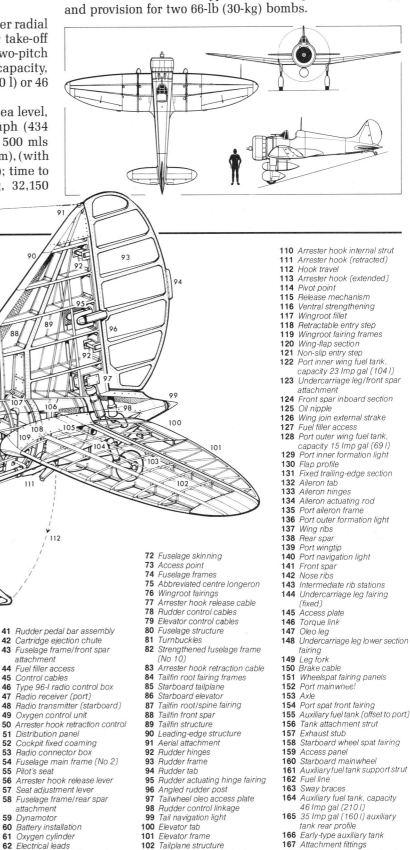

20 Cowling forward ring
21 Panel fasteners
22 Nakajima Kotobuki nine-cylinder radial engine
23 Exhaust pipes
24 Cowling frame
25 Cooling gills
26 Engine bearer upper supports
27 Engine accessories
28 Engine bearer lower supports
29 Ammunition magazines
30 Exhaust/cooling slot

31 Engine support/bulkhead upper attachment
32 Ammunition feed
33 Machine-gun barrel sleeve
34 Starboard 0·303-in (7·7-mm) Type 89 (Vickers) machine-gun
35 Windscreen frames

36 Flat panels
37 Port machine-gun charging mechanism
38 Fuselage forward main frame (No 1)
39 Fishtail external plating
40 Control column
41 Rudder pedal bar assembly
42 Cartridge ejection chute
43 Fuselage frame/front spar attachment
44 Fuel filler access
45 Control cables
46 Type 96-I radio control box
47 Radio receiver (port)
48 Radio transmitter (starboard)
49 Oxygen control unit
50 Arrester hook retraction control
51 Distribution panel
52 Cockpit fixed coaming
53 Radio connector box
54 Fuselage main frame (No 2)
55 Pilot's seat
56 Arrester hook release lever
57 Seat adjustment lever
58 Fuselage frame/rear spar attachment
59 Dynamotor
60 Battery installation
61 Oxygen cylinder
62 Electrical leads
63 Strengthened pick-up point
64 Fuselage upper longeron
65 Pilot's headrest
66 Turn-over frame fairing
67 Aerial lead-in
68 Aerial mast
69 Aerial
70 Dorsal spine
71 Spine former frames

72 Fuselage skinning
73 Access point
74 Fuselage frames
75 Abbreviated centre longeron
76 Wingroot fairings
77 Arrester hook release cable
78 Rudder control cables
79 Elevator control cables
80 Fuselage structure
81 Turnbuckles
82 Strengthened fuselage frame (No 10)
83 Arrester hook retraction cable
84 Tailfin root fairing frames
85 Starboard tailplane
86 Starboard elevator
87 Tailfin root/spine fairing
88 Tailfin front spar
89 Tailfin structure
90 Leading-edge structure
91 Aerial attachment
92 Rudder hinges
93 Rudder frame
94 Rudder tab
95 Rudder actuating hinge fairing
96 Angled rudder post
97 Fuselage oleo access plate
98 Rudder control linkage
99 Tail navigation light
100 Elevator tab
101 Elevator frame
102 Tailplane structure
103 Non-retractable tailwheel
104 Tailwheel leg fairing
105 Elevator torque tube
106 Fuselage aft frame
107 Arrester hook retraction cable guide
108 Fuselage frame/tailplane spar attachment
109 Centre brace

110 Arrester hook internal strut
111 Arrester hook (retracted)
112 Hook travel
113 Arrester hook (extended)
114 Pivot point
115 Release mechanism
116 Ventral strengthening
117 Wingroot fillet
118 Retractable entry step
119 Wingroot fairing frames
120 Wing-flap section
121 Non-slip entry step
122 Port inner wing fuel tank, capacity 23 Imp gal (104 l)
123 Undercarriage leg/front spar attachment
124 Front spar inboard section
125 Oil nipple
126 Wing join external strake
127 Fuel filler access
128 Port outer wing fuel tank, capacity 15 Imp gal (69 l)
129 Port inner formation light
130 Flap profile
131 Fixed trailing-edge section
132 Aileron tab
133 Aileron hinges
134 Aileron actuating rod
135 Port aileron frame
136 Port outer formation light
137 Wing ribs
138 Rear spar
139 Port wingtip
140 Port navigation light
141 Front spar
142 Nose ribs
143 Intermediate rib stations
144 Undercarriage leg fairing (fixed)
145 Access plate
146 Torque link
147 Oleo leg
148 Undercarriage leg lower section fairing
149 Leg fork
150 Brake cable
151 Wheelspat fairing panels
152 Port mainwheel
153 Axle
154 Port spat front fairing
155 Auxiliary fuel tank (offset to port)
156 Tank attachment strut
157 Exhaust stub
158 Starboard wheel spat fairing
159 Access panel
160 Starboard mainwheel
161 Auxiliary fuel tank support strut
162 Fuel line
163 Sway braces
164 Auxiliary fuel tank, capacity 46 Imp gal (210 l)
165 35 Imp gal (160 l) auxiliary tank rear profile
166 Early-type auxiliary tank
167 Attachment fittings
168 Camera gun (attached under inner starboard wing)
169 Attachment fairing
170 Operating cable (to cockpit)
171 Underwing (outboard of under-carriage leg) bomb-rack
172 Shackles
173 Arming mechanism
174 30 kg. underwing bomb load

# Grumman F3F (March 1935)

By a quirk of fate, carrier-based biplane fighter performance was to be carried to its ultimate by *force majeure* rather than intent; the aircraft to achieve the peak performance levels being the last of the barrel-like biplane progeny of Leroy Grumman and his associates of the youthful Grumman Aircraft Engineering Corporation. When the first of the genre, the F2F-1, had made its debut aboard the USS *Lexington* in February 1935, it carried US naval aviation a major step forward in fighter technology; when the definitive F3F-3 went aboard USS *Yorktown* in May 1939, it was an anachronism and was phased out of first line service in 1941.

The corpulent F2F-1 had introduced to the shipboard single-seat fighter such embellishments as a cockpit canopy and retractable undercarriage. It demonstrated an outstanding performance by contemporary standards, but the advances that it had betokened had extracted penalties in the form of poor directional stability and a tendency to wind-up in a spin. In an attempt to mate further performance enhancement with more acceptable handling characteristics, the basic design was aerodynamically refined and the fuselage marginally stretched, and as the XF3F-1, the modified aircraft flew on 20 March 1935.

Notably more manoeuvrable, with exceptional handling characteristics, very light stick forces and much improved directional stability, albeit retaining what were considered to be dangerous spinning traits, the refined model was ordered into production as the F3F-1, 54 being delivered in 1936. Replacement of the Twin Wasp Junior engine with the higher-powered Cyclone resulted in delivery of 81 F3F-2s from mid-1937: here manufacture of the shipboard fighter biplane for the US Navy and USMC *should* have ended.

In the event, the successful coalescence of nautical and aeronautical requirements in so far as the new generation of fighter monoplanes was concerned— an endeavour in which Japan had, incidentally, taken the vanguard with the A5M —was proving more time-consuming than had been anticipated. Thus, a further order was placed for the now conceptually obsolete Grumman biplane. This called for 27 F3F-3s embodying various drag-reducing refinements.

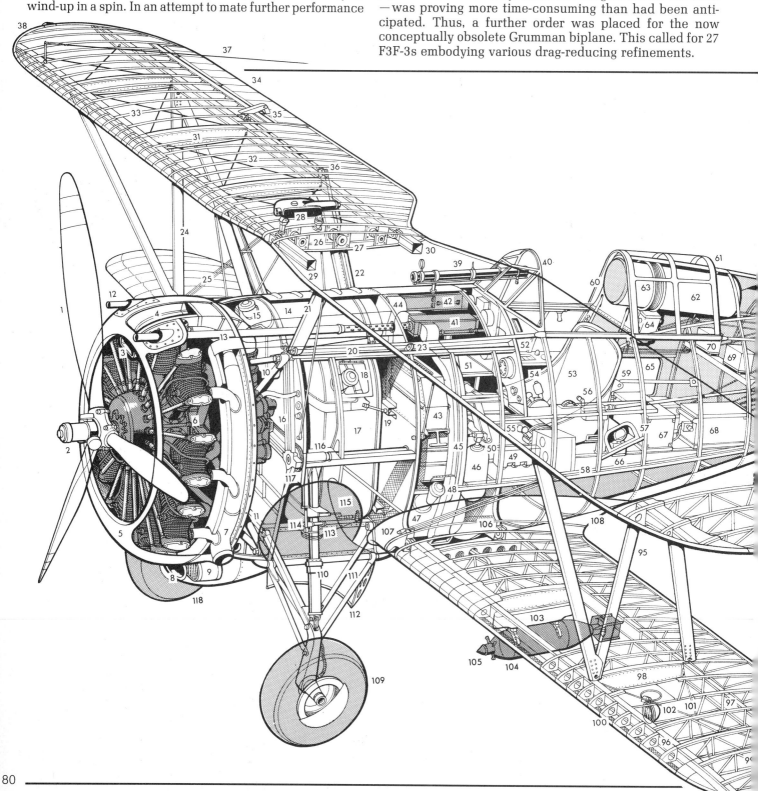

## SPECIFICATION: F3F-3

**Power Plant:** One Wright R-1820-22 Cyclone nine-cylinder radial air-cooled engine rated at 950 hp at 2,200 rpm for take-off and 750 hp at 15,200 ft (4 635 m). Three-blade Hamilton Standard metal controllable-pitch propeller. Internal fuel capacity, 108 Imp gal (492 l), including 39 Imp gal (178 l) reserve tank.

**Performance:** Max speed, 239 mph (384 km/h) at sea level, 264 mph (425 km/h) at 15,200 ft (4 635 m); normal range, 980 mls (1 577 km) at 128 mph (206 km/h), (with reserve tank), 1,150 mls (1 850 km); initial climb, 2,750 ft/min (13,97 m/sec); service ceiling, 33,200 ft (10 120 m).

**Weights:** Empty equipped, 3,285 lb (1 490 kg); normal loaded, 4,543 lb (2 061 kg); max, 4,795 lb (2 175 kg).

**Dimensions:** Span, 32 ft 0 in (9,75 m); length, 23 ft 0 in (7,01 m); height (propeller vertical), 9 ft 4 in (2,84 m); wing area, 260·6 sq ft (24,21 m²).

**Armament:** One 0·50-in (12,7-mm) Browning Mod 2 machine gun with 200 rounds and one 0·30-in (7,62-mm) Browning Mod 2 machine gun with 500 rounds. Provision for two 116-lb (52,6-kg) Mk IV bombs.

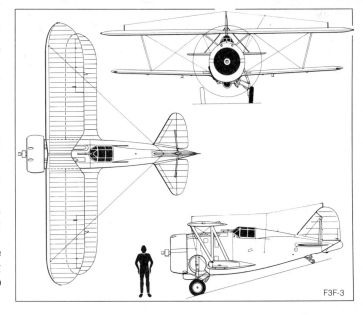

F3F-3

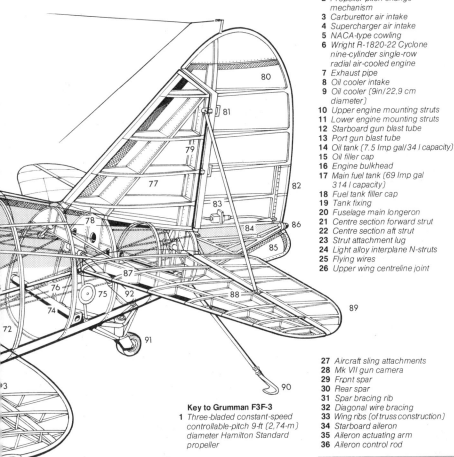

2 Propeller pitch change mechanism
3 Carburettor air intake
4 Supercharger air intake
5 NACA-type cowling
6 Wright R-1820-22 Cyclone nine-cylinder single-row radial air-cooled engine
7 Exhaust pipe
8 Oil cooler intake
9 Oil cooler (9in/22,9 cm diameter)
10 Upper engine mounting struts
11 Lower engine mounting struts
12 Starboard gun blast tube
13 Port gun blast tube
14 Oil tank (7.5 Imp gal/34 l capacity)
15 Oil filler cap
16 Engine bulkhead
17 Main fuel tank (69 Imp gal 314 l capacity)
18 Fuel tank filler cap
19 Tank fixing
20 Fuselage main longeron
21 Centre section forward strut
22 Centre section aft strut
23 Strut attachment lug
24 Light alloy interplane N-struts
25 Flying wires
26 Upper wing centreline joint

27 Aircraft sling attachments
28 Mk VII gun camera
29 Front spar
30 Rear spar
31 Spar bracing rib
32 Diagonal wire bracing
33 Wing ribs (of truss construction)
34 Starboard aileron
35 Aileron actuating arm
36 Aileron control rod

37 Aerial cable
38 Starboard navigation light
39 Mk III Mod 4 telescopic sight
40 Windscreen frame
41 Port 0·3-in (7,62-mm) Browning machine gun
42 Starboard 0·5-in (12,7-mm) Browning machine gun
43 Ammunition tanks (500 rounds 0·3-in/7,62-mm and 200 rounds 0·5-in/12,7-mm)
44 Ammunition feed chute
45 Cartridge case ejector chute
46 Pressure fire extinguisher
47 Auxiliary fuel tank (39 Imp gal/178 l capacity)
48 Auxiliary tank filler
49 Very pistol cartridge holder
50 Rudder pedal
51 Chartboard
52 Instrument panel
53 Pilot's seat
54 Throttle and propeller controls
55 Bomb release levers
56 Tailplane trim control
57 Access step
58 Cockpit floor structure
59 Adjustable seat support structure
60 Headrest
61 Aft-sliding canopy
62 Life raft
63 D/F loop
64 Junction Box
65 Equipment bay access door
66 Dynamotor unit
67 Radio transmitter
68 Radio receiver
69 First aid kit
70 Emergency rations and water supply
71 Dorsal light
72 Fuselage frames (Z section)
73 Tailplane incidence control rod
74 Lift/hoist tube
75 Controls access cover
76 Rudder and elevator control cables

77 Fin structure (solid section ribs)
78 Fin/fuselage attachment
79 Rudder post
80 Rudder structure (fabric covered)
81 Rudder hinge
82 Trim tab
83 Trim actuator
84 Tailcone
85 Arrestor hook fairing
86 Tail light
87 Variable-incidence tailplane
88 Tailplane structure
89 Elevator (fabric covered)
90 Arrestor hook (extended)
91 Retractable tailwheel (solid rubber tyre)
92 Tailwheel shock absorber strut
93 Port upper wing structure
94 Port navigation light
95 Interplane "N" struts
96 Lower wing front spar
97 Lower wing rear spar
98 Spar bracing rib
99 Wing ribs
100 Leading edge construction
101 Wire bracing
102 Retractable landing light
103 Mk XLI bomb rack
104 Mk IV 116-lb (52,7-kg) demolition bomb
105 Fuse unit
106 Wing spar root fitting
107 Flying wire attachment
108 Wing root fillet
109 Port mainwheel (26 in × 6 in/66 cm × 15 cm)
110 Oleo strut
111 Radius arms
112 Fairing door
113 Retraction strut
114 Lock actuator
115 Wheel well
116 Retraction strut axle mounting
117 Retraction chain drive
118 Starboard mainwheel

**Key to Grumman F3F-3**
1 Three-bladed constant-speed controllable-pitch 9-ft (2,74-m) diameter Hamilton Standard propeller

**Right:** An F3F-2 of VF-6 "Fighting Six" which was deployed aboard the USS *Enterprise* late 1937. The F3F-2 was the first version of the fighter to be powered by the Wright Cyclone engine and was essentially similar externally to the definitive F3F-3, apart from the revised engine cowling and forward fuselage decking, new windscreen and various more minor changes of the latter aimed at reducing drag on the later version of the fighter.

# Curtiss Hawk 75A (April 1935)

To claim for the Allies the first aerial victories of WWII in both European (when flown by the Armée de l'Air) and Pacific (flown by the USAF) conflicts, the Hawk 75A, alias P-36, had represented something of a watershed in US fighter development when flown as a prototype in mid-April 1935. Few fighters were ever to carry a wider diversity of national markings or demonstrate greater ubiquity.

Designed by Donovan Reese Berlin as the Curtiss contender in a US Army pursuit contest that, originally scheduled for May 1935, was to prove a positive catalyst in US fighter design, the new warplane owed nothing to the company's long experience with this combat aircraft category. Combining low-wing cantilever monoplane configuration with aluminium alloy semi-monocoque fuselage and multi-spar metal wing with flush-riveted smooth Alclad skinning, hydraulically-actuated split flaps and retractable undercarriage, and an aft-sliding cockpit canopy, Berlin's design represented an advance in the state of the art.

The combination of individual features was not, in itself, revolutionary—similar lines of development were being pursued contemporaneously in Europe—but was undeni-

ably audacious and resulted in a truly classic design which was arguably the most advanced fighter in the world at the time of its début. Withal, such was the fantastic tempo of fighter development in the second half of the 'thirties, that the Hawk 75A was to prove inferior in vital performance aspects to the majority of its antagonists. Offering superlative manoeuvrability, delightful handling characteristics and beautifully harmonised controls, it nevertheless lacked the climb-and-dive performance, acceleration and level speed to enable it to compete on even terms within two years of its service entry.

While the original contest was to be lost to the less advanced Seversky contender (see pages 90-91), the Curtiss fighter was the winner in the long run, with 227 being sold to the US Army as P-36s and a further 753 being exported as the Hawk 75A, the largest single recipient being the Armée de l'Air which ordered it with both two-row Pratt & Whitney Twin Wasp and single-row Wright Cyclone radial engines, those undelivered at the time of France's capitulation being inherited by Britain where they promptly received the appellation of Mohawk (Mohawk III with Pratt & Whitney

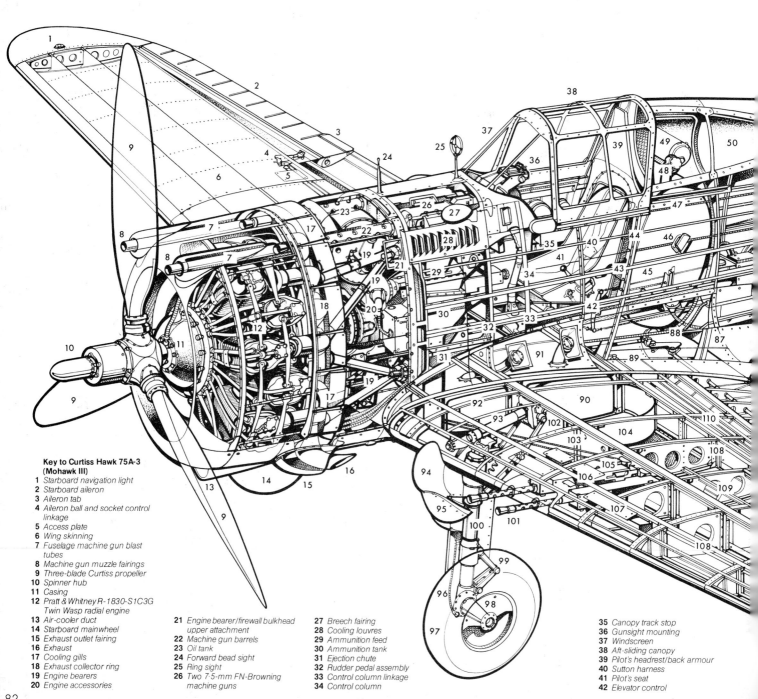

**Key to Curtiss Hawk 75A-3 (Mohawk III)**

1 Starboard navigation light
2 Starboard aileron
3 Aileron tab
4 Aileron ball and socket control linkage
5 Access plate
6 Wing skinning
7 Fuselage machine gun blast tubes
8 Machine gun muzzle fairings
9 Three-blade Curtiss propeller
10 Spinner hub
11 Casing
12 Pratt & Whitney R-1830-S1C3G Twin Wasp radial engine
13 Air-cooler duct
14 Starboard mainwheel
15 Exhaust outlet fairing
16 Exhaust
17 Cooling gills
18 Exhaust collector ring
19 Engine bearers
20 Engine accessories
21 Engine bearer/firewall bulkhead upper attachment
22 Machine gun barrels
23 Oil tank
24 Forward bead sight
25 Ring sight
26 Two 7·5-mm FN-Browning machine guns
27 Breech fairing
28 Cooling louvres
29 Ammunition feed
30 Ammunition tank
31 Ejection chute
32 Rudder pedal assembly
33 Control column linkage
34 Control column
35 Canopy track stop
36 Gunsight mounting
37 Windscreen
38 Aft-sliding canopy
39 Pilot's headrest/back armour
40 Sutton harness
41 Pilot's seat
42 Elevator control

Twin Wasp; Mohawk IV with Wright Cyclone), serving in the Middle East, India and Burma until the beginning of 1944.

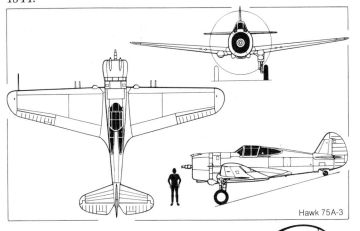

Hawk 75A-3

**SPECIFICATION: Hawk 75A-4 (Mohawk IV)**

**Power Plant:** One Wright GR-1820-G205A (R-1820-87) Cyclone nine-cylinder radial air-cooled engine rated at 1,200 hp at 2,500 rpm for take-off, 1,200 hp at 4,200 ft (1 280 m) and 1,000 hp at 14,200 ft (4 330 m). Three-blade constant-speed Curtiss propeller. Internal fuel capacity, 87 Imp gal (397 l), including 48 Imp gal (217 l) in optional fuselage tank.

**Performance:** Max speed, 323 mph (520 km/h) at 15,100 ft (4 600 m), 272 mph (438 km/h) at sea level; typical cruise, 262 mph (422 km/h) at 10,000 ft (3 050 m); normal range, 670 mls (1 078 km), (with fuselage tank), 1,010 mls (1 625 km); initial climb, 2,820 ft/min (14,32 m/sec); service ceiling, 32,700 ft (9 965 m).

**Weights:** Empty equipped, 4,541 lb (2 060 kg); normal loaded, 5,750 lb (2 608 kg).

**Dimensions:** Span, 37 ft 4 in (11,38 m); length, 28 ft 7¾ in (8,74 m); height, 9 ft 3 in (2,82 m); wing area, 236 sq ft (21,92 m²).

**Armament:** Six 7,5-mm FN-Browning Mle 38 machine guns with 600 rpg (fuselage) and 500 rpg (wing).

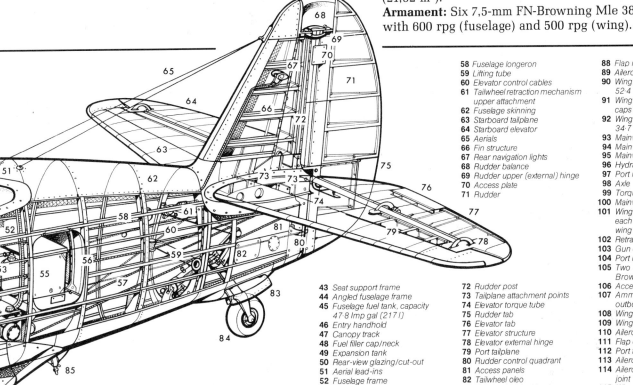

58 Fuselage longeron
59 Lifting tube
60 Elevator control cables
61 Tailwheel retraction mechanism upper attachment
62 Fuselage skinning
63 Starboard tailplane
64 Starboard elevator
65 Aerials
66 Fin structure
67 Rear navigation lights
68 Rudder balance
69 Rudder upper (external) hinge
70 Access plate
71 Rudder

43 Seat support frame
44 Angled fuselage frame
45 Fuselage fuel tank, capacity 47·8 Imp gal (217 l)
46 Entry handhold
47 Canopy track
48 Fuel filler cap/neck
49 Expansion tank
50 Rear-view glazing/cut-out
51 Aerial lead-ins
52 Fuselage frame
53 Hydraulic reservoir
54 Hydraulic pump
55 Radio equipment
56 Access/service panel
57 Rudder control cables

72 Rudder post
73 Tailplane attachment points
74 Elevator torque tube
75 Rudder tab
76 Elevator tab
77 Elevator structure
78 Elevator external hinge
79 Port tailplane
80 Rudder control quadrant
81 Access panels
82 Tailwheel oleo
83 Tailwheel fairing doors
84 Retractable tailwheel
85 Fuel vent/dump
86 Wingroot fairing
87 Former

88 Flap rod control link
89 Aileron control link
90 Wing aft fuel tank, capacity 52·4 Imp gal (2,39 l)
91 Wing centre section fuel filler caps
92 Wing forward fuel tank, capacity 34·7 Imp gal (1,58 l)
93 Mainwheel retraction cylinder
94 Mainwheel leg fairing
95 Mainwheel leg fairing door
96 Hydraulic brake line
97 Port mainwheel
98 Axle
99 Torque links
100 Mainwheel oleo
101 Wing machine gun barrels (one each wing in 75A-3, two each wing in 75A-4)
102 Retraction strut attachment
103 Gun charging cables
104 Port mainwheel well
105 Two 0·303-in (7,7-mm) Browning machine guns
106 Access panels
107 Ammunition bays (inboard/outboard)
108 Wing spars
109 Wing ribs
110 Aileron control rod
111 Flap control push rod rollers
112 Port flap structure
113 Aileron tab
114 Aileron control ball and socket joint
115 Wing skinning
116 Port aileron
117 Wingtip structure
118 Port navigation light
119 Pitot tube

**Right:** Hawk 75A-7s of the Royal Netherlands Indies Army Air Corps over Java mid-1941. These operated against the Japanese from Madioen between 21 December 1941 and 5 February 1942.

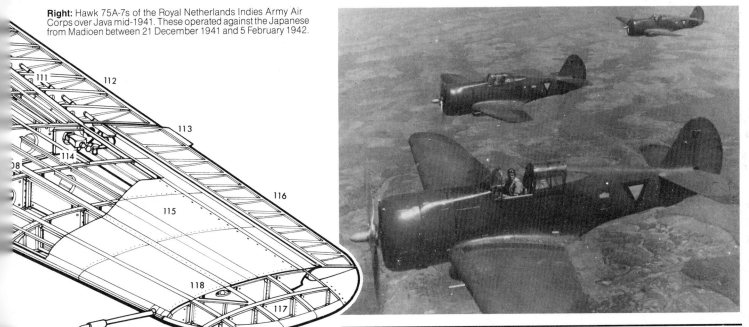

# Messerschmitt Bf 109 (May 1935)

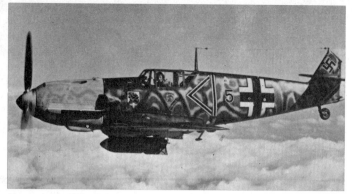

**Above:** A Bf 109E-4/B fighter-bomber of II Gruppe of Jagdgeschwader 54 flying over the Leningrad Sector of the Eastern Front in 1942.

When the first prototype Bf 109 commenced flight testing late in May 1935 as the first single-seat fighter to combine with the low-wing cantilever monoplane configuration a flush-riveted all-metal stressed-skin monocoque structure, a retractable undercarriage and an enclosed cockpit, it was evolutionary rather than revolutionary. Its features had all

been used individually by other aircraft but not previously combined in one airframe.

Willy Messerschmitt and his co-designer, Robert Lusser, took full advantage of the most advanced aerodynamics and structural techniques of the day; the result was an inspired creation. By comparison with its contemporary and future antagonist, the Spitfire (see pages 96-99), it possessed a much higher wing loading, but compensated for this to some extent by use of the then-radical combination of automatic leading-edge slots and slotted trailing-edge flaps; its creators had made no concessions to the traditionalists.

A well-conceived, soundly-designed fighter, the Bf 109 was to maintain in maturity the success that was to attend its infancy; its fundamental concept facilitating the introduction of progressively more powerful engines and armament enabling it to stay in the forefront of its class for three-quarters of the decade that witnessed the most dramatic increase in the tempo of fighter evolution.

The first prototype, the Bf 109 V1, was powered by a Rolls-Royce Kestrel V engine; the V2 and V3, flown in January and June 1936 respectively, had the Jumo 210, retained for the Bf

continued on page 86 ▶

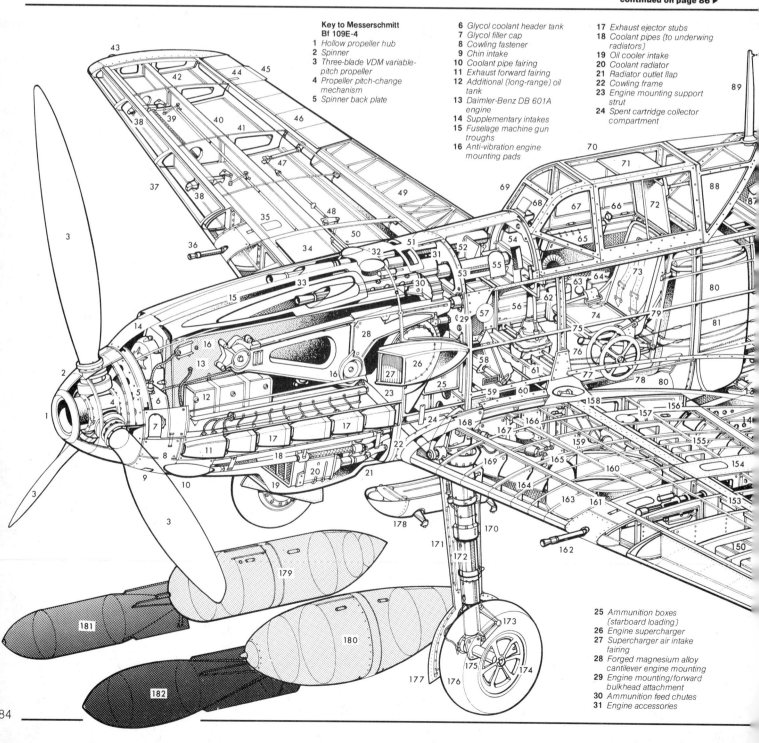

**Key to Messerschmitt Bf 109E-4**
1. Hollow propeller hub
2. Spinner
3. Three-blade VDM variable-pitch propeller
4. Propeller pitch-change mechanism
5. Spinner back plate
6. Glycol coolant header tank
7. Glycol filler cap
8. Cowling fastener
9. Chin intake
10. Coolant pipe fairing
11. Exhaust forward fairing
12. Additional (long-range) oil tank
13. Daimler-Benz DB 601A engine
14. Supplementary intakes
15. Fuselage machine gun troughs
16. Anti-vibration engine mounting pads
17. Exhaust ejector stubs
18. Coolant pipes (to underwing radiators)
19. Oil cooler intake
20. Coolant radiator
21. Radiator outlet flap
22. Cowling frame
23. Engine mounting support strut
24. Spent cartridge collector compartment
25. Ammunition boxes (starboard loading)
26. Engine supercharger
27. Supercharger air intake fairing
28. Forged magnesium alloy cantilever engine mounting
29. Engine mounting/forward bulkhead attachment
30. Ammunition feed chutes
31. Engine accessories

## SPECIFICATION: Bf 109E-3

**Power Plant:** One Daimler-Benz DB 601Aa 12-cylinder inverted-vee liquid-cooled engine rated at 1,175 hp at 2,480 rpm for take-off and 990 hp at 12,140 ft (3 700 m). Three-blade VDM constant-speed metal propeller. Internal fuel capacity, 88 Imp gal (400 l).

**Performance:** Max speed, 290 mph (467 km/h) at sea level, 307 mph (494 km/h) at 3,280 ft (1 000 m), 348 mph (560 km/h) at 14,560 ft (4 440 m); max cruise, 300 mph (483 km/h) at 13,120 ft (4 000 m); range cruise, 210 mph (338 km/h) at 6,560 ft (2 000 m); max range, 410 mls (660 km); initial climb (at 5,400 lb/2 450 kg), 3,280 ft/min (16.66 m /sec); time to 9,840 ft (3 000 m), 3·6 min, to 19,685 ft (6 000 m), 7·75 min; service ceiling, 34,450 ft (10 500 m).

**Weights:** Empty, 4,189 lb (1 900 kg); empty equipped, 4,685 lb (2 125 kg); loaded, 5,875 lb (2 665 kg).

**Dimensions:** Span, 32 ft 4½ in (9,87 m); length 28 ft 4½ in (8,64 m); height, 8 ft 2¹/₃ in (23,50 m); wing area, 174·05 sq ft.

**Armament:** Two 20-mm MG FF (Oerlikon) cannon with 60 rpg and two 7,9-mm Rheinmetall Borsig MG 17 machine guns with 1,000 rpg.

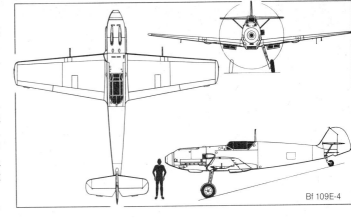

Bf 109E-4

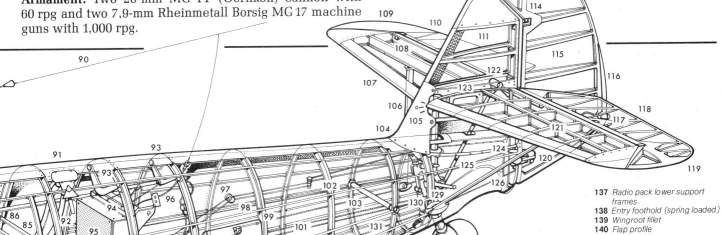

32 Two fuselage-mounted MG-17 machine guns
33 Blast tube muzzles
34 Wing skinning
35 Starboard cannon access
36 20-mm MG FF wing cannon
37 Leading-edge automatic slot
38 Slot tracks
39 Slot actuating linkage
40 Wing main spar
41 Intermediate rib station
42 Wing end rib
43 Starboard navigation light
44 Aileron outer hinge
45 Aileron metal trim tab
46 Starboard aileron
47 Aileron/flap link connection
48 Combined control linkage
49 Starboard flap frame
50 Cannon ammunition drum access
51 Fuselage machine gun cooling slots
52 Gun mounting frame
53 Firewall/bulkhead
54 Instrument panel near face (fabric covered)
55 Oil dipstick cover
56 Control column

57 Oil filler cap (tank omitted for clarity)
58 Rudder pedal assembly
59 Aircraft identity data plate (external)
60 Main spar centre-section carry-through
61 Underfloor control linkage
62 Oxygen regulator
63 Harness adjustment lever
64 Engine priming pump
65 Circuit breaker panel
66 Hood catch
67 Starboard hinged cockpit canopy
68 Revi gunsight (offset to starboard)
69 Windscreen panel frame
70 Canopy section frame
71 Pilot's head armour
72 Pilot's back armour
73 Seat harness
74 Pilot's seat
75 Seat adjustment lever
76 Tailplane incidence handwheel
77 Cockpit floor diaphragm
78 Landing flaps control handwheel
79 Seat support frame
80 Contoured ("L"-shape) fuel tank
81 Tailplane incidence cables
82 Fuselage frame
83 Rudder cable
84 Oxygen cylinders (2)
85 Fuel filler/overspill pipes
86 Baggage compartment
87 Entry handhold (spring loaded)
88 Canopy fixed aft section
89 Aerial mast
90 Aerial
91 Fuel filler cap
92 Fuel vent line
93 Radio pack support brackets
94 Anti-vibration bungee supports

95 FuG VII transmitter/receiver radio pack.
96 Aerial lead-in
97 Tailplane incidence cable pulley
98 Rudder control cable
99 Monocoque fuselage structure
100 Radio access/first aid kit panel
101 Elevator control cables
102 Fuselage frame
103 Lifting tube
104 Tailfin root fillet
105 Tailplane incidence gauge (external)
106 Tailplane support strut
107 Starboard tailplane
108 Elevator outer-hinge
109 Elevator balance
110 Starboard elevator
111 Tailfin structure
112 Aerial stub
113 Rudder balance
114 Rudder upper hinge
115 Rudder frame
116 Rudder trim tab
117 Tail navigation light
118 Port elevator frame
119 Elevator balance
120 Rudder control quadrant
121 Tailplane structure
122 Elevator torque tube sleeve
123 Tailplane end rib attachment
124 Fuselage end post
125 Elevator control rod
126 Port tailplane support strut
127 Non-retractable tailwheel
128 Tailwheel leg
129 Elevator control cable/rod link
130 Tailwheel leg shock-absorber
131 Rudder control cable
132 Fuselage stringer
133 Accumulator
134 Fuselage half ventral join
135 Electrical leads
136 Fuselage panels

137 Radio pack lower support frames
138 Entry foothold (spring loaded)
139 Wingroot fillet
140 Flap profile
141 Port flap frame
142 Port aileron frame
143 Aileron metal trim tab
144 Rear spar
145 Port wingtip
146 Port navigation light
147 Wing main spar outer section
148 Solid ribs
149 Leading-edge automatic slot
150 Rib cut-outs
151 Control link access plate
152 Wing rib stations
153 Port wing 20-mm MG FF cannon installation
154 Ammunition drum access panel
155 Inboard rib cut-outs
156 Flap visual position indicator
157 Control access panel
158 Main spar/fuselage attachment fairing
159 Wing control surface cable pulleys
160 Port mainwheel well
161 Wheel well (zipped) fabric shield
162 20-mm MG FF wing cannon
163 Wing front spar
164 Undercarriage leg tunnel rib cut-outs
165 Undercarriage lock mechanism
166 Wing/fuselage end rib
167 Undercarriage actuating cylinder
168 Mainwheel leg/fuselage attachment bracket
169 Leg pivot point
170 Mainwheel oleo leg
171 Mainwheel leg door
172 Brake lines
173 Torque links
174 Mainwheel hub
175 Axle
176 Port mainwheel
177 Mainwheel half-door
178 Ventral ETC centre-line stores pylon, possible loads inc:
179 Early-type (wooden) drop tank
180 66 Imp gal (300 l) (Junkers) metal drop tank
181 551-lb (250-kg) HE bomb, or
182 551-lb (250-kg) SAP bomb

# Messerschmitt Bf 109

cont ▶ 109B, C and D series. The first Bf 109Bs left the assembly lines in February 1937 and by March were in Spain with the Legion Condor, establishing an enviable reputation. Late in 1938 the Bf 109E entered service, mating the basic airframe with the more powerful DB 601 engine and, as the Bf 109E-3, introducing wing-mounted cannon armament.

The Bf 109E offered excellent handling characteristics and response at low and medium speeds, a good low-speed climb angle and a gentle stall without any tendency to spin. Climb and dive were second to none, but the controls heavied up with speed, and manoeuvrability was found wanting in the "Battle of Britain", this epic conflict having a salutary effect on the Messerschmitt fighter's evolution. Aerodynamic refinement and an uprated engine characterised the Bf 109F, which appeared operationally spring 1941, and carried, according to some Luftwaffe pilots, the basic design to the zenith of its development cycle, higher weight and power loadings thereafter being accompanied by progressive deterioration of handling qualities and manoeuvrability, although, by consensus, these were considered acceptable penalties in exchange for higher speeds and increased versatility.

A significant further stage in this weight escalation was provided by the DB 605-powered Bf 109G, which achieved operational status in the spring of 1942, and was to be built in infinitely larger numbers than any other Bf 109 sub-type. Built in multifarious forms, the immense differences between late models, such as the Bf 109G-14 of early 1944, and the Bf 109E-4 of mid-1940, dramatically reflected the changing demands of the air war. In September 1944, as the war in Europe drew to its close, the ultimate production variant of the Messerschmitt fighter made its appearance. This, the Bf 109K, employed the very much more powerful DB 605D series engine and incorporated all the progressive developments introduced piecemeal by Bf 109G versions.

Built in larger numbers than any other combat aeroplane before or since and employed on every front to which the Luftwaffe was committed, the Bf 109 was an extraordinarily durable warplane and a true classic.

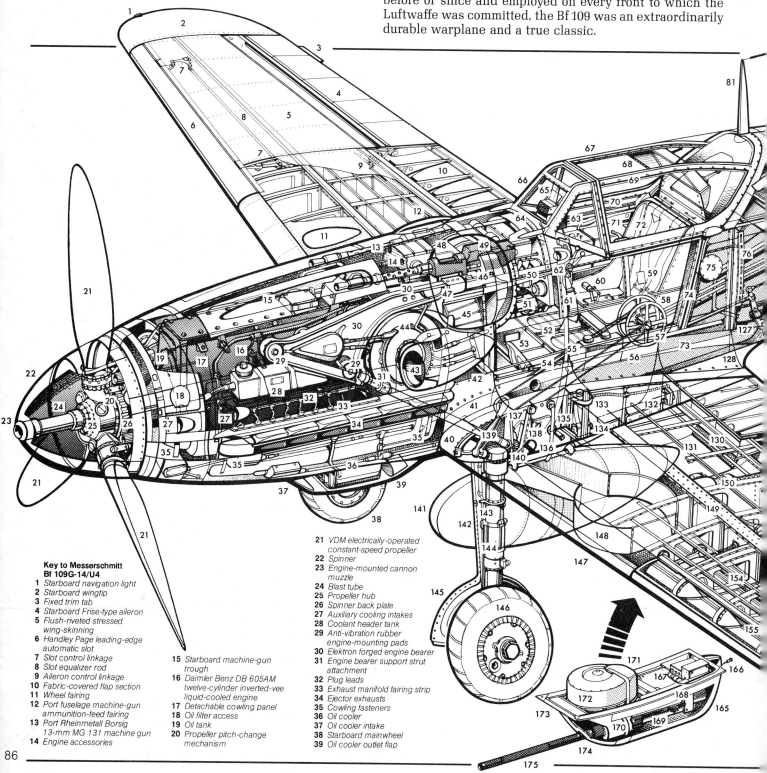

**Key to Messerschmitt Bf 109G-14/U4**

1 Starboard navigation light
2 Starboard wingtip
3 Fixed trim tab
4 Starboard Frise-type aileron
5 Flush-riveted stressed wing-skinning
6 Handley Page leading-edge automatic slot
7 Slot control linkage
8 Slot equalizer rod
9 Aileron control linkage
10 Fabric-covered flap section
11 Wheel fairing
12 Port fuselage machine-gun ammunition-feed fairing
13 Port Rheinmetall Borsig 13-mm MG 131 machine gun
14 Engine accessories
15 Starboard machine-gun trough
16 Daimler Benz DB 605AM twelve-cylinder inverted-vee liquid-cooled engine
17 Detachable cowling panel
18 Oil filter access
19 Oil tank
20 Propeller pitch-change mechanism
21 VDM electrically-operated constant-speed propeller
22 Spinner
23 Engine-mounted cannon muzzle
24 Blast tube
25 Propeller hub
26 Spinner back plate
27 Auxiliary cooling intakes
28 Coolant header tank
29 Anti-vibration rubber engine-mounting pads
30 Elektron forged engine bearer
31 Engine bearer support strut attachment
32 Plug leads
33 Exhaust manifold fairing strip
34 Ejector exhausts
35 Cowling fasteners
36 Oil cooler
37 Oil cooler intake
38 Starboard mainwheel
39 Oil cooler outlet flap

## SPECIFICATION: Bf 109G-6

**Power Plant:** One Daimler-Benz DB 605AM 12-cylinder inverted-vee liquid-cooled engine rated at 1,475 hp at 2,800 rpm (or 1,800 hp with MW 50 methanol-water injection) for take-off. Three-blade VDM constant-speed metal propeller. Internal fuel capacity, 88 Imp gal (400 l) with provision for one 66 Imp gal (300 l) auxiliary fuel tank.

**Performance:** Max speed, 340 mph (547 km/h) at sea level, 366 mph (590 km/h) at 6,560 ft (2 000 m), 380 mph (611 km/h) at 13,120 ft (4 000 m), 386 mph (621 km/h) at 22,640 ft (6 900 m); range (internal fuel), 350 mls (563 km) at 330 mph (530 km/h) at 19,030 ft (5 800 m), (with auxiliary tank), 620 mls (998 km) at 317 mph (510 km/h) at 19,685 ft (6 000m); initial climb, 3,346 ft/min (17 m/sec); time to 9,840 ft (3 000 m), 2·9 min; service ceiling, 37,890 ft (11 550 m).

**Weights:** Empty equipped, 5,893 lb (2 673 kg); normal loaded, 6,940 lb (3 148 kg); max overload, 7,496 lb (3 400 kg).

**Dimensions:** Span, 32 ft 6½ in (9,92 m); length 29 ft 0½ in (8,85 m); height 8 ft 2½ in (2,50 m); wing area, 173·3 sq ft (16,10 m²).

**Armament:** One 30-mm Rheinmetall Borsig MK 108 cannon with 60 rounds (or 20-mm Mauser MG 151 with 150 rounds) and two 13-mm Rheinmetall Borsig MG 131 machine guns with 300 rounds per gun.

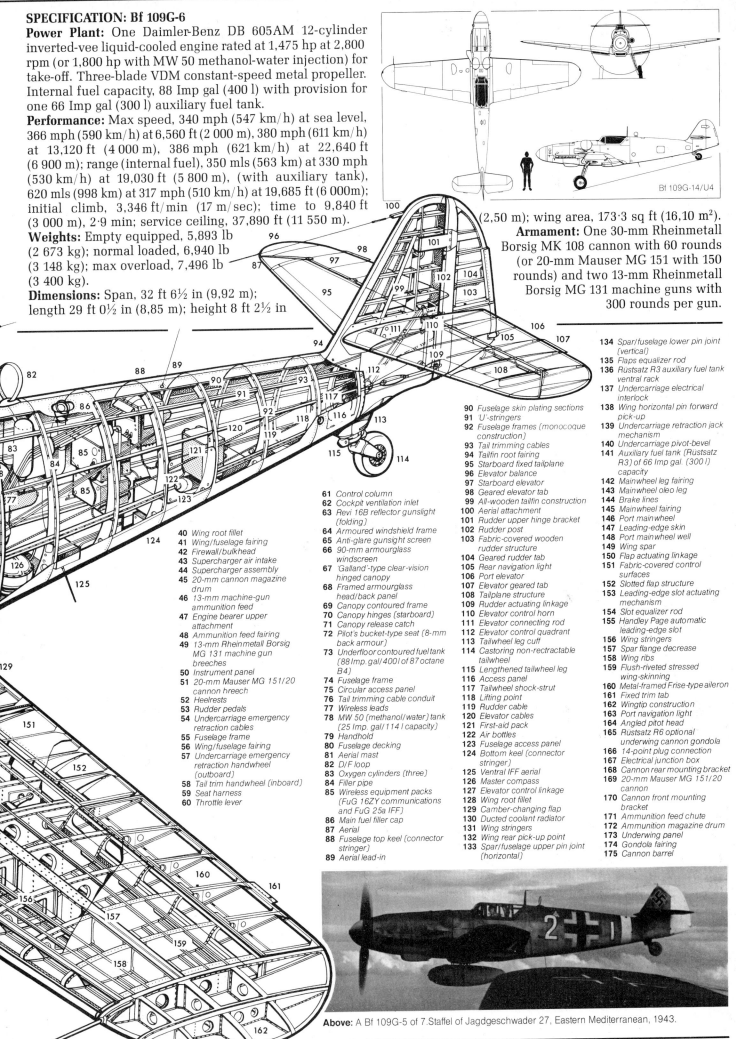

Bf 109G-14/U4

40 Wing root fillet
41 Wing/fuselage fairing
42 Firewall/bulkhead
43 Supercharger air intake
44 Supercharger assembly
45 20-mm cannon magazine drum
46 13-mm machine-gun ammunition feed
47 Engine bearer upper attachment
48 Ammunition feed fairing
49 13-mm Rheinmetall Borsig MG 131 machine gun breeches
50 Instrument panel
51 20-mm Mauser MG 151/20 cannon breech
52 Heelrests
53 Rudder pedals
54 Undercarriage emergency retraction cables
55 Fuselage frame
56 Wing/fuselage fairing
57 Undercarriage emergency retraction handwheel (outboard)
58 Tail trim handwheel (inboard)
59 Seat harness
60 Throttle lever
61 Control column
62 Cockpit ventilation inlet
63 Revi 16B reflector gunslight (folding)
64 Armoured windshield frame
65 Anti-glare gunsight screen
66 90-mm armourglass windscreen
67 'Galland'-type clear-vision hinged canopy
68 Framed armourglass head/back panel
69 Canopy contoured frame
70 Canopy hinges (starboard)
71 Canopy release catch
72 Pilot's bucket-type seat (8-mm back armour)
73 Underfloor contoured fuel tank (88 Imp.gal/400 l of 87 octane B4)
74 Fuselage frame
75 Circular access panel
76 Tail trimming cable conduit
77 Wireless leads
78 MW 50 (methanol/water) tank (25 Imp. gal/114 l capacity)
79 Handhold
80 Fuselage decking
81 Aerial mast
82 D/F loop
83 Oxygen cylinders (three)
84 Filler pipe
85 Wireless equipment packs (FuG 16ZY communications and FuG 25a IFF)
86 Main fuel filler cap
87 Aerial
88 Fuselage top keel (connector stringer)
89 Aerial lead-in
90 Fuselage skin plating sections
91 'U'-stringers
92 Fuselage frames (monocoque construction)
93 Tail trimming cables
94 Tailfin root fairing
95 Starboard fixed tailplane
96 Elevator balance
97 Starboard elevator
98 Geared elevator tab
99 All-wooden tailfin construction
100 Aerial attachment
101 Rudder upper hinge bracket
102 Rudder post
103 Fabric-covered wooden rudder structure
104 Geared rudder tab
105 Rear navigation light
106 Port elevator
107 Elevator geared tab
108 Tailplane structure
109 Rudder actuating linkage
110 Elevator control horn
111 Elevator connecting rod
112 Elevator control quadrant
113 Tailwheel leg cuff
114 Castoring non-rectractable tailwheel
115 Lengthened tailwheel leg
116 Access panel
117 Tailwheel shock-strut
118 Lifting point
119 Rudder cable
120 Elevator cables
121 First-aid pack
122 Air bottles
123 Fuselage access panel
124 Bottom keel (connector stringer)
125 Ventral IFF aerial
126 Master compass
127 Elevator control linkage
128 Wing root fillet
129 Camber-changing flap
130 Ducted coolant radiator
131 Wing stringers
132 Wing rear pick-up point
133 Spar/fuselage upper pin joint (horizontal)
134 Spar/fuselage lower pin joint (vertical)
135 Flaps equalizer rod
136 Rüstsatz R3 auxiliary fuel tank ventral rack
137 Undercarriage electrical interlock
138 Wing horizontal pin forward pick-up
139 Undercarriage retraction jack mechanism
140 Undercarriage pivot-bevel
141 Auxiliary fuel tank (Rüstsatz R3) of 66 Imp gal. (300 l) capacity
142 Mainwheel leg fairing
143 Mainwheel oleo leg
144 Brake lines
145 Mainwheel fairing
146 Port mainwheel
147 Leading-edge skin
148 Port mainwheel well
149 Wing spar
150 Flap actuating linkage
151 Fabric-covered control surfaces
152 Slotted flap structure
153 Leading-edge slot actuating mechanism
154 Slot equalizer rod
155 Handley Page automatic leading-edge slot
156 Wing stringers
157 Spar flange decrease
158 Wing ribs
159 Flush-riveted stressed wing-skinning
160 Metal-framed Frise-type aileron
161 Fixed trim tab
162 Wingtip construction
163 Port navigation light
164 Angled pitot head
165 Rüstsatz R6 optional underwing cannon gondola
166 14-point plug connection
167 Electrical junction box
168 Cannon rear mounting bracket
169 20-mm Mauser MG 151/20 cannon
170 Cannon front mounting bracket
171 Ammunition feed chute
172 Ammunition magazine drum
173 Underwing panel
174 Gondola fairing
175 Cannon barrel

**Above:** A Bf 109G-5 of 7.Staffel of Jagdgeschwader 27, Eastern Mediterranean, 1943.

# Morane-Saulnier M.S. 406 (August 1935)

Contemporary with the Hurricane (see pages 92-93) and likewise a synthesis of years of fighter design experience translated into terms of low-wing cantilever monoplane, the M.S.406 provided an outstanding example of the rapidity with which, in the 'thirties, an indifferent design could translate to the patently obsolescent. An aesthetically unattractive aeroplane with few pretensions to elegance, the M.S.406, by the standards of the day, could lay claim to no more than a certain functional sturdiness and pleasant handling characteristics reminiscent of those of the fighter generation that it was intended to supplant.

Designed by R. Gauthier to fulfil a specification issued in September 1934, the Morane-Saulnier fighter represented a more conservative structural approach to the requirement than its more fashionable competitors, retaining classic steel-tube construction, with, apart from fabric-covered aft fuselage and control surfaces, Plymax—okoumé plywood bonded to aluminium—stressed skinning. It was first flown on 8 August 1935 as the M.S.405, being ordered into production as the M.S.406, and the last of 16 pre-series aircraft being completed and flown on 21 June 1938 as a pattern aircraft for the production model—almost three years after the initiation of flight testing!

Production aircraft were slow to follow, fewer than a dozen having been taken on charge by 1 January 1939, by which time the M.S.406 had already been rendered thoroughly obsolescent by fighter development abroad. However, a production tempo of six daily had been attained by April and 11 daily four months later, the M.S.406 being numerically the most important Armée de l'Air fighter by the time France went to war in September 1939, 12 M.S.406-equipped Groupes de Chasse being included in the Order of Battle.

It was soon abundantly clear that the M.S.406 was ineffectual in combat with the Bf 109E. It was seriously underpowered; at anything approaching its alleged maximum speed, the ethylene-glycol radiator was retracted and the engine rapidly overheated; a lack of up-locks resulted in the mainwheels popping out of their wells with application of positive g, and the cold of altitude resulted in the pneumatic machine gun actuation and propeller pitch change freezing solid. Production (1,080) ended March 1940.

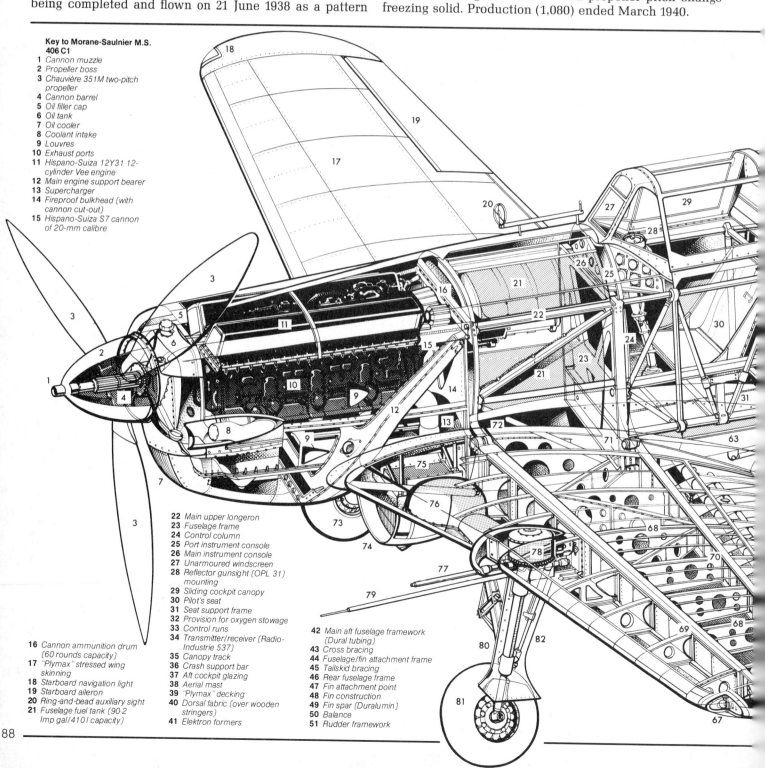

**Key to Morane-Saulnier M.S. 406 C1**

1 Cannon muzzle
2 Propeller boss
3 Chauvière 351M two-pitch propeller
4 Cannon barrel
5 Oil filler cap
6 Oil tank
7 Oil cooler
8 Coolant intake
9 Louvres
10 Exhaust ports
11 Hispano-Suiza 12Y31 12-cylinder Vee engine
12 Main engine support bearer
13 Supercharger
14 Fireproof bulkhead (with cannon cut-out)
15 Hispano-Suiza S7 cannon of 20-mm calibre
16 Cannon ammunition drum (60 rounds capacity)
17 "Plymax" stressed wing skinning
18 Starboard navigation light
19 Starboard aileron
20 Ring-and-bead auxiliary sight
21 Fuselage fuel tank (90·2 Imp gal/410l capacity)
22 Main upper longeron
23 Fuselage frame
24 Control column
25 Port instrument console
26 Main instrument console
27 Unarmoured windscreen
28 Reflector gunsight (OPL 31) mounting
29 Sliding cockpit canopy
30 Pilot's seat
31 Seat support frame
32 Provision for oxygen stowage
33 Control runs
34 Transmitter/receiver (Radio-Industrie 537)
35 Canopy track
36 Crash support bar
37 Aft cockpit glazing
38 Aerial mast
39 "Plymax" decking
40 Dorsal fabric (over wooden stringers)
41 Elektron formers
42 Main aft fuselage framework (Dural tubing)
43 Cross bracing
44 Fuselage/fin attachment frame
45 Tailskid bracing
46 Rear fuselage frame
47 Fin attachment point
48 Fin construction
49 Fin spar (Duralumin)
50 Balance
51 Rudder framework

## SPECIFICATION: M.S.406

**Power Plant:** One Hispano-Suiza 12Y 31 12-cylinder vee liquid-cooled engine rated at 830 hp at 2,400 rpm for take-off and 860 hp at 10,335 ft (3 150 m). Three-bladed two-pitch metal Chauvière 351M propeller. Internal fuel capacity, 90·2 Imp gal (410 l).

**Performance:** Max speed, 249 mph (401 km/h) at sea level, 271 mph (437 km/h) at 6,560 ft (2 000 m), 289 mph (465 km/h) at 13,125 ft (4 000 m); econ cruise, 199 mph (320 km/h); max range, 565 mls (910 km) at 196 mph (315 km/h) at 19,685 ft (6 000 m), 621 mls (1 000 km) at 166 mph (267 km/h) at 3,280 ft (1 000 m); initial climb, 2,559 ft/min (13 m/sec); service ceiling, 30,840 ft (9 400 m).

**Weights:** Empty equipped, 4,173 lb (1 893 kg); normal loaded, 5,348 lb (2 426 kg); max, 5,511 lb (2 500 kg).

**Dimensions:** Span, 34 ft 9⅝ in (10,62 m); length, 26 ft 9⅓ in (8,17 m); height (tail down), 8 ft 10¾ in (2,71 m); wing area, 184·07 sq ft (17,10 m²).

**Armament:** One 20-mm Hispano-Suiza S9 or HS 404 cannon with 60 rounds and two 7,5-mm MAC 1934 machine guns with 300 rpg.

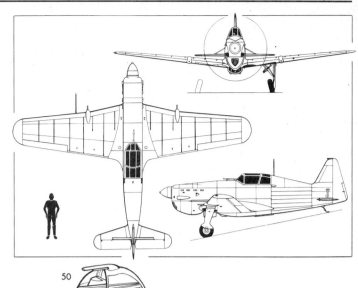

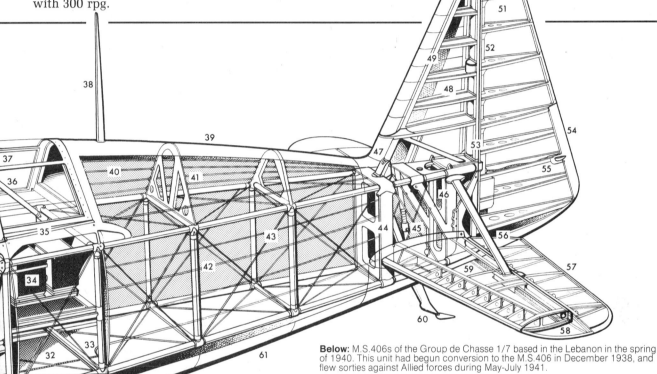

52 Rudder post
53 Rudder hinge
54 Rudder tab
55 Tab cable
56 Tailplane strut
57 Elevator construction
58 Elevator balance
59 Tailplane structure
60 Tail skid
61 Ventral fabric
62 Hinged ventral aerial
63 Wing roof fairing
64 Flap construction
65 Port aileron
66 Wingtip construction
67 Port navigation light
68 Wing ribs
69 Forward (main) wing spar
70 Aft wing spar
71 Rear spar/fuselage attachment point
72 Front spar/fuselage attachment points (two)
73 Starboard mainwheel
74 Retractable radiator
75 Radiator retraction links
76 Undercarriage well inner shell
77 Port 7,5-mm MAC 1934 machine gun
78 Ammunition drum (300 round capacity)
79 Pitot tube
80 Mainwheel leg
81 Port mainwheel (low-pressure tyre shown at ground angle)
82 Mainwheel leg fairing

**Below:** M.S.406s of the Group de Chasse 1/7 based in the Lebanon in the spring of 1940. This unit had begun conversion to the M.S.406 in December 1938, and flew sorties against Allied forces during May-July 1941.

# Seversky P-35 (August 1935)

If the P-35 had any title to fame it was the somewhat tenuous claim of having introduced to US Army Air Corps fighter aviation such refinements as an enclosed cockpit, a constant-speed propeller and a retractable undercarriage. The end product of a strange series of metamorphoses imposed on a fundamental design that saw birth as a three-seat commercial twin-float amphibian, the P-35 had an extraordinarily convoluted development history.

Its progenitor, the SEV-3, conceived by Alexander P de Seversky and translated into practicality by Alexander Kart-veli, fully reflected the dramatic advances in aeronautical technology taking place in the early 'thirties, few aircraft of the day combining more of these innovatory developments. Rolled out in June 1933, the basic design soon demonstrated remarkable changeling propensities, progressing to military basic trainer (SEV-3XAR), two-seat fighter (SEV-2XP) and even single-seat fighter (SEV-1XP), all without fundamental structural re-design.

In SEV-1XP form, as first flown in August 1935, it was winning contender in a US Army single-seat pursuit contest—effectively a straight competition between the

**Above:** Two EP-1s of Flygflottilj 3 serving in the tactical recce role shortly after the end of WWII. Sixty EP-1s reached Sweden.

**Above:** A P-35 after withdrawal from the first-line strength serving in the fighter training role circa 1942.

**Below:** The P-35 of the CO of the 27th Pursuit Squadron, 1st Pursuit Group, at Selfridge Field, Michigan, 1938-39. The 1st PG was the initial P-35 operator and began to re-equip with the P-36 in 1939.

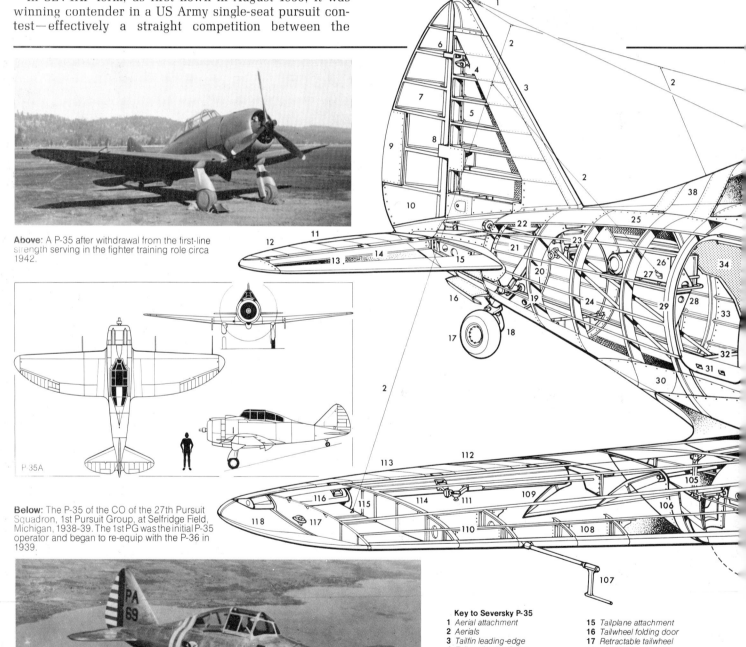

### Key to Seversky P-35

| | |
|---|---|
| 1 Aerial attachment | 15 Tailplane attachment |
| 2 Aerials | 16 Tailwheel folding door |
| 3 Tailfin leading-edge | 17 Retractable tailwheel |
| 4 Tail navigation lights | 18 Axle fork |
| 5 Tailfin structure | 19 Lifting point |
| 6 Rudder upper hinge | 20 Fuselage frame |
| 7 Rudder structure | 21 Tailwheel shock absorber |
| 8 Rudder centre hinge fairing | 22 Control rods |
| 9 Rudder tab | 23 Elevator control linkage |
| 10 Rudder lower section | 24 Fuselage longerons |
| 11 Elevator tab | 25 Skinning |
| 12 Starboard elevator | 26 Radio equipment |
| 13 Starboard tailplane | 27 Aerial lead-in |
| 14 Elevator hinge | 28 Radio support tray |

Seversky fighter and the Curtiss Model 75 (see pages 82-83)—and recipient of an order for 77 production models with deliveries commencing as P-35s in May 1937. Offering a roomy, comfortable cockpit and pleasant handling characteristics, the P-35 was a well-designed and robust aircraft, but it was inadequate as a fighter, lacking the two most important attributes: adequate performance and firepower. It was extremely stable—too much so for its intended role—and it tended to fall away in a spin when approaching its *official* service ceiling. Inverted flight and outside loops were prohibited, and the P-35 was already viewed as outmoded before the completion of deliveries in August 1938.

Despite the innate shortcomings of the design, a more heavily-armed and marginally more powerful export version, the EP-1, was sold to Sweden, orders being placed for 120 aircraft. In the event, only 60 were delivered, the remainder being requisitioned by the US government and 48 of these being sent to the Philippines as P-35As to see brief and inauspicious action at the beginning of the Pacific War, many of the US aircraft deployed in the Philippines being destroyed in a surprise attack by Japanese aircraft on the Luzon airfields on 8 December 1941.

## SPECIFICATION: P-35

**Power Plant:** One Pratt & Whitney R-1830-9 Twin Wasp 14-cylinder two-row radial air-cooled engine rated at 950 hp at 2,600 rpm for take-off and 850 hp at 8,000 ft (2 440 m). Three-bladed Hamilton Standard constant-speed metal propeller. Internal fuel capacity, 166·5 Imp gal.

**Performance:** Max speed, 281 mph (452 km/h) at 10,000 ft (3 050 m); max continuous cruise, 259 mph (417 km/h); range (max continuous cruise), 1,150 mls (1 850 km); initial climb, 2,440 ft/min (12,39 m/sec); time to 5,000 ft (1 525 m), 2·05 min, to 15,000 ft (4 570 m), 6·9 min; service ceiling 30,600 ft (9 325 m).

**Weights:** Empty equipped, 4,315 lb (1 957 kg); normal loaded, 5,599 lb (2 540 kg); max, 6,295 lb (2 855 kg).

**Dimensions:** Span, 36 ft 0 in (10,97 m); length, 25 ft 2 in (7,67 m); height, 9 ft 1 in (2,77 m); wing area, 220 sq ft (20,44 m²).

**Armament:** One 0·30-in (7,62-mm) and one 0·50-in (12,7-mm) machine gun.

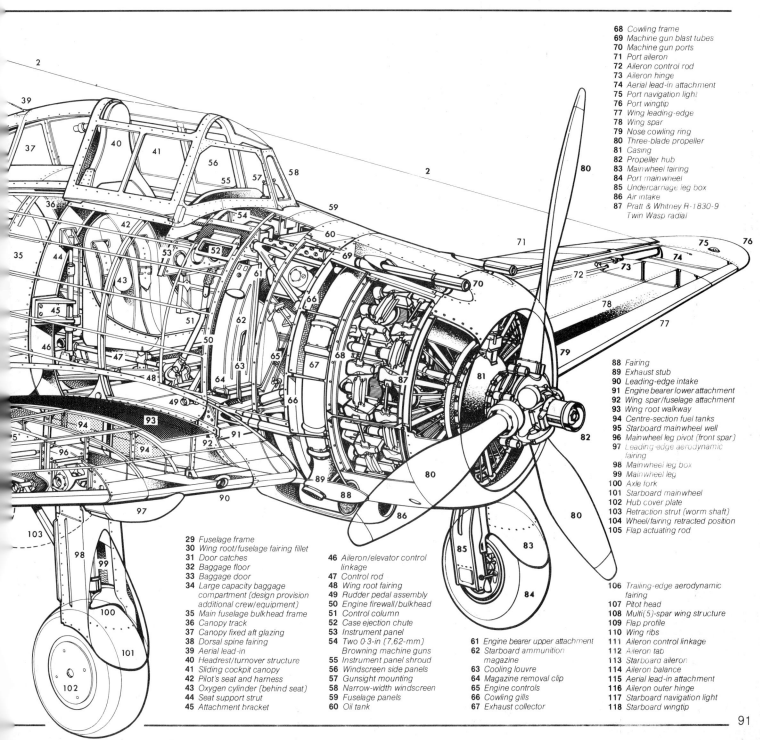

68 Cowling frame
69 Machine gun blast tubes
70 Machine gun ports
71 Port aileron
72 Aileron control rod
73 Aileron hinge
74 Aerial lead-in attachment
75 Port navigation light
76 Port wingtip
77 Wing leading-edge
78 Wing spar
79 Nose cowling ring
80 Three-blade propeller
81 Casing
82 Propeller hub
83 Mainwheel fairing
84 Port mainwheel
85 Undercarriage leg box
86 Air intake
87 Pratt & Whitney R-1830-9 Twin Wasp radial

88 Fairing
89 Exhaust stub
90 Leading-edge intake
91 Engine bearer lower attachment
92 Wing spar/fuselage attachment
93 Wing root walkway
94 Centre-section fuel tanks
95 Starboard mainwheel well
96 Mainwheel leg pivot (front spar)
97 Leading-edge aerodynamic fairing
98 Mainwheel leg box
99 Mainwheel leg
100 Axle fork
101 Starboard mainwheel
102 Hub cover plate
103 Retraction strut (worm shaft)
104 Wheel/fairing retracted position
105 Flap actuating rod

106 Trailing-edge aerodynamic fairing
107 Pitot head
108 Multi (5)-spar wing structure
109 Flap profile
110 Wing ribs
111 Aileron control linkage
112 Aileron tab
113 Starboard aileron
114 Aileron balance
115 Aerial lead-in attachment
116 Aileron outer hinge
117 Starboard navigation light
118 Starboard wingtip

29 Fuselage frame
30 Wing root/fuselage fairing fillet
31 Door catches
32 Baggage floor
33 Baggage door
34 Large capacity baggage compartment (design provision additional crew/equipment)
35 Main fuselage bulkhead frame
36 Canopy track
37 Canopy fixed aft glazing
38 Dorsal spine fairing
39 Aerial lead-in
40 Headrest/turnover structure
41 Sliding cockpit canopy
42 Pilot's seat and harness
43 Oxygen cylinder (behind seat)
44 Seat support strut
45 Attachment bracket

46 Aileron/elevator control linkage
47 Control rod
48 Wing root fairing
49 Rudder pedal assembly
50 Engine firewall/bulkhead
51 Control column
52 Case ejection chute
53 Instrument panel
54 Two 0·3-in (7,62-mm) Browning machine guns
55 Instrument panel shroud
56 Windscreen side panels
57 Gunsight mounting
58 Narrow-width windscreen
59 Fuselage panels
60 Oil tank

61 Engine bearer upper attachment
62 Starboard ammunition magazine
63 Cooling louvre
64 Magazine removal clip
65 Engine controls
66 Cowling gills
67 Exhaust collector

# Hawker Hurricane (November 1935)

The logical outcome of a long line of single-seat fighting aircraft and a compromise in mating the requirements born of the new fighter monoplane era with traditional constructional methods, the Hurricane was the RAF's first combat aircraft capable of exceeding 300 mph (482 km/h). Destined to carry the larger part of the burden of Britain's defence in the most significant aerial conflict ever fought, the "Battle of Britain", the Hurricane complemented the Spitfire to a remarkable degree.

Designed by Sydney Camm and first flown on 6 November 1935, the Hurricane retained the classic tubular-metal cross-braced fabric-covered Warren-type structure, despite the international trend towards the light metal stressed-skin monocoque. This conservatism was, in fact, viewed in some quarters with misgivings, resulting in design of a metal stressed-skin wing commencing before the prototype trials had begun.

An initial production contract was placed on 20 July 1936, the first aircraft flying on 12 October 1937, and the Hurricane proving itself very much a pilot's aeroplane. It was gentle and forgiving, control harmony was fairly good throughout the speed range, and aerobatics were pleasant and easy to execute. The controls heavied up with speed, although this was a characteristic that the Hurricane shared with most of its contemporaries, and it became somewhat tail heavy in a dive. It was to be found inferior in most performance respects to its principal adversary in the "Battle", the Bf 109E, but it enjoyed a clear edge in low-altitude manoeuvrability and in turning circle at all altitudes. Furthermore, as a result of the robust nature of its structure, it could absorb much battle damage and remain airborne.

Early in the Hurricane's career, the two-pitch propeller gave place to a constant-speed unit, the fabric-covered wing was supplanted by that of all-metal stressed skin, and pilot armour was progressively introduced. Installation of the uprated Merlin XX engine resulted in the Hurricane II with tremendously expanded versatility, the Mk IID being an anti-armour version with 40-mm cannon, and production terminating in September 1944 with the "universal armament wing" Mk IV, 12,780 Hurricanes having been built in the UK and a further 1,451 in Canada.

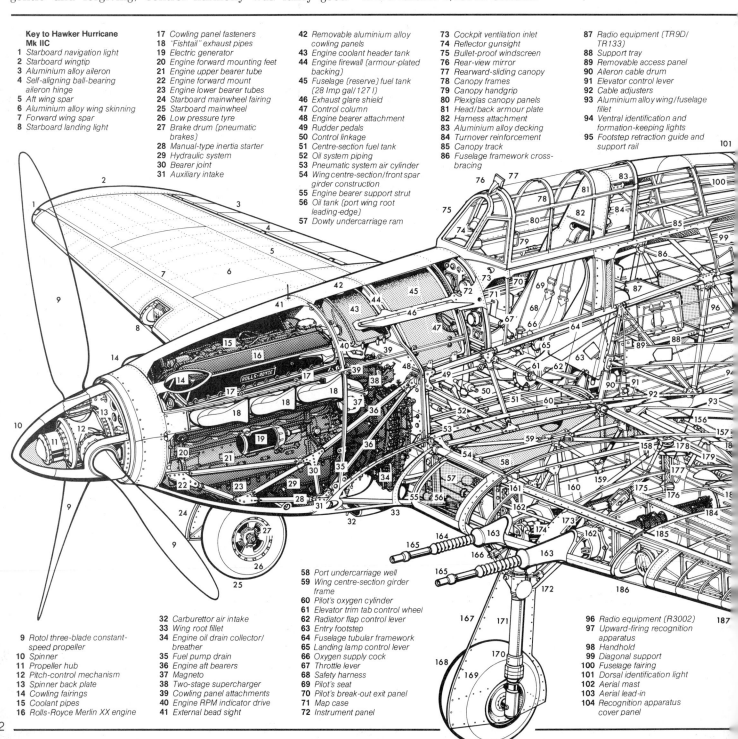

**Key to Hawker Hurricane Mk IIC**

1 Starboard navigation light
2 Starboard wingtip
3 Aluminium alloy aileron
4 Self-aligning ball-bearing aileron hinge
5 Aft wing spar
6 Aluminium alloy wing skinning
7 Forward wing spar
8 Starboard landing light
9 Rotol three-blade constant-speed propeller
10 Spinner
11 Propeller hub
12 Pitch-control mechanism
13 Spinner back plate
14 Cowling fairings
15 Coolant pipes
16 Rolls-Royce Merlin XX engine
17 Cowling panel fasteners
18 "Fishtail" exhaust pipes
19 Electric generator
20 Engine forward mounting feet
21 Engine upper bearer tube
22 Engine forward mount
23 Engine lower bearer tubes
24 Starboard mainwheel fairing
25 Starboard mainwheel
26 Low pressure tyre
27 Brake drum (pneumatic brakes)
28 Manual-type inertia starter
29 Hydraulic system
30 Bearer joint
31 Auxiliary intake
32 Carburettor air intake
33 Wing root fillet
34 Engine oil drain collector/breather
35 Fuel pump drain
36 Engine aft bearers
37 Magneto
38 Two-stage supercharger
39 Cowling panel attachments
40 Engine RPM indicator drive
41 External bead sight
42 Removable aluminium alloy cowling panels
43 Engine coolant header tank
44 Engine firewall (armour-plated backing)
45 Fuselage (reserve) fuel tank (28 Imp gal/127 l)
46 Exhaust glare shield
47 Control column
48 Engine bearer attachment
49 Rudder pedals
50 Control linkage
51 Centre-section fuel tank
52 Oil system piping
53 Pneumatic system air cylinder
54 Wing centre-section/front spar girder construction
55 Engine bearer support strut
56 Oil tank (port wing root leading-edge)
57 Dowty undercarriage ram
58 Port undercarriage well
59 Wing centre-section girder frame
60 Pilot's oxygen cylinder
61 Elevator trim tab control wheel
62 Radiator flap control lever
63 Entry footstep
64 Fuselage tubular framework
65 Landing lamp control lever
66 Oxygen supply cock
67 Throttle lever
68 Safety harness
69 Pilot's seat
70 Pilot's break-out exit panel
71 Map case
72 Instrument panel
73 Cockpit ventilation inlet
74 Reflector gunsight
75 Bullet-proof windscreen
76 Rear-view mirror
77 Rearward-sliding canopy
78 Canopy frames
79 Canopy handgrip
80 Plexiglas canopy panels
81 Head/back armour plate
82 Harness attachment
83 Aluminium alloy decking
84 Turnover reinforcement
85 Canopy track
86 Fuselage framework cross-bracing
87 Radio equipment (TR9D/TR133)
88 Support tray
89 Removable access panel
90 Aileron cable drum
91 Elevator control lever
92 Cable adjusters
93 Aluminium alloy wing/fuselage fillet
94 Ventral identification and formation-keeping lights
95 Footstep retraction guide and support rail
96 Radio equipment (R3002)
97 Upward-firing recognition apparatus
98 Handhold
99 Diagonal support
100 Fuselage fairing
101 Dorsal identification light
102 Aerial mast
103 Aerial lead-in
104 Recognition apparatus cover panel

## SPECIFICATION: Hurricane IIC

**Power Plant:** One Rolls-Royce Merlin XX 12-cylinder liquid-cooled vee engine rated at 1,280 hp at 3,000 rpm for take-off and 1,460 hp at 6,250 ft (1 905 m). Three-bladed Rotol constant-speed propeller. Internal fuel capacity, 97 Imp gal (441 l), and provision for two 45 Imp gal (205 l) drop tanks.

**Performance:** Max speed, 327 mph (526 km/h) at 18,000 ft (5 485 m), (with tropical filter), 301 mph (484 km/h); range, 460 mls (740 km) at 178 mph (286 km/h), (with tropical filter), 426 mls (685 km), (with drop tanks), 920 mls (1 480 km); initial climb, 2,750 ft/min (13,9 m/sec); time to 15,000 ft (4 575 m), 5·5 min, to 25,000 ft (7 620 m), 10 min; service ceiling, 35,600 ft (10 850 m).

**Weights:** Empty equipped, 6,577 lb (2 983 kg); normal loaded, 7,544 lb (3 422 kg); max, 8,044 lb (3 648 kg).

**Dimensions:** Span, 40 ft 0 in (12,19 m); length, 32 ft 3 in (9,83 m); height, 13 ft 3 in (4,04 m); wing area, 258 sq ft (23,97 m²).

**Armament:** Four 20-mm Hispano Mk I or II cannon with 90 rpg and provision for two 250-lb (113,5-kg) or 500-lb (227-kg) bombs under wings.

Mk IIC

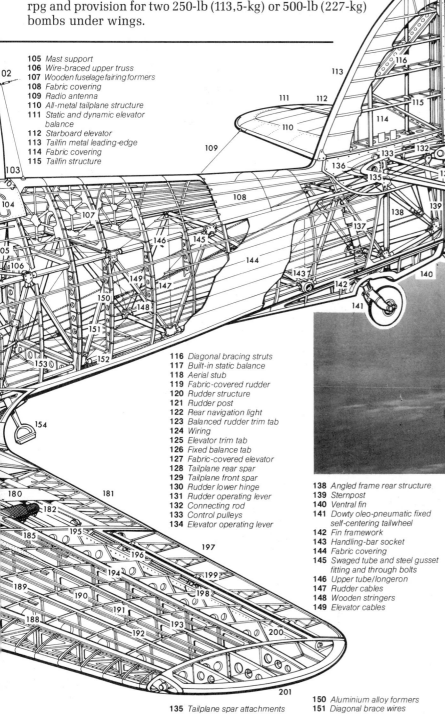

**Below:** Hurricane IICs of No 94 Sqdn, RAF, operating from El Gamil in the Western Desert in late 1942. Some of these aircraft have two of the cannon removed.

105 Mast support
106 Wire-braced upper truss
107 Wooden fuselage fairing formers
108 Fabric covering
109 Radio antenna
110 All-metal tailplane structure
111 Static and dynamic elevator balance
112 Starboard elevator
113 Tailfin metal leading-edge
114 Fabric covering
115 Tailfin structure

116 Diagonal bracing struts
117 Built-in static balance
118 Aerial stub
119 Fabric-covered rudder
120 Rudder structure
121 Rudder post
122 Rear navigation light
123 Balanced rudder trim tab
124 Wiring
125 Elevator trim tab
126 Fixed balance tab
127 Fabric-covered elevator
128 Tailplane rear spar
129 Tailplane front spar
130 Rudder lower hinge
131 Rudder operating lever
132 Connecting rod
133 Control pulleys
134 Elevator operating lever

135 Tailplane spar attachments
136 Aluminium alloy tailplane/ fuselage fairing
137 Tailwheel shock-strut

138 Angled frame rear structure
139 Sternpost
140 Ventral fin
141 Dowty oleo-pneumatic fixed self-centering tailwheel
142 Fin framework
143 Handling-bar socket
144 Fabric covering
145 Swaged tube and steel gusset fitting and through bolts
146 Upper tube/longeron
147 Rudder cables
148 Wooden stringers
149 Elevator cables

150 Aluminium alloy formers
151 Diagonal brace wires
152 Lower tube/longeron
153 Aluminium alloy former bottom section

154 Retractable entry footstep
155 Wingroot fillet
156 Flap rod universal joint
157 Aileron cables
158 Fuselage/wing rear spar girder attachment
159 Main wing fuel tank (port and starboard: 33 Imp gal/150 l each)
160 Ventral Glycol radiator and oil cooler
161 Front spar wing fixings
162 Cannon forward mounting bracket
163 Canon fairing
164 Recoil spring
165 Cannon barrels
166 Undercarriage retraction jack
167 Undercarriage fairing
168 Low pressure tyre
169 Port mainwheel
170 Mainwheel shock-strut
171 Oleo-pneumatic cylinder
172 Landing gear drag strut
173 Leading-edge armament access doors
174 Landing gear pivot point
175 Undercarriage sliding joint

176 Upper wing surface armament access plates
177 Rear spar wing fixing
178 Magazine blister fairings
179 Gun heating manifold
180 Breech-block access plates
181 Metal flaps
182 Cannon breech-blocks
183 Ammunition magazine drum
184 Port outer 20-mm Hispano cannon
185 Spar section change
186 Port landing light
187 Leading-edge structure
188 Front main spar
189 Forward intermediate spar
190 Stringers
191 Rib formers
192 Aluminium alloy wing skinning
193 Rear intermediate spar
194 Rear spar
195 Aileron control pulley
196 Aileron inboard hinge
197 Aluminium alloy aileron
198 Aileron control gear main pulley
199 Self-aligning ball-bearing hinge
200 Aileron outboard hinge
201 Detachable wingtip

# Fokker D XXI (February 1936)

The D XXI may be viewed as a compromise between the long accepted and the newly fashionable in fighter design. It retained Fokker's time-proven constructional recipe—a welded steel-tube fuselage and wooden wings primarily fabric covered—and such passé features as a fixed undercarriage and two-pitch propeller; it incorporated, however, certain concessions to modernity, notably a cantilever low wing and also an enclosed cockpit.

If Dr Ir E. Schatzki and his team were unambitious in their approach to fighter design by international standards already established in the mid 'thirties, and the D XXI was, in consequence, uninspired, this reflected the unpretentious specification, formulated by the Air Division of the Royal Netherlands Indies Army, that had resulted in its conception. Furthermore, all-metal, stressed-skin monocoque structures were, at the time, beyond Fokker's capability. The specification placed emphasis on ease of maintenance in the field and simplicity of operation, and although retractable undercarriages had become vogue, the disadvantages that such incurred seemed, to the Fokker team, to outweigh gains

at the performance levels sought, the reduced drag would have resulted in a three-four per cent speed gain and the increased weight would have reduced climb.

The prototype D XXI was flown on 27 February 1936, 36 being ordered for the home-based Army's Air Division, production acceptances commencing July 1938. The D XXI proved to possess somewhat unforgiving characteristics. Overly vigorous aft movement of the stick would result in the fighter rolling left and falling away in a spin, and an inadvertent flick roll at the top of a loop was almost inevitable if the rudder bar was even slightly off centre. The landing speed and glide angle were high, and there was a disconcerting tendency to drop a wing at the last moment and a habit of groundlooping if the tailwheel was unlocked. Conversely, the D XXI had light controls, was extremely sturdy and provided a stable gun platform.

An export order (for seven) was obtained from Finland, where the licence-manufacturer of 35 was subsequently undertaken, with the first flying in October 1938, and Denmark, too, licence-built the fighter, completing 10 after procuring two as pattern aircraft. In 1940, after

**Key to Fokker D XXI**
1 Starboard navigation light
2 Starboard wingtip
3 Wing skinning (bakelite plywood)
4 Starboard aileron (steel tube structure with fabric skinning)
5 Aileron tab
6 Gun and ammunition bay access panels
7 Starboard landing light
8 Machine gun barrels
9 Three-blade two-pitch propeller
10 Propeller hub
11 Pitch change mechanism
12 Reduction gear housing
13 Cowling ring
14 Exhaust gas collector ring profile
15 Bristol Mercury VIII nine-cylinder radial air-cooled engine
16 Oil cooler air intake tubes
17 Engine cowling clips
18 Engine mounting ring
19 Starboard wheel spat
20 Starboard mainwheel
21 Carburettor air intake
22 Lower engine bearer
23 Carburettor
24 Oil cooler
25 Oil cooler air outlet
26 Engine control linkage
27 Oxygen bottles (two)
28 Upper engine bearers
29 Accessories
30 Rod-mounted half-ring and bead sight
31 Fuel filler point
32 Fuel tank of 77 Imp gal (350 l) capacity
33 Forward fuselage longeron brace
34 Front spar/fuselage attachment point
35 Oil tank
36 Rear spar/fuselage attachment point
37 Cockpit floor step
38 Rudder pedals
39 Instrument panel
40 Engine control levers
41 Control column
42 Windscreen
43 Fixed canopy section
44 Centreline canopy hinge
45 Hinged canopy and side flap
46 Vertically-adjustable pilot's seat
47 Elevator trim wheel
48 Flap setting lever
49 Recessed foothold
50 First aid kit stowage
51 Equipment bay
52 Steel roll-over pylon
53 Radio mast
54 Cockpit aft glazing
55 Radio transmitter/receiver
56 Battery
57 Elevator control cable
58 Radio compartment hinged access cover
59 Handhold
60 Detachable dural dorsal panels
61 Welded chrome-molybdenum fuselage frame
62 Dorsal hoop formers
63 Fuselage stringers (fabric covered)
64 Signal lamp
65 Starboard tailpane
66 Elevator mass balance
67 Fin/tailplane bracing wire
68 Radio aerial
69 Starboard elevator
70 Elevator tab
71 Control pulley
72 Elevator control linkage
73 Fabric-coverd fin
74 Fin structure
75 Tail navigation light
76 Aerial stub mast
77 Rudder upper hinge
78 Fin/tailplane bracing wire

the Fokker fighters had given good service in the Soviet-Finnish conflict (as the D XXIs of the home-based Air Division were to do during the invasion of the Netherlands in May 1940), Finland reinstated D XXI production, building a further 55 with the R-1535 Twin Wasp engine, for which Fokker had previously adapted the basic airframe.

## SPECIFICATION: D XXI

**Power Plant:** One Bristol Mercury VIII nine-cylinder radial air-cooled engine rated at 730 hp at 2,650 rpm for take-off and 825 hp at 13,000 ft (3 960 m). Three-blade two-pitch metal propeller. Internal fuel capacity, 77 Imp gal (350 l).
**Performance:** Max speed, 286 mph (460 km/h) at 16,730 ft (5 100 m); cruise (66% power), 240 mph (386 km/h), (55% power), 228 mph (368 km/h); range (55% power), 590 mls (950 km); initial climb, 3,937 ft/min (20 m/sec); time to 6,560 ft (2 000 m), 2·3 min, to 9,840 ft (3 000 m), 4·05 min; service ceiling, 36,090 ft (11 000 m).
**Weights:** Empty equipped, 3,197 lb (1 450 kg); max loaded, 4,519 lb (2 050 kg).
**Dimensions:** Span, 36 ft 1 in (11,00 m); length, 26 ft 10¾ in (8,20 m); height, 9 ft 8 in (2,95 m); wing area, 174·37 sq ft (16,20 m²).
**Armament:** Four 7,9-mm FN-Browning M-36 machine guns with 300 rounds of ammunition for each gun.

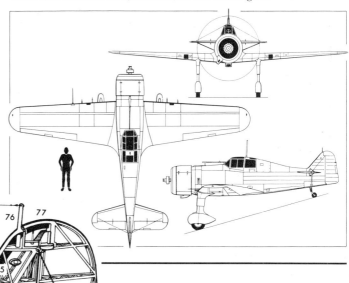

**Below:** D XXIs of the 1e JaVa of the LVA photographed during a neutrality patrol immediately prior to the involvement of the Netherlands in WWII. The D XXI was sturdy and simple in the best Fokker tradition.

| | | |
|---|---|---|
| 79 Rudder tab | 82 Tailplane structure | 100 Mainwheel leg fairing |
| 80 Rudder (metal framed and fabric covered) | 83 Tailplane lower bracing strut | 101 Oleopneumatic strut |
| 81 Port elevator (metal framed and fabric covered) | 84 Elevator mass balance | 102 Fairing overlap |
| | 85 Tailplane/fuselage attachment | 103 Ground-servicing footrest |
| | 86 Tailwheel strut housing | 104 Axle fork |
| | 87 Control pulley | 105 Port mainwheel |
| | 88 Compressed rubber shock absorber | 106 Port wheel spat |
| | 89 Steerable tailwheel | 107 Pitot head |
| | 90 Rudder control cables | 108 Machine gun barrels |
| | 91 Ventral formers | 109 Port landing light |
| | 92 Recessed foothold | 110 FN/Browning M-36 machine guns (7,9-mm calibre) |
| | 93 Control pulley | 111 Ammunition boxes |
| | 94 Wing root fairing | 112 Flap construction |
| | 95 Flap profile | 113 Aileron construction |
| | 96 Rear spar | 114 Aileron tab |
| | 97 Front spar | 115 Wing rib structure |
| | 98 Wing leading edge construction | 116 Port navigation light |
| | 99 Undercarriage/front spar anchorage | 117 Reinforcement for ground handling |

# Supermarine Spitfire (March 1936)

Occasionally a fighter appears that enjoys charisma, attended by success in infancy and consolidating that success in maturity. Very rarely, such a fighter achieves a truly legendary status but the Spitfire was destined to be just such a rarity. It was to be more than just a highly successful fighter, however, for it was to be the material symbol of final victory to the British at a time when the nation's fortunes were at their nadir.

The success of the Spitfire was not fortuitous. It was both an inspired design and the distillation of past experience. Its sires included the S.6B, which, in 1931, had won the Schneider Trophy outright, and in no fighter was breeding more clearly discernible. With such a pedigree, nothing less than a true thoroughbred could have resulted when, late in 1934, Reginald J. Mitchell defined the new fighter, which was to fly as a prototype on 6 March 1936, and receive a production contract three months later.

Like the Bf 109 (see pages 84-87), flown 10 months earlier, the Spitfire employed state-of-the-art all-metal stressed-skin monocoque structural techniques, and, similarly, it was the smallest practicable airframe that could be designed around a pilot, the chosen power plant and the specified armament. Mitchell's approach was perhaps more conservative than that of his German contemporaries in that he sought modest wing loadings whereas Messerschmitt and Lusser gambled on appreciably higher loadings with a sophisticated arrangement of leading-edge slots and slotted trailing-edge flaps.

Mk VB

**Key to Supermarine Spitfire VB**

1 Aerial stub attachment
2 Rudder upper hinge
3 Fabric-covered rudder
4 Rudder tab
5 Sternpost
6 Rudder tab hinge
7 Rear navigation light
8 Starboard elevator tab
9 Starboard elevator structure
10 Elevator balance
11 Tailplane front spar
12 IFF aerial
13 Castoring non-retractable tailwheel
14 Tailwheel strut
15 Fuselage double frame
16 Elevator control lever
17 Tailplane spar/fuselage attachment
18 Fin rear spar (fuselage frame extension)
19 Fin front spar (fuselage frame extension)
20 Port elevator tab hinge
21 Port elevator
22 IFF aerial
23 Port tailplane
24 Rudder control lever
25 Cross shaft
26 Tailwheel oleo access plate
27 Tailwheel oleo shock-absorber
28 Fuselage angled frame
29 Battery compartment
30 Lower longeron
31 Elevator control cables
32 Fuselage construction
33 Rudder control cables
34 Radio compartment
35 Radio support tray
36 Flare chute
37 Oxygen bottle
38 Auxiliary long-range fuel tank (29 gal/132 l)
39 Dorsal formation light
40 Aerial lead-in
41 HF aerial
42 Aerial mast
43 Cockpit aft glazing
44 Voltage regulator
45 Canopy track
46 Structural bulkhead
47 Headrest
48 Plexiglas canopy
49 Rear-view mirror
50 Entry flap (port)
51 Air bottles (alternative rear fuselage stowage)
52 Sutton harness
53 Pilot's seat (moulded Bakelite)
54 Datum longeron
55 Seat support frame
56 Wingroot fillet
57 Seat adjustment lever
58 Rudder pedal frame
59 Elevator control connecting tube
60 Control column spade grip
61 Trim wheel

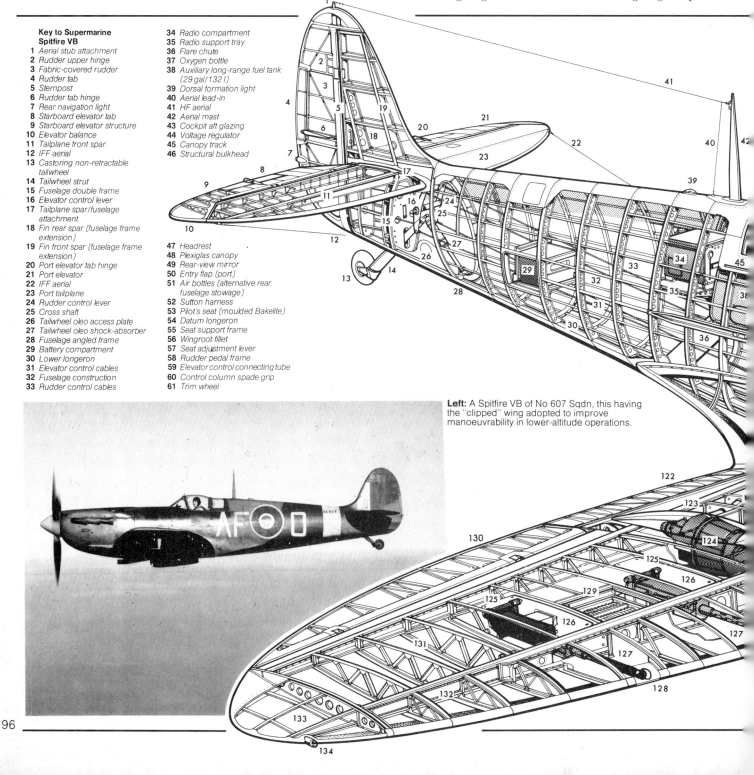

**Left:** A Spitfire VB of No 607 Sqdn, this having the "clipped" wing adopted to improve manoeuvrability in lower-altitude operations.

The Bf 109 concept *was* the more advanced: it was to place the German fighter at a disadvantage to the Spitfire in agility, but it gave an edge in climbing, diving and in level speed below 20,000 ft (6 095 m). The respective advantages accruing from these differing philosophies were largely to cancel each other out, however, when the two fighters met as adversaries in the epic "Battle of Britain" which was to bring immortality to the Spitfire.

Flown on 14 May 1938, the production Spitfire I began to reach RAF squadrons in the following August, and 19 squadrons had been equipped by the time that the new fighter was committed to the "Battle". From this point, the basic fighter was to be subjected to the intensive development and incremental redesign resulting in three distinct generations, each closely linked with the availability of more powerful engines, and when this genealogical process had run its course, little remained unaltered. Perhaps surprisingly, the Spitfire, aesthetically one of the most elegant fighters ever to grace an airfield, lost little beauty through its three generations and was to remain throughout fundamentally Mitchell's original design.

continued on page 98 ▶

**SPECIFICATION: Spitfire IA**

**Power Plant:** One Rolls-Royce Merlin II 12-cylinder vee liquid-cooled engine rated at 880 hp at 3,000 rpm for take-off and 1,030 hp at 16,250 ft (4 955 m). Three-bladed de Havilland two-pitch metal propeller. Internal fuel capacity, 84 Imp gal (382 l).

**Performance:** Max speed, 346 mph (557 km/h) at 15,000 ft (4 575 m); max cruise, 304 mph (489 km/h) at 15,000 ft (4 575 m); range, 415 mls (668 km) at max cruise, 630 mls (1 014 km) at 175 mph (282 km/h); climb to 15,000 ft (4 575 m), 6·85 min; service ceiling, 30,500 ft (9 295 m); endurance at maximum power, 43 min; maximum endurance, 3·6 hours.

**Weights:** Empty equipped, 4,517 lb (2 049 kg); normal loaded, 5,844 lb (2 651 kg).

**Dimensions:** Span, 36 ft 10 in (11,23 m); length, 29 ft 11 in (9,12 m); height, 12 ft 7¾ in (3,86 m); wing area, 242 sq ft (22,48 m²).

**Armament:** Eight 0·303-in (7.7-mm) Browning Mk II machine guns with 300 rounds of ammunition per gun. (Mk IB) Two 20-mm British Hispano cannon with 120 rounds of ammunition per gun.

---

62 Reflector gunsight
63 External windscreen armour
64 Instrument panel
65 Main fuselage fuel tank (48 gal/ 218 l)
66 Fuel tank/longeron attachment fittings
67 Rudder pedals
68 Rudder bar
69 King post
70 Fuselage lower fuel tank (37 gal[168 l])
71 Firewall/bulkhead
72 Engine bearer attachment
73 Steel tube bearers
74 Magneto

75 'Fishtail" exhaust manifold
76 Gun heating 'intensifier"
77 Hydraulic tank
78 Fuel filler cap
79 Air compressor intake
80 Air compressor
81 Rolls-Royce Merlin 45 engine
82 Coolant piping
83 Port cannon wing fairing
84 Flaps
85 Aileron control cables
86 Aileron push tube
87 Bellcrank
88 Aileron hinge
89 Port aileron
90 Machine-gun access panels

91 Port wingtip
92 Port navigation light
93 Leading-edge skinning
94 Machine-gun ports (protected)
95 20-mm cannon muzzle
96 Thre-blade constant-speed propeller
97 Spinner
98 Propeller hub
99 Coolant tank
100 Cowling fastening
101 Engine anti-vibration mounting pad
102 Engine accessories
103 Engine bearers
104 Main engine support member

105 Coolant pipe
106 Exposed oil tank
107 Port mainwheel
108 Mainwheel fairing
109 Carburettor air intake
110 Stub/spar attachment
111 Mainwheel leg pivot point
112 Main spar
113 Leading-edge ribs (diagonals deleted for clarity)
114 Mainwheel leg shock-absorber
115 Mainwheel fairing
116 Starboard mainwheel
117 Angled axle
118 Cannon barrel support fairing
119 Spar cut-out

120 Mainwheel well
121 Gun heating pipe
122 Flap structure
123 Cannon wing fairing
124 Cannon magazine drum (120 rounds)
125 Machine-gun support brackets
126 Gun access panels
127 0·303-in machine-gun barrels
128 Machine-gun ports
129 Ammunition boxes (350 rpg)
130 Starboard aileron construction
131 Wing ribs
132 Single-tube outer spar section
133 Wingtip structure
134 Starboard navigation light

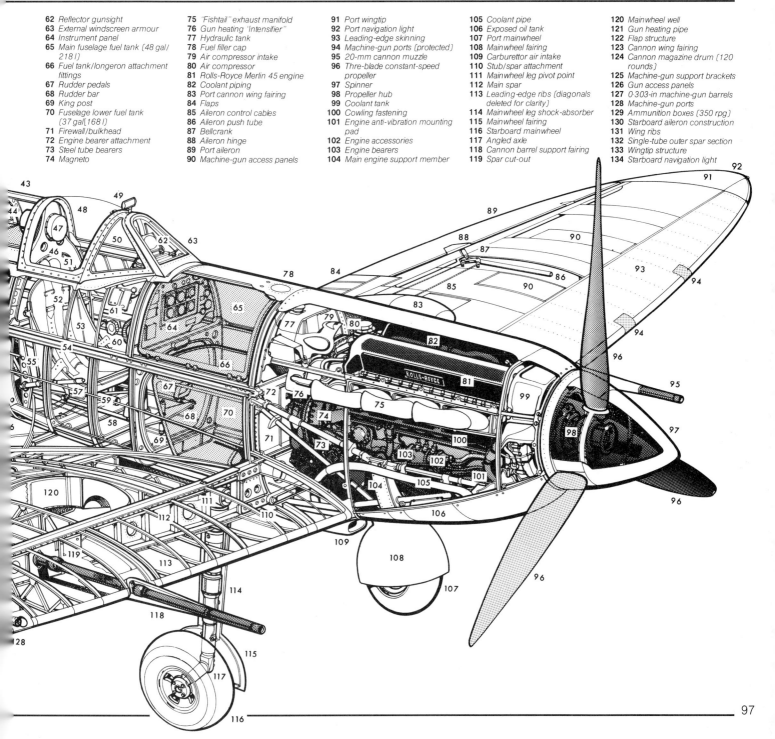

# Supermarine Spitfire

cont ▶

From August 1940, an improved sub-type, the Spitfire II with a Merlin XII engine and pilot armour, began to reach the squadrons, initiating the evolution that was to allow the Spitfire to retain its position among the best fighters available to any of the warring nations. Thirty of the 1,567 Mk Is built had been the initial recipients of the "B" type wing in which four of the machine guns were supplanted by a pair of 20-mm cannon, and this wing was to be applied to 170 of the 921 Mk IIs completed. The Mk II was superseded in turn by the Mk V, which, built in larger numbers (6,487) than any variant, started life essentially as a Mk II with uprated Merlin 45 engine.

The two-speed, two-stage supercharged Merlin 60 series launched the second-generation Spitfire, the first of which was the Mk IX, which, basically a Mk V airframe, was a Merlin 61-powered interim model introduced hurriedly to counter the Fw190 (see pages 128-129), while the pressurized Mk VII and unpressurized Mk VIII intended to take full advantage of the new series engines were brought to fruition. The Mk IX made its

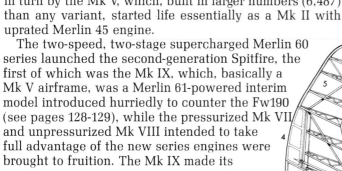

F Mk21

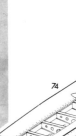

### Key to Supermarine Spitfire 21

1. Starboard elevator construction
2. Elevator tab
3. Tail navigation light
4. Rudder trim tab
5. Fabric covered rudder construction
6. Sternpost
7. Rudder balance weight
8. Fin main spar
9. Tailfin construction
10. Tail ballast weights
11. Fin secondary spar
12. Rudder trim jack
13. Tailplane trim jack
14. Tailplane construction
15. Tailwheel doors
16. Mudguard
17. Tailwheel retraction jack
18. Tailplane control rods
19. Tailwheel
20. Fuselage double bulkhead
21. Port elevator
22. Port tailplane
23. Fin root fillet fairing
24. Tail assembly joint frame
25. Oxygen cylinder
26. Six-cartridge signal flare launcher
27. Tailplane control cables
28. Access door
29. Fuselage ballast weights
30. Battery
31. R.3067 radio receiver
32. Radio access door
33. Whip aerial
34. Harness release
35. TR.1143 radio transmitter
36. Radio track
37. Fuselage frame and stringer construction
38. Wing root trailing edge fillet
39. Control cable runs
40. Fuselage main longeron
41. Port side access door
42. Canopy aft glazing
43. Sliding canopy rail
44. Voltage regulator
45. Fuselage double frame
46. Seat support framework
47. Back armour
48. Pilot's seat
49. Sutton harness
50. Head armour
51. Sliding cockpit canopy cover
52. Rear-view mirror
53. Windscreen framing
54. Bullet proof windscreen
55. Reflector gunsight
56. Port side entry hatch
57. Instrument panel
58. Control column
59. Compass mounting
60. Undercarriage control lever
61. Seat adjusting handle
62. Seat pan armour plate
63. Wing root rib
64. Radiator shutter jack
65. Coolant radiator, oil cooler on port side
66. Gun heating duct
67. Wing rear spar
68. Flap hydraulic jack
69. Flap shroud ribs
70. Tubular flap spar
71. Starboard split trailing edge flap
72. Aileron control bellcrank
73. Aileron hinge
74. Aileron tab
75. Aluminium skinned aileron construction
76. Wing tip fairing
77. Starboard navigation light
78. Wing tip construction
79. Aileron outer hinge rib
80. Wing rib construction
81. Main spar
82. Leading edge nose ribs
83. Ammunition boxes, 150 rounds per gun
84. Mainwheel fairing door
85. Ammunition feed drums
86. Blister fairings
87. Ammunition belt feed
88. 20-mm British Hispano Mk II cannon barrels
89. Cannon barrel support fairing
90. Recoil springs
91. Fuel filler cap
92. Leading edge fuel tank, capacity 17 Imp gal (77 l)
93. Main undercarriage wheel well
94. Mainwheel blister fairing
95. Undercarriage retraction link
96. Undercarriage leg pivot
97. Shock absorber leg strut
98. Hydraulic brake pipe
99. Starboard mainwheel
100. Mainwheel leg fairing door
101. Undercarriage torque scissors

**Left:** A Spitfire F Mk 24 of No 80 Sqdn, RAF, operating from Kai Tak, Hong Kong, 1949-51. Note identification striping introduced with Korean War.

service debut in June 1942, no fewer than 5,646 being built, the Mk VII (140 built) and Mk VIII (1,658 built) following from September and the end of the year respectively.

Mating of the airframe with the Griffon engine produced a third and final Spitfire generation, and after the interim Mk XII (a Mk V adaption), the Mk XIV was built from the ground up for the new power plant, entering service January 1944 (957 being produced). Its lineal successor was the Mk XVIII with lengthened fuselage and rear-view hood, the latter having been applied to late Mk XIVs, but evolution did not reach its apex until the appearance of the Mks 21 and 22, with a new extended wing, five-bladed propeller and other changes. The Mk 21 became operational in April 1945 (120 built), the Mk 22 (287 built) differing primarily in having the rear-view cockpit canopy, late examples featuring an enlarged tail.

A decade of Spitfire production came to its close in March 1948 with delivery of the last of 54 Mk 24s which embodied revised fuel tankage. These aircraft brought the grand total of all types of Supermarine Spitfire built (excluding prototypes) to no less than 20,346.

## SPECIFICATION: Spitfire F Mk 22

**Power Plant:** One Rolls-Royce Griffon 64 12-cylinder vee liquid-cooled engine rated at 1,520 hp at 2,750 rpm for take-off and 2,375 hp at 1,250 ft (380 m). Five-bladed Rotol constant-speed propeller. Internal fuel capacity, 186 Imp gal (845 l) with provision for 90 Imp gal (409 l) drop tank.

**Performance:** Max speed, 390 mph (628 km/h) at sea level, 450 mph (724 km/h) at 19,600 ft (5 975 m); average cruise, 230-245 mph (370-394 km/h) at 20,000 ft (6 095 m); range (max internal fuel), 580 mls (933 km), (with drop tank), 965 mls (1 553 km); initial climb, 4,880 ft/min (24,79 m/sec); service ceiling, 43,000 ft (13 105 m).

**Weights:** Empty equipped, 7,160 lb (3 247 kg); normal, 9,900 lb (4 490 kg); max, 11,290 lb (5 121 kg).

**Dimensions:** Span, 36 ft 11 in (11,26 m); length, 32 ft 11 in (10,04 m); height, 13 ft 6 in (4,12 m); wing area, 243·6 sq ft (22,63 m²).

**Armament:** Four 20-mm British Hispano Mk II cannon with 175 rpg inboard and 150 rpg outboard. Provision for one 250-lb (113,5-kg) bomb beneath each wing and a 500-lb (227-kg) bomb beneath the fuselage.

102 Fuel pipe runs
103 Main spar stub attachment
104 Lower main fuel tank, capacity 48 Imp gal (218 l)
105 Upper main fuel tank, capacity 36 Imp gal (164 l)
106 Fuel filler cap
107 Oil tank vent
108 Oil tank, capacity 9 Imp gal (41 l)
109 Oil tank access door
110 Engine compartment fireproof bulkhead
111 Port split trailing edge flap
112 Flap hydraulic jack
113 Flap synchronising jack
114 Port twin 20-mm Hispano cannon
115 Spent cartridge case ejector chute
116 Ammunition feed drums
117 Ammunition belt feeds
118 Ammunition boxes, 150 rounds per gun
119 Aileron control bellcrank
120 Aileron tab
121 Port aileron
122 Wing tip fairing
123 Port navigation light
124 Pitot tube
125 Cannon barrel fairings
126 Cannon barrels
127 Port leading edge fuel tank, capacity 17 Imp gal (77 l)
128 Upper engine cowling
129 Hydraulic fluid tank
130 Intercooler
131 Compressor intake
132 Generator
133 Heywood compressor
134 Engine bearer attachment
135 Hydraulic pump
136 Coolant pipes
137 Gun camera
138 Camera port
139 Engine air intake duct
140 Port mainwheel
141 Engine bearer
142 Cartridge starter
143 Exhaust stubs
144 2,035 hp Rolls-Royce Griffon 61 engine
145 Engine magnetoes
146 Coolant header tank
147 Front engine mounting
148 Lower engine cowling
149 Spinner backplate
150 Propeller hub pitch change mechanism
151 Spinner
152 Rotol five-bladed constant speed propeller

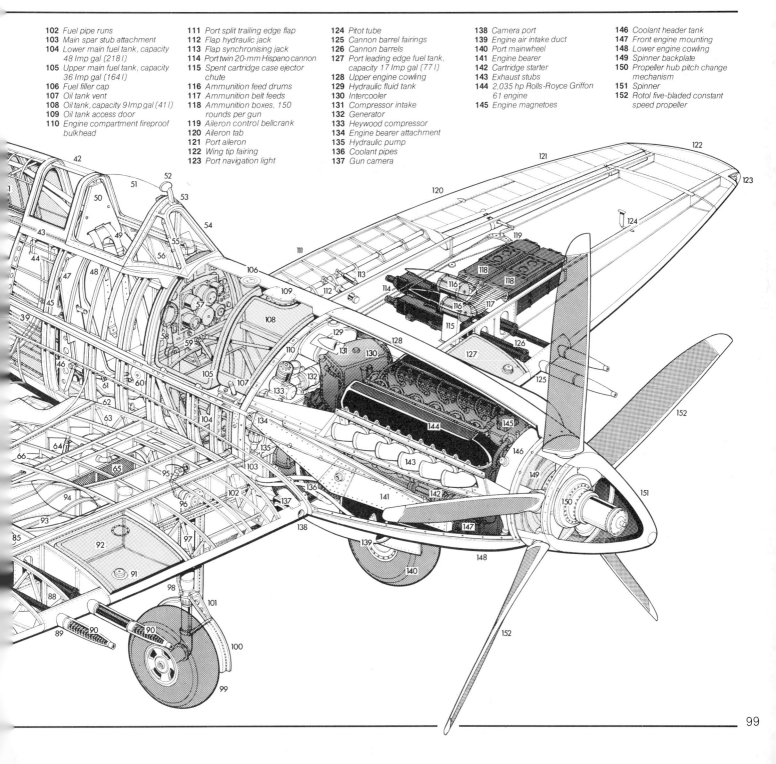

# Messerschmitt Bf 110 (May 1936)

The strategic fighter concept—a warplane coupling high performance and heavy armament with endurance for deep-penetration offensive sorties over enemy territory—saw birth in WWI, but it was not until the second half of the 'thirties that it took really practicable form in the shape of the Bf 110. Referred to as a *Zerstörer,* a term borrowed from naval parlance, the Bf 110 flew on 12 May 1936, its initial large-scale production sub-type, the Bf 110C, entering service with the Luftwaffe from January 1939 onward.

A supremely elegant warplane for which a formidable reputation was assiduously fostered by German propagandists, the Bf 110 proved an abysmal failure when committed to the "Battle of Britain". It was not the indifferent warplane that this debacle suggested, however, but the victim of an inadequate understanding of the limitations of the strategic fighter concept and its incorrect deployment as a consequence. No designer, however talented, could create a large and heavy twin-engined fighter capable of competing in agility with single-engined contemporaries.

Once the limitations of the Bf 110 were appreciated, it was to serve throughout the remainder of WWII with distinction in a variety of diurnal and nocturnal roles. An eminently soundly designed warplane with pleasant handling characteristics, a very good performance and surprisingly manoeuvrable for its size and twin-engined configuration, the Bf 110 was the backbone of German night defence; production, ending March 1945, totalled some 6,050. Its basic design proved amenable to engine changes and application of equipment beyond any envisaged by its designers.

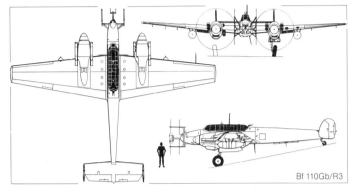

Bf 110Gb/R3

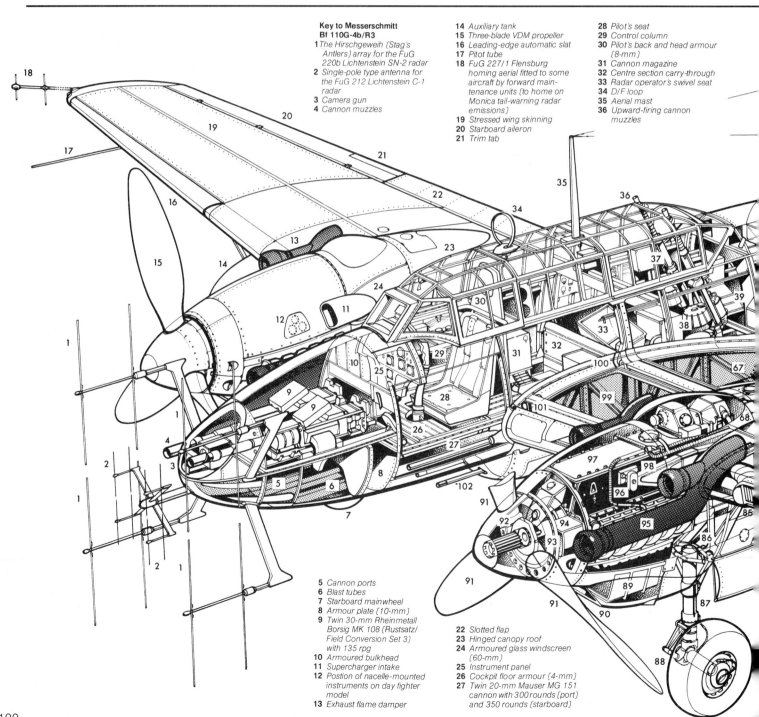

**Key to Messerschmitt Bf 110G-4b/R3**

1 The Hirschgeweih (Stag's Antlers) array for the FuG 220b Lichtenstein SN-2 radar
2 Single-pole type antenna for the FuG 212 Lichtenstein C-1 radar
3 Camera gun
4 Cannon muzzles
5 Cannon ports
6 Blast tubes
7 Starboard mainwheel
8 Armour plate (10-mm)
9 Twin 30-mm Rheinmetall Borsig MK 108 (Rustsatz/ Field Conversion Set 3) with 135 rpg
10 Armoured bulkhead
11 Supercharger intake
12 Postion of nacelle-mounted instruments on day fighter model
13 Exhaust flame damper
14 Auxiliary tank
15 Three-blade VDM propeller
16 Leading-edge automatic slat
17 Pitot tube
18 FuG 227/1 Flensburg homing aerial fitted to some aircraft by forward maintenance units (to home on Monica tail-warning radar emissions)
19 Stressed wing skinning
20 Starboard aileron
21 Trim tab
22 Slotted flap
23 Hinged canopy roof
24 Armoured glass windscreen (60-mm)
25 Instrument panel
26 Cockpit floor armour (4-mm)
27 Twin 20-mm Mauser MG 151 cannon with 300 rounds (port) and 350 rounds (starboard)
28 Pilot's seat
29 Control column
30 Pilot's back and head armour (8-mm)
31 Cannon magazine
32 Centre section carry-through
33 Radar operator's swivel seat
34 D/F loop
35 Aerial mast
36 Upward-firing cannon muzzles

## SPECIFICATION: Bf 110G-4c/R3

**Power Plant:** Two Daimler-Benz DB 605B-1 12-cylinder inverted-vee liquid-cooled engines each rated at 1,475 hp at 2,800 rpm for take-off and 1,355 hp at 18,700 ft (5 700 m). Three-blade VDM controllable-pitch propellers. Internal fuel capacity, 279 Imp gal (1 270 l) with provision for two 66 Imp gal (300 l) drop tanks.

**Performance:** Max speed, 311 mph (500 km/h) at sea level, 342 mph (550 km/h) at 22,900 ft (6 980 m); max continuous cruise, 317 mph (510 km/h) at 19,685 ft (6 000 m); max range (internal fuel), 560 mls (900 km), (with two drop tanks), 808 mls (1 300 km); max climb rate, 2,170 ft/min (11 m/sec); service ceiling, 26,250 ft (8 000 m).

**Weights:** Empty equipped, 11,230 lb (5 094 kg); normal loaded, 20,701 lb (9 390 kg); max, 21,799 lb (9 888 kg).

**Dimensions:** Span, 53 ft 3¼ in (16,25 m); length (excluding radar antennae), 39 ft 6¼ in (12,07 m), (including antennae), 42 ft 9¾ in (13,05 m); height, 13 ft 8½ in (4,18 m); wing area, 413·33 sq ft (38,40 m²).

**Armament:** Two 30-mm Rheinmetall Borsig MK 108 cannon with 135 rpg and two 20-mm Mauser MG 151 cannon with 300 (port) and 350 (starboard) rounds, plus one 7,9-mm MG 81Z twin machine gun with 800 rounds, or twin 20-mm MG 151 or MG FF cannon in "schräge Musik" installation.

**Above:** Bf 110D-3s of 9. Staffel of Zerstörergeschwader 26 over the Mediterranean, summer 1941, and (immediately above) Bf 110G-4d/R3 night fighters of a home-based Nachtjagdgruppe.

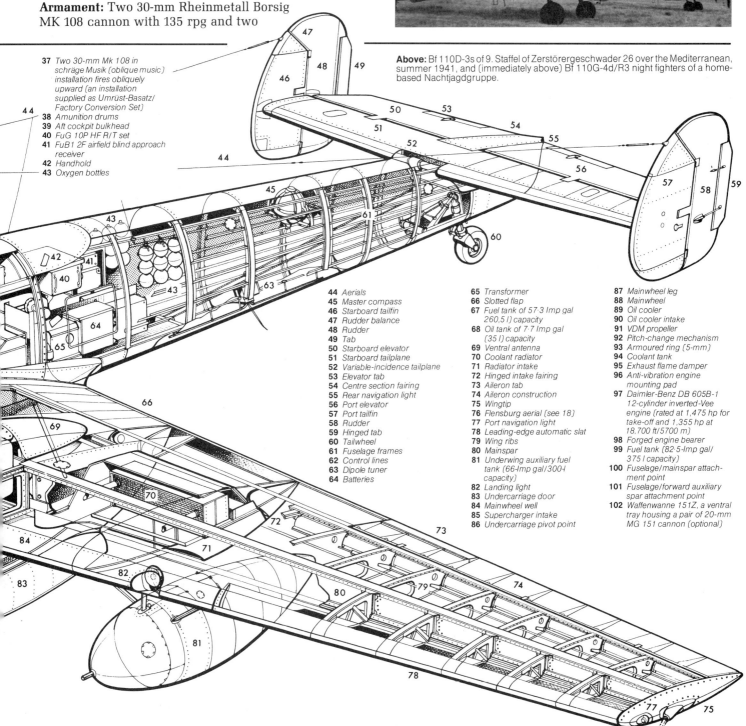

37 Two 30-mm Mk 108 in schräge Musik (oblique music) installation fires obliquely upward (an installation supplied as Umrüst-Basatz/Factory Conversion Set)
38 Amunition drums
39 Aft cockpit bulkhead
40 FuG 10P HF R/T set
41 FuB1 2F airfield blind approach receiver
42 Handhold
43 Oxygen bottles

44 Aerials
45 Master compass
46 Starboard tailfin
47 Rudder balance
48 Rudder
49 Tab
50 Starboard elevator
51 Starboard tailplane
52 Variable-incidence tailplane
53 Elevator tab
54 Centre section fairing
55 Rear navigation light
56 Port elevator
57 Port tailfin
58 Rudder
59 Hinged tab
60 Tailwheel
61 Fuselage frames
62 Control lines
63 Dipole tuner
64 Batteries

65 Transformer
66 Slotted flap
67 Fuel tank of 57·3 Imp gal (260,5 l) capacity
68 Oil tank of 7·7 Imp gal (35 l) capacity
69 Ventral antenna
70 Coolant radiator
71 Radiator intake
72 Hinged intake fairing
73 Aileron tab
74 Aileron construction
75 Wingtip
76 Flensburg aerial (see 18)
77 Port navigation light
78 Leading-edge automatic slat
79 Wing ribs
80 Mainspar
81 Underwing auxiliary fuel tank (66-Imp gal/300-l capacity)
82 Landing light
83 Undercarriage door
84 Mainwheel well
85 Supercharger intake
86 Undercarriage pivot point

87 Mainwheel leg
88 Mainwheel
89 Oil cooler
90 Oil cooler intake
91 VDM propeller
92 Pitch-change mechanism
93 Armoured ring (5-mm)
94 Coolant tank
95 Exhaust flame damper
96 Anti-vibration engine mounting pad
97 Daimler-Benz DB 605B-1 12-cylinder inverted-Vee engine (rated at 1,475 hp for take-off and 1,355 hp at 18,700 ft/5700 m)
98 Forged engine bearer
99 Fuel tank (82·5-Imp gal/375 l capacity)
100 Fuselage/mainspar attachment point
101 Fuselage/forward auxiliary spar attachment point
102 Waffenwanne 151Z, a ventral tray housing a pair of 20-mm MG 151 cannon (optional)

# Nakajima Ki.27 (October 1936)

**Above:** A Ki.27otsu of the 1st Chutai of the 64th Sentai photographed over southern China after the so-called "Nomonhan Incident".

Configurationally similar to the Fokker D XXI (see pages 94-95) flown seven-and-a-half months earlier, but of very much more advanced structural concept, the Ki.27 was indisputably an inspired design, but its very success performed a disservice for Japan in that it overly influenced subsequent fighter development policy, generating complacency which resulted in insufficient attention being given to fighter development trends elsewhere.

Imperial Army pilots were encouraged to compare their dexterity in dogfighting with the skilled used of the bamboo Shinai by masters of the ancient martial art of Kendo. Thus, qualities of manoeuvre were accorded pre-eminence in a fighter and a somewhat bigoted attitude was adopted towards other attributes if they could be emphasized only at some expense to agility. The Ki.27, however, was a supremely successful compromise between the demands of these traditionalists and those of the visionaries in respect of speed and climb.

Designed by Prof Hideo Itokawa and Yasumi Koyama and first flown on 15 October 1936, the Ki.27 represented the smallest practicable airframe that could be designed around

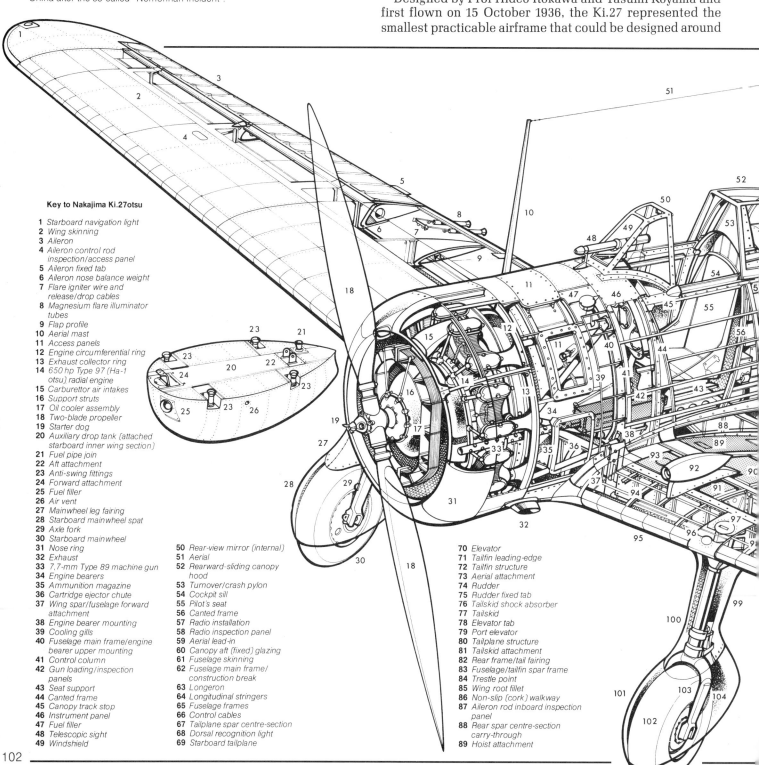

**Key to Nakajima Ki.27otsu**

1 Starboard navigation light
2 Wing skinning
3 Aileron
4 Aileron control rod inspection/access panel
5 Aileron fixed tab
6 Aileron nose balance weight
7 Flare igniter wire and release/drop cables
8 Magnesium flare illuminator tubes
9 Flap profile
10 Aerial mast
11 Access panels
12 Engine circumferential ring
13 Exhaust collector ring
14 650 hp Type 97 (Ha-1 otsu) radial engine
15 Carburettor air intakes
16 Support struts
17 Oil cooler assembly
18 Two-blade propeller
19 Starter dog
20 Auxiliary drop tank (attached starboard inner wing section)
21 Fuel pipe join
22 Aft attachment
23 Anti-swing fittings
24 Forward attachment
25 Fuel filler
26 Air vent
27 Mainwheel leg fairing
28 Starboard mainwheel spat
29 Axle fork
30 Starboard mainwheel
31 Nose ring
32 Exhaust
33 7,7-mm Type 89 machine gun
34 Engine bearers
35 Ammunition magazine
36 Cartridge ejector chute
37 Wing spar/fuselage forward attachment
38 Engine bearer mounting
39 Cooling gills
40 Fuselage main frame/engine bearer upper mounting
41 Control column
42 Gun loading/inspection panels
43 Seat support
44 Canted frame
45 Canopy track stop
46 Instrument panel
47 Fuel filler
48 Telescopic sight
49 Windshield

50 Rear-view mirror (internal)
51 Aerial
52 Rearward-sliding canopy hood
53 Turnover/crash pylon
54 Cockpit sill
55 Pilot's seat
56 Canted frame
57 Radio installation
58 Radio inspection panel
59 Aerial lead-in
60 Canopy aft (fixed) glazing
61 Fuselage skinning
62 Fuselage main frame/ construction break
63 Longeron
64 Longitudinal stringers
65 Fuselage frames
66 Control cables
67 Tailplane spar centre-section
68 Dorsal recognition light
69 Starboard tailplane

70 Elevator
71 Tailfin leading-edge
72 Tailfin structure
73 Aerial attachment
74 Rudder
75 Rudder fixed tab
76 Tailskid shock absorber
77 Tailskid
78 Elevator tab
79 Port elevator
80 Tailplane structure
81 Tailskid attachment
82 Rear frame/tail fairing
83 Fuselage/tailfin spar frame
84 Trestle point
85 Wing root fillet
86 Non-slip (cork) walkway
87 Aileron rod inboard inspection panel
88 Rear spar centre-section carry-through
89 Hoist attachment

a Kotobuki (Congratulation) radial engine. Emulating the Imperial Navy's A5M (see pages 78-79), it was of all-metal flush-riveted stressed-skin semi-monocoque construction, and fitted with hydraulically-operated split flaps. Extraordinarily light and possessing superlative agility, the Ki.27 was ordered into production as the Army Type 97 Fighter, making its operational debut over China in April 1938. Lacking in firepower, armour and fuel tank protection—and *what* fighters of the period possessed these desirable features in combination—the Ki.27 was without doubt the fastest fighter in the Orient and bore favourable comparison with fighters being produced contemporaneously by the most technologically advanced western countries.

At an early production stage, the initial Ki.27ko gave place to the Ki.27otsu featuring minor cockpit changes, and when the type was phased out by the parent company late 1940, production transferred to the Mansyu Hikoki Seizo K.K. (Manchurian Aeroplane Manufacturing Co Ltd) at Harbin, in Japan's puppet state of Manchukuo, northeast China. There it continued for a further 18 months, finally bringing the total of this type manufactured to 3,396 aircraft.

## SPECIFICATION: Ki.27otsu

**Power Plant:** One Nakajima Ha-1otsu (Kotobuki) nine-cylinder radial air-cooled engine rated at 710 hp at 2,600 rpm for take-off and 780 hp at 9,515 ft (2 900 m). Two-bladed Sumitomo PE metal two-pitch (ground adjustable) propeller. Internal fuel capacity, 72·6 Imp gal (330 l), with provision for two 28·6 Imp gal (130 l) auxiliary tanks.

**Performance:** Max speed, 265 mph (427 km/h) at 3,280 ft (1 000 m), 276 mph (445 km/h) at 6,560 ft (2 000 m), 292 mph (470 km/h) at 11,480 ft (3 500 m); max continuous cruise, 217 mph (350 km/h) at 11,480 ft (3 500 m); range (internal fuel), 390 mls (630 km), (with auxiliary tanks), 683 mls (1 100 km); time to 3,280 ft (1 000 m), 1·16 min, to 9,840 ft (3 000 m), 2·98 min; service ceiling, 40,190 ft (12 250 m).

**Weights:** Empty equipped, 2,447 lb (1 110 kg); normal loaded, 3,410 lb (1 547 kg); max, 3,946 lb (1 790 kg).

**Dimensions:** Span 37 ft 1¼ in (11,31 m); length, 24 ft 8½ in (7,53 m); height, 10 ft 8 in (3,28 m); wing area, 199·78 sq ft (18,56 m²).

**Armament:** Two 7,7-mm Type 89 machine guns with 500 rpg; provision for four 55-lb (25-kg) bombs under wing.

**Above:** Ki.27otsu fighters serving in the advanced training role at the Akeno school in 1942, by the end of which year this type had been virtually withdrawn from operations.

Ki.27otsu

90 Aft fuel tank (14·3 Imp gal/65 l capacity)
91 Forward fuel tank (16·5 Imp gal/75 l capacity)
92 Gun camera bullet fairing
93 Fuel filler
94 Front spar
95 Leading-edge
96 Anti-corrosive filler
97 Landing gear strut
98 Strut/front spar attachment
99 Mainwheel leg fairing
100 Mainwheel leg oleo
101 Spat
102 Port mainwheel
103 Axle fork
104 Brake cable
105 Leading-edge ribs
106 Main spar
107 Wing ribs
108 Aileron control rod
109 Flaps
110 Aileron tab
111 Port aileron
112 Stiffeners
113 Pitot head
114 Wing skinning
115 Port navigation light

# Junkers Ju 88 (December 1936)

There can be little doubt that fortuity influences the success or failure of many aircraft; there can be no doubt whatsoever that the success of what was to rank as arguably the most outstanding long-range heavy fighter and night fighter of WWII was purely fortuitous. This, the Ju 88, had been conceived solely as a *Schnellbomber*—a high-speed bomber in the design of which performance was uncompromised by the needs of alternative roles. In the event, this strictly dedicated design was to evolve as perhaps the most versatile warplane ever produced; it was to excel in all the roles of a very wide repertoire and in none more so than that of fighter.

Intended to meet a *Schnellbomber* requirement formulated in the spring of 1935, and designed by W. H. Evers and A. Gassner, both having gained experience in light metal stressed-skin constructional techniques in the USA, the Ju 88 owed nothing to any preceding design from the Junkers drawing boards. The first prototype, the Ju 88 V1, flew on 21 December 1936, immediately demonstrating a quantum performance advance. Its potential in the heavy fighter, or *Zerstörer*, role was apparent before the bomber attained service, the Ju 88 V7 being modified for *Zerstörer* trials in

the summer of 1939. The possibilities of the Ju 88 for the nocturnal intercept task, too, were foreseen early in WWII, but with all priority assigned to the bomber, fighter capability was of little more than academic interest.

A rudimentary *Zerstörer* adaptation of the bomber, the Ju 88C-2, did appear in 1940, however, and in the autumn of 1941, the Ju 88C-4, built "from the ground up" as a heavy fighter, began to enter service. The first *Zerstörer* manufactured in really large numbers was to be the Ju 88C-6, and late in 1942, this began to play a part in the nocturnal defence of Germany. Changing operational requirements produced successive sub-types, the liquid-cooled Jumo engines of the C-series giving place to BMW radials in early G-series aircraft, which, with enlarged tail surfaces, appeared in the spring of 1944, 700-800 subsequently being manufactured in parallel with the C-series of which about 3,200 were delivered to the Luftwaffe.

An outstanding pilot's aeroplane, the Ju 88 demanded some degree of skill in handling, offering excellent performance and a high level of agility for an aeroplane of its size and weight.

**Key to Junkers Ju 88G-1**

1 Starboard navigation light
2 Wingtip profile
3 FuG 227 'Flensburg' radar receiver antenna
4 Starboard aileron
5 Aileron control runs
6 Starboard flaps
7 Flap-fairing strip
8 Wing ribs
9 Starboard outer fuel tank (91 Imp gal/415 l capacity)
10 Fuel filler cap
11 Leading edge structure
12 Annular exhaust slot
13 Cylinder head fairings
14 Adjustable nacelle nose ring
15 Twelve-blade cooling fan
16 Propeller boss
17 Variable-pitch VS 111 wooden propeller
18 Leading-edge radar array
19 FuG 220 'Lichtenstein' SN-2 intercept radar array
20 Nose cone
21 Forward armoured bulkhead
22 Gyro compass
23 Instrument panel
24 Armour-glass windscreen
25 Folding seat
26 Control column
27 Rudder pedal brake cylinder
28 Control runs
29 Pilot's armoured seat
30 Sliding window section
31 Headrest
32 Jettisonable canopy roof section
33 Gun restraint
34 Wireless operator-gunner's seat
35 Rheinmetall Borsig MG 131 machine gun (13-mm calibre)
36 Radio equipment (FuG 10P HF, FuG 16ZY VHF, FuG 25 IFF)
37 Ammunition box (500 rounds of 13-mm)
38 FuG 220 'Lichtenstein' SN-2 indicator box
39 FuG 227 'Flensburg' indicator box
40 Control linkage
41 Bulkhead
42 Armoured gun mount
43 Aerial post traverse check
44 Fuel filler cap
45 Whip aerial
46 Forward fuselage fuel tank (105 Imp gal/480 l capacity)
47 Fuselage horizontal construction joint
48 Bulkhead
49 Fuel filler cap
50 Aft fuselage fuel tank (230 Imp gal/1 045 l capacity)
51 Access hatch
52 Bulkhead
53 Control linkage access plate
54 Fuselage stringers
55 Upper longeron
56 Maintenance walkway
57 Control linkage
58 Horizontal construction joint
59 Z-section fuselage frames
60 Dinghy stowage
61 Fuel vent pipe
62 Master compass
63 Spherical oxygen bottles
64 Accumulator
65 Tailplane centre section carry-through
66 Starboard tailplane
67 Elevator balance
68 Aerial
69 Starboard elevator
70 Elevator tab
71 Tailfin forward spar/fuselage attachment
72 Tailfin structure

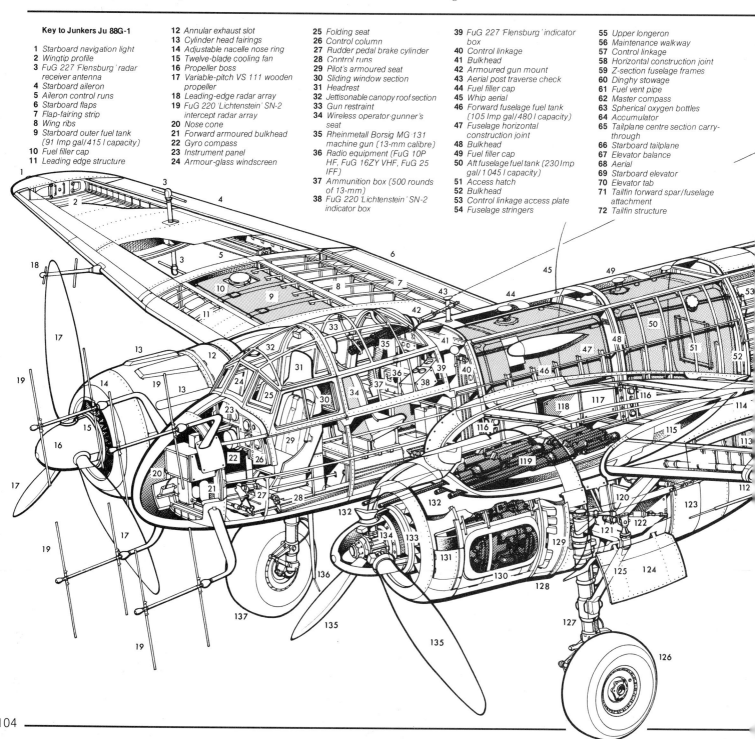

## SPECIFICATION: Ju 88G-7b

**Power Plant:** Two Junkers Jumo 213E 12-cylinder inverted-vee liquid-cooled engines each rated at 1,750 hp at 3,200 rpm for take-off and 1,320 hp at 31,990 ft (9 750 m). Three-bladed VS 19 constant-speed wooden propellers. Internal fuel capacity, 704 Imp gal (3 200 l). Provision for one 198 Imp gal (900 l) drop tank.

**Performance:** Max speed, 270 mph (435 km/h) at sea level, 363 mph (584 km/h) at 33,465 ft (10 200 m), (with MW 50 water-methanol injection), 389 mph (626 km/h) or (without flame dampers) 402 mph (647 km/h) at 29,855 ft (9 100 m); endurance (including one hour at emergency power with MW 50 boost), 3·72 hrs; initial climb, 1,655 ft/min (8,4 m/sec); time to 32,315 ft (9 850 m), 26·4 min.

**Weights:** Normal loaded, 28,900 lb (13 110 kg); max, 32,350 lb (14 674 kg).

**Dimensions:** Span, 65 ft 10½ in (20,08 m); length, 51 ft 0¼ in (15,55 m); height, 15 ft 11 in (4,85 m); wing area, 586·6 sq ft (54,50 m²).

**Armament:** Two fixed forward-firing 20-mm MG 151 cannon with 200 rounds for each cannon, two fixed obliquely-upward-firing 20-mm MG 151 cannon with 200 rounds of ammunition for each cannon, and one flexibly-mounted aft-firing 13-mm MG 131 machine gun with 500 rounds of ammunition.

**Above:** A Ju 88C-6b night fighter with FuG 202 Lichtenstein BC radar array, this being the first radar-equipped version of the Ju 88 and essentially an adaptation of the Ju 88C-6 heavy diurnal fighter. The Ju 88C-6b appeared in service late in 1942.

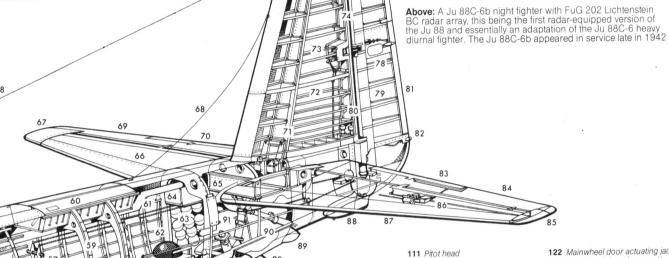

111 Pitot head
112 Landing lamp
113 Mainwheel well rear bulkhead
114 Port outer fuel tank location (91 Imp gal/415 l capacity)
115 Ventral gun pack (offset to port)
116 Ball-and-socket fuselage/wing attachment points
117 Port inner fuel tank location (93·4 Imp gal/425 l capacity)
118 Ammunition boxes for MG 151 cannon (200 rpg)
119 Mauser MG 151/20 cannon (four) of 20-mm calibre
120 Mainwheel leg retraction yoke
121 Leg pivot member
122 Mainwheel door actuating jack
123 Mainwheel door (rear section)
124 Mainwheel door (forward section)
125 Leg support strut
126 Port mainwheel
127 Mainwheel leg
128 Annular exhaust slot
129 Exhaust stubs (internal)
130 BMW 801D air-cooled radial engine (partly omitted for clarity)
131 Annular oil tank
132 Cannon muzzles (depressed five degrees)
133 Twelve-blade cooling fan
134 Propeller mechanism
135 Variable-pitch wooden VS 111 propeller
136 FuG 16ZY antenna
137 Starboard mainwheel

73 Rudder actuator
74 Rudder post
75 Rudder mass balance
76 Rudder upper hinge
77 Rudder tab (upper section)
78 Inspection/maintenance handhold
79 Rudder structure
80 Tailfin aft spar/fuselage attachment
81 Rudder tab (lower section)
82 Rear navigation light
83 Elevator tab
84 Port elevator
85 Elevator balance
86 Elevator tab actuator
87 Heated leading edge
88 Tail bumper/fuel vent outlet
89 Tailwheel doors
90 Tailwheel retraction mechanism
91 Shock absorber leg
92 Mudguard
93 Tailwheel
94 Access hatch
95 Fixed antenna
96 D/F loop
97 Lower longeron
98 Nacelle/flap fairing
99 Port flap
100 Wing centre/outer section attachment point
101 Aileron controls
102 Aileron tab (port only)
103 Aileron hinges
104 Rear spar
105 Port aileron
106 Port navigation light
107 FuG 101a radio altimeter antenna
108 Wing structure
109 Leading-edge radar array
110 Forward spar

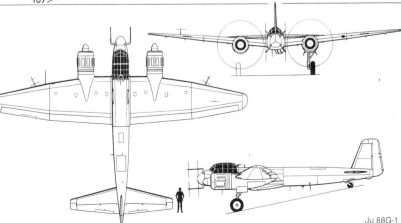

Ju 88G-1

# Bloch 152 (May 1937)

Probably the least auspicious chapter in the story of French fighter development was that provided by the production derivatives of the Bloch 150. These burly, inelegant fighters were sturdily built and capable of sustaining considerable battle damage. They were viceless, they possessed excellent dive characteristics and their agility, if perhaps lacking in vivacity and somewhat demanding on pilot muscle, was superior to that of the Messerschmitt Bf 109 against which they were to be pitted in combat. Conversely, they were too large and heavy for the power available to them and, in consequence, lacked the acceleration, level speed and climb rate necessary to compete effectively over France in the summer of 1940, these deficiencies being compounded by manifestly inadequate ammunition capacity.

Bedevilled from birth by problems associated with their fundamental design, these fighters stemmed from the Bloch 150, which, designed by Maurice Roussel, was conceived as a private venture. Almost a year elapsed between completion of the Bloch 150 prototype and its successful first flight on 4 May 1937, and then a complete structural redesign was found necessary in order to render series production practical. The re-structured and aerodynamically-refined Bloch 151 flew on 18 August 1938, the first production example being taken on charge by the Armée de l'Air on 7 March 1939, but this sub-type had already been overtaken by the Bloch 152, first flown on 15 December 1938, embodying changes intended to reduce drag and improve low-speed behaviour. In consequence, production of the Bloch 151 was restricted to 144 aircraft which were declared by the Armée de l'Air unsuited for first-line duties—although the exigencies of 1940 were to dictate their use in combat.

The Bloch 151 and 152 were externally barely distinguishable, the latter differing, apart from the GR 14N engine variant installed, in having a revised wing, which, while retaining the same torsion box, possessed 5·6 per cent more area. Teething problems were numerous, not least of these being achievement of satisfactory engine cooling with acceptable drag. Seven Groupes de Chasse were operating Bloch 151s and 152s on 10 May 1940, and of the 363 of the latter taken on charge to that time, only 80 embodied all the modifications that were at that time considered necessary to render them fully operational.

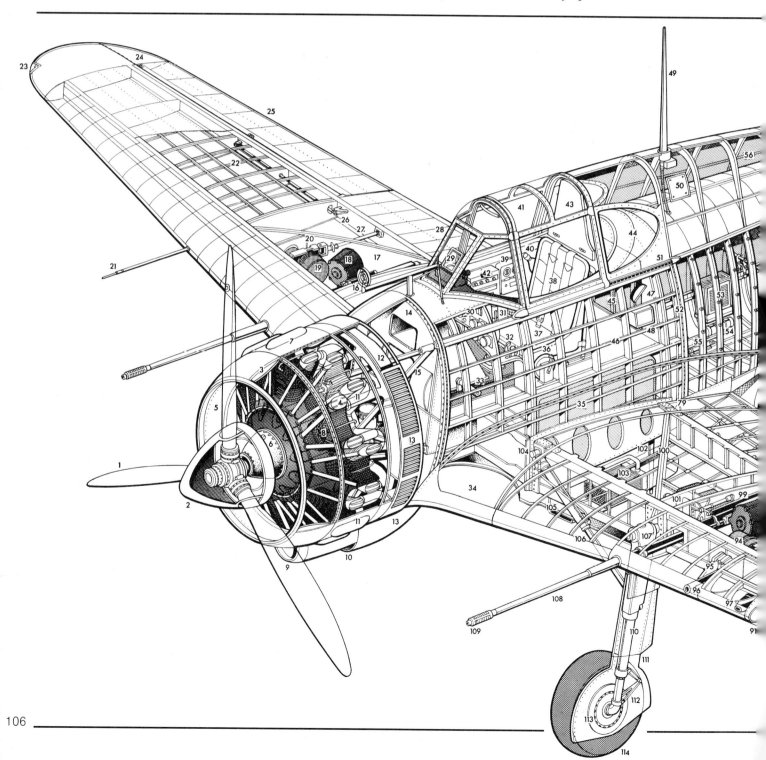

## SPECIFICATION: Bloch 152

**Power Plant:** One Gnôme-Rhône 14 N 49 14-cylinder two-row radial air-cooled engine rated at 1,180 hp at 2,400 rpm for take-off and 1,070 hp at 12,140 ft (3 700 m). Three-blade metal variable-pitch Chauvière 371 propeller. Internal fuel capacity, 93·5 Imp gal (425 l).

**Performance:** Max speed, 310 mph (500 km/h) at 18,045 ft (5 500 m); max continuous cruise, 261 mph (420 km/h); econ cruise, 211 mph (340 km/h); max range, 360 mls (580 km); time to 26,245 ft (8 000 m), 14·3 min; service ceiling, 32,810 ft (10 000 m).

**Weights:** Empty equipped, 5,066 lb (2 298 kg); normal loaded, 5,966 lb (2 706 kg).

**Dimensions:** Span, 34 ft 8⅛ in (10,57 m); length, 29 ft 10⅔ in (9,11 m); height (tail up), 11 ft 11¼ in (3,64 m); wing area, 195·58 sq ft (18,17 m²).

**Armament:** Two 20-mm Hispano-Suiza HS 404 cannon with 60 rpg and two 7,5-mm MAC 1934 machine guns with 300 or 500 rpg.

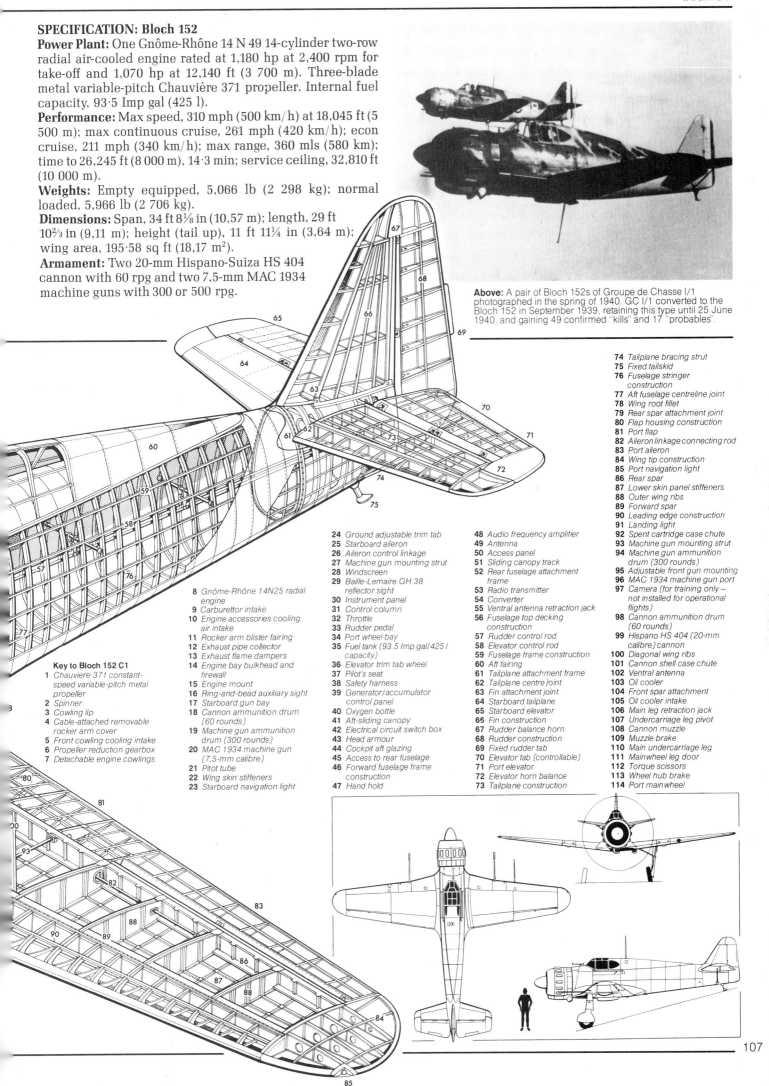

**Above:** A pair of Bloch 152s of Groupe de Chasse I/1 photographed in the spring of 1940. GC I/1 converted to the Bloch 152 in September 1939, retaining this type until 25 June 1940, and gaining 49 confirmed "kills" and 17 "probables".

**Key to Bloch 152 C1**

1 Chauviere 371 constant-speed variable-pitch metal propeller
2 Spinner
3 Cowling lip
4 Cable-attached removable rocker arm cover
5 Front cowling cooling intake
6 Propeller reduction gearbox
7 Detachable engine cowlings
8 Gnôme-Rhône 14N25 radial engine
9 Carburettor intake
10 Engine accessories cooling air intake
11 Rocker arm blister fairing
12 Exhaust pipe collector
13 Exhaust flame dampers
14 Engine bay bulkhead and firewall
15 Engine mount
16 Ring-and-bead auxiliary sight
17 Starboard gun bay
18 Cannon ammunition drum (60 rounds)
19 Machine gun ammunition drum (300 rounds)
20 MAC 1934 machine gun (7,5-mm calibre)
21 Pitot tube
22 Wing skin stiffeners
23 Starboard navigation light
24 Ground adjustable trim tab
25 Starboard aileron
26 Aileron control linkage
27 Machine gun mounting strut
28 Windscreen
29 Baille-Lemaire GH 38 reflector sight
30 Instrument panel
31 Control column
32 Throttle
33 Rudder pedal
34 Port wheel bay
35 Fuel tank (93.5 Imp gal/425 l capacity)
36 Elevator trim tab wheel
37 Pilot's seat
38 Safety harness
39 Generator/accumulator control panel
40 Oxygen bottle
41 Aft-sliding canopy
42 Electrical circuit switch box
43 Head armour
44 Cockpit aft glazing
45 Access to rear fuselage
46 Forward fuselage frame construction
47 Hand hold
48 Audio frequency amplifier
49 Antenna
50 Access panel
51 Sliding canopy track
52 Rear fuselage attachment frame
53 Radio transmitter
54 Converter
55 Ventral antenna retraction jack
56 Fuselage top decking construction
57 Rudder control rod
58 Elevator control rod
59 Fuselage frame construction
60 Aft fairing
61 Tailplane attachment frame
62 Tailplane centre joint
63 Fin attachment joint
64 Starboard tailplane
65 Starboard elevator
66 Fin construction
67 Rudder balance horn
68 Rudder construction
69 Fixed rudder tab
70 Elevator tab (controllable)
71 Port elevator
72 Elevator horn balance
73 Tailplane construction
74 Tailplane bracing strut
75 Fixed tailskid
76 Fuselage stringer construction
77 Aft fuselage centreline joint
78 Wing root fillet
79 Rear spar attachment joint
80 Flap housing construction
81 Port flap
82 Aileron linkage connecting rod
83 Port aileron
84 Wing tip construction
85 Port navigation light
86 Rear spar
87 Lower skin panel stiffeners
88 Outer wing ribs
89 Forward spar
90 Leading edge construction
91 Landing light
92 Spent cartridge case chute
93 Machine gun mounting strut
94 Machine gun ammunition drum (300 rounds)
95 Adjustable front gun mounting
96 MAC 1934 machine gun port
97 Camera (for training only – not installed for operational flights)
98 Cannon ammunition drum (60 rounds)
99 Hispano HS 404 (20-mm calibre) cannon
100 Diagonal wing ribs
101 Cannon shell case chute
102 Ventral antenna
103 Oil cooler
104 Front spar attachment
105 Oil cooler intake
106 Main leg retraction jack
107 Undercarriage leg pivot
108 Cannon muzzle
109 Muzzle brake
110 Main undercarriage leg
111 Mainwheel leg door
112 Torque scissors
113 Wheel hub brake
114 Port mainwheel

# Grumman F4F Wildcat (September 1937)

The design of any fighter must perforce involve a measure of compromise between conflicting requirements and that of a shipboard fighter more than most, a balance having to be struck between combat demands and operational venue dictates. When the Grumman F4F first appeared on carrier decks it represented what was almost certainly the best compromise achievable at that time between aeronautical and nautical requirements in a fighter monoplane.

Clearly showing lineal descent from the F3F (see pages 80-81) in its corpulence, the F4F lacked any pretensions to elegance. Designed to an outline specification drawn up by the US Navy late in 1935, the prototype, the XF4F-2, flew on 2 September 1937, being ordered into production two years later, in August 1939, as the F4F-3, soon to be emotively dubbed Wildcat. The F4F-3 began to enter US Navy service late 1940, being preceded into service by an export equivalent, which, built against French contracts, joined the Royal Navy in the previous summer as Martlet I.

Whereas both the F4F-3 and Martlet I had fixed wings, their successors, the F4F-4 and Martlet II, incorporated an ingenious method of wing folding in which the mainplanes pivoted around the mainspar. The first folding-wing Martlet IIs were deployed operationally by the Royal Navy in September 1941, and F4F-4s had entered US Navy service by April 1942, serving in strength from the carriers *Yorktown*, *Enterprise* and *Hornet* at the Battle of Midway, June 1942.

The F4F possessed an extremely good rate of climb, an excellent patrol range, superb ditching characteristics and the sturdiness necessary for intensive carrier operations. More stable to fly and therefore heavier to manoeuvre than many of its shore-based contemporaries, it nevertheless had a small turning circle and a good roll rate. Its stalling behaviour was innocuous, but operation of the undercarriage handcrank tended to result in "rollercoaster" climb-outs and acceptable spinning characteristics were not to be achieved until the advent of the definitive (FM-2) production model.

Production was eventually entrusted to Eastern Motors who built 5,460 as FM-1s and FM-2s to bring the grand total of fighters of this series built to 7,815 aircraft, of which more than 920 went to the Royal Navy, that service eventually also adopting the name Wildcat for the aircraft.

**Key to Grumman F4F-4 Wildcat**

1 Starboard navigation light
2 Wingtip
3 Starboard formation light
4 Rear spar
5 Aileron construction
6 Fixed aileron tab
7 All riveted wing construction
8 Lateral stiffeners
9 Forward canted main spar
10 'Crimped' leading edge ribs
11 Solid web forward ribs
12 Starboard outer gun blast tube
13 Carburettor air duct
14 Intake
15 Curtiss three-blade constant-speed propeller
16 Propeller cuffs
17 Propeller hub
18 Engine front face
19 Pressure baffle
20 Forward cowling ring
21 Cooler intake
22 Cooler air duct
23 Pratt & Whitney R-1830-86 radial engine
24 Rear cowling ring/flap support
25 Controllable cowling flaps
26 Downdraft ram air duct
27 Engine mounting ring
28 Anti-detonant regulator unit
29 Cartridge starter
30 Generator
31 Intercooler
32 Engine accessories
33 Bearer assembly welded cluster joint
34 Main beam
35 Lower cowl flap
36 Exhaust stub
37 Starboard mainwheel
38 Undercarriage fairing
39 Lower drag link
40 Hydraulic brake
41 Port mainwheel
42 Detachable hub cover
43 Low pressure tyre
44 Axle forging
45 Upper drag link
46 Oleo shock strut
47 Ventral fairing
48 Wheel well
49 Pivot point
50 Landing light
51 Main forging
52 Compression link

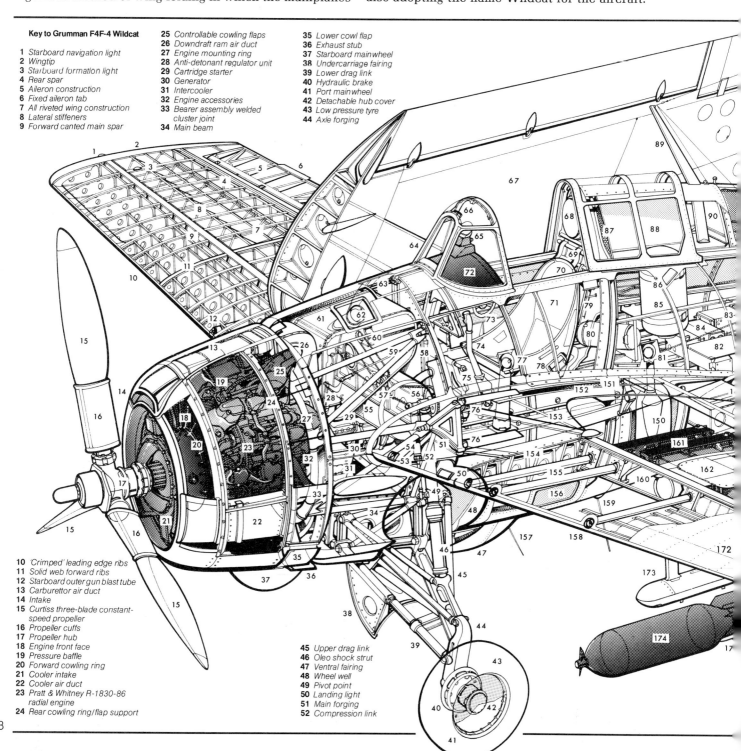

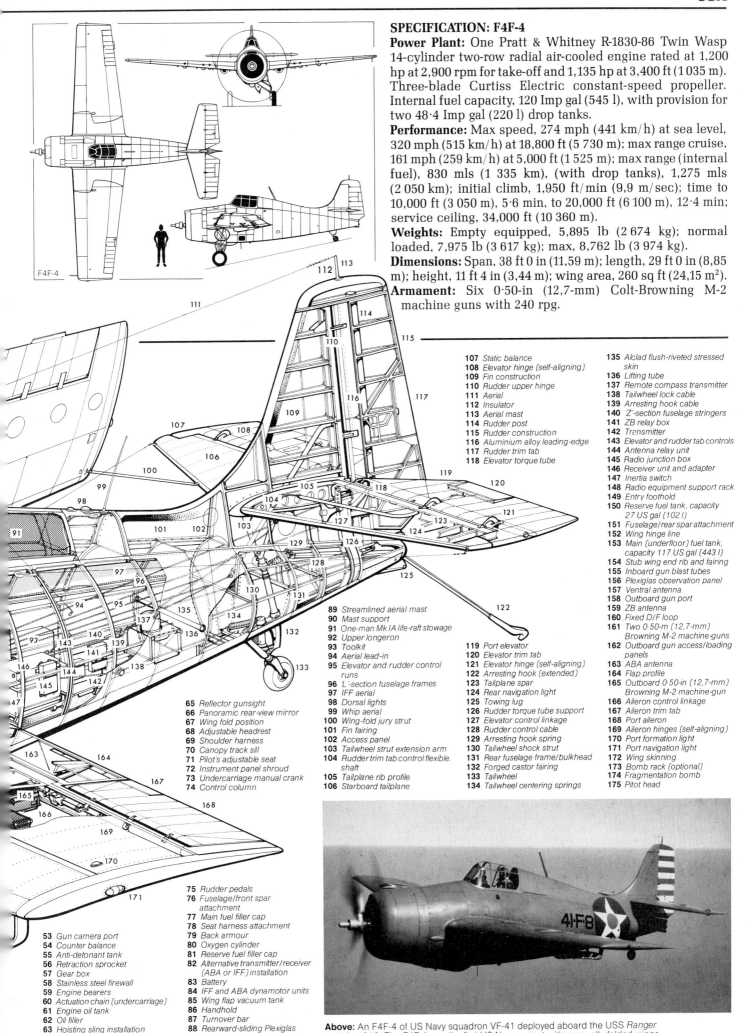

## SPECIFICATION: F4F-4

**Power Plant:** One Pratt & Whitney R-1830-86 Twin Wasp 14-cylinder two-row radial air-cooled engine rated at 1,200 hp at 2,900 rpm for take-off and 1,135 hp at 3,400 ft (1 035 m). Three-blade Curtiss Electric constant-speed propeller. Internal fuel capacity, 120 Imp gal (545 l), with provision for two 48·4 Imp gal (220 l) drop tanks.

**Performance:** Max speed, 274 mph (441 km/h) at sea level, 320 mph (515 km/h) at 18,800 ft (5 730 m); max range cruise, 161 mph (259 km/h) at 5,000 ft (1 525 m); max range (internal fuel), 830 mls (1 335 km), (with drop tanks), 1,275 mls (2 050 km); initial climb, 1,950 ft/min (9,9 m/sec); time to 10,000 ft (3 050 m), 5·6 min, to 20,000 ft (6 100 m), 12·4 min; service ceiling, 34,000 ft (10 360 m).

**Weights:** Empty equipped, 5,895 lb (2 674 kg); normal loaded, 7,975 lb (3 617 kg); max, 8,762 lb (3 974 kg).

**Dimensions:** Span, 38 ft 0 in (11,59 m); length, 29 ft 0 in (8,85 m); height, 11 ft 4 in (3,44 m); wing area, 260 sq ft (24,15 m²).

**Armament:** Six 0·50-in (12,7-mm) Colt-Browning M-2 machine guns with 240 rpg.

107 Static balance
108 Elevator hinge (self-aligning)
109 Fin construction
110 Rudder upper hinge
111 Aerial
112 Insulator
113 Aerial mast
114 Rudder post
115 Rudder construction
116 Aluminium alloy leading-edge
117 Rudder trim tab
118 Elevator torque tube

135 Alclad flush-riveted stressed skin
136 Lifting tube
137 Remote compass transmitter
138 Tailwheel lock cable
139 Arresting hook cable
140 'Z'-section fuselage stringers
141 ZB relay box
142 Transmitter
143 Elevator and rudder tab controls
144 Antenna relay unit
145 Radio junction box
146 Receiver unit and adapter
147 Inertia switch
148 Radio equipment support rack
149 Entry foothold
150 Reserve fuel tank, capacity 27 US gal (102 l)
151 Fuselage/rear spar attachment
152 Wing hinge line
153 Main (underfloor) fuel tank, capacity 117 US gal (443 l)
154 Stub wing end rib and fairing
155 Inboard gun blast tubes
156 Plexiglas observation panel
157 Ventral antenna
158 Outboard gun port
159 ZB antenna
160 Fixed D/F loop
161 Two 0·50-in (12,7-mm) Browning M-2 machine-guns
162 Outboard gun access/loading panels
163 ABA antenna
164 Flap profile
165 Outboard 0·50-in (12,7-mm) Browning M-2 machine-gun
166 Aileron control linkage
167 Aileron trim tab
168 Port aileron
169 Aileron hinges (self-aligning)
170 Port formation light
171 Port navigation light
172 Wing skinning
173 Bomb rack (optional)
174 Fragmentation bomb
175 Pitot head

89 Streamlined aerial mast
90 Mast support
91 One-man Mk IA life-raft stowage
92 Upper longeron
93 Toolkit
94 Aerial lead-in
95 Elevator and rudder control runs
96 'L'-section fuselage frames
97 IFF aerial
98 Dorsal lights
99 Whip aerial
100 Wing-fold jury strut
101 Fin fairing
102 Access panel
103 Tailwheel strut extension arm
104 Rudder trim tab control flexible shaft
105 Tailplane rib profile
106 Starboard tailplane

119 Port elevator
120 Elevator trim tab
121 Elevator hinge (self-aligning)
122 Arresting hook (extended)
123 Tailplane spar
124 Rear navigation light
125 Towing lug
126 Rudder torque tube support
127 Elevator control linkage
128 Rudder control cable
129 Arresting hook spring
130 Tailwheel shock strut
131 Rear fuselage frame/bulkhead
132 Forged castor fairing
133 Tailwheel
134 Tailwheel centering springs

65 Reflector gunsight
66 Panoramic rear-view mirror
67 Wing fold position
68 Adjustable headrest
69 Shoulder harness
70 Canopy track sill
71 Pilot's adjustable seat
72 Instrument panel shroud
73 Undercarriage manual crank
74 Control column

75 Rudder pedals
76 Fuselage/front spar attachment
77 Main fuel filler cap
78 Seat harness attachment
79 Back armour
80 Oxygen cylinder
81 Reserve fuel filler cap
82 Alternative transmitter/receiver (ABA or IFF) installation
83 Battery
84 IFF and ABA dynamotor units
85 Wing flap vacuum tank
86 Handhold
87 Turnover bar
88 Rearward-sliding Plexiglas canopy

53 Gun camera port
54 Counter balance
55 Anti-detonant tank
56 Retraction sprocket
57 Gear box
58 Stainless steel firewall
59 Engine bearers
60 Actuation chain (undercarriage)
61 Engine oil tank
62 Oil filler
63 Hoisting sling installation
64 Bullet resistant windscreen

**Above:** An F4F-4 of US Navy squadron VF-41 deployed aboard the USS *Ranger* early in 1942. The F4F-4 was the first US Navy variant with manually-folded wings.

# Macchi C.200 Saetta (December 1937)

**Above:** Late production C.200s of the 81ª squadriglia, 6º Gruppo, flying over Sicily in 1941 before the unit converted to the C.202.

The rate of fighter evolution in each country was, in the 'thirties, inevitably paced by that of indigenous power plant development. The successful creation in Britain, France and Germany of a series of high-powered low-drag liquid-cooled engines had a profound effect on fighter design in those countries, but the tardiness of the Italian aero engine industry in evolving comparable power plants placed Italian fighter designers at a distinct disadvantage when developing their first generation of all-metal stressed-skin cantilever monoplanes. One of these new-generation fighters was the C.200 Saetta (Lightning) designed by Ing Mario Castoldi.

First flown on 24 December 1937, the C.200 revealed little of its distinguished pedigree of aerodynamically superlative racing floatplanes. Its contours were essentially ungainly owing to the necessity of using a bulky drag-evoking radial engine in combination with a humped fuselage profile resulting from emphasis on pilot vision. Aesthetic appeal apart, the C.200 was a soundly conceived, innately robust fighter, the first production examples of which were completed in July 1939. It offered viceless handling and excellent response in all flight régimes. Its beautifully harmonised controls were finger-light; its climb-and-dive performance was outstanding and it provided a stable gun platform. But the C.200 was lacking in level speed and firepower.

Production of C.200s finally totalled 1,153, but only 156 were on strength when Italy declared war, 10 June 1940. With the 241st C.200, the unpopular cockpit canopy was dis-

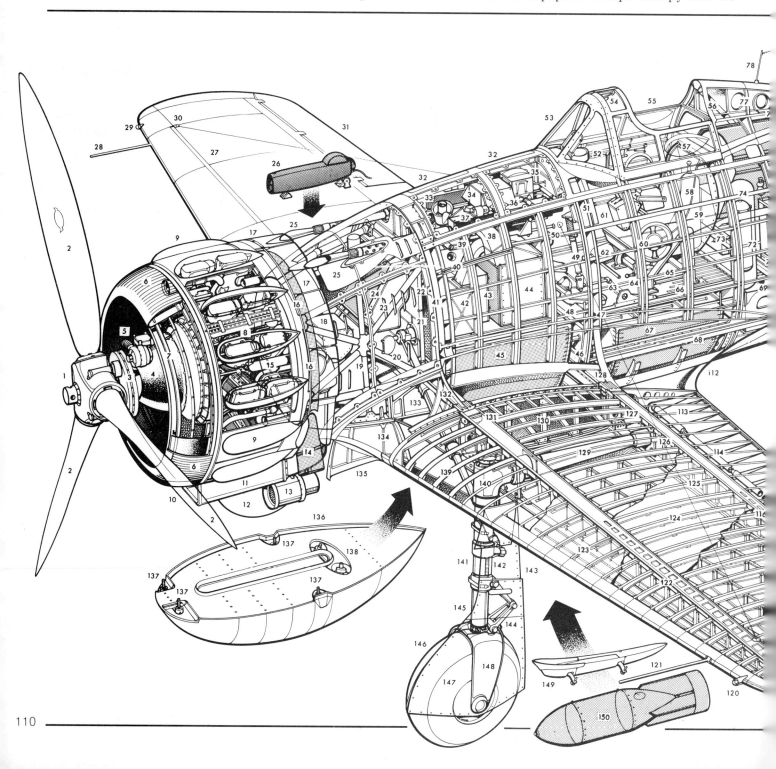

carded. The basic design, adapted for Daimler-Benz engines, spawned the excellent C.202 Folgore and C.205 Veltro.

## SPECIFICATION: C.200 Saetta

**Power Plant:** One Fiat A.74 RC.38 14-cylinder two-row radial air-cooled engine rated at 870 hp at 2,520 rpm for take-off and 840 hp at 12,465 ft (3 800 m). Three-bladed Piaggio P.1001 constant-speed propeller. Internal fuel capacity, 68 Imp gal (313 l) plus 18 Imp gal (83 l) internal overload tank and provision for 33 Imp gal (150 l) auxiliary tank.

**Performance:** (At 5,070 lb/2 300 kg) Max speed, 312 mph (503 km/h) at 14,765 ft (4 500 m); range (standard internal fuel), 354 mls (570 km) at 289 mph (465 km/h) at 19,685 ft (6 000 m), (with overload fuel and auxiliary tank), 540 mls (870 km); time to 3,280 ft (1 000 m), 1·05 min, to 16,405 ft (5 000 m), 5·85 min; ceiling, 29,200 ft (8 900 m).

**Weights:** Empty equipped, 4,451 lb (2 019 kg); normal loaded, 5,597 lb (2 539 kg).

**Dimensions:** Span, 34 ft 8½ in (10,50 m); length, 26 ft 10½ in (8,19 m); wing area 180·94 sq ft (16,81 m²).

**Armament:** Two 12,7-mm SAFAT machine guns with 370 rpg, and provision for two 110-lb (50-kg), 220-lb (100-kg) or 352-lb (160-kg) bombs under wings.

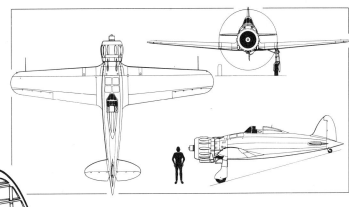

**Below:** C.200s of the 362ª squadriglia, 22º Gruppo, which spearheaded Regia Aeronautica participation in the air war over the Soviet Union in August 1941.

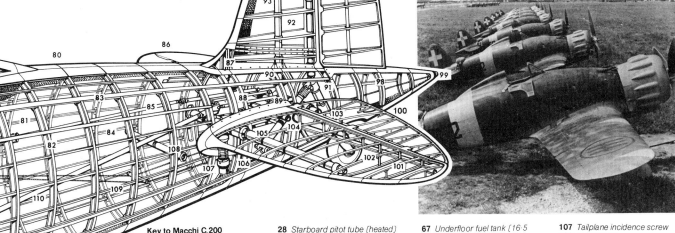

**Key to Macchi C.200 (Serie XIX) Saetta**

1 Propeller hub
2 Variable-pitch Piaggio 1001 propeller
3 Hub plate
4 Casing
5 Pitch control mechanism
6 Oil radiator
7 Cowling ring
8 Fiat A.74 R.C.38 14-cylinder radial air-cooled engine
9 Cowling rocker arm fairings
10 Carburettor intake
11 Intake housing
12 Starboard mainwheel
13 Intake filter
14 Exhaust outlet
15 Engine mounting ring
16 Exhaust collector ring
17 Adjustable cowling gills
18 Zenith compressor
19 Engine ring bearer frames
20 Oil filler access
21 Undercarriage retraction jack attachment
22 Firewall bulkhead
23 Cooling louvres
24 Oil tank (9·2 Imp gal/42 l capacity)
25 Machine gun muzzle ports
26 F.M.62 gun camera (mounted mid-chord starboard wing join)
27 Starboard mainplane

28 Starboard pitot tube (heated)
29 Starboard navigation light
30 Aerial attachment
31 Starboard aileron
32 Cowling access panels
33 Fuel filler cap
34 Allocchio Bacchini B.30 R/T set
35 Battery
36 Twin 12,7-mm Breda-SAFAT machine guns
37 Gun synchronization mechanism
38 Link and case ejector chute
39 Gun mounting arm
40 Ammunition feed chute
41 Fuselage forward frame (Frame 0)
42 Supplementary magazine
43 Ammunition magazine
44 Link/spent case collector
45 Main fuel tank (52·3 Imp gal/238 l capacity)
46 Centre-section rear spar carry-through
47 Fuselage frame (Frame 4)
48 Rudder pedal/heel rest assembly
49 Control column
50 Aerial attachment
51 Instrument panel
52 San Giorgio reflector gunsight
53 Windscreen
54 Canopy side-panel lock/release
55 Cutaway canopy side-panels
56 Turnover pylon structure
57 Side vision blisters
58 SILMCA CO₂ fire-extinguisher bottle (fuselage starboard wall)
59 Pilot's seat
60 Adjustable tailplane trim wheel
61 Throttle quadrant
62 Pilot's oxygen cylinder (to right of seat)
63 Control linkage
64 Seat adjustment handle
65 Seat mounting frame
66 Cockpit floor

67 Underfloor fuel tank (16·5 Imp gal/75 l capacity)
68 Lower longeron
69 Entry foothold
70 Cylinder support frame
71 Compressed air cylinder (2·2 Imp gal/10 l capacity)
72 Hydraulic reservoir (flap actuation)
73 Garelli compressor (fuselage starboard wall)
74 Hydraulic reservoir (undercarriage actuation)
75 Auxiliary fuel tank (18·26 Imp gal/83 l capacity)
76 Fuel filler access cut-out
77 Fairing formers
78 Stub aerial mast
79 Aerial
80 Fuselage skin
81 Fuselage structure
82 Frame
83 Upper longeron
84 Stringer
85 Rudder control rod
86 Starboard horizontal tail surfaces
87 Tailfin front attachment
88 Fuselage frame (Frame 16)
89 Elevator control horns
90 Tailplane attachment (Frame 17)
91 Fuselage aft frame (Frame 18)
92 Tailfin structure
93 Support tube
94 Rudder post
95 Aerial attachment
96 Rudder balance
97 Rudder frame
98 Tail cone
99 Tail navigation light
100 Port elevator
101 Port tailplane structure
102 Non-retractable tailwheel
103 Tailwheel shock strut
104 Tailplane incidence torque tube (+1°45" to −5°30")
105 Tailplane support tube
106 Tailwheel strut attachment

107 Tailplane incidence screw
108 Lifting tube
109 Tailplane incidence control cables
110 Elevator control rod
111 Lower longeron
112 Wing root fillet
113 Flap profile
114 Flap-operating rod
115 Flap structure
116 Wing rear spar
117 Port aileron structure
118 Wing outer section ribs
119 Port wingtip structure
120 Port navigation light
121 Port pitot tube (unheated)
122 Wing front spar
123 Leading-edge rib sections
124 Wing skin
125 Aerial
126 Undercarriage/rear spar attachment
127 Wing outer/inner section rear spar join
128 Wing root fairing former
129 Undercarriage rotation spindle
130 Centre-section outer rib
131 Wing outer/inner section front spar join
132 Frame O carry-through
133 Undercarriage retraction strut
134 Port mainwheel well
135 Mainwheel door inner section
136 Auxiliary jettisonable fuel tank (33 Imp gal/150 l capacity)
137 Attachment lugs
138 Fuel connections
139 Mainwheel leg well
140 Undercarriage pivot
141 Mainwheel leg
142 Retraction strut attachment
143 Leg doors (hinged)
144 Torque tinks
145 Shock strut
146 Port mainwheel
147 Mainwheel door outer section
148 Axle fork
149 Underwing stores pylon
150 Bomb

# Fiat CR.42 Falco (May 1938)

Possessing the dubious distinction of having been both the last single-seat fighter of biplane configuration manufactured and the last to see extensive active service, the CR.42 Falco (Falcon) brought to a close the distinguished line of fighters created by Celestino Rosatelli. Extremely light on the controls, universally viewed as a delight to fly and superbly agile, the CR.42 carried the fighting biplane to its development apex, but had the misfortune to be conceived at a time when the biplane had already been eclipsed by the monoplane as the standard international fighter configuration.

Featuring the distinctive Warren truss interplane bracing that was the unmistakable hallmark of the Rosatelli fighters, the CR.42 first flew on 23 May 1938, and was already conceptually obsolete. Nevertheless, deliveries to the Regia Aeronautica began in April 1939, export orders were obtained from Belgium, Hungary and Sweden, and production was to continue into 1943, a total of 1,781 CR.42s being delivered. It fought virtually throughout WWII, and, curiously, it fought against the Luftwaffe (with the Aéronautique Militaire Belge), alongside the Luftwaffe (with

**Above:** A CR.42 operated by the Swedish Flygflottilj 9 from Säve, near Gothenburg, from 1940 until 1944.

## Key to Fiat CR.42 Falco

1 Rudder balance
2 Rudder upper hinge
3 Rudder frame
4 Rudder post
5 Rudder hinge
6 Tailfin structure
7 Tailfin front spar
8 Tailfin frame support
9 Rudder actuating hinge
10 Tailcone
11 Tail navigation light
12 Elevator tab
13 Starboard elevator
14 Elevator balance
15 Tailplane structure
16 Fixed tailwheel
17 Hinged tailwheel spat
18 Tailwheel leg assembly
19 Tailwheel shock absorber
20 Fuselage end post frame
21 Fuselage/tailfin frames
22 Tailfin leading edge
23 Port elevator
24 Elevator balance
25 Port tailplane
26 Rudder cable turnbuckles
27 Fuselage dorsal decking formers
28 Elevator tab control cables
29 Fuselage upper frame
30 Fuselage fabric stringers
31 Lifting point
32 Starboard aileron
33 Aileron hinge
34 Aileron leading edge balances
35 Aileron control cable
36 Wing fabric covering
37 Starboard upper wingtip
38 Starboard navigation light
39 Aileron control cable turnbuckle
40 Aileron control cable run
41 Wing ribs
42 Wing rear spar
43 Fuselage framework
44 Elevator control rod linkage
45 Rudder cables
46 Fuselage cross-frame members
47 Pilot's headrest fairing
48 Pilot's headrest
49 Cockpit coaming
50 Oxygen cylinder
51 Fire extinguisher
52 Pilot's seat
53 Compressed air cylinder
54 Air cleansing filter
55 Compressor
56 Pilot's seat support frame
57 Rudder bar assembly
58 Control column
59 Instrument panel
60 Gunsight
61 Windscreen
62 Windshield frame
63 Pilot's entry handhold
64 Wing structure
65 Generator for underwing searchlights (night-fighter variant)
66 Fuselage/upper wing rear strut (aileron cable run)
67 Interplane strut attachment
68 Upper wing rear spar

69 Internal cross-brace wires
70 Wing ribs
71 Port aileron
72 Aileron leading edge balances
73 Aileron hinge
74 Interplane outer strut attachment
75 Wing outer ribs
76 Port upper wingtip

77 Port navigation light
78 Wing leading edge
79 Upper wing front spar
80 Aileron control cable turn-buckle
81 Interplane cross-brace wires
82 Pitot head
83 Interplane outer struts
84 Port lower wing
85 Strut lower attachment

86 Lower wing rear spring
87 Wing skinning
88 Gun muzzles
89 Fuselage/upper wing strut assembly
90 Strut/upper wing centre join
91 Internal brace
92 Upper wing centre-section profile
93 0·50-in (12·7-mm) machine gun
94 Ammunition feed chute
95 Ammunition magazine
96 Fuselage supplementary fuel tank, capacity 24 Imp gal (110 l)
97 Cartridge collector box
98 Fuselage main fuel tank, capacity 77 Imp gal (350 l)
99 Fuselage frame
100 Strut attachment point
101 Machine gun blast tube
102 Access panels
103 Fuel filler point
104 Oil filler point
105 Gun muzzle troughs
106 Gun synchronization control
107 Supplementary oil tank
108 Engine bearer attachment
109 Compressor
110 Main oil tank
111 Firewall/bulkhead
112 Cooling gills
113 Filter
114 Engine cowling ring
115 Exhaust collector ring
116 Cowling panelling
117 Fiat A.74R radial engine

118 Cylinder head fairings
119 Cowling nose profile
120 Propeller control mechanism
121 Propeller hub
122 Fiat three-blade propeller
123 Spinner
124 Wheelspat strakes (servicing access)
125 Carburettor intake
126 Port wheelspat
127 Port mainwheel
128 Carburettor intake trunking

129 Exhaust outlet
130 Radiator wing root intake
131 Intake duct
132 Starboard oil radiator assembly
133 Wing root exhaust
134 Lower wing end rib/fuselage attachment
135 Undercarriage attachment
136 Undercarriage rear strut attachment
137 Lower wing structure
138 Interplane inner struts
139 Pitot head
140 Interplane outer struts
141 Lower wing trailing edge
142 Rear spar
143 Interplane strut attachment
144 Wing ribs

145 Front spar
146 Undercarriage leg rear strut
147 Undercarriage leg
148 Brace strut
149 Leg/trouser attachment
150 Undercarriage trouser join
151 Torque strut
152 Axle
153 Brake line
154 Wheelspat strakes (servicing access)
155 Hub access panel
156 Mainwheel spat
157 Starboard mainwheel
158 Underwing searchlights (night-fighter variant)

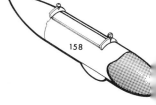

the Regia Aeronautica) and with the Luftwaffe itself, singing the swan-song of the fighting biplane while so doing.

### SPECIFICATION: CR.42 Falco

**Power Plant:** One Fiat A.74 R1C.38 14-cylinder two-row radial air-cooled engine rated at 858 hp at 2,500 rpm (for three minutes) for take-off and 840 hp at 12,465 ft (3 800 m). Three-bladed variable-pitch Fiat 3D 41-1 propeller. Internal fuel capacity, 101 Imp gal (460 l).

**Performance:** Max speed, 212 mph (342 km/h) at sea level, 247 mph (397 km/h) at 9,840 ft (3 000 m), 267 mph (430 km/h) at 16,405 ft (5 000 m); climb to 3,280 ft (1 000 m), 1·4 min, to 9,840 ft (3 000 m), 4·25 min, to 16,405 ft (5 000 m), 7·33 min; service ceiling 33,465 ft (10 200 m); range, 481 mls (775 km) at 236 mph (380 km/h) at 18,045 ft (5 500 m).

**Weights:** Empty equipped, 3,929 lb (1 782 kg); normal loaded, 5,059 lb (2 295 kg).

**Dimensions:** Span, 31 ft 9⅞ in (9,70 m); length, 27 ft 1²/₃ in (8,27 m); height, 11 ft 9¹/₃ in (3,59 m); wing area, 241·11 sq ft (22,40 m²).

**Armament:** Two 12,7-mm SAFAT machine guns with 400 rpg.

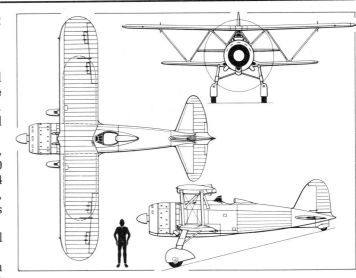

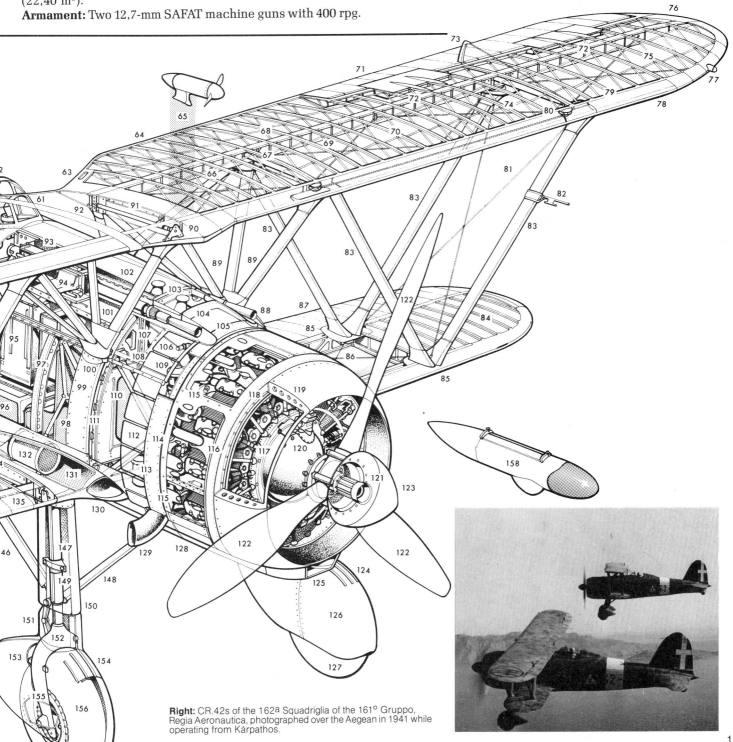

**Right:** CR.42s of the 162ª Squadriglia of the 161° Gruppo, Regia Aeronautica, photographed over the Aegean in 1941 while operating from Kàrpathos.

# Polikarpov I-153 (mid 1938)

With the dawn of the 'forties, the fighter biplane possessed barely more relevance to aerial warfare than did cavalry to a land battle. Nevertheless, the Soviet Union, which, paradoxically, had been in the vanguard of the development of cantilever monoplane fighters with retractable undercarriages, had persisted, like Italy, in its belief in the biplane long after this configuration for fighters had been discarded by the other major air powers.

Some difficulties experienced by I-16 pilots in combating the supremely agile Fiat CR.32 biplane had led to a Soviet decision to continue pursuit of fighter biplane development, Nikolai N. Polikarpov being assigned the task of evolving as expeditiously as possible a new and more potent warplane of this type. Responsibility for the project was given by Polikarpov to one of his principal design team leaders, Aleksei Ya Shcherbakov, who, in order to accelerate development, based the new fighter on the existing I-152 (I-15bis), the basic structure of which, albeit refined in detail and extensively re-stressed, was retained. The drag-evoking centre section cabane of the I-152 was rejected, the upper wing roots being neatly "gulled" into the fuselage,

**Above:** An I-153 of the Chinese Nationalist Air Force, circa 1941, 93 having been sent to China early 1940.

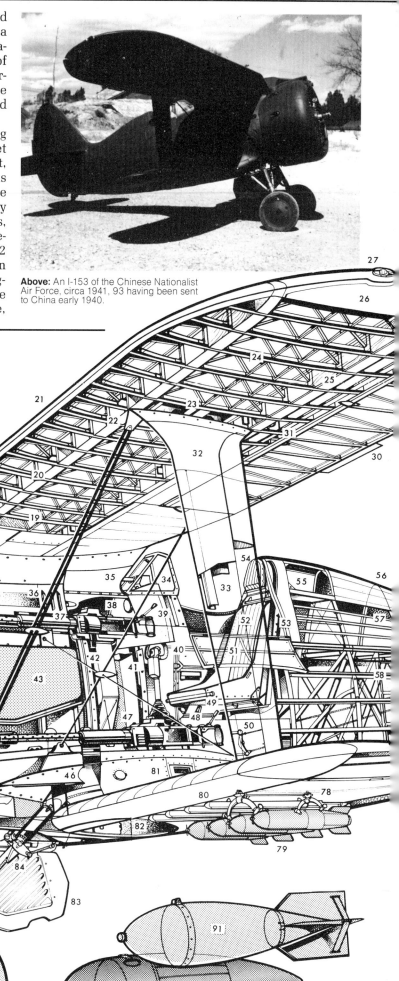

and a complex but ingenious main undercarriage retraction system was adopted.

The project received official approval on 11 October 1937 as the I-153 (alternatively I-15ter), prototypes completing State Acceptance Tests in the autumn of 1938. Production was immediately begun at Factories Nos 1 and 156 in the Moscow area, initial deliveries commencing during the late spring of 1939. The first I-153s were hurriedly sent to participate in the so-called "Nomonhan" fighting between Russo-Mongolian and Japanese forces in the summer of 1939, the results achieved being sufficient to disillusion the most ardent biplane protagonists; it was manifestly obvious that the reasoning behind the I-153 had been fundamentally unsound.

Two factories were already engaged in large-scale I-153 production, however, so the programme—during the 18-month production life of the I-153 deliveries averaged 48 weekly—had to be continued until the last weeks of 1940, when 3,437 had been built. The I-153 was thus numerically the second most important fighter in the Soviet inventory when the Wehrmacht attacked, June 1941.

## SPECIFICATION: I-153

**Power Plant:** One Shvetsov M-62 nine-cylinder radial air-cooled engine rated at 1,000 hp at 2,200 rpm for take-off and 850 hp at 5,020 ft (1 530 m). Two-bladed two-pitch metal AV-1D or -2 propeller. Internal fuel capacity, 68 Imp gal (310 l) with provision also for two 17.6 Imp gal (80 l) auxiliary fuel tanks.

**Performance:** Max speed, 227 mph (366 km/h) at sea level, 280 mph (450 km/h) at 15,090 ft (4 600 m); normal cruise, 184 mph (297 km/h) at 6,560 ft (2 000 m); range (internal fuel), 292 mls (470 km) at 184 mph (297 km/h), (with auxiliary tanks), 497 mls (800 km) at 168 mph (270 km/h); time to 3,280 ft (1 000 m), 0.85 min, to 9,840 ft (3 000 m), 3.0 min, to 16,400 ft (5 000 m), 5.3 min.

**Weights:** Empty equipped, 3,201 lb (1 452 kg); normal loaded, 4,221 lb (1 960 kg); max, 4,652 lb (2 110 kg).

**Dimensions:** Span, 32 ft 9½ in (10,00 m); length, 20 ft 3 in (6,17 m); height (tail down), 9 ft 2¼ in (2,80 m); wing area, 238.31 sq ft (22,14 m²).

**Armament:** Four 7,62-mm Shpital'ny-Komaritsky ShKAS machine guns with 650 rpg.

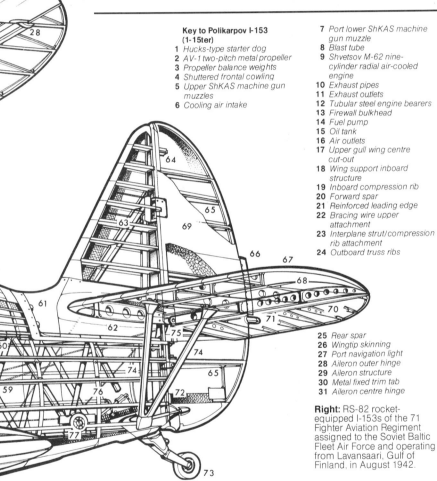

**Key to Polikarpov I-153 (I-15ter)**
1 Hucks-type starter dog
2 AV-1 two-pitch metal propeller
3 Propeller balance weights
4 Shuttered frontal cowling
5 Upper ShKAS machine gun muzzles
6 Cooling air intake
7 Port lower ShKAS machine gun muzzle
8 Blast tube
9 Shvetsov M-62 nine-cylinder radial air-cooled engine
10 Exhaust pipes
11 Exhaust outlets
12 Tubular steel engine bearers
13 Firewall bulkhead
14 Fuel pump
15 Oil tank
16 Air outlets
17 Upper gull wing centre cut-out
18 Wing support inboard structure
19 Inboard compression rib
20 Forward spar
21 Reinforced leading edge
22 Bracing wire upper attachment
23 Interplane strut/compression rib attachment
24 Outboard truss ribs
25 Rear spar
26 Wingtip skinning
27 Port navigation light
28 Aileron outer hinge
29 Aileron structure
30 Metal fixed trim tab
31 Aileron centre hinge
32 Aerofoil-section interplane strut
33 Main strut member
34 Three-piece windscreen
35 OP type gun sight
36 Cooling air louvres
37 Port upper 7,62-mm Shpital'ny-Komaritsky machine gun
38 Instrument panel
39 Manual gun cocking mechanism
40 Control column spade grip
41 Ammunition tanks (650 rpg)
42 Interplane bracing wires spacer
43 Contoured fuselage fuel tank (68 Imp gal/310 l capacity)
44 Engine bearer support frame
45 Bracing wire lower attachment
46 Lower mainplane fairing
47 Port lower 7,62-mm Shpital'ny-Komaritsky machine gun
48 Seat support frame
49 Manual gun cocking mechanism
50 Elevator control cables
51 Hinged entry/access flap
52 Pilot's seat
53 Back armour (9-mm)
54 Pilot's headrest
55 Stowage compartment
56 Dorsal decking
57 Formers
58 L-section light alloy stringers
59 Elevator control cables
60 Chrome-molybdenum tubular steel fuselage frame
61 Tail fin/fuselage fairing
62 Tailplane inboard rib
63 Tail fin structure
64 Rudder upper hinge
65 Rudder structure
66 Adjustable trim tab
67 Port tailplane
68 Tailplane spar
69 Fabric skinning
70 Port elevator
71 Rear navigation light
72 Rudder lower hinge
73 Non-retractable solid-type tailwheel
74 Light alloy tailplane bracing struts
75 Elevator control horn
76 Tailwheel shock-absorber
77 Lifting point
78 Outboard bomb/tank shackles
79 82-mm RS-82 rocket missiles
80 RS-82 launch rails
81 Entry step
82 Port mainwheel well
83 Mainwheel well fairing plate
84 Mainwheel retraction/rotation strut
85 Mainwheel leg/door actuation rod
86 Starboard mainwheel oleo leg
87 Starboard light-alloy wheel fairing panel
88 Port wheel fairing panel
89 Starboard mainwheel
90 Wheel cover
91 Alternative 110-lb/50-kg bomb, or
92 Auxiliary drop tank (17.6 Imp gal/80 l capacity)

**Right:** RS-82 rocket-equipped I-153s of the 71 Fighter Aviation Regiment assigned to the Soviet Baltic Fleet Air Force and operating from Lavansaari, Gulf of Finland, in August 1942.

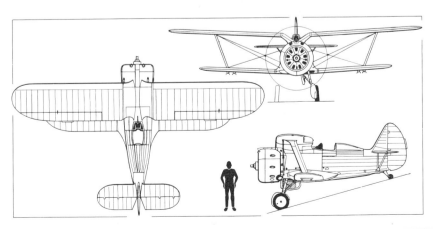

# Curtiss P-40 (October 1938)

In developing the P-40, Donovan Berlin and his team were capitalising on investment in an existing design rather than attempting an advance in the state of the fighter art; an unaspiring evolutive growth of an already proven airframe to produce a comparatively modest performance increment. In short, the P-40 was a straightforward extrapolation of its predecessor, the P-36 alias Hawk 75A (see pages 82-83), and, as such, was to prove itself an indifferent and controversial fighter, lauded for its delightful handling characteristics and vilified for its lack of agility; praised for its sturdiness and abused for its inability to compete with its principal adversaries on anything like equal terms.

The shortcomings of the P-40 reflected unfavourably on the outmoded tactical concepts that gave it birth rather than the competence of the Curtiss design team. From the mid 'thirties, the "ascendancy of bombardment over pursuit" doctrine had inhibited US fighter development. The US Army Air Corps saw the primary missions of the fighter as coastal defence and close air support, emphasis thus being placed on sturdiness and low altitude capability, the P-40's characteristics being a consequence of this concept.

The prototype, ordered in July 1937 as a rework of the 10th production P-36 with an Allison V-1710 liquid-cooled engine, flew as the XP-40 on 14 October 1938, being dubbed Hawk 81A by its manufacturer. An order for 524 was placed on 27 April 1939, and the first production P-40 flew on 4 April 1940. The P-40 was extraordinarily robust and possessed light and very effective ailerons, thanks largely to which its handling characteristics were delightful, but it was lamentably lacking in practical capability by European standards —it possessed no protective armour or self-sealing tanks and its armament was restricted to a pair of 'fifties!

With delivery of the 200th aircraft as the first P-40B, self-sealing fuel tanks and some armour were provided, and armament was augmented by a pair of 0·30-in (7,62-mm) wing guns, the wing armament being doubled for the final 324 of the contract delivered as P-40Cs. Weight escalation had a deleterious effect on performance of these more battleworthy P-40s, with the result that their operational career was inauspicious. Despite their manifest shortcomings, however, the RAF

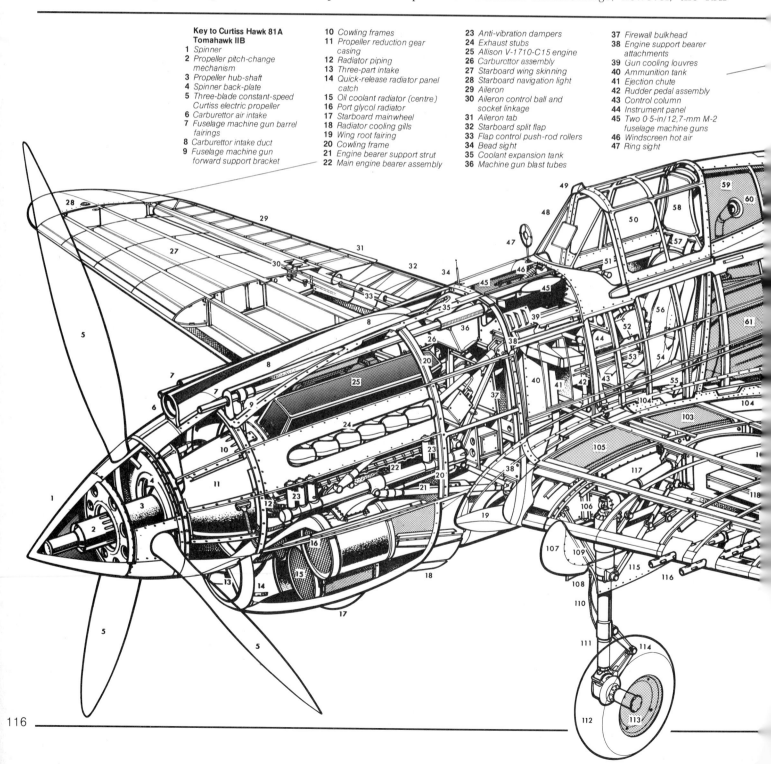

**Key to Curtiss Hawk 81A Tomahawk IIB**
1 Spinner
2 Propeller pitch-change mechanism
3 Propeller hub-shaft
4 Spinner back-plate
5 Three-blade constant-speed Curtiss electric propeller
6 Carburettor air intake
7 Fuselage machine gun barrel fairings
8 Carburettor intake duct
9 Fuselage machine gun forward support bracket
10 Cowling frames
11 Propeller reduction gear casing
12 Radiator piping
13 Three-part intake
14 Quick-release radiator panel catch
15 Oil coolant radiator (centre)
16 Port glycol radiator
17 Starboard mainwheel
18 Radiator cooling gills
19 Wing root fairing
20 Cowling frame
21 Engine bearer support strut
22 Main engine bearer assembly
23 Anti-vibration dampers
24 Exhaust stubs
25 Allison V-1710-C15 engine
26 Carburettor assembly
27 Starboard wing skinning
28 Starboard navigation light
29 Aileron
30 Aileron control ball and socket linkage
31 Aileron tab
32 Starboard split flap
33 Flap control push-rod rollers
34 Bead sight
35 Coolant expansion tank
36 Machine gun blast tubes
37 Firewall bulkhead
38 Engine support bearer attachments
39 Gun cooling louvres
40 Ammunition tank
41 Ejection chute
42 Rudder pedal assembly
43 Control column
44 Instrument panel
45 Two 0·5-in/12,7-mm M-2 fuselage machine guns
46 Windscreen hot air
47 Ring sight

took on charge a total of 1,180 similar aircraft (including 230 from ex-French contracts) which it designated as Tomahawk Is, IIAs and IIBs (Hawk 81A-1s and -2s).

Availability of an uprated version of the V-1710 engine with an external spur reduction gear prompted redesign of the basic Hawk 81A as the Hawk 87A. The new

continued on page 119 ▶

## SPECIFICATION: P-40C

**Power Plant:** One Allison V-1710-33 12-cylinder vee liquid-cooled engine rated at 1,090 hp at 3,000 rpm for take-off and 1,090 hp at 15,000 ft (4 570 m). Three-bladed Curtiss constant-speed metal propeller. Internal fuel capacity, 132·6 Imp gal (603 l), including 33·7 Imp gal (153 l) reserve tank.

**Performance:** Max speed (at 7,327 lb/3 323 kg), 345 mph (555 km/h) at 15,000 ft (4 572 m); max continuous cruise, 270 mph (434 km/h); initial climb, 2,690 ft/min (13,66 m/sec); service ceiling, 29,500 ft (8 990 m); range (max internal fuel), 800 mls (1 287 km).

**Weights:** Empty equipped, 5,812 lb (2 636 kg); normal loaded, 7,549 lb (3 424 kg); max, 8,058 lb (3 655 kg).

**Dimensions:** Span, 37 ft 3½ in (11,37 m); length, 31 ft 8½ in (9,66 m); ht, 10 ft 7 in (3,22 m); wing area, 236 sq ft (21,92 m²).

**Armament:** Two 0·50-in (12,7-mm) Colt-Browning machine guns with 380 rpg and four 0·30-in (7,62-mm) Colt-Browning machine guns with 490 rpg.

Hawk 81A

48  Clear vision windscreen
49  Faired rear-view mirror
50  Aft-sliding Plexiglas canopy
51  Cockpit ventilation control
52  Throttle quadrant
53  Engine control rods
54  Pilot's seat
55  Control linkage
56  Harness
57  Seat support frame

58  Pilot's headrest
59  Rear-view vision cut-out
60  Fuselage fuel tank filler cap
61  Fuselage auxiliary fuel tank, capacity 41 Imp gal (218 l)
62  Control cables
63  Hydraulics tank
64  Oil tank, capacity 9.6 Imp gal (43,6 l)
65  Oil tank filler cap
66  Aerials
67  Dorsal (offset) identification light
68  Aerial lead-in
69  TR9D radio receiver/transmitter equipment
70  Fuselage stringers
71  Fuselage frame

72  Starboard tailplane
73  Starboard elevator
74  Tailfin structure
75  Tail navigation lights
76  Aerial attachment
77  Rudder upper (external) hinge bracket
78  Rudder structure
79  Rudder centre hinge
80  Rudder trim tab
81  Elevator tab
82  Port elevator
83  Tailplane structure
84  Rudder lower hinge
85  Tailwheel door
86  Retractable tailwheel
87  Tailwheel oleo leg
88  Access plates
89  Elevator control horn linkage
90  Tailplane attachments
91  Trim tab control chains
92  Tailwheel retraction mechanism
93  Elevator control cables
94  Lifting tube
95  Rudder control cables
96  Battery
97  Fuselage compartment access door
98  Oxygen cylinders
99  Hydraulics pump

100  Wing root fillet
101  Port split flap
102  Port mainwheel well
103  Wing main (aft) fuel tank, capacity 51 Imp gal (232 l)
104  Wing/fuselage attachment plates
105  Wing reserve (forward) fuel tank, capacity 33.6 Imp gal (153 l)
106  Rotation bevel gears
107  Undercarriage leg fairing
108  Fairing doors
109  Brace strut
110  Brake cable
111  Mainwheel oleo pneumatic leg
112  Smooth contour tyre
113  Hub cover
114  Torque links
115  Retraction drag struts
116  Wing machine gun barrels
117  Undercarriage-retraction cylinder
118  Inboard wing gun ammunition box (490 rounds)
119  Blast tubes
120  Outboard wing gun ammunition box (490 rounds)
121  Two 0.3-in (7.62-mm) Colt MG-40 wing machine guns
122  Outboard wing structure
123  Aileron control link access
124  Aileron trim tab
125  Port aileron
126  Port wingtip structure
127  Aerial attachment
128  Port navigation light
129  Leading-edge ribs
130  Pitot tube

**Right:** A Tomahawk IIB (Hawk 81A) of No 414 Sqdn, RAF, and (below right) one of the original P-40s (no wing guns) with the 21st Pursuit Sqdn, 35th Pursuit Group, in 1941.

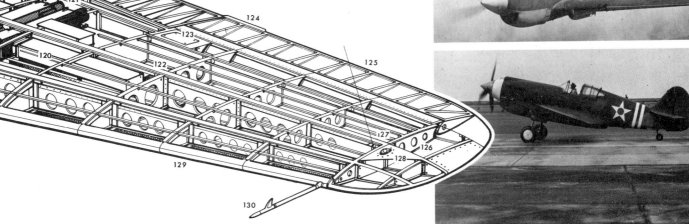

# Curtiss P-40

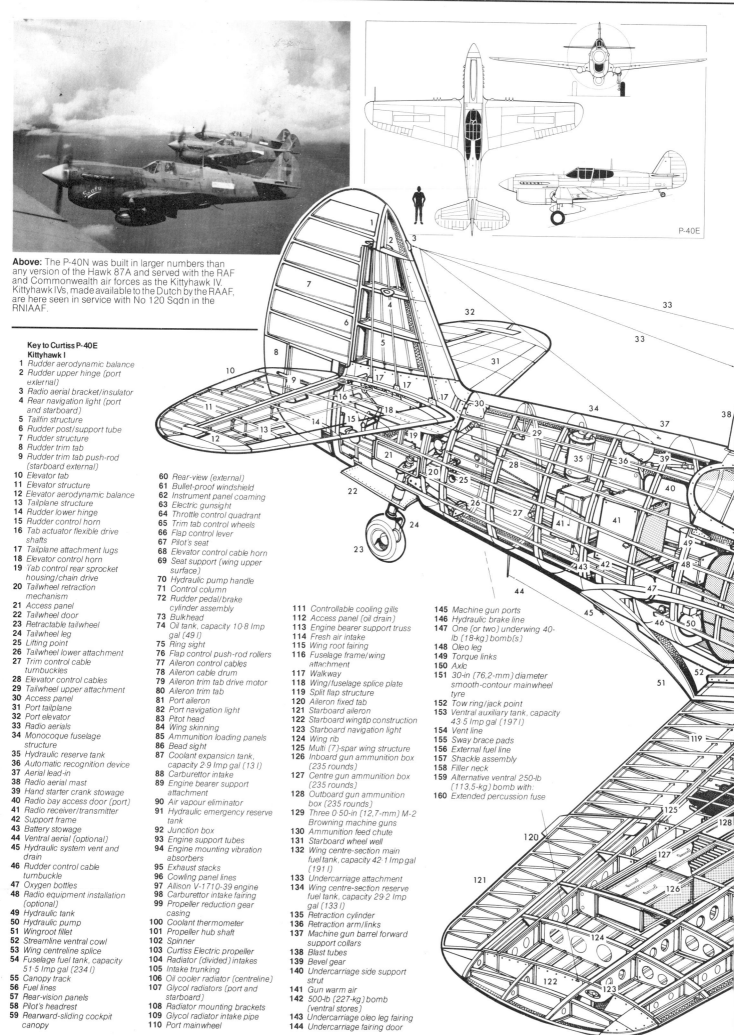

**Above:** The P-40N was built in larger numbers than any version of the Hawk 87A and served with the RAF and Commonwealth air forces as the Kittyhawk IV. Kittyhawk IVs, made available to the Dutch by the RAAF, are here seen in service with No 120 Sqdn in the RNIAAF.

P-40E

**Key to Curtiss P-40E Kittyhawk I**

1 Rudder aerodynamic balance
2 Rudder upper hinge (port external)
3 Radio aerial bracket/insulator
4 Rear navigation light (port and starboard)
5 Tailfin structure
6 Rudder post/support tube
7 Rudder structure
8 Rudder trim tab
9 Rudder trim tab push-rod (starboard external)
10 Elevator tab
11 Elevator structure
12 Elevator aerodynamic balance
13 Tailplane structure
14 Rudder lower hinge
15 Rudder control horn
16 Tab actuator flexible drive shafts
17 Tailplane attachment lugs
18 Elevator control horn
19 Tab control rear sprocket housing/chain drive
20 Tailwheel retraction mechanism
21 Access panel
22 Tailwheel door
23 Retractable tailwheel
24 Tailwheel leg
25 Lifting point
26 Tailwheel lower attachment
27 Trim control cable turnbuckles
28 Elevator control cables
29 Tailwheel upper attachment
30 Access panel
31 Port tailplane
32 Port elevator
33 Radio aerials
34 Monocoque fuselage structure
35 Hydraulic reserve tank
36 Automatic recognition device
37 Aerial lead-in
38 Radio aerial mast
39 Hand starter crank stowage
40 Radio bay access door (port)
41 Radio receiver/transmitter
42 Support frame
43 Battery stowage
44 Ventral aerial (optional)
45 Hydraulic system vent and drain
46 Rudder control cable turnbuckle
47 Oxygen bottles
48 Radio equipment installation (optional)
49 Hydraulic tank
50 Hydraulic pump
51 Wingroot fillet
52 Streamline ventral cowl
53 Wing centreline splice
54 Fuselage fuel tank, capacity 51·5 Imp gal (234 l)
55 Canopy track
56 Fuel lines
57 Rear-vision panels
58 Pilot's headrest
59 Rearward-sliding cockpit canopy

60 Rear-view (external)
61 Bullet-proof windshield
62 Instrument panel coaming
63 Electric gunsight
64 Throttle control quadrant
65 Trim tab control wheels
66 Flap control lever
67 Pilot's seat
68 Elevator control cable horn
69 Seat support (wing upper surface)
70 Hydraulic pump handle
71 Control column
72 Rudder pedal/brake cylinder assembly
73 Bulkhead
74 Oil tank, capacity 10·8 Imp gal (49 l)
75 Ring sight
76 Flap control push-rod rollers
77 Aileron control cables
78 Aileron cable drum
79 Aileron trim tab drive motor
80 Aileron trim tab
81 Port aileron
82 Port navigation light
83 Pitot head
84 Wing skinning
85 Ammunition loading panels
86 Bead sight
87 Coolant expansion tank, capacity 2·9 Imp gal (13 l)
88 Carburettor intake
89 Engine bearer support attachment
90 Air vapour eliminator
91 Hydraulic emergency reserve tank
92 Junction box
93 Engine support tubes
94 Engine mounting vibration absorbers
95 Exhaust stacks
96 Cowling panel lines
97 Allison V-1710-39 engine
98 Carburettor intake fairing
99 Propeller reduction gear casing
100 Coolant thermometer
101 Propeller hub shaft
102 Spinner
103 Curtiss Electric propeller
104 Radiator (divided) intakes
105 Intake trunking
106 Oil cooler radiator (centreline)
107 Glycol radiators (port and starboard)
108 Radiator mounting brackets
109 Glycol radiator intake pipe
110 Port mainwheel

111 Controllable cooling gills
112 Access panel (oil drain)
113 Engine bearer support truss
114 Fresh air intake
115 Wing root fairing
116 Fuselage frame/wing attachment
117 Walkway
118 Wing/fuselage splice plate
119 Split flap structure
120 Aileron fixed tab
121 Starboard aileron
122 Starboard wingtip construction
123 Starboard navigation light
124 Wing rib
125 Multi (7)-spar wing structure
126 Inboard gun ammunition box (235 rounds)
127 Centre gun ammunition box (235 rounds)
128 Outboard gun ammunition box (235 rounds)
129 Three 0·50-in (12,7-mm) M-2 Browning machine guns
130 Ammunition feed chute
131 Starboard wheel well
132 Wing centre-section main fuel tank, capacity 42·1 Imp gal (191 l)
133 Undercarriage attachment
134 Wing centre-section reserve fuel tank, capacity 29·2 Imp gal (133 l)
135 Retraction cylinder
136 Retraction arm/links
137 Machine gun barrel forward support collars
138 Blast tubes
139 Bevel gear
140 Undercarriage side support strut
141 Gun warm air
142 500-lb (227-kg) bomb (ventral stores)
143 Undercarriage oleo leg fairing
144 Undercarriage fairing door

145 Machine gun ports
146 Hydraulic brake line
147 One (or two) underwing 40-lb (18-kg) bomb(s)
148 Oleo leg
149 Torque links
150 Axle
151 30-in (76,2-mm) diameter smooth-contour mainwheel tyre
152 Tow ring/jack point
153 Ventral auxiliary tank, capacity 43·5 Imp gal (197 l)
154 Vent line
155 Sway brace pads
156 External fuel line
157 Shackle assembly
158 Filler neck
159 Alternative ventral 250-lb (113,5-kg) bomb with:
160 Extended percussion fuse

cont ▶ engine was shorter with a higher thrust line, necessitating redesign of the nose, the radiator was relocated, the fuselage cross section was reduced and the rear fuselage recontoured to improve pilot view aft and down. The new model flew as the Hawk 87A on 22 May 1941, and was already recipient of a British contract for 560 aircraft (Kittyhawk I). Parallel production was undertaken for the USAAF as the P-40D (first 22 aircraft) and P-40E, the latter having armament increased from four to six 'fifties, the name Warhawk being adopted.

The Warhawk was faster at altitude and more combatworthy, but take-off performance, climb and manoeuvrability proved inferior. Orders were placed for 2,320 E-model fighters, 1,500 of these being purchased from Lend-Lease funds. Development of the Allison-engined version continued with the P-40K (a longer fuselage being introduced with the K-10 batch) and P-40M, parallel production being undertaken of the P-40F and P-40L with the Packard-built Merlin. Production terminated with the Allison-engined P-40N (5,216 completed) to bring the grand total of Hawk 81A and 87A fighters built to 13,738 aircraft.

## SPECIFICATION: P-40E-1

**Power Plant:** One Allison V-1710-39 12-cylinder vee liquid-cooled engine rated at 1,150 hp at 3,000 rpm for take-off and as military power at 11,700 ft (3 570 m). Three-bladed Curtiss Electric constant-speed metal propeller. Internal fuel capacity, 124 Imp gal (564 l) and provision for one 43 Imp gal (197 l) drop tank.
**Performance:** Max speed, 335 mph (539 km/h) at 5,000 ft (1 525 m), 362 mph (582 km/h) at 15,000 ft (4 575 m); max continuous cruise, 296 mph (476 km/h) at 5,000 ft (1 525 m), 312 mph (502 km/h) at 15,000 ft (4 575 m); time to 5,000 ft (1 525 m), 2·4 min, to 15,000 ft (4 575 m), 7·6 min; range (internal fuel at max continuous cruise), 525 mls (845 km).
**Weights:** Empty equipped, 6,350 lb (2 880 kg); normal loaded 8,400 lb (3 814 kg); max, 9,100 lb (4 131 kg).
**Dimensions:** Span, 37 ft 4 in (11,38 m); length, 31 ft 9 in (9,68 m); height, 12 ft 4 in (3,76 m); wing area, 236 sq ft (21,92 m²).
**Armament:** Six 0·50-in (12,7-mm) Colt-Browning M2 machine guns with (average of) 281 rpg. Provision for one bomb (up to 500 lb/227 kg) on fuselage centreline and two 100-lb (45-kg) bombs under wings.

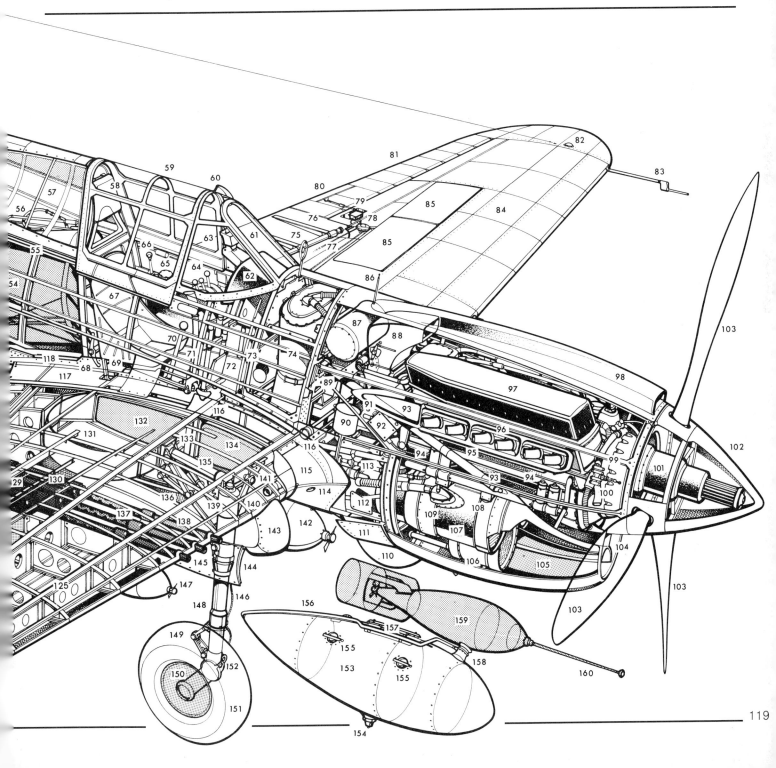

# Dewoitine D 520 (October 1938)

It was France's misfortune that, when WWII commenced, her aircraft industry had only just begun to recover the creativity in fighter design displayed in the early 'thirties. The M.S.406 (see pages 88-89) had proved pedestrian in both concept and capability, and the Bloch 152 (see pages 106-107), as the end product of an unduly protracted gestation, was to lack some qualities vital for success in fighter-versus-fighter combat. The D 520, on the other hand, fully restored French fighter design to international standards; the tragedy was that quantity availability came too late seriously to affect the issue in French skies in the summer of 1942.

Designed by Emile Dewoitine in collaboration with Robert Castello and Jacques Henrat, the D 520 met a requirement formulated in June 1936. Of all-metal stressed-skin monocoque construction with a monospar wing, it placed emphasis on manufacturing economy by minimizing machined parts and sub-assemblies and stressing component interchangeability. Aerodynamically refined and structurally robust, the first of three D 520 prototypes flew on 2 October 1938, and an initial production order was placed on the following 14 March. The first production example was flown seven months later, on 31 October 1939, but, regrettably, difficulties with the H-S 12Y 45 engine and various technical shortcomings, such as inadequate engine cooling and an unsatisfactory pneumatic machine gun control system were to frustrate delivery schedules. In consequence, only one Groupe de Chasse was to be mounted on the D 520 when the Wehrmacht launched its assault on 10 May 1940.

While incapable of competing with its principal opponent, the Bf 109E, in level speed and low-altitude climb, the D 520 enjoyed a marked edge in manoeuvrability and offered excellent diving characteristics. Its most serious shortcomings were a lack of damping in yaw, oversensitivity to turbulence and abrupt use of the throttle, and a tendency to ground loop. Further Groupes were hurriedly converted during summer 1940, and acquitted themselves honourably despite their pilots' unfamiliarity with the D 520, 403 (of 437 completed) having been taken on charge by the Armée de l'Air at the time of the Armistice, and 478 more being built before and after German occupation of Vichy France.

### Key to Dewoitine D.520

1 Cannon port
2 Spinner
3 Three-blade Ratier Electric propeller
4 Cannon barrel blast tube
5 Coolant water tank
6 Safety vent
7 Cowling forward frame
8 Auxiliary intake
9 Chin intake
10 Coolant piping
11 Oil cooler intake
12 Intake duct
13 Oil radiator
14 Engine bearer frames
15 Engine accessories
16 Exhaust stubs
17 Hispano-Suiza 12 Y 45 engine
18 Cowling rear frame
19 Cannon ammunition drum (60 rounds)
20 Oil tank
21 Starboard wing fuel tank
22 Wing skinning
23 Starboard navigation light
24 Starboard aileron
25 Aileron hinge
26 Emergency ring and bead gunsight
27 Fuselage main fuel tank
28 Fuselage main frame upper member
29 Engine bearer upper attachment
30 Bulkhead
31 20-mm HS 404 cannon breech
32 Compressor outlet
33 Extinguisher
34 Szydlowski compressor
35 Engine bearer support frame
36 Wing root fairing
37 Starboard mainwheel
38 Port mainwheel well
39 Ventral radiator bath intake
40 Undercarriage retraction mechanism
41 Mainwheel leg pivot
42 Wing machine gun blast tubes
43 Machine gun ports
44 Mainwheel leg
45 Port mainwheel
46 Mainwheel cover
47 Mainwheel leg door
48 Port wing fuel tank
49 Wing nose ribs
50 Pitot head
51 Port navigation light
52 Wingtip
53 Port aileron frame
54 Aileron hinge
55 Wing rear false spar
56 Wing skinning
57 Wing ribs
58 Two 7·5-mm MAC 1934 machine guns
59 Ammunition feed
60 Wing main spar
61 Ammunition boxes (675 rpg)
62 Gun hot air
63 Radiator bath
64 Wing flap inboard profile
65 Radiator outlet flap
66 Port wing flap
67 Hinged receiver antenna (extended)
68 Wing root fairing
69 Fuselage main frame lower member
70 Wing flap control linkage
71 Rudder pedal bar
72 Instrument panel
73 Command radio receiver
74 Control column grip
75 HF receiver
76 Windscreen
77 OPL RX 39 gunsight
78 Canopy track
79 Pilot's seat
80 Seat adjustment lever
81 Seat mounting frame
82 Tailplane incidence adjustment handwheel
83 Ventral antenna actuation jack
84 Oxygen cylinder
85 Fuselage frame
86 Tailplane incidence cable
87 Oleo reservoirs (2)
88 Sliding canopy (open)
89 Radio equipment (Radio-Industrie 537)
90 Aft canopy fixed glazing
91 Radio relay/lead-in
92 Transmitter antenna (fixed)
93 Dorsal decking
94 Fuselage frames
95 Stringers
96 Equipment/baggage compartment door
97 Compressed air cylinders
98 Elevator control linkage
99 Elevator cables
100 Lift point
101 Rudder cables
102 Fuselage main frame/tailfin spar attachment
103 Tailplane root fairing
104 Fuselage frame
105 Rudder linkage
106 Tailwheel shock absorber
107 Fixed tailwheel
108 Rudder lower hinge
109 Tailplane structure
110 Port elevator frame
111 Rudder tab hinge fairing
112 Rudder tab
113 Elevator control horn
114 Elevator torque tube
115 Tailplane attachment
116 Rudder frame
117 Rudder post
118 Tailfin structure
119 Tailfin front spar
120 Starboard tailplane
121 Tailfin leading-edge
122 Tail navigation light
123 Rudder internal balance
124 Rudder upper hinge

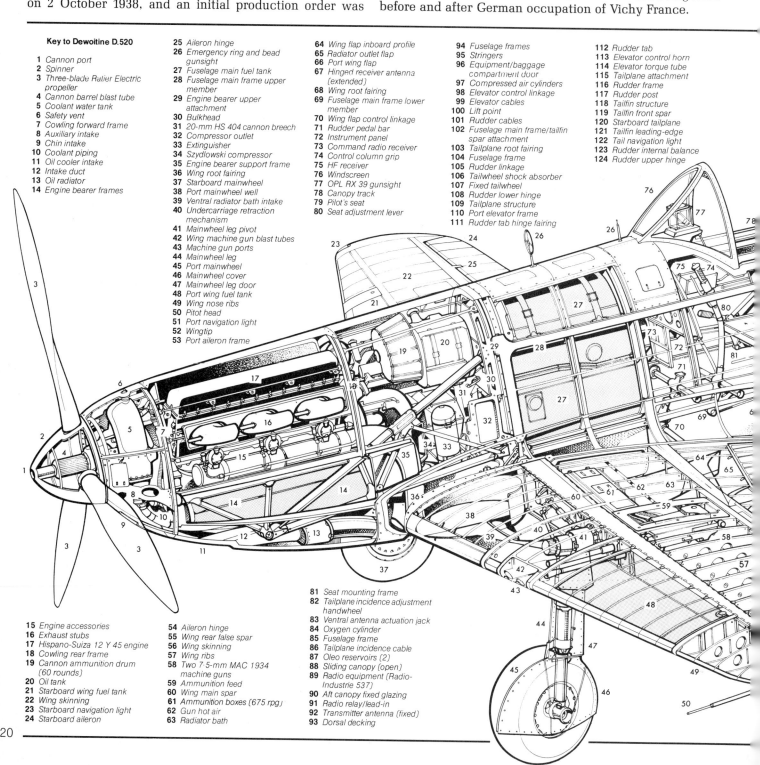

**SPECIFICATION: D 520**

**Power Plant:** One Hispano-Suiza 12 Y 45 12-cylinder vee liquid-cooled engine rated at 947 bhp at 2,520 rpm for take-off, 838 bhp at sea level and 907 bhp at 13,780 ft (4 200 m). Ratier 1606M or Chauvière three-bladed constant-speed propeller. Internal fuel capacity, 140 Imp gal (636 l).

**Performance:** Max speed, 264 mph (425 km/h) at sea level, 314 mph (505 km/h) at 13,125 ft (4 000 m), 332 mph (535 km/h) at 18,045 ft (5 500 m); range (max internal fuel), 957 mls (1 540 km) at 230 mph (370 km/h) at 16,730 ft (5 100 m); time to 13,125 ft (4 000 m), 5·82 min, to 19,680 ft (6 000 m), 8·98 min; service ceiling, 33,620 ft (10 245 m).

**Weights:** Empty, 4,488 lb (2 036 kg); normal loaded (wing tanks empty), 5,902 lb (2 677 kg); max take-off, 6,144 lb (2 787 kg).

**Dimensions:** Span, 33 ft 5½ in (10,20 m); length, 28 ft 2²⁄₃ in (8,60 m); height (tail down), 8 ft 5⅛ in (2,57 m); wing area, 171·9 sq ft (15,97 m²).

**Armament:** One 20-mm Hispano-Suiza HS 404 cannon with 60 rounds    and four 7,5-mm machine guns with 675 rpg.

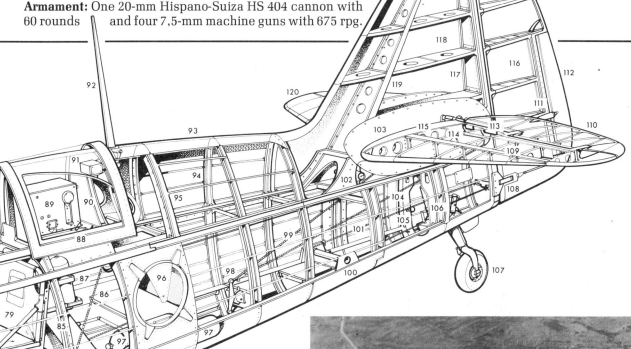

**Above right:** D 520 No 248 of the 2ᵉ Escadrille. Groupe de Chasse II/7, in July-August of 1940, the white fuselage stripe signifying Vichy use.

**Below right:** An early production D 520 (No 14) which was not brought up to full operational standards and was used successively for the training of pilots of Groupes de Chasse I/3 and II/3.

# Lockheed P-38 Lightning (January 1939)

Uniquity can rarely be ascribed with justification to a fighter, but the combination of features embodied by the P-38 assuredly rendered it unique. Born of a reawakening of interest in the twin-engined single-seat fighter configuration — conceived in WWI and resurrected in the mid 'thirties virtually simultaneously in Britain, Germany and France — the P-38 was destined to be the *only* such warplane powered by piston engines to achieve large-scale production and extensive service in WWII.

The P-38 was the first fighter with a nosewheel undercarriage and the first single-seat fighter of twin-boom arrangement to achieve service; it was the first squadron fighter with turbo-superchargers; it was to become the first aircraft known to have encountered the compressibility phenomenon and the first fighter equipped (from the late-series P-38J) with power-boosted controls.

Designed by H. L. Hibbard to meet a far-sighted proposal for an innovatory twin-engined *interceptor* circulated early in 1936, the prototype Lightning, the XP-38 — weighing more than a bombed-up Blenheim, then Britain's standard medium bomber, and possessing a wing loading almost twice that of contemporary fighters — flew on 27 January 1939, deliveries of the first "battle-worthy" model (P-38D) commencing in August 1941. Four years later, in August 1945 when production ended, 9,923 P-38s had been delivered.

## SPECIFICATION: P-38J-25 Lightning

**Power Plant:** Two Allison V-1710-89/91 12-cylinder vee liquid-cooled engines each rated at 1,425 hp at 3,000 rpm for take-off and 1,425 hp at 26,500 ft (8 075 m). Three-bladed Curtiss Electric constant-speed metal propellers. Internal fuel capacity, 341 Imp gal (1 552 l) and provision for two drop tanks of from 62·5 Imp gal (284 l) to 250 Imp gal (1 136 l) capacity.

**Performance:** Max speed, 360 mph (579 km/h) at 5,000 ft (1 525 m), 390 mph (628 km/h) at 15,000 ft (4 575 m), 414 mph (666 km/h) at 25,000 ft (7 625 m); range (internal fuel), 840 mls (1 352 km), (max external fuel), 1,880 mls (3 025 km); max climb, 3,670 ft/min (18,6 m/sec) at 5,000 ft (1 525 m); time to 30,000 ft (9 150 m), 12·0 min.

**Weights:** Empty equipped, 14,100 lb (6 401 kg); normal loaded, 17,500 lb (7 945 kg); max, 21,600 lb (9 806 kg).

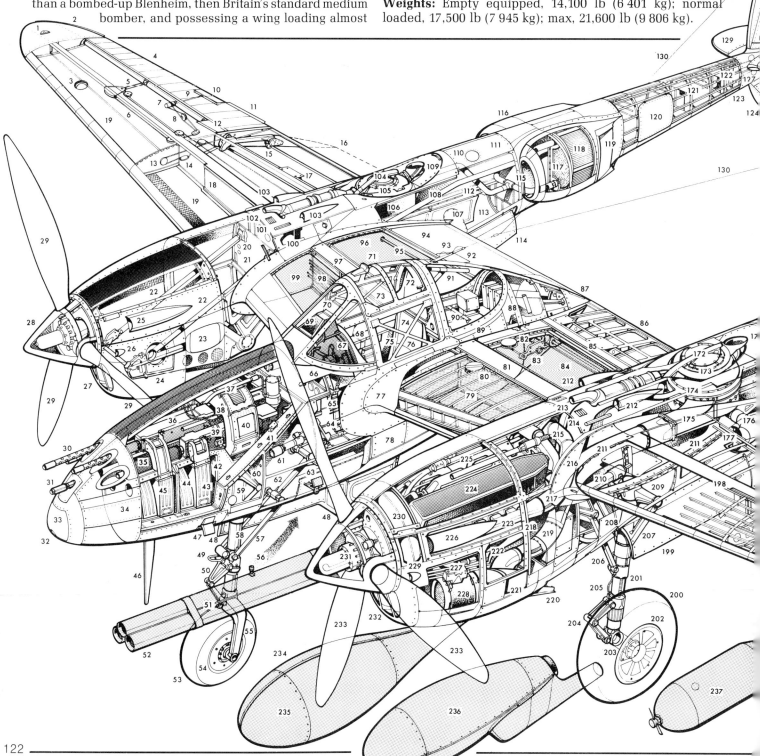

**Dimensions:** Span, 52 ft 0 in (15,85 m); length, 37 ft 10 in (11,53 m); height, 12 ft 10 in (3,91 m); wing area, 328 sq ft (30,50 m²).

**Armament:** One 20-mm AN-M2 "C" cannon with 150 rounds and four 0·50-in (12,7-mm) machine guns with 500 rpg.

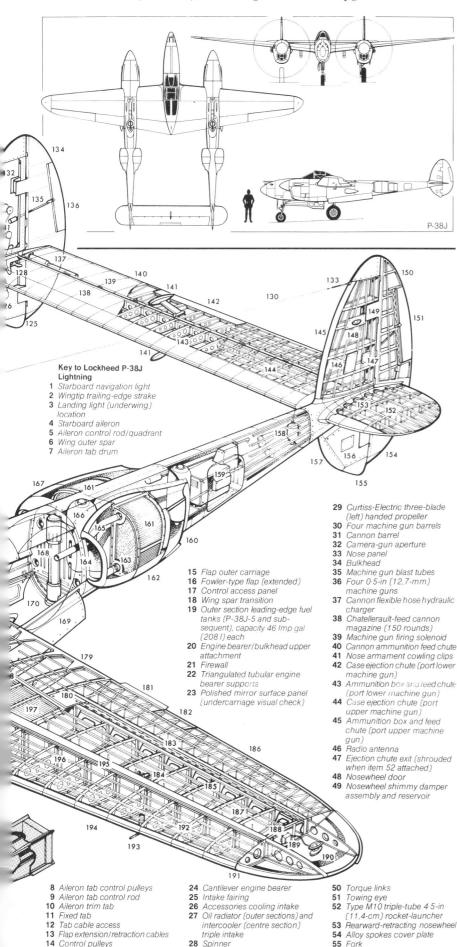

P-38J

**Key to Lockheed P-38J Lightning**

1 Starboard navigation light
2 Wingtip trailing-edge strake
3 Landing light (underwing) location
4 Starboard aileron
5 Aileron control rod/quadrant
6 Wing outer spar
7 Aileron tab drum

8 Aileron tab control pulleys
9 Aileron tab control rod
10 Aileron trim tab
11 Fixed tab
12 Tab cable access
13 Flap extension/retraction cables
14 Control pulleys

15 Flap outer carriage
16 Fowler-type flap (extended)
17 Control access panel
18 Wing spar transition
19 Outer section leading-edge fuel tanks (P-38J-5 and subsequent), capacity 46 Imp gal (208 l) each
20 Engine bearer/bulkhead upper attachment
21 Firewall
22 Triangulated tubular engine bearer supports
23 Polished mirror surface panel (undercarriage visual check)
24 Cantilever engine bearer
25 Intake fairing
26 Accessories cooling intake
27 Oil radiator (outer sections) and intercooler (centre section) triple intake
28 Spinner

29 Curtiss-Electric three-blade (left) handed propeller
30 Four machine gun barrels
31 Cannon barrel
32 Camera-gun aperture
33 Nose panel
34 Bulkhead
35 Machine gun blast tubes
36 Four 0·5-in (12,7-mm) machine guns
37 Cannon flexible hose hydraulic charger
38 Chatellerault-feed cannon magazine (150 rounds)
39 Machine gun firing solenoid
40 Cannon ammunition feed chute
41 Nose armament cowling clips
42 Case ejection chute (port lower machine gun)
43 Ammunition box and feed chute (port lower machine gun)
44 Case ejection chute (port upper machine gun)
45 Ammunition box and feed chute (port upper machine gun)
46 Radio antenna
47 Ejection chute exit (shrouded when item 52 attached)
48 Nosewheel door
49 Nosewheel shimmy damper assembly and reservoir

50 Torque links
51 Towing eye
52 Type M10 triple-tube 4·5-in (11,4-cm) rocket-launcher
53 Rearward-retracting nosewheel
54 Alloy spokes cover plate
55 Fork

56 Rocket-launcher forward attachment (to 63)
57 Nosewheel lower drag struts
58 Nosewheel oleo leg
59 Nosewheel pin access
60 Side struts and fulcrum
61 Actuating cylinder
62 Upper drag strut
63 Rocket-launcher forward attachment bracket
64 Rudder pedal assembly
65 Engine controls quadrant
66 Instrument panel
67 "Spectacle grip" cantilevered control wheel
68 Non-reflective shroud
69 Lynn-3 reflector sight mounting
70 Optically-flat bullet-proof windscreen (P-38J-10 and later)
71 External rear-view mirror
72 Armoured headrest
73 Rearward-hinged canopy
74 Pilot's armoured seat back
75 Canopy bracing
76 Downward-winding side windows
77 Wing root fillets
78 Nosewheel well
79 Port reserve fuel tank, capacity 50 Imp gal (227 l)
80 Fuel filler cap
81 Main (double I-beam) spar
82 Fuel filler cap
83 Flap inner carriage
84 Port main fuel tank, capacity 75 Imp gal (341 l)
85 Flap control access
86 Flap structure
87 Entry ladder release
88 Flap drive motor
89 Fuel surge tank and main hydraulic reservoir in aft nacelle
90 Radio equipment compartment
91 Turnover support pylon
92 Flap control access
93 Aerial attachment
94 Starboard inner flap
95 Flap push-pull rod
96 Starboard main fuel tank, capacity as 84
97 Main spar
98 Engine control runs
99 Starboard reserve fuel tank, capacity as 79
100 Starboard oil tank
101 Cooling louvres
102 Cabin heater intake
103 Turbo-supercharger cooling intakes
104 Turbine cooling duct
105 Exhaust turbine
106 Supercharger housing
107 Wingroot/boom fillet
108 Coolant/radiator return pipe (left and right)
109 Exhaust waste gate outlet
110 Access panel
111 Boom Joint (Station 265)
112 Radiator/coolant supply pipe
113 Mainwheel well
114 Mainwheel doors
115 Radiator intake
116 Starboard outer radiator fairing
117 Radiator grille
118 Engine coolant radiator assembly
119 Exit flap
120 Tool and baggage compartment
121 Boom structure
122 D/R master compass housing
123 Boom/tail attachment joint (Station 393)
124 Starboard lower fin
125 Tail bumper skid shoe
126 Elevator control pulley
127 Rudder stop
128 Elevator control horn
129 Fixed tip
130 Radio aerials
131 Tail surface control pulleys
132 Aerodynamic mass balance
133 Aerial attachments
134 Starboard rudder
135 Tab control rod and drum
136 Rudder trim tab
137 Elevator abbreviated torque tube
138 Tailplane stressed skin
139 Elevator pin hinges (eight off)
140 Elevator
141 Upper and lower mass balances
142 Elevator trim tab
143 Tailplane structure
144 Stiffeners
145 Port fin structure
146 Elevator pulley access

147 Rudder tab drum access
148 Tail running light (port)
149 Aerodynamic mass balance
150 Rudder framework
151 Rudder trim tab
152 Fixed tip structure
153 Tail surfaces/boom (quatrefoil bulkhead) attachment flanges
154 Rudder lower section
155 Tail bumper skid shoe
156 Elevator pulley access
157 Port lower fin
158 Elevator, rudder, and tab cables
159 Battery compartment
160 Radiator exit flap
161 Engine coolant radiator assembly
162 Radiator housing
163 Radiator/coolant supply pipe
164 Radiator intake
165 Coolant/radiator return pipe
166 Oxygen cylinder
167 Port inner radiator fairing
168 Flare tube (port and starboard booms)
169 Mainwheel doors
170 Mainwheel well
171 Exhaust waste gate outlet
172 Turbine cooling duct
173 Exhaust turbine
174 Supercharger assembly
175 Supercharger/intercooler duct
176 Carburettor intake duct
177 Carburettor air intake
178 Abbreviated rear spar
179 Flap outer section
180 Tab cable access
181 Fixed tab
182 Aileron trim tab
183 Aileron full-span piano-wire hinge
184 Underwing pitot attachment
185 Raked web stiffener (outboard of rear spar)
186 Aileron structure
187 Outer wing pressed sheet ribs
188 Aileron counterweight
189 Junction box
190 Port navigation lights
191 Port wingtip structure
192 Leading-edge ribs
193 Pitot head
194 Wing leading-edge skin join (fabric-covered piano-wire hinge)
195 Wing outer section I-beam box spar
196 Leading-edge stringers (no fuel tanks in early P-38 Js)
197 Wing inner surface corrugation
198 Spar single/double I-beam box spar transition
199 Mainwheel leg doors
200 Rearward-retracting mainwheel
201 Mainwheel oleo leg
202 Alloy spoked hub
203 Cantilever axle
204 Torque links
205 Hydraulic brake cable
206 Drag strut
207 Side strut
208 Drag links
209 Fulcrum
210 Actuating cylinder
211 Multi-bolt outer wing fixings
212 Turbo-supercharger cooling intakes
213 Cabin heater intake
214 Cooling louvres
215 Carburettor duct
216 Outer section wing fillet
217 Insulated exhaust shroud duct
218 Intercooler/carburettor duct
219 Supercharger/intercooler duct
220 Outlet
221 Oil radiator shutter
222 Intercooler
223 Exhausts
224 Allison V-1710-89/91 twelve-cylinder Vee engine
225 Magnetos/distributors
226 Intake fairing
227 Header feed pipes
228 Port outer oil radiator
229 Spark-plug and magneto cooling intake
230 Coolant header tank
231 Propeller hub
232 Oil radiator (outer sections) and intercooler (centre section) triple intake
233 Curtiss-Electric three-blade (right) handed propeller
234 Outer section underwing stores, including
235 Jettisonable auxiliary fuel tank, or
236 Smoke generator, or
237 1,000-lb (454-kg) bomb

# Nakajima Ki.43 Hayabusa (January 1939)

Effectively an extrapolation of the preceding Ki.27 (see pages 102-103) in adhering to the same design precepts, so closely did the Ki.43 follow the established formula that its only concessions to contemporary fashion were a modest increase in power and an hydraulically-retractable under-carriage. The Army specification formulated at the end of 1937 and to the requirements of which the Ki.43 was developed had been singular in its lack of imagination and total disregard for international fighter trends. The Ki.43 was, in consequence, to be overshadowed by obsolescence from the moment of its birth.

Designed by the team responsible for the Ki.27 and with similar structural weight consciousness, the Ki.43 flew early in January 1939, but two years were to elapse owing to a combination of development difficulties and tardiness on the part of the procurement authority before, on 9 January 1941, it was finally to be ordered into production as the Army Type 1 Fighter. Acceptances of the initial model, the Ki.43-I-ko, commenced in the following June, but only two Sentais had converted when the Pacific War began.

Insofar as agility was concerned, the Ki.43 knew no peer.

It could be looped and Immelmanned at airspeeds of 168 mph (270 km/h) and lower, acceleration from low airspeeds was exceptional, stall recovery was impeccable, and its so-called "butterfly" combat flaps endowed it with an aston-ishing rate of turn. On the other hand, it lacked firepower, armour and fuel tank protection, and its structure, while not fragile could not absorb much punishment. Furthermore, it could be out-dived and out-zoomed by most Allied fighters.

The fundamental components of the Ki.43's structure did not permit power or armament increases commensurate with the demands of the air war, and thus, although pro-duction was to continue until the end of the conflict, despite obsolescence, only modest improvements were made. The Ki.43-I-ko soon gave place to the Ki.43-I-hei which sup-planted the 7,7-mm guns with 12,7-mm weapons, and the Ki.43-II-ko, introduced in November 1942, received the marginally more powerful Ha-115 engine with two-speed supercharger and a three-blade constant-speed propeller. As the war progressed, the Ki.43 was invariably outclassed, but, committed on every front, it soldiered on as numerically the most important Army fighter with a total of 5,919 built.

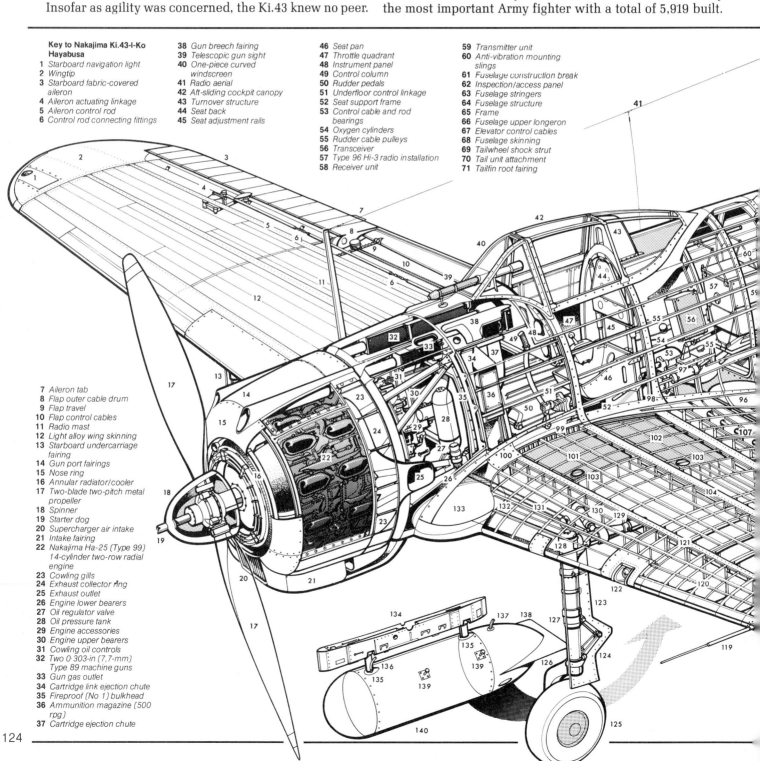

**Key to Nakajima Ki.43-I-Ko Hayabusa**

1 Starboard navigation light
2 Wingtip
3 Starboard fabric-covered aileron
4 Aileron actuating linkage
5 Aileron control rod
6 Control rod connecting fittings
7 Aileron tab
8 Flap outer cable drum
9 Flap travel
10 Flap control cables
11 Radio mast
12 Light alloy wing skinning
13 Starboard undercarriage fairing
14 Gun port fairings
15 Nose ring
16 Annular radiator/cooler
17 Two-blade two-pitch metal propeller
18 Spinner
19 Starter dog
20 Supercharger air intake
21 Intake fairing
22 Nakajima Ha-25 (Type 99) 14-cylinder two-row radial engine
23 Cowling gills
24 Exhaust collector ring
25 Exhaust outlet
26 Engine lower bearers
27 Oil regulator valve
28 Oil pressure tank
29 Engine accessories
30 Engine upper bearers
31 Cowling oil controls
32 Two 0.303-in (7,7-mm) Type 89 machine guns
33 Gun gas outlet
34 Cartridge link ejection chute
35 Fireproof (No 1) bulkhead
36 Ammunition magazine (500 rpg)
37 Cartridge ejection chute

38 Gun breech fairing
39 Telescopic gun sight
40 One-piece curved windscreen
41 Radio aerial
42 Aft-sliding cockpit canopy
43 Turnover structure
44 Seat back
45 Seat adjustment rails
46 Seat pan
47 Throttle quadrant
48 Instrument panel
49 Control column
50 Rudder pedals
51 Underfloor control linkage
52 Seat support frame
53 Control cable and rod bearings
54 Oxygen cylinders
55 Rudder cable pulleys
56 Transceiver
57 Type 96 Hi-3 radio installation
58 Receiver unit

59 Transmitter unit
60 Anti-vibration mounting slings
61 Fuselage construction break
62 Inspection/access panel
63 Fuselage stringers
64 Fuselage structure
65 Frame
66 Fuselage upper longeron
67 Elevator control cables
68 Fuselage skinning
69 Tailwheel shock strut
70 Tail unit attachment
71 Tailfin root fairing

## SPECIFICATION: Ki.43-I-hei

**Power Plant:** One Nakajima Ha-25 14-cylinder air-cooled engine rated at 990 hp at 2,700 rpm for take-off and 970 hp at 11,155 ft (3 400 m). Two-bladed two-pitch metal propeller. Internal fuel capacity, 125 Imp gal (564 l), plus two internal (wing) 33 Imp gal (150 l) overload tanks and provision for two 44 Imp gal (200 l) drop tanks.

**Performance:** Max speed, 274 mph (441 km/h) at 3,280 ft (1 000 m), 286 mph (460 km/h) at 6,560 ft (2 000 m), 298 mph (479 km/h) at 9,840 ft (3 000 m), 306 mph (492 km/h) at 16,405 ft (5 000 m); normal cruise, 236 mph (380 km/h) at 8,200 ft (2 500 m); range (internal fuel including overload tanks), 746 mls (1 200 km) at 217 mph (350 km/h), 808 mls (1 300 km) at 202 mph (325 km/h); time to 16,405 ft (5 000 m), 5·5 min; service ceiling, 38,550 ft (11 750 m).

**Weights:** Empty equipped, 3,505 lb (1 509 kg); normal loaded, 4,516 lb (2 048 kg); max, 5,694 lb (2 583 kg).

**Dimensions:** Span, 37 ft 6 in (11,44 m); length, 28 ft 11¾ in (8,83 m); height, 10 ft 8¾ in (3,27 m); wing area, 236·81 sq ft (22,00 m²).

**Armament:** Two 12,7-mm Ho-103 (Type 1) machine guns with 250 rpg and provision for two 33-lb (15-kg) bombs under wing.

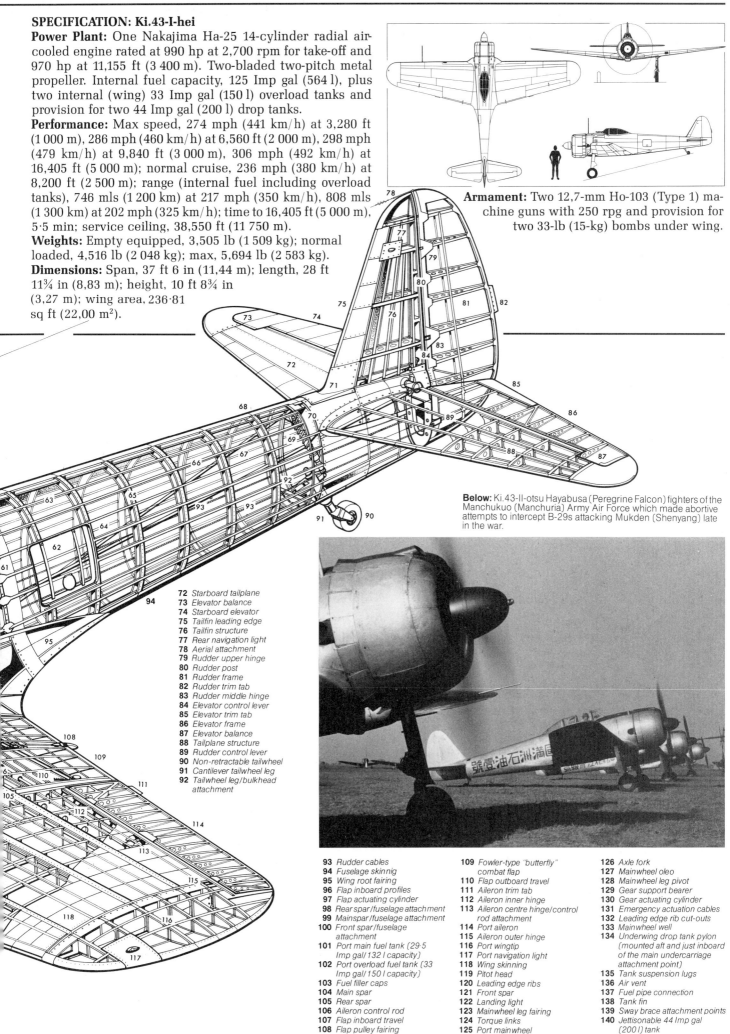

**Below:** Ki.43-II-otsu Hayabusa (Peregrine Falcon) fighters of the Manchukuo (Manchuria) Army Air Force which made abortive attempts to intercept B-29s attacking Mukden (Shenyang) late in the war.

72 Starboard tailplane
73 Elevator balance
74 Starboard elevator
75 Tailfin leading edge
76 Tailfin structure
77 Rear navigation light
78 Aerial attachment
79 Rudder upper hinge
80 Rudder post
81 Rudder frame
82 Rudder trim tab
83 Rudder middle hinge
84 Elevator control lever
85 Elevator trim tab
86 Elevator frame
87 Elevator balance
88 Tailplane structure
89 Rudder control lever
90 Non-retractable tailwheel
91 Cantilever tailwheel leg
92 Tailwheel leg/bulkhead attachment

93 Rudder cables
94 Fuselage skinnig
95 Wing root fairing
96 Flap inboard profiles
97 Flap actuating cylinder
98 Rear spar/fuselage attachment
99 Mainspar/fuselage attachment
100 Front spar/fuselage attachment
101 Port main fuel tank (29·5 Imp gal/132 l capacity)
102 Port overload fuel tank (33 Imp gal/150 l capacity)
103 Fuel filler caps
104 Main spar
105 Rear spar
106 Aileron control rod
107 Flap inboard travel
108 Flap pulley fairing

109 Fowler-type "butterfly" combat flap
110 Flap outboard travel
111 Aileron trim tab
112 Aileron inner hinge
113 Aileron centre hinge/control rod attachment
114 Port aileron
115 Aileron outer hinge
116 Port wingtip
117 Port navigation light
118 Wing skinning
119 Pitot head
120 Leading edge ribs
121 Front spar
122 Landing light
123 Mainwheel leg fairing
124 Torque links
125 Port mainwheel

126 Axle fork
127 Mainwheel oleo
128 Mainwheel leg pivot
129 Gear support bearer
130 Gear actuating cylinder
131 Emergency actuation cables
132 Leading edge rib cut-outs
133 Mainwheel well
134 Underwing drop tank pylon (mounted aft and just inboard of the main undercarriage attachment point)
135 Tank suspension lugs
136 Air vent
137 Fuel pipe connection
138 Tank fin
139 Sway brace attachment points
140 Jettisonable 44 Imp gal (200 l) tank

# Mitsubishi A6M Reisen (April 1939)

The philosophy of exercising the most rigid weight consciousness in order to achieve the characteristics demanded of a pure air superiority fighter employed with success by Jiro Horikoshi in the A5M (see pages 78-79) was again to be pursued in the development of a successor, the A6M Reisen (Zero Fighter). Within little more than two years of the operational deployment of the new fighter, however, it was to be realised that its concept was already atrophic; its structural design strictures rendered it insufficiently amenable to the changes demanded by combat experience. The Reisen, which briefly enjoyed aerial mastery over the Pacific, thus rapidly declined in effectiveness.

Designed to a 12-Shi (1937) specification and first flown on 1 April 1939, the A6M was ordered into series production as the Navy Type O Carrier Fighter in July 1940, the same month in which pre-series A6M2s appeared operationally over China, and when the Pacific War commenced, 328 A6M2s were on Imperial Navy strength. At normal close-in high-g dogfighting speeds, the A6M was superlatively manoeuvrable—the Allies credited it with almost mystical powers of manoeuvre—but in all other respects it was

rapidly outclassed by the newer Allied fighters.

The failure of the succeeding generation of Navy fighters to achieve service rapidly dictated retention of the Reisen in production despite its obsolescence. successive versions embodying various palliatives intended to mitigate its inferiority in combat with strictly limited success, but production continued until the end of hostilities when a total of 11,800 had been delivered.

## SPECIFICATION: A6M2b Reisen Model 21
**Power Plant:** One Nakajima NK1C Sakae 14-cylinder radial air-cooled engine rated at 940 hp at 2,600 rpm for take-off and 950 hp at 13,780 ft (4 200 m). Three-bladed Mitsubishi-Hamilton constant-speed metal propeller. Internal fuel capacity, 114 Imp gal (518 l), with provision for a 72·5 Imp gal (330 l) drop tank.

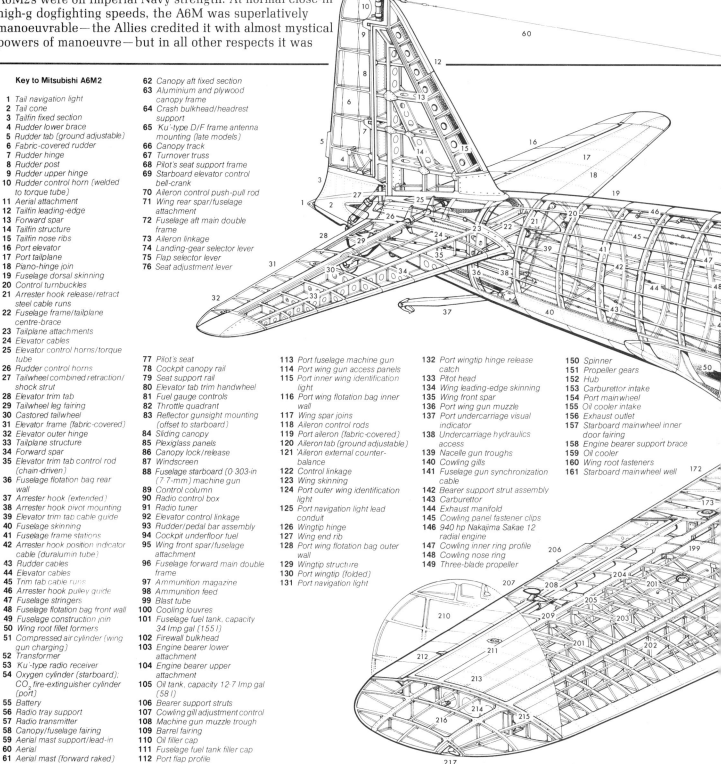

**Key to Mitsubishi A6M2**

1 Tail navigation light
2 Tail cone
3 Tailfin fixed section
4 Rudder lower brace
5 Rudder tab (ground adjustable)
6 Fabric-covered rudder
7 Rudder hinge
8 Rudder post
9 Rudder upper hinge
10 Rudder control horn (welded to torque tube)
11 Aerial attachment
12 Tailfin leading-edge
13 Forward spar
14 Tailfin structure
15 Tailfin nose ribs
16 Port elevator
17 Port tailplane
18 Piano-hinge join
19 Fuselage dorsal skinning
20 Control turnbuckles
21 Arrester hook release/retract steel cable runs
22 Fuselage frame/tailplane centre-brace
23 Tailplane attachments
24 Elevator cables
25 Elevator control horns/torque tube
26 Rudder control horns
27 Tailwheel combined retraction/shock strut
28 Elevator trim tab
29 Tailwheel leg fairing
30 Castored tailwheel
31 Elevator frame (fabric-covered)
32 Elevator outer hinge
33 Tailplane structure
34 Forward spar
35 Elevator trim tab control rod (chain-driven)
36 Fuselage flotation bag rear wall
37 Arrester hook (extended)
38 Arrester hook pivot mounting
39 Elevator trim tab cable guide
40 Fuselage skinning
41 Fuselage frame stations
42 Arrester hook position indicator cable (duralumin tube)
43 Rudder cables
44 Elevator cables
45 Trim tab cable runs
46 Arrester hook pulley guide
47 Fuselage stringers
48 Fuselage flotation bag front wall
49 Fuselage construction join
50 Wing root fillet formers
51 Compressed air cylinder (wing gun charging)
52 Transformer
53 'Ku'-type radio receiver
54 Oxygen cylinder (starboard); CO$_2$ fire-extinguisher cylinder (port)
55 Battery
56 Radio tray support
57 Radio transmitter
58 Canopy/fuselage fairing
59 Aerial mast support/lead-in
60 Aerial
61 Aerial mast (forward raked)

62 Canopy aft fixed section
63 Aluminium and plywood canopy frame
64 Crash bulkhead/headrest support
65 'Ku'-type D/F frame antenna mounting (late models)
66 Canopy track
67 Turnover truss
68 Pilot's seat support frame
69 Starboard elevator control bell-crank
70 Aileron control push-pull rod
71 Wing rear spar/fuselage attachment
72 Fuselage aft main double frame
73 Aileron linkage
74 Landing-gear selector lever
75 Flap selector lever
76 Seat adjustment lever

77 Pilot's seat
78 Cockpit canopy rail
79 Seat support rail
80 Elevator tab trim handwheel
81 Fuel gauge controls
82 Throttle quadrant
83 Reflector gunsight mounting (offset to starboard)
84 Sliding canopy
85 Plexiglass panels
86 Canopy lock/release
87 Windscreen
88 Fuselage starboard (0·303-in (7·7-mm) machine gun
89 Control column
90 Radio control box
91 Radio tuner
92 Elevator control linkage
93 Rudder/pedal bar assembly
94 Cockpit underfloor fuel
95 Wing front spar/fuselage attachment
96 Fuselage forward main double frame
97 Ammunition magazine
98 Ammunition feed
99 Blast tube
100 Cooling louvres
101 Fuselage fuel tank, capacity 34 Imp gal (155 l)
102 Firewall bulkhead
103 Engine bearer lower attachment
104 Engine bearer upper attachment
105 Oil tank, capacity 12·7 Imp gal (58 l)
106 Bearer support struts
107 Cowling gill adjustment control
108 Machine gun muzzle trough
109 Barrel fairing
110 Oil filler cap
111 Fuselage fuel tank filler cap
112 Port flap profile

113 Port fuselage machine gun
114 Port wing gun access panels
115 Port inner wing identification light
116 Port wing flotation bag inner wall
117 Wing spar joins
118 Aileron control rods
119 Port aileron (fabric-covered)
120 Aileron tab (ground adjustable)
121 Aileron external counter-balance
122 Control linkage
123 Wing skinning
124 Port outer wing identification light
125 Port navigation light lead conduit
126 Wingtip hinge
127 Wing end rib
128 Port wing flotation bag outer wall
129 Wingtip structure
130 Port wingtip (folded)
131 Port navigation light

132 Port wingtip hinge release catch
133 Pitot head
134 Wing leading-edge skinning
135 Wing front spar
136 Port wing gun muzzle
137 Port undercarriage visual indicator
138 Undercarriage hydraulics access
139 Nacelle gun troughs
140 Cowling gills
141 Fuselage gun synchronization cable
142 Bearer support strut assembly
143 Carburettor
144 Exhaust manifold
145 Cowling panel fastener clips
146 940 hp Nakajima Sakae 12 radial engine
147 Cowling inner ring profile
148 Cowling nose ring
149 Three-blade propeller

150 Spinner
151 Propeller gears
152 Hub
153 Carburettor intake
154 Port mainwheel
155 Oil cooler intake
156 Exhaust outlet
157 Starboard mainwheel inner door fairing
158 Engine bearer support brace
159 Oil cooler
160 Wing root fasteners
161 Starboard mainwheel well

**Performance:** Max speed, 332 mph (534 km/h) at 14,930 ft (4 550 m), 282 mph (454 km/h) at sea level; max continuous cruise, 207 mph (333 km/h); range (internal fuel), 1,160 mls (1 866 km) at 146 mph (235 km/h) at 1,500 ft (455 m), (with drop tank), 1,930 mls (3 105 km); initial climb, 3,100 ft/min (15,75 m/sec); time to 19,685 ft (6 000 m), 7·45 min; service ceiling, 33,790 ft (10 300 m).

**Weights:** Empty equipped, 3,704 lb (1 680 kg); normal loaded, 5,313 lb (2 410 kg); max, 6,164 lb (2 796 kg).

**Dimensions:** Span, 39 ft 4½ in (12,00 m); length, 29 ft 8¾ in (9,06 m); height 10 ft 0⅛ in (3,05 m); wing area, 241·54 sq ft (22,44 m²).

**Armament:** Two 20-mm Navy Type 99 Mk 1 (Oerlikon) cannon with 60 rpg and two 7,7-mm Type 97 (Vickers) machine guns with 500 rpg.

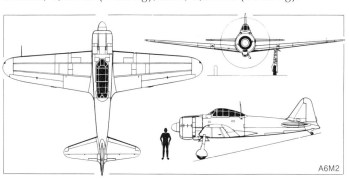

A6M2

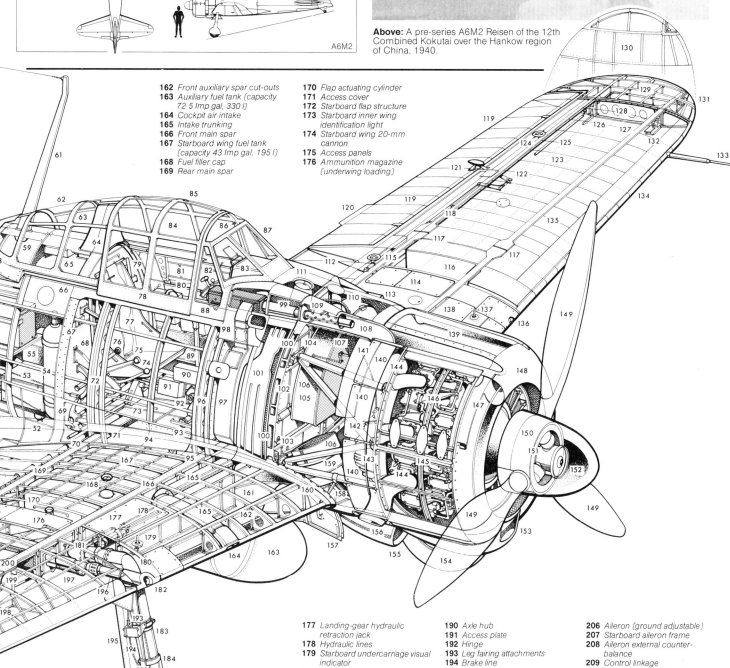

**Above:** A pre-series A6M2 Reisen of the 12th Combined Kokutai over the Hankow region of China, 1940.

162 Front auxiliary spar cut-outs
163 Auxiliary fuel tank (capacity 72·5 Imp gal, 330 l)
164 Cockpit air intake
165 Intake trunking
166 Front main spar
167 Starboard wing fuel tank (capacity 43 Imp gal, 195 l)
168 Fuel filler cap
169 Rear main spar
170 Flap actuating cylinder
171 Access cover
172 Starboard flap structure
173 Starboard inner wing identification light
174 Starboard wing 20-mm cannon
175 Access panels
176 Ammunition magazine (underwing loading)

177 Landing-gear hydraulic retraction jack
178 Hydraulic lines
179 Starboard undercarriage visual indicator
180 Landing-gear pivot axis
181 Undercarriage/spar mounting
182 Starboard wing gun muzzle
183 Starboard undercarriage leg
184 Oleo travel
185 Welded steel wheel fork
186 Wheel uplock latch
187 Starboard mainwheel
188 Wheel door fairing ball and swivel closure
189 Mainwheel door fairing

190 Axle hub
191 Access plate
192 Hinge
193 Leg fairing attachments
194 Brake line
195 Leg fairing
196 Leg fairing upper flap
197 Wing gun barrel support collar
198 Wing nose ribs
199 Wing spar joins
200 Cartridge ejection chute
201 Wing outer structure
202 Front spar outer section
203 Inter-spar ribs
204 Rear spar outer section
205 Aileron control access

206 Aileron (ground adjustable)
207 Starboard aileron frame
208 Aileron external counter-balance
209 Control linkage
210 Starboard wingtip (folded)
211 Starboard outer wing identification light
212 Aileron outer hinge
213 Starboard wing flotation bag outer wall
214 Wing end rib
215 Starboard wingtip hinge release catch
216 Wingtip structure
217 Starboard navigation light

# Focke-Wulf Fw 190 (June 1939)

**Above:** Fw 190G-3s of II Gruppe of Schlachtgeschwader 10 over Rumania early in 1944. The Fw 190G was a dedicated fighter-bomber version.

If any fighter has, at the time of its operational debut, ever been able to lay claim to coming close to perfection, then that fighter was arguably the Fw 190 designed by Dipl-Ing Kurt Tank. It was not, of course, perfect—no fighter yet designed had been devoid of defects—but it certainly came closer to that state of grace than any contemporary.

Forsaking the liquid-cooled engine, then considered *de rigeur* for fighters in Germany, in favour of an air-cooled radial, and first flown on 1 June 1939, the Fw 190 was a compact, well-proportioned warplane, possessing superlative control harmony, and being both a good dogfighter and a good gun platform. Its debut caused widespread RAF consternation in 1941; it could out-perform the contemporary Spitfire V on every count apart from turning circle— its manoeuvre margins were limited by rather harsh stalling characteristics. The balance was to be redressed in part by the Spitfire IX, but even this redoubtable fighter was left standing by the Fw 190's half-roll and dive.

The Fw 190 established a broad operational repertoire, and 16,724 were to be delivered by the end of 1944, with a futher 2,700 or so thereafter.

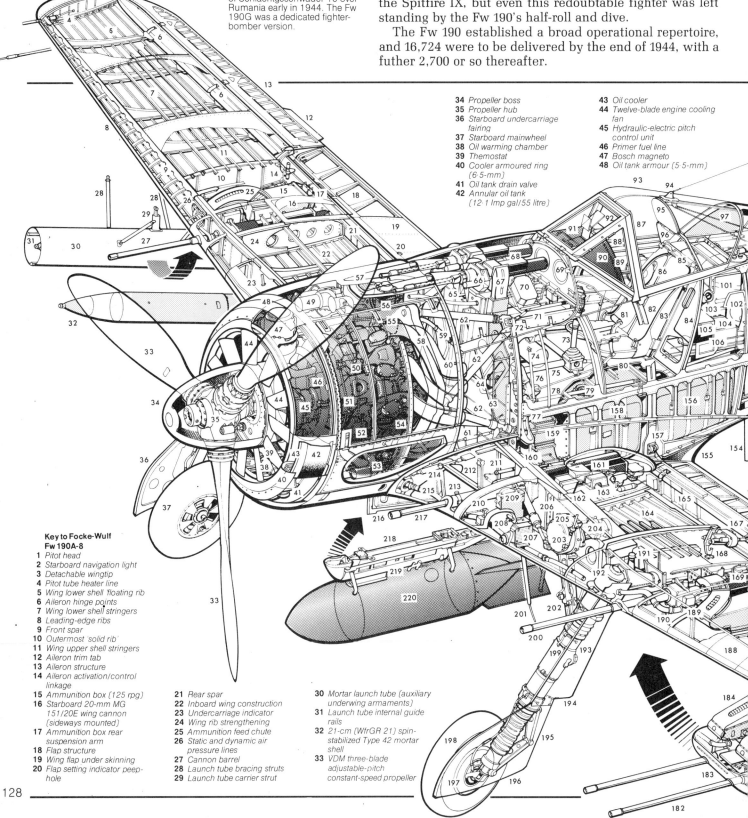

34 Propeller boss
35 Propeller hub
36 Starboard undercarriage fairing
37 Starboard mainwheel
38 Oil warming chamber
39 Themostat
40 Cooler armoured ring (6·5-mm)
41 Oil tank drain valve
42 Annular oil tank (12·1 Imp gal/55 litre)

43 Oil cooler
44 Twelve-blade engine cooling fan
45 Hydraulic-electric pitch control unit
46 Primer fuel line
47 Bosch magneto
48 Oil tank armour (5·5-mm)

**Key to Focke-Wulf Fw 190A-8**

1 Pitot head
2 Starboard navigation light
3 Detachable wingtip
4 Pitot tube heater line
5 Wing lower shell 'floating rib
6 Aileron hinge points
7 Wing lower shell stringers
8 Leading-edge ribs
9 Front spar
10 Outermost 'solid rib'
11 Wing upper shell stringers
12 Aileron trim tab
13 Aileron structure
14 Aileron activation/control linkage
15 Ammunition box (125 rpg)
16 Starboard 20-mm MG 151/20E wing cannon (sideways mounted)
17 Ammunition box rear suspension arm
18 Flap structure
19 Wing flap under skinning
20 Flap setting indicator peep-hole

21 Rear spar
22 Inboard wing construction
23 Undercarriage indicator
24 Wing rib strengthening
25 Ammunition feed chute
26 Static and dynamic air pressure lines
27 Cannon barrel
28 Launch tube bracing struts
29 Launch tube carrier strut

30 Mortar launch tube (auxiliary underwing armaments)
31 Launch tube internal guide rails
32 21-cm (WfrGR 21) spin-stabilized Type 42 mortar shell
33 VDM three-blade adjustable-pitch constant-speed propeller

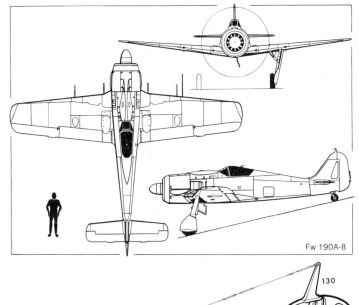

Fw 190A-8

## SPECIFICATION: Fw 190A-8

**Power Plant:** One BMW 801D 14-cylinder two-row radial air-cooled engine rated at 1,700 hp at 2,700 rpm for take-off and 1,440 hp at 18,700 ft (5 700 m). Three-bladed VDM constant-speed propeller. Internal fuel, 115·5 Imp gal (524 l).

**Performance:** Max speed, 355 mph (571 km/h) at sea level, 402 mph (647 km/h) at 18,045 ft (5 500 m), (with GM 1 nitrous oxide boost), 408 mph (656 km/h) at 20,670 ft (6 300 m); normal cruise, 298 mph (480 km/h) at 6,560 ft (2 000 m); max range (internal fuel), 644 mls (1 035 km), (with drop tank), 915 mls (1 470 km); initial climb, 3,450 ft/min (17,5 m/sec); service ceiling, 33,800 ft (10 300 m), (with GM 1), 37,400 ft (11 400 m).

**Weights:** Empty equipped, 7,652 lb (3 470 kg); normal loaded, 9,660 lb (4 380 kg); max, 10,724 lb (4 865 kg).

**Dimensions:** Span, 34 ft 5½ in (10,51 m); length, 29 ft 4¼ in (8,95 m); height, 12 ft 11½ in (3,95 m); wing area, 196·98 sq ft (18,30 m²).

**Armament:** Two 13-mm Rheinmetall-Borsig MG 131 machine guns with 475 rpg and four 20-mm Mauser MG 151/20E cannon with 250 rpg (inboard pair) and 140 rpg (outboard).

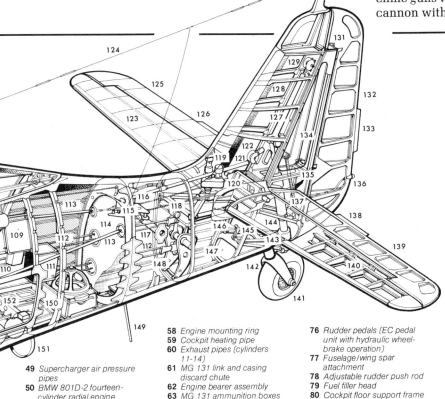

49 Supercharger air pressure pipes
50 BMW 801D-2 fourteen-cylinder radial engine
51 Cowling support ring
52 Cowling quick-release fasteners
53 Oil pump
54 Fuel pump (engine rear face)
55 Oil filter (starboard)
56 Wing root cannon synchronization gear
57 Gun troughs/cowling upper panel attachment
58 Engine mounting ring
59 Cockpit heating pipe
60 Exhaust pipes (cylinders 11-14)
61 MG 131 link and casing discard chute
62 Engine bearer assembly
63 MG 131 ammunition boxes (400 rpg)
64 Fuel filter recess housing
65 MG 131 ammunition cooling pipes
66 MG 131 synchronization gear
67 Ammunition feed chute
68 Twin fuselage 13-mm MG 131 machine guns
69 Windscreen mounting frame
70 Emergency power fuse and distributor box
71 Rear hinged gun access panel
72 Engine bearer/bulkhead attachmenmt
73 Control column
74 Transformer
75 Aileron control torsion bar
76 Rudder pedals (EC pedal unit with hydraulic wheel-brake operation)
77 Fuselage/wing spar attachment
78 Adjustable rudder push rod
79 Fuel filler head
80 Cockpit floor support frame
81 Throttle lever
82 Pilot's seat back plate armour (8-mm)
83 Seat guide rails
84 Side-section back armour (5-mm)
85 Shoulder armour (5-mm)
86 Oxygen supply valve
87 Steel frame turnover pylon
88 Windscreen spray pipes
89 Instrument panel shroud
90 30-mm armoured glass quarterlights
91 50-mm armoured glass windscreen
92 Revi 16B reflector gunsight
93 Canopy
94 Aerial attachment
95 Headrest
96 Head armour (12-mm)
97 Head armour support strut
98 Explosive charge canopy emergency jettison unit
99 Canopy channel side
100 Auxiliary tank: fuel (25·3 Imp gal/115 litre) or GM-1 (18·7 Imp gal/85 litre)
101 FuG 16ZY transmitter-receiver unit
102 Handhold cover
103 Primer fuel filler cap
104 Autopilot steering unit (PKS 12)
105 FuG 16ZY power transformer
106 Entry step cover plate
107 Two tri-spherical oxygen bottles (starboard fuselage wall)
108 Auxiliary fuel tank filler point
109 FuG 25a transponder unit
110 Autopilot position integration unit
111 FuG 16ZY homer bearing converter
112 Elevator control cables
113 Rudder control DUZ-flexible rods
114 Fabric panel (Bulkhead 12)
115 Rudder differential unit
116 Aerial lead-in
117 Rear fuselage lift tube
118 Triangular stress frame
119 Tailplane trim unit
120 Tailplane attachment fitting
121 Tailwheel retraction guide tube
122 Retraction cable lower pulley
123 Starboard tailplane
124 Aerial
125 Starboard elevator
126 Elevator trim tab
127 Tailwheel shock strut guide
128 Fin construction
129 Retraction cable under pulley
130 Aerial attachment stub
131 Rudder upper hinge
132 Rudder structure
133 Rudder trim tab
134 Tailwheel retraction mechanism access panel
135 Rudder attachment/actuation fittings
136 Rear navigation light
137 Extension spring
138 Elevator trim tab
139 Port elevator structure
140 Tailplane construction
141 Semi-retracting tailwheel
142 Forked wheel housing
143 Drag yoke
144 Tailwheel shock strut
145 Tailwheel locking linkage
146 Elevator actuation lever linkage
147 Angled frame spar
148 elevator differential bellcrank
149 FuG 25a ventral antenna
150 Master compass sensing unit
151 FuG 16ZY fixed loop homing antenna
152 Radio compartment access hatch
153 Single tri-spherical oxygen bottle (port fuselage wall)
154 Retractable entry step
155 Wing root fairing
156 Fuselage rear fuel tank (64·5 Imp gal/293 litre)
157 Fuselage/rear spar attachment
158 Fuselage forward fuel tank (51 Imp gal/232 litre)
159 Port wing root cannon ammunition box (250 rpg)
160 Ammunition feed chute
161 Port wing root MG 151/20E cannon
162 Link and casing discard chute
163 Cannon rear mount support bracket
164 Upper and lower wing shell stringers
165 Rear spar
166 Spar construction
167 Flap position indicator scale and peep-hole
168 Flap actuating electric motor
169 Port 20-mm MG 151/20E wing cannon (sideways mounted)
170 Aileron transverse linkage
171 Ammunition box (125 rpg)
172 Ammunition box rear suspension arm
173 Aileron control linkage
174 Aileron control unit
175 Aileron trim tab
176 Port aileron structure
177 Port navigation light
178 Outboard wing stringers
179 Detachable wingtip
180 A-8/R1 variant underwing gun pack (in place of outboard wing cannon)
181 Link and casing discard chute
182 Twin unsynchronized 20-mm MG 151/20E cannon
183 Light metal fairing (gondola)
184 Ammunition feed chutes
185 Ammunition boxes (125 rpg)
186 Carrier frame restraining cord
187 Ammunition box rear suspension arms
188 Leading-edge skining
189 Ammunition feed chute
190 Ammunition warming pipe
191 Aileron bellcrank
192 Mainwheel strut mounting assembly
193 EC-oleo shock strut
194 Mainwheel leg fairing
195 Scissors unit
196 Mainwheel fairing
197 Axle housing
198 Port mainwheel
199 Brake lines
200 Cannon barrel
201 FuG 16ZY Morane antenna
202 Radius rods
203 Rotating drive unit
204 Mainwheel retraction electric motor housing
205 Undercarriage indicator
206 Sealed air-jack
207 BSK 16 gun camera
208 Retraction locking hooks
209 Undercarriage locking unit
210 Armament collimation tube
211 Camera wiring conduits
212 Wheel well
213 Cannon barrel blast tube
214 Wheel cover actuation strut
215 Ammunition hot air
216 Port inboard wheel cover
217 Wing root cannon barrel
218 ETC 501 carrier unit
219 ETC 501 bomb-rack
220 SC 500 bomb load

# Bristol Beaufighter (July 1939)

Many were to be the adaptations for fighter roles of aircraft conceived purely as bombers, the supreme example of such aeronautical versatility being provided by the Junkers Ju 88 (pages 104-105). This outstandingly polymorphous German aircraft was paralleled in the UK by another such example of improvisation, albeit a somewhat more dedicated fighter adaptation of an existing bomber. This, the Bristol Beaufighter, was, like its German counterpart, to be numbered among WWII's most versatile warplanes.

To overcome the RAF's embarrassing lack of long-range heavy fighters, Leslie G. Frise and his team conceived, late in 1938, a "minimum change" fighter derivative of the Beaufort torpedo-bomber. Featuring more powerful engines and a redesigned forward fuselage, this flew as the Beaufighter on 17 July 1939. An inelegant aeroplane, brutally powerful in appearance, the Beaufighter was an aircraft towards which no pilot could be indifferent; it was either liked or heartily disliked.

Entering service in the nocturnal intercept role in September 1940 as the only RAF aircraft capable of carrying AI Mk IV radar without sacrificing either endur-

ance or firepower, the Beaufighter displayed a measure of handling precocity. Extreme care had to be exercised to avoid an incipient swing during take-off; a side-to-side yawing during undercarriage retraction was not easily controllable, and prior to adoption of tailplane dihedral it suffered pronounced fore-and-aft instability, particularly noticeable in the climb and landing approach. It tended to pitch nose down when the cannon were fired and its controls were heavy. But the Beaufighter was an immensely strong, outstandingly robust aeroplane.

In the spring of 1941, the Beaufighter was introduced by RAF Coastal Command as a long-range fighter, 915 Mk Is being delivered before replacement of the Hercules III or XI engines by the Hercules VI resulted in the Beaufighter VI of which 1,682 were built, 60 of these as interim torpedo fighters with an 18-in (46-cm) or 22·5-in (57-cm) torpedo to enter service late 1942. With Hercules XVII engines, the definitive Beaufighter X torpedo fighter followed from 1943, 2,205 being built, together with 163 Beaufighter XICs lacking torpedo-carrying provision, production ending on 21 September 1945 with 5,562 Beaufighters built.

**Key to Bristol Beaufighter I**

1 Starboard navigation light (fore) and formation-keeping light (aft)
2 Wing structure
3 Aileron adjustable tab
4 Starboard aileron
5 Four Browning 0·303-in (7,7-mm) machine guns
6 Machine gun ports
7 Starboard outer wing fuel tank, capacity 87 Imp gal (395 l)
8 Split trailing-edge flaps, hydraulically actuated
9 Starboard flap
10 Flap operating jack
11 Starboard nacelle tail fairing
12 Oil tank, capacity 17 Imp gal (77 l)
13 Starboard inner wing fuel tank, capacity 188 Imp gal (855 l)
14 Cabin air duct
15 Hinged leading-edge sections
16 Engine bulkhead
17 Engine bearers
18 Auxiliary intake
19 Supercharger air intake

20 Engine cooling flaps
21 1,560 hp Bristol Hercules III radial engine
22 De Havilland Hydromatic propeller
23 Propeller spinner
24 Lockheed oleo-pneumatic shock-absorber
25 Starboard mainwheel, with Dunlop brakes
26 Forward identification lamp in nose cap
27 Rudder pedals
28 Control column
29 Cannon ports
30 Seat adjusting lever
31 Pilot's seat
32 Instrument panel
33 Clear-vision panel
34 Flat bullet-proof windscreen
35 Fixed canopy (sideways-hinged on later aircraft)
36 Spar carry-through step
37 Nose centre section attachment point

38 Fuselage/centre section attachment point
39 Pilot's entry/emergency escape hatchway
40 Underfloor cannon blast tubes
41 Fuselage/centre section attachment points
42 Centre section attachment longeron reinforcement
43 Cabin air duct
44 Cannon heating duct
45 Rear spar carry-through
46 Bulkhead cut-out (observer access to front hatch)
47 Bulkhead
48 Hydraulic header tank
49 Aerial mast
50 Monocoque fuselage construction
51 Starboard cannon (two 20-mm)
52 Floor level
53 Steps
54 Observer's swivel seat (normally forward-facing)
55 Radio controls and intercom

56 Observer's cupola
57 Hinged panel
58 Aerial
59 Oxygen bottles
60 Vertical control cable shaft
61 Sheet metal bulkhead
62 Control cables
63 Tailplane structure
64 Elevator
65 Elevator balance tab
66 Fin structure
67 Rudder balance
68 Rudder framework
69 Tail formation keeping (upper) and navigation lamps
70 Rudder
71 Rudder trim tab
72 Elevator trim tab
73 Elevator balance tab

74 Elevator structure
75 Port tailplane (12 deg dihedral on later aircraft)
76 Rudder hinge (lower)
77 Tailwheel retraction mechanism
78 Retracting tailwheel
79 Tailwheel bay
80 Tail-unit joint ring
81 Control cables
82 Parachute flare chute
83 Fuselage skinning — flush riveted Alclad

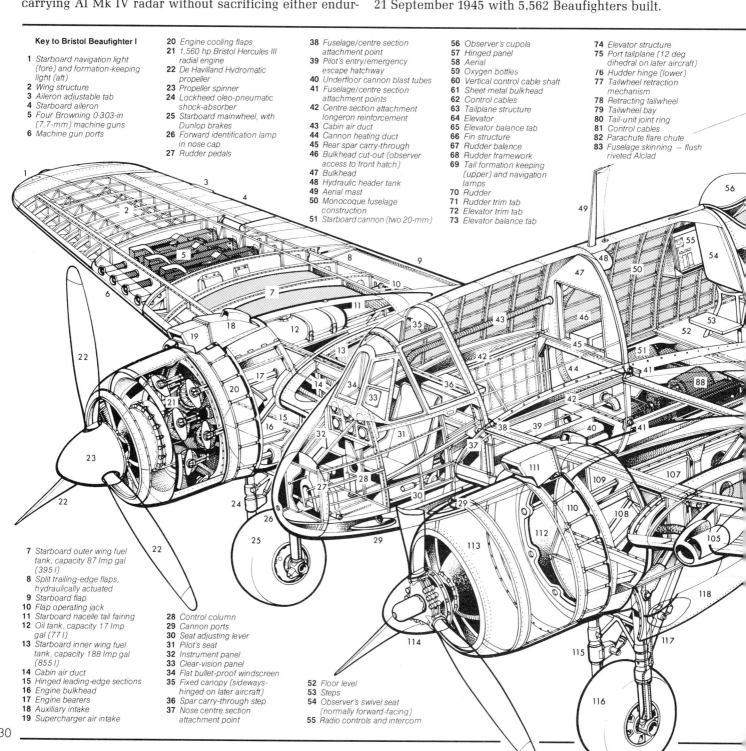

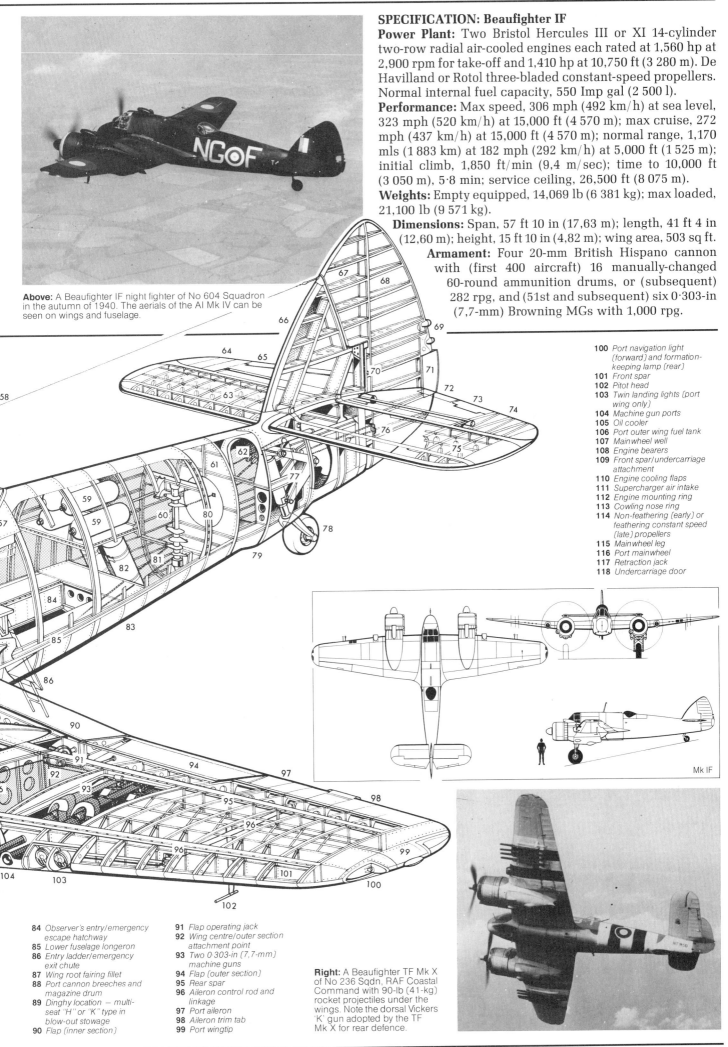

**Above:** A Beaufighter IF night fighter of No 604 Squadron in the autumn of 1940. The aerials of the AI Mk IV can be seen on wings and fuselage.

## SPECIFICATION: Beaufighter IF

**Power Plant:** Two Bristol Hercules III or XI 14-cylinder two-row radial air-cooled engines each rated at 1,560 hp at 2,900 rpm for take-off and 1,410 hp at 10,750 ft (3 280 m). De Havilland or Rotol three-bladed constant-speed propellers. Normal internal fuel capacity, 550 Imp gal (2 500 l).

**Performance:** Max speed, 306 mph (492 km/h) at sea level, 323 mph (520 km/h) at 15,000 ft (4 570 m); max cruise, 272 mph (437 km/h) at 15,000 ft (4 570 m); normal range, 1,170 mls (1 883 km) at 182 mph (292 km/h) at 5,000 ft (1 525 m); initial climb, 1,850 ft/min (9,4 m/sec); time to 10,000 ft (3 050 m), 5·8 min; service ceiling, 26,500 ft (8 075 m).

**Weights:** Empty equipped, 14,069 lb (6 381 kg); max loaded, 21,100 lb (9 571 kg).

**Dimensions:** Span, 57 ft 10 in (17,63 m); length, 41 ft 4 in (12,60 m); height, 15 ft 10 in (4,82 m); wing area, 503 sq ft.

**Armament:** Four 20-mm British Hispano cannon with (first 400 aircraft) 16 manually-changed 60-round ammunition drums, or (subsequent) 282 rpg, and (51st and subsequent) six 0·303-in (7,7-mm) Browning MGs with 1,000 rpg.

100 Port navigation light (forward) and formation-keeping lamp (rear)
101 Front spar
102 Pitot head
103 Twin landing lights (port wing only)
104 Machine gun ports
105 Oil cooler
106 Port outer wing fuel tank
107 Mainwheel well
108 Engine bearers
109 Front spar/undercarriage attachment
110 Engine cooling flaps
111 Supercharger air intake
112 Engine mounting ring
113 Cowling nose ring
114 Non-feathering (early) or feathering constant speed (late) propellers
115 Mainwheel leg
116 Port mainwheel
117 Retraction jack
118 Undercarriage door

Mk IF

84 Observer's entry/emergency escape hatchway
85 Lower fuselage longeron
86 Entry ladder/emergency exit chute
87 Wing root fairing fillet
88 Port cannon breeches and magazine drum
89 Dinghy location – multi-seat "H" or "K" type in blow-out stowage
90 Flap (inner section)
91 Flap operating jack
92 Wing centre/outer section attachment point
93 Two 0·303-in (7,7-mm) machine guns
94 Flap (outer section)
95 Rear spar
96 Aileron control rod and linkage
97 Port aileron
98 Aileron trim tab
99 Port wingtip

**Right:** A Beaufighter TF Mk X of No 236 Sqdn, RAF Coastal Command with 90-lb (41-kg) rocket projectiles under the wings. Note the dorsal Vickers 'K' gun adopted by the TF Mk X for rear defence.

# Hawker Typhoon (February 1940)

Aviation's history abounds with aircraft designed for one function only to find their *métier* in another. Fighters have certainly not been immune to such role transposition, several having been intended to operate in one specialised band of the fighter spectrum but establishing a true forté in a disparate arena. One such was the Typhoon—an abysmal failure in its intended role of high-altitude interceptor but a ground attack fighter *par excellence*.

Heaviest and most powerful single-seat single-engined warplane envisaged at the time of its inception and an object lesson in the danger of committing to production an undeveloped aeroplane, the Typhoon was ordered in quantity late in 1939, but did not fly as a prototype until 24 February 1940. From the outset, it suffered tribulations, which, although not stemming from fundamental airframe design, were of such serious nature that, on more than one occasion, the entire programme came within an ace of cancellation. The problems of a notoriously unreliable engine were compounded by rear fuselage failures, and answers had still to be found when the Typhoon was committed to squadron service from September 1941.

An innately rugged aeroplane, with a thick, high-lift wing of generous area, the Typhoon offered reasonable and precise aerobatic handling. Its stability was excellent and it was a good gun platform, but its controls were heavy, its low-speed handling left much to be desired, and it manifested a disappointing climb rate and an exceedingly poor performance above 20,000 ft (6 095 m). At lower altitudes it was very fast—it was the first RAF fighter capable of exceeding 400 mph (644 km/h)—and it achieved some success in intercepting Fw 190s engaged in low-altitude high-speed intrusions over the United Kingdom which could not be countered by Spitfires.

The Typhoon's low-altitude potential was not to be fully exploited, however, until it was fitted with bombs and rockets, and employed as a ground attack fighter, a task in which it excelled, being transformed from a fighter of dubious reliability into a highly potent weapon that turned the scales in several land battles and upset many land warfare concepts. Although production was to total 3,317, the Typhoon, in spite of its later successes, never completely recovered from its early vicissitudes.

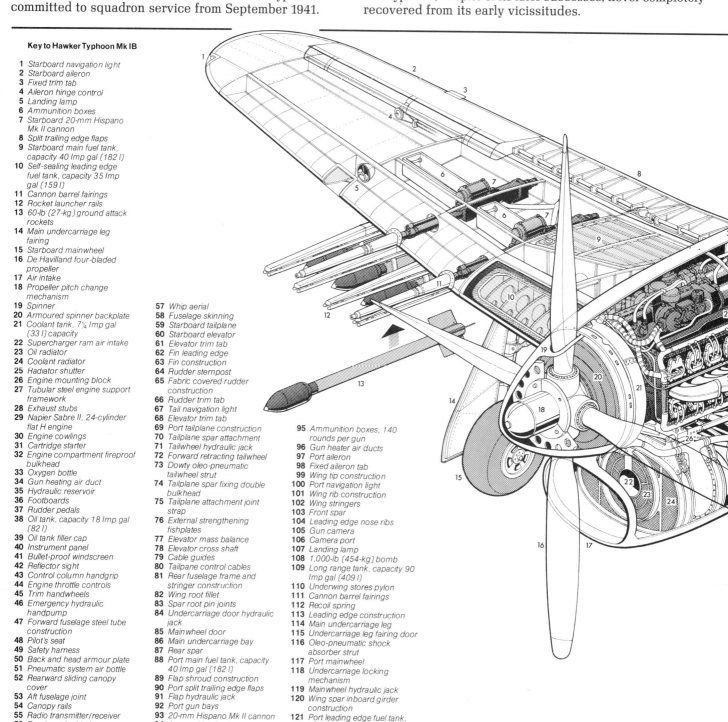

**Key to Hawker Typhoon Mk IB**

1 Starboard navigation light
2 Starboard aileron
3 Fixed trim tab
4 Aileron hinge control
5 Landing lamp
6 Ammunition boxes
7 Starboard 20-mm Hispano Mk II cannon
8 Split trailing edge flaps
9 Starboard main fuel tank, capacity 40 Imp gal (182 l)
10 Self-sealing leading edge fuel tank, capacity 35 Imp gal (159 l)
11 Cannon barrel fairings
12 Rocket launcher rails
13 60-lb (27-kg) ground attack rockets
14 Main undercarriage leg fairing
15 Starboard mainwheel
16 De Havilland four-bladed propeller
17 Air intake
18 Propeller pitch change mechanism
19 Spinner
20 Armoured spinner backplate
21 Coolant tank, 7¼ Imp gal (33 l) capacity
22 Supercharger ram air intake
23 Oil radiator
24 Coolant radiator
25 Radiator shutter
26 Engine mounting block
27 Tubular steel engine support framework
28 Exhaust stubs
29 Napier Sabre II, 24-cylinder flat H engine
30 Engine cowlings
31 Cartridge starter
32 Engine compartment fireproof bulkhead
33 Oxygen bottle
34 Gun heating air duct
35 Hydraulic reservoir
36 Footboards
37 Rudder pedals
38 Oil tank, capacity 18 Imp gal (82 l)
39 Oil tank filler cap
40 Instrument panel
41 Bullet-proof windscreen
42 Reflector sight
43 Control column handgrip
44 Engine throttle controls
45 Trim handwheels
46 Emergency hydraulic handpump
47 Forward fuselage steel tube construction
48 Pilot's seat
49 Safety harness
50 Back and head armour plate
51 Pneumatic system air bottle
52 Rearward sliding canopy cover
53 Aft fuselage joint
54 Canopy rails
55 Radio transmitter/receiver
56 Fuselage double frame

57 Whip aerial
58 Fuselage skinning
59 Starboard tailplane
60 Starboard elevator
61 Elevator trim tab
62 Fin leading edge
63 Fin construction
64 Rudder sternpost
65 Fabric covered rudder construction
66 Rudder trim tab
67 Tail navigation light
68 Elevator trim tab
69 Port tailplane construction
70 Tailplane spar attachment
71 Tailwheel hydraulic jack
72 Forward retracting tailwheel
73 Dowty oleo-pneumatic tailwheel strut
74 Tailplane spar fixing double bulkhead
75 Tailplane attachment joint strap
76 External strengthening fishplates
77 Elevator mass balance
78 Elevator cross shaft
79 Cable guides
80 Tailpane control cables
81 Rear fuselage frame and stringer construction
82 Wing root fillet
83 Spar root pin joints
84 Undercarriage door hydraulic jack
85 Mainwheel door
86 Main undercarriage bay
87 Rear spar
88 Port main fuel tank, capacity 40 Imp gal (182 l)
89 Flap shroud construction
90 Port split trailing edge flaps
91 Flap hydraulic jack
92 Port gun bays
93 20-mm Hispano Mk II cannon
94 Ammunition feed drum

95 Ammunition boxes, 140 rounds per gun
96 Gun heater air ducts
97 Port aileron
98 Fixed aileron tab
99 Wing tip construction
100 Port navigation light
101 Wing rib construction
102 Wing stringers
103 Front spar
104 Leading edge nose ribs
105 Gun camera
106 Camera port
107 Landing lamp
108 1,000-lb (454-kg) bomb
109 Long range tank, capacity 90 Imp gal (409 l)
110 Underwing stores pylon
111 Cannon barrel fairings
112 Recoil spring
113 Leading edge construction
114 Main undercarriage leg
115 Undercarriage leg fairing door
116 Oleo-pneumatic shock absorber strut
117 Port mainwheel
118 Undercarriage locking mechanism
119 Mainwheel hydraulic jack
120 Wing spar inboard girder construction
121 Port leading edge fuel tank, capacity 35 Imp gal (159 l)

## SPECIFICATION: Typhoon IB

**Power Plant:** One Napier Sabre IIA 24-cylinder H-type liquid-cooled engine rated at 2,180 hp at 3,650 rpm for take-off and 1,830 hp at 11,500 ft (3 505 m). Three- or four-bladed de Havilland Hydromatic constant-speed propeller. Internal fuel capacity, 150 Imp gal (682 l) with provision for two 45 Imp gal (205 l) drop tanks.

**Performance:** Max speed, 405 mph (652 km/h) at 18,000 ft (5 485 m), 374 mph (602 km/h) at 5,500 ft (1 675 m); econ cruise, 354 mph (409 km/h) at 15,000 ft (4 570 m); range (internal fuel), 610 mls (982 km), (with drop tanks), 1,000 mls (1 610 km), (with max external ordnance), 510 mls (821 km); time to 15,000 ft (4 570 m), 6·2 min; service ceiling, 34,000 ft (10 363 m).

**Weights:** Empty equipped, 9,800 lb (4 445 kg); normal loaded, 11,777 lb (5 342 kg); max, 13,980 lb (6 341 kg).

**Dimensions:** Span, 41 ft 7 in (12,67 m); length, 31 ft 11 in (9,73 m); ht, 15 ft 3½ in (4,66 m); wing area, 249 sq ft (23,13 m²).

**Armament:** Four 20-mm Hispano Mk II cannon with 140 rpg and up to two 1,000-lb (454-kg) bombs or eight 60-lb (27,2-kg) rocket projectiles.

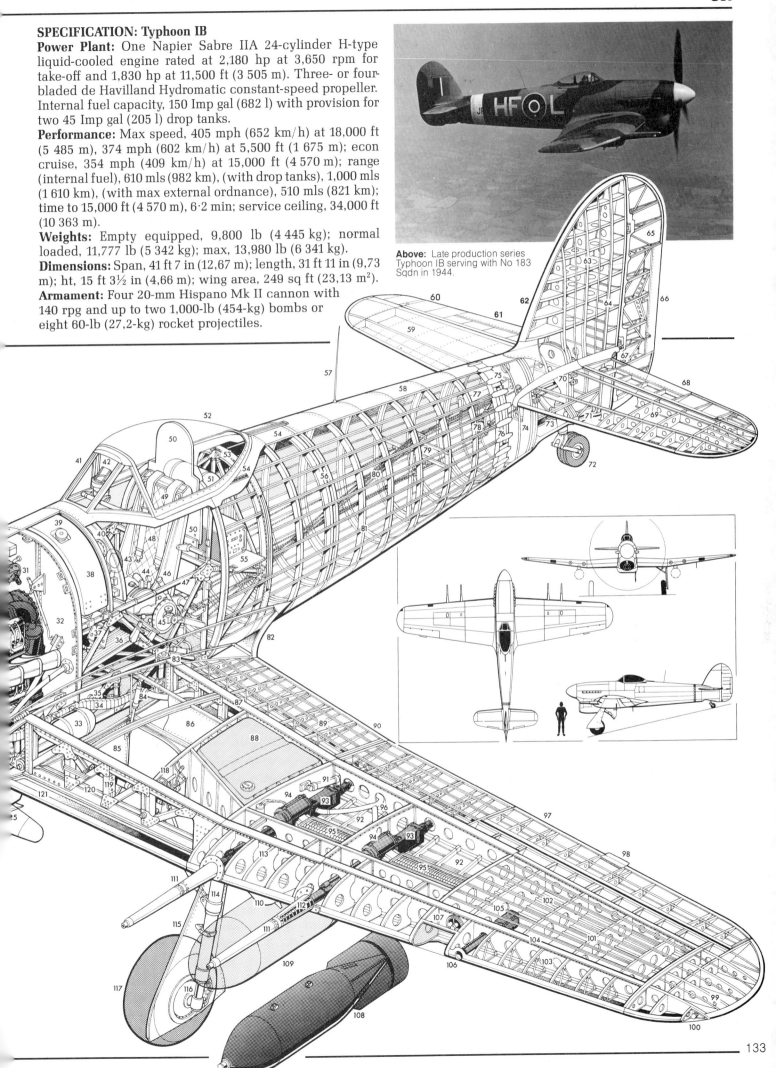

**Above:** Late production series Typhoon IB serving with No 183 Sqdn in 1944.

# Mikoyan-Gurevich MiG-3 (April 1940)

First in the generation of single-seat fighters evolving immediately prior to WWII to be optimised for high-altitude intercept, the MiG-3 was small, heavy and very fast. Its speed capability was counterbalanced, however, by poor longitudinal stability and sluggish control response under virtually all conditions; poor spinning characteristics, and a proclivity for spinning out of a steep banking turn; strictly limited visibility for taxying and take-off, and a dauntingly high landing speed—defects compounded by inadequate firepower and endurance.

Conceptual development began late in 1938 as 'Project K' within the design brigade headed by Nikolai Polikarpov, primary responsibility being assigned to two deputies, Artem Mikoyan and Mikhail Gurevich. Speed at altitude took precedence over all other capabilities, the aim being to design the smallest practical airframe around the most powerful available liquid-cooled engine. With the concept defined, Mikoyan and Gurevich established an independent bureau and the first of three prototypes of the aircraft was flown on 5 April 1940.

The initial model—for which a Stalin Prize was awarded in which Polikarpov shared—was designated MiG-1. Poor handling and unacceptably short range dictated major changes introduced with the 101st aircraft in February 1941,

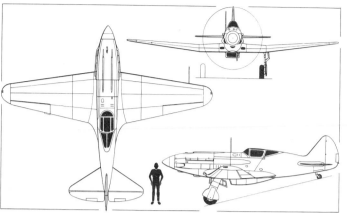

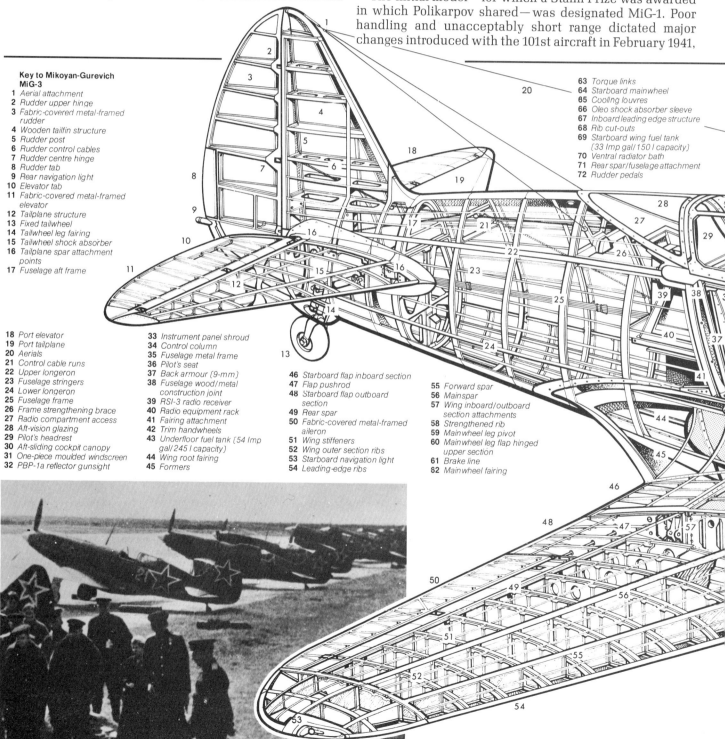

**Key to Mikoyan-Gurevich MiG-3**

1 Aerial attachment
2 Rudder upper hinge
3 Fabric-covered metal-framed rudder
4 Wooden tailfin structure
5 Rudder post
6 Rudder control cables
7 Rudder centre hinge
8 Rudder tab
9 Rear navigation light
10 Elevator tab
11 Fabric-covered metal-framed elevator
12 Tailplane structure
13 Fixed tailwheel
14 Tailwheel leg fairing
15 Tailwheel shock absorber
16 Tailplane spar attachment points
17 Fuselage aft frame

18 Port elevator
19 Port tailplane
20 Aerials
21 Control cable runs
22 Upper longeron
23 Fuselage stringers
24 Lower longeron
25 Fuselage frame
26 Frame strengthening brace
27 Radio compartment access
28 Aft-vision glazing
29 Pilot's headrest
30 Aft-sliding cockpit canopy
31 One-piece moulded windscreen
32 PBP-1a reflector gunsight

33 Instrument panel shroud
34 Control column
35 Fuselage metal frame
36 Pilot's seat
37 Back armour (9-mm)
38 Fuselage wood/metal construction joint
39 RSI-3 radio receiver
40 Radio equipment rack
41 Fairing attachment
42 Trim handwheels
43 Underfloor fuel tank (54 Imp gal/245 l capacity)
44 Wing root fairing
45 Formers

46 Starboard flap inboard section
47 Flap pushrod
48 Starboard flap outboard section
49 Rear spar
50 Fabric-covered metal-framed aileron
51 Wing stiffeners
52 Wing outer section ribs
53 Starboard navigation light
54 Leading-edge ribs

55 Forward spar
56 Mainspar
57 Wing inboard/outboard section attachments
58 Strengthened rib
59 Mainwheel leg pivot
60 Mainwheel leg flap hinged upper section
61 Brake line
62 Mainwheel fairing
63 Torque links
64 Starboard mainwheel
65 Cooling louvres
66 Oleo shock absorber sleeve
67 Inboard leading edge structure
68 Rib cut-outs
69 Starboard wing fuel tank (33 Imp gal/150 l capacity)
70 Ventral radiator bath
71 Rear spar/fuselage attachment
72 Rudder pedals

**Left:** MiG-3s of the 7 IAP (Fighter Aviation Regt) of the Black Sea Fleet Air Force in 1944.

the designation MiG-3 being simultaneously adopted. Fuel capacity was almost doubled, but in the absence of fundamental redesign, the changes made to improve flying qualities could be no more than palliatives, the MiG-3 remaining a fatiguing aircraft to fly and one demanding a high degree of piloting skill.

Entering service in March 1941, no fewer than 1,269 MiG-3s had been completed by mid-year, but they were soon found too highly specialised in capability for the type of combat that ensued, this mostly taking place at lower altitudes than those at which the MiG-3 was designed to operate. This specialised interceptor was at a distinct disadvantage in fighter-versus-fighter combat. It had resulted from an incorrect assessment of the timescale of the Luftwaffe high-altitude bomber development programme, and the optimised warplane that took to the air was a luxury that the Soviet Union could ill afford at that time. Fortuitously, the AM-35A engine had to be withdrawn from production, MiG-3 manufacture thus being terminated by *force majeure* spring 1942, 3,322 having rolled off the assembly lines and assignment to less important sectors following from early 1943.

## SPECIFICATION: MiG-3

**Power Plant:** One Mikulin AM-35A 12-cylinder vee liquid cooled engine rated at 1,350 hp at 2,050 rpm for take-off, 1,200 hp at 19,685 ft (6 000 m) and 1,150 hp at 22,965 ft (7 000 m). VISh-61Shch three-bladed constant-speed metal propeller. Internal fuel capacity, 114 Imp gal (519 l).
**Performance:** Max speed, 298 mph (480 km/h) at sea level, 325 mph (523 km/h) at 6,560 ft (2 000 m), 351 mph (565 km/h) at 13,125 ft (4 000 m), 398 mph (640 km/h) at 25,590 ft (7 800 m); max continuous cruise, 342 mph (550 km/h); range (max continuous cruise and 10% reserves), 510 mls (820 km), (long-range cruise), 742 mls (1 195 km); time to 16,400 ft (5 000 m), 5·7 min; ceiling, 39,370 ft (12 000 m).
**Weights:** Empty, 5,721 lb (2 595 kg); normal loaded, 7,385 lb (3 350 kg).
**Dimensions:** Span, 33 ft 5²/₃ in (10,20 m); length, 27 ft 0¾ in (8,25 m); height (tail up), 12 ft 2½ in (3,72 m); wing area, 187·72 sq ft (17,44 m²).
**Armament:** One 12.7-mm Berezin UB machine gun with 300 rounds and two 7,62-mm Shpital'ny-Komaritsky ShKAS machine guns with 375 (later 750) rpg.

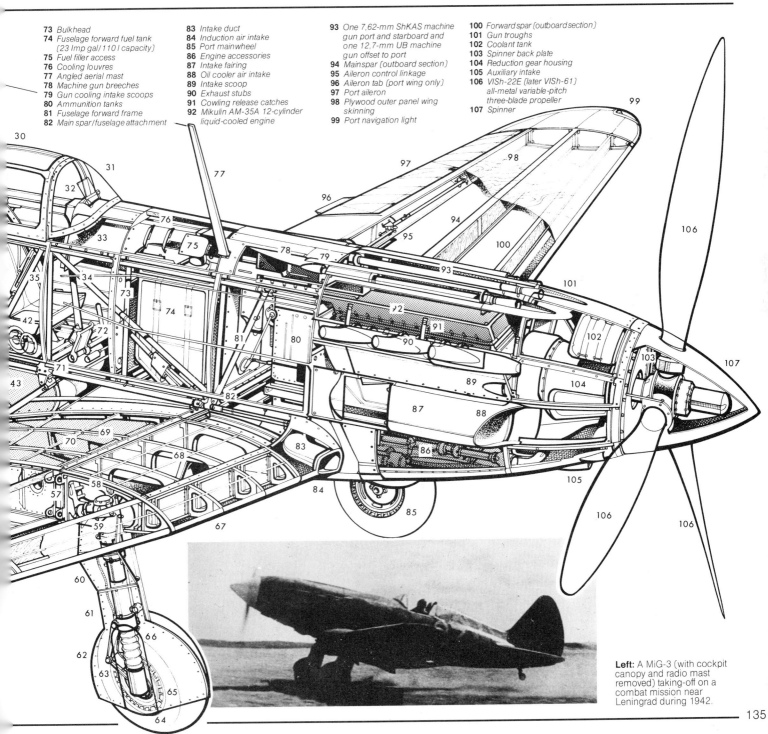

73 Bulkhead
74 Fuselage forward fuel tank (23 Imp gal/110 l capacity)
75 Fuel filler access
76 Cooling louvres
77 Angled aerial mast
78 Machine gun breeches
79 Gun cooling intake scoops
80 Ammunition tanks
81 Fuselage forward frame
82 Main spar/fuselage attachment
83 Intake duct
84 Induction air intake
85 Port mainwheel
86 Engine accessories
87 Intake fairing
88 Oil cooler air intake
89 Intake scoop
90 Exhaust stubs
91 Cowling release catches
92 Mikulin AM-35A 12-cylinder liquid-cooled engine
93 One 7,62-mm ShKAS machine gun port and starboard and one 12,7-mm UB machine gun offset to port
94 Mainspar (outboard section)
95 Aileron control linkage
96 Aileron tab (port wing only)
97 Port aileron
98 Plywood outer panel wing skinning
99 Port navigation light
100 Forward spar (outboard section)
101 Gun troughs
102 Coolant tank
103 Spinner back plate
104 Reduction gear housing
105 Auxiliary intake
106 VISh-22E (later VISh-61) all-metal variable-pitch three-blade propeller
107 Spinner

**Left:** A MiG-3 (with cockpit canopy and radio mast removed) taking-off on a combat mission near Leningrad during 1942.

# Vought F4U Corsair (May 1940)

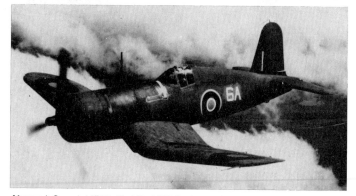

**Above:** A Corsair I (F4U-1) of No 1830 Sqdn, the Royal Navy's first Corsair unit which operated from HMS *Illustrious* in 1944.

Corsair heralded a quantum advance in shipboard fighter capability as a result of the considerable ingenuity exercised by Rex B. Beisel and his design team.

The production model, flown on 25 June 1942, demonstrated a regrettable lack of shipboard finesse which was to exclude it from US carrier decks until the summer of 1944, although the Royal Navy, perhaps less fastidious than its US counterpart, was to clear the Corsair for shipboard operations nine months earlier. The Corsair suffered an incipient landing bounce and an almost unheralded torque stall in landing configuration, shortcomings compounded by some directional instability after touchdown. Its control harmony was poor, but its acceleration was dramatic; in the cruise and at high speeds stability was positive at all times; it had a good range, adequate firepower and great strength.

Of unparalleled appearance by virtue of a reverse-gulled wing — which resolved the clearance problem of the largest propeller ever used to that time by a fighter and kept the undercarriage within manageable length — the Corsair mated innovatory airframe design with the world's first 2,000 hp engine. Flown as a prototype (XF4U-1) on 29 May 1940, the

Shore-based operations with the US Marine Corps began early in 1943, and if a qualified success when flown from carriers, the Corsair established an enviable reputation from shore bases, production continuing until December 1952, by which time 7,829 had been delivered.

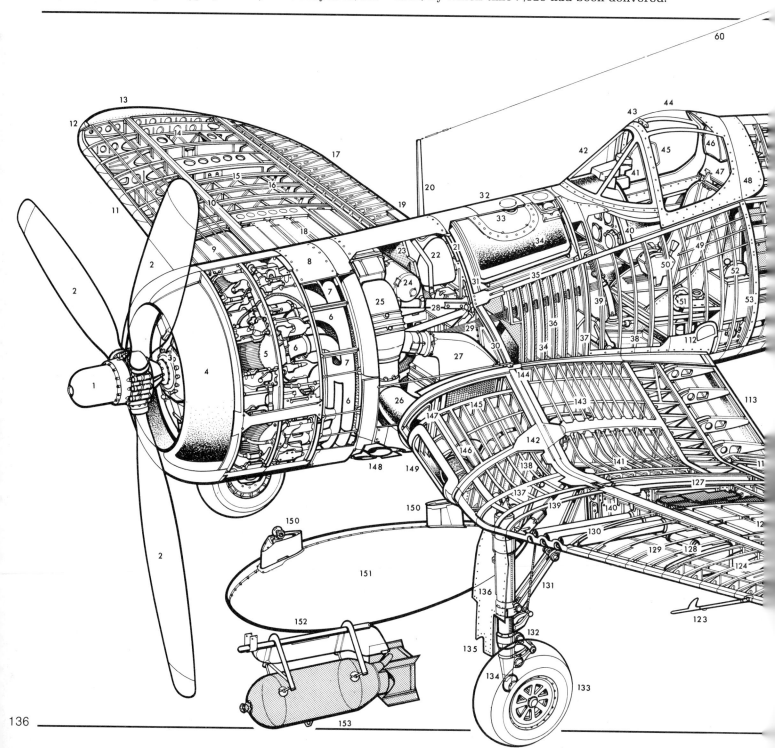

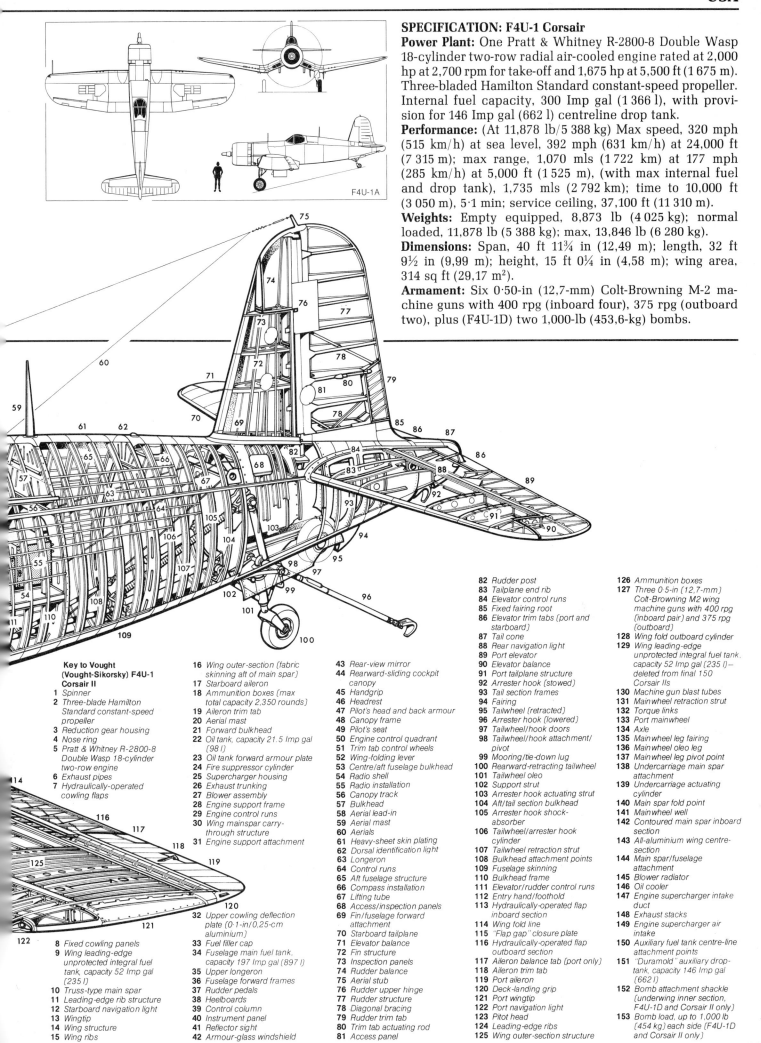

F4U-1A

## SPECIFICATION: F4U-1 Corsair

**Power Plant:** One Pratt & Whitney R-2800-8 Double Wasp 18-cylinder two-row radial air-cooled engine rated at 2,000 hp at 2,700 rpm for take-off and 1,675 hp at 5,500 ft (1 675 m). Three-bladed Hamilton Standard constant-speed propeller. Internal fuel capacity, 300 Imp gal (1 366 l), with provision for 146 Imp gal (662 l) centreline drop tank.

**Performance:** (At 11,878 lb/5 388 kg) Max speed, 320 mph (515 km/h) at sea level, 392 mph (631 km/h) at 24,000 ft (7 315 m); max range, 1,070 mls (1 722 km) at 177 mph (285 km/h) at 5,000 ft (1 525 m), (with max internal fuel and drop tank), 1,735 mls (2 792 km); time to 10,000 ft (3 050 m), 5·1 min; service ceiling, 37,100 ft (11 310 m).

**Weights:** Empty equipped, 8,873 lb (4 025 kg); normal loaded, 11,878 lb (5 388 kg); max, 13,846 lb (6 280 kg).

**Dimensions:** Span, 40 ft 11¾ in (12,49 m); length, 32 ft 9½ in (9,99 m); height, 15 ft 0¼ in (4,58 m); wing area, 314 sq ft (29,17 m²).

**Armament:** Six 0·50-in (12,7-mm) Colt-Browning M-2 machine guns with 400 rpg (inboard four), 375 rpg (outboard two), plus (F4U-1D) two 1,000-lb (453,6-kg) bombs.

**Key to Vought (Vought-Sikorsky) F4U-1 Corsair II**

1 Spinner
2 Three-blade Hamilton Standard constant-speed propeller
3 Reduction gear housing
4 Nose ring
5 Pratt & Whitney R-2800-8 Double Wasp 18-cylinder two-row engine
6 Exhaust pipes
7 Hydraulically-operated cowling flaps
8 Fixed cowling panels
9 Wing leading-edge unprotected integral fuel tank, capacity 52 Imp gal (235 l)
10 Truss-type main spar
11 Leading-edge rib structure
12 Starboard navigation light
13 Wingtip
14 Wing structure
15 Wing ribs
16 Wing outer-section (fabric skinning aft of main spar)
17 Starboard aileron
18 Ammunition boxes (max total capacity 2,350 rounds)
19 Aileron trim tab
20 Aerial mast
21 Forward bulkhead
22 Oil tank, capacity 21.5 Imp gal (98 l)
23 Oil tank forward armour plate
24 Fire suppressor cylinder
25 Supercharger housing
26 Exhaust trunking
27 Blower assembly
28 Engine support frame
29 Engine control runs
30 Wing mainspar carry-through structure
31 Engine support attachment
32 Upper cowling deflection plate (0·1-in/0,25-cm aluminium)
33 Fuel filler cap
34 Fuselage main fuel tank, capacity 197 Imp gal (897 l)
35 Upper longeron
36 Fuselage forward frames
37 Rudder pedals
38 Heelboards
39 Control column
40 Instrument panel
41 Reflector sight
42 Armour-glass windshield
43 Rear-view mirror
44 Rearward-sliding cockpit canopy
45 Handgrip
46 Headrest
47 Pilot's head and back armour
48 Canopy frame
49 Pilot's seat
50 Engine control quadrant
51 Trim tab control wheels
52 Wing-folding lever
53 Centre/aft fuselage bulkhead
54 Radio shell
55 Radio installation
56 Canopy track
57 Bulkhead
58 Aerial lead-in
59 Aerial mast
60 Aerials
61 Heavy-sheet skin plating
62 Dorsal identification light
63 Longeron
64 Control runs
65 Aft fuselage structure
66 Compass installation
67 Lifting tube
68 Access/inspection panels
69 Fin/fuselage forward attachment
70 Starboard tailplane
71 Tailplane balance
72 Fin structure
73 Inspection panels
74 Aerial support frame
75 Aerial stub
76 Rudder upper hinge
77 Rudder structure
78 Diagonal bracing
79 Rudder trim tab
80 Trim tab actuating rod
81 Access panel
82 Rudder post
83 Tailplane end rib
84 Elevator control runs
85 Fixed fairing root
86 Elevator trim tabs (port and starboard)
87 Tail cone
88 Rear navigation light
89 Port elevator
90 Elevator balance
91 Port tailplane structure
92 Arrester hook (stowed)
93 Tail section frames
94 Fairing
95 Tailwheel (retracted)
96 Arrester hook (lowered)
97 Tailwheel/hook doors
98 Tailwheel/hook attachment/ pivot
99 Mooring/tie-down lug
100 Rearward-retracting tailwheel
101 Tailwheel oleo
102 Support strut
103 Arrester hook actuating strut
104 Aft/tail section bulkhead
105 Arrester hook shock-absorber
106 Tailwheel/arrester hook cylinder
107 Tailwheel retraction strut
108 Bulkhead attachment points
109 Fuselage skinning
110 Bulkhead frame
111 Elevator/rudder control runs
112 Entry hand/foothold
113 Hydraulically-operated flap inboard section
114 Wing fold line
115 "Flap gap" closure plate
116 Hydraulically-operated flap outboard section
117 Aileron balance tab (port only)
118 Aileron trim tab
119 Port aileron
120 Deck-landing grip
121 Port wingtip
122 Port navigation light
123 Pitot head
124 Leading-edge ribs
125 Wing outer-section structure
126 Ammunition boxes
127 Three 0·5-in (12,7-mm) Colt-Browning M2 wing machine guns with 400 rpg (inboard pair) and 375 rpg (outboard)
128 Wing fold outboard cylinder
129 Wing leading-edge unprotected integral fuel tank, capacity 52 Imp gal (235 l) — deleted from final 150 Corsair IIs
130 Machine gun blast tubes
131 Mainwheel retraction strut
132 Torque links
133 Port mainwheel
134 Axle
135 Mainwheel leg fairing
136 Mainwheel oleo leg
137 Mainwheel leg pivot point
138 Undercarriage main spar attachment
139 Undercarriage actuating cylinder
140 Main spar fold point
141 Mainwheel well
142 Contoured main spar inboard section
143 All-aluminium wing centre-section
144 Main spar/fuselage attachment
145 Blower radiator
146 Oil cooler
147 Engine supercharger intake duct
148 Exhaust stacks
149 Engine supercharger air intake
150 Auxiliary fuel tank centre-line attachment points
151 "Duramold" auxiliary drop-tank, capacity 146 Imp gal (662 l)
152 Bomb attachment shackle (underwing inner section, F4U-1D and Corsair II only)
153 Bomb load, up to 1,000 lb (454 kg) each side (F4U-1D and Corsair II only)

# Reggiane Re 2001 Falco II (July 1940)

The fact that fighter capability enhancement was paced primarily by power plant availability was demonstrated in no country more profoundly than in Italy. Here, in the late 'thirties, fighter development began to fall behind international standards through no lack of talent on the part of Italian practitioners of the art of fighter design, but through a manifest lack of engines capable of meeting the performance demands of the new generation of fighters.

The availability to the Italian fighter manufacturers of the excellent Daimler-Benz series of liquid-cooled engines radically transformed the situation, however, and resulted in an interim generation of fighters. These, essentially adaptations of existing designs to take advantage of the newly-available German engines, coupled the excellent handling characteristics and manoeuvrability of their progenitors with appreciably improved performances, raising Italian fighter standards once more to international levels.

Representative of this interim generation was the Re 2001 Falco (Falcon) II designed by Roberto G. Longhi

and produced by the "Reggiane" subsidiary of the Caproni organisation as an adaptation of the radial-engined Re 2000, aerodynamically the most refined of pre-WWII Italian fighters. Flown mid-July 1940, the Re 2001 entered service late in 1941, night fighter (Caccia Notturno) and fighter-bomber (Caccia Bombardiere) versions being produced. The Re 2001 retained the delightful flying qualities of the preceding Re 2000, but engine availability inhibited production and only 237 were to be delivered to the Regia Aeronautica.

## SPECIFICATION: Re 2001 Series I

**Power Plant:** One Alfa Romeo R.A.1000 RC.41 Ia Monsonie (DB 601A) 12-cylinder inverted-vee liquid-cooled engine rated at 1,175 hp at 2,500 rpm for take-off and 1,100 hp at 12,140 ft (3 700 m). Three-bladed Alfa Romeo R.A.1000 constant-speed propeller. Internal fuel capacity, 119·65 Imp gal (544 l).

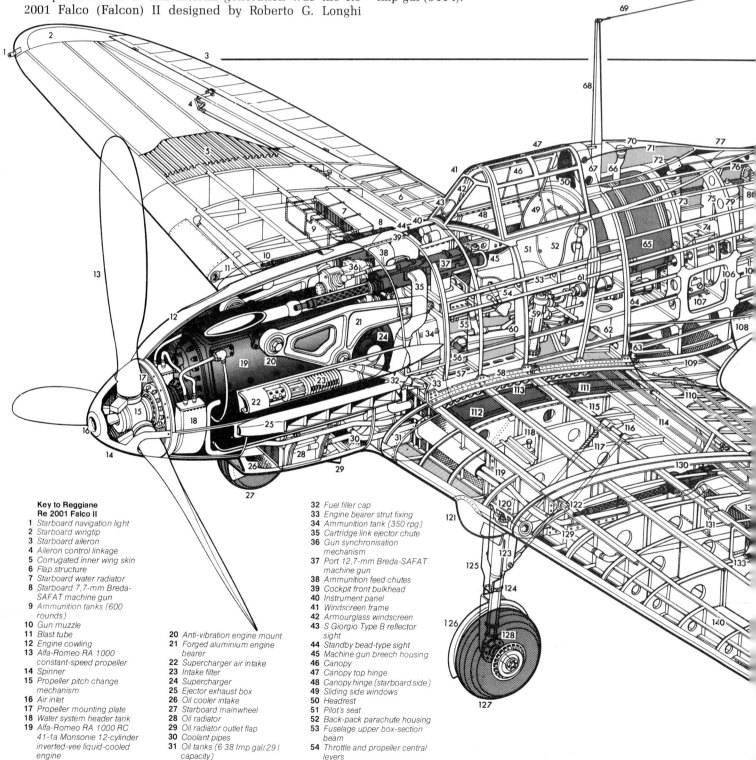

**Key to Reggiane Re 2001 Falco II**
1 Starboard navigation light
2 Starboard wingtip
3 Starboard aileron
4 Aileron control linkage
5 Corrugated inner wing skin
6 Flap structure
7 Starboard water radiator
8 Starboard 7,7-mm Breda-SAFAT machine gun
9 Ammunition tanks (600 rounds)
10 Gun muzzle
11 Blast tube
12 Engine cowling
13 Alfa-Romeo RA 1000 constant-speed propeller
14 Spinner
15 Propeller pitch change mechanism
16 Air inlet
17 Propeller mounting plate
18 Water system header tank
19 Alfa-Romeo RA 1000 RC 41-1a Monsonie 12-cylinder inverted-vee liquid-cooled engine

20 Anti-vibration engine mount
21 Forged aluminium engine bearer
22 Supercharger air intake
23 Intake filter
24 Supercharger
25 Ejector exhaust box
26 Oil cooler intake
27 Starboard mainwheel
28 Oil radiator
29 Oil radiator outlet flap
30 Coolant pipes
31 Oil tanks (6·38 Imp gal/29 l capacity)

32 Fuel filler cap
33 Engine bearer strut fixing
34 Ammunition tank (350 rpg)
35 Cartridge link ejector chute
36 Gun synchronisation mechanism
37 Port 12,7-mm Breda-SAFAT machine gun
38 Ammunition feed chutes
39 Cockpit front bulkhead
40 Instrument panel
41 Windscreen frame
42 Armourglass windscreen
43 S Giorgio Type B reflector sight
44 Standby bead-type sight
45 Machine gun breech housing
46 Canopy
47 Canopy top hinge
48 Canopy hinge (starboard side)
49 Sliding side windows
50 Headrest
51 Pilot's seat
52 Back-pack parachute housing
53 Fuselage upper box-section beam
54 Throttle and propeller central levers

138

**Performance:** Max speed, 273 mph (440 km/h) at sea level, 320 mph (515 km/h) at 9,845 ft (3 000 m), 339 mph (545 km/h) at 17,945 ft (5 470 m); range, 646 mls (1 040 km) at 233 mph (375 km/h) at 19,685 ft (6 000 m), 553 mls (890 km) at 273 mph (440 km/h) at 26,245 ft (8 000 m); time to 13,125 ft (4 000 m), 4·17 min, to 19,685 ft (6 000 m), 6·5 min; service ceiling, 39,205 ft (11 950 m).
**Weights:** Empty equipped, 5,265 lb (2 388 kg), loaded, 6,989 lb (3 170 kg).
**Dimensions:** Span, 36 ft 1 in (11,00 m); length, 27 ft 5⅛ in (8,36 m); height, 10 ft 2⅞ in (3,12 m); wing area, 219·58 sq ft (20,40 m²).

**Armament:** Two 12,7-mm Breda-SAFAT machine guns with 350 rpg and two 7,7-mm Breda-SAFAT machine guns with 600 rpg.

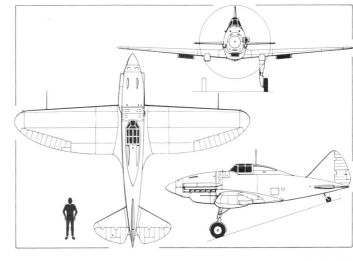

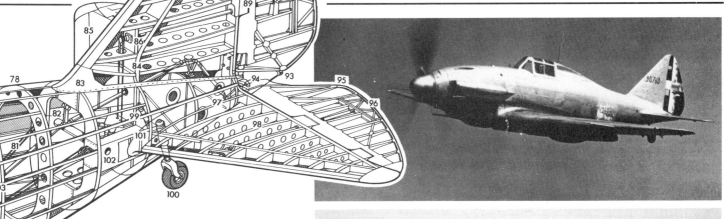

**Top right:** A IIIa Series Re 2001 completed as a night fighter with underwing 20-mm cannon, and (immediately right) a similarly-armed Series IV° Re 2001 C.N. of the 82ᵃ squadriglia, 21° Gruppo, of the Italian Co-Belligerent Air Force.

55 Control condition
56 Rudder pedal
57 Fuselage lower box-section beam
58 Wing attachment angle beam
59 Flap and under-carriage gearbox
60 Emergency hand pump
61 Electric flap motor
62 Flap drive shaft
63 Bevel drive to flap linkage

64 Electric undercarriage motor
65 Fuselage fuel tank (17·6 Imp gals/80 l)
66 Tank filler pipe
67 Headrest support structure
68 Aerial mast
69 Aerial
70 Fuel filler cap
71 Rearward vision cut-out
72 Hydraulic reservoir access panel
73 Hydraulic reservoir
74 Modulator
75 Fuselage frames
76 Z-section stringers
77 Cockpit aft fairing
78 Fuselage upper skin plating
79 Pneumatic reservoir
80 $CO_2$ fire extinguisher bottle
81 Rudder cables
82 Elevator rod linkage
83 Fin fairing
84 Fin spar mounting
85 Starboard tailplane
86 Rudder trim linkage
87 Fin structure
88 Rudder post
89 Hinge box
90 Rudder structure
91 Aerial attachment
92 Rudder trim tab
93 Rear navigation light
94 Rudder operating arm

95 Port elevator
96 Elevator trim tab
97 Elevator control linkage
98 Tailplane structure
99 Tailwheel shock absorber
100 Castoring tailwheel
101 Tailplane attachment box-beam
102 Lifting point
103 Trim control cables
104 Fuselage lower skin plating
105 Batteries
106 Access hatch
107 TBR 30 radio transmitter and receiver
108 Wing root fillet
109 Port flap structure
110 Trailing edge structure
111 Aft wing fuel tank (44 Imp gal/200 l capacity)
112 Forward wing fuel tank (58 Imp gal/264 l capacity)
113 Wing upper skin (corrugated sandwich construction)
114 Port mainwheel well
115 Undercarriage drive shaft
116 Bevel gear housing
117 Undercarriage retraction screw jacks
118 Undercarriage 'pop-up' position indicator
119 Coolant pipes in leading edge

120 Undercarriage pivot mounting
121 Undercarriage leg fairing
122 Port gun muzzle
123 Main undercarriage leg
124 Shock absorber strut
125 Leg fairing door
126 Wheel cover plate
127 Port mainwheel
128 Pneumatic brake
129 Wing outer panel bolted joint
130 Port 7,7-mm Breda-SAFAT machine gun
131 Ammunition tanks (800 rounds)
132 Port wing radiator
133 Cooling air inlet
134 Radiator fairing
135 Cooling air outlet flap
136 Flap shroud construction
137 Multi-spar wing structure
138 Cranked rear spar
139 Intermediate spars
140 Front spar
141 Aileron control linkage
142 Port aileron
143 Aileron hinge mounting
144 Aileron trim tab
145 Lower wing skin
146 L-section stringers
147 Leading edge structure
148 Pitot head
149 Port navigation light
150 Wingtip construction

# North American P-51 Mustang (October 1940)

Fighter history demonstrates frequently that service success does not necessarily equate with time expended on the drawing board, an outstanding case in point being the P-51. This was translated from outline concept to completed prototype within 122 days, yet was to emerge as arguably the best all-round single-seat piston-engined fighter of a WWII combatant.

Designed under the leadership of Raymond H. Rice and Edgar Schmued, and conceived in response to an RAF rather than USAAF requirement, the Mustang was an inspired design, an innovatory feature of which was the use of a low-drag laminar-flow aerofoil section. Flown (as the NA-73X) on 26 October 1940, the Mustang underwent very rapid genealogical processes, although its basic structure was subjected to no fundamental changes.

The initial model, known as the Mustang I to the RAF and P-51A to the USAAF, was powered by a low-altitude Allison V-1710 engine which rendered it unsuited for the air-to-air role, since most combat took place above the altitude at which engine

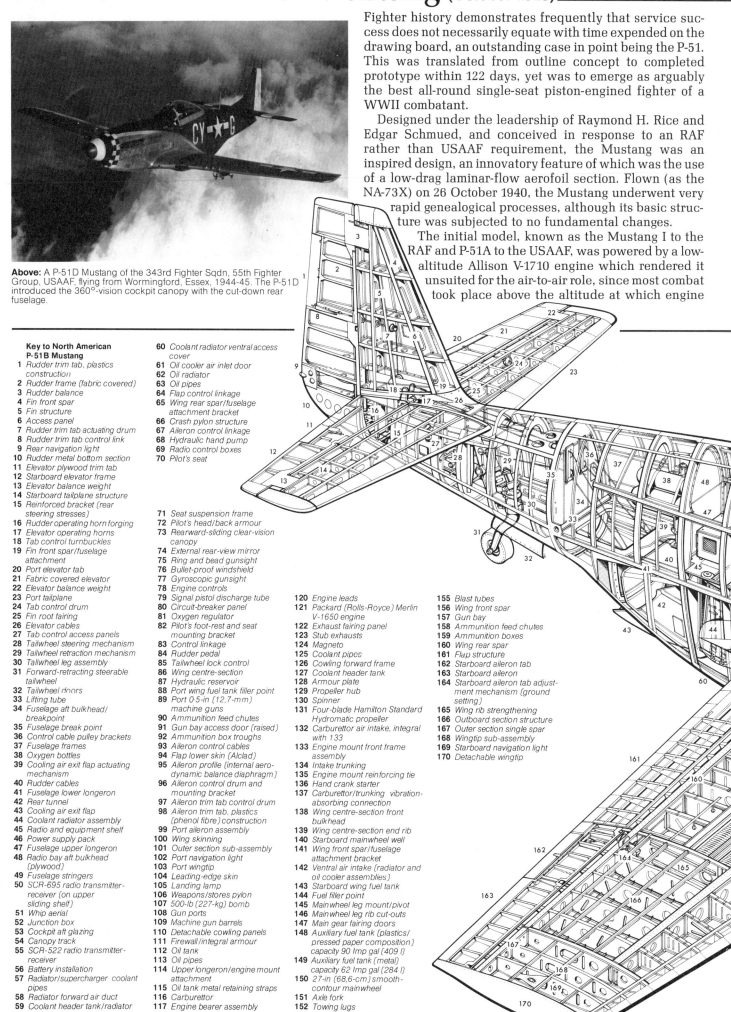

**Above:** A P-51D Mustang of the 343rd Fighter Sqdn, 55th Fighter Group, USAAF, flying from Wormingford, Essex, 1944-45. The P-51D introduced the 360°-vision cockpit canopy with the cut-down rear fuselage.

**Key to North American P-51B Mustang**

1 Rudder trim tab, plastics construction
2 Rudder frame (fabric covered)
3 Rudder balance
4 Fin front spar
5 Fin structure
6 Access panel
7 Rudder trim tab actuating drum
8 Rudder trim tab control link
9 Rear navigation light
10 Rudder metal bottom section
11 Elevator plywood trim tab
12 Starboard elevator frame
13 Elevator balance weight
14 Starboard tailplane structure
15 Reinforced bracket (rear steering stresses)
16 Rudder operating horn forging
17 Elevator operating horns
18 Tab control turnbuckles
19 Fin front spar/fuselage attachment
20 Port elevator tab
21 Fabric covered elevator
22 Elevator balance weight
23 Port tailplane
24 Tab control drum
25 Fin root fairing
26 Elevator cables
27 Tab control access panels
28 Tailwheel steering mechanism
29 Tailwheel retraction mechanism
30 Tailwheel leg assembly
31 Forward-retracting steerable tailwheel
32 Tailwheel doors
33 Lifting tube
34 Fuselage aft bulkhead/ breakpoint
35 Fuselage break point
36 Control cable pulley brackets
37 Fuselage frames
38 Oxygen bottles
39 Cooling air exit flap actuating mechanism
40 Rudder cables
41 Fuselage lower longeron
42 Rear tunnel
43 Cooling air exit flap
44 Coolant radiator assembly
45 Radio and equipment shelf
46 Power supply pack
47 Fuselage upper longeron
48 Radio bay aft bulkhead (plywood)
49 Fuselage stringers
50 SCR-695 radio transmitter-receiver (on upper sliding shelf)
51 Whip aerial
52 Junction box
53 Cockpit aft glazing
54 Canopy track
55 SCR-522 radio transmitter-receiver
56 Battery installation
57 Radiator/supercharger coolant pipes
58 Radiator forward air duct
59 Coolant header tank/radiator pipe

60 Coolant radiator ventral access cover
61 Oil cooler air inlet door
62 Oil radiator
63 Oil pipes
64 Flap control linkage
65 Wing rear spar/fuselage attachment bracket
66 Crash pylon structure
67 Aileron control linkage
68 Hydraulic hand pump
69 Radio control boxes
70 Pilot's seat

71 Seat suspension frame
72 Pilot's head/back armour
73 Rearward-sliding clear-vision canopy
74 External rear-view mirror
75 Ring and bead gunsight
76 Bullet-proof windshield
77 Gyroscopic gunsight
78 Engine controls
79 Signal pistol discharge tube
80 Circuit-breaker panel
81 Oxygen regulator
82 Pilot's foot-rest and seat mounting bracket
83 Control linkage
84 Rudder pedal
85 Tailwheel lock control
86 Wing centre-section
87 Hydraulic reservoir
88 Port wing fuel tank filler point
89 Port 0.5-in (12.7-mm) machine guns
90 Ammunition feed chutes
91 Gun bay access door (raised)
92 Ammunition box troughs
93 Aileron control cables
94 Flap lower skin (Alclad)
95 Aileron profile (internal aerodynamic balance diaphragm)
96 Aileron control drum and mounting bracket
97 Aileron trim tab control drum
98 Aileron trim tab, plastics (phenol fibre) construction
99 Port aileron assembly
100 Wing skinning
101 Outer section sub-assembly
102 Port navigation light
103 Port wingtip
104 Leading-edge skin
105 Landing lamp
106 Weapons/stores pylon
107 500-lb (227-kg) bomb
108 Gun ports
109 Machine gun barrels
110 Detachable cowling panels
111 Firewall/integral armour
112 Oil tank
113 Oil pipes
114 Upper longeron/engine mount attachment
115 Oil tank metal retaining straps
116 Carburettor
117 Engine bearer assembly
118 Cowling panel frames
119 Engine aftercooler

120 Engine leads
121 Packard (Rolls-Royce) Merlin V-1650 engine
122 Exhaust fairing panel
123 Stub exhausts
124 Magneto
125 Coolant pipes
126 Cowling forward frame
127 Coolant header tank
128 Armour plate
129 Propeller hub
130 Spinner
131 Four-blade Hamilton Standard Hydromatic propeller
132 Carburettor air intake, integral with 133
133 Engine mount front frame assembly
134 Intake trunking
135 Engine mount reinforcing tie
136 Hand crank starter
137 Carburettor/trunking vibration-absorbing connection
138 Wing centre-section front bulkhead
139 Wing centre-section end rib
140 Starboard mainwheel well
141 Wing front spar/fuselage attachment bracket
142 Ventral air intake (radiator and oil cooler assemblies)
143 Starboard wing fuel tank
144 Fuel filler point
145 Mainwheel leg mount/pivot
146 Mainwheel leg rib cut-outs
147 Main gear fairing doors
148 Auxiliary fuel tank (plastics/ pressed paper composition) capacity 90 Imp gal (409 l)
149 Auxiliary fuel tank (metal) capacity 62 Imp gal (284 l)
150 27-in (68,6-cm) smooth-contour mainwheel
151 Axle fork
152 Towing lugs
153 Landing gear fairing
154 Main gear shock strut

155 Blast tubes
156 Wing front spar
157 Gun bay
158 Ammunition feed chutes
159 Ammunition boxes
160 Wing rear spar
161 Flap structure
162 Starboard aileron tab
163 Starboard aileron
164 Starboard aileron tab adjustment mechanism (ground setting)
165 Wing rib strengthening
166 Outboard section structure
167 Outer section single spar
168 Wingtip sub-assembly
169 Starboard navigation light
170 Detachable wingtip

output began to fall off rapidly. The airframe proved readily amenable to installation of the Merlin, however, and this engine, with which it first flew on 13 October 1942, dramatically enhanced altitude performance, being adopted for the P-51B (Mustang II). A total of 15,367 was built, 7,956 of these were the P-51D model having a cut-down rear fuselage with all-round vision canopy.

### SPECIFICATION: P-51D Mustang

**Power Plant:** One Packard V-1650-7 (Merlin) 12-cylinder vee liquid-cooled engine rated at 1,450 hp at 3,000 rpm for take-off and 1,695 hp at 10,300 ft (3 140 m). Four-bladed Hamilton Standard constant-speed propeller. Internal fuel capacity, 224 Imp gal (1 018 l), and provision for two 62.5 or 91.5 Imp gal (284 or 416 l) drop tanks.

**Performance:** Max speed, 395 mph (636 km/h) at 5,000 ft (1 525 m), 413 mph (665 km/h) at 15,000 ft (4 570 m), 437 mph (703 km/h) at 25,000 ft (7 620 m); range (internal fuel), 950 mls (1 529 km) at 25,000 ft (7 620 m), (max external fuel), 1,650 mls (2 655 km); initial climb, 3,475 ft/min (17,7 m/sec); time to 20,000 ft (6 100 m), 7·3 min.

**Weights:** Empty, 7,635 lb (3 463 kg); normal loaded, 10,100 lb (4 580 kg); max, 12,100 lb (5 490 kg).

**Dimensions:** Span, 37 ft 0 in (11,28 m); length, 32 ft 3 in (9,83 m); height, 13 ft 8 in (4,16 m); wing area, 235 sq ft (21,83 m²).

**Armament:** Four 0·50-in (12,7-mm) Colt-Browning machine guns with 400 rpg, or two with 400 rpg and four with 270 rpg. Provision for two bombs of up to 1,000 lb (454 kg) each, plus (later aircraft) six 5-in (12,7-cm) rockets.

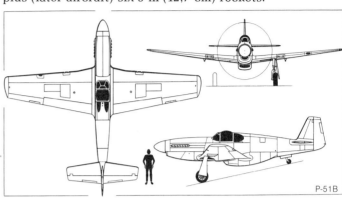

P-51B

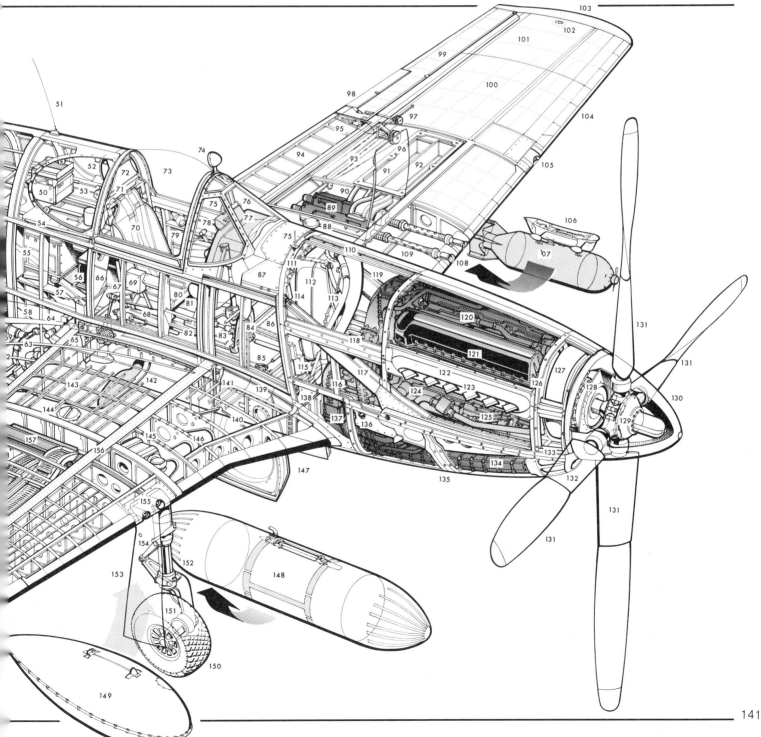

# De Havilland Mosquito (November 1940)

The Mosquito affords an example of that phenomenon rarely encountered in military aviation annals: the warplane based on precepts directly contrary to those of officialdom and persisted with despite profound official scepticism. Radical in its initial concept as an unarmed bomber capable of out-flying all contemporary *fighters*, the Mosquito was to find its true métier as a fighter. Indeed, it was to become one of the most versatile fighters of WWII, its prodigious repertoire spanning the spectrum from nocturnal intercept and intrusion to diurnal long-range fighter-bomber and anti-shipping strike missions.

Ostensibly retrograde in utilising a wooden structure at a time when such were, by consensus, unequivocally superseded, the Mosquito was designed under the leadership of R.E. Bishop, and although devised as an unarmed bomber, its fighter potential had been appreciated by the time that basic design was defined, sufficient space accordingly being provided beneath the cockpit for a battery of cannon. In fact, five months before the bomber prototype was to fly, on 25 November 1940, a prototype fighter was ordered, this flying on 15 May 1941.

**Above:** A Mosquito II with AI Mk V radar, operated by No 456 Sqdn from Middle Wallop, in day fighter colours in mid-1943.

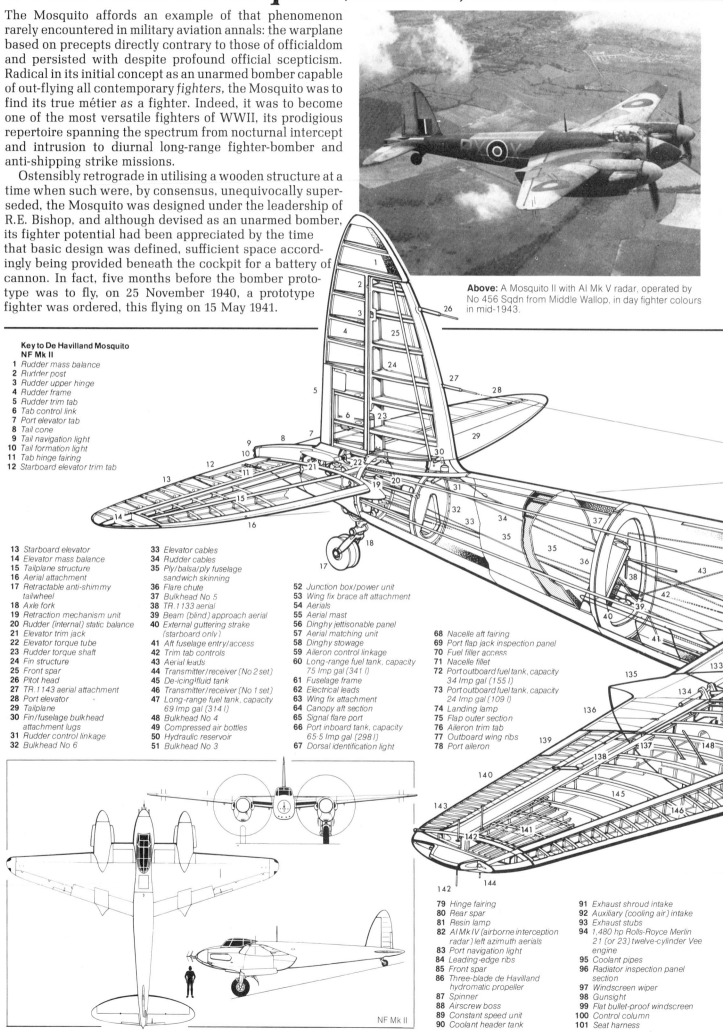

**Key to De Havilland Mosquito NF Mk II**

1 Rudder mass balance
2 Rudder post
3 Rudder upper hinge
4 Rudder frame
5 Rudder trim tab
6 Tab control link
7 Port elevator tab
8 Tail cone
9 Tail navigation light
10 Tail formation light
11 Tab hinge fairing
12 Starboard elevator trim tab
13 Starboard elevator
14 Elevator mass balance
15 Tailplane structure
16 Aerial attachment
17 Retractable anti-shimmy tailwheel
18 Axle fork
19 Retraction mechanism unit
20 Rudder (internal) static balance
21 Elevator trim jack
22 Elevator torque tube
23 Rudder torque shaft
24 Fin structure
25 Front spar
26 Pitot head
27 TR.1143 aerial attachment
28 Port elevator
29 Tailplane
30 Fin/fuselage bulkhead attachment lugs
31 Rudder control linkage
32 Bulkhead No 6

33 Elevator cables
34 Rudder cables
35 Ply/balsa/ply fuselage sandwich skinning
36 Flare chute
37 Bulkhead No 5
38 TR.1133 aerial
39 Beam (blind) approach aerial
40 External guttering strake (starboard only)
41 Aft fuselage entry/access
42 Trim tab controls
43 Aerial leads
44 Transmitter/receiver (No 2 set)
45 De-icing fluid tank
46 Transmitter/receiver (No 1 set)
47 Long-range fuel tank, capacity 69 Imp gal (314 l)
48 Bulkhead No 4
49 Compressed air bottles
50 Hydraulic reservoir
51 Bulkhead No 3

52 Junction box/power unit
53 Wing fix brace aft attachment
54 Aerials
55 Aerial mast
56 Dinghy jettisonable panel
57 Aerial matching unit
58 Dinghy stowage
59 Aileron control linkage
60 Long-range fuel tank, capacity 75 Imp gal (341 l)
61 Fuselage frame
62 Electrical leads
63 Wing fix attachment
64 Canopy aft section
65 Signal flare port
66 Port inboard tank, capacity 65·5 Imp gal (298 l)
67 Dorsal identification light

68 Nacelle aft fairing
69 Port flap jack inspection panel
70 Fuel filler access
71 Nacelle fillet
72 Port outboard fuel tank, capacity 34 Imp gal (155 l)
73 Port outboard fuel tank, capacity 24 Imp gal (109 l)
74 Landing lamp
75 Flap outer section
76 Aileron trim tab
77 Outboard wing ribs
78 Port aileron

79 Hinge fairing
80 Rear spar
81 Resin lamp
82 AI Mk IV (airborne interception radar) left azimuth aerials
83 Port navigation light
84 Leading-edge ribs
85 Front spar
86 Three-blade de Havilland hydromatic propeller
87 Spinner
88 Airscrew boss
89 Constant speed unit
90 Coolant header tank

91 Exhaust shroud intake
92 Auxiliary (cooling air) intake
93 Exhaust stubs
94 1,480 hp Rolls-Royce Merlin 21 (or 23) twelve-cylinder Vee engine
95 Coolant pipes
96 Radiator inspection panel section
97 Windscreen wiper
98 Gunsight
99 Flat bullet-proof windscreen
100 Control column
101 Seat harness

NF Mk II

Differing from the bomber solely in having strengthened wing mainspar, a side door replacing a ventral entry hatch, armament and AI Mk IV radar, with its characteristic "arrowhead" aerials, the fighter entered service as the Mosquito NF Mk II in May 1942. Installation of centimetric AI Mk VIII radar or the US SCR 720 (AI Mk X) radar was to transform Mk II into Mks XII or (new-build) XIII and Mk XVII respectively, while success of the Mk II in the intruder role with radar deleted prompted the FB Mk VI, which fully realised the potential of the Mosquito as a fighter-bomber, entering service in the first half of 1943. With a strengthened "basic" wing, the Mk VI carried full cannon and machine gun armament and up to 2,000 lb (907 kg) of ordnance.

The Mosquito, while at times demonstrating mild precocity in taking-off and landing, was essentially a well-bred aircraft with extremely pleasant flying characteristics. A grand total of 7,781 Mosquitoes was to be built, with the last leaving the assembly line in November 1950. Of these, 1,134 were to be built in Canada and 212 in Australia, the fighter variants being by far the most proliferous, some 4,650 being completed as night fighters or fighter-bombers.

**SPECIFICATION: Mosquito F Mk II**

**Power Plant:** Two Rolls-Royce Merlin 21 12-cylinder vee liquid-cooled engines each rated at 1,280 hp at 3,000 rpm for take-off and 1,480 hp at 12,250 ft (3 730 m). Three-bladed de Havilland constant-speed propellers. Internal fuel capacity, 547 Imp gal (2 487 l).

**Performance:** Max speed, 356 mph (573 km/h) at 9,000 ft (2 745 m), 370 mph (595 km/h) at 14,000 ft (4 265 m); max cruise, 283 mph (455 km/h) at sea level, 341 mph (549 km/h) at 20,000 ft (6 100 m); cruise range, 780-890 mls (1 255-1 432 km) according to altitude; time to 15,000 ft (4 570 m), 6·75 min; service ceiling, 34,500 ft (10 515 m).

**Weights:** Empty, 14,300 lb (6 490 kg); typical loaded, 18,100 lb (8 210 kg); max, 20,000 lb (9 070 kg).

**Dimensions:** Span, 54 ft 2 in (16,51 m); length, 40 ft 10 in (12,44 m); height, 15 ft 3 in (4,65 m); wing area, 454 sq ft (42,18 m²).

**Armament:** Four 20-mm Hispano Mk I cannon with 150 rounds of ammunition for each gun and four 0·303-in (7,7-mm) Browning Mk II star machine guns with 500 rounds of ammunition for each gun.

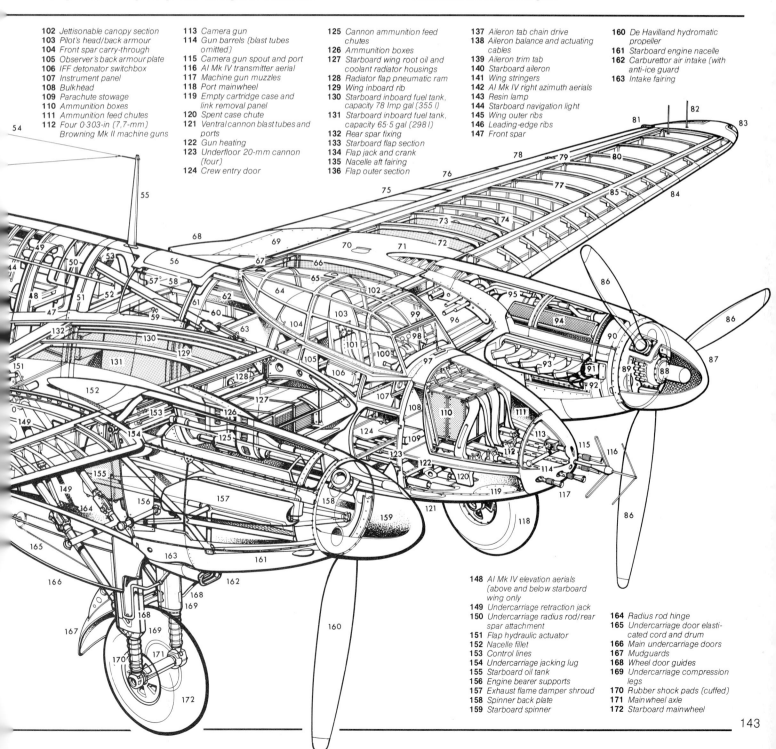

102 Jettisonable canopy section
103 Pilot's head/back armour
104 Front spar carry-through
105 Observer's back armour plate
106 IFF detonator switchbox
107 Instrument panel
108 Bulkhead
109 Parachute stowage
110 Ammunition boxes
111 Ammunition feed chutes
112 Four 0·303-in (7,7-mm) Browning Mk II machine guns
113 Camera gun
114 Gun barrels (blast tubes omitted)
115 Camera gun spout and port
116 AI Mk IV transmitter aerial
117 Machine gun muzzles
118 Port mainwheel
119 Empty cartridge case and link removal panel
120 Spent case chute
121 Ventral cannon blast tubes and ports
122 Gun heating
123 Underfloor 20-mm cannon (four)
124 Crew entry door
125 Cannon ammunition feed chutes
126 Ammunition boxes
127 Starboard wing root oil and coolant radiator housings
128 Radiator flap pneumatic ram
129 Wing inboard rib
130 Starboard inboard fuel tank, capacity 78 Imp gal (355 l)
131 Starboard inboard fuel tank, capacity 65·5 gal (298 l)
132 Rear spar fixing
133 Starboard flap section
134 Flap jack and crank
135 Nacelle aft fairing
136 Flap outer section
137 Aileron tab chain drive
138 Aileron balance and actuating cables
139 Aileron trim tab
140 Starboard aileron
141 Wing stringers
142 AI Mk IV right azimuth aerials
143 Resin lamp
144 Starboard navigation light
145 Wing outer ribs
146 Leading-edge ribs
147 Front spar
160 De Havilland hydromatic propeller
161 Starboard engine nacelle
162 Carburettor air intake (with anti-ice guard)
163 Intake fairing

148 AI Mk IV elevation aerials (above and below starboard wing only)
149 Undercarriage retraction jack
150 Undercarriage radius rod/rear spar attachment
151 Flap hydraulic actuator
152 Nacelle fillet
153 Control lines
154 Undercarriage jacking lug
155 Starboard oil tank
156 Engine bearer supports
157 Exhaust flame damper shroud
158 Spinner back plate
159 Starboard spinner
164 Radius rod hinge
165 Undercarriage door elasticated cord and drum
166 Main undercarriage doors
167 Mudguards
168 Wheel door guides
169 Undercarriage compression legs
170 Rubber shock pads (cuffed)
171 Mainwheel axle
172 Starboard mainwheel

# Republic P-47 Thunderbolt (May 1941)

Traditionally small and agile, the single-engined single-seat fighter took on an entirely new aspect with emergence of the P-47. By far the heaviest and largest such warplane created to that time, its great weight and generous proportions dwarfed all predecessors. While ostensibly an enlarged extrapolation of the less-than-successful P-43 Lancer, the P-47, designed by Alexander Kartveli and flown (as the XP-47B) on 6 May 1941, was effectively conceived around a turbo-supercharger system. The lengthy, space-consuming ducting accepted in order to submerge the blower itself in the rear fuselage, together with the R-2800 engine and the chosen armament, governed its physical characteristics.

Weight and size inevitably evoked penalties. The climb rate was overly sedate, zoom capability poor and turning circle wide. Controls were light laterally but heavy fore and aft; it mushed in high-speed turns, and stalled at any speed it invariably snapped into a vicious spin. But the P-47 had been devised primarily as a high-altitude bomber interceptor rather than a dogfighter; what it lacked in agility it compensated for with excellent altitude capability, formidable diving performance, extremely effective firepower

**Above:** A P-47D-25 of 82nd Fighter Sqdn, 78th Fighter Group, based at Duxford, 1944. The -25 was first of D-series with "bubble" hood.

**Key to Republic P-47D-10 Thunderbolt**

1 Rudder upper hinge
2 Aerial attachment
3 Fin flanged ribs
4 Rudder post/fin aft spar
5 Fin front spar
6 Rudder trim tab worm and screw actuating mechanism chain driven)
7 Rudder centre hinge
8 Rudder trim tab
9 Rudder structure
10 Tail navigation light
11 Elevator fixed tab
12 Elevator trim tab
13 Starboard elevator structure
14 Elevator outboard hinge
15 Elevator torque tube
16 Elevator trim tab worm and screw actuating mechanism
17 Chain drive
18 Starboard tailplane
19 Tail jacking point
20 Rudder control cables
21 Elevator control rod and linkage
22 Fin spar/fuselage attachment points
23 Port elevator
24 Aerial
25 Port tailplane structure (two spars and flanged ribs)
26 Tailwheel retraction worm gear
27 Tailwheel anti-shimmy damper
28 Tailwheel oleo
29 Tailwheel doors
30 Retractable and steerable tailwheel
31 Tailwheel fork
32 Tailwheel mount and pivot
33 Rudder cables
34 Rudder and elevator trim control cables
35 Lifting tube
36 Elevator rod linkage
37 Semi-monocoque all-metal fuselage construction
38 Fuselage dorsal "razorback" profile
39 Aerial lead-in
40 Fuselage stringers
41 Supercharger air filter
42 Supercharger
43 Turbine casing
44 Turbosupercharger compartment air vent
45 Turbosupercharger exhaust hood fairing (stainless steel)
46 Outlet louvres
47 Intercooler exhaust doors (port and starboard)
48 Exhaust pipes
49 Cooling air ducts
50 Intercooler unit (cooling and supercharged air)
51 Radio transmitter and receiver packs (Detrola)
52 Canopy track
53 Elevator rod linkage
54 Aerial mast
55 Formation light

56 Rearward-vision frame cutout and glazing
57 Oxygen bottles
58 Supercharged and cooling air pipe (supercharger to carburettor) port
59 Elevator linkage
60 Supercharged and cooling air pipe (supercharger to carburettor) starboard
61 Central duct (to intercooler unit)
62 Wing root air louves
63 Wing root fillet
64 Auxiliary fuel tank (83 Imp gal/379 l)
65 Auxiliary fuel filler point

66 Rudder cable turnbuckle
67 Cockpit floor support
68 Seat adjustment lever
69 Pilot's seat
70 Canopy emergency release (port and starboard)
71 Trim tab controls
72 Back and head armour
73 Headrest
74 Rearward-sliding canopy
75 Rear-view mirror fairing
76 "Vee" windshields with central pillar
77 Internal bulletproof glass screen
78 Gunsight
79 Engine control quadrant (cockpit port wall)
80 Control column
81 Rudder pedals
82 Oxygen regulator
83 Underfloor elevator control quadrant
84 Rudder cable linkage
85 Wing rear spar/fuselage attachment (tapered bolts/bushings)
86 Wing supporting lower bulkhead section
87 Main fuel tank (170 Imp gal/776 l)
88 Fuselage forward structure
89 Stainless steel/Alclad firewall bulkhead
90 Cowl flap valve
91 Main fuel filler point
92 Anti-freeze fluid tank
93 Hydraulic reservoir
94 Aileron control rod
95 Aileron trim tab control cables
96 Aileron hinge access panels
97 Aileron and tab control linkage
98 Aileron trim tab (port wing only)
99 Frise-type aileron
100 Wing rear (No 2) spar
101 Port navigation light
102 Pitot head

103 Wing front (No 1) spar
104 Wing stressed skin
105 Four-gun ammunition troughs (individual bays)
106 Staggered gun barrels
107 Removable panel
108 Inter-spar gun bay access panel
109 Forward gunsight bead
110 Oil feed pipes
111 Oil tank (24 Imp gal/108 l)
112 Hydraulic pressure line
113 Engine upper bearers
114 Engine control correlating cam
115 Eclipse pump (anti-icing)
116 Fuel level transmitter
117 Generator
118 Battery junction box
119 Storage battery
120 Exhaust collector ring
121 Cowl flap actuating cylinder
122 Exhaust outlets to collector ring
123 Cowl flaps
124 Supercharged and cooling air ducts to carburettor (port and starboard)
125 Exhaust upper outlets
126 Cowling frame
127 Pratt & Whitney R-2800-59 eighteen-cylinder twin-row engine
128 Cowling nose panel
129 Magnetos
130 Propeller governor
131 Propeller hub
132 Reduction gear casing
133 Spinner
134 Propeller cuffs
135 Four-blade Curtiss constant-speed electric propeller
136 Oil cooler intakes (port and starboard)
137 Supercharger intercooler (central) air intake
138 Ducting
139 Oil cooler feed pipes
140 Starboard oil cooler
141 Engine lower bearers
142 Oil cooler exhaust variable shutter

143 Fixed deflector
144 Excess exhaust gas gate
145 Belly stores/weapons shackles
146 Metal auxiliary drop tank (62.5 Imp gal/284 l)
147 Inboard mainwheel well door
148 Mainwheel well door actuating cylinder
149 Camera gun port
150 Cabin air-conditioning intake (starboard wing only)
151 Wing root fairing
152 Wing front spar/fuselage attachment (tapered bolts/bushings)
153 Wing inboard rib mainwheel well recess
154 Wing front (No 1 spar)
155 Undercarriage pivot point
156 Hydraulic retraction cylinder
157 Auxiliary (undercarriage mounting) wing spar
158 Gun bay warm air flexible duct
159 Wing rear (No 2) spar
160 Landing flap inboard hinge
161 Auxiliary (No 3) wing spar inboard section (flap mounting)
162 NACA slotted trailing-edge landing flaps
163 Landing flap centre hinge
164 Landing flap hydraulic cylinder

165 Four 0·5-in (12,7-mm) Browning machine guns
166 Inter-spar gun bay inboard rib
167 Ammunition feed chutes

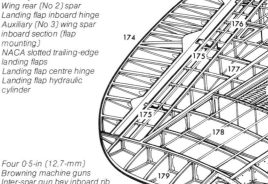

180

and incredible sturdiness and ability to absorb damage.

Perhaps surprisingly, it was to find its true forté in the role of fighter-bomber. Of 15,683 P-47s manufactured, predominant was the D-series of which 12,602 were built.

### SPECIFICATION: P-47D-30 Thunderbolt

**Power Plant:** One Pratt & Whitney R-2800-59 Double Wasp 18-cylinder two-row air-cooled radial engine rated at 2,000 hp at 2,700 rpm for take-off and 2,535 hp at 27,000 ft (8 230 m) with water-methanol injection. Four-bladed Curtiss Electric constant-speed propeller. Internal fuel capacity, 308 Imp gal (1 400 l), with provision for one 62·5 or 91·5 Imp gal (284 or 416 l) drop tank under the fuselage and two 125 Imp gal (568 l) underwing drop tanks.

**Performance:** Max speed, 363 mph (584 km/h) at 5,000 ft (1 525 m), 398 mph (640 km/h) at 15,000 ft (4 570 m), 428 mph (689 km/h) at 25,000 ft (7 620 m); range (internal fuel), 560 mls (900 km) at max continuous power at 25,000 ft (7 620 m), (max external fuel), 1,800 mls (2 896 km) at long-range cruise at 10,000 ft (3 050 m); initial climb, 3,120 ft/min (15,85 m/sec); time to 15,000 ft (4 570 m), 6·2 min.

**Weights:** Empty, 10,600 lb (4 810 kg); loaded, 14,500 lb (6 580 kg); max, 17,400 lb (7 890 kg).

**Dimensions:** Span, 40 ft 9 in (12,42 m); length, 36 ft 1 in (10,99 m); height, 14 ft 7 in (4,44 m); wing area, 300 sq ft.

**Armament:** Eight 0·50-in (12,7-mm) Colt-Browning machine guns with (normal) 267 or (max) 425 rpg. Provision for max bomb load of 2,500 lb (1 135 kg).

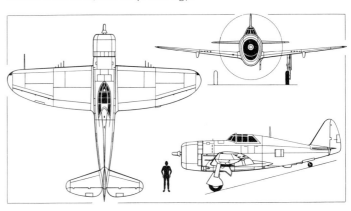

168 Individual ammunition troughs
169 Underwing stores/weapons pylon
170 Landing flap outboard hinge
171 Flap door
172 Landing flap profile
173 Aileron fixed tab (starboard wing only)
174 Frise-type aileron structure
175 Aileron hinge/steel forging spar attachments
176 Auxiliary (No 3) wing spar outboard section (aileron mounting)
177 Multi-cellular wing construction
178 Wing outboard ribs
179 Wingtip structure
180 Starboard navigation light
181 Leading-edge rib sections
182 Bomb shackles
183 500-lb (227-kg) M-43 demolition bomb
184 Undercarriage leg fairing (overlapping upper section)
185 Mainwheel fairing (lower section)
186 Wheel fork
187 Starboard mainwheel
188 Brake lines
189 Landing gear air-oil shock strut
190 Machine gun barrel blast tubes
191 Staggered gun barrels
192 Rocket-launcher slide bar
193 Centre strap
194 Front mount (attached below front spar between inboard pair of guns)
195 Deflector arms
196 Triple-tube 4·5-in (11,5-cm) rocket-launcher (Type M10)
197 Front retaining band
198 4·5 in (11,5-cm) M8 rocket projectile

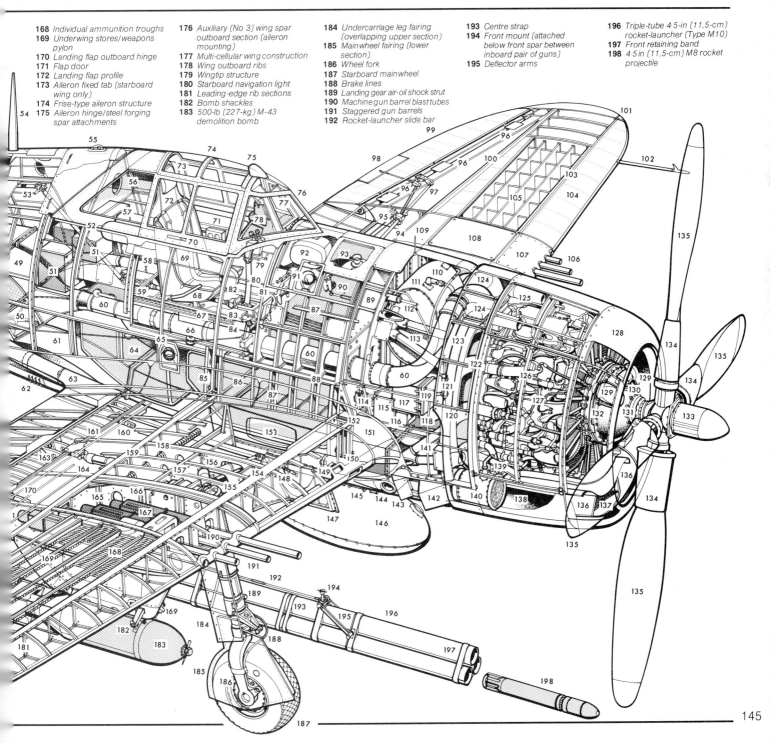

# Messerschmitt Me 163 (August 1941)

Conceptually certainly the most audacious fighter ever to achieve service status and remarkable for the number and variety of its innovations, the Me 163 was to claim uniquity in being the only manned warplane solely rocket powered to be deployed operationally. Other fighters similar in concept were to evolve, but none was to attain production, and the rocket-driven interceptor, like the triplane fighter of WWI, was to prove merely an aberration from the mainstream of fighter evolution.

Conceived rather as a vehicle for transonic research than for a combat role, the Me 163 was designed by Dr Alexander M. Lippisch and no thought was given to operational potential until seven weeks after the first powered flight test (Me 163A V1) on 13 August 1941. The aircraft then underwent total redesign to adapt it as an interceptor, a role for which it was predestined by its high speed and phenomenal climb rate. No more than the basic configuration was retained and the first powered flight of the redesigned model (Me 163B V2) took place on 23 June 1943.

With a stressed-skin light alloy semi-monocoque fuselage and plywood-covered wooden wings, the Me 163B relied on differentially-operated elevons for lateral and longitudinal control, taking-off with the aid of a jettisonable two-wheel dolly and landing on a centreline skid. Its handling and stability characteristics were good, control harmony being outstanding, but unless the CG was well forward, the stall was unheralded and abrupt, the port wing dropping sharply and a steep spiral dive ensuing. Considerable precision was necessary in taking-off and even more so in landing, and operation of the Me 163B was rendered hazardous by the lethal propensities of its highly volatile rocket fuels.

The operational début of the Me 163 was awaited with something akin to trepidation by RAF and USAAF alike. In the event, this alarm was to prove unjustified owing to the shortcomings inherent in the basic operational concept of the rocket-propelled interceptor. Only 279 production aircraft were to be delivered and the service record of the Me 163B was to prove dismal. Its successes were few and 80 per cent of the losses that it sustained resulted from take-off or landing accidents, while 15 per cent were due to fire in the air or loss of control in a dive. Operations were limited by shortages of rocket fuel and trained pilots.

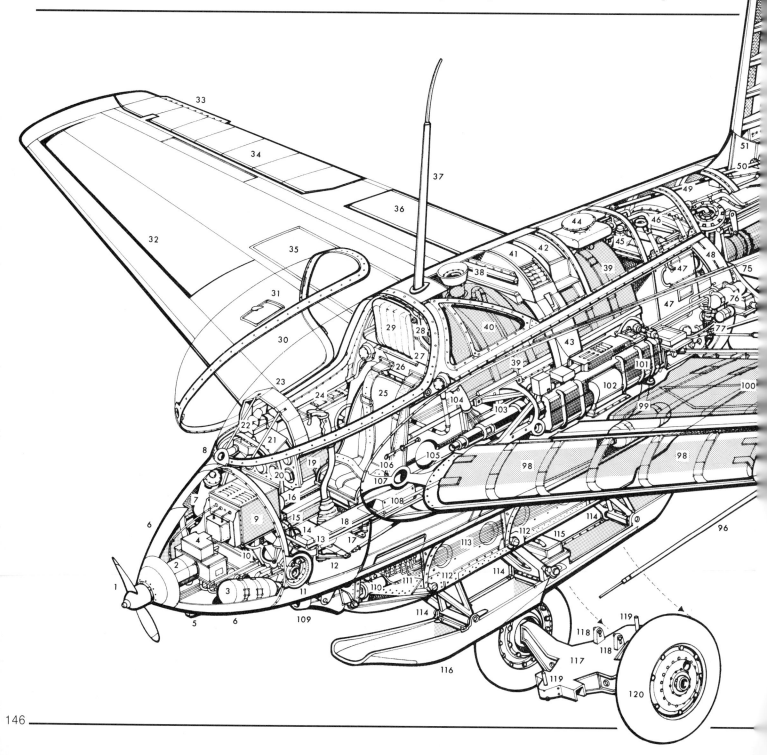

**Above:** An Me 163B-1a of Erprobungskommando (Proving Detachment) 16 at Bad Zwischenahn, Oldenburg, this unit forming in 1944 for training and tactical evaluation tasks.

**SPECIFICATION: Me 163B-1a**

**Power Plant:** One Walter HWK 509A-1 or -2 bi-fuel rocket motor rated at 3,748 lb (1 700 kg) max thrust. Internal fuel capacity, 255 Imp gal (1 160 l) T-stoff (hydrogen peroxide plus oxyquinoline) and 108 Imp gal (490 l) C-stoff (hydrazine hydrate solution in methanol).

**Performance:** Max speed, 516 mph (830 km/h) at sea level, 593 mph (955 km/h) between 9,850 and 29,500 ft (3 000 and 9 000 m); max powered endurance, 7·5 min; powered endurance after climb to 29,500 ft (9 000 m) at 497 mph (800 km/h), 2·5 min; normal radius of action, 22 mls (35·5 km); initial climb, 15,950 ft/min (81 m/sec); time to 29,500 ft (9 000 m), 2·5 min, to 39,370 ft (12 000 m), 3·35 min; service ceiling, 39,500 ft (12 040 m).

**Weights:** Empty equipped, 4,206 lb (1 908 kg); loaded, 9,502 lb (4 310 kg).

**Dimensions:** Span, 30 ft 7$\frac{1}{3}$ in (9,33 m); length 19 ft 2$\frac{1}{3}$ in (5,85 m); height (on dolly), 9 ft 0$\frac{2}{3}$ in (2,76 m); wing area, 199·13 sq ft (18,50 m²).

**Armament:** Two 30-mm Rheinmetall Borsig MK 108 cannon with 60 rpg.

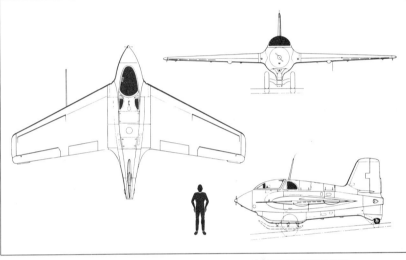

19 Control column
20 Hinged instrument panel
21 Armourglass windscreen brace
22 Revi 16B gunsight
23 Armourglass internal windscreen (90-mm)
24 Armament and radio switches (starboard console)
25 Pilot's seat
26 Back armour (8-mm)
27 Head and shoulder armour (13-mm)
28 Radio frequency selector pack
29 Headrest
30 Mechanically-jettisonable hinged canopy
31 Ventilation panel
32 Fixed leading-edge wing slot
33 Trim tab
34 Fabric-covered starboard elevon
35 Position of underwing landing flap
36 Inboard trim flap
37 FuG 16zy radio receiving aerial
38 T-Stoff filler cap

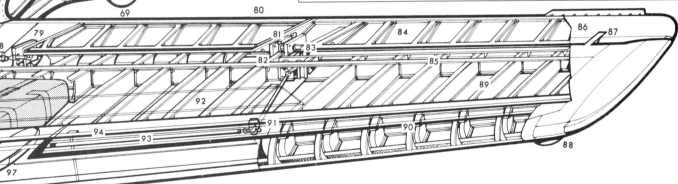

**Key to Messerschmitt Me 163B-1a**

1 Generator drive propeller
2 Generator
3 Compressed air bottle
4 Battery and electronics packs
5 Cockpit ventilation intake
6 Solid armour (15-mm) nose cone
7 Accumulator pressuriser
8 Direct cockpit air intake
9 FuG 25a radio pack
10 Rudder control assembly
11 Hydraulic and compressed air points
12 Elevon control rocker-bar
13 Control relay
14 Flying controls assembly box
15 Plastic rudder pedals
16 Radio tuning controls
17 Torque shaft
18 Port T-stoff cockpit tank (13 Imp gal/60 l capacity)

39 Main unprotected T-Stoff fuselage tank (229 Imp gal/1,040 l capacity)
40 Aft cockpit glazing
41 Port cannon ammunition box (60 rounds)
42 Starboard cannon ammunition box (60 rounds)
43 Ammunition feed chute
44 T-Stoff starter tank
45 Rocket motor upper bell crank
46 C-Stoff filler cap
47 HWK 509A-1 motor turbine housing
48 Main rocket motor mounting frame
49 Rudder control rod
50 Disconnect point
51 Aerial matching unit
52 Fin front spar/fuselage attachment point
53 Tailfin construction
54 Rudder horn balance
55 Rudder upper hinge
56 Rudder frame
57 Rudder trim tab

58 Rudder control rocker-bar
59 Linkage fairing
60 Fin rear spar/fuselage attachment point
61 Rocket motor combustion chamber
62 Tailpipe
63 Rudder root fairing
64 Rocket thrust orifice
65 Vent pipe outlet
66 Hydraulic cylinder
67 Lifting point
68 Tailwheel fairing
69 Steerable tailwheel
70 Tailwheel axle fork
71 Tailwheel oleo
72 Tailwheel steering linkage
73 Coupling piece/vertical lever
74 Wing root fillet
75 Combustion chamber support brace
76 Gun-cocking mechanism
77 Trim flap control angle gear (bulkhead mounted)
78 Worm gear
79 Trim flap mounting

80 Port inboard trim flap
81 Elevon mounting
82 Rocker-bar
83 Elevon actuation push-rod
84 Port elevon
85 Wing rear spar
86 Trim tab
87 Elevon outboard hinge
88 Wingtip bumper
89 Wing construction
90 Fixed leading-edge wing slot
91 Elevon control bell crank
92 Position of port underwing landing flap
93 Push-rod in front spar
94 Front spar
95 FuG 25a aerial
96 Pitot head
97 Wing tank connecting pipe fairing
98 C-Stoff leading-edge tank (16 Imp gal/73 l capacity)
99 Gun-cocking compressed air bottle
100 Main C-Stoff wing tank (38 Imp gal/173 l capacity)

101 Port 30-mm Mk 108 short-barrel cannon
102 Expanding shell and link chute
103 Gun forward mounting frame
104 Pressure-tight gun-control passage
105 Blast tube
106 Gun alignment mechanism
107 Cannon port
108 FuG 23a FF pack
109 Tow-bar attachment point
110 Compressed-air ram for landing skid
111 Hydraulics and compressed-air pipes
112 Landing skid pivots
113 Landing skid keel mounting
114 Landing skid mounting bracketrs
115 Trolley jettison mechanism
116 Landing skid
117 Take-off trolley frame
118 Take-off trolley retaining lugs
119 Take-off trolley alignment pins
120 Low-pressure tyre

# Kawasaki Ki.61 Hien (December 1941)

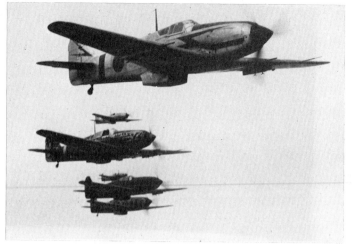

**Above:** Ki.61-I-otsu fighters of the 244th Sentai based at Chofu, Tokyo Defence Area.

The advent in Japanese Army service in 1943 of the Ki.61 Hien (Swallow) signified a radical change in fighter design thinking in Japan; it reflected the final rejection of the almost pathological belief in the paramouncy of agility above all else that previously dominated Japanese fighter evolution. Primarily as an outcome of analyses of combat with the Soviet I-16 over the Khalkin-Gol during the "Nomonhan Incident" of 1939, level speed and climb-and-dive characteristics were accorded equal importance with manoeuvrability, and some attention was finally given to firepower, self-sealing fuel tanks and pilot protection.

Designed by Takeo Doi and Shin Owada around the Daimler-Benz DB 601 engine, which had been adapted for Japanese manufacture, the Ki.61 was flown mid-December 1941. Although at first compared disparagingly by some Army pilots with the Ki.43 (see pages 124-125), which conformed more closely with established Japanese values, the Ki.61 was a thoroughly competent design from virtually every aspect. It retained a measure of traditional manoeuvrability combined with some of the better characteristics that, prior to its début, were exclusive to western fighters.

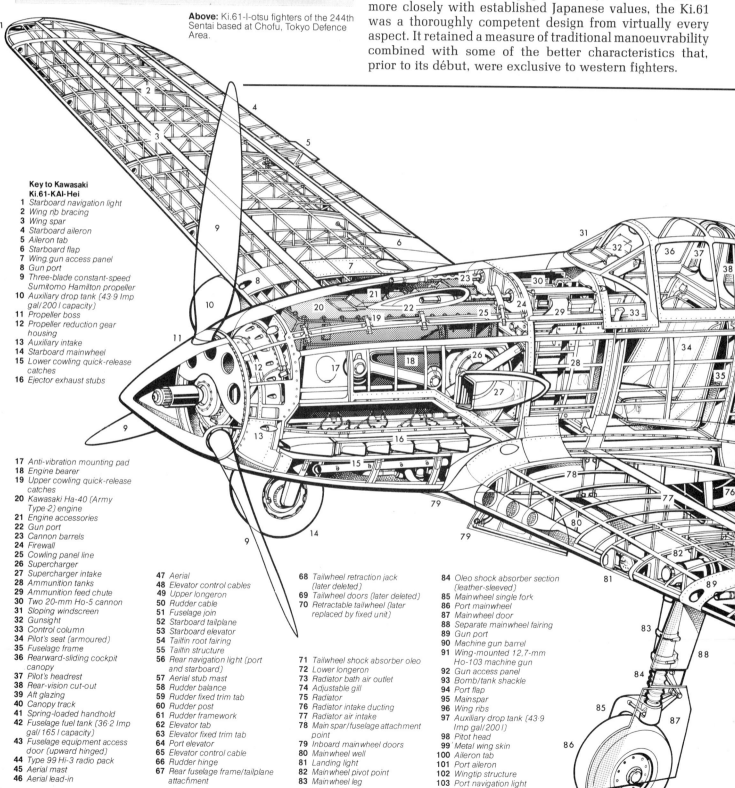

**Key to Kawasaki Ki.61-KAI-Hei**

1 Starboard navigation light
2 Wing rib bracing
3 Wing spar
4 Starboard aileron
5 Aileron tab
6 Starboard flap
7 Wing gun access panel
8 Gun port
9 Three-blade constant-speed Sumitomo Hamilton propeller
10 Auxiliary drop tank (43·9 Imp gal/200 l capacity)
11 Propeller boss
12 Propeller reduction gear housing
13 Auxiliary intake
14 Starboard mainwheel
15 Lower cowling quick-release catches
16 Ejector exhaust stubs
17 Anti-vibration mounting pad
18 Engine bearer
19 Upper cowling quick-release catches
20 Kawasaki Ha-40 (Army Type 2) engine
21 Engine accessories
22 Gun port
23 Cannon barrels
24 Firewall
25 Cowling panel line
26 Supercharger
27 Supercharger intake
28 Ammunition tanks
29 Ammunition feed chute
30 Two 20-mm Ho-5 cannon
31 Sloping windscreen
32 Gunsight
33 Control column
34 Pilot's seat (armoured)
35 Fuselage frame
36 Rearward-sliding cockpit canopy
37 Pilot's headrest
38 Rear-vision cut-out
39 Aft glazing
40 Canopy track
41 Spring-loaded handhold
42 Fuselage fuel tank (36·2 Imp gal/165 l capacity)
43 Fuselage equipment access door (upward hinged)
44 Type 99 Hi-3 radio pack
45 Aerial mast
46 Aerial lead-in

47 Aerial
48 Elevator control cables
49 Upper longeron
50 Rudder cable
51 Fuselage join
52 Starboard tailplane
53 Starboard elevator
54 Tailfin root fairing
55 Tailfin structure
56 Rear navigation light (port and starboard)
57 Aerial stub mast
58 Rudder balance
59 Rudder fixed trim tab
60 Rudder post
61 Rudder framework
62 Elevator tab
63 Elevator fixed trim tab
64 Port elevator
65 Elevator control cable
66 Rudder hinge
67 Rear fuselage frame/tailplane attachment

68 Tailwheel retraction jack (later deleted)
69 Tailwheel doors (later deleted)
70 Retractable tailwheel (later replaced by fixed unit)
71 Tailwheel shock absorber oleo
72 Lower longeron
73 Radiator bath air outlet
74 Adjustable gill
75 Radiator
76 Radiator intake ducting
77 Radiator air intake
78 Main spar/fuselage attachment point
79 Inboard mainwheel doors
80 Mainwheel well
81 Landing light
82 Mainwheel pivot point
83 Mainwheel leg

84 Oleo shock absorber section (leather-sleeved)
85 Mainwheel single fork
86 Port mainwheel
87 Mainwheel door
88 Separate mainwheel fairing
89 Gun port
90 Machine gun barrel
91 Wing-mounted 12,7-mm Ho-103 machine gun
92 Gun access panel
93 Bomb/tank shackle
94 Port flap
95 Mainspar
96 Wing ribs
97 Auxiliary drop tank (43·9 Imp gal/200 l)
98 Pitot head
99 Metal wing skin
100 Aileron tab
101 Port aileron
102 Wingtip structure
103 Port navigation light

While it could not be flown with the abandon of the Ki.43, tending to stall and spin out to port with any overly violent use of the ailerons and rudder, the Ki.61 responded quickly and positively to smooth use of the controls and could hold its own in a dive against its heavier US adversaries. Appearing in combat over New Guinea in June 1943, it demanded some reassessment by the Allies of Japanese fighter capabilities and major rethinking of tactics once it was appreciated that it possessed attributes not found in its predecessors.

The initial Ki.61-I-ko and -otsu mounted machine gun armament—although 388 were re-armed with 20-mm MG 151 cannon—while the armament of the Ki.61-I-KAI-hei was more efficacious, incorporating Ho-5 cannon. A total of 2,660 Ki.61-I fighters (including prototypes) was built, their intended successor, the Ki.61-II-KAI with the more powerful but notoriously unreliable Ha-140 engine, failing to achieve service in any substantial quantity. More than any other type, the Hien dispelled the former widely-held belief among the Allies that all Japanese fighters were "lightweights".

### SPECIFICATION: Ki.61-I-KAI-hei Hien

**Power Plant:** One Kawasaki Ha-40 (Army Type 2) 12-cylinder inverted-vee liquid-cooled engine rated at 1,175 hp at 2,500 rpm for take-off and 1,100 hp at 13,780 ft (4 200 m). Three-bladed Sumitomo constant-speed propeller. Internal fuel capacity, 121 Imp gal (550 l) with provision for two 44 Imp gal (200 l) drop tanks.

**Performance:** Max speed, 360 mph (580 km/h) at 16,405 ft (5 000 m), 302 mph (486 km/h) at sea level; normal cruise, 242 mph (390 km/h) at 13,125 ft (4 000 m); range (internal fuel), 360 mls (580 km), (with drop tanks), 671 mls (1 080 km); time to 16,405 ft (5 000 m), 7·0 min; service ceiling, 32,810 ft (10 000 m).

**Weights:** Empty equipped, 5,798 lb (2 630 kg); normal loaded, 7,650 lb (3 470 kg).

**Dimensions:** Span, 39 ft 4½ in (12,00 m); length, 29 ft 2¾ in (8,94 m); height, 12 ft 1¾ in (3,70 m); wing area, 215·28 sq ft (20,00 m²).

**Armament:** Two 20-mm Ho-5 cannon with 120 rpg and two 12,7-mm Ho-103 machine guns with 200 rpg. Provision for two 551-lb (250-kg) bombs.

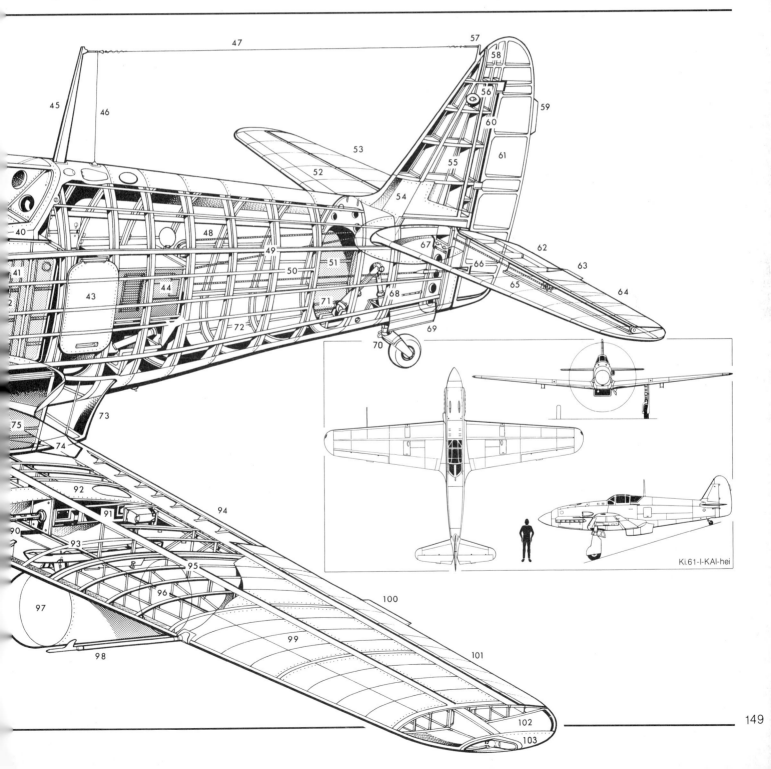

Ki.61-I-KAI-hei

# Fairey Firefly (December 1941)

Carrying British two-seat piston-engined shipboard fighter development to its apex, the Firefly synthesized its parent company's years of expertise in mating aeronautical with nautical demands. Conceived as a multi-role aeroplane with emphasis on the Fleet fighter mission, it was to combine supreme versatility with tractability and reliability, coupling these attributes with a sound performance, good firepower and exceptional agility. It was to fulfil an unprecedentedly broad mission spectrum and this amenability was to result in a life span of a quarter of a century, during which it participated in two major wars.

While a very real advance in two-seat carrier fighters, the Firefly was essentially orthodox, its one really innovatory feature being its retractable Youngmann area-increasing flaps. With these at take-off setting, it could turn with the best of its single-seat contemporaries near the stall and turn inside most of them. Extended but undrooped, these flaps gave an invaluable lift increment in the cruise.

Superficially resembling the earlier Fulmar, the Firefly first flew on 22 December 1941, there being no prototype as such, and first equipped a squadron in October 1943, first

production aeroplanes being F Mk I day fighters. The versatility of the design began to become apparent with the debut of night fighting NF Mk I and fighter-reconnaissance FR Mk I versions, 140 of the former and 236 of the latter supplementing 459 straight day fighters.

In the Far East, its principal operational venue, the Firefly established an enviable reputation, and by the time WWII ended, extensive development was under way. The single-stage Griffon of the Mk I gave place to a two-stage engine, which, mated with wing leading-edge radiators, clipped wingtips and redesigned vertical tail, resulted in the more elegant Mk 4 flown on 25 May 1946. One hundred and sixty Mk 4s preceded externally similar Mks 5 and 6 which added anti-submarine warfare to their repertoire, 352 Mk 5s and 133 Mk 6s being built between January 1947 and September 1951, with power-folding wings replacing manual folding early in 1949.

Six squadrons of Mks 4 and 5 were involved in the Korean War, from 25 June 1950, when North Korean forces invaded the South, until the armistice of 27 July 1953. Production ended on 20 April 1956, when 1,702 Fireflies had been delivered.

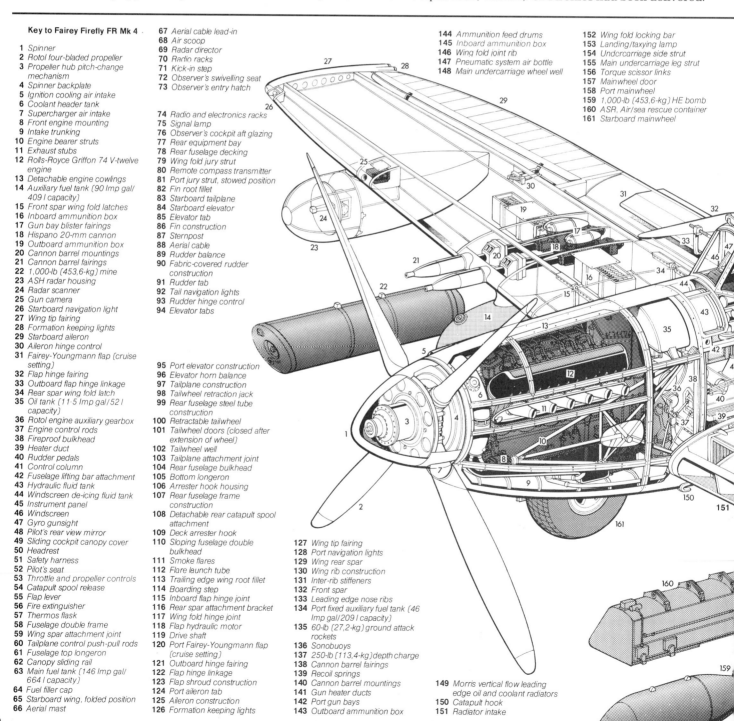

**Key to Fairey Firefly FR Mk 4**

1 Spinner
2 Rotol four-bladed propeller
3 Propeller hub pitch-change mechanism
4 Spinner backplate
5 Ignition cooling air intake
6 Coolant header tank
7 Supercharger air intake
8 Front engine mounting
9 Intake trunking
10 Engine bearer struts
11 Exhaust stubs
12 Rolls-Royce Griffon 74 V-twelve engine
13 Detachable engine cowlings
14 Auxiliary fuel tank (90 Imp gal/409 l capacity)
15 Front spar wing fold latches
16 Inboard ammunition box
17 Gun bay blister fairings
18 Hispano 20-mm cannon
19 Outboard ammunition box
20 Cannon barrel mountings
21 Cannon barrel fairings
22 1,000-lb (453,6-kg) mine
23 ASH radar housing
24 Radar scanner
25 Gun camera
26 Starboard navigation light
27 Wing tip fairing
28 Formation keeping lights
29 Starboard aileron
30 Aileron hinge control
31 Fairey-Youngmann flap (cruise setting)
32 Flap hinge fairing
33 Outboard flap hinge linkage
34 Rear spar wing fold latch
35 Oil tank (11·5 Imp gal/52 l capacity)
36 Rotol engine auxiliary gearbox
37 Engine control rods
38 Fireproof bulkhead
39 Heater duct
40 Rudder pedals
41 Control column
42 Fuselage lifting bar attachment
43 Hydraulic fluid tank
44 Windscreen de-icing fluid tank
45 Instrument panel
46 Windscreen
47 Gyro gunsight
48 Pilot's rear view mirror
49 Sliding cockpit canopy cover
50 Headrest
51 Safety harness
52 Pilot's seat
53 Throttle and propeller controls
54 Catapult spool release
55 Flap lever
56 Fire extinguisher
57 Thermos flask
58 Fuselage double frame
59 Wing spar attachment joint
60 Tailplane control push-pull rods
61 Fuselage top longeron
62 Canopy sliding rail
63 Main fuel tank (146 Imp gal/664 l capacity)
64 Fuel filler cap
65 Starboard wing, folded position
66 Aerial mast

67 Aerial cable lead-in
68 Air scoop
69 Radar director
70 Radio racks
71 Kick-in step
72 Observer's swivelling seat
73 Observer's entry hatch

74 Radio and electronics racks
75 Signal lamp
76 Observer's cockpit aft glazing
77 Rear equipment bay
78 Rear fuselage decking
79 Wing fold jury strut
80 Remote compass transmitter
81 Port jury strut, stowed position
82 Fin root fillet
83 Starboard tailplane
84 Starboard elevator
85 Elevator tab
86 Fin construction
87 Sternpost
88 Aerial cable
89 Rudder balance
90 Fabric-covered rudder construction
91 Rudder tab
92 Tail navigation lights
93 Rudder hinge control
94 Elevator tabs

95 Port elevator construction
96 Elevator horn balance
97 Tailplane construction
98 Tailwheel retraction jack
99 Rear fuselage steel tube construction
100 Retractable tailwheel
101 Tailwheel doors (closed after extension of wheel)
102 Tailwheel well
103 Tailplane attachment joint
104 Rear fuselage bulkhead
105 Bottom longeron
106 Arrester hook housing
107 Rear fuselage frame construction
108 Detachable rear catapult spool attachment
109 Deck arrester hook
110 Sloping fuselage double bulkhead
111 Smoke flares
112 Flare launch tube
113 Trailing edge wing root fillet
114 Boarding step
115 Inboard flap hinge joint
116 Rear spar attachment bracket
117 Wing fold hinge joint
118 Flap hydraulic motor
119 Drive shaft
120 Port Fairey-Youngmann flap (cruise setting)
121 Outboard hinge fairing
122 Flap hinge linkage
123 Flap shroud construction
124 Port aileron tab
125 Aileron construction
126 Formation keeping lights

127 Wing tip fairing
128 Port navigation lights
129 Wing rear spar
130 Wing rib construction
131 Inter-rib stiffeners
132 Front spar
133 Leading edge nose ribs
134 Port fixed auxiliary fuel tank (46 Imp gal/209 l capacity)
135 60-lb (27,2-kg) ground attack rockets
136 Sonobuoys
137 250-lb (113,4-kg) depth charge
138 Cannon barrel fairings
139 Recoil springs
140 Cannon barrel mountings
141 Gun heater ducts
142 Port gun bays
143 Outboard ammunition box

144 Ammunition feed drums
145 Inboard ammunition box
146 Wing fold joint rib
147 Pneumatic system air bottle
148 Main undercarriage wheel well

149 Morris vertical flow leading edge oil and coolant radiators
150 Catapult hook
151 Radiator intake

152 Wing fold locking bar
153 Landing/taxiing lamp
154 Undercarriage side strut
155 Main undercarriage leg strut
156 Torque scissor links
157 Mainwheel door
158 Port mainwheel
159 1,000-lb (453,6-kg) HE bomb
160 ASR, Air/sea rescue container
161 Starboard mainwheel

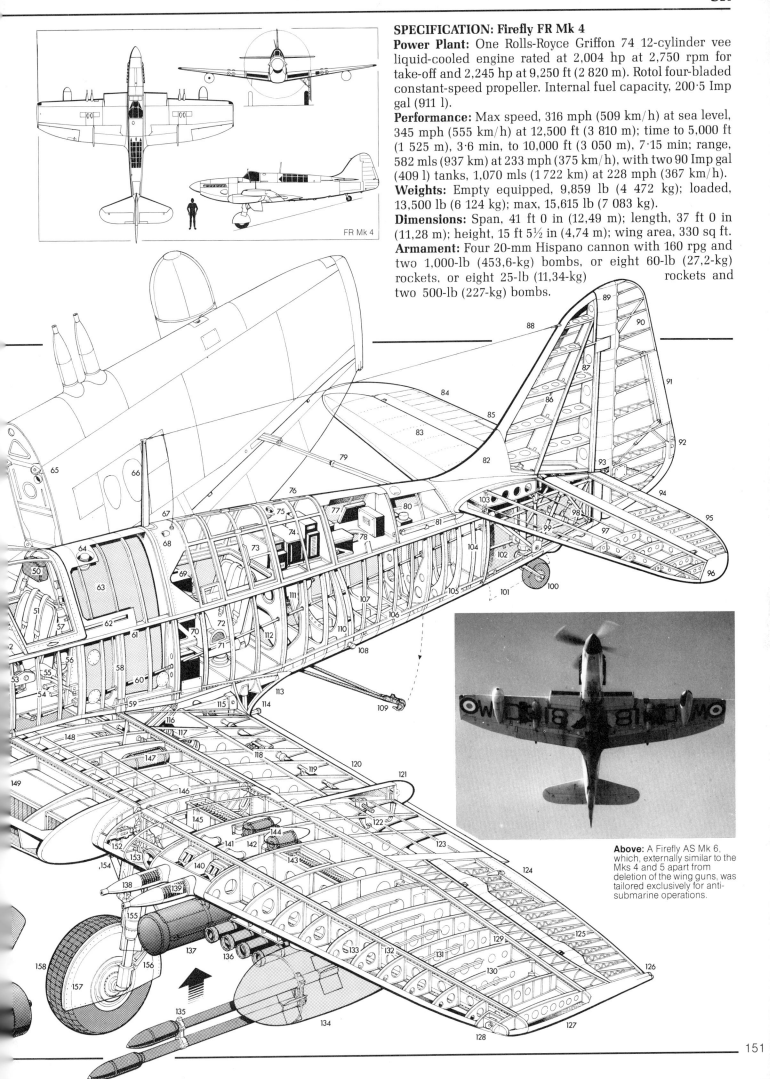

## SPECIFICATION: Firefly FR Mk 4

**Power Plant:** One Rolls-Royce Griffon 74 12-cylinder vee liquid-cooled engine rated at 2,004 hp at 2,750 rpm for take-off and 2,245 hp at 9,250 ft (2 820 m). Rotol four-bladed constant-speed propeller. Internal fuel capacity, 200·5 Imp gal (911 l).

**Performance:** Max speed, 316 mph (509 km/h) at sea level, 345 mph (555 km/h) at 12,500 ft (3 810 m); time to 5,000 ft (1 525 m), 3·6 min, to 10,000 ft (3 050 m), 7·15 min; range, 582 mls (937 km) at 233 mph (375 km/h), with two 90 Imp gal (409 l) tanks, 1,070 mls (1 722 km) at 228 mph (367 km/h).

**Weights:** Empty equipped, 9,859 lb (4 472 kg); loaded, 13,500 lb (6 124 kg); max, 15,615 lb (7 083 kg).

**Dimensions:** Span, 41 ft 0 in (12,49 m); length, 37 ft 0 in (11,28 m); height, 15 ft 5½ in (4,74 m); wing area, 330 sq ft.

**Armament:** Four 20-mm Hispano cannon with 160 rpg and two 1,000-lb (453,6-kg) bombs, or eight 60-lb (27,2-kg) rockets, or eight 25-lb (11,34-kg) rockets and two 500-lb (227-kg) bombs.

FR Mk 4

**Above:** A Firefly AS Mk 6, which, externally similar to the Mks 4 and 5 apart from deletion of the wing guns, was tailored exclusively for anti-submarine operations.

# Lavochkin La-5 (March 1942)

The mating with an air-cooled radial engine of a fighter airframe designed expressly for a liquid-cooled inline power plant as a result of *force majeure* has not been unknown. Without the redesign of fundamental components, however, few such enforced marital unions have enjoyed success. One such metamorphosis that did prosper was the La-5 which was conceived as a result of re-engining the decidedly pedestrian LaGG-3 from the design bureau headed by Semyon A. Lavochkin.

The adaptation of the LaGG-3 airframe for the Shvetsov radial engine was the responsibility of Lavochkin's deputy S.M. Alekseyev, and the first conversion was flown successfully in March 1942. The reworking for the new power plant of all LaGG-3 airframes existing on the assembly lines commenced in July of that year, and production continued with new-build airframes featuring cut-down aft-fuselage decking and all-round vision canopy until late 1944. The M-82 of the La-5 and improved M-82F of the La-5F gave place from the end of March 1943 to the fuel-injection M-82FN (La-5FN)—FN standing for *Forsirovannii Nyeposredstvenny*, "boosted engine"—which soon proved its worth

during the crucial battle of Kursk, July-August 1943. A total of 9,920 La-5 fighters was manufactured.

The La-5 was, incidentally, the last single-seat fighter of wooden construction to see large-scale production and service. Its structure, inherited from the LaGG-3, employed a plastic-impregnated wood possessing special strength and fire-resistance properties, this being used in conjunction with bakelite ply (layers of birch strip bonded with bakelite film) for skinning. From the late spring of 1944, however, metal wing spars were introduced, these both saving weight and permitting a modest increase in internal fuel capacity.

The La-5 was a superlative low-to-medium altitude air superiority fighter, excelling in close-in high-g manoeuvring combat. Control was sensitive, climb-and-dive qualities were good, stall recovery was of a high order, turn rate was second to none and the aircraft could be looped and Immelmanned at low airspeeds. It did display some capriciousness during landing, however, demonstrating an incipient bounce and, if power was applied, frequently turning over.

**Key to Lavochkin La-5FN**

1 Hucks-type starter dog
2 Spinner
3 Propeller balance
4 Controllable frontal intake louvres
5 VISh-105V metal controllable-pitch three-bladed propeller
6 Nose ring profile
7 Intake centrebody

17 Outlet cover panel
18 Engine accessories
19 Mainspar/fuselage attachment
20 Ammunition tanks (200 rpg)
21 Link and cartridge ejection chutes
22 Engine bearer upper support bracket
23 Cannon breech fairing
24 Paired 20-mm ShVAK cannon
25 Supercharger intake trunking

35 Cockpit air
36 Control column
37 Outlet louvres
38 Rudder pedal assembly
39 Underfloor control linkage
40 Rear spar/fuselage attachment
41 Rudder and elevator trim handwheels
42 Seat height adjustment
43 Boost controls

54 Dural fuselage side panels
55 Control cables
56 Plywood-sheathed birch frames with triangular-section wooden stringers
57 Stressed plywood skinning
58 Accumulator
59 Accumulator access panel
60 Tailfin front spar attachment
61 Aerial mast

62 Radio aerials
63 Starboard tailplane
64 Elevator hinge
65 Metal-framed fabric-covered elevator
66 Tailfin leading edge
67 Tailfin wooden structure (plywood skinning)
68 Aerial stub
69 Rudder balance

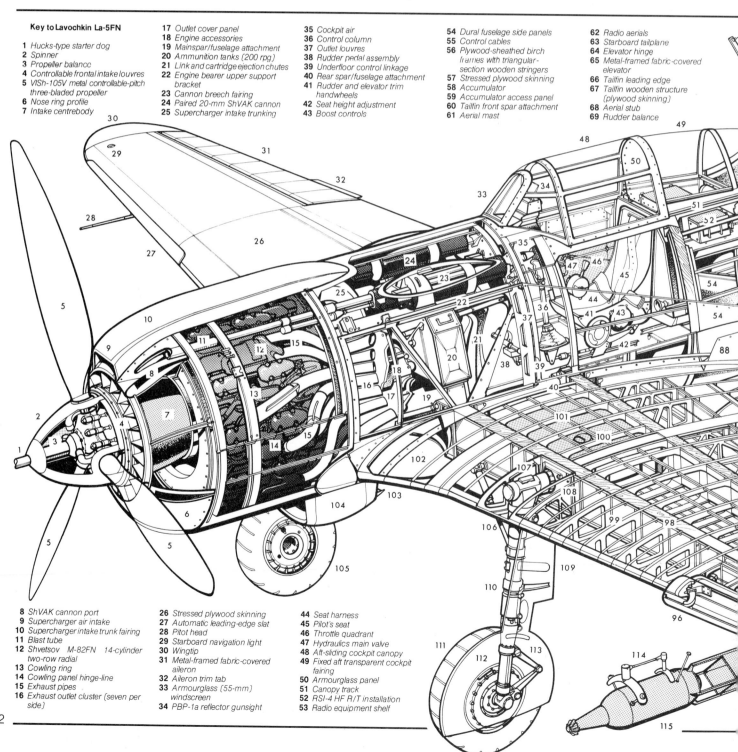

8 ShVAK cannon port
9 Supercharger air intake
10 Supercharger intake trunk fairing
11 Blast tube
12 Shvetsov M-82FN 14-cylinder two-row radial
13 Cowling ring
14 Cowling panel hinge-line
15 Exhaust pipes
16 Exhaust outlet cluster (seven per side)

26 Stressed plywood skinning
27 Automatic leading-edge slat
28 Pitot head
29 Starboard navigation light
30 Wingtip
31 Metal-framed fabric-covered aileron
32 Aileron trim tab
33 Armourglass (55-mm) windscreen
34 PBP-1a reflector gunsight

44 Seat harness
45 Pilot's seat
46 Throttle quadrant
47 Hydraulics main valve
48 Aft-sliding cockpit canopy
49 Fixed aft transparent cockpit fairing
50 Armourglass panel
51 Canopy track
52 RSI-4 HF R/T installation
53 Radio equipment shelf

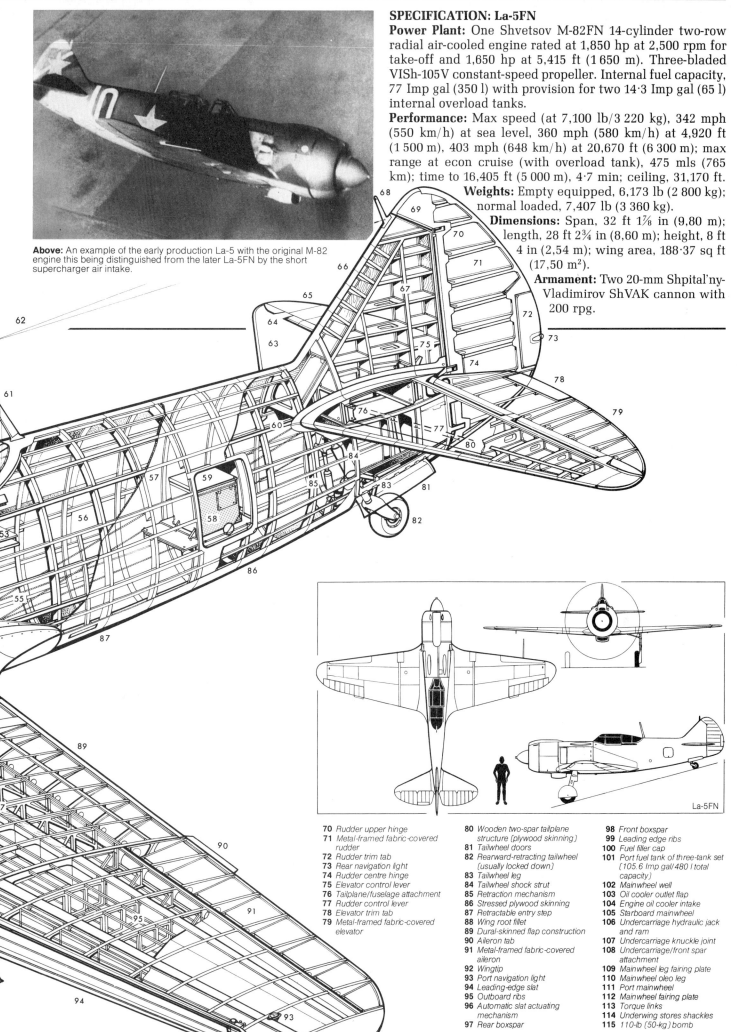

**SPECIFICATION: La-5FN**

**Power Plant:** One Shvetsov M-82FN 14-cylinder two-row radial air-cooled engine rated at 1,850 hp at 2,500 rpm for take-off and 1,650 hp at 5,415 ft (1 650 m). Three-bladed VISh-105V constant-speed propeller. Internal fuel capacity, 77 Imp gal (350 l) with provision for two 14·3 Imp gal (65 l) internal overload tanks.

**Performance:** Max speed (at 7,100 lb/3 220 kg), 342 mph (550 km/h) at sea level, 360 mph (580 km/h) at 4,920 ft (1 500 m), 403 mph (648 km/h) at 20,670 ft (6 300 m); max range at econ cruise (with overload tank), 475 mls (765 km); time to 16,405 ft (5 000 m), 4·7 min; ceiling, 31,170 ft.

**Weights:** Empty equipped, 6,173 lb (2 800 kg); normal loaded, 7,407 lb (3 360 kg).

**Dimensions:** Span, 32 ft 1⅛ in (9,80 m); length, 28 ft 2¾ in (8,60 m); height, 8 ft 4 in (2,54 m); wing area, 188·37 sq ft (17,50 m²).

**Armament:** Two 20-mm Shpital'ny-Vladimirov ShVAK cannon with 200 rpg.

**Above:** An example of the early production La-5 with the original M-82 engine this being distinguished from the later La-5FN by the short supercharger air intake.

La-5FN

70 Rudder upper hinge
71 Metal-framed fabric-covered rudder
72 Rudder trim tab
73 Rear navigation light
74 Rudder centre hinge
75 Elevator control lever
76 Tailplane/fuselage attachment
77 Rudder control lever
78 Elevator trim tab
79 Metal-framed fabric-covered elevator
80 Wooden two-spar tailplane structure (plywood skinning)
81 Tailwheel doors
82 Rearward-retracting tailwheel (usually locked down)
83 Tailwheel leg
84 Tailwheel shock strut
85 Retraction mechanism
86 Stressed plywood skinning
87 Retractable entry step
88 Wing root fillet
89 Dural-skinned flap construction
90 Aileron tab
91 Metal-framed fabric-covered aileron
92 Wingtip
93 Port navigation light
94 Leading-edge slat
95 Outboard ribs
96 Automatic slat actuating mechanism
97 Rear boxspar
98 Front boxspar
99 Leading edge ribs
100 Fuel filler cap
101 Port fuel tank of three-tank set (105.6 Imp gal/480 l total capacity)
102 Mainwheel well
103 Oil cooler outlet flap
104 Engine oil cooler intake
105 Starboard mainwheel
106 Undercarriage hydraulic jack and ram
107 Undercarriage knuckle joint
108 Undercarriage/front spar attachment
109 Mainwheel leg fairing plate
110 Mainwheel oleo leg
111 Port mainwheel
112 Mainwheel fairing plate
113 Torque links
114 Underwing stores shackles
115 110-lb (50-kg) bomb

# Messerschmitt Me 262 (March 1942)

One of the few truly epoch-marking fighters in aviation's annals and arguably the most formidable warplane of WWII, the Me 262 launched a new era in aerial warfare. Such was its performance that, at the eleventh hour, it *could* have regained for the Luftwaffe some measure of ascendancy; fortunately for the Allies, the Me 262 was plagued by vacillation and irresolution.

Despite its radical nature and even if marginally underpowered, the Me 262 was a pilot's aeroplane and, in many respects, easier to fly than the piston-engined Bf 109G. Responsive and docile, with pleasant harmony of control, it enjoyed a marked speed advantage over every contemporary. Aileron control at all altitudes was effective, stalling characteristics were good, and if unable to turn as tightly as piston-engined opponents, it could hold speed in tight turns for much longer. It was demanding on runway length, however, and its pilot had to exercise care not to exceed limiting Mach number in a dive, while a low-speed flame-out of one of its temperamental turbojets was almost invariably disastrous: the Me 262 flew fairly well on one engine, but landing thus presented major problems.

Project studies for the Me 262 began (as P 1065) in October 1938, when the intended power plant was still largely theoretical. Definitive configuration was not reached until May 1940, when increased engine weight at a late airframe design stage dictated wing sweep to compensate for the forward CG shift—at that time, the Messerschmitt team was unaware of the potential aerodynamic advantages of sweepback and it was thus largely fortuitous that the Me 262 became the world's first operational swept-wing fighter.

The first prototype, the Me 262 V1, flew on 18 April 1941 with a Jumo 210G piston engine, this being retained for the initial flight with turbojets operating on 25 March 1942. The first flight on turbojets alone (Me 262 V3) took place three months later, on 18 July, and Luftwaffe acceptances of pre-series aircraft began in April 1944, with the first production aircraft following in June. The basic model was the Me 262A-1a, a fighter-bomber variant being the Me 262A-2a, 513 being completed July-December 1944, and a further 865 following January-April 1945. Piecemeal deployment, fuel shortages and inadequate pilot training largely nullified the Me 262's threat.

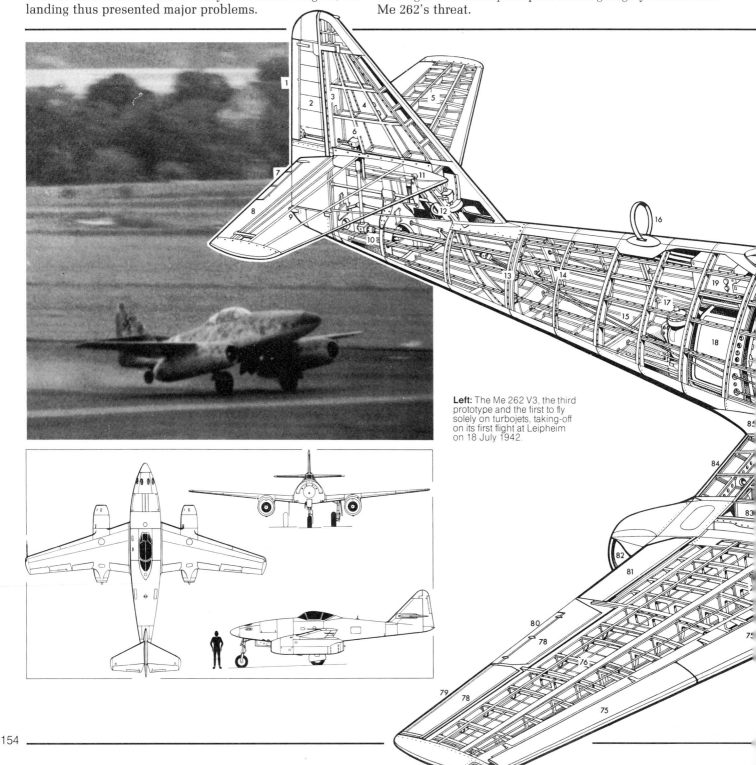

**Left:** The Me 262 V3, the third prototype and the first to fly solely on turbojets, taking-off on its first flight at Leipheim on 18 July 1942.

**Above:** The Me 262A-1a had the distinction of being the first production fighter to employ wing sweepback, although this was not adopted to reduce compressibility effects but to rectify a shift in centre of gravity.

## SPECIFICATION: Me 262A-1a

**Power Plant:** Two Junkers Jumo 004B-1, -2 or -3 axial-flow turbojets each rated at 1,984 lb (900 kg) thrust. Max internal fuel capacity, 565 Imp gal (2 570 l).

**Performance:** (At normal loaded weight) Max speed, 514 mph (827 km/h) at sea level, 530 mph (853 km/h) at 9,840 ft (3 000 m), 540 mph (870 km/h) at 19,685 ft (6 000 m), 532 mph (856 km/h) at 26,245 ft (8 000 m), 510 mph (820 km/h) at 32,810 ft (10 000 m); range (main tanks only— 396 Imp gal/1 800 l), 298 mls (480 km) at sea level, 528 mls (850 km) at 19,685 ft (6 000 m), 652 mls (1 050 km) at 29,530 ft (9 000 m); initial climb, 3,939 ft/min (19,99 m/sec).

**Weights:** Empty, 8,378 lb (3 800 kg); equipped, 9,742 lb (4 420 kg); normal loaded (main tanks only), 14,101 lb (6 396 kg), (max internal fuel), 15,720 lb (7 130 kg).

**Dimensions:** Span, 41 ft 0½ in (12,51 m); length, 34 ft 9½ in (10,60 m); height, 11 ft 6¾ in (3,52 m); wing area, 233·58 sq ft (21,70 m²).

**Armament:** Four 30-mm Rheinmetall Borsig MK 108 cannon with 100 rounds per gun for the upper pair and 80 rounds per gun for the lower pair.

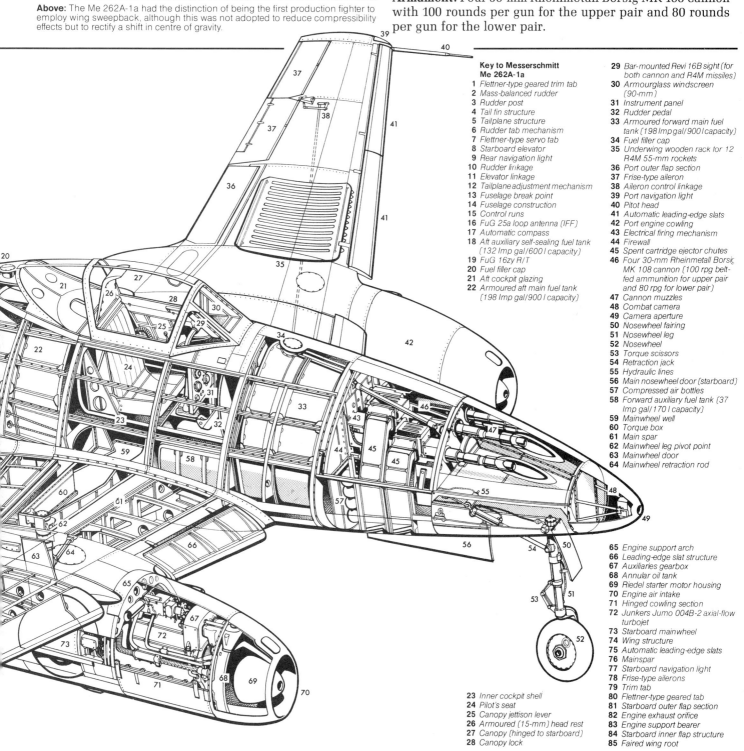

**Key to Messerschmitt Me 262A-1a**

1 Flettner-type geared trim tab
2 Mass-balanced rudder
3 Rudder post
4 Tail fin structure
5 Tailplane structure
6 Rudder tab mechanism
7 Flettner-type servo tab
8 Starboard elevator
9 Rear navigation light
10 Rudder linkage
11 Elevator linkage
12 Tailplane adjustment mechanism
13 Fuselage break point
14 Fuselage construction
15 Control runs
16 FuG 25a loop antenna (IFF)
17 Automatic compass
18 Aft auxiliary self-sealing fuel tank (132 Imp gal/600 l capacity)
19 FuG 16zy R/T
20 Fuel filler cap
21 Aft cockpit glazing
22 Armoured aft main fuel tank (198 Imp gal/900 l capacity)
23 Inner cockpit shell
24 Pilot's seat
25 Canopy jettison lever
26 Armoured (15-mm) head rest
27 Canopy (hinged to starboard)
28 Canopy lock

29 Bar-mounted Revi 16B sight (for both cannon and R4M missiles)
30 Armourglass windscreen (90-mm)
31 Instrument panel
32 Rudder pedal
33 Armoured forward main fuel tank (198 Imp gal/900 l capacity)
34 Fuel filler cap
35 Underwing wooden rack for 12 R4M 55-mm rockets
36 Port outer flap section
37 Frise-type aileron
38 Aileron control linkage
39 Port navigation light
40 Pitot head
41 Automatic leading-edge slats
42 Port engine cowling
43 Electrical firing mechanism
44 Firewall
45 Spent cartridge ejector chutes
46 Four 30-mm Rheinmetall Borsig MK 108 cannon (100 rpg belt-fed ammunition for upper pair and 80 rpg for lower pair)
47 Cannon muzzles
48 Combat camera
49 Camera aperture
50 Nosewheel fairing
51 Nosewheel leg
52 Nosewheel
53 Torque scissors
54 Retraction jack
55 Hydraulic lines
56 Main nosewheel door (starboard)
57 Compressed air bottles
58 Forward auxiliary fuel tank (37 Imp gal/170 l capacity)
59 Mainwheel well
60 Torque box
61 Main spar
62 Mainwheel leg pivot point
63 Mainwheel door
64 Mainwheel retraction rod

65 Engine support arch
66 Leading-edge slat structure
67 Auxiliaries gearbox
68 Annular oil tank
69 Riedel starter motor housing
70 Engine air intake
71 Hinged cowling section
72 Junkers Jumo 004B-2 axial-flow turbojet
73 Starboard mainwheel
74 Wing structure
75 Automatic leading-edge slats
76 Mainspar
77 Starboard navigation light
78 Frise-type ailerons
79 Trim tab
80 Flettner-type geared tab
81 Starboard outer flap section
82 Engine exhaust orifice
83 Engine support bearer
84 Starboard inner flap structure
85 Faired wing root

# Northrop P-61 Black Widow (May 1942)

Until the advent on operations in 1944 of the P-61, all fighters dedicated to the nocturnal intercept task had been adaptations of aircraft designed primarily for other operational roles. The P-61 was thus unique at the time of its début in being the first warplane designed from the outset for night fighting to achieve service status.

As large as a medium bomber and possessing a crew of three, comprising pilot, gunner and radar operator, the P-61 had its conception in a British rather than American requirement. In 1940, British resources could not be stretched to the design and development of a fighter expressly for nocturnal operation. Thus, Northrop was approached with a British specification for a heavily-armed night fighter equipped with radar and capable of mounting standing patrols from dusk to dawn if necessary. Before negotiations reached a decisive stage, however, the US Army prepared a broadly similar specification and it was to this that the P-61 was developed, the prototype (XP-61) flying on 26 May 1942.

The P-61 embodied several innovatory features, the most novel of which was the use of the then-radical spoiler-type aileron permitting inclusion of near full-span flaps and thus expanding the speed range and permitting operation from comparatively small airfields. Deliveries of the initial production model, the P-61A, commenced in October 1943, and, for an aircraft of its size and weight, the P-61 proved remarkably manoeuvrable. It could be looped, Immelmanned, slow-rolled or barrel-rolled, and perform any other precision or semi-precision manoeuvre with ease. It could even be slow-rolled with one engine out in the direction of the dead engine! It possessed an outstanding turn ability at speeds down to as low as 90 mph (145 km/h), and the stall under any condition—power on, power off or asymmetric—was straightforward with no tendency for a wing to drop.

The P-61 achieved operational status almost simultaneously in both Europe and the Pacific in the early months of 1944. The P-61A was succeeded by the P-61B with minor but operationally important modifications, and the P-61C which introduced turbo-superchargers. When production terminated with the surrender of Japan in August 1945, a total of 706 P-61s had been delivered.

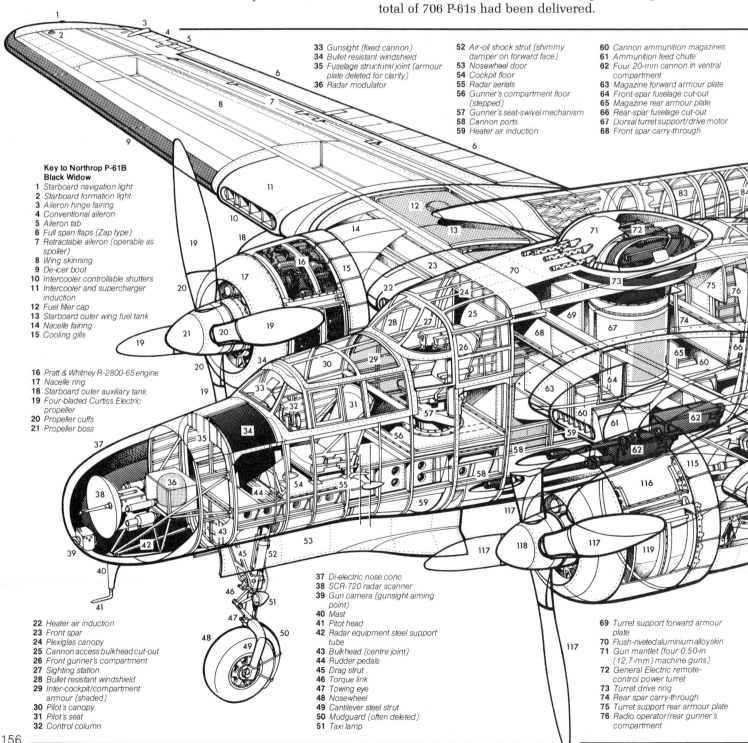

**Key to Northrop P-61B Black Widow**

1 Starboard navigation light
2 Starboard formation light
3 Aileron hinge fairing
4 Conventional aileron
5 Aileron tab
6 Full span flaps (Zap type)
7 Retractable aileron (operable as spoiler)
8 Wing skinning
9 De-icer boot
10 Intercooler controllable shutters
11 Intercooler and supercharger induction
12 Fuel filler cap
13 Starboard outer wing fuel tank
14 Nacelle fairing
15 Cooling gills
16 Pratt & Whitney R-2800-65 engine
17 Nacelle ring
18 Starboard outer auxiliary tank
19 Four-bladed Curtiss Electric propeller
20 Propeller cuffs
21 Propeller boss

22 Heater air induction
23 Front spar
24 Plexiglas canopy
25 Cannon access bulkhead cut-out
26 Front gunner's compartment
27 Sighting station
28 Bullet resistant windshield
29 Inter-cockpit/compartment armour (shaded)
30 Pilot's canopy
31 Pilot's seat
32 Control column

33 Gunsight (fixed cannon)
34 Bullet resistant windshield
35 Fuselage structural joint (armour plate deleted for clarity)
36 Radar modulator

37 Di-electric nose cone
38 SCR-720 radar scanner
39 Gun camera (gunsight aiming point)
40 Mast
41 Pitot head
42 Radar equipment steel support tube
43 Bulkhead (centre joint)
44 Rudder pedals
45 Drag strut
46 Torque link
47 Towing eye
48 Nosewheel
49 Cantilever steel strut
50 Mudguard (often deleted)
51 Taxi lamp

52 Air-oil shock strut (shimmy damper on forward face)
53 Nosewheel door
54 Cockpit floor
55 Radar aerials
56 Gunner's compartment floor (stepped)
57 Gunner's seat-swivel mechanism
58 Cannon ports
59 Heater air induction

60 Cannon ammunition magazines
61 Ammunition feed chute
62 Four 20-mm cannon in ventral compartment
63 Magazine forward armour plate
64 Front-spar fuselage cut-out
65 Magazine rear armour plate
66 Rear-spar fuselage cut-out
67 Dorsal turret support/drive motor
68 Front spar carry-through

69 Turret support forward armour plate
70 Flush-riveted aluminium alloy skin
71 Gun mantlet (four 0.50-in (12.7-mm) machine guns)
72 General Electric remote-control power turret
73 Turret drive ring
74 Rear spar carry-through
75 Turret support rear armour plate
76 Radio operator/rear gunner's compartment

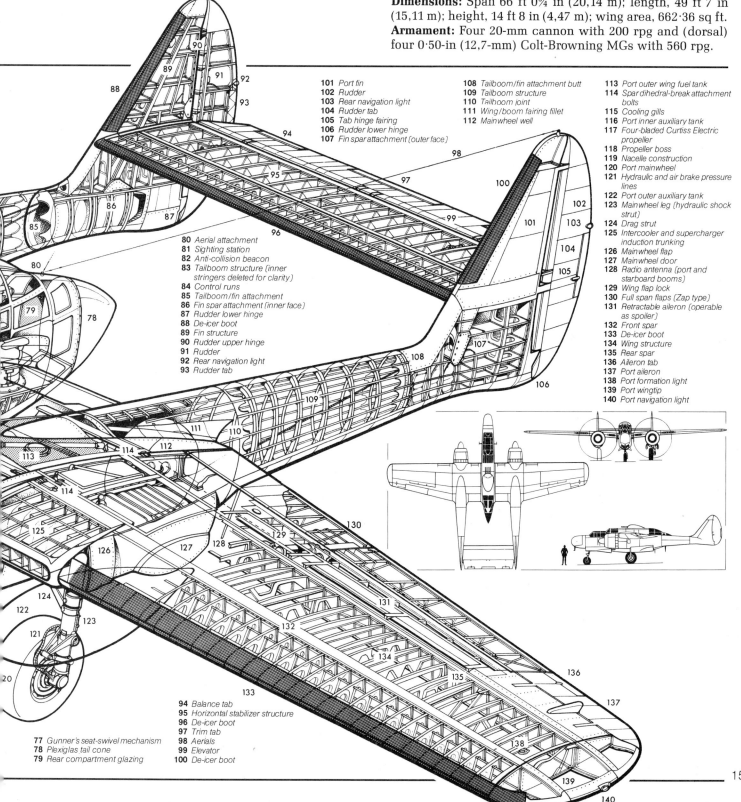

**Above:** A P-61A-5 of the 422nd Night Fighter Sqdn, USAAF, based at Scorton, Yorks, in the summer of 1944 as first UK-based P-61 squadron.

## SPECIFICATION: P-61B-20 Black Widow

**Power Plant:** Two Pratt & Whitney R-2800-65 Double Wasp 18-cylinder two-row radial air-cooled engines each rated at 1,850 hp at 2,700 rpm for take-off and 2,000 hp at 2,300 ft (700 m). Four-bladed Curtiss Electric propellers. Internal fuel capacity, 525 Imp gal (2 385 l) and provision for two or four 137·5 Imp gal (625 l) or 258 Imp gal (1 173 l) drop tanks.

**Performance:** Max speed, 330 mph (531 km/h) at sea level, 352 mph (566 km/h) at 10,000 ft (3 050 m), 366 mph (589 km/h) at 20,000 ft (6 100 m); range (max continuous power), 550 mls (885 km) at 305 mph (491 km/h) at 10,000 ft (3 050 m), 610 mls (982 km) at 339 mph (545 km/h) at 25,000 ft (7 620 m); initial climb, 2,550 ft/min (12,9 m/sec); time to 5,000 ft (1 525 m), 2·7 min, to 10,000 ft (3 050 m), 5·6 min, to 15,000 ft (4 570 m), 8·6 min.

**Weights:** Empty equipped, 23,450 lb (10 637 kg); normal loaded, 29,700 lb (13 472 kg); max, 36,200 lb (16 420 kg).

**Dimensions:** Span 66 ft 0¾ in (20,14 m); length, 49 ft 7 in (15,11 m); height, 14 ft 8 in (4,47 m); wing area, 662·36 sq ft.

**Armament:** Four 20-mm cannon with 200 rpg and (dorsal) four 0·50-in (12,7-mm) Colt-Browning MGs with 560 rpg.

77 Gunner's seat-swivel mechanism
78 Plexiglas tail cone
79 Rear compartment glazing
80 Aerial attachment
81 Sighting station
82 Anti-collision beacon
83 Tailboom structure (inner stringers deleted for clarity)
84 Control runs
85 Tailboom/fin attachment
86 Fin spar attachment (inner face)
87 Rudder lower hinge
88 De-icer boot
89 Fin structure
90 Rudder upper hinge
91 Rudder
92 Rear navigation light
93 Rudder tab
94 Balance tab
95 Horizontal stabilizer structure
96 De-icer boot
97 Trim tab
98 Aerials
99 Elevator
100 De-icer boot
101 Port fin
102 Rudder
103 Rear navigation light
104 Rudder tab
105 Tab hinge fairing
106 Rudder lower hinge
107 Fin spar attachment (outer face)
108 Tailboom/fin attachment butt
109 Tailboom structure
110 Tailboom joint
111 Wing/boom fairing fillet
112 Mainwheel well
113 Port outer wing fuel tank
114 Spar dihedral-break attachment bolts
115 Cooling gills
116 Port inner auxiliary tank
117 Four-bladed Curtiss Electric propeller
118 Propeller boss
119 Nacelle construction
120 Port mainwheel
121 Hydraulic and air brake pressure lines
122 Port outer auxiliary tank
123 Mainwheel leg (hydraulic shock strut)
124 Drag strut
125 Intercooler and supercharger induction trunking
126 Mainwheel flap
127 Mainwheel door
128 Radio antenna (port and starboard booms)
129 Wing flap lock
130 Full span flaps (Zap type)
131 Retractable aileron (operable as spoiler)
132 Front spar
133 De-icer boot
134 Wing structure
135 Rear spar
136 Aileron tab
137 Port aileron
138 Port formation light
139 Port wingtip
140 Port navigation light

# Grumman F6F Hellcat (June 1942)

The inexorable growth in the size and weight of US Navy single-seat shipboard fighters that had begun its immoderate upward spiral with the F4U Corsair (see pages 136-137) was to attain its apex for the single piston-engined warplane of this category with the appearance of the F6F Hellcat. Possessing the biggest wing of any single-seat fighter to see combat in WWII and weighing 60 per cent more than its predecessor, the F4F Wildcat, the F6F was conceived primarily as an air superiority weapon with the range to seek out the enemy so that he could be brought to battle. It was the product of a design philosophy diametrically opposed to that pursued by the designers of its principal adversaries, in that agility and speed were not permitted to compromise structural strength, armour protection and firepower. It was thus not the fastest shipboard fighter of WWII, nor the most manoeuvrable, but it was undoubtedly the most efficacious.

The F6F was an astonishing fighter, not so much for its intrinsic qualities but for the rapidity of its translation from drawing board to operational deployment. No fighter of its era had a briefer gestation; none progressed from prototype test to squadron service within a shorter timespan. Designed by a team headed by Leroy R. Grumman and William T. Schwendler, the F6F was hurriedly conceived, engineered and manufactured, but it was to display no evidence of that haste. The contract for two prototypes had been placed on 30 June 1941, and a year later, on 26 June 1942,

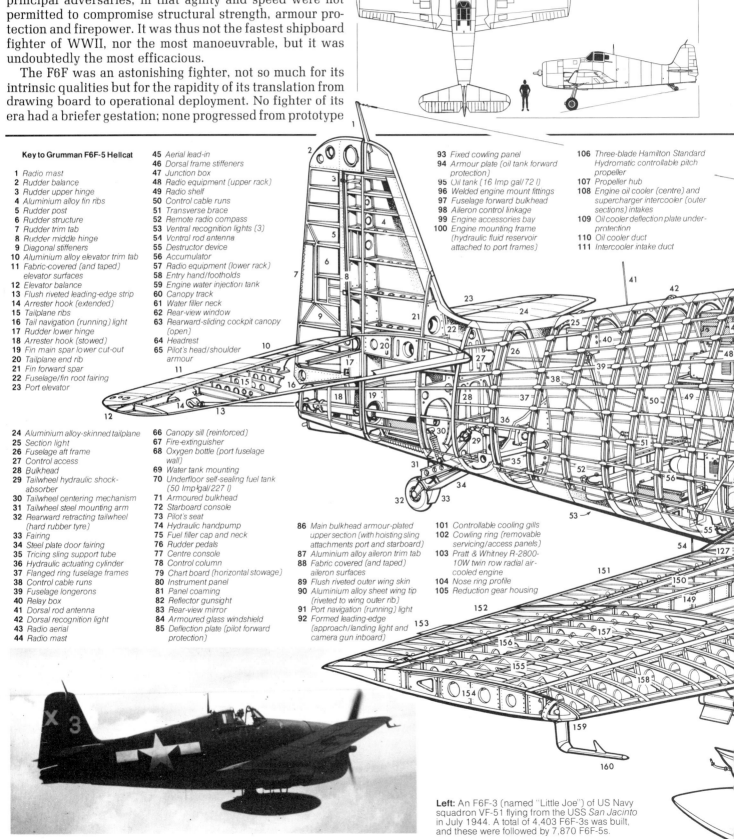

**Key to Grumman F6F-5 Hellcat**

1 Radio mast
2 Rudder balance
3 Rudder upper hinge
4 Aluminium alloy fin ribs
5 Rudder post
6 Rudder structure
7 Rudder trim tab
8 Rudder middle hinge
9 Diagonal stiffeners
10 Aluminium alloy elevator trim tab
11 Fabric-covered (and taped) elevator surfaces
12 Elevator balance
13 Flush riveted leading-edge strip
14 Arrester hook (extended)
15 Tailplane ribs
16 Tail navigation (running) light
17 Rudder lower hinge
18 Arrester hook (stowed)
19 Fin main spar lower cut-out
20 Tailplane end rib
21 Fin forward spar
22 Fuselage/fin root fairing
23 Port elevator

24 Aluminium alloy-skinned tailplane
25 Section light
26 Fuselage aft frame
27 Control access
28 Bulkhead
29 Tailwheel hydraulic shock-absorber
30 Tailwheel centering mechanism
31 Tailwheel steel mounting arm
32 Rearward retracting tailwheel (hard rubber tyre)
33 Fairing
34 Steel plate door fairing
35 Tricing sling support tube
36 Hydraulic actuating cylinder
37 Flanged ring fuselage frames
38 Control cable runs
39 Fuselage longerons
40 Relay box
41 Dorsal rod antenna
42 Dorsal recognition light
43 Radio aerial
44 Radio mast

45 Aerial lead-in
46 Dorsal frame stiffeners
47 Junction box
48 Radio equipment (upper rack)
49 Radio shelf
50 Control cable runs
51 Transverse brace
52 Remote radio compass
53 Ventral recognition lights (3)
54 Ventral rod antenna
55 Destructor device
56 Accumulator
57 Radio equipment (lower rack)
58 Entry hand/footholds
59 Engine water injection tank
60 Canopy track
61 Water filler neck
62 Rear-view window
63 Rearward-sliding cockpit canopy (open)
64 Headrest
65 Pilot's head/shoulder armour
66 Canopy sill (reinforced)
67 Fire-extinguisher
68 Oxygen bottle (port fuselage wall)
69 Water tank mounting
70 Underfloor self-sealing fuel tank (50 Imp gal/227 l)
71 Armoured bulkhead
72 Starboard console
73 Pilot's seat
74 Hydraulic handpump
75 Fuel filler cap and neck
76 Rudder pedals
77 Centre console
78 Control column
79 Chart board (horizontal stowage)
80 Instrument panel
81 Panel coaming
82 Reflector gunsight
83 Rear-view mirror
84 Armoured glass windshield
85 Deflection plate (pilot forward protection)

86 Main bulkhead armour-plated upper section (with hoisting sling attachments port and starboard)
87 Aluminium alloy aileron trim tab
88 Fabric covered (and taped) aileron surfaces
89 Flush riveted outer wing skin
90 Aluminium alloy sheet wing tip (riveted to wing outer rib)
91 Port navigation (running) light
92 Formed leading-edge (approach/landing light and camera gun inboard)

93 Fixed cowling panel
94 Armour plate (oil tank forward protection)
95 Oil tank (16 Imp gal/72 l)
96 Welded engine mount fittings
97 Fuselage forward bulkhead
98 Aileron control linkage
99 Engine accessories bay
100 Engine mounting frame (hydraulic fluid reservoir attached to port frames)

101 Controllable cooling gills
102 Cowling ring (removable servicing/access panels)
103 Pratt & Whitney R-2800-10W twin row radial air-cooled engine
104 Nose ring profile
105 Reduction gear housing
106 Three-blade Hamilton Standard Hydromatic controllable pitch propeller
107 Propeller hub
108 Engine oil cooler (centre) and supercharger intercooler (outer sections) intakes
109 Oil cooler deflection plate under-protection
110 Oil cooler duct
111 Intercooler intake duct

**Left:** An F6F-3 (named "Little Joe") of US Navy squadron VF-51 flying from the USS *San Jacinto* in July 1944. A total of 4,403 F6F-3s was built, and these were followed by 7,870 F6F-5s.

testing of the first prototype (XF6F-1) commenced. Within 14 weeks, on 3 October, the first production aircraft (F6F-3) was flown; the first US Navy squadron began to equip on 16 January 1943, and fifteen squadrons were to be mounted on the fighter by the year's end, with a total of 2,555 F6F Hellcats then delivered!

The F6F could not manoeuvre with its Japanese adversaries, but it was faster, it could out-dive its opponents, it possessed superior firepower and it could withstand far more punishment. In flight, the F6F was stable about all axes, although it displayed marked changes in directional and lateral trim with speed and power changes. It stalled with little warning and the drop of either wing, but recovery was straightforward, and the controls heavied up at high speeds until the introduction of spring tabs on the F6F-5 model rendered the ailerons light and effective throughout the speed range.

When production terminated in November 1945, no fewer than 12,275 F6F Hellcats had been manufactured and no fighter had done more to wrest aerial ascendancy over the Pacific from the Japanese.

## SPECIFICATION: F6F-3 Hellcat

**Power Plant:** One Pratt & Whitney R-2800-10 Double Wasp 18-cylinder two-row radial air-cooled engine rated at 2,000 hp at 2,700 rpm for take-off and 1,800 hp at 15,700 ft (4 785 m). Three-bladed Hamilton Standard constant-speed propeller. Internal fuel capacity, 208 Imp gal (946 l), with provision for one 125 Imp gal (568 l) centreline drop tank.

**Performance:** (At 11,381 lb/5 162 kg) max speed, 324 mph (521 km/h) at sea level, 376 mph (605 km/h) at 22,800 ft (6 950 m); range (max internal fuel), 1,085 mls (1 746 km) at 179 mph (288 km/h) at 5,000 ft (1 525 m), (with drop tank), 1,620 mls (2 607 km) at 177 mph (285 km/h); initial climb, 3,650 ft/min (18,5 m/sec); time to 15,000 ft (4 570 m), 6·0 min, to 25,000 ft (7 620 m), 11·3 min; service ceiling, 35,500 ft (10 820 m).

**Weights:** Empty, 9,042 lb (4 101 kg); loaded, 12,186 lb (5 528 kg); max, 13,221 lb (5 997 kg).

**Dimensions:** Span, 42 ft 10 in (13,08 m); length, 33 ft 4 in (10,17 m); height, 14 ft 5 in (4,40 m); wing area, 334 sq ft.

**Armament:** Six 0·50-in (12,7-mm) Colt-Browning machine guns with 400 rpg.

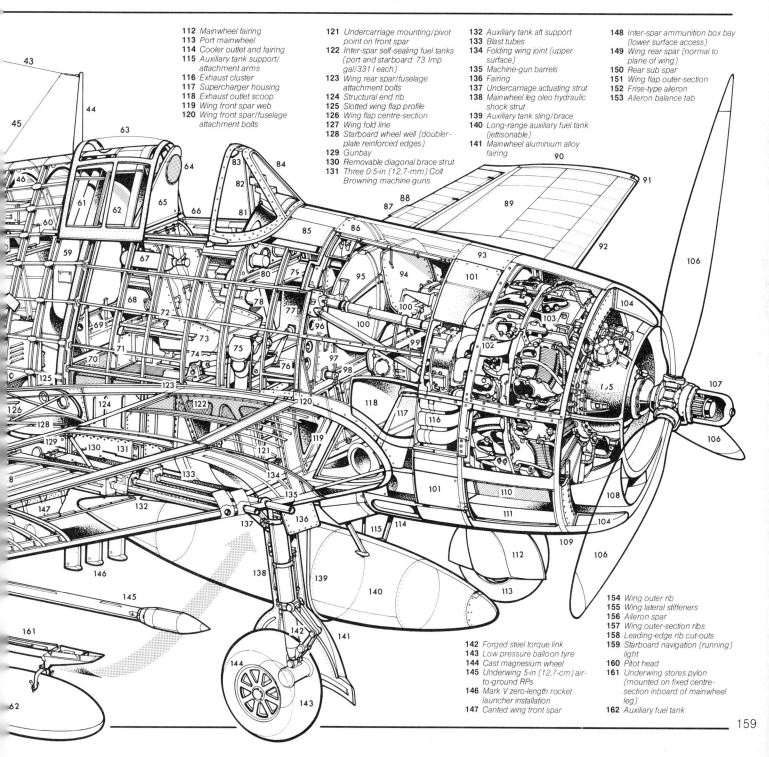

112 Mainwheel fairing
113 Port mainwheel
114 Cooler outlet and fairing
115 Auxiliary tank support/attachment arms
116 Exhaust cluster
117 Supercharger housing
118 Exhaust outlet scoop
119 Wing front spar web
120 Wing front spar/fuselage attachment bolts
121 Undercarriage mounting/pivot point on front spar
122 Inter-spar self-sealing fuel tanks (port and starboard: 73 Imp gal/331 l each)
123 Wing rear spar/fuselage attachment bolts
124 Structural end rib
125 Slotted wing flap profile
126 Wing flap centre-section
127 Wing fold line
128 Starboard wheel well (doubler-plate reinforced edges)
129 Gunbay
130 Removable diagonal brace strut
131 Three 0·5-in (12,7-mm) Colt Browning machine guns
132 Auxiliary tank aft support
133 Blast tubes
134 Folding wing joint (upper surface)
135 Machine-gun barrels
136 Fairing
137 Undercarriage actuating strut
138 Mainwheel leg oleo hydraulic shock strut
139 Auxiliary tank sling/brace
140 Long-range auxiliary fuel tank (jettisonable)
141 Mainwheel aluminium alloy fairing
142 Forged steel torque link
143 Low pressure balloon tyre
144 Cast magnesium wheel
145 Underwing 5-in (12,7-cm) air-to-ground RPs
146 Mark V zero-length rocket launcher installation
147 Canted wing front spar
148 Inter-spar ammunition box bay (lower surface access)
149 Wing rear spar (normal to plane of wing)
150 Rear sub spar
151 Wing flap outer-section
152 Frise-type aileron
153 Aileron balance tab
154 Wing outer rib
155 Wing lateral stiffeners
156 Aileron spar
157 Wing outer-section ribs
158 Leading-edge rib cut-outs
159 Starboard navigation (running) light
160 Pitot head
161 Underwing stores pylon (mounted on fixed centre-section inboard of mainwheel leg)
162 Auxiliary fuel tank

# Yakovlev Yak-9 (July 1942)

No more astonishing an example of genealogical progression can be found in fighter development annals than that offered by the WWII fighter progeny of Alexander S. Yakovlev. One fundamental fighter design of thoroughly orthodox concept and prosaic capability was to spawn, via a bewildering succession of component, equipment, armament, engine and, eventually, structural changes, an entire *family* of combat aircraft; a family that was to provide in excess of 58 per cent of *all* fighters built in the Soviet Union during 1941-45.

Lightly armed, rudimentarily equipped and lacking refinements common to their western contemporaries, these fighters were deserving of respect nonetheless. Simple to build and to maintain under austere field conditions, they were ideally suited for the combat scenario to which they were committed; they were low-to-medium altitude fighters *par excellence,* their common virtues being good stability under all conditions and outstanding controllability at high attack angles.

From the basic Yak-1, phasing into service immediately prior to the German assault on the Soviet Union, two distinct lines of development emerged, albeit more by circumstance than intent. These were categorised as "heavy" and "light", the former materialising as the Yak-9 and the latter as the Yak-3 (see pages 166-167). The Yak-9 flew (as the Yak-7DI) in July 1942, appearing in small numbers operationally late in November. Subjected to a constant evolutionary process, the basic general-purpose "frontal" fighter was developed in several dedicated versions. These included the nocturnal intercept Yak-9PVO, the pinpoint bombing Yak-9B with internal bomb stowage, and the anti-armour Yak-9T and -9K with 37-mm and 45-mm engine-mounted cannon respectively.

The Yak-9D featured increased internal fuel and the Yak-9DD was an even longer-ranging model for escort duties, while the late-war Yak-9U, all-metal -9UT and post-WWII Yak-9P were to receive the more powerful M-107 engine. Production was to continue into the postwar years, 16,769 Yak-9 fighters in a variety of sub-types — including 3,900 "third generation" Yak-9Us—having rolled off the assembly lines when manufacture finally terminated in 1947.

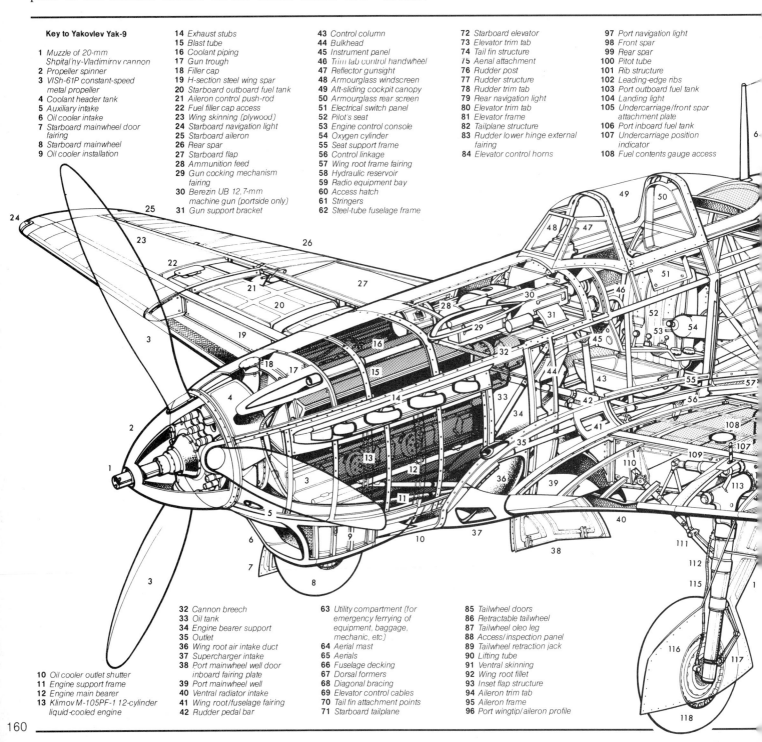

**Key to Yakovlev Yak-9**

1 Muzzle of 20-mm Shpital'ny-Vladimirov cannon
2 Propeller spinner
3 VISh-61P constant-speed metal propeller
4 Coolant header tank
5 Auxiliary intake
6 Oil cooler intake
7 Starboard mainwheel door fairing
8 Starboard mainwheel
9 Oil cooler installation
10 Oil cooler outlet shutter
11 Engine support frame
12 Engine main bearer
13 Klimov M-105PF-1 12-cylinder liquid-cooled engine
14 Exhaust stubs
15 Blast tube
16 Coolant piping
17 Gun trough
18 Filler cap
19 H-section steel wing spar
20 Starboard outboard fuel tank
21 Aileron control push-rod
22 Fuel filler cap access
23 Wing skinning (plywood)
24 Starboard navigation light
25 Starboard aileron
26 Rear spar
27 Starboard flap
28 Ammunition feed
29 Gun cocking mechanism fairing
30 Berezin UB 12,7-mm machine gun (portside only)
31 Gun support bracket
32 Cannon breech
33 Oil tank
34 Engine bearer support
35 Outlet
36 Wing root air intake duct
37 Supercharger intake
38 Port mainwheel well door inboard fairing plate
39 Port mainwheel well
40 Ventral radiator intake
41 Wing root/fuselage fairing
42 Rudder pedal bar
43 Control column
44 Bulkhead
45 Instrument panel
46 Trim tab control handwheel
47 Reflector gunsight
48 Armourglass windscreen
49 Aft-sliding cockpit canopy
50 Armourglass rear screen
51 Electrical switch panel
52 Pilot's seat
53 Engine control console
54 Oxygen cylinder
55 Seat support frame
56 Control linkage
57 Wing root frame fairing
58 Hydraulic reservoir
59 Radio equipment bay
60 Access hatch
61 Stringers
62 Steel-tube fuselage frame
63 Utility compartment (for emergency ferrying of equipment, baggage, mechanic, etc)
64 Aerial mast
65 Aerials
66 Fuselage decking
67 Dorsal formers
68 Diagonal bracing
69 Elevator control cables
70 Tail fin attachment points
71 Starboard tailplane
72 Starboard elevator
73 Elevator trim tab
74 Tail fin structure
75 Aerial attachment
76 Rudder post
77 Rudder structure
78 Rudder trim tab
79 Rear navigation light
80 Elevator trim tab
81 Elevator frame
82 Tailplane structure
83 Rudder lower hinge external fairing
84 Elevator control horns
85 Tailwheel doors
86 Retractable tailwheel
87 Tailwheel oleo leg
88 Access/inspection panel
89 Tailwheel retraction jack
90 Lifting tube
91 Ventral skinning
92 Wing root fillet
93 Inset flap structure
94 Aileron trim tab
95 Aileron frame
96 Port wingtip/aileron profile
97 Port navigation light
98 Front spar
99 Rear spar
100 Pitot tube
101 Rib structure
102 Leading-edge ribs
103 Port outboard fuel tank
104 Landing light
105 Undercarriage/front spar attachment plate
106 Port inboard fuel tank
107 Undercarriage position indicator
108 Fuel contents gauge access

**Above:** Yak-9s of the 6th Guards Fighter Aviation Regiment photographed June 1944. No 22 is flown by Lt Col M.V. Avdeyev.

## SPECIFICATION: Yak-9D

**Power Plant:** One Klimov M-105PF-3 12-cylinder vee liquid-cooled engine rated at 1,240 hp at 2,600 rpm for take-off and 1,360 hp at 2,625 ft (800 m). Three-bladed VISh-105SV constant-speed propeller. Internal fuel capacity, 143 Imp gal (650 l).

**Performance:** Max speed, 332 mph (534 km/h) at sea level, 347 mph (558 km/h) at 3,280 ft (1 000 m), 354 mph (570 km/h) at 6,560 ft (2 000 m), 374 mph (602 km/h) at 10,170 ft (3 100 m); max range, 870 mls (1 400 km) at 186 mph (300 km/h), 733 mls (1 180 km) at 242 mph (390 km/h), 603 mls (970 km) at 264 mph (425 km/h); time to 16,405 ft (5 000 m), 6·0 min.

**Weights:** Empty equipped, 5,269 lb (2 390 kg); normal loaded, 6,867 lb (3 115 kg).

**Dimensions:** Span, 31 ft 11½ in (9,74 m); length, 28 ft 0¾ in (8,55 m); height (tail up), 9 ft 10 in (3,00 m); wing area, 184·6 sq ft (17,15 m²).

**Armament:** One 20-mm Shpital'ny-Vladimirov ShVAK cannon with 120 rounds and one 12,7-mm Berezin UB machine gun with 180-220 rounds.

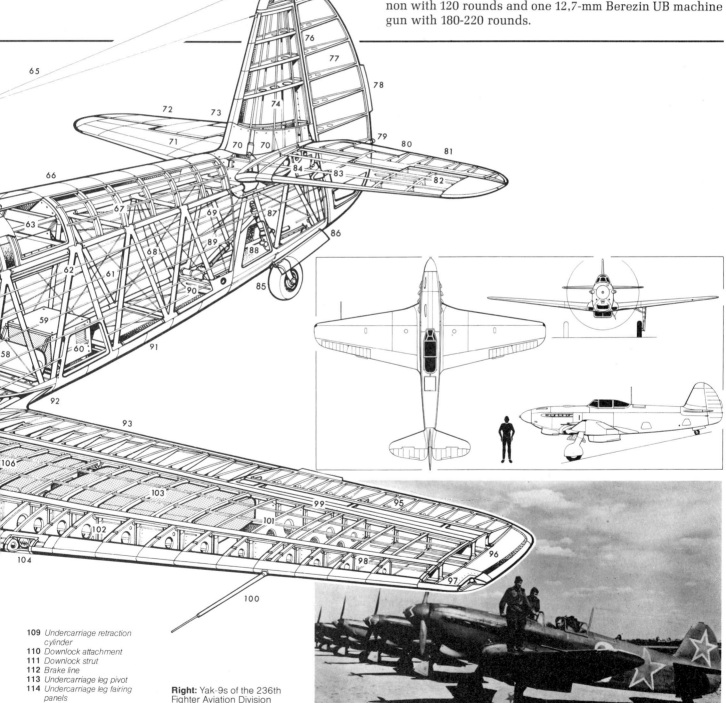

109 *Undercarriage retraction cylinder*
110 *Downlock attachment*
111 *Downlock strut*
112 *Brake line*
113 *Undercarriage leg pivot*
114 *Undercarriage leg fairing panels*
115 *Mainwheel oleo leg*
116 *Mainwheel door fairing plate*
117 *Torque links*
118 *Port mainwheel*

**Right:** Yak-9s of the 236th Fighter Aviation Division photographed at Bari, Italy, when operating in support of Yugoslav partisan units during 1944.

# Gloster Meteor (March 1943)

Once the foundations for a technical breakthrough have been laid through pure research, its practical application is frequently pursued independently and simultaneously in several countries. So it was with the aircraft gas turbine and its application to the fighter, which developed into a race between Germany and Britain that the former won by a short head.

Operations with the Me 262 (see pages 154-155) had just begun when, in July 1944, its British counterpart, the Meteor, made its RAF service début. Twelve prototypes, the first of which flew on 5 March 1943, were followed by 20 Meteor Is, but their 1,700 lb (771 kg) Welland turbojets were insufficiently powerful to realise the full airframe potential, the 2,000 lb (907 kg) Derwent I being adopted for the initial series model, the Meteor III—although the first 15 perforce kept the Welland—flown September 1944.

Two hundred and ten Meteor IIIs were followed by the Derwent 5-powered F Mk 4, which, with strengthened airframe, began to enter service in 1948. Unlike its German contemporary, the Meteor was not a pilot's aeroplane in the traditional sense; its faults were common enough among first-generation jet fighters. Controls were well balanced and reasonably effective, but heavied up above Mach=0·72 until they became almost "solid", coarse use of trimmers being necessary to produce any marked effect. A strong nose-up trim change needed to be countered around Mach=0·75 and became barely manageable at Mach=0·82, while there was a tendency to snake at speed and the Meteor was handicapped in flying a pursuit curve above 460 mph (740 km/h) by its high aileron stick forces.

The Meteor was, nevertheless, arguably the most successful of western first-generation jet fighters. Early in the production run of 753 F Mk 4s, the wing span was reduced to provide a more acceptable roll rate, and, to improve somewhat inadequate directional stability, the fuselage of its successor, the F Mk 8, was lengthened. This variant entered service from 1950, 1,183 being built. In first-line RAF service for 17 years, the Meteor was exported to a dozen countries, a total of 3,850 being built in all versions.

**SPECIFICATION: Meteor F Mk 4**
**Power Plant:** Two Rolls-Royce Derwent 5 centrifugal-flow

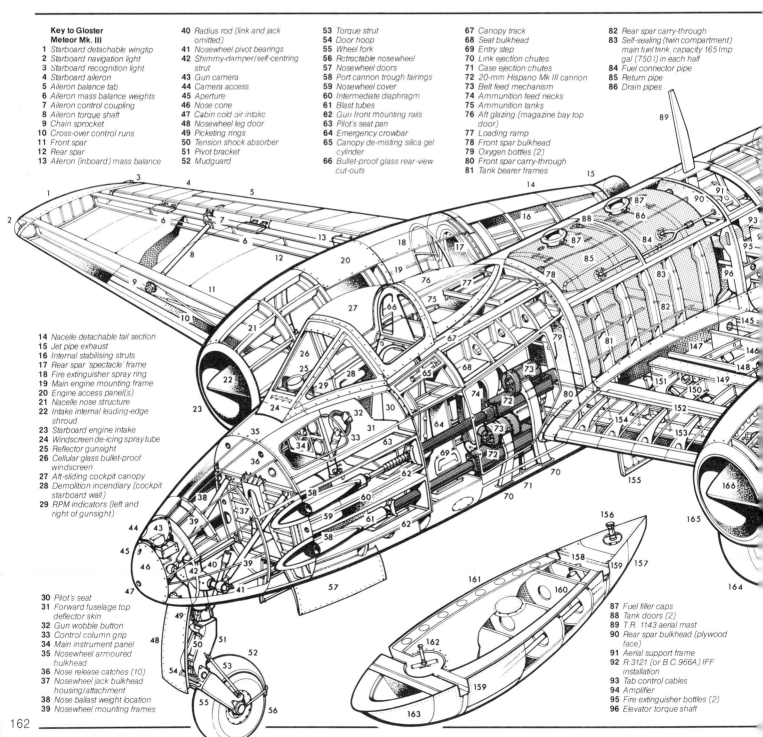

**Key to Gloster Meteor Mk. III**
1 Starboard detachable wingtip
2 Starboard navigation light
3 Starboard recognition light
4 Starboard aileron
5 Aileron balance tab
6 Aileron mass balance weights
7 Aileron control coupling
8 Aileron torque shaft
9 Chain sprocket
10 Cross-over control runs
11 Front spar
12 Rear spar
13 Aileron (inboard) mass balance
14 Nacelle detachable tail section
15 Jet pipe exhaust
16 Internal stabilising struts
17 Rear spar 'spectacle' frame
18 Fire extinguisher spray ring
19 Main engine mounting frame
20 Engine access panel(s)
21 Nacelle nose structure
22 Intake internal leading-edge shroud
23 Starboard engine intake
24 Windscreen de-icing spray tube
25 Reflector gunsight
26 Cellular glass bullet-proof windscreen
27 Aft-sliding cockpit canopy
28 Demolition incendiary (cockpit starboard wall)
29 RPM indicators (left and right of gunsight)
30 Pilot's seat
31 Forward fuselage top deflector skin
32 Gun wobble button
33 Control column grip
34 Main instrument panel
35 Nosewheel armoured bulkhead
36 Nose release catches (10)
37 Nosewheel jack bulkhead housing/attachment
38 Nose ballast weight location
39 Nosewheel mounting frames

40 Radius rod (link and jack omitted)
41 Nosewheel pivot bearings
42 Shimmy-damper/self-centring strut
43 Gun camera
44 Camera access
45 Aperture
46 Nose cone
47 Cabin cold air intake
48 Nosewheel leg door
49 Picketing rings
50 Tension shock absorber
51 Pivot bracket
52 Mudguard

53 Torque strut
54 Door hoop
55 Wheel fork
56 Retractable nosewheel
57 Nosewheel doors
58 Port cannon trough fairings
59 Nosewheel cover
60 Intermediate diaphragm
61 Blast tubes
62 Gun front mounting rails
63 Pilot's seat pan
64 Emergency crowbar
65 Canopy de-misting silica gel cylinder
66 Bullet-proof glass rear-view cut-outs

67 Canopy track
68 Seat bulkhead
69 Entry step
70 Link ejection chutes
71 Case ejection chutes
72 20-mm Hispano Mk III cannon
73 Belt feed mechanism
74 Ammunition feed necks
75 Ammunition tanks
76 Aft glazing (magazine bay top door)
77 Loading ramp
78 Front spar bulkhead
79 Oxygen bottles (2)
80 Front spar carry-through
81 Tank bearer frames

82 Rear spar carry-through
83 Self-sealing (twin compartment) main fuel tank, capacity 165 imp gal (750 l) in each half
84 Fuel connector pipe
85 Return pipe
86 Drain pipes
87 Fuel filler caps
88 Tank doors (2)
89 T.R. 1143 aerial mast
90 Rear spar bulkhead (plywood face)
91 Aerial support frame
92 R.3121 (or B.C.966A) IFF installation
93 Tab control cables
94 Amplifier
95 Fire extinguisher bottles (2)
96 Elevator torque shaft

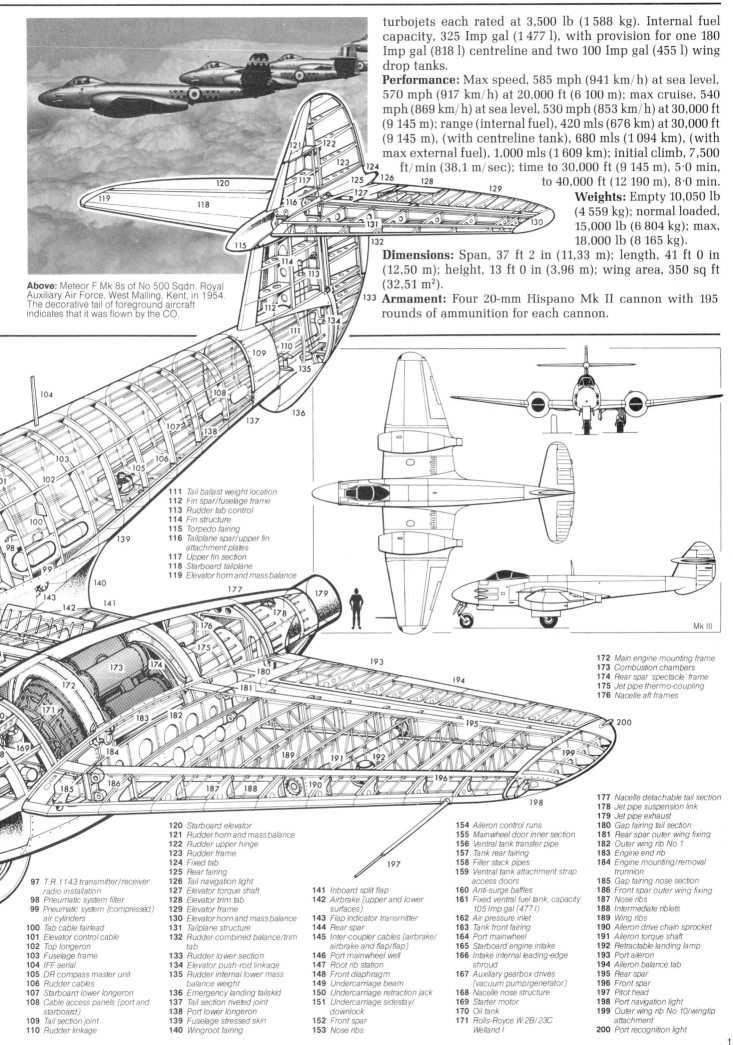

turbojets each rated at 3,500 lb (1 588 kg). Internal fuel capacity, 325 Imp gal (1 477 l), with provision for one 180 Imp gal (818 l) centreline and two 100 Imp gal (455 l) wing drop tanks.

**Performance:** Max speed, 585 mph (941 km/h) at sea level, 570 mph (917 km/h) at 20,000 ft (6 100 m); max cruise, 540 mph (869 km/h) at sea level, 530 mph (853 km/h) at 30,000 ft (9 145 m); range (internal fuel), 420 mls (676 km) at 30,000 ft (9 145 m), (with centreline tank), 680 mls (1 094 km), (with max external fuel), 1,000 mls (1 609 km); initial climb, 7,500 ft/min (38,1 m/sec); time to 30,000 ft (9 145 m), 5·0 min, to 40,000 ft (12 190 m), 8·0 min.

**Weights:** Empty 10,050 lb (4 559 kg); normal loaded, 15,000 lb (6 804 kg); max, 18,000 lb (8 165 kg).

**Dimensions:** Span, 37 ft 2 in (11,33 m); length, 41 ft 0 in (12,50 m); height, 13 ft 0 in (3,96 m); wing area, 350 sq ft (32,51 m²).

**Armament:** Four 20-mm Hispano Mk II cannon with 195 rounds of ammunition for each cannon.

**Above:** Meteor F Mk 8s of No 500 Sqdn, Royal Auxiliary Air Force, West Malling, Kent, in 1954. The decorative tail of foreground aircraft indicates that it was flown by the CO.

97 T.R.1143 transmitter/receiver radio installation
98 Pneumatic system filter
99 Pneumatic system (compressed) air cylinders
100 Tab cable fairlead
101 Elevator control cable
102 Top longeron
103 Fuselage frame
104 IFF aerial
105 DR compass master unit
106 Rudder cables
107 Starboard lower longeron
108 Cable access panels (port and starboard)
109 Tail section joint
110 Rudder linkage
111 Tail ballast weight location
112 Fin spar/fuselage frame
113 Rudder tab control
114 Fin structure
115 Torpedo fairing
116 Tailplane spar/upper fin attachment plates
117 Upper fin section
118 Starboard tailplane
119 Elevator horn and mass balance
120 Starboard elevator
121 Rudder horn and mass balance
122 Rudder upper hinge
123 Rudder frame
124 Fixed tab
125 Rear fairing
126 Tail navigation light
127 Elevator torque shaft
128 Elevator trim tab
129 Elevator frame
130 Elevator horn and mass balance
131 Tailplane structure
132 Rudder combined balance/trim tab
133 Rudder lower section
134 Elevator push-rod linkage
135 Rudder internal lower mass balance weight
136 Emergency landing tailskid
137 Tail section riveted joint
138 Port lower longeron
139 Fuselage stressed skin
140 Wingroot fairing
141 Inboard split flap
142 Airbrake (upper and lower surfaces)
143 Flap indicator transmitter
144 Rear spar
145 Inter-coupler cables (airbrake/airbrake and flap/flap)
146 Port mainwheel well
147 Root rib station
148 Front diaphragm
149 Undercarriage beam
150 Undercarriage retraction jack
151 Undercarriage sidestay/downlock
152 Front spar
153 Nose ribs
154 Aileron control runs
155 Mainwheel door inner section
156 Ventral tank transfer pipe
157 Tank rear fairing
158 Filler stack pipes
159 Ventral tank attachment strap access doors
160 Anti-surge baffles
161 Fixed ventral fuel tank, capacity 105 Imp gal (477 l)
162 Air pressure inlet
163 Tank front fairing
164 Port mainwheel
165 Starboard engine intake
166 Intake internal leading-edge shroud
167 Auxiliary gearbox drives (vacuum pump/generator)
168 Nacelle nose structure
169 Starter motor
170 Oil tank
171 Rolls-Royce W.2B/23C Welland I
172 Main engine mounting frame
173 Combustion chambers
174 Rear spar 'spectacle' frame
175 Jet pipe thermo-coupling
176 Nacelle aft frames
177 Nacelle detachable tail section
178 Jet pipe suspension link
179 Jet pipe exhaust
180 Gap fairing tail section
181 Rear spar outer wing fixing
182 Outer wing rib No 1
183 Engine end rib
184 Engine mounting/removal trunnion
185 Gap fairing nose section
186 Front spar outer wing fixing
187 Nose ribs
188 Intermediate riblets
189 Wing ribs
190 Aileron drive chain sprocket
191 Aileron torque shaft
192 Retractable landing lamp
193 Port aileron
194 Aileron balance tab
195 Rear spar
196 Front spar
197 Pitot head
198 Port navigation light
199 Outer wing rib No 10/wingtip attachment
200 Port recognition light

Mk III

163

# Nakajima Ki.84 Hayate (April 1943)

Carrying Japanese WWII single-seat fighter evolution to its peak, the Ki.84 Hayate (Gale) mirrored the metamorphosis in Imperial Army offensive air superiority fighter demands that had taken place since introduction of the Ki.43 Hayabusa (see pages 124-125). The Ki.43 had featured a well-designed but decidedly lightly constructed airframe mated with a low-powered engine, rudimentary pilot and fuel tank protection, and the lightest of armament. The Ki.84, in dramatic contrast, was characterised by an extremely robust structure with all the advantages of a really powerful engine utilising water-methanol injection, self-sealing fuel tanks, adequate pilot protection and a highly destructive armament.

Designed under the direction of Yasumi Koyama, the Ki.84 was flown during the first week of April 1943, within 11 months of the acceptance by the Army Air Headquarters of Nakajima's design study. No fewer than 83 service trials aircraft were built, largely by hand, and the first production example of the Ki.84-I-ko (Type 4 Fighter Model 1-ko) was delivered in April 1944. Production rose quickly and widespread regimental service was rapidly achieved.

Although possessing somewhat temperamental ground handling characteristics, the Ki.84 displayed exceptionally tractable flying qualities, comparatively inexperienced pilots converting after the briefest of training. In common with most of its contemporaries, the elevators tended to heavy up at high speeds and the rudder became somewhat mushy at low speeds, but in all other respects the Ki.84 offered superlative handling; it could out-climb and out-manoeuvre any adversary, and it was never to be outclassed.

By the beginning of 1945, the Ki.84 had become the most numerous of Japanese Army fighters, and acceptances of this redoubtable warplane (both pre-production and production) were to total 3,470 aircraft.

**SPECIFICATION: Ki.84-I-ko Hayate**
**Power Plant:** One Nakajima Ha-45-21 18-cylinder radial air-cooled engine rated at 2,000 hp at 3,000 rpm for take-off and 1,860 hp at 5,905 ft (1 800 m). Four-bladed Pe-32 constant-speed propeller. Internal fuel, 153 Imp gal (696 l), with provision for two 44 Imp gal (200 l) drop tanks.

**Key to Nakajima Ki.84-1-Ko Hayate**
1 Starter dog
2 Spinner
3 Constant-speed electrically-operated Pe-32 propeller
4 Propeller reduction gear housing
5 Carburettor air intake
6 Starboard 20-mm Ho 5 cannon muzzle
7 Gun camera port
8 Starboard leading-edge fuel tank (14·7 Imp gal/67 l capacity)
9 Mainspar
10 Starboard navigation light
11 Starboard wingtip
12 Fabric-covered aileron
13 Aileron control link fairing
14 Aileron trim tab
15 Flap track extension fairing
16 Starboard Fowler-type "butterfly" combat flap
17 Wing cannon ammunition box access
18 Wing cannon access covers
19 Carburettor intake trunking
20 Machine gun blast tube
21 Machine gun trough
22 Nakajima Ha-45-21 engine
23 Cowling fasteners
24 Aluminium cylinder fans
25 Oil cooler intake
26 Starboard mainwheel
27 Oil cooler housing
28 Ejector exhaust stubs
29 Cowling grills
30 Engine bearers
31 Oil tank (11 Imp gal/50 l capacity)
32 Vent
33 Gun cooling muffle
34 Firewall/bulkhead
35 Ho-103 machine gun (two) of 12·7-mm calibre
36 Main fuel tank (47·7 Imp gal/217 l capacity)
37 Port ammunition tank (350 rounds)
38 Fuel filler cap
39 Rudder pedals
40 Control column
41 Instrument panel
42 Fuselage flush-riveted stressed-skin panels
43 Reflector sight (offset to starboard)
44 Armourglass (65-mm) windscreen
45 Aft-sliding cockpit canopy
46 Canopy lock/release
47 Pilot's headrest
48 Pilot's head armour/turnover support
49 Canopy fixed aft fairing
50 Canopy track
51 Entry handgrip
52 Pilot's 13-mm back armour
53 Elevator trim handwheel
54 Pilot's seat (adjustable vertically)
55 Throttle quadrant
56 Flap setting lever
57 Undercarriage selector lever
58 Underfloor control runs
59 Flap-rod linkage
60 Water-methanol tank
61 Mid-fuselage construction break
62 Radio equipment tray
63 Type 4 Hi-3 radio pack
64 Aerial lead-in
65 Aerial mast
66 Aerials
67 Light alloy semi-monocoque fuselage structure
68 Fuselage upper longeron
69 Oval-section fuselage and frames
70 Aft fuselage construction break
71 Starboard tailplane
72 Elevator balance
73 Starboard elevator (fabric-covered)
74 Elevator trim tab
75 Tailfin leading edge
76 Tailfin structure
77 Rear navigation/formation light
78 Aerial stub attachment
79 Rudder upper hinge
80 Rudder frame (fabric covered)
81 Rudder trim tab
82 Rudder centre hinge
83 Rudder lower section
84 Elevator trim tab
85 Elevator frame (fabric covered)
86 Tailplane structure
87 Tailwheel doors
88 Solid rudder tyre
89 Aft-retracting tailwheel
90 Fuselage lower longeron
91 Tail surface control cables
92 Oxygen cylinders
93 Radio access
94 Retractable entry step
95 Wing root fairing
96 Fairing former
97 Port main wing tank (40 Imp gal/173 l capacity)
98 Fuel filler cap
99 Wing spar
100 Undercarriage leg cut-outs
101 Mainwheel wells
102 Mainwheel doors
103 Port 20-mm Ho-5 cannon muzzle
104 Wheel brake hydraulic lines
105 Shock absorber links
106 Port mainwheel
107 Axle
108 Mainwheel leg fairing
109 Auxiliary fuel tank (43·9 Imp gal/200 l capacity)
110 Landing light
111 Cannon blast tube
112 Cannon access cover
113 Flap tracks
114 Flap track extension fairings
115 Fowler-type "butterfly" flap structure
116 Rear auxiliary spar
117 Cannon ammunition tank (150 rounds)
118 Spar join
119 Port auxiliary leading-edge tank (14·7 Imp gal/67 l capacity)
120 Fuel filler cap
121 Pitot tube
122 Leading-edge structure
123 Main spar outer section
124 Wing ribs
125 Aileron control rod link fairing
126 Aileron trim tab
127 Aileron frame (fabric covered)
128 Wing skinning
129 Port wingtip
130 Port navigation light

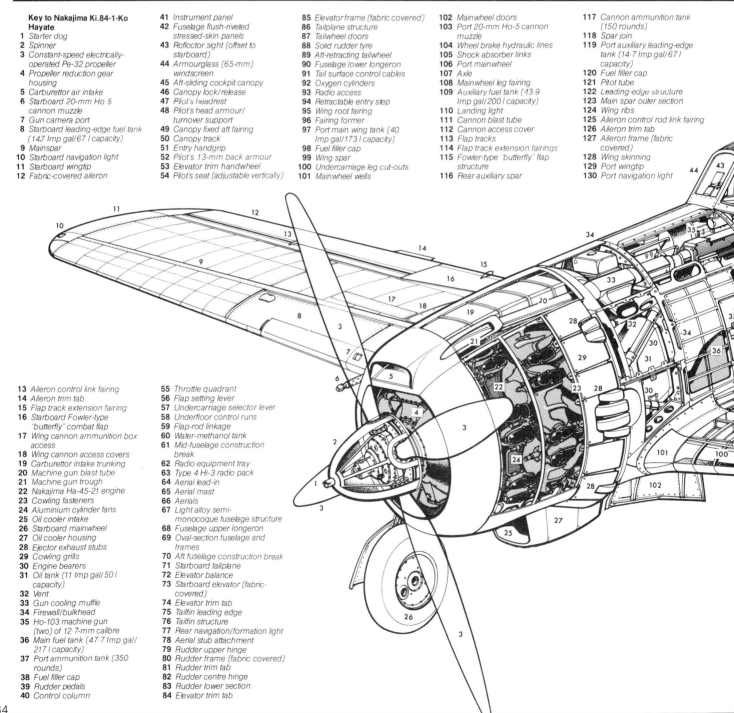

**Performance:** Max speed, 325 mph (523 km/h) at sea level, 362 mph (582 km/h) at 9,840 ft (3 000 m), 388 mph (624 km/h) at 21,325 ft (6 500 m); range (max internal fuel), 1,025 mls (1 650 km) at 178 mph (286 km/h) at 11,640 ft (3 550 m), 780 mls (1 255 km) at 254 mph (408 km/h), (with drop tanks), 1,815 mls (2 920 km) at 173 mph (278 km/h), 1,410 mls (2 270 km) at 241 mph (388 km/h); initial climb, 3,790 ft/min (19,25 m/sec); time to 16,405 ft (5 000 m), 6·42 min, to 26,245 ft (8 000 m), 11·66 min; service ceiling, 36,090 ft (11 000 m).

**Weights:** Empty equipped, 5,864 lb (2 660 kg); normal loaded, 8,192 lb (3 716 kg); max, 9,195 lb (4 171 kg).

**Dimensions:** Span, 36 ft 2 in (11,02 m); length, 32 ft 6½ in (9,92 m); height, 11 ft 1 in (3,38 m); wing area, 226·04 sq ft.

**Armament:** Two 20-mm Ho-5 cannon with 150 rpg and two 13-mm Ho-103 machine guns with 350 rpg. Provision for two bombs of up to 551 lb (250 kg) weight each.

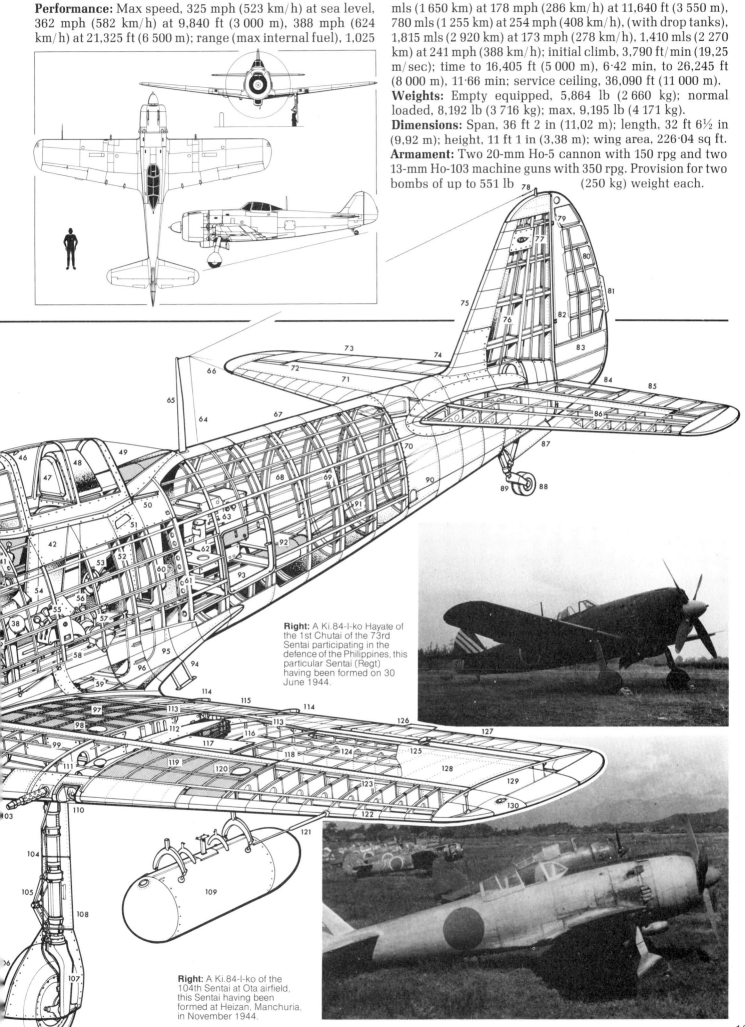

**Right:** A Ki.84-I-ko Hayate of the 1st Chutai of the 73rd Sentai participating in the defence of the Philippines, this particular Sentai (Regt) having been formed on 30 June 1944.

**Right:** A Ki.84-I-ko of the 104th Sentai at Ota airfield, this Sentai having been formed at Heizan, Manchuria, in November 1944.

# Yakovlev Yak-3 (April 1943)

With the changing requirements of aerial warfare as WWII evolved, the practice of developing versions of existing aircraft optimised to cater for one specific portion of the overall fighter combat spectrum was pursued with increasing vigour by all the principal combatants. A noteworthy example of this practice was provided by Aleksandr Yakovlev's bureau as a result of a 1942 order calling for delivery, in the shortest possible time, of an advanced-performance fighter dedicated to the battlefield low-altitude air superiority task.

The time factor left no option but to develop the basic Yak-1 for this specialised role, and one of Yakovlev's team leaders, K.V. Sinelshchikov, was given the task of ascertaining the means of endowing this fighter with the attributes called for. The Klimov bureau was asked to boost the low-altitude performance of its M-105PF engine — a requirement that was to be fulfilled by raising the revs at considerable expense to the TBO — and Sinelshchikov undertook a thorough weight analysis of the design, simultaneously introducing a variety of aerodynamic improvements. The section and basic planform of the Yak-1

wing were retained, but aspect ratio, span and area were reduced; a shallower cockpit canopy with frameless windscreen was designed, and engine cowling contours were refined by transferring the oil cooler intake to the wing root.

Yak-3U

**Key to Yakovlev Yak-3U**

1 Rudder trim tab
2 Rudder structure
3 Rudder post
4 Tail fin structure
5 Aerial attachment
6 Tail fin leading edge spar
7 Spar attachment points
8 Tail fin root fairing
9 Elevator control horns
10 Rudder lower hinge
11 Elevator torque tube
12 Rear navigation light
13 Elevator trim tab
14 Elevator structure
15 Tailplane construction
16 Tailwheel doors
17 Retractable tailwheel
18 Tailwheel oleo
19 Tailwheel well
20 Wheel-impact door-closure struts
21 Tailwheel retraction jack
22 Lifting tube
23 Tubular steel fuselage framework
24 Ventral former
25 Elevator control cables
26 Diagonal brace wires
27 Dorsal former
28 Decking
29 Aerial
30 Aerial attachment/lead-in
31 Canopy fixed aft glazing
32 Armourglass screen
33 Canopy track
34 HF (RSI-6M) radio equipment
35 Accumulator

36 Equipment rack
37 Hydraulic reservoir
38 Ventral coolant radiator housing
39 Control rod linkage
40 Radiator bath aft fairing
41 Radiator
42 Seat support frame
43 Pilot's seat pan
44 Trim tab control console (port)
45 Padded (armoured) seat back
46 Switchbox
47 Aft-sliding cockpit canopy
48 Reflector sight

49 One-piece moulded armourglass windscreen
50 Instrument panel coaming
51 Control column
52 Instrument panel starboard console
53 Control linkage
54 Rudder pedal bar
55 Bulkhead
56 Frame
57 Gun support tray
58 Bracket
59 Shpital'ny-Vladimirov B-20 (MP-20) 20-mm cannon (port and starboard)
60 Port flap

61 Guide rollers
62 Aileron push-rod control linkage
63 Aileron trim tab
64 Port aileron
65 Port wingtip
66 Port navigation light
67 Pitot tube

68 Forward spar
69 Port outboard fuel tank
70 Fuel filler cap
71 Supercharger intake scoop
72 Intake ducting
73 Gun cocking mechanism fairings
74 Supercharger housing

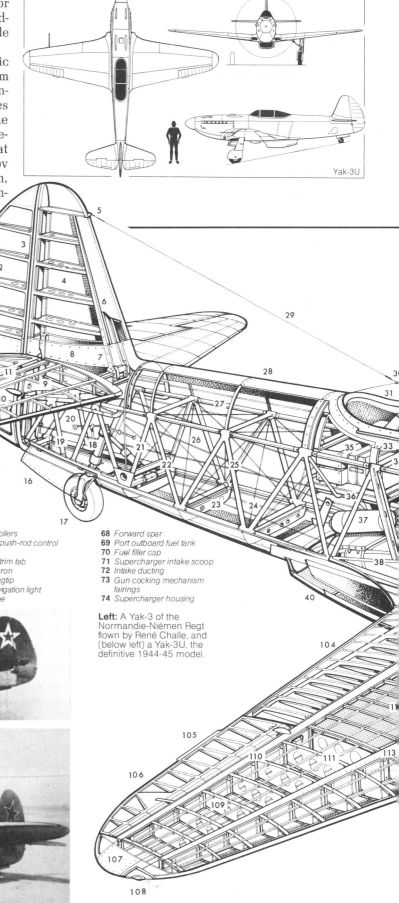

**Left:** A Yak-3 of the Normandie-Niémen Regt flown by René Challe, and (below left) a Yak-3U, the definitive 1944-45 model.

The result, the Yak-3, was flown in April 1943, reaching frontline regiments in quantity early summer 1944. Exceptionally light on the ailerons, light stick pressures producing fast and accurate snap rolls, the Yak-3 proved outstandingly manoeuvrable. It could complete a full 360 deg combat turn in 18·5 seconds, starting at 3,280 ft (1 000 m) and gaining 3,940 ft (1 200 m) in the process. Stalling speed was high, however, and there was a marked tendency to drop a wing on the approach unless speed was kept up.

In the late autumn of 1943, the Yak-3 airframe was mated with the 1,650 hp M-107A engine, production commencing a year later as the Yak-3U, and, three months later still, the mixed structure giving place to one of metal throughout with light alloy stressed skinning. Production of this definitive Yak-3U was to continue until early 1946, when 4,848 Yak-3s of all types had been built. The Yak-3U was the fastest of all production piston-engined Yakovlev fighters, its speed ranging from 386 mph (622 km/h) at 1,640 ft (500 m) to 447 mph (720 km/h) at 18,045 ft (5 500 m), but it entered service too late to achieve operational deployment during World War II.

**SPECIFICATION: Yak-3**
**Power Plant:** One Klimov M-105PF-2 12-cylinder vee liquid-cooled engine rated at 1,244 hp at 2,700 rpm for take-off and 1,300 hp at 2,625 ft (800 m). Three-bladed VISh-105SV constant-speed propeller. Internal fuel capacity, 60·5 Imp gal (275 l).
**Performance:** Max speed, 367 mph (590 km/h) at sea level, 384 mph (618 km/h) at 3,280 ft (1 000 m), 390 mph (628 km/h) at 6,560 ft (2 000 m), 407 mph (655 km/h) at 10,170 ft (3 100 m); range, 416 mls (670 km) at 332 mph (534 km/h), 560 mls (900 km) at 193 mph (310 km/h); initial climb, 3,800 ft/min (19,3 m/sec); time to 16,405 ft (5 000 m), 4·1 min; service ceiling, 35,450 ft (10 800 m).
**Weights:** Empty equipped, 4,641 lb (2 105 kg); normal loaded, 5,864 lb (2 660 kg).
**Dimensions:** Span, 30 ft 2¼ in (9,20 m); length, 27 ft 10¼ in (8,49 m); height, 7 ft 11¼ in (2,42 m); wing area, 159·63 sq ft (14,83 m²).
**Armament:** One 20-mm Shpital'ny-Vladimirov ShVAK cannon with 120 rounds and two 12,7-mm Berezin UB machine guns with 250 rpg.

75 Cowling frame
76 Engine bearer/firewall attachment
77 Oil tank
78 Ammunition boxes
79 Cowling aft frame
80 Exhaust stubs
81 Blast tubes
82 Gun muzzle troughs
83 Filler cap
84 Coolant header tank
85 Propeller pitch mechanism
86 VISh-107 variable-pitch metal propeller
87 Propeller spinner

88 Propeller hub
89 Auxiliary intake
90 Cowling attachment frames
91 Klimov M-107A (VK-107A) 12-cylinder liquid-cooled Vee engine
92 Coolant ducting
93 Port mainwheel
94 Engine bearer
95 Oil cooler intake
96 Ducting
97 Mainwheel well door inboard section
98 Wheel-impact door-closure struts

99 Mainspar cut-out
100 Oil cooler housing
101 Oil cooler outlet fairing
102 Radiator intake
103 Radiator grill
104 Inset flap structure
105 Aileron trim tab
106 Aileron frame
107 Starboard wingtip

108 Starboard navigation light
109 Outboard wing ribs
110 Rear spar
111 Stringers
112 Starboard outboard fuel tank
113 Front spar
114 Undercarriage/spar attachment plate
115 Undercarriage retraction cylinder

116 Mainwheel leg well
117 Undercarriage downlock strut
118 Brake lines
119 Torque links
120 Mainwheel oleo leg
121 Mainwheel leg fairing plate
122 Mainwheel fairing plate
123 Axle fork
124 Starboard mainwheel

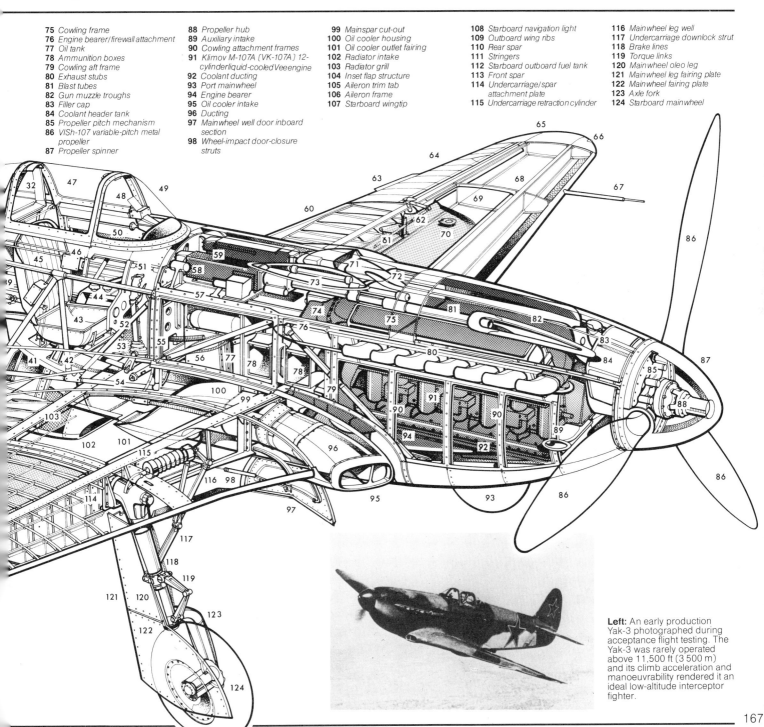

**Left:** An early production Yak-3 photographed during acceptance flight testing. The Yak-3 was rarely operated above 11,500 ft (3 500 m) and its climb acceleration and manoeuvrability rendered it an ideal low-altitude interceptor fighter.

# De Havilland Vampire (September 1943)

In view of the comparatively low thrusts afforded by early turbojets, the friction losses that were the inevitable consequence of long intake ducts and tailplanes could be ill afforded by designers of first-generation jet fighters. As a means of overcoming the problem in a single-engined arrangement, R.E. Bishop and his team opted, in designing the Vampire, for a twin-boom configuration, the turbojet being mounted in a short central nacelle drawing air from wing root intakes and exhausting between the tailbooms. While this configuration was not to see general acceptance, it was to characterise all de Havilland jet fighters, being retained successively for the Venom and Sea Vixen.

The Vampire was flown on 26 September 1943, the production F Mk 1 flying 19 months later, on 20 April 1945, and 268 being built. With the 41st aircraft, the 2,700 lb (1 225 kg) Goblin 1 turbojet gave place to the 3,100 lb (1 406 kg) Goblin 2, the 51st aircraft introducing cabin pressuriza-tion. The F Mk 1 was superseded by the F Mk 3, which, with increased internal fuel and redesigned tail, flew on 4 November 1946, 209 being built plus 80 essentially similar F Mk 30s in Australia.

Unquestionably one of the most aerobatic jet fighters ever to enter service, the Vampire was particularly note-worthy for the outstanding lightness and sensitivity of its controls at speed, remarkable manoeuvrability being demonstrated within the 400-500 mph (645-805 km/h) speed range. Between Mach=0·71 and 0·76, however, the Vampire tended to porpoise with marked wing buffet. At lower speeds, coarse use of the small rudders was neces-sary to maintain height in steep turns and the Vampire stalled easily in comparatively shallow turns, a wing dropping sharply. The power response of the Goblin was leisurely and rapid throttle movements could result in engine surge or flame out. No relight system was provided and thus a flame out rendered a forced landing inevitable.

Introduced in 1948 as a fighter-bomber, the FB Mk 5 was to prove the most proliferous version of the Vampire and was widely exported. In addition to 1,149 built in the

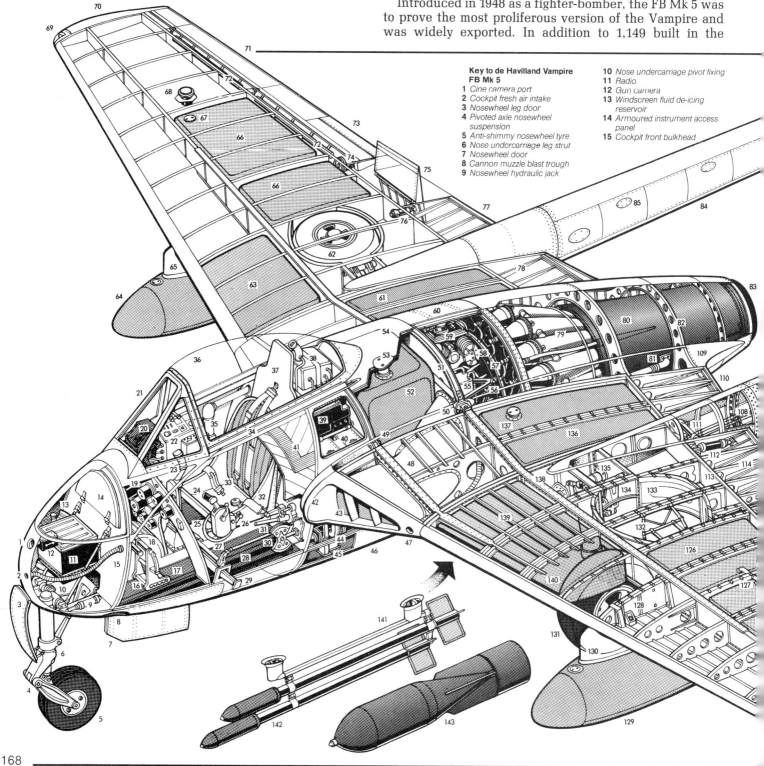

Key to de Havilland Vampire
FB Mk 5
1 Cine camera port
2 Cockpit fresh air intake
3 Nosewheel leg door
4 Pivoted axle nosewheel suspension
5 Anti-shimmy nosewheel tyre
6 Nose undercarriage leg strut
7 Nosewheel door
8 Cannon muzzle blast trough
9 Nosewheel hydraulic jack
10 Nose undercarriage pivot fixing
11 Radio
12 Gun camera
13 Windscreen fluid de-icing reservoir
14 Armoured instrument access panel
15 Cockpit front bulkhead

UK—plus 302 examples of the tropicalised FB Mk 9—it was licence-built in France (67), Italy (80) and India (281) as the FB Mk 52, and in Switzerland (100) as the FB Mk 6.

## SPECIFICATION: Vampire FB Mk 5

**Power Plant:** One de Havilland Goblin 2 centrifugal-flow turbojet rated at 3,100 lb (1 406 kg) thrust. Internal fuel capacity, 330 Imp gal (1 500 l), with provision for two 100 Imp gal (455 l) drop tanks.

**Performance:** Max speed, 531 mph (854 km/h) at sea level, 525 mph (845 km/h) at 17,500 ft (5 335 m), 505 mph (813 km/h) at 30,000 ft (9 145 m); range (with drop tanks), 590 mls (950 km) at 350 mph (563 km/h) at sea level, 1,145 mls (1 843 km) at 30,000 ft (9 145 m); initial climb, 4,050 ft/min (20,57 m/sec); service ceiling, 43,500 ft (13 255 m).

**Weights:** Empty, 7,253 lb (3 290 kg); normal loaded, 10,520 lb (4 772 kg); max, 12,360 lb (5 606 kg).

**Dimensions:** Span, 38 ft 0 in (11,58 m); length, 30 ft 9 in (9,37 m); height, 6 ft 2 in (1,88 m); wing area, 262 sq ft (24,34 m²).

**Armament:** Four 20-mm Hispano cannon with 125 rpg, plus one 500-lb (226,8-kg) or 1,000-lb (453,6-kg) bombs.

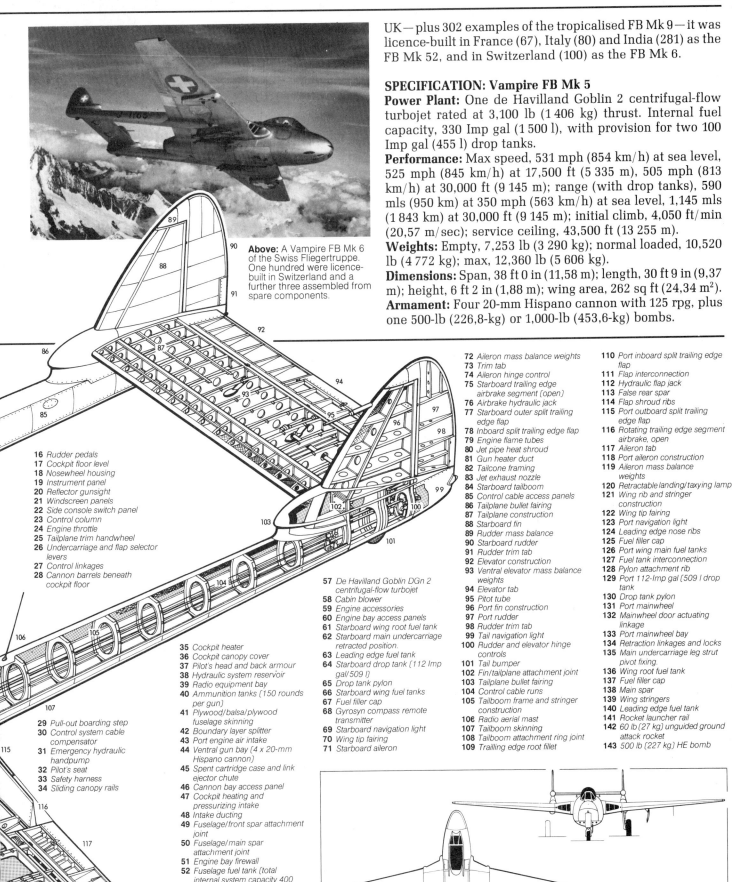

**Above:** A Vampire FB Mk 6 of the Swiss Fliegertruppe. One hundred were licence-built in Switzerland and a further three assembled from spare components.

16 Rudder pedals
17 Cockpit floor level
18 Nosewheel housing
19 Instrument panel
20 Reflector gunsight
21 Windscreen panels
22 Side console switch panel
23 Control column
24 Engine throttle
25 Tailplane trim handwheel
26 Undercarriage and flap selector levers
27 Control linkages
28 Cannon barrels beneath cockpit floor
29 Pull-out boarding step
30 Control system cable compensator
31 Emergency hydraulic handpump
32 Pilot's seat
33 Safety harness
34 Sliding canopy rails
35 Cockpit heater
36 Cockpit canopy cover
37 Pilot's head and back armour
38 Hydraulic system reservoir
39 Radio equipment bay
40 Ammunition tanks (150 rounds per gun)
41 Plywood/balsa/plywood fuselage skinning
42 Boundary layer splitter
43 Port engine air intake
44 Ventral gun bay (4 x 20-mm Hispano cannon)
45 Spent cartridge case and link ejector chute
46 Cannon bay access panel
47 Cockpit heating and pressurizing intake
48 Intake ducting
49 Fuselage/front spar attachment joint
50 Fuselage/main spar attachment joint
51 Engine bay firewall
52 Fuselage fuel tank (total internal system capacity 400 Imp gal/1818 l)
53 Fuel filler cap
54 Wooden skin section fabric covering
55 Cockpit air heat exchanger
56 Engine bearer struts
57 De Havilland Goblin DGn 2 centrifugal-flow turbojet
58 Cabin blower
59 Engine accessories
60 Engine bay access panels
61 Starboard wing root fuel tank
62 Starboard main undercarriage retracted position.
63 Leading edge fuel tank
64 Starboard drop tank (112 Imp gal/509 l)
65 Drop tank pylon
66 Starboard wing fuel tanks
67 Fuel filler cap
68 Gyrosyn compass remote transmitter
69 Starboard navigation light
70 Wing tip fairing
71 Starboard aileron
72 Aileron mass balance weights
73 Trim tab
74 Aileron hinge control
75 Starboard trailing edge airbrake segment (open)
76 Airbrake hydraulic jack
77 Starboard outer split trailing edge flap
78 Inboard split trailing edge flap
79 Engine flame tubes
80 Jet pipe heat shroud
81 Gun heater duct
82 Tailcone framing
83 Jet exhaust nozzle
84 Starboard tailboom
85 Control cable access panels
86 Tailplane bullet fairing
87 Tailplane construction
88 Starboard fin
89 Rudder mass balance
90 Starboard rudder
91 Rudder trim tab
92 Elevator construction
93 Ventral elevator mass balance weights
94 Elevator tab
95 Pitot tube
96 Port fin construction
97 Port rudder
98 Rudder trim tab
99 Tail navigation light
100 Rudder and elevator hinge controls
101 Tail bumper
102 Fin/tailplane attachment joint
103 Tailplane bullet fairing
104 Control cable runs
105 Tailboom frame and stringer construction
106 Radio aerial mast
107 Tailboom skinning
108 Tailboom attachment ring joint
109 Trailling edge root fillet
110 Port inboard split trailing edge flap
111 Flap interconnection
112 Hydraulic flap jack
113 False rear spar
114 Flap shroud ribs
115 Port outboard split trailing edge flap
116 Rotating trailing edge segment airbrake, open
117 Aileron tab
118 Port aileron construction
119 Aileron mass balance weights
120 Retractable landing/taxying lamp
121 Wing rib and stringer construction
122 Wing tip fairing
123 Port navigation light
124 Leading edge nose ribs
125 Fuel filler cap
126 Port wing main fuel tanks
127 Fuel tank interconnection
128 Pylon attachment rib
129 Port 112-Imp gal (509 l) drop tank
130 Drop tank pylon
131 Port mainwheel
132 Mainwheel door actuating linkage
133 Port mainwheel bay
134 Retraction linkages and locks
135 Main undercarriage leg strut pivot fixing.
136 Wing root fuel tank
137 Fuel filler cap
138 Main spar
139 Wing stringers
140 Leading edge fuel tank
141 Rocket launcher rail
142 60 lb (27 kg) unguided ground attack rocket
143 500 lb (227 kg) HE bomb

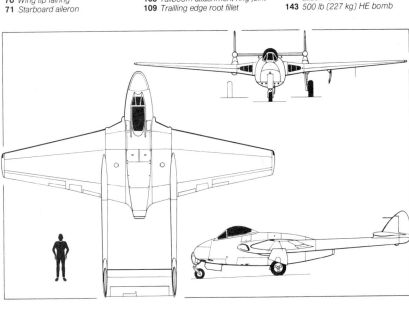

# Lockheed F-80 Shooting Star (January 1944)

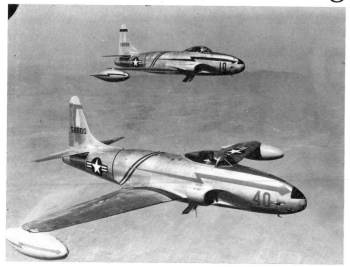

**Above:** P-80B Shooting Stars of the 36th Fighter Group, USAF, which were deployed to Europe and are seen here flying over West Germany.

More advanced conceptually and aerodynamically than either of its British contemporaries, the Shooting Star was, nevertheless, to suffer the indignity, within five years of service entry, of establishing that the legacy of advanced aerodynamic data left by Germany had already rendered first-generation jet fighters patently obsolete. This was to be demonstrated dramatically over Korea late in 1950, when the Shooting Star encountered the MiG-15 in the first jet-versus-jet mêlées. The Shooting Star was totally outclassed. Too late for WWII, it was already outdated when the Korean conflict commenced a mere half-decade later!

The first jet fighter accepted for operational use by the US forces, the Shooting Star was designed by Clarence L. Johnson around the British Halford H-1B turbojet, and the XP-80 flew with this power plant on 8 January 1944. Allis-Chalmers' inability to deliver a licence-built version of the H-1B within an acceptable timescale dictated fundamental redesign for the General Electric I-40 (J33-GE-11), and as the XP-80A, with increased overall dimensions and fuel tankage, a further prototype flew on 10 June 1944, 138 days from commencement of redesign.

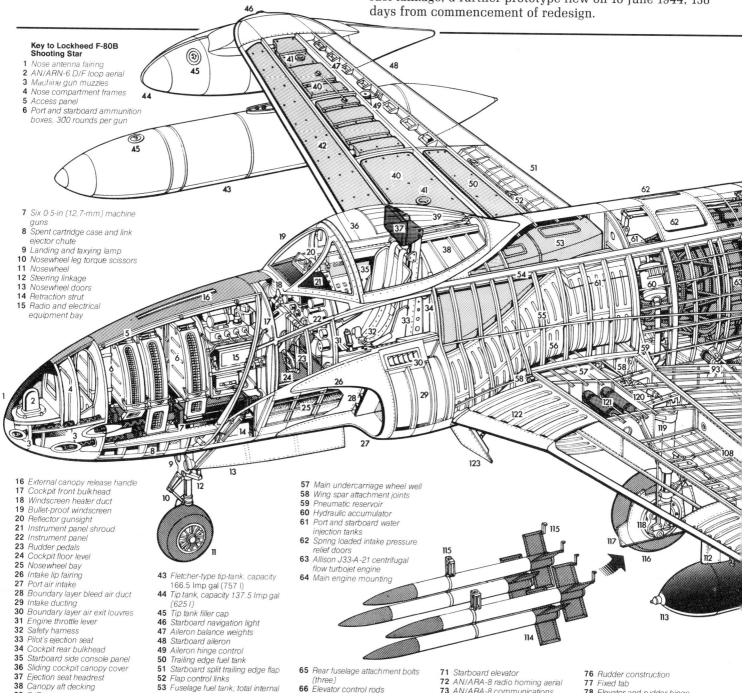

**Key to Lockheed F-80B Shooting Star**

1 Nose antenna fairing
2 AN/ARN-6 D/F loop aerial
3 Machine gun muzzles
4 Nose compartment frames
5 Access panel
6 Port and starboard ammunition boxes, 300 rounds per gun
7 Six 0.5-in (12,7-mm) machine guns
8 Spent cartridge case and link ejector chute
9 Landing and taxying lamp
10 Nosewheel leg torque scissors
11 Nosewheel
12 Steering linkage
13 Nosewheel doors
14 Retraction strut
15 Radio and electrical equipment bay
16 External canopy release handle
17 Cockpit front bulkhead
18 Windscreen heater duct
19 Bullet-proof windscreen
20 Reflector gunsight
21 Instrument panel shroud
22 Instrument panel
23 Rudder pedals
24 Cockpit floor level
25 Nosewheel bay
26 Intake lip fairing
27 Port air intake
28 Boundary layer bleed air duct
29 Intake ducting
30 Boundary layer air exit louvres
31 Engine throttle lever
32 Safety harness
33 Pilot's ejection seat
34 Cockpit rear bulkhead
35 Starboard side console panel
36 Sliding cockpit canopy cover
37 Ejection seat headrest
38 Canopy aft decking
39 D/F sense antenna
40 Starboard wing fuel tanks
41 Fuel filler caps
42 Leading edge tank

43 Fletcher-type tip-tank, capacity 166.5 Imp gal (757 l)
44 Tip tank, capacity 137.5 Imp gal (625 l)
45 Tip tank filler cap
46 Starboard navigation light
47 Aileron balance weights
48 Starboard aileron
49 Aileron hinge control
50 Trailing edge fuel tank
51 Starboard split trailing edge flap
52 Flap control links
53 Fuselage fuel tank; total internal capacity 354 Imp gal (1609 l)
54 Fuselage main longeron
55 Centre fuselage frames
56 Intake trunking

57 Main undercarriage wheel well
58 Wing spar attachment joints
59 Pneumatic reservoir
60 Hydraulic accumulator
61 Port and starboard water injection tanks
62 Spring loaded intake pressure relief doors
63 Allison J33-A-21 centrifugal flow turbojet engine
64 Main engine mounting

65 Rear fuselage attachment bolts (three)
66 Elevator control rods
67 Jet pipe bracing cables
68 Fin root fillet
69 Elevator control link
70 Starboard tailplane

71 Starboard elevator
72 AN/ARA-8 radio homing aerial
73 AN/ARA-8 communications aerial
74 Pitot tube
75 AN/ARC-3 radio "pick-axe" antenna

76 Rudder construction
77 Fixed tab
78 Elevator and rudder hinge controls
79 Tail navigation light
80 Jet pipe nozzle
81 Elevator tabs

Exceptionally clean aerodynamically, the P-80 set several design precedents; it featured hydraulically-boosted control surfaces, fuselage-mounted airbrakes and a detachable aft fuselage. Thirteen YP-80As preceded delivery in February 1945 of the first production P-80A, 677 of which were built (including 114 as photo-recce FP-80As), to be followed by 240 P-80Bs with thinner wing, ejection seat and a water-injection-boosted J33-A-21 turbojet. The definitive model was the J33-A-23-powered P-80C of which 798 were built during 1948-49, a further 254 A- and B-models being converted to similar standards.

The P-80 was redesignated F-80 in June 1948, and with the appearance of the MiG-15 over Korea was relegated to the fighter-bomber role until April 1953, being withdrawn from first-line USAF squadrons within eight months of the end of the Korean conflict.

## SPECIFICATION: P-80A-1 Shooting Star

**Power Plant:** One General Electric (Allison-built) J33-A-9 or GE-11 centrifugal-flow turbojet rated at 3,850 lb (1 746 kg) thrust. Internal fuel capacity, 354 Imp gal (1 609 l), with provision for two 137·5 Imp gal (625 l) or 191·5 Imp gal (871 l) wingtip drop tanks.

**Performance:** Max speed, 558 mph (898 km/h) at sea level, 548 mph (882 km/h) at 10,000 ft (3 050 m), 533 mph (858 km/h) at 20,000 ft (6 100 m); range (internal fuel), 780 mls (1 255 km) at 410 mph (660 km/h) at 35,000 ft (10 670 m), (two 137·5 Imp gal/625 l drop tanks), 1,100 mls (1 770 km) at 407 mph (655 km/h) at 25,000 ft (7 620 m); time to 5,000 ft (1 525 m), 1·2 min, to 10,000 ft (3 050 m), 2·4 min, to 20,000 ft (6 100 m), 5·5 min; service ceiling, 45,000 ft (13 715 m).

**Weights:** Empty, 7,920 lb (3 593 kg); normal loaded, 11,700 lb (5 307 kg); max, 14,000 lb (6 350 kg).

**Dimensions:** Span, 38 ft 10½ in (11,85 m); length, 34 ft 6 in (10,51 m); height, 11 ft 4 in (3,45 m); wing area, 237·6 sq ft.

**Armament:** Six 0·50-in (12,7-mm) Colt-Browning M-2 machine guns with 300 rpg; provision for 2 × 500-lb (226,8-kg) or 1,000-lb (453,6-kg) bombs, or 10 × 5-in (12,7-cm) rockets.

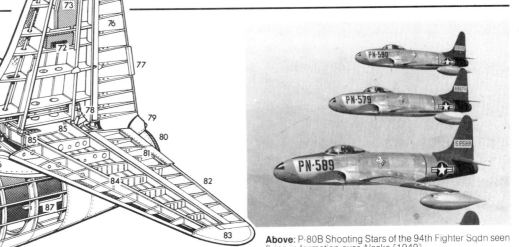

**Above:** P-80B Shooting Stars of the 94th Fighter Sqdn seen flying in formation over Alaska (1949).

| | | |
|---|---|---|
| 82 Port elevator construction | 87 Jet pipe mounting rail | 106 Tip tank mounting and jettison control |
| 83 Elevator mass balance | 88 Gyrosyn radio compass flux valve | 107 Detachable lower wing skin/fuel tank bay panels |
| 84 Tailplane construction | 89 Rear fuselage frame and stringer construction | 108 Port wing fuel tank bays |
| 85 Fin/tailplane attachment joints | 90 Fuselage skin plating | 109 Inter tank bay ribs |
| 86 Tailplane fillet fairing | 91 Jet pipe support frame | 110 Front spar |
| | 92 Trailing edge wing root fillet | 111 Corrugated leading edge inner skin |
| | 93 Flap drive motor | 112 Port stores pylon |
| | 94 Port split trailing edge flap | 113 1,000-lb (454-kg) HE bomb |
| | 95 Flap shroud ribs | 114 5-in (12,7-cm) HVAR ground attack rockets (10 rockets maximum load) |
| | 96 Trailing edge fuel tank bay | 115 HVAR rocket mountings |
| | 97 Rear spar | 116 Port mainwheel |
| | 98 Trailing edge ribs | 117 Mainwheel doors |
| | 99 Port aileron tab | 118 Wheel brake pad |
| | 100 Aileron hinge control | 119 Main undercarriage leg strut |
| | 101 Upper skin panel aileron hinge line | 120 Retraction jack |
| | 102 Aileron construction | 121 Oxygen tanks |
| | 103 Wing tip fairing construction | 122 Wing root leading edge extension |
| | 104 Tip tank | 123 Port ventral airbrake |
| | 105 Port navigation light | |

# Grumman F8F Bearcat (August 1944)

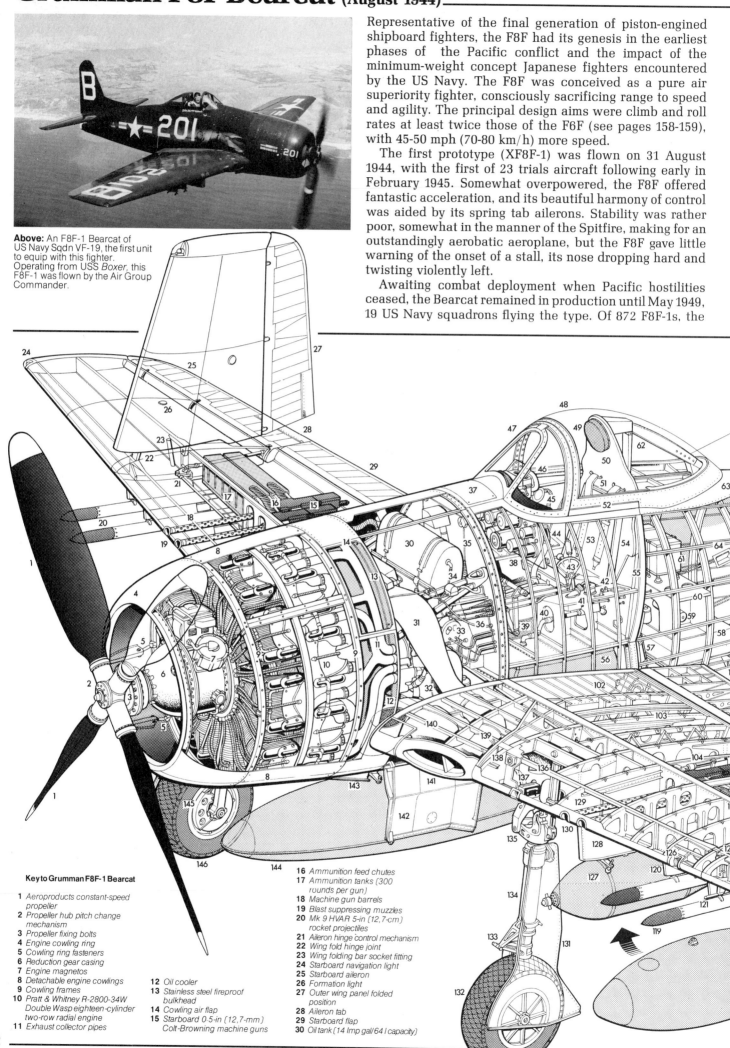

**Above:** An F8F-1 Bearcat of US Navy Sqdn VF-19, the first unit to equip with this fighter. Operating from USS *Boxer*, this F8F-1 was flown by the Air Group Commander.

Representative of the final generation of piston-engined shipboard fighters, the F8F had its genesis in the earliest phases of the Pacific conflict and the impact of the minimum-weight concept Japanese fighters encountered by the US Navy. The F8F was conceived as a pure air superiority fighter, consciously sacrificing range to speed and agility. The principal design aims were climb and roll rates at least twice those of the F6F (see pages 158-159), with 45-50 mph (70-80 km/h) more speed.

The first prototype (XF8F-1) was flown on 31 August 1944, with the first of 23 trials aircraft following early in February 1945. Somewhat overpowered, the F8F offered fantastic acceleration, and its beautiful harmony of control was aided by its spring tab ailerons. Stability was rather poor, somewhat in the manner of the Spitfire, making for an outstandingly aerobatic aeroplane, but the F8F gave little warning of the onset of a stall, its nose dropping hard and twisting violently left.

Awaiting combat deployment when Pacific hostilities ceased, the Bearcat remained in production until May 1949, 19 US Navy squadrons flying the type. Of 872 F8F-1s, the

**Key to Grumman F8F-1 Bearcat**

1 Aeroproducts constant-speed propeller
2 Propeller hub pitch change mechanism
3 Propeller fixing bolts
4 Engine cowling ring
5 Cowling ring fasteners
6 Reduction gear casing
7 Engine magnetos
8 Detachable engine cowlings
9 Cowling frames
10 Pratt & Whitney R-2800-34W Double Wasp eighteen-cylinder two-row radial engine
11 Exhaust collector pipes
12 Oil cooler
13 Stainless steel fireproof bulkhead
14 Cowling air flap
15 Starboard 0.5-in (12.7-mm) Colt-Browning machine guns
16 Ammunition feed chutes
17 Ammunition tanks (300 rounds per gun)
18 Machine gun barrels
19 Blast suppressing muzzles
20 Mk 9 HVAR 5-in (12.7-cm) rocket projectiles
21 Aileron hinge control mechanism
22 Wing fold hinge joint
23 Wing folding bar socket fitting
24 Starboard navigation light
25 Starboard aileron
26 Formation light
27 Outer wing panel folded position
28 Aileron tab
29 Starboard flap
30 Oil tank (14 Imp gal/64 l capacity)

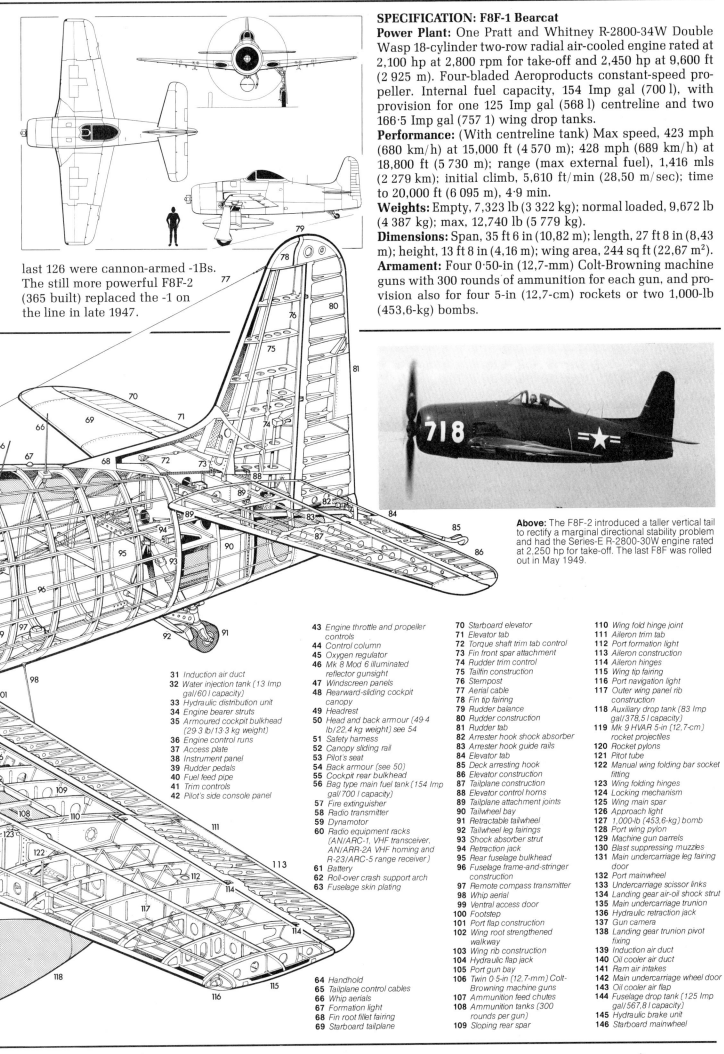

**SPECIFICATION: F8F-1 Bearcat**

**Power Plant:** One Pratt and Whitney R-2800-34W Double Wasp 18-cylinder two-row radial air-cooled engine rated at 2,100 hp at 2,800 rpm for take-off and 2,450 hp at 9,600 ft (2 925 m). Four-bladed Aeroproducts constant-speed propeller. Internal fuel capacity, 154 Imp gal (700 l), with provision for one 125 Imp gal (568 l) centreline and two 166·5 Imp gal (757 1) wing drop tanks.

**Performance:** (With centreline tank) Max speed, 423 mph (680 km/h) at 15,000 ft (4 570 m); 428 mph (689 km/h) at 18,800 ft (5 730 m); range (max external fuel), 1,416 mls (2 279 km); initial climb, 5,610 ft/min (28,50 m/sec); time to 20,000 ft (6 095 m), 4·9 min.

**Weights:** Empty, 7,323 lb (3 322 kg); normal loaded, 9,672 lb (4 387 kg); max, 12,740 lb (5 779 kg).

**Dimensions:** Span, 35 ft 6 in (10,82 m); length, 27 ft 8 in (8,43 m); height, 13 ft 8 in (4,16 m); wing area, 244 sq ft (22,67 m²).

**Armament:** Four 0·50-in (12,7-mm) Colt-Browning machine guns with 300 rounds of ammunition for each gun, and provision also for four 5-in (12,7-cm) rockets or two 1,000-lb (453,6-kg) bombs.

last 126 were cannon-armed -1Bs. The still more powerful F8F-2 (365 built) replaced the -1 on the line in late 1947.

**Above:** The F8F-2 introduced a taller vertical tail to rectify a marginal directional stability problem and had the Series-E R-2800-30W engine rated at 2,250 hp for take-off. The last F8F was rolled out in May 1949.

31 Induction air duct
32 Water injection tank (13 Imp gal/60 l capacity)
33 Hydraulic distribution unit
34 Engine bearer struts
35 Armoured cockpit bulkhead (29·3 lb/13·3 kg weight)
36 Engine control runs
37 Access plate
38 Instrument panel
39 Rudder pedals
40 Fuel feed pipe
41 Trim controls
42 Pilot's side console panel

43 Engine throttle and propeller controls
44 Control column
45 Oxygen regulator
46 Mk 8 Mod 6 illuminated reflector gunsight
47 Windscreen panels
48 Rearward-sliding cockpit canopy
49 Headrest
50 Head and back armour (49·4 lb/22,4 kg weight) see 54
51 Safety harness
52 Canopy sliding rail
53 Pilot's seat
54 Back armour (see 50)
55 Cockpit rear bulkhead
56 Bag type main fuel tank (154 Imp gal/700 l capacity)
57 Fire extinguisher
58 Radio transmitter
59 Dynamotor
60 Radio equipment racks (AN/ARC-1, VHF transceiver, AN/ARR-2A VHF homing and R-23/ARC-5 range receiver)
61 Battery
62 Roll-over crash support arch
63 Fuselage skin plating
64 Handhold
65 Tailplane control cables
66 Whip aerials
67 Formation light
68 Fin root fillet fairing
69 Starboard tailplane

70 Starboard elevator
71 Elevator tab
72 Torque shaft trim tab control
73 Fin front spar attachment
74 Rudder trim control
75 Tailfin construction
76 Sternpost
77 Aerial cable
78 Fin tip fairing
79 Rudder balance
80 Rudder construction
81 Rudder tab
82 Arrester hook shock absorber
83 Arrester hook guide rails
84 Elevator tab
85 Deck arresting hook
86 Elevator construction
87 Tailplane construction
88 Elevator control horns
89 Tailplane attachment joints
90 Tailwheel bay
91 Retractable tailwheel
92 Tailwheel leg fairings
93 Shock absorber strut
94 Retraction jack
95 Rear fuselage bulkhead
96 Fuselage frame-and-stringer construction
97 Remote compass transmitter
98 Whip aerial
99 Ventral access door
100 Footstep
101 Port flap construction
102 Wing root strengthened walkway
103 Wing rib construction
104 Hydraulic flap jack
105 Port gun bay
106 Twin 0·5-in (12,7-mm) Colt-Browning machine guns
107 Ammunition feed chutes
108 Ammunition tanks (300 rounds per gun)
109 Sloping rear spar

110 Wing fold hinge joint
111 Aileron trim tab
112 Port formation light
113 Aileron construction
114 Aileron hinges
115 Wing tip fairing
116 Port navigation light
117 Outer wing panel rib construction
118 Auxiliary drop tank (83 Imp gal/378,5 l capacity)
119 Mk 9 HVAR 5-in (12,7-cm) rocket projectiles
120 Rocket pylons
121 Pitot tube
122 Manual wing folding bar socket fitting
123 Wing folding hinges
124 Locking mechanism
125 Wing main spar
126 Approach light
127 1,000-lb (453,6-kg) bomb
128 Port wing pylon
129 Machine gun barrels
130 Blast suppressing muzzles
131 Main undercarriage leg fairing door
132 Port mainwheel
133 Undercarriage scissor links
134 Landing gear air-oil shock strut
135 Main undercarriage trunion
136 Hydraulic retraction jack
137 Gun camera
138 Landing gear trunion pivot fixing
139 Induction air duct
140 Oil cooler air duct
141 Ram air intakes
142 Main undercarriage wheel door
143 Oil cooler air flap
144 Fuselage drop tank (125 Imp gal/567,8 l capacity)
145 Hydraulic brake unit
146 Starboard mainwheel

# Hawker Sea Fury (September 1944)

A contemporary of the Bearcat (see pages 172-173), with much the same installed power, but rather larger and 20 per cent heavier, the Sea Fury was similarly representative of the zenith of long years of propeller-driven fighter development overtaken by technological advances while still in infancy. As with the Bearcat, the Sea Fury's arrival aboard the carriers signified the beginning of the end of the piston-engined shipboard fighter era. It was to write the finalé to its genre in the skies above Korea during 1950-1952.

Initially evolved in both shipboard and land-based versions, the first prototype flown on 1 September 1944 represented the land-based variant, with the fundamentally similar "semi-navalised" (in that it lacked wing folding facilities) prototype following on 21 February 1945, and a "fully-navalised" prototype flying eight months later, on 12 October. The initial production version, the Sea Fury F Mk 10, entered service from the spring of 1947. Only 50 F Mk 10s were built before replacement by the more versatile FB Mk 11, 615 of which had been built when production ended in November 1950. The FB Mk 11 constituted the principal Royal Navy single-seat fighter equipment until the advent

of its lineal successor, the Sea Hawk (see pages 180-181) in late 1953.

Compact, sturdy and tractable, the Sea Fury was a true pilot's aeroplane. Marginally stable about all three axes, it had light and effective controls, and while a comparison with the Bearcat assuredly gave an edge in climb and manoeuvrability to the US Navy fighter, the Sea Fury was the better weapons platform and the superior aircraft under instrument flight conditions.

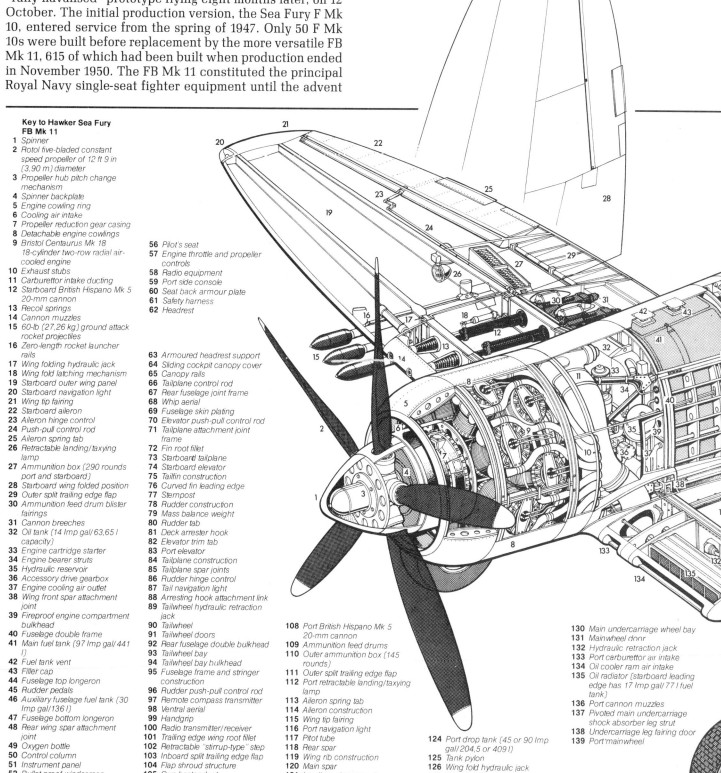

**Key to Hawker Sea Fury FB Mk 11**

1 Spinner
2 Rotol five-bladed constant speed propeller of 12 ft 9 in (3,90 m) diameter
3 Propeller hub pitch change mechanism
4 Spinner backplate
5 Engine cowling ring
6 Cooling air intake
7 Propeller reduction gear casing
8 Detachable engine cowlings
9 Bristol Centaurus Mk 18 18-cylinder two-row radial air-cooled engine
10 Exhaust stubs
11 Carburettor intake ducting
12 Starboard British Hispano Mk 5 20-mm cannon
13 Recoil springs
14 Cannon muzzles
15 60-lb (27,26 kg) ground attack rocket projectiles
16 Zero-length rocket launcher rails
17 Wing folding hydraulic jack
18 Wing fold latching mechanism
19 Starboard outer wing panel
20 Starboard navigation light
21 Wing tip fairing
22 Starboard aileron
23 Aileron hinge control
24 Push-pull control rod
25 Aileron spring tab
26 Retractable landing/taxiing lamp
27 Ammunition box (290 rounds port and starboard)
28 Starboard wing folded position
29 Outer split trailing edge flap
30 Ammunition feed drum blister fairings
31 Cannon breeches
32 Oil tank (14 Imp gal/63,65 l capacity)
33 Engine cartridge starter
34 Engine bearer struts
35 Hydraulic reservoir
36 Accessory drive gearbox
37 Engine cooling air outlet
38 Wing front spar attachment joint
39 Fireproof engine compartment bulkhead
40 Fuselage double frame
41 Main fuel tank (97 Imp gal/441 l)
42 Fuel tank vent
43 Filler cap
44 Fuselage top longeron
45 Rudder pedals
46 Auxiliary fuselage fuel tank (30 Imp gal/136 l)
47 Fuselage bottom longeron
48 Rear wing spar attachment joint
49 Oxygen bottle
50 Control column
51 Instrument panel
52 Bullet proof windscreen
53 Mk 4B reflector sight
54 Windscreen framing
55 Pilot's starboard side console

56 Pilot's seat
57 Engine throttle and propeller controls
58 Radio equipment
59 Port side console
60 Seat back armour plate
61 Safety harness
62 Headrest

63 Armoured headrest support
64 Sliding cockpit canopy cover
65 Canopy rails
66 Tailplane control rod
67 Rear fuselage joint frame
68 Whip aerial
69 Fuselage skin plating
70 Elevator push-pull control rod
71 Tailplane attachment joint frame
72 Fin root fillet
73 Starboard tailplane
74 Starboard elevator
75 Tailfin construction
76 Curved fin leading edge
77 Sternpost
78 Rudder construction
79 Mass balance weight
80 Rudder tab
81 Deck arrester hook
82 Elevator trim tab
83 Port elevator
84 Tailplane construction
85 Tailplane spar joints
86 Rudder hinge control
87 Tail navigation light
88 Arresting hook attachment link
89 Tailwheel hydraulic retraction jack
90 Tailwheel
91 Tailwheel doors
92 Rear fuselage double bulkhead
93 Tailwheel bay
94 Tailwheel bay bulkhead
95 Fuselage frame and stringer construction
96 Rudder push-pull control rod
97 Remote compass transmitter
98 Ventral aerial
99 Handgrip
100 Radio transmitter/receiver
101 Trailing edge wing root fillet
102 Retractable "stirrup-type" step
103 Inboard split trailing edge flap
104 Flap shroud structure
105 Gun heater duct
106 Inboard ammunition box (145 rounds)
107 Ammunition guide track

108 Port British Hispano Mk 5 20-mm cannon
109 Ammunition feed drums
110 Outer ammunition box (145 rounds)
111 Outer split trailing edge flap
112 Port retractable landing/taxiing lamp
113 Aileron spring tab
114 Aileron construction
115 Wing tip fairing
116 Port navigation light
117 Pitot tube
118 Rear spar
119 Wing rib construction
120 Main spar
121 Leading edge nose ribs
122 1,000-lb (453,6-kg) HE bomb
123 60-lb (27,26-kg) ground attack rockets

124 Port drop tank (45 or 90 Imp gal/204,5 or 409 l)
125 Tank pylon
126 Wing fold hydraulic jack
127 Wing fold hinge joints
128 Cannon barrel mountings
129 Port interspar fuel tank (28 Imp gal/127 l)

130 Main undercarriage wheel bay
131 Mainwheel door
132 Hydraulic retraction jack
133 Port carburettor air intake
134 Oil cooler ram air intake
135 Oil radiator (starboard leading edge has 17 Imp gal/77 l fuel tank)
136 Port cannon muzzles
137 Pivoted main undercarriage shock absorber leg strut
138 Undercarriage leg fairing door
139 Port mainwheel

139

## SPECIFICATION: Sea Fury FB Mk 11

**Power Plant:** One Bristol Centaurus 18 18-cylinder two-row radial air-cooled engine rated at 2,480 hp at 2,700 rpm for take-off and 2,550 hp at 4,000 ft (1 220 m). Five-bladed Rotol constant-speed propeller. Internal fuel capacity, 200 Imp gal (909 l), with provision for two 45 Imp gal (204 l) or 90 Imp gal (409 l) drop tanks.

**Performance:** Max speed, 460 mph (740 km/h) at 18,000 ft (5 485 m), 415 mph (668 km/h) at 30,000 ft (9 145 m); initial climb, 4,320 ft/min (21,94 m/sec); time to 20,000 ft (6 095 m), 5·7 min, to 30,000 ft (9 145 m), 10·8 min; service ceiling, 35,800 ft (10 910 m); range (internal fuel), 700 mls (1 126 km), (two 90 Imp gal/409 l drop tanks), 1,040 mls (1 674 km).

**Weights:** Empty, 9,240 lb (4 191 kg); normal loaded, 12,350 lb (5 602 kg); max, 14,650 lb (6 645 kg).

**Dimensions:** Span 38 ft 4¾ in (11,69 m); length, 34 ft 8 in (10,56 m); height, 15 ft 10½ in (4,84 m); wing area, 280 sq ft.

**Armament:** Four 20-mm British Hispano Mk 5 cannon with 145 rpg; provision for 2 500-lb (226,8-kg) or 1,000-lb (453,6-kg) bombs, or 12 3-in (7,62-cm) or 5-in (12,7-cm) rockets.

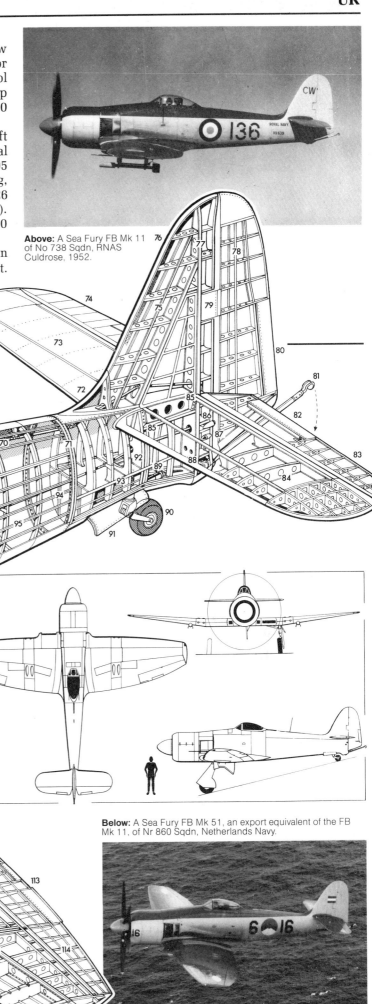

**Above:** A Sea Fury FB Mk 11 of No 738 Sqdn, RNAS Culdrose, 1952.

**Below:** A Sea Fury FB Mk 51, an export equivalent of the FB Mk 11, of Nr 860 Sqdn, Netherlands Navy.

# McDonnell FH-1 Phantom (January 1945)

Use of the turbojet as an aircraft prime mover was to arouse US Navy interest from the beginning of the 'forties, but application of pure jet aircraft to shipboard operations posed numerous problems. Turbojet-powered aircraft consumed prodigious quantities of fuel; they called for the use of a nosewheel undercarriage with which no flight deck experience existed; their take-off run was excessive by carrier standards, rendering catapult launching a necessity, and their high landing speed demanded improved arresting techniques.

Despite these problems, on 7 January 1943, development began of a single-seat shipboard fighter, which, to be powered solely by turbojets, was to emerge two years later as the Phantom. The Phantom was to make two claims to fame in fighter annals, one substantive and the other vicarious. It was the first pure jet fighter designed from the outset for the shipboard operation and it was to be the sire of the Phantom II (see pages 216-217), the most significant and efficacious fighter of the 'sixties.

Comparatively conservative and fundamentally simple in design, the Phantom was created by a team led by Kendall Perkins, and the first of two prototypes was flown as the XFD-1 on 26 January 1945 (with only one turbojet installed as delivery of the second was still awaited). Production was initiated 40 days later, on 7 March, with deliveries of 60 aircraft commencing as FH-1s in January 1947. The Phantom was operated from a carrier deck for the first time on 21 July 1946, emulating the feat of a "hooked Vampire" seven-and-a-half months earlier which had proved the feasibility of carrier-based jet operations.

Decidedly underpowered, the Phantom was stable under all conditions, but stick forces tended to become unacceptably light with aft movement of the CG, as when ammunition was expended. Power variations resulted in only small trim changes, and extension of the undercarriage and flaps produced only a mild nose heaviness. At higher speeds, however, harsh buffeting, a strong nose-up tendency and rolling instability strictly limited performance.

The sole US Navy squadron to equip with the Phantom became carrier qualified on 5 May 1948. Two US Marine Corps squadrons also flew the Phantom, which was finally withdrawn from service mid-1950.

**Key to McDonnell FH-1 Phantom**

1 Nose cone
2 Forward radio bay
3 Access/connection
4 Support brace
5 Fuselage forward frame
6 Gun muzzle ports (4)
7 Forward vane
8 Gun bay upper hinge line
9 Gun barrels
10 Four 0·50-in (12,7-mm) nose guns
11 Starboard guns ejection chutes
12 Port guns ammunition feeds
13 Starboard guns ammunition boxes
14 Port guns ammunition boxes
15 Ammunition box tray handles
16 Support frame
17 Nosewheel steering/shimmy damper
18 Nosewheel leg
19 Rearward-retracting nosewheel
20 Hub
21 Torque links
22 Nosewheel well door
23 Auxiliary intake scoop
24 Bulkhead
25 Gun charging mechanism
26 Armoured deflector plate
27 Gun breeches
28 Gun firing control
29 Windscreen frame
30 Mk 23 gunsight
31 Armoured glass windscreen
32 Standby compass
33 Cockpit starboard sill
34 Radio control panels
35 Control column
36 Instrument panel
37 Starboard panel segment
38 Port panel segment
39 Control linkage
40 Rudder pedal assembly
41 Cockpit floor support
42 Underfloor control run links
43 Nosewheel well
44 Bulkhead
45 Chute pack seat pan
46 Port control console
47 Throttle quadrant
48 Trim tab controls
49 Oxygen controls
50 Oxygen regulator
51 Seat support frame
52 Pilot's seat
53 Canopy lock/release
54 Back armour/turnover frame support
55 Padded headrest
56 Clear vision bubble canopy
57 Starboard wing fold hinges
58 Front spar
59 Intermediate rib station
60 Wing skinning
61 Starboard navigation light
62 End rib
63 Wingtip
64 Starboard aileron
65 Actuating link
66 Aileron trim tab
67 Control runs
68 Aileron profile
69 Starboard flap (outer section)
70 Flap control mechanism
71 Centre-section end rib/wing fold
72 Rearward-sliding canopy
73 Bulkhead/upper longeron attachment
74 Fuselage forward self-sealing fuel tank
75 Fuel filler caps
76 Fuselage forward main frame/centre-section pick-up
77 Leads
78 Fuselage centre self-sealing fuel tank
79 Fuselage aft main frame/centre-section pick-up
80 Fuselage aft self-sealing fuel tank
81 Rear frame/bulkhead
82 Access
83 Aft electrics
84 Aerial lead-in
85 Antenna
86 Dorsal identification light (offset to port)
87 Equipment bay
88 Fixed aerial
89 Aerial
90 Fuselage/tailfin root fillet
91 Attachment bolt plate
92 Starboard tailplane
93 Rear spar
94 End rib
95 Starboard elevator
96 Elevator actuating link
97 Elevator trim tab
98 Tailfin leading-edge
99 Aerial attachment
100 Pitot tube
101 Rudder upper hinge
102 Tailfin structure
103 Rudder
104 Tailfin front spar
105 Rudder post
106 Rudder trim tab
107 Tab actuating link
108 Rudder control
109 Horn/actuating link
110 Port elevator
111 Elevator trim tab
112 Port tailplane structure
113 Tail navigation light
114 Tailplane leading-edge
115 Elevator torque tube
116 Tailplane attachment points
117 Fillet
118 Aft fuselage skinning
119 Rear frames
120 Tail bumper
121 Arrester hook
122 Control runs/leads
123 Aft fuselage structure
124 Upper longeron
125 Lower longeron
126 Arrester hook pivot
127 Arrester hook mechanism
128 Wingroot fillet
129 Jet tail pipe
130 Exhaust
131 Wing/jet pipe fairing
132 Port flap (inner cut-out section)
133 Auxiliary spar
134 Rear spar
135 Engine rear mounting links (wing deflection)
136 Port Westinghouse J30 turbojet (buried in centre-section)
137 Centre-section structure
138 Reinforced ribs
139 Front spar
140 Turbojet inlet duct
141 Shut-off valve
142 Engine front mounting links (wing deflection)
143 Intake surround
144 Port engine intake
145 Wing inboard ribs
146 Port (non self-sealing) oil tank
147 Contoured spar section
148 Mainwheel well inner door
149 Landing gear intercostals

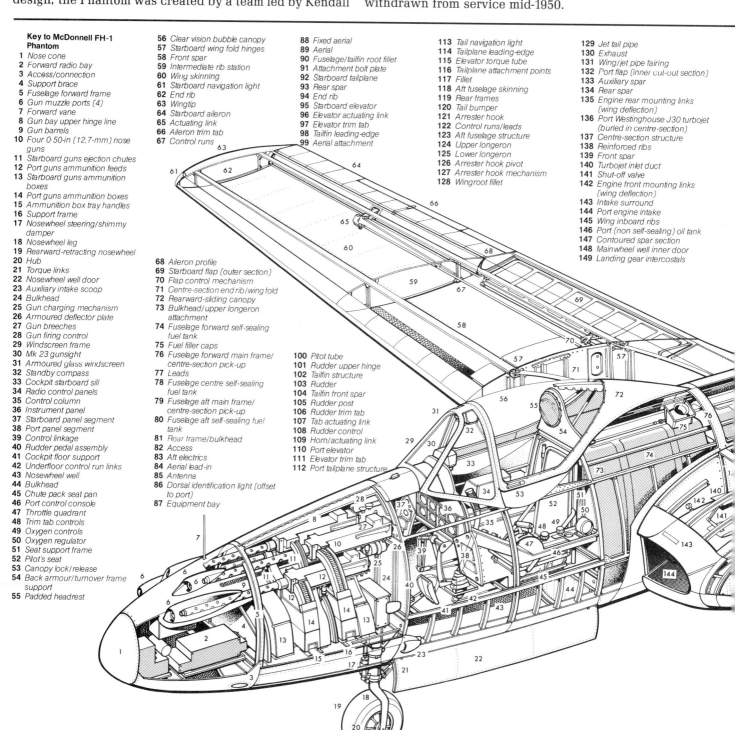

## SPECIFICATION: FH-1 Phantom

**Power Plant:** Two Westinghouse J30-WE-20 axial-flow turbojets each rated at 1,560 lb (708 kg) thrust. Internal fuel capacity, 312 Imp gal (1 418 l), with provision made for one 158 Imp gal (718 l) or one 245·6 Imp gal (1 117 l) centreline drop tank.

**Performance:** Max speed, 472 mph (760 km/h) at sea level, 485 mph (780 km/h) at 15,000 ft (4 570 m); initial climb, 4,800 ft/min (24,38 m/sec); time to 30,000 ft (9 145 m), 11·0 min; service ceiling, 34,500 ft (10 515 m); range (with 158 Imp gal/718 l drop tank), 771 mls (1 241 km) at 312 mph (502 km/h) at 20,000 ft (6 095 m); ferry range (with 245·6 Imp gal/1 117 l drop tank), 910 mls (1 464 km) at 307 mph (494 km/h).

**Weights:** Empty, 6,699 lb (3 039 kg); normal loaded, 9,974 lb (4 524 kg); max, 12,500 lb (5 670 kg).

**Dimensions:** Span, 40 ft 9 in (12,42 m); length, 38 ft 9 in (11,81 m); height, 14 ft 2 in (4,32 m); wing area, 274 sq ft (25,45 m²).

**Armament:** Four 0·50-in (12,7-mm) Colt-Browning machine guns with 325 rpg.

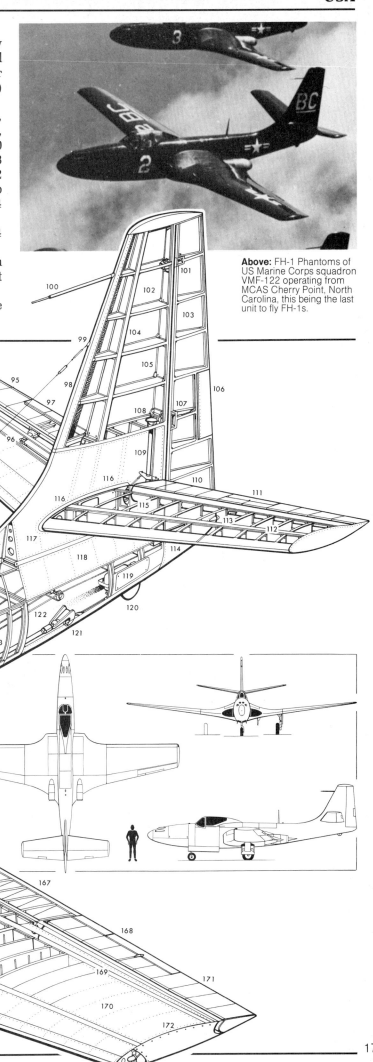

**Above:** FH-1 Phantoms of US Marine Corps squadron VMF-122 operating from MCAS Cherry Point, North Carolina, this being the last unit to fly FH-1s.

150 Port mainwheel well
151 Wing fold hinge fittings
152 Wing fold line
153 Wing fold pin fittings
154 Wing fold push point
155 Landing gear retraction links
156 Attachment frame
157 Electric drive motor
158 Mainwheel leg
159 Mainwheel leg door
160 Port mainwheel cover flap
161 Torque links
162 Port mainwheel
163 Brake lines
164 Outer leading-edge
165 Outer front spar
166 Wing rib stations
167 Port flap (outer section)
168 Aileron trim tab
169 Rear spar
170 Wing skinning
171 Port aileron
172 Wingtip/end rib
173 Port navigation light

# Republic F-84 Thunderjet (February 1946)

The first turbojet-powered fighter conceived specifically for the radii of action demanded for the penetration mission, the Thunderjet also represented the culmination of first-generation US single-seat land-based jet fighter evolution. Designed under the aegis of Alexander Kartveli, it was distinctive among combat aircraft at the time of its début in utilising the straight-through airflow concept, which, while penalising internal capacity, simplified induction and exhaust, and was conducive to low internal pressure losses. A simple pitot-type intake combined maximum flow efficiency with the highest possible critical Mach number, minimum fuselage cross section combining with a comparatively high fineness ratio to result in exceptionally low drag. The wing, mounted in low-mid position to minimize interference drag, employed a comparatively thick (12 per cent) constant-section aerofoil in order to accommodate the main undercarriage members and the bulk of the fuel.

The first of three (XP-84) prototypes flew on 28 February 1946, the initial production model, the F-84B, flying in June 1947, introducing an ejection seat and a 4,000 lb (1 814 kg)

J35-A-15C turbojet. Two hundred and twenty-six F-84Bs were followed by 191 F-84Cs with minor changes and 154 F-84Ds with thicker skin gauges and the 5,000 lb (2 268 kg) J35-A-17D. With the F-84E, the Thunderjet emulated its lineal predecessor, the P-47, in finding its true forté as a fighter-bomber, a role in which it excelled. Offering exceptional load-carrying ability, it provided a very stable weapons platform and had good instrument flying characteristics, and the sturdiness to withstand rough airfield conditions and battle damage.

The Thunderjet was exceptionally demanding on runway length and lacked the agility for effectiveness in fighter-versus-fighter combat. Without external stores it accelerated rapidly owing to its low drag characteristics, quickly attaining its Mach=0·82 limitation when, below 15,000 ft (4 570 m), it produced a sudden and uncontrollable pitch-up and, at higher altitudes, extreme buffeting.

Following 843 F-84Es, under the impetus of the Korean conflict, 3,025 of the definitive F-84G model were built,

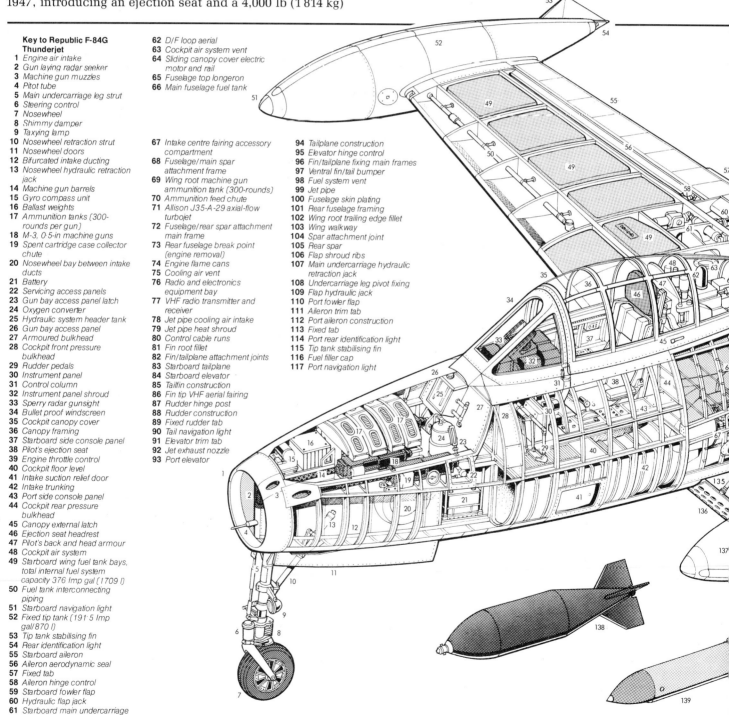

**Key to Republic F-84G Thunderjet**

1 Engine air intake
2 Gun laying radar seeker
3 Machine gun muzzles
4 Pitot tube
5 Main undercarriage leg strut
6 Steering control
7 Nosewheel
8 Shimmy damper
9 Taxying lamp
10 Nosewheel retraction strut
11 Nosewheel doors
12 Bifurcated intake ducting
13 Nosewheel hydraulic retraction jack
14 Machine gun barrels
15 Gyro compass unit
16 Ballast weights
17 Ammunition tanks (300-rounds per gun)
18 M-3, 0·5-in machine guns
19 Spent cartridge case collector chute
20 Nosewheel bay between intake ducts
21 Battery
22 Servicing access panels
23 Gun bay access panel latch
24 Oxygen converter
25 Hydraulic system header tank
26 Gun bay access panel
27 Armoured bulkhead
28 Cockpit front pressure bulkhead
29 Rudder pedals
30 Instrument panel
31 Control column
32 Instrument panel shroud
33 Sperry radar gunsight
34 Bullet proof windscreen
35 Cockpit canopy cover
36 Canopy framing
37 Starboard side console panel
38 Pilot's ejection seat
39 Engine throttle control
40 Cockpit floor level
41 Intake suction relief door
42 Intake trunking
43 Port side console panel
44 Cockpit rear pressure bulkhead
45 Canopy external latch
46 Ejection seat headrest
47 Pilot's back and head armour
48 Cockpit air system
49 Starboard wing fuel tank bays, total internal fuel system capacity 376 Imp gal (1709 l)
50 Fuel tank interconnecting piping
51 Starboard navigation light
52 Fixed tip tank (191·5 Imp gal/870 l)
53 Tip tank stabilising fin
54 Rear identification light
55 Starboard aileron
56 Aileron aerodynamic seal
57 Fixed tab
58 Aileron hinge control
59 Starboard fowler flap
60 Hydraulic flap jack
61 Starboard main undercarriage pivot fixing

62 D/F loop aerial
63 Cockpit air system vent
64 Sliding canopy cover electric motor and rail
65 Fuselage top longeron
66 Main fuselage fuel tank
67 Intake centre fairing accessory compartment
68 Fuselage/main spar attachment frame
69 Wing root machine gun ammunition tank (300-rounds)
70 Ammunition feed chute
71 Allison J35-A-29 axial-flow turbojet
72 Fuselage/rear spar attachment main frame
73 Rear fuselage break point (engine removal)
74 Engine flame cans
75 Cooling air vent
76 Radio and electronics equipment bay
77 VHF radio transmitter and receiver
78 Jet pipe cooling air intake
79 Jet pipe heat shroud
80 Control cable runs
81 Fin root fillet
82 Fin/tailplane attachment joints
83 Starboard tailplane
84 Starboard elevator
85 Tailfin construction
86 Fin tip VHF aerial fairing
87 Rudder hinge post
88 Rudder construction
89 Fixed rudder tab
90 Tail navigation light
91 Elevator trim tab
92 Jet exhaust nozzle
93 Port elevator

94 Tailplane construction
95 Elevator hinge control
96 Fin/tailplane fixing main frames
97 Ventral fin/tail bumper
98 Fuel system vent
99 Jet pipe
100 Fuselage skin plating
101 Rear fuselage framing
102 Wing root trailing edge fillet
103 Wing walkway
104 Spar attachment joint
105 Rear spar
106 Flap shroud ribs
107 Main undercarriage hydraulic retraction jack
108 Undercarriage leg pivot fixing
109 Flap hydraulic jack
110 Port fowler flap
111 Aileron trim tab
112 Port aileron construction
113 Fixed tab
114 Port rear identification light
115 Tip tank stabilising fin
116 Fuel filler cap
117 Port navigation light

1,936 of these being supplied with MAP funding to foreign air forces, production ending in July 1953.

## SPECIFICATION: F-84G Thunderjet

**Power Plant:** One Allison J35-A-29 axial-flow turbojet rated at 5,600 lb (2 540 kg) thrust. Internal fuel capacity, 376 Imp gal (1 709 l), with provision for two wingtip and two underwing 191·5 Imp gal (870 l) drop tanks.

**Performance:** Max speed, 622 mph (1 001 km/h) at sea level, 575 mph (925 km/h) at 20,000 ft (6 095 m), 540 mph (869 km/h) at 36,000 ft (10 970 m); continuous cruise, 483 mph (777 km/h) at 35,000 ft (10 670 m); time to 35,000 ft (10 670 m), 7·9 min, (with external tanks), 9·4 min; service ceiling, 40,500 ft (12 345 m); range (internal fuel), 670 mls (1 078 km), (with wingtip tanks), 1,330 mls (2 140 km), (with max external fuel), 2,000 mls (3 217 km).

**Weights:** Empty, 11,095 lb (5 033 kg); normal loaded, 18,645 lb (8 457 kg); max, 23,525 lb (10 670 kg).

**Dimensions:** Span, 36 ft 5 in (11,09 m); length, 38 ft 1 in (11,60 m); height, 12 ft 7 in (3,83 m); wing area, 260 sq ft (24,15 m²).

**Armament:** Six 0·50-in (12,7-mm) Colt-Browning M-3 machine guns with 300 rpg, with provision for up to 4,000 lb (1 184 kg) of external ordnance.

118 Fixed tip tank (191·5 Imp gal/870 l)
119 Port wing fuel tank bays
120 Wing stringers
121 Main spar
122 Fuel tank interconnecting piping
123 Leading edge nose ribs
124 Mainwheel doors
125 Port mainwheel
126 Hydraulic brake unit
127 Main undercarriage leg strut
128 Inflight refuelling probe (alternative to item 133)
129 Leading edge fuel tank
130 Main undercarriage wheel well
131 Mainwheel door
132 Wing root M-3 0·5-in (12,7-mm) machine gun
133 Boom type in-flight refuelling probe (alternative to item 128)
134 Stores pylon
135 Airbrake hydraulic jack
136 Perforated ventral airbrake
137 191·5 Imp gal (870 l) drop tank
138 500-lb (227-kg) HE bomb
139 'Tiny Tim' 30-cm air to ground rocket
140 Rocket fixing shackles
141 HVAR ground attack rockets

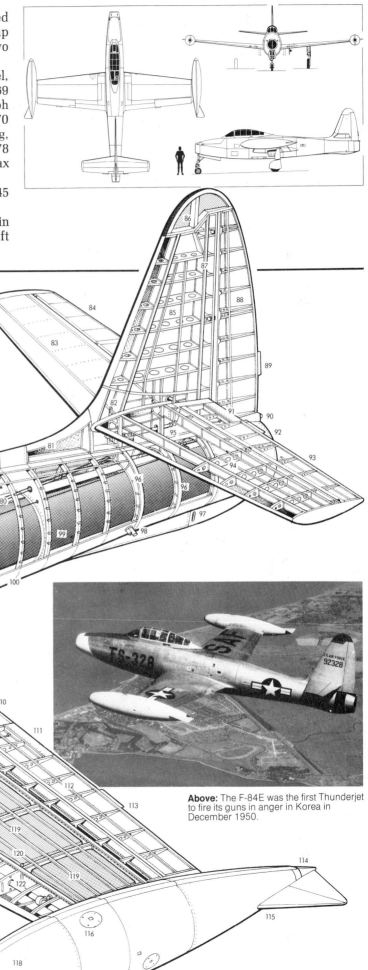

**Above:** The F-84E was the first Thunderjet to fire its guns in anger in Korea in December 1950.

# Hawker Sea Hawk (September 1947)

Arguably the pre-eminent example of post-WWII combat aircraft pulchritude, the supremely graceful Sea Hawk shipboard fighter was noteworthy for its ingenious arrangement of bifurcated intakes and exhaust orifices. Aesthetically an outstandingly elegant aircraft and aerodynamically extraordinarily clean, the Sea Hawk laid claim to originality not in its wing root leading-edge air intakes but in their mating with similarly bifurcated exhaust pipes via a constant-thickness root chord. This arrangement left the fuselage virtually free of ducting and catered for large-capacity fuel tanks fore and aft of the turbojet and, therefore, symmetrical about the CG.

Conceived as the P.1040 land-based interceptor and flown on 2 September 1947, the design was readily adaptable for shipboard use and a "navalised" prototype flew almost exactly a year later, on 3 September 1948. The production Sea Hawk F Mk 1 (95 built) flew on 14 November 1951, aileron oscillation which caused a loss of lateral control being corrected by the introduction of power actuation on the F Mk 2 (40 built). A strengthened wing for external loads produced the FB Mk 3 (116 built), this being succeeded by the close air support FGA Mk 4 (97 built). The definitive production FGA Mk 6 replaced the 5,000 lb (2 268 kg) thrust Nene 101 with the 103, 86 being built for the Royal Navy, with deliveries completed early 1956, followed by 22 similar FGA Mk 50s for the Netherlands and 68 (Mks 100 and 101) for Federal Germany, production terminating in 1961 with a batch of 14 FGA Mk 6s for the Indian Navy.

## SPECIFICATION: Sea Hawk FGA Mk 6

**Power Plant:** One Rolls-Royce Nene 103 centrifugal-flow turbojet rated at 5,200 lb (2 359 kg) thrust. Internal fuel capacity, 395 Imp gal (1 796 l), with provision for up to four 90 Imp gal (409 l) drop tanks.

**Performance:** Max speed, 599 mph (964 km/h)

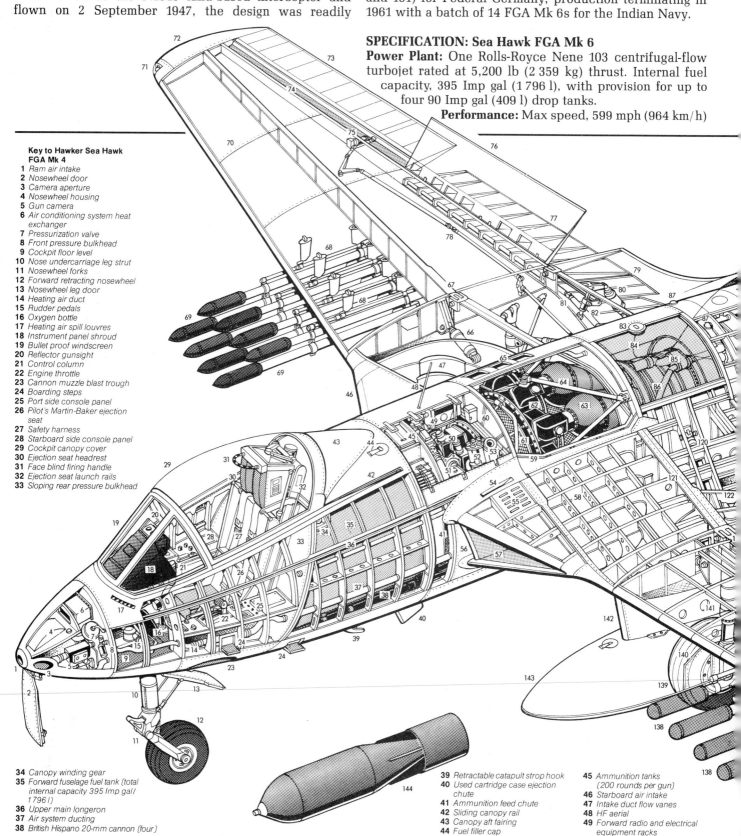

**Key to Hawker Sea Hawk FGA Mk 4**

1 Ram air intake
2 Nosewheel door
3 Camera aperture
4 Nosewheel housing
5 Gun camera
6 Air conditioning system heat exchanger
7 Pressurization valve
8 Front pressure bulkhead
9 Cockpit floor level
10 Nose undercarriage leg strut
11 Nosewheel forks
12 Forward retracting nosewheel
13 Nosewheel leg door
14 Heating air duct
15 Rudder pedals
16 Oxygen bottle
17 Heating air spill louvres
18 Instrument panel shroud
19 Bullet proof windscreen
20 Reflector gunsight
21 Control column
22 Engine throttle
23 Cannon muzzle blast trough
24 Boarding steps
25 Port side console panel
26 Pilot's Martin-Baker ejection seat
27 Safety harness
28 Starboard side console panel
29 Cockpit canopy cover
30 Ejection seat headrest
31 Face blind firing handle
32 Ejection seat launch rails
33 Sloping rear pressure bulkhead

34 Canopy winding gear
35 Forward fuselage fuel tank (total internal capacity 395 Imp gal/ 1796 l)
36 Upper main longeron
37 Air system ducting
38 British Hispano 20-mm cannon (four)

39 Retractable catapult strop hook
40 Used cartridge case ejection chute
41 Ammunition feed chute
42 Sliding canopy rail
43 Canopy aft fairing
44 Fuel filler cap

45 Ammunition tanks (200 rounds per gun)
46 Starboard air intake
47 Intake duct flow vanes
48 HF aerial
49 Forward radio and electrical equipment racks

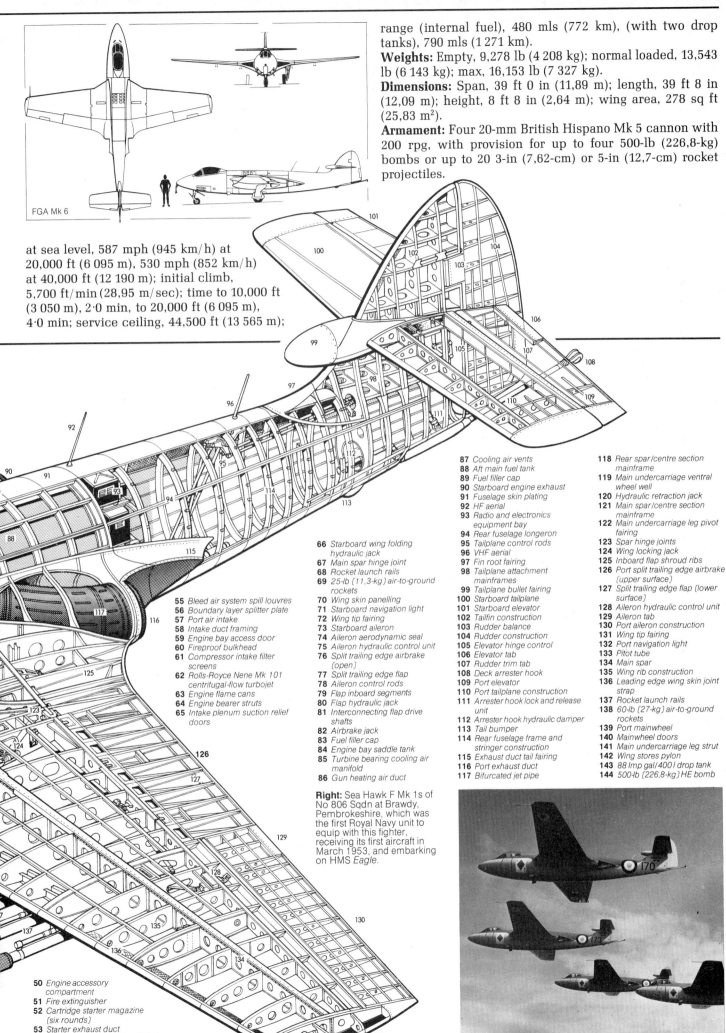

range (internal fuel), 480 mls (772 km), (with two drop tanks), 790 mls (1 271 km).
**Weights:** Empty, 9,278 lb (4 208 kg); normal loaded, 13,543 lb (6 143 kg); max, 16,153 lb (7 327 kg).
**Dimensions:** Span, 39 ft 0 in (11,89 m); length, 39 ft 8 in (12,09 m); height, 8 ft 8 in (2,64 m); wing area, 278 sq ft (25,83 m²).
**Armament:** Four 20-mm British Hispano Mk 5 cannon with 200 rpg, with provision for up to four 500-lb (226,8-kg) bombs or up to 20 3-in (7,62-cm) or 5-in (12,7-cm) rocket projectiles.

FGA Mk 6

at sea level, 587 mph (945 km/h) at 20,000 ft (6 095 m), 530 mph (852 km/h) at 40,000 ft (12 190 m); initial climb, 5,700 ft/min (28,95 m/sec); time to 10,000 ft (3 050 m), 2·0 min, to 20,000 ft (6 095 m), 4·0 min; service ceiling, 44,500 ft (13 565 m);

50 Engine accessory compartment
51 Fire extinguisher
52 Cartridge starter magazine (six rounds)
53 Starter exhaust duct
54 Boundary layer bleed air spill duct

55 Bleed air system spill louvres
56 Boundary layer splitter plate
57 Port air intake
58 Intake duct framing
59 Engine bay access door
60 Fireproof bulkhead
61 Compressor intake filter screens
62 Rolls-Royce Nene Mk 101 centrifugal-flow turbojet
63 Engine flame cans
64 Engine bearer struts
65 Intake plenum suction relief doors

66 Starboard wing folding hydraulic jack
67 Main spar hinge joint
68 Rocket launch rails
69 25-lb (11,3-kg) air-to-ground rockets
70 Wing skin panelling
71 Starboard navigation light
72 Wing tip fairing
73 Starboard aileron
74 Aileron aerodynamic seal
75 Aileron hydraulic control unit
76 Split trailing edge airbrake (open)
77 Split trailing edge flap
78 Aileron control rods
79 Flap inboard segments
80 Flap hydraulic jack
81 Interconnecting flap drive shafts
82 Airbrake jack
83 Fuel filler cap
84 Engine bay saddle tank
85 Turbine bearing cooling air manifold
86 Gun heating air duct

87 Cooling air vents
88 Aft main fuel tank
89 Fuel filler cap
90 Starboard engine exhaust
91 Fuselage skin plating
92 HF aerial
93 Radio and electronics equipment bay
94 Rear fuselage longeron
95 Tailplane control rods
96 VHF aerial
97 Fin root fairing
98 Tailplane attachment mainframes
99 Tailplane bullet fairing
100 Starboard tailplane
101 Starboard elevator
102 Tailfin construction
103 Rudder balance
104 Rudder construction
105 Elevator hinge control
106 Elevator tab
107 Rudder trim tab
108 Deck arrester hook
109 Port elevator
110 Port tailplane construction
111 Arrester hook lock and release unit
112 Arrester hook hydraulic damper
113 Tail bumper
114 Rear fuselage frame and stringer construction
115 Exhaust duct tail fairing
116 Port exhaust duct
117 Bifurcated jet pipe

118 Rear spar/centre section mainframe
119 Main undercarriage ventral wheel well
120 Hydraulic retraction jack
121 Main spar/centre section mainframe
122 Main undercarriage leg pivot fairing
123 Spar hinge joints
124 Wing locking jack
125 Inboard flap shroud ribs
126 Port split trailing edge airbrake (upper surface)
127 Split trailing edge flap (lower surface)
128 Aileron hydraulic control unit
129 Aileron tab
130 Port aileron construction
131 Wing tip fairing
132 Port navigation light
133 Pitot tube
134 Main spar
135 Wing rib construction
136 Leading edge wing skin joint strap
137 Rocket launch rails
138 60-lb (27-kg) air-to-ground rockets
139 Port mainwheel
140 Mainwheel doors
141 Main undercarriage leg strut
142 Wing stores pylon
143 88 Imp gal/400 l drop tank
144 500-lb (226,8-kg) HE bomb

**Right:** Sea Hawk F Mk 1s of No 806 Sqdn at Brawdy, Pembrokeshire, which was the first Royal Navy unit to equip with this fighter, receiving its first aircraft in March 1953, and embarking on HMS Eagle.

# North American F-86 Sabre (October 1947)

An outstanding technological milestone in fighter development was reached with the adoption of wing sweepback. While the Me 262 (see pages 154-155) claimed the distinction of having been the *first* jet fighter featuring swept wings to attain service, it had utilised sweepback to compensate for a forward *CG* shift rather than as a means of delaying the onset of compressibility. The F-86 Sabre, on the other hand, was conceived with full knowledge of the aerodynamic advantages to be gained from sweeping wing surfaces. It could thus be claimed to have inaugurated a second generation in jet fighter development, albeit an honour gained by a mere 13-week lead over the Soviet MiG-15 (see pages 184-185).

Designed by a team led by Raymond H. Rice, the Sabre flew as a prototype (XP-86) on 1 October 1947, the first production model (F-86A) flying only five months later, on 18 May 1948, entering USAF service from February 1949, a few weeks before its Soviet contemporary joined the V-VS. By this time, the Sabre had already been committed to a process of development and incremental redesign which, over the years, was to result in a dozen major model

changes and adaptation for five different turbojets. To be licence-built in four countries, it was to serve with more than two dozen air forces and it was to be manufactured continuously for 13 years—the last being assembled in Japan in February 1961—with 8,732 being built in its multifarious land-based forms, plus 1,112 examples of shipboard models.

The first production fighter capable of attaining supersonic speed in a dive—Mach=1·0 being reached easily within about 5,000 ft (1 525 m) from a dive commenced at 36,000 ft (10 975 m)—the Sabre was, nevertheless, somewhat underpowered, and while a good gun platform, in perpetuating the use of six fifties it was deficient in firepower. Committed to the Korean conflict with the operational début of the MiG-15, its superlative handling qualities and genuine transonic capabilities compensated for inferiority in acceleration, manoeuvrability and altitude performance by comparison with its Soviet adversary.

The F-86E model with "all-flying" tail, which appeared in 1951, eliminated many of the F-86A's undesirable compressibility effects. Its g limitation was its pilot's tolerance

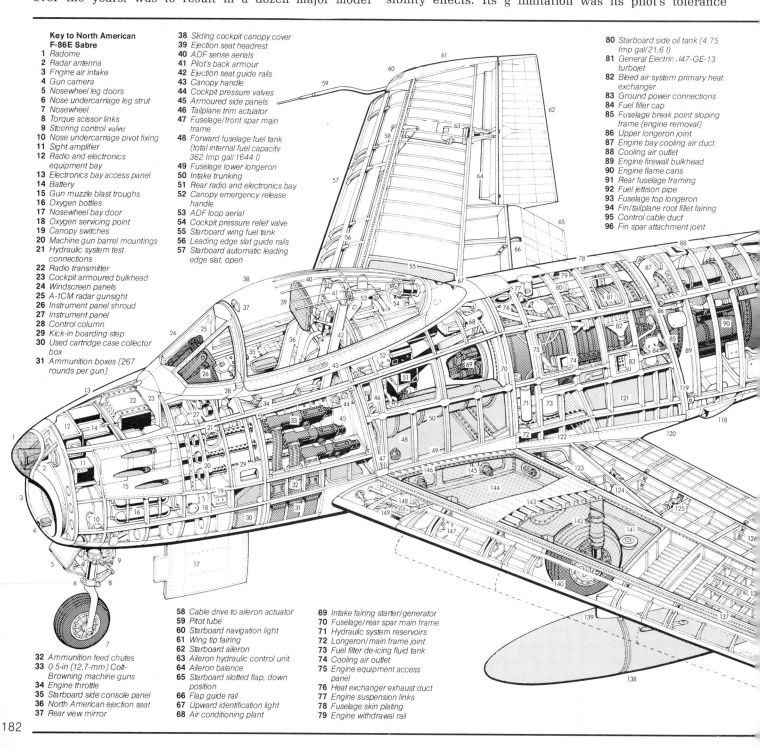

**Key to North American F-86E Sabre**
1 Radome
2 Radar antenna
3 Engine air intake
4 Gun camera
5 Nosewheel leg doors
6 Nose undercarriage leg strut
7 Nosewheel
8 Torque scissor links
9 Steering control valve
10 Nose undercarriage pivot fixing
11 Sight amplifier
12 Radio and electronics equipment bay
13 Electronics bay access panel
14 Battery
15 Gun muzzle blast troughs
16 Oxygen bottles
17 Nosewheel bay door
18 Oxygen servicing point
19 Canopy switches
20 Machine gun barrel mountings
21 Hydraulic system test connections
22 Radio transmitter
23 Cockpit armoured bulkhead
24 Windscreen panels
25 A-1CM radar gunsight
26 Instrument panel shroud
27 Instrument panel
28 Control column
29 Kick-in boarding step
30 Used cartridge case collector box
31 Ammunition boxes (267 rounds per gun)

38 Sliding cockpit canopy cover
39 Ejection seat headrest
40 ADF sense aerials
41 Pilot's back armour
42 Ejection seat guide rails
43 Canopy handle
44 Cockpit pressure valves
45 Armoured side panels
46 Tailplane trim actuator
47 Fuselage/front spar main frame
48 Forward fuselage fuel tank (total internal fuel capacity 362 Imp gall/1644 l)
49 Fuselage lower longeron
50 Intake trunking
51 Rear radio and electronics bay
52 Canopy emergency release handle
53 ADF loop aerial
54 Cockpit pressure relief valve
55 Starboard wing fuel tank
56 Leading edge slat guide rails
57 Starboard automatic leading edge slat, open

80 Starboard side oil tank [4.75 Imp gal/21,6 l]
81 General Electric J47-GE-13 turbojet
82 Bleed air system primary heat exchanger
83 Ground power connections
84 Fuel filler cap
85 Fuselage break point sloping frame (engine removal)
86 Upper longeron joint
87 Engine bay cooling air duct
88 Cooling air outlet
89 Engine firewall bulkhead
90 Engine flame cans
91 Rear fuselage framing
92 Fuel jettison pipe
93 Fuselage top longeron
94 Fin/tailplane root fillet fairing
95 Control cable duct
96 Fin spar attachment joint

58 Cable drive to aileron actuator
59 Pitot tube
60 Starboard navigation light
61 Wing tip fairing
62 Starboard aileron
63 Aileron hydraulic control unit
64 Aileron balance
65 Starboard slotted flap, down position
66 Flap guide rail
67 Upward identification light
68 Air conditioning plant

69 Intake fairing starter/generator
70 Fuselage/rear spar main frame
71 Hydraulic system reservoirs
72 Longeron/main frame joint
73 Fuel filter de-icing fluid tank
74 Cooling air outlet
75 Engine equipment access panel
76 Heat exchanger exhaust duct
77 Engine suspension links
78 Fuselage skin plating
79 Engine withdrawal rail

32 Ammunition feed chutes
33 0·5-in (12,7-mm) Colt-Browning machine guns
34 Engine throttle
35 Starboard side console panel
36 North American ejection seat
37 Rear view mirror

rather than that of the airframe, and it was one of the few fighters of its generation that could be termed viceless.

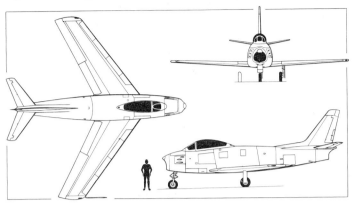

## SPECIFICATION: F-86E Sabre

**Power Plant:** One General Electric J47-GE-13 axial-flow turbojet rated at 5,200 lb (2 359 kg). Internal fuel capacity, 379·5 Imp gal (1 725 l), with provision for two 173·7 Imp gal (790 l) drop tanks.

**Performance:** Max speed, 679 mph (1 093 km/h) at sea level, 601 mph (967 km/h) at 35,000 ft (10 670 m); average cruise, 537 mph (864 km/h); initial climb, 7,250 ft/min (36,83 m/sec); time to 30,000 ft (9 145 m), 6·3 min; service ceiling, 47,200 ft (14 385 m); combat radius (internal fuel), 321 mls (517 km), (with drop tanks), 424 mls (682 km); ferry range, 1,022 mls (1 645 km).

**Weights:** Empty, 10,845 lb (4 919 kg); loaded (clean), 14,856 lb (6 739 kg); max, 17,806 lb (8 077 kg).

**Dimensions:** Span, 37 ft 1½ in (11, 31 m); length, 37 ft 6½ in (11,44 m); height, 14 ft 9½ in (4,51 m); wing area, 287·9 sq ft (26,74 m²).

**Armament:** Six 0·50-in (12,7-mm) Colt-Browning M-3 machine guns with 267 rounds of ammunition for each gun, with provision for two 1,000-lb (453,6-kg) bombs or sixteen 5-in (12,7-cm) rockets.

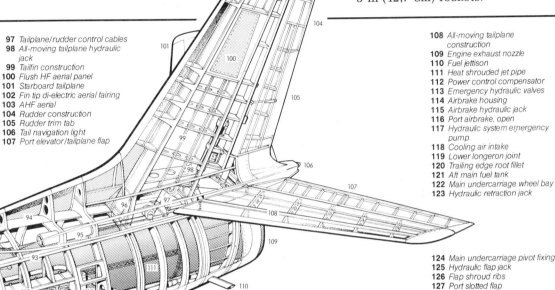

97 Tailplane/rudder control cables
98 All-moving tailplane hydraulic jack
99 Tailfin construction
100 Flush HF aerial panel
101 Starboard tailplane
102 Fin tip di-electric aerial fairing
103 AHF aerial
104 Rudder construction
105 Rudder trim tab
106 Tail navigation light
107 Port elevator/tailplane flap

108 All-moving tailplane construction
109 Engine exhaust nozzle
110 Fuel jettison
111 Heat shrouded jet pipe
112 Power control compensator
113 Emergency hydraulic valves
114 Airbrake housing
115 Airbrake hydraulic jack
116 Port airbrake, open
117 Hydraulic system emergency pump
118 Cooling air intake
119 Lower longeron joint
120 Trailing edge root fillet
121 Aft main fuel tank
122 Main undercarriage wheel bay
123 Hydraulic retraction jack

124 Main undercarriage pivot fixing
125 Hydraulic flap jack
126 Flap shroud ribs
127 Port slotted flap
128 Port aileron construction

129 Aileron hydraulic power control unit
130 Gyrosyn compass remote transmitter
131 Wing tip fairing
132 Port navigation light
133 Port automatic leading-edge slat open position
134 Leading-edge slat rib construction
135 Front spar
136 Wing rib and stringer construction
137 Wing skin/leading edge piano hinge attachment joint
138 100 Imp gal (454 l) drop tank
139 Drop tank pylon
140 Port mainwheel
141 Fuel filler cap
142 Main undercarriage leg strut
143 Fuel tank bay corrugated double skin
144 Port wing fuel tank
145 Tank interconnectors
146 Skin panel attachment joint strap
147 Slat guide rails
148 Fuel feed pipe
149 Aileron cable drive

**Right:** F-86F-35 Sabre of the "Skyblazers" aerobatic team based at Chaumont, France, in October 1955. The F-86F introduced the 5,970 lb (2 708 kg) J47-GE-27 turbojet, late production examples (as illustrated) discarding the wing slats in favour of extended wing leading edges and small boundary layer fences at threequarters span.

# Mikoyan-Gurevich MiG-15 (December 1947)

To be numbered among the most significant warplanes in the history of military aviation, the MiG-15, together with its US counterpart, the F-86 Sabre (see pages 182-183), represented a radical advance in fighter technology and initiated what was to be seen as a second generation in jet fighter development. Both were brilliant designs evolved contemporaneously, the prototype of the US fighter flying exactly 13 weeks before the Soviet fighter. Both were to manifest clear advantages and disadvantages when compared one with the other, but the comparative losses that they were to sustain when pitted in combat over Korea were to give a misleading impression of their relative capabilities.

In Korea, the overriding factor was the higher standard of training of the Sabre-mounted USAF pilots. Flown by equally proficient pilots, the outcome of any encounter between Sabre and MiG-15 would have depended on a combination of altitude and opportunity to exploit their differing characteristics. Smaller and lighter than its US counterpart, with an appreciably better thrust-to-weight ratio, the MiG-15 was the less sophisticated aeroplane from the equipment viewpoint, and conceived for high-altitude bomber interception

with armament optimised for this task, it was not ideally suited for fighter-versus-fighter combat and was thus at a disadvantage in the type of *mêlée* to which it was committed in the Korean War, 1950-1953.

It was capable of out-climbing and out-manoeuvring the Sabre, however, and it offered better acceleration. Furthermore, it had several thousand feet in hand when the US fighter ran out of ceiling. Conversely, the MiG-15 suffered directional snaking above Mach 0·86 and displayed a tendency to drop a wing and flick into a spin if forced to manoeuvre at medium altitudes. The F-86 Sabre, unlike its Soviet counterpart, did possess a genuinely transonic airframe; its handling at transonic speeds endowed it with a definite superiority as a gun platform and the ability to lose its opponent in a dive.

Conceived to meet a specification formulated in March 1946, the first prototype of the MiG-15 flew on 30 December 1947 as the I-310 with an imported Rolls-Royce Nene 2 engine. Various design revisions resulted in the Type S, this series entering production mid-March 1948, with service deliveries commencing in spring 1949. Many variants of the

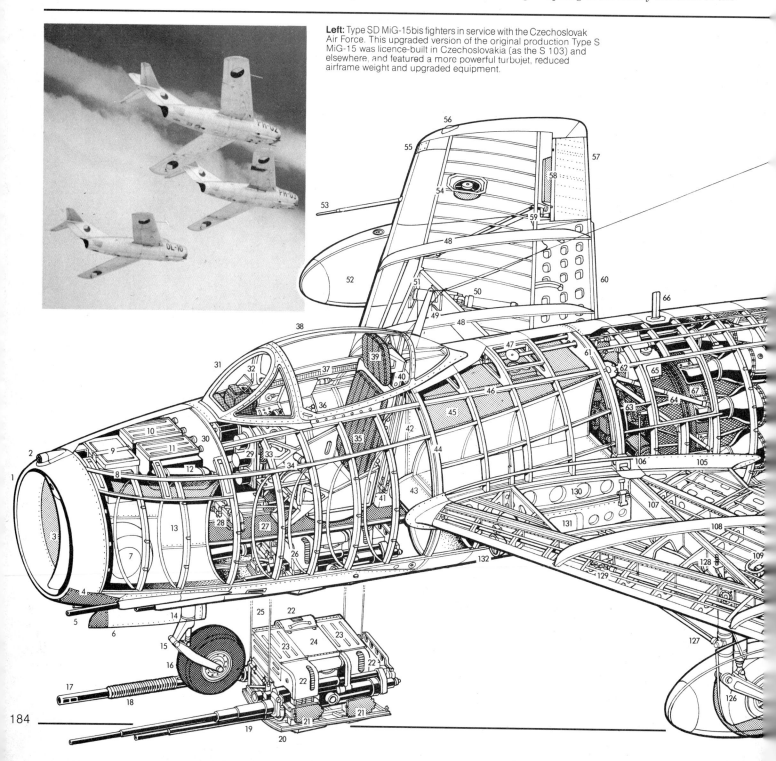

**Left:** Type SD MiG-15bis fighters in service with the Czechoslovak Air Force. This upgraded version of the original production Type S MiG-15 was licence-built in Czechoslovakia (as the S 103) and elsewhere, and featured a more powerful turbojet, reduced airframe weight and upgraded equipment.

basic Type S MiG-15 followed, most important being the Type SD MiG-15bis with the RD-45F-derived 5,952 lb (2 700 kg) VK-1 engine which was to be built in larger numbers than any jet fighter before or since.

## SPECIFICATION: MiG-15 (Type S)

**Power Plant:** One Klimov RD-45F (Rolls-Royce Nene derivative) centrifugal turbojet rated at 5,005 lb (2 270 kg) static thrust. Internal fuel capacity, 321 Imp gal (1 460 l).

**Performance:** Max speed, 652 mph (1 050 km/h) at sea level, 648 mph (1 043 km/h) at 9,840 ft (3 000 m), 640 mph (1 031 km/h) at 16,405 ft (5 000 m), 623 mph (1 004 km/h) at 26,245 ft (8 000 m); range, 882 mls (1 420 km) at 236 mph (380 km/h) at 39,370 ft (12 000 m), with two 54·4 Imp gal (247,5 l) drop tanks, 1,192 mls (1 920 km); initial climb, 8,268 ft/min (42 m/sec).

**Weights:** Empty equipped, 7,456 lb (3 382 kg); normal loaded (clean), 10,595 lb (4 806 kg).

**Dimensions:** Span, 33 ft 0⅞ in (10,08 m); length, 32 ft 11¼ in (10,04 m); height, 12 ft 1⅝ in (3,70 m); wing area, 221·74 sq ft (20,60 m²).

**Armament:** One 37-mm Nudelman N-37 cannon with 40 rounds and two 23-mm Nudelman-Suranov NS-23KM cannon with 80 rpg.

MiG-15bis

**Key to Mikoyan-Gurevich MiG-15bis**

1. Engine air intake
2. Gun camera aperture
3. Intake centre divider
4. Cannon blast shield
5. Cannon muzzles
6. Nosewheel doors
7. Nosewheel well between intake ducts
8. Forward fuselage equipment bay
9. Battery
10. RSIU-3M VHF transmitter
11. VHF radio receiver
12. Oxygen bottle
13. Bifurcated intake ducting
14. Nosewheel leg strut
15. Pivoted axle beam
16. Nosewheel
17. Starboard 37-mm N-37 cannon
18. Recoil spring
19. Port twin NR-23 23-mm cannon
20. Gun pack ventral door
21. Cartridge case ejection chutes
22. Ammunition feed chutes
23. 23-mm ammunition boxes (80-rounds per gun)
24. 37-mm ammunition box (40 rounds)
25. Gun pack winching cables
26. Ventral gun pack in position beneath cockpit floor
27. Cockpit floor level
28. Rudder pedals
29. Instrument panel
30. Cockpit front pressure bulkhead
31. Bullet proof windscreen
32. Reflector-type gunsight
33. Control column
34. Engine throttle
35. Pilot's ejection seat
36. Canopy handles
37. Sliding canopy rail
38. Cockpit canopy cover
39. Ejection seat headrest
40. Seat guide rails
41. Control rod runs
42. Cockpit rear pressure bulkhead
43. Wing centre-section carry through
44. Front spar/fuselage main frame
45. Main fuel tank (total internal fuel capacity 310 Imp gal/1410 l)
46. Fuselage upper longeron
47. Fuel filler cap access panel
48. Starboard wing fences
49. Radio aerial mast
50. Starboard flap jack
51. Main undercarriage pivot fixing
52. Slipper-type drop tank, 54·8 Imp gal/250 l)
53. Pitot tube
54. Remote compass transmitter
55. Anti-flutter weight
56. Starboard navigation light
57. Starboard aileron
58. Aileron balance
59. Aileron hinge control
60. Starboard Fowler-type flap
61. Rear spar/fuselage main frame
62. Rear fuselage break point (engine removal)
63. Engine accessories
64. Engine mounting struts
65. Oil tanks
66. VHF aerial
67. Klimov VK-1 centrifugal turbojet
68. Engine flame cans (9)
69. Rear engine mounting bulkhead
70. Rear fuselage fuel tank filler cap access
71. Fin mounting main frames
72. Heat shrouded jet pipe
73. Sloping fin spar bulkhead
74. Fin attachment joints
75. Tail control rods
76. Fin construction
77. Tailplane attachment joint
78. HF aerial cable
79. Starboard tailplane
80. Fin tip fairing
81. Rudder anti-flutter weight
82. Upper rudder segment
83. Tail navigation light
84. Elevator trim tab (port only)
85. Port elevator
86. Elevator anti-flutter weight
87. Tailplane construction
88. Elevator mass balance
89. Fin/tailplane spar joint
90. Elevator control rod
91. Rudder lower segment
92. Fixed rudder tab
93. Jet pipe shroud
94. Rudder mass balance
95. Engine exhaust nozzle
96. Airbrake housing
97. Pneumatic airbrake jack
98. Port airbrake, open
99. Tail bumper
100. Fuselage frame and stringer construction
101. Rear fuselage fuel tank
102. Fuel tank access panel
103. Fuselage skin plating
104. Lower fuselage longeron
105. Wing root fillet
106. Rear spar attachment joint
107. Diagonal spar/undercarriage mounting beam
108. Inboard wing fence
109. Flap hydraulic jack
110. Port fowler flap
111. Outboard wing fence
112. Aileron operating rod
113. Aileron tab, port only
114. Aileron balance
115. Port aileron construction
116. Wing tip fairing
117. Port navigation light
118. Anti-flutter weight
119. Wing rib and stringer construction
120. Main spar
121. Leading edge nose ribs
122. Slipper tank fixing
123. Port slipper-type drop tank
124. Fuel filler cap
125. Port mainwheel
126. Levered suspension axle beam
127. Hydraulic retraction jack (pneumatic standby)
128. Undercarriage position indicator
129. Leading edge, control rod runs
130. Main undercarriage wheel well
131. Wheel well door
132. Retractable landing lamp

# Avro Canada CF-100 Canuck (January 1950)

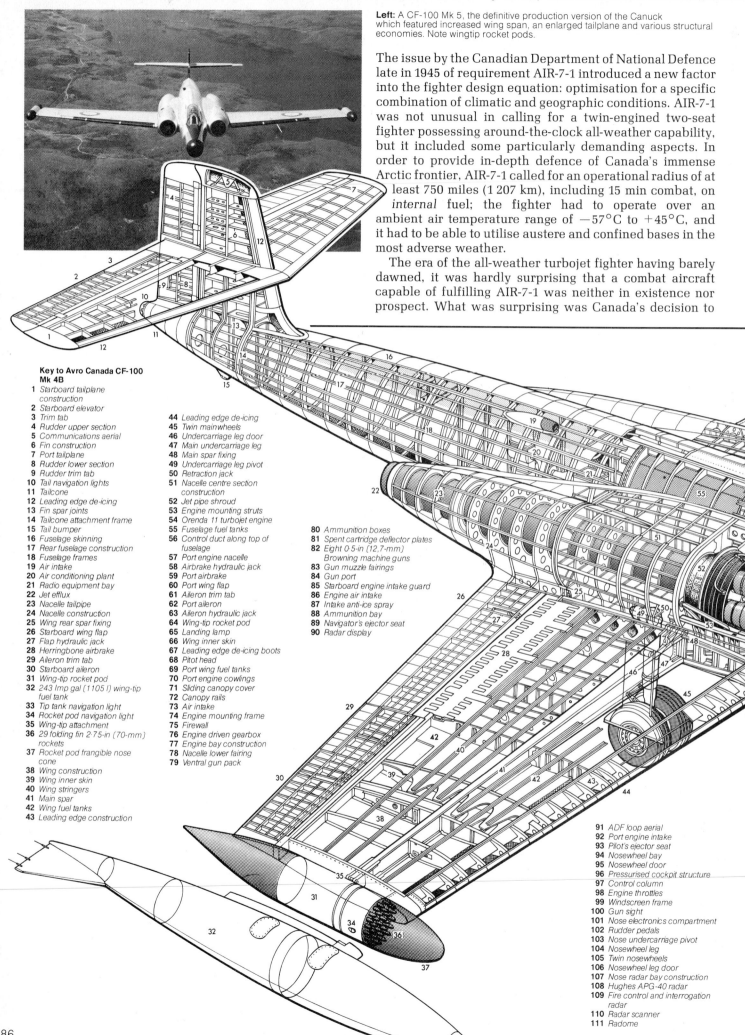

**Left:** A CF-100 Mk 5, the definitive production version of the Canuck which featured increased wing span, an enlarged tailplane and various structural economies. Note wingtip rocket pods.

The issue by the Canadian Department of National Defence late in 1945 of requirement AIR-7-1 introduced a new factor into the fighter design equation: optimisation for a specific combination of climatic and geographic conditions. AIR-7-1 was not unusual in calling for a twin-engined two-seat fighter possessing around-the-clock all-weather capability, but it included some particularly demanding aspects. In order to provide in-depth defence of Canada's immense Arctic frontier, AIR-7-1 called for an operational radius of at least 750 miles (1 207 km), including 15 min combat, on *internal* fuel; the fighter had to operate over an ambient air temperature range of $-57^\circ$C to $+45^\circ$C, and it had to be able to utilise austere and confined bases in the most adverse weather.

The era of the all-weather turbojet fighter having barely dawned, it was hardly surprising that a combat aircraft capable of fulfilling AIR-7-1 was neither in existence nor prospect. What was surprising was Canada's decision to

### Key to Avro Canada CF-100 Mk 4B

1. Starboard tailplane construction
2. Starboard elevator
3. Trim tab
4. Rudder upper section
5. Communications aerial
6. Fin construction
7. Port tailplane
8. Rudder lower section
9. Rudder trim tab
10. Tail navigation lights
11. Tailcone
12. Leading edge de-icing
13. Fin spar joints
14. Tailcone attachment frame
15. Tail bumper
16. Fuselage skinning
17. Rear fuselage construction
18. Fuselage frames
19. Air intake
20. Air conditioning plant
21. Radio equipment bay
22. Jet efflux
23. Nacelle tailpipe
24. Nacelle construction
25. Wing rear spar fixing
26. Starboard wing flap
27. Flap hydraulic jack
28. Herringbone airbrake
29. Aileron trim tab
30. Starboard aileron
31. Wing-tip rocket pod
32. 243 Imp gal (1105 l) wing-tip fuel tank
33. Tip tank navigation light
34. Rocket pod navigation light
35. Wing-tip attachment
36. 29 folding fin 2·75-in (70-mm) rockets
37. Rocket pod frangible nose cone
38. Wing construction
39. Wing inner skin
40. Wing stringers
41. Main spar
42. Wing fuel tanks
43. Leading edge construction
44. Leading edge de-icing
45. Twin mainwheels
46. Undercarriage leg door
47. Main undercarriage leg
48. Main spar fixing
49. Undercarriage leg pivot
50. Retraction jack
51. Nacelle centre section construction
52. Jet pipe shroud
53. Engine mounting struts
54. Orenda 11 turbojet engine
55. Fuselage fuel tanks
56. Control duct along top of fuselage
57. Port engine nacelle
58. Airbrake hydraulic jack
59. Port airbrake
60. Port wing flap
61. Aileron trim tab
62. Port aileron
63. Aileron hydraulic jack
64. Wing-tip rocket pod
65. Landing lamp
66. Wing inner skin
67. Leading edge de-icing boots
68. Pitot head
69. Port wing fuel tanks
70. Port engine cowlings
71. Sliding canopy cover
72. Canopy rails
73. Air intake
74. Engine mounting frame
75. Firewall
76. Engine driven gearbox
77. Engine bay construction
78. Nacelle lower fairing
79. Ventral gun pack
80. Ammunition boxes
81. Spent cartridge deflector plates
82. Eight 0·5-in (12,7-mm) Browning machine guns
83. Gun muzzle fairings
84. Gun port
85. Starboard engine intake guard
86. Engine air intake
87. Intake anti-ice spray
88. Ammunition bay
89. Navigator's ejector seat
90. Radar display
91. ADF loop aerial
92. Port engine intake
93. Pilot's ejector seat
94. Nosewheel bay
95. Nosewheel door
96. Pressurised cockpit structure
97. Control column
98. Engine throttles
99. Windscreen frame
100. Gun sight
101. Nose electronics compartment
102. Rudder pedals
103. Nose undercarriage pivot
104. Nosewheel leg
105. Twin nosewheels
106. Nosewheel leg door
107. Nose radar bay construction
108. Hughes APG-40 radar
109. Fire control and interrogation radar
110. Radar scanner
111. Radome

develop a warplane tailored to AIR-7-1 as a national programme. This was to emerge four years later in the shape of the CF-100 which was to be deceptively conservative in aerodynamic configuration.

Designed by a team headed by John Frost and first flown on 19 January 1950, the CF-100 featured twin turbojets surmounting a thin, unswept wing and flanking a slim, circular-section fuselage into which they were faired to produce an almost aerofoil-section central body contributing 30 per cent of the total lift. The first series version, the Mk 3 (70 built) flew on 11 October 1952, and was succeeded by the 6,355 lb (2 882 kg) Orenda 9-powered Mk 4A and 7,275 lb (3 300 kg) Orenda 11-powered Mk 4B, the former (137 built) retaining the Mk 3's ventral tray of eight 0.50-in (12,7-mm) M-3 guns, and the latter (144 built) having a ventral rocket pack as an option, both mounting wingtip rocket pods. The definitive model, the Mk 5 (329 built), featured a 6-ft (1,83-m) wing extension and discarded the ventral pack in favour of larger wingtip pods, production ending late 1958.

## SPECIFICATION: CF-100 Mk 5

**Power Plant:** Two Avro Orenda Mk 14 axial-flow turbojets each rated at 7,275 lb (3 700 kg). Internal fuel capacity, 1,350 Imp gal (6 137 l), with provision for two 243 Imp gal (1 105 l) wingtip tanks.

**Performance:** Max speed, 624 mph (1 004 km/h) or M=0.8 at sea level, 590 mph (949 km/h) at 5,000 ft (1 525 m), 560 mph (901 km/h) or M=0.85 at 40,000 ft (12 190 m); range cruise, 447 mph (722 km/h) or M=0.68 at 36,000 ft (10 975 m); initial climb, 8,500 ft/min (43,2 m/sec); time to 40,000 ft (12 190 m), 8.0 min; combat radius (internal fuel), 700 mls (1 126 km); max range (with wingtip tanks), 2,300 mls (3 700 km).

**Weights:** Empty, 23,100 lb (10 478 kg); normal loaded, 33,600 lb (15 240 kg); max, 36,465 lb (16 540 kg).

**Dimensions:** Span (over pods), 60 ft 10¼ in (18,55 m), (without pods), 57 ft 2½ in (17,42 m); length, 54 ft 1¾ in (16,50 m); height, 14 ft 6 in (4,42 m); wing area, 579.14 sq ft (53,80 m²).

**Armament:** Fifty-two 2.75-in (70-mm) folding-fin rockets in each of two wingtip pods.

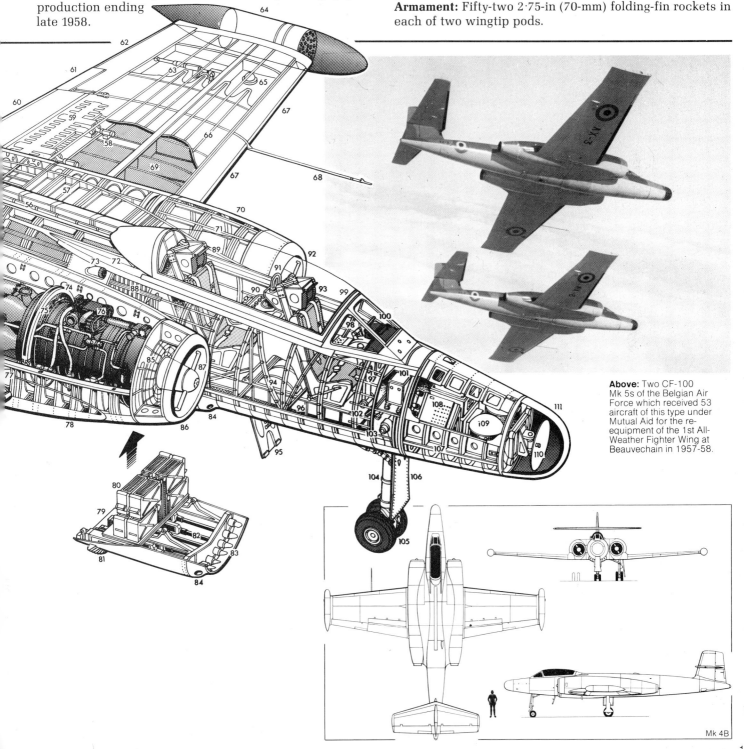

**Above:** Two CF-100 Mk 5s of the Belgian Air Force which received 53 aircraft of this type under Mutual Aid for the re-equipment of the 1st All-Weather Fighter Wing at Beauvechain in 1957-58.

# Republic F-84F Thunderstreak (June 1950)

With practicability of wing sweepback proven as a means of delaying compressibility onset, studies were made of its application to a variety of existing straight-wing fighters as potentially economical means of enhancing performance. Most such were of dubious feasibility, and, in the event, only two of US origin were pursued to the extent that production derivatives resulted: the F9F Cougar (see pages 192-193) and the F-84F Thunderstreak. Insofar as the latter was concerned, however, incremental redesign prior to production was to produce a fundamentally new aeroplane, retaining no commonality with its precursor, the F-84E Thunderjet (see pages 178-179).

Conceived during a period of acute governmental parsimony towards new warplane development, the F-84F stemmed from a late 1949 proposal to mate the fuselage of the existing F-84E with new swept surfaces, thus offering a substantial performance increment yet utilising up to 60 per cent of existing tooling. This union was duly flown as the XF-84F on 3 June 1950, but in order to take full advantage of its more advanced aerodynamic characteristics, redesign of the fuselage was undertaken to permit installation of the more powerful Wright J65 turbojet, equipped with which a further prototype, designated the YF-84F, flew on 14 February 1951.

Numerous additional changes eradicated the last commonality with the F-84E before the first production F-84F flew on 14 February 1951, service phase-in by the USAF commencing in 1954. Optimised for the fighter-bomber mission, the F-84F proved exceptionally demanding on field length, and, at the time of its service dèbut, its landing speed was considered dauntingly high. Underpowered with external loads, the F-84F tended to wallow in the climb-out, lacked acceleration and was particularly susceptible to high-speed stalling. Some of its less pleasant handling characteristics were alleviated with the introduction of an "all-flying" tail with the 276th (F-86F-25) and subsequent aircraft, and it was to prove an exceptionally rugged aircraft, a stable weapons platform and capable of lifting formidable stores loads.

A total of 2,711 F-84F Thunderstreaks was built, 1,301 of these being supplied to NATO air forces from 1955 and serving until the early 'seventies.

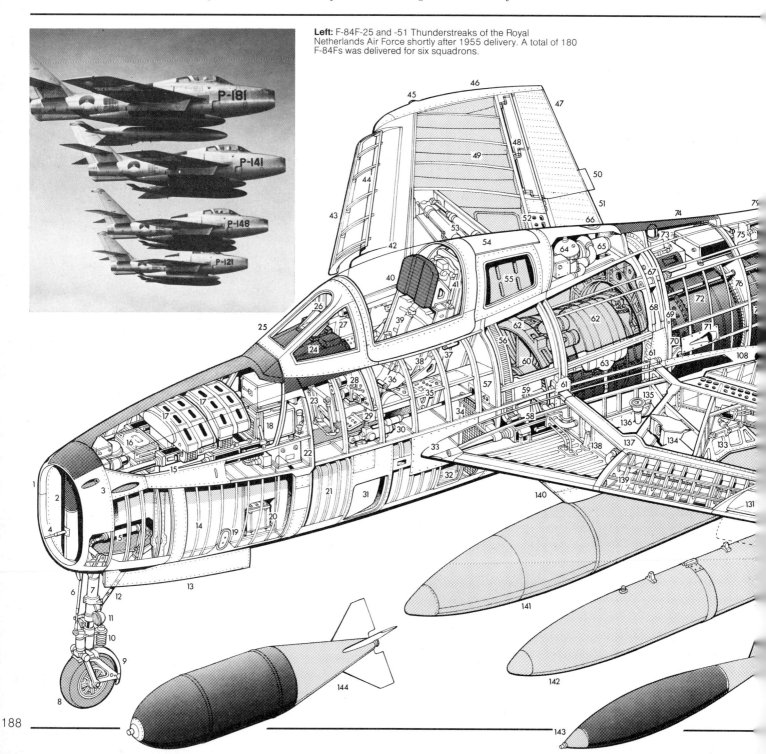

**Left:** F-84F-25 and -51 Thunderstreaks of the Royal Netherlands Air Force shortly after 1955 delivery. A total of 180 F-84Fs was delivered for six squadrons.

## SPECIFICATION: F-84F-50 Thunderstreak

**Power Plant:** One Wright J65-W-7 axial-flow turbojet rated at 7,800 lb (3 538 kg). Internal fuel capacity, 475 Imp gal (2 159 l), with provision for two 191·5 Imp gal (870 l) or 375 Imp gal (1 705 l) drop tanks, or (for ferrying) two of each.

**Performance:** Max speed, 658 mph (1 059 km/h) or M=0·864 at sea level 612 mph (985 km/h) or M=0·92 at 35,000 ft (10 670 m); max cruise, 539 mph (867 km/h); combat radius (two 375 Imp gal/1 705 l drop tanks), 856 mls (1 378 km); ferry range (max external fuel), 2,343 mls (3 770 km); initial climb, 7,400 ft/min (37,59 m/sec); time to 35,000 ft (10 670 m), 7·2 min; combat ceiling, 44,850 ft (13 670 m).

**Weights:** Empty, 13,645 lb (6 189 kg); combat, 18,700 lb (8 482 kg); normal loaded, 25,226 lb (11 442 kg); max, 27,000 lb (12 247 kg).

**Dimensions:** Span, 33 ft 7¼ in (10,24 m); length, 43 ft 4¾ in (13,23 m); height, 15 ft 0 in (4,57 m); wing area, 325 sq ft (30,19 m²).

**Armament:** Six 0·50-in (12,7-mm) Colt-Browning M-3 machine guns with 300 rpg, and provision for up to 6,000 lb (2 722 kg) of external ordnance.

**Key to Republic F-84F Thunderstreak**

1 Engine air intake
2 Gun tracking radar antenna
3 Machine gun muzzles
4 Pitot tube
5 Nose undercarriage hydraulic retraction jack
6 Leg compression link
7 Nosewheel leg strut
8 Nosewheel
9 Mudguard
10 Steering jack
11 Taxying lamp
12 Nose undercarriage leg rear strut
13 Nosewheel doors
14 Intake duct framing
15 Nose compartment 0·05-in (12,7-mm) Colt-Browning M-3 machine guns (four)
16 Radar electronics equipment
17 Ammunition tanks, total 1,800 rounds
18 Forward avionics bay including LABS bombing computer
19 Static ports
20 Battery
21 Intake ducting
22 Cockpit front pressure bulkhead
23 Rudder pedals
24 Instrument panel shroud
25 Windscreen panels
26 A-4 Radar gunsight
27 Stand-by compass
28 Instrument panel
29 Ejection seat footrests
30 Aileron hydraulic booster
31 Intake suction relief door
32 Duct screen clearance access panel
33 Wing root machine gun muzzle
34 Intake duct screen
35 Port side console panel
36 Engine throttle
37 External canopy release handle
38 Pilot's ejection seat
39 Safety harness
40 Headrest
41 Ejection seat guide rails
42 Cockpit canopy cover
43 Starboard automatic leading edge slat, open
44 Slat guide rails
45 Starboard navigation light
46 Wing tip fairing
47 Starboard aileron
48 Aileron control rods
49 Starboard wing integral fuel tank; maximum internal fuel capacity 475 Imp gal (2 159 l)
50 Aileron fixed tab
51 Starboard flap
52 Spoiler
53 Starboard main undercarriage leg (retracted position)
54 Canopy rear hinge arm
55 Cockpit aft glazing
56 Ammunition feed chute
57 Cockpit rear pressure bulkhead
58 Wing root 0·50-in (12,7-mm) Colt-Browning M-3 machine gun
59 Engine electric starter/generator
60 Intake compressor face
61 Wing/fuselage spar lug attachment bolts (total four)
62 Fuselage main fuel tanks
63 Engine oil tank
64 Oxygen bottle
65 Air conditioning and pressurization pack
66 Fuselage fuel tank filler cap
67 Tail section attachment bolts (four)
68 Fuselage double main frames
69 Fuselage break point
70 Main engine mounting
71 Engine bay cooling intake
72 Wright J65-W-7 turbojet engine
73 Radio compass antenna
74 Flush aerial fairing
75 Aft radio equipment bay
76 Engine firewall
77 Engine turbine section
78 Fuselage frame and stringer construction
79 Dorsal spine fairing
80 Anti collision light
81 VHF aerial
82 Tailpipe cooling intake
83 Rear fuselage framing
84 Jet pipe
85 Rudder control rod, elevator on starboard side
86 Fin root fillet
87 Aerial tuning units
88 All-moving tailplane control jack
89 Tailplane pivot fixing
90 Fin/tailplane sealing plates
91 Starboard all-moving tailplane
92 Fin leading edge
93 Tailfin construction
94 Rudder mass balance weight
95 Fin tip aerial fairing
96 Tail navigation lights
97 Rudder construction
98 Rudder fixed tab
99 Parallel chord all-moving tailplane construction
100 Jet pipe exhaust nozzle
101 Rudder hinge control
102 Tailfin attachment frames
103 Brake parachute fairing doors
104 Parachute stowage
105 Parachute release link
106 Airbrake hydraulic jack
107 Port perforated airbrake
108 Trailing edge wing root fillet
109 Port plain flap construction
110 Port spoiler
111 Drop tank stabilising fins
112 Aileron fixed tab
113 Port aileron construction
114 Aileron control rods
115 Rear spar
116 Port wing integral fuel tank
117 Wing tip fairing
118 Port navigaton light
119 Retractable landing lamp
120 5-in (12,7-cm) HVAR ground attack rockets
121 Wing stringers
122 Wing rib construction
123 Port outer wing pylon
124 Undercarriage leg torque scissors
125 Mainwheel doors
126 Port mainwheel
127 Main undercarriage leg strut
128 Undercarriage leg pivot fixing
129 Hydraulic retraction jack
130 Main undercarriage mounting beam
131 Port automatic leading edge slat (closed position)
132 Mainwheel well
133 Inner wheel door
134 Fuselage boom' in-flight refuelling adaptor (open)
135 Wing tank fuel filler cap
136 Ventral engine access doors
137 Front spar
138 Pylon fixing
139 Fixed leading edge construction
140 Inboard pylon
141 312 Imp gal (1420-l) ferry tank
142 191.5 Imp gal (870 l) drop tank
143 Mk 84 1,000-lb (454-kg) HE bomb
144 2,000-lb (907-kg) free fall nuclear weapon

# Hawker Hunter (July 1951)

Acknowledged as *the* classic single-seat fighter of the 'fifties, the aesthetically-unsurpassed Hunter was the first genuinely transonic British service aircraft. First flown on 21 July 1951, the Hunter suffered a somewhat protracted gestation and did not enter the RAF in its initial F Mk 1 service form for three years, until July 1954. Even then, serious teething problems remained to be resolved, such as pitch-up, ineffectual longitudinal control at high speed, and engine surging and pitch-down during gun firing, but its fundamental shortcoming, inadequate internal fuel tankage, was insoluble.

The principal problems were eradicated and the fuel problem was mitigated with the F Mk 4, which flew on 20 October 1954, by a nominal increase in internal capacity and provision for drop tanks, and the Hunter began to establish a reputation as a "pilot's aeroplane" in every respect. It was to prove tolerant to most kinds of abuse, offering flawless handling with very few limitations, and its relatively low wing loading and, for its day, comparatively high power-to-weight ratio rendered it an exhilarating aircraft to fly.

Extraordinarily robust, a fact belied by its fine contours, the Hunter was to see almost two decades of first-line RAF service, its last operational roles being those of ground attack and tactical reconnaissance as the FGA Mk 9 and FR Mk 10 respectively, these both being conversions of the definitive F Mk 6 single-seat production model which had entered service from June 1956. Production of the Hunter was to continue into 1959, with a total of 1,972 being completed of which 445 were licence-built in Belgium and the Netherlands. Of these, almost one-third were later to be refurbished and converted for a variety of roles for the RAF and a dozen overseas customers.

**SPECIFICATION: Hunter F Mk 6**
**Power Plant:** One Rolls-Royce Avon 207 axial-flow turbojet rated at 10,150 lb (4 605 kg) static thrust. Internal fuel capacity, 392 Imp gal (1 782 l), with provision for four 100

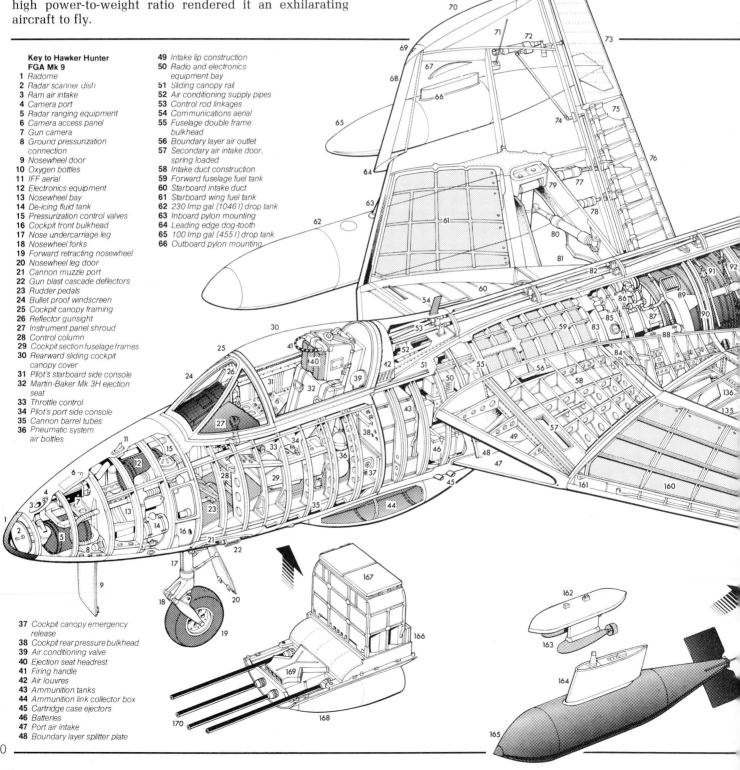

**Key to Hawker Hunter FGA Mk 9**
1 Radome
2 Radar scanner dish
3 Ram air intake
4 Camera port
5 Radar ranging equipment
6 Camera access panel
7 Gun camera
8 Ground pressurization connection
9 Nosewheel door
10 Oxygen bottles
11 IFF aerial
12 Electronics equipment
13 Nosewheel bay
14 De-icing fluid tank
15 Pressurization control valves
16 Cockpit front bulkhead
17 Nose undercarriage leg
18 Nosewheel forks
19 Forward retracting nosewheel
20 Nosewheel leg door
21 Cannon muzzle port
22 Gun blast cascade deflectors
23 Rudder pedals
24 Bullet proof windscreen
25 Cockpit canopy framing
26 Reflector gunsight
27 Instrument panel shroud
28 Control column
29 Cockpit section fuselage frames
30 Rearward sliding cockpit canopy cover
31 Pilot's starboard side console
32 Martin-Baker Mk 3H ejection seat
33 Throttle control
34 Pilot's port side console
35 Cannon barrel tubes
36 Pneumatic system air bottles
37 Cockpit canopy emergency release
38 Cockpit rear pressure bulkhead
39 Air conditioning valve
40 Ejection seat headrest
41 Firing handle
42 Air louvres
43 Ammunition tanks
44 Ammunition link collector box
45 Cartridge case ejectors
46 Batteries
47 Port air intake
48 Boundary layer splitter plate

49 Intake lip construction
50 Radio and electronics equipment bay
51 Sliding canopy rail
52 Air conditioning supply pipes
53 Control rod linkages
54 Communications aerial
55 Fuselage double frame bulkhead
56 Boundary layer air outlet
57 Secondary air intake door, spring loaded
58 Intake duct construction
59 Forward fuselage fuel tank
60 Starboard intake duct
61 Starboard wing fuel tank
62 230 Imp gal (1046 l) drop tank
63 Inboard pylon mounting
64 Leading edge dog-tooth
65 100 Imp gal (455 l) drop tank
66 Outboard pylon mounting

Imp gal (455 l) or two 230 Imp gal (1 046 l) and two 100 Imp gal (455 l) drop tanks.

**Performance:** Max speed, 715 mph (1 150 km/h) or M=0·938 at sea level, 623 mph (1 002 km/h) or M=0·945 at 36,000 ft (10 975 m); tactical radius (internal fuel/high-altitude intercept mission), 228 mls (367 km), HI-LO-HI with 24 x 3-in/7,62-cm rockets and two 230 Imp gal/1 046 l drop tanks), 443 mls (713 km); ferry range (max external fuel), 1,900 mls (3 058 km); initial climb, 17,200 ft/min (87,37 m/sec); time to 40,000 ft (12 190 m), 4·95 min.

**Weights:** Empty equipped, 14,122 lb (6 405 kg); loaded (clean), 17,750 lb (8 051 kg); max, 23,800 lb (10 796 kg).

**Dimensions:** Span, 33 ft 8 in (10,25 m); length, 45 ft 10½ in (13,98 m); height, 13 ft 2 in (4,02 m); wing area, 349 sq ft (32,42 m²).

**Armament:** Four 30-mm Aden cannon with 100 rounds of ammunition for each cannon and up to 3,600 lb (1 633 kg) of external ordnance (for example, two 1,000-lb/454-kg bombs and 24 3-in/7,62-cm rockets).

FGA Mk 9

67 Wing fence
68 Leading edge extension
69 Starboard navigation light
70 Starboard wing tip
71 Whip aerial
72 Fairey hydraulic aileron booster jack
73 Starboard aileron
74 Aileron control rod linkage
75 Flap cut-out section for drop tank clearance
76 Starboard flap construction
77 Flap hydraulic jack
78 Flap synchronising jack
79 Starboard main undercarriage mounting
80 Retraction jack
81 Starboard undercarriage bay
82 Dorsal spine fairing
83 Main wing attachment frames
84 Main spar attachment joint
85 Engine starter fuel tank
86 Air conditioning system
87 Engine intake compressor face
88 Air conditioning pre-cooler
89 Cooling air outlet louvres
90 Rear spar attachment frames
91 Aileron control rods
92 Front engine mountings
93 Rolls-Royce Avon 207 turbojet
94 Bleed air duct
95 Engine bay cooling flush air intake
96 Rear engine mounting
97 Rear fuselage joint ring
98 Joint ring attachment bolts
99 Tailplane control rods
100 Fuel piping from rear tank
101 Rear fuselage fuel tank
102 Fuel collector tank
103 Hydraulic accumulator
104 Fin root fairing
105 Hydraulic accumulator
106 Tailplane trim jack
107 Fairey hydraulic elevator booster
108 Tailplane mounting pivot
109 Rudder hinge control rods
110 Starboard tailplane
111 Starboard elevator
112 Tailfin construction
113 Fin tip aerial fairing
114 Rudder construction
115 Rudder trim tab
116 Trim tab control jack
117 Tailplane anti-buffet fairing
118 Tail navigation light
119 Brake parachute housing
120 Tailpipe fairing
121 Port elevator construction
122 Tailplane construction
123 Detachable tailcone
124 Tailplane spar mounting frames
125 Jetpipe
126 Jetpipe access doors
127 Rear fuselage frame and stringer construction
128 Airbrake jack housing
129 Airbrake retracted position
130 Airbrake operating jack
131 Airbrake open position
132 Engine bearing cooling air outlet
133 Wing root trailing edge fillet
134 Flap housing construction
135 Port main undercarriage bay
136 Mainwheel door
137 Port main undercarriage retraction jack
138 Main undercarriage leg pivot mounting
139 Flap synchronising jack
140 Hydraulic flap jack
141 Port flap
142 Rear spar
143 Aileron control rod
144 Aileron trim tab
145 Port aileron construction
146 Fairey hydraulic aileron booster
147 Wing tip construction
148 Port navigation light
149 Pitot tube
150 3-in (7,62-cm) rocket projectiles
151 Leading edge extension ribs
152 Wing rib construction
153 Main spar
154 Dowty main undercarriage leg
155 Shock absorber torque links
156 Leading edge dog tooth
157 Mainwheel doors
158 Dunlop-Maxaret anti-skid wheel brakes
159 Port mainwheel
160 Port wing fuel tank: total internal fuel capacity 392 Imp gal (1782 l)
161 Leading edge pin joint
162 M.L. twin stores carrier
163 20-lb (9-kg) practice bombs
164 Inboard wing pylon
165 1,000-lb (454-kg) bomb
166 Four × 30-mm Aden gun pack
167 Ammunition boxes, 100 rounds per gun
168 Link collector box
169 Gun gas purging air duct
170 Cannon barrels remaining in aircraft when pack is withdrawn

**Right:** A Hunter FGA Mk 9 of the Rhodesian Air Force at Thornhill in 1964. Twelve ex-RAF F Mk 6s were brought up to FGA Mk 9 standards for Rhodesia.

# Grumman F9F (F-9) Cougar (September 1951)

With the adoption of wing sweepback for land-based fighters, designers of shipboard counterparts began to evaluate the effects of this development on their future progeny. The swept wing at first appeared incompatible with carrier requirements. It increased dihedral effect, decreased damping in roll, and it adversely affected the relationship between adverse yaw due to rolling and the stability of the aircraft. Furthermore, there seemed little likelihood that the swept wing could offer acceptable carrier approach speeds.

After protracted evaluation of the problems, Grumman Aircraft Engineering decided to adopt the most economical and low-risk solution to the development of a swept-wing carrier fighter by emulating Republic Aviation and applying sweep-back to an existing aircraft with unswept surfaces. The subject of this development was the F9F-5 Panther, which had become the first naval jet fighter to see combat when it began Korean operations on 3 July 1950. The problem of approach speeds had been resolved with the Panther by combining leading-edge slats with trailing-edge flaps. This arrangement was retained for its swept-wing derivative,

but the chord of the slats was increased and the flaps were extended along three-quarters of the span. The ailerons were supplanted by upper-surface spoilers and fences were added to reduce spanwise flow.

Within the phenomenally short time of six months, a swept-wing prototype, the XF9F-6, was completed and flown on 20 September 1951. This retained the fuselage and vertical tail surfaces of the F9F-5 Panther, and the first production deliveries to the US Navy began as the F9F-6 Cougar barely more than three months later.

The flying characteristics of the Cougar remained essentially similar to those of the Panther. Handling was pleasant, control response was good, it was relatively agile and there were no significant restrictions on flight manoeuvres, and stalling speeds were virtually indentical. But whereas the Panther had a critical Mach number of 0·83, which it could only reach in a dive accompanied by severe buffet and almost uncontrollable pitch-up, its more practical limitation being Mach =0·79, the F9F-6 could attain

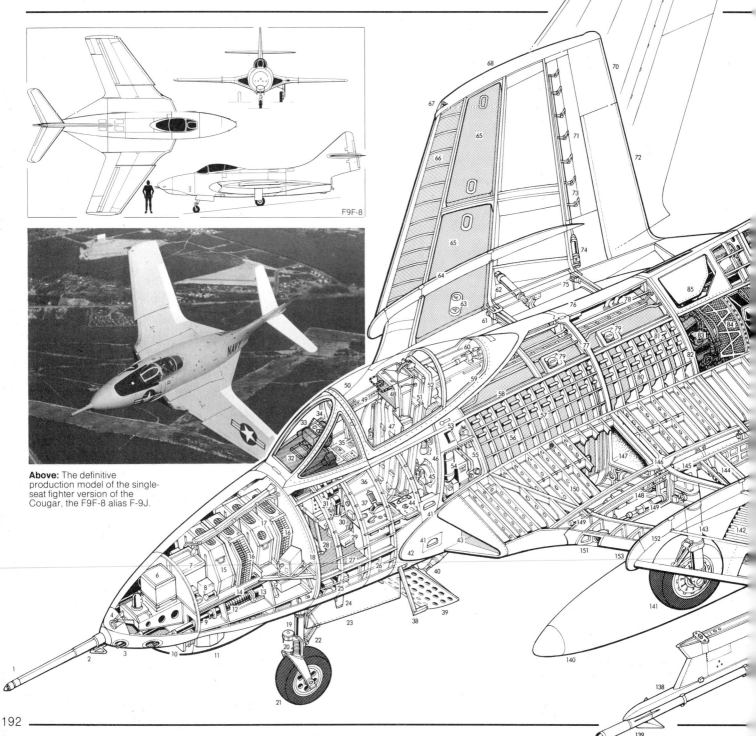

F9F-8

**Above:** The definitive production model of the single-seat fighter version of the Cougar, the F9F-8 alias F-9J.

Mach = 0·86 at sea level and 0·895 at 35,000 ft (10 670 m) in level flight.

The first service shipboard swept-wing fighter, the F9F-6 (753 built) was followed by the F9F-7 (178 built) with the 6,950 lb (3 152 kg) Allison J33-A-16, the definitive fighter model being the F9F-8 (601 built), which, first flown on 18 December 1953, introduced an 8-in (20-cm) fuselage extension to increase internal fuel capacity, discarded the slats to permit installation of leading-edge tanks, and had a 15 per cent wing chord increase to improve the critical Mach number by providing a relatively thinner section. In 1962, the F9F was redesignated F-9. A training variant (TF-9J) remained in service until early in 1974.

## SPECIFICATION: F9F-8 (F-9J) Cougar

**Power Plant:** One Pratt & Whitney J48-P-8 centrifugal-flow turbojet rated at 7,250 lb (3 289 kg) static thrust. Internal fuel capacity, 885 Imp gal (4 024 l), with provision for two 125 Imp gal (568 l) drop tanks.

**Performance:** Max speed, 642 mph (1 033 km/h) or M = 0·84; combat radius, 443 mls (713 km); range (internal fuel), 1,209 mls (1 946 km) at 516 mph (830 km/h) at 38,000-42,000 ft (11 580-12 800 m); initial climb, 4,800 ft/min (24,36 m/sec); time to 20,000 ft (6 095 m), 4·8 min, to 30,000 ft (9 145 m), 8·3 min; service ceiling, 42,000 ft (12 800 m).

**Weights:** Empty, 11,866 lb (5 382 kg); normal loaded (clean), 20,098 lb (9 116 kg); maximum gross weight, 24,763 lb (11 232 kg).

**Dimensions:** Span, 34 ft 6 in (10,51 m); length, 42 ft 2 in (12,85 m); height, 12 ft 2½ in (3,72 m); wing area, 337 sq ft (31,30 m²).

**Armament:** Four 20-mm M-3 cannon with 190 rounds of ammunition per gun and provision for two AIM-9 Sidewinder air-to-air missiles or up to four 500-lb (226,8-kg) bombs.

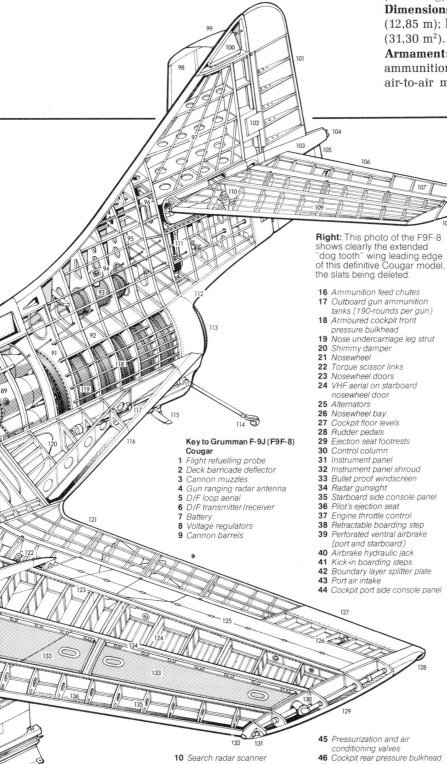

**Right:** This photo of the F9F-8 shows clearly the extended "dog tooth" wing leading edge of this definitive Cougar model, the slats being deleted.

**Key to Grumman F-9J (F9F-8) Cougar**

1 Flight refuelling probe
2 Deck barricade deflector
3 Cannon muzzles
4 Gun ranging radar antenna
5 D/F loop aerial
6 D/F transmitter/receiver
7 Battery
8 Voltage regulators
9 Cannon barrels
10 Search radar scanner
11 Radar scanner housing
12 Cannon recoil spring
13 M-3 20-mm cannon (4)
14 Nose cone withdrawal rail
15 Inboard gun ammunition tanks (190-rounds per gun)
16 Ammunition feed chutes
17 Outboard gun ammunition tanks (190-rounds per gun)
18 Armoured cockpit front pressure bulkhead
19 Nose undercarriage leg strut
20 Shimmy damper
21 Nosewheel
22 Torque scissor links
23 Nosewheel doors
24 VHF aerial on starboard nosewheel door
25 Alternators
26 Nosewheel bay
27 Cockpit floor levels
28 Rudder pedals
29 Ejection seat footrests
30 Control column
31 Instrument panel
32 Instrument panel shroud
33 Bullet proof windscreen
34 Radar gunsight
35 Starboard side console panel
36 Pilot's ejection seat
37 Engine throttle control
38 Retractable boarding step
39 Perforated ventral airbrake (port and starboard)
40 Airbrake hydraulic jack
41 Kick-in boarding steps
42 Boundary layer splitter plate
43 Port air intake
44 Cockpit port side console panel
45 Pressurization and air conditioning valves
46 Cockpit rear pressure bulkhead
47 Safety harness
48 Face blind firing handle
49 Sliding canopy rail
50 Cockpit canopy cover
51 Ejection seat launch rails
52 Pilot's back armour
53 Canopy external latch
54 Oxygen bottle
55 Equipment bay access door
56 Forward fuselage fuel tank
57 Fuselage frame and stringer construction
58 Main longeron
59 Canopy aft glazing
60 Sliding canopy jack
61 Wing-fold spar hinge joint
62 Wing-fold hydraulic jack
63 Fuel filler cap
64 Starboard wing fence
65 Wing main fuel tanks (total internal capacity 885 Imp gal/4024 l)
66 Leading edge integral fuel tank
67 Starboard navigation light
68 Wing tip fairing
69 Starboard wing folded position
70 Fixed portion of trailing edge
71 Starboard roll control spoilers
72 Starboard flap
73 Spoiler hinge control links
74 Spoiler hydraulic jack
75 Rear spar hinge joint
76 Fuselage skin plating
77 Wing spar/fuselage main frame
78 Fuel system piping
79 Fuel filler caps
80 Fuselage rear fuel tank
81 Control cable ducts
82 Rear spar/fuselage main frame
83 Engine accessory compartment
84 Compressor intake screen
85 Supplementary air intake doors (open)
86 Pratt & Whitney J48-P-8A centrifugal-flow turbojet
87 Rear fuselage break point (engine removal)
88 Engine mounting main frame
89 Engine flame cans
90 Secondary air intake door, open
91 Fireproof bulkhead
92 Jet pipe heat shroud
93 Water injection tank
94 Water filler cap
95 Fuselage/fin root frame construction
96 Fin attachment joint
97 Tailfin construction
98 Starboard tailplane
99 Starboard elevator
100 Fin tip VHF aerial
101 Rudder construction
102 Rudder mass balance
103 Fin/tailplane fairing
104 Tail navigation lights
105 Lower rudder segment trim tab
106 Elevator trim tab
107 Port elevator
108 Elevator horn balance
109 Port tailplane construction
110 Trimming tailplane hinge joint
111 Tailplane trim jack
112 Exhaust nozzle shroud
113 Jet exhaust nozzle
114 Sting-type deck arrester hook
115 Retractable tail bumper
116 Wing root trailing edge fillet
117 Arrester hook damper and retraction jack
118 Rear fuselage framing
119 Jet pipe
120 Intake duct aft fairing
121 Port fowler flap
122 Spoiler hydraulic jack
123 Rear spar
124 Wing rib construction
125 Port roll control spoilers
126 Trim tab electric actuator
127 Roll control trim tab (port only)
128 Fuel jettison vent
129 Port wing tip fairing
130 Fuel vent valve
131 Port navigation light
132 Fuel venting ram air intake
133 Port wing main fuel tanks
134 Main spar
135 Cambered leading edge ribs
136 Leading edge integral fuel tank
137 Wing stores pylon (4)
138 Missile launch rail
139 AIM-9 Sidewinder air-to-air missile
140 125 Imp Gal (568 l) auxiliary fuel tank
141 Port mainwheel
142 Fuel tank bay corrugated double skin
143 Main undercarriage leg strut
144 Wing fold hydraulic jack
145 Main undercarriage pivot housing
146 Main spar hinge joint
147 Intake duct
148 Undercarriage hydraulic retraction jack
149 Wing-fold locking cylinders
150 Intake duct framing
151 Landing/taxiing lamp
152 Port wing fence
153 Leading-edge dog-tooth

# Mikoyan-Gurevich MiG-19 (May 1952)

If overshadowed by ancestors which saw combat over Korea and descendants capable of bi-sonic performance, the MiG-19, as the first Soviet production fighter capable of sustained supersonic speed in level flight justifies a position of some importance in combat aircraft development annals. Flown appreciably before its US contemporary, the F-100 Super Sabre (see pages 198-199), its development for production was, owing to the then existing technological limitations of the Soviet aircraft industry, perforce more leisurely. Thus, the US fighter, subjected to an accelerated development tempo previously unsurpassed, was to gain the distinction of being both the first genuine supersonic fighter and the first to achieve service status.

The MiG-19 evolved from a series of experimental aeroplanes, its first genuine prototype being considered the I-360 (SM-2) flown on 27 May 1952. It mated the centre and rear fuselage, tail assembly and twin AM-5 engine installation of the I-340 (SM-1) MiG-17 derivative with the 55 deg swept wing and forward fuselage of the I-350(M). The latter, with a single Lyulka TR-3A engine, had first flown on 16 June 1951, but poor engine reliability had confined testing to five flights. The paired AM-5s afforded insufficient power for supersonic speed in level flight, this not being achieved until the late summer of 1953, when Mach 1·12 was attained with the aid of afterburning AM-5A engines. By this time, the low-set horizontal tail arrangement first flown on the I-350(M) had been adopted and pre-series production initiated as the MiG-19F.

The pre-series aircraft presented numerous problems, the most serious being elevator ineffectiveness at high speeds and engine unreliability. Various changes were progressively introduced in a further prototype, the SM-9 flown on 5 January 1954, the incremental modifications including more powerful RD-9 engines and a slab-type all-flying horizontal tail, large-scale production being ordered on 31 August 1955 as the MiG-19S. This basic model emerged as an extremely agile and effective day interceptor, with outstanding acceleration and manoeuvrability up to medium altitudes, although suffering somewhat critical low-speed handling and stability. Production was phased out in the Soviet Union late 1957, and in Czechoslovakia in 1961, but continues in China (as the F-6).

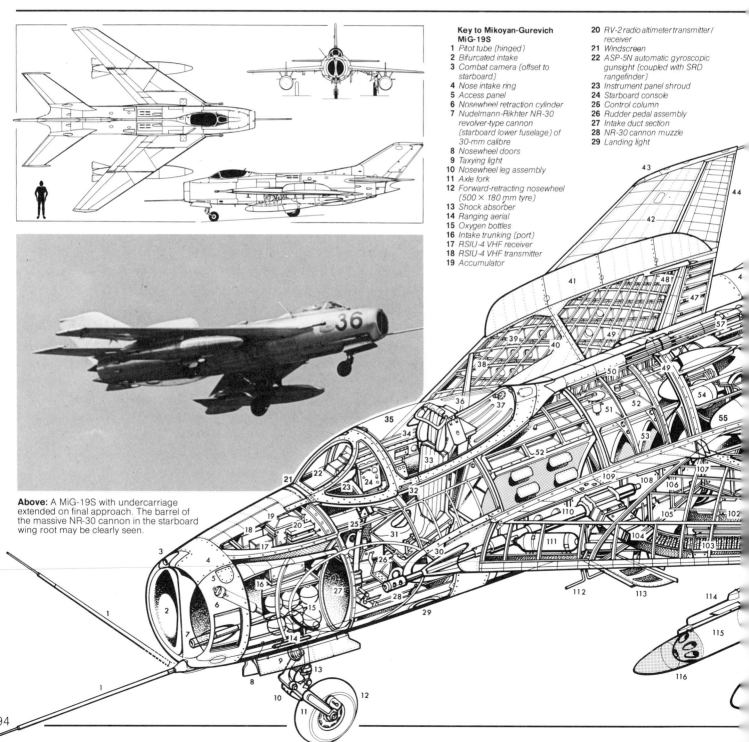

**Key to Mikoyan-Gurevich MiG-19S**
1 Pitot tube (hinged)
2 Bifurcated intake
3 Combat camera (offset to starboard)
4 Nose intake ring
5 Access panel
6 Nosewheel retraction cylinder
7 Nudelmann-Rikhter NR-30 revolver-type cannon (starboard lower fuselage) of 30-mm calibre
8 Nosewheel doors
9 Taxying light
10 Nosewheel leg assembly
11 Axle fork
12 Forward-retracting nosewheel (500 × 180 mm tyre)
13 Shock absorber
14 Ranging aerial
15 Oxygen bottles
16 Intake trunking (port)
17 RSIU-4 VHF receiver
18 RSIU-4 VHF transmitter
19 Accumulator
20 RV-2 radio altimeter transmitter/receiver
21 Windscreen
22 ASP-5N automatic gyroscopic gunsight (coupled with SRD rangefinder)
23 Instrument panel shroud
24 Starboard console
25 Control column
26 Rudder pedal assembly
27 Intake duct section
28 NR-30 cannon muzzle
29 Landing light

**Above:** A MiG-19S with undercarriage extended on final approach. The barrel of the massive NR-30 cannon in the starboard wing root may be clearly seen.

## SPECIFICATION: MiG-19S

**Power Plant:** Two Tumansky RD-9B turbojets each rated at 5,732 lb (2 600 kg) thrust dry and 7,165 lb (3 250 kg) thrust with afterburning. Internal fuel capacity, 808 Imp gal (3 675 l), provision for two 167 Imp gal (760 l) drop tanks.

**Performance:** Max speed (clean), 902 mph at 32,810 ft (10 000 m), or M=1·35, (with two drop tanks), 715 mph (1 150 km/h), or M=1·12; range cruise, 590 mph (950 km/h) at 32,810 ft (10 000 m); max range (clean), 863 mls (1 390 km) at 45,920 ft (14 000 m), 310 mls (500 km) at 3,280 ft (1 000 m), (with drop tanks), 1,366 mls (2 200 km) at 45,920 ft (14 000 m); initial climb (max take-off weight), 22,640 ft/min (115 m/sec); time to 32,810 ft (10 000 m), 1·85 min.

**Weights:** Empty equipped, 11,399 lb (5 172 kg); loaded, 16,314 lb (7 400 kg); max, 19,621 lb (8 900 kg).

**Dimensions:** Span, 29 ft 6¹/₃ in (9,00 m); length (excluding pitot), 41 ft 4 in (12,60 m); height, 12 ft 9½ in (3,90 m); wing area, 269·1 sq ft (25,00 m²).

**Armament:** Three 30-mm Nudelmann-Rikhter NR-30 cannon with 55 rounds for fuselage-mounted gun and 75 rpg for wing root weapons.

**Above:** Two Chinese-built MiG-19S (F-6) fighters in service with the Pakistan Air Forces No 19 Sqdn.

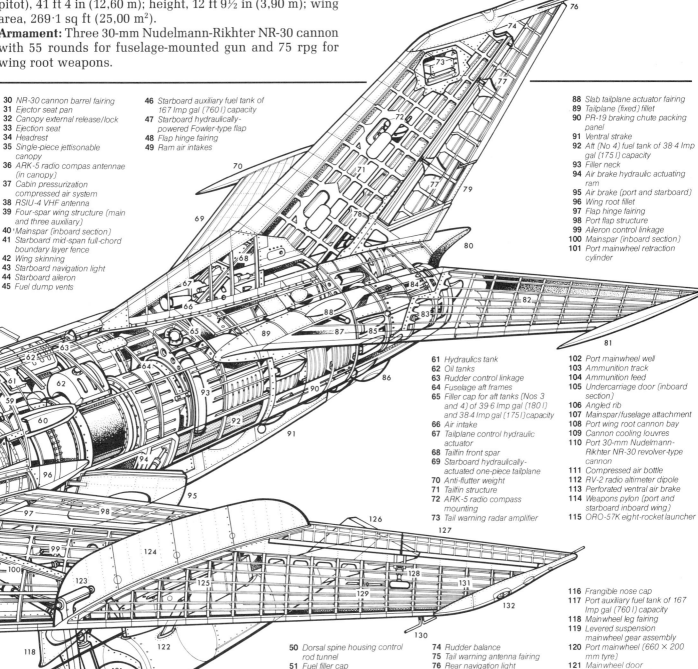

30 NR-30 cannon barrel fairing
31 Ejector seat pan
32 Canopy external release/lock
33 Ejection seat
34 Headrest
35 Single-piece jettisonable canopy
36 ARK-5 radio compas antennae (in canopy)
37 Cabin pressurization compressed air system
38 RSIU-4 VHF antenna
39 Four-spar wing structure (main and three auxiliary)
40 Mainspar (inboard section)
41 Starboard mid-span full-chord boundary layer fence
42 Wing skinning
43 Starboard navigation light
44 Starboard aileron
45 Fuel dump vents

46 Starboard auxiliary fuel tank of 167 Imp gal (760 l) capacity
47 Starboard hydraulically-powered Fowler-type flap
48 Flap hinge fairing
49 Ram air intakes

50 Dorsal spine housing control rod tunnel
51 Fuel filler cap
52 Main (Nos 1 and 2) fuel tanks of 323 Imp gal (1 470 l) and 72·6 Imp gal (330 l) capacity
53 Intake cut-out frames
54 Hydraulics accumulator
55 Port Tumanski RD-9B turbojet
56 Slot intakes
57 Air conditioning system
58 Slab-type tailplane control rod linkage
59 Fuselage break point
60 Air intake

61 Hydraulics tank
62 Oil tanks
63 Rudder control linkage
64 Fuselage aft frames
65 Filler cap for aft tanks (Nos 3 and 4) of 39·6 Imp gal (180 l) and 38·4 Imp gal (175 l) capacity
66 Air intake
67 Tailplane control hydraulic actuator
68 Tailfin front spar
69 Starboard hydraulically-actuated one-piece tailplane
70 Anti-flutter weight
71 Tailfin structure
72 ARK-5 radio compass mounting
73 Tail warning radar amplifier

74 Rudder balance
75 Tail warning antenna fairing
76 Rear navigation light
77 Rudder hinges
78 Tailfin rear spar
79 Rudder tab
80 Pen-nib exhaust fairing
81 Anti-flutter weight
82 One-piece tailplane structure
83 Exhaust nozzle (three position) hydraulic control
84 Afterburner
85 Afterburner cooling air intakes
86 Tail bumper
87 Slab tailplane spigot

88 Slab tailplane actuator fairing
89 Tailplane (fixed) fillet
90 PR-19 braking chute packing panel
91 Ventral strake
92 Aft (No 4) fuel tank of 38·4 Imp gal (175 l) capacity
93 Filler neck
94 Air brake hydraulic actuating ram
95 Air brake (port and starboard)
96 Wing root fillet
97 Flap hinge fairing
98 Port flap structure
99 Aileron control linkage
100 Mainspar (inboard section)
101 Port mainwheel retraction cylinder

102 Port mainwheel well
103 Ammunition track
104 Ammunition feed
105 Undercarriage door (inboard section)
106 Angled rib
107 Mainspar/fuselage attachment
108 Port wing root cannon bay
109 Cannon cooling louvres
110 Port 30-mm Nudelmann-Rikhter NR-30 revolver-type cannon
111 Compressed air bottle
112 RV-2 radio altimeter dipole
113 Perforated ventral air brake
114 Weapons pylon (port and starboard inboard wing)
115 ORO-57K eight-rocket launcher

116 Frangible nose cap
117 Port auxiliary fuel tank of 167 Imp gal (760 l) capacity
118 Mainwheel leg fairing
119 Levered suspension mainwheel gear assembly
120 Port mainwheel (660 × 200 mm tyre)
121 Mainwheel door
122 Auxiliary tank bracing struts
123 Mainwheel leg pivot
124 Port mid-span full-chord boundary layer fence
125 Auxiliary tank pylon
126 Fuel dump vents
127 Port aileron
128 Inspection/access panel
129 Aileron control rod linkage
130 Radio altimeter dipole
131 Wing outboard structure
132 Port navigation light

# Dassault Mystère IV (September 1952)

Reflecting the renaissance of French combat aircraft design expertise after the lapse of a decade, the series of single-seat fighters evolved by Avions Marcel Dassault in the late 'forties and early 'fifties was destined to be overshadowed by the company's delta-winged fighter progeny that were to emerge late in the latter decade. Nevertheless, with the Mystère IVA, French fighter design could be considered to have regained international stature.

Dassault had pursued a low-risk policy of incremental development in mating the fuselage of the straight-wing Ouragan, the first French jet fighter of indigenous design to attain production, with moderately swept surfaces to produce the Mystère in 1951. This was to be manufactured in limited numbers for the Armée de l'Air, but possessed little more than a conceptual similarity to the Mystère IV, the appellation "Mystère" having been adopted by Dassault as a generic designation for a series of swept-wing fighters. Designed to achieve genuine transonic performance, the Mystère IV, by comparison with the Mystère II, had quarter-chord sweepback increased from 30 to 38 degrees and the wing thickness-chord ratio

reduced from 9·0 to 7·5 per cent, a prototype powered by a 6,283 lb (2 850 kg) Tay 250A turbojet flying on 28 September 1952.

In April 1953, 225 examples of the new fighter were ordered under the off-shore procurement programme as Mystère IVAs for the Armée de l'Air and a supplementary order for a further 100 was placed by the French government. In the event, this order was to be cut back and 60 of the aircraft were to be delivered to Israel, an additional 110 being ordered by India to bring total production to 411 aircraft with completion late 1958.

The Mystère IVA possessed the shortcomings of most of its contemporaries. It was underpowered and possessed inadequate internal fuel capacity; it could exceed Mach unity in a dive, transonic speeds being accompanied by buffeting and barely controllable pitch-up; climb and acceleration were poor and directional snaking at speed reduced its value as a gun platform. When flown in combat by the Israelis in the 1956 Middle East conflict it proved inferior in climb and manoeuvrability to the MiG-15, pilot quality playing a major part in the success of the French

**Key to Dassault Mystère IVA**

1 Engine air intake
2 Radar rangefinder antenna
3 Intake divider
4 Gun camera
5 Nose electronics compartment access door
6 Radar transmitter
7 Radar receiver
8 Nose undercarriage wheel bay
9 Hydraulic retraction jack
10 Battery
11 Cockpit front pressure bulkhead
12 Rudder pedals
13 Cockpit floor level
14 Nose undercarriage pivot fixing
15 Cannon blast trough
16 Cannon muzzle
17 Nosewheel leg door
18 Landing/taxiing lamp
19 Nose undercarriage leg strut
20 Nosewheel
21 Torque scissor links
22 Bifurcated intake duct framing
23 Control column
24 Cockpit coaming
25 Instrument panel shroud
26 Gyro gunsight
27 Windscreen panels
28 Cockpit canopy cover
29 Ejection seat face blind firing handle
30 Headrest
31 Pilot's ejection seat
32 Canopy emergency release lever
33 Engine throttle lever
34 Port side console panel
35 Cockpit pressurised enclosure
36 Cannon mounting
37 DEFA 30-mm cannon
38 Spent cartridge case collector box
39 Gun bay access panel
40 Ammunition feed chute
41 Ammunition box (150 rounds per gun)
42 Control rod runs
43 Cockpit armoured rear pressure bulkhead
44 Sliding canopy rail
45 Oxygen bottle
46 Forward fuselage fuel tank (total internal capacity 396 Imp gal/1800 l)
47 Wing root fillet
48 Aileron hydraulic booster
49 Intake duct framing
50 Radio and electronics equipment bay
51 UHF aerial
52 Starboard wing fuel cells
53 Aileron push-pull control rods
54 Pitot tube
55 Starboard navigation light
56 Wing tip fairing
57 Starboard aileron
58 Aileron hinge control
59 Split trailing edge flap
60 Flap torque shaft actuator
61 Fuel tank access door

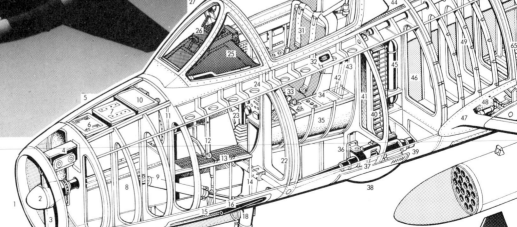

**Above:** A Mystère IVA of the 12e Escadre de Chasse of the Armée de l'Air. The Mystère IVA was the service's first transonic fighter, the initial 75 aircraft retaining the Tay 250A turbojet of the prototype, all subsequent aircraft having the later Verdon.

fighter, and in the Indo-Pakistan war of September 1965, the Mystère IVA was largely relegated to the close air support role particularly suited to its robust structure.

## SPECIFICATION: Mystère IVA

**Power Plant:** One Hispano-Suiza Verdon 350 centrifugal-flow turbojet rated at 7,716 lb (3 500 kg) static thrust. Internal capacity, 396 Imp gal (1 800 l), provision for two 137·5 Imp gal (625 l) or 181·5 Imp gal (825 l) drop tanks.

**Performance:** Max speed, 661 mph (1 063 km/h) or M=0·867 at sea level, 601 mph (967 km/h) or M=0·91 at 36,000 ft (10 975 m); tactical radius (internal fuel/high-altitude intercept mission), 205 mls (330 km); range (internal fuel), 547 mls (880 km), (max external fuel), 1,019 mls (1 640 km); initial climb, 8,415 ft/min (42,75 m/sec); service ceiling, 42,980 ft (13 100 m).

**Weights:** Empty equipped, 12,950 lb (5 874 kg); normal loaded, 16,530 lb (7 498 kg); max, 20,050 lb (9 095 kg).

**Dimensions:** Span, 36 ft 5¾ in (11,12 m); length, 42 ft 1¾ in (12,85 m); height, 15 ft 1 in (4,60 m); wing area, 344·45 sq ft (32,00 m²).

**Armament:** Two 30-mm DEFA 541 cannon with 150 rpg and provision for two 19 x 68-mm rocket pods or two 1,000-lb (453,6-kg) bombs.

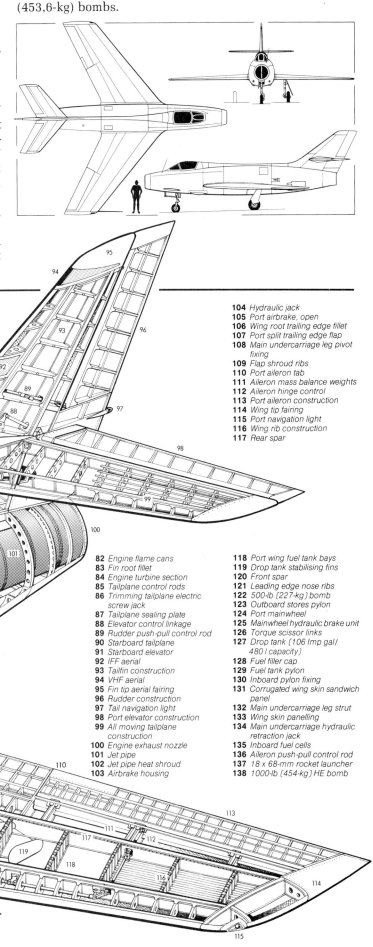

62 Fuel filler cap
63 Control rod duct
64 Centre fuselage fuel tank
65 Wing front spar/fuselage main frame
66 Wing centre-section carry-through
67 Wing skin bolted root joint
68 Rear spar/fuselage main frame
69 Main undercarriage wheel bay
70 Hydraulic reservoir
71 Engine accessory compartment
72 Fuel system piping
73 Control rod runs
74 Dorsal spine fairing
75 Engine bay access door
76 Generator
77 Compressor intake filter screens
78 Intake plenum chamber
79 Main engine mounting
80 Hispano-Suiza Verdon 350 centrifugal-flow turbojet
81 Rear fuselage break point (engine removal)

82 Engine flame cans
83 Fin root fillet
84 Engine turbine section
85 Tailplane control rods
86 Trimming tailplane electric screw jack
87 Tailplane sealing plate
88 Elevator control linkage
89 Rudder push-pull control rod
90 Starboard tailplane
91 Starboard elevator
92 IFF aerial
93 Tailfin construction
94 VHF aerial
95 Fin tip aerial fairing
96 Rudder construction
97 Tail navigation light
98 Port elevator construction
99 All moving tailplane construction
100 Engine exhaust nozzle
101 Jet pipe
102 Jet pipe heat shroud
103 Airbrake housing

104 Hydraulic jack
105 Port airbrake, open
106 Wing root trailing edge fillet
107 Port split trailing edge flap
108 Main undercarriage leg pivot fixing
109 Flap shroud ribs
110 Port aileron tab
111 Aileron mass balance weights
112 Aileron hinge control
113 Port aileron construction
114 Wing tip fairing
115 Port navigation light
116 Wing rib construction
117 Rear spar

118 Port wing fuel tank bays
119 Drop tank stabilising fins
120 Front spar
121 Leading edge nose ribs
122 500-lb (227-kg) bomb
123 Outboard stores pylon
124 Port mainwheel
125 Mainwheel hydraulic brake unit
126 Torque scissor links
127 Drop tank (106 Imp gal/ 480 l capacity)
128 Fuel filler cap
129 Fuel tank pylon
130 Inboard pylon fixing
131 Corrugated wing skin sandwich panel
132 Main undercarriage leg strut
133 Wing skin panelling
134 Main undercarriage hydraulic retraction jack
135 Inboard fuel cells
136 Aileron push-pull control rod
137 18 x 68-mm rocket launcher
138 1000-lb (454-kg) HE bomb

# North American F-100 Super Sabre (May 1953)

**Above:** An F-100C-5 of the 36th Fighter Day Wing based at Bitburg, Germany in 1956. Increases in vertical fin and wing areas overcame initial inertia coupling problems which had resulted in uncontrollable yaw.

Signifying a quantum advance in fighter performance when it achieved operational capability with the USAF late in September 1954, the F-100, as the world's first combat aircraft capable of sustained level-flight supersonic performance, was one of the true epoch-markers in fighter development annals. Noteworthy also for the brevity of its prototype-to-production cycle, it was first flown (as the YF-100A) on 25 May 1953, with the first production model (F-100A) following barely five months later, on 14 October. Its Soviet counterpart, which was to evolve as the MiG-19 (see pages 194-195), in fact flew a year earlier, but the F-100 was nevertheless to be both the first combat aircraft to achieve level-flight supersonic speeds and also the first to achieve service status.

Whereas the F-100A was essentially an air superiority fighter, its successor, the F-100C featured six external ordnance stations for the fighter-bomber mission, and the definitive production model, the more sophisticated and versatile F-100D, was optimised for this role. When production terminated in October 1959, a total of 2,192 Super Sabres had been delivered.

**Key to North American F-100D Super Sabre**

1. Pitot tube, folded for ground handling
2. Engine air intake
3. Pitot tube hinge point
4. Radome
5. IFF aerial
6. AN/APR-25(v) gun tracking radar
7. Intake bleed air electronics cooling duct
8. Intake duct framing
9. Cooling air exhaust duct
10. Cannon muzzle port
11. UHF aerial
12. Nose avionics compartment
13. Hinged, nose compartment access door
14. In-flight re-fuelling probe
15. Windscreen panels
16. A-4 radar gunsight
17. Instrument panel shroud
18. Cockpit front pressure bulkhead
19. Rudder pedals
20. Gunsight power supply
21. Armament relay panel
22. Intake ducting
23. Cockpit canopy emergency operating controls
24. Nosewheel leg door
25. Torque scissors
26. Twin nosewheels
27. Nose undercarriage leg strut
28. Philco-Cord M-39 20-mm cannon (four)
29. 'Kick-in' boarding steps
30. Ejection seat footrests
31. Instrument panel
32. Engine throttle
33. Canopy external handle
34. Starboard side console panel
35. Pilot's ejection seat
36. Headrest
37. Cockpit canopy cover
38. Ejection seat guide rails
39. Cockpit rear pressure bulkhead
40. Port side console panel
41. Cockpit floor level
42. Control cable runs
43. Gun bay access panel
44. Ammunition feed chutes
45. Ammunition tanks, 200-rpg
46. Power supply amplifier
47. Rear electrical and electronics bay
48. Cockpit pressurization valve
49. Anti-collision light
50. Air conditioning plant
51. Radio compass aerial
52. Intake bleed air heat exchanger
53. Heat exchanger exhaust duct
54. Secondary air turbine
55. Air turbine exhaust duct (open)
56. Starboard wing integral fuel tank, capacity 174 Imp gal (791 l)
57. Starboard automatic leading edge slat, open
58. Slat guide rails
59. Wing fence
60. Starboard navigation light
61. Wing tip fairing

62. Fixed portion of trailing edge
63. Starboard aileron
64. Aileron hydraulic jack
65. Starboard outer plain flap
66. Flap hydraulic jack
67. UHF aerial
68. Engine intake centre-body
69. Wing attachment fuselage main frames
70. Fuselage fuel tanks; total internal capacity 641 Imp gal (2 915 l)
71. Wing spar centre section carry through beams
72. Main engine intake compressor face
73. Main engine mounting
74. Pratt & Whitney J57-P-21A afterburning turbojet engine
75. Dorsal spine fairing
76. Fuel vent pipe
77. Engine oil tank
78. Fuselage upper longeron
79. Engine accessory gearbox
80. Compressor bleed air 'blow-off' valve
81. Fuselage break point
82. Rear fuselage attachment bolts (four)
83. Fin root fillet
84. Engine turbine section
85. Engine rear mounting ring
86. Afterburner fuel spray manifold
87. Fin attachment sloping frame
88. Rudder hydraulic jack
89. Fin stub attachment joint
90. Tailfin construction
91. Fin leading edge
92. Fin tip aerial fairing
93. Upper UHF aerial
94. Fixed portion of trailing edge
95. AN/APR-26(v) radar warning antenna
96. Tail navigation light
97. Fuel jettison pipe
98. Rudder construction
99. Rudder trim control jack
100. Externally braced trailing edge section

101. Brake parachute cable fixing
102. Variable area afterburner, exhaust nozzle
103. Parachute cable 'pull-out' flaps
104. Afterburner nozzle control jacks
105. Brake parachute housing
106. Port all-moving tailplane
107. Tailplane spar box construction
108. Pivot fixing
109. Tailplane mounting fuselage double frames
110. Engine afterburner duct
111. Tailplane hydraulic jack
112. Fuselage lower longeron
113. Rear fuselage fuel tank
114. Port inner plain flap
115. Flap rib construction
116. Main undercarriage wheel bay
117. Undercarriage leg pivot fixing
118. Flap hydraulic jack
119. Flap interconnecting linkage
120. Port outer flap
121. Flap hydraulic jack
122. Aileron jack
123. Wing fence
124. Port aileron
125. Fixed portion of trailing edge
126. Wing tip fairing
127. Port navigation light
128. Compass master transmitter
129. 750-lb (340-kg) HE bomb
130. SUU 7A CBU 19-round bomblet dispenser
131. Outboard wing pylon
132. Leading edge slat rib construction
133. Hinged leading edge attachment joint
134. Outboard pylon fixing
135. Wing rib construction
136. Rear spar

137. Port wing integral fuel tank, 174 Imp gal (791 l)
138. Multi-spar inner wing panel construction
139. Centre pylon fixing
140. Multi-plate disc brake
141. Port mainwheel
142. Main undercarriage leg strut
143. Undercarriage mounting rib
144. Front spar
145. Wing/fuselage attachment skin joint
146. Aileron cable control run
147. Inboard pylon
148. Airbrake hydraulic jacks (two)
149. Retractable landing/taxying lamps, port and starboard
150. Ventral airbrake
151. 166·5 Imp gal (757 l) drop tank or napalm container
152. AGM-12C Bullpup B tactical missile
153. Centre wing pylon
154. 279 Imp gal (1 268 l) air refuellable 'supersonic' fuel tank
155. Tank side bracing strut

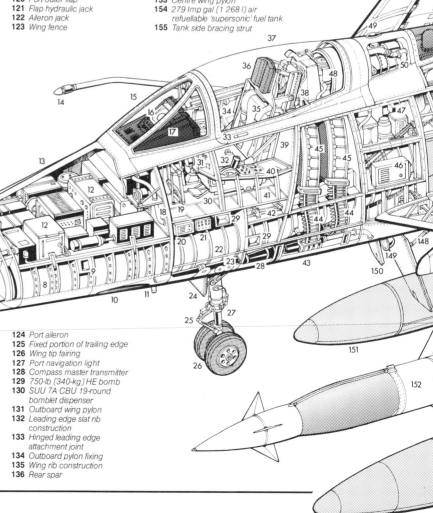

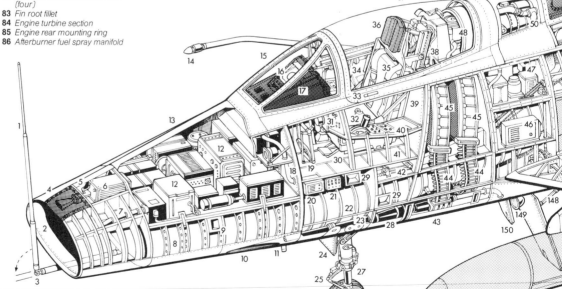

## SPECIFICATION: F-100D Super Sabre

**Power Plant:** One Pratt & Whitney J57-P-21 or -21A axial-flow turbojet rated at 10,200 lb (4 627 kg) military dry thrust and 16,000 lb (7 258 kg) with afterburning. Internal fuel capacity, 990 Imp gal (4 500 l), with provision for two 279 Imp gal (1 268 l) and two 166·5 Imp gal (757 l) drop tanks.

**Performance:** Max speed, 927 mph (1 492 km/h) or M=1·39 at 35,000 ft (10 670 m), 739 mph (1 190 km/h) or M=0·97 at sea level; max initial climb, 22,400 ft/min (113,79 m/sec); combat ceiling, 51,300 ft (15 636 m); combat radius (max external fuel), 599 mls (964 km) at 587 mph (945 km/h) at 30,500-39,000 ft (9 295-11 885 m), (internal fuel and six Mk 82 Snakeye bombs), 279 mls (448 km); ferry range (max external fuel), 1,971 mls (3 172 km).

**Weights:** Empty, 20,638 lb (9 361 kg); combat, 30,061 lb (13 636 kg); max, 38,048 lb (17 258 kg).

**Dimensions:** Span, 38 ft 9½ in (11,82 m); length (excluding pitot), 49 ft 3½ in (15.03 m); height, 16 ft 2½ in (4,94 m); wing area, 400·18 sq ft (37,18 m²).

**Armament:** Four 20-mm M-39 cannon with 200 rpg and up to 6,000 lb (2 722 kg) of external ordnance.

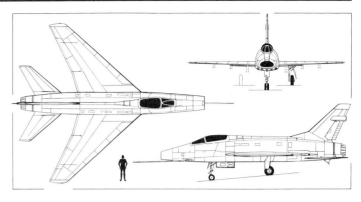

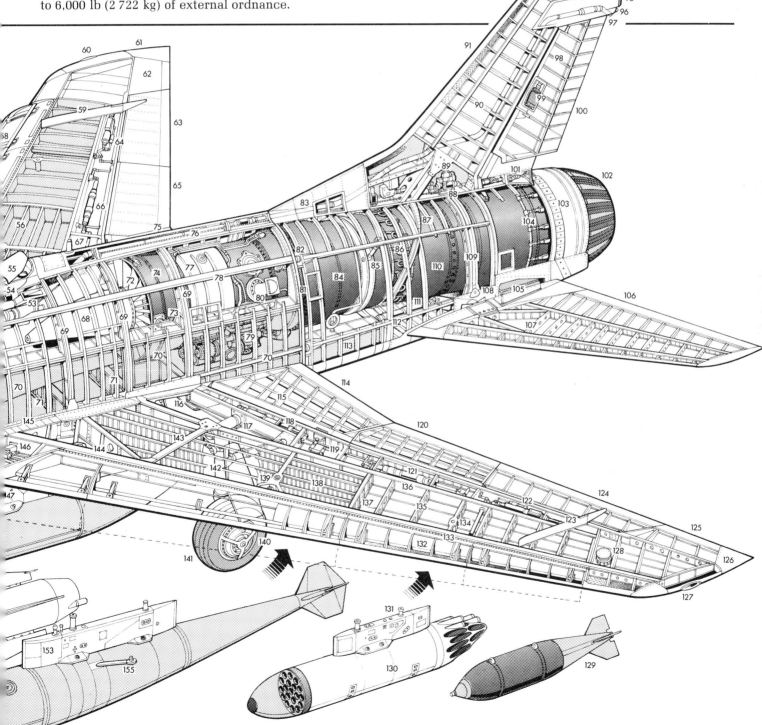

# Lockheed F-104 Starfighter (February 1954)

With its genesis in the Korean War, the Starfighter was first of the bi-sonic fighters generated by experience of that conflict. Original in concept, it represented a radical advance in the state of the art and few aircraft have had greater impact on fighter technology. Conceived by Clarence Johnson purely as a high-altitude air superiority fighter, the Starfighter was to undergo an extraordinary metamorphosis for multi-role operation, being entirely restressed to meet new strength requirements with full external loads and to permit low-altitude missions without placard restrictions. In the process, it was to become one of the most controversial war-planes ever manufactured in quantity.

First flown (as the XF-104) on 7 February 1954, the Starfighter was characterised by a diminutive unswept wing of thin (3·4 per cent) thickness-chord ratio mounted immoderately far aft on an inordinately long, slim fuselage. Penalties were to be paid for its role transformation, wing loading increasing from the 96 lb/sq ft (468,71 kg/m²) of the clean F-104A interceptor to no less than 158 lb/sq ft (771,42 kg/m²) for the ultimate multi-role derivative, the F-104S, in fully laden condition.

Despite fundamental unsuitability for tactical strike, the Starfighter became the subject of an immense multi-national manufacturing programme (as the F-104G), being built in Europe, Canada (as the CF-104) and Japan (in the F-104J dedicated interceptor variant). The final model, the F-104S developed jointly by Lockheed and Aeritalia, was first flown in 1966, having a 17,900 lb (8 120 kg) J79-GE-19 engine, additional stores pylons, provision for AIM-7 Sparrow III air-to-air missiles and a maximum weight of 31,000 lb (14 062 kg). The production of 205 aircraft was completed in Italy in the latter part of 1978. This brought the overall total of Starfighters built to 2,536, of which 737 were built by Lockheed.

## SPECIFICATION: F-104G Starfighter
**Power Plant:** One General Electric J79-GE-11A turbojet rated at 10,000 lb (4 536 kg) dry thrust and 15,600 lb (7 076 kg) with afterburning. Internal fuel capacity, 847·5 Imp gal (3 853 l), including 101·5 Imp gal (462 l) gun bay tank, with provision for two 283 Imp gal (1 287 l) wingtip and two 324·7 Imp gal (1 476 l) underwing drop tanks.

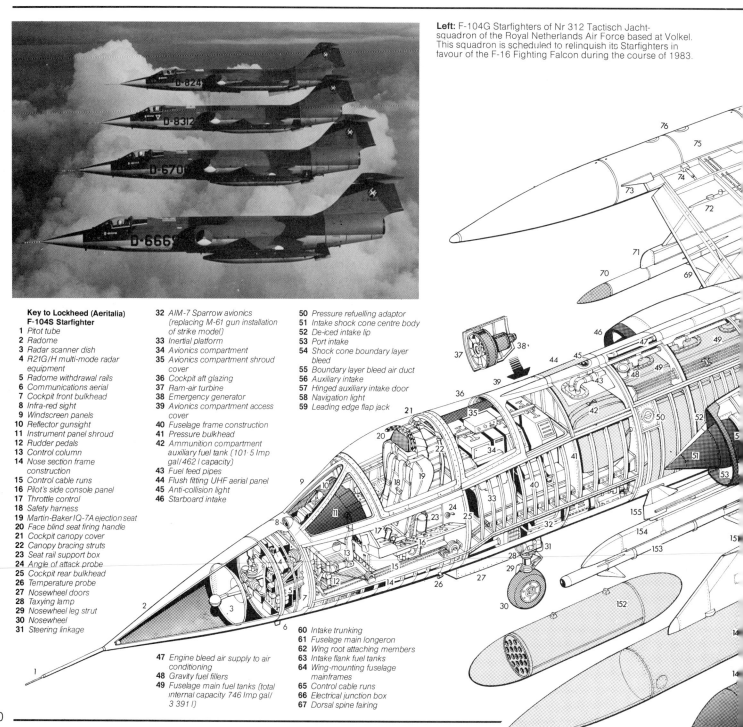

**Left:** F-104G Starfighters of Nr 312 Tactisch Jachtsquadron of the Royal Netherlands Air Force based at Volkel. This squadron is scheduled to relinquish its Starfighters in favour of the F-16 Fighting Falcon during the course of 1983.

**Key to Lockheed (Aeritalia) F-104S Starfighter**

1 Pitot tube
2 Radome
3 Radar scanner dish
4 R21G/H multi-mode radar equipment
5 Radome withdrawal rails
6 Communications aerial
7 Cockpit front bulkhead
8 Infra-red sight
9 Windscreen panels
10 Reflector gunsight
11 Instrument panel shroud
12 Rudder pedals
13 Control column
14 Nose section frame construction
15 Control cable runs
16 Pilot's side console panel
17 Throttle control
18 Safety harness
19 Martin-Baker IQ-7A ejection seat
20 Face blind seat firing handle
21 Cockpit canopy cover
22 Canopy bracing struts
23 Seat rail support box
24 Angle of attack probe
25 Cockpit rear bulkhead
26 Temperature probe
27 Nosewheel doors
28 Taxying lamp
29 Nosewheel leg strut
30 Nosewheel
31 Steering linkage

32 AIM-7 Sparrow avionics (replacing M-61 gun installation of strike model)
33 Inertial platform
34 Avionics compartment
35 Avionics compartment shroud cover
36 Cockpit aft glazing
37 Ram-air turbine
38 Emergency generator
39 Avionics compartment access cover
40 Fuselage frame construction
41 Pressure bulkhead
42 Ammunition compartment auxiliary fuel tank (101·5 Imp gal/462 l capacity)
43 Fuel feed pipes
44 Flush fitting UHF aerial panel
45 Anti-collision light
46 Starboard intake

47 Engine bleed air supply to air conditioning
48 Gravity fuel fillers
49 Fuselage main fuel tanks (total internal capacity 746 Imp gal/3 391 l)

50 Pressure refuelling adaptor
51 Intake shock cone centre body
52 De-iced intake lip
53 Port intake
54 Shock cone boundary layer bleed
55 Boundary layer bleed air duct
56 Auxiliary intake
57 Hinged auxiliary intake door
58 Navigation light
59 Leading edge flap jack
60 Intake trunking
61 Fuselage main longeron
62 Wing root attaching members
63 Intake flank fuel tanks
64 Wing-mounting fuselage mainframes
65 Control cable runs
66 Electrical junction box
67 Dorsal spine fairing

**Performance:** Max speed, 1,328 mph (2 137 km/h) or M=2·0 at 35,000 ft (10 670 m), 860 mph (1 384 km/h) or M=1·13 at sea level; max initial climb, 48,000 ft/min (243,8 m/sec); combat ceiling 50,000 ft (15,240 m); combat radius (basic support mission with four drop tanks and two 1,000-lb/453,6-kg bombs), 619 mls (996 km) at 586 mph (943 km/h) at 21,900-33,700 ft (6 675-10 270 m), (M=2·0 intercept mission with four drop tanks), 296 mls (476 km); ferry range, 1,875 mls (3 017 km).

**Weights:** Empty (interceptor), 13,996 lb (6 349 kg), (fighter-bomber), 14,054 lb (6 375 kg); combat (interceptor), 20,002 lb (9 073 kg), (fighter-bomber), 20,640 lb (9 362 kg); max, 29,038 lb (13 172 kg).

**Dimensions:** Span, 21 ft 10¾ in (6,67 m); length, 54 ft 9½ in (16,70 m); height, 13 ft 6 in (4,11 m); wing area, 196·1 sq ft (18,22 m²).

**Armament:** One 20-mm M-61 rotary cannon with 725 rounds and up to 4,000 lb (1 814 kg) of external ordnance.

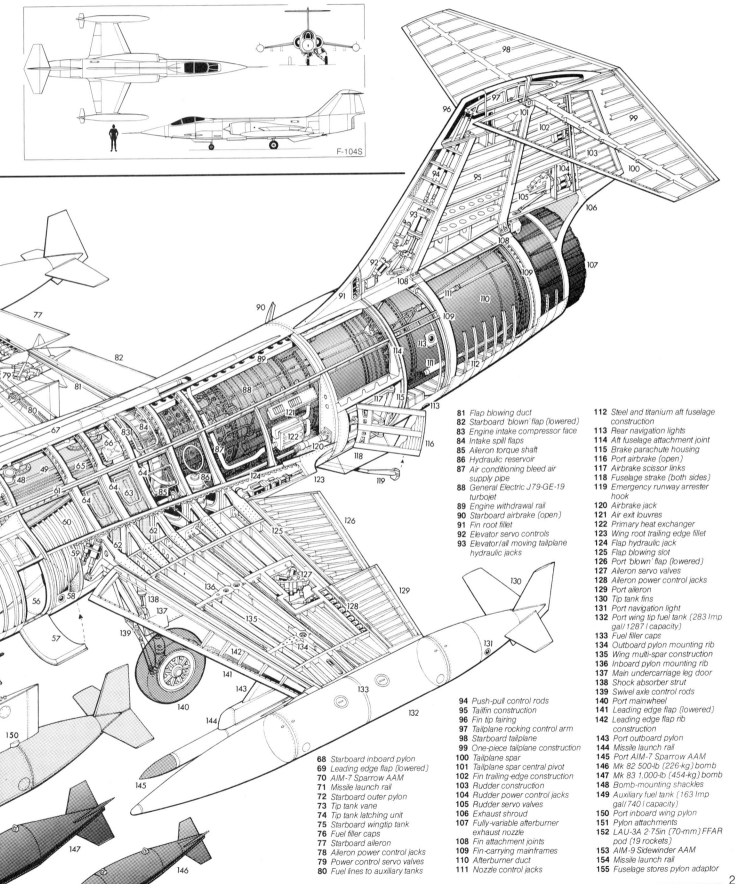

F-104S

68 Starboard inboard pylon
69 Leading edge flap (lowered)
70 AIM-7 Sparrow AAM
71 Missile launch rail
72 Starboard outer pylon
73 Tip tank vane
74 Tip tank latching unit
75 Starboard wingtip tank
76 Fuel filler caps
77 Starboard aileron
78 Aileron power control jacks
79 Power control servo valves
80 Fuel lines to auxiliary tanks

81 Flap blowing duct
82 Starboard 'blown' flap (lowered)
83 Engine intake compressor face
84 Intake spill flaps
85 Aileron torque shaft
86 Hydraulic reservoir
87 Air conditioning bleed air supply pipe
88 General Electric J79-GE-19 turbojet
89 Engine withdrawal rail
90 Starboard airbrake (open)
91 Fin root fillet
92 Elevator servo controls
93 Elevator/all moving tailplane hydraulic jacks

94 Push-pull control rods
95 Tailfin construction
96 Fin tip fairing
97 Tailplane rocking control arm
98 Starboard tailplane
99 One-piece tailplane construction
100 Tailplane spar
101 Tailplane spar central pivot
102 Fin trailing-edge construction
103 Rudder construction
104 Rudder power control jacks
105 Rudder servo valves
106 Exhaust shroud
107 Fully-variable afterburner exhaust nozzle
108 Fin attachment joints
109 Fin-carrying mainframes
110 Afterburner duct
111 Nozzle control jacks

112 Steel and titanium aft fuselage construction
113 Rear navigation lights
114 Aft fuselage attachment joint
115 Brake parachute housing
116 Port airbrake (open)
117 Airbrake scissor links
118 Fuselage strake (both sides)
119 Emergency runway arrester hook
120 Airbrake jack
121 Air exit louvres
122 Primary heat exchanger
123 Wing root trailing edge fillet
124 Flap hydraulic jack
125 Flap blowing slot
126 Port 'blown' flap (lowered)
127 Aileron servo valves
128 Aileron power control jacks
129 Port aileron
130 Tip tank fins
131 Port navigation light
132 Port wing tip fuel tank (283 Imp gall/1287 l capacity)
133 Fuel filler caps
134 Outboard pylon mounting rib
135 Wing multi-spar construction
136 Inboard pylon mounting rib
137 Main undercarriage leg door
138 Shock absorber strut
139 Swivel axle control rods
140 Port mainwheel
141 Leading edge flap (lowered)
142 Leading edge flap rib construction
143 Port outboard pylon
144 Missile launch rail
145 Port AIM-7 Sparrow AAM
146 Mk 82 500-lb (226-kg) bomb
147 Mk 83 1,000-lb (454-kg) bomb
148 Bomb-mounting shackles
149 Auxiliary fuel tank (163 Imp gall/740 l capacity)
150 Port inboard wing pylon
151 Pylon attachments
152 LAU-3A 2·75in (70-mm) FFAR pod (19 rockets)
153 AIM-9 Sidewinder AAM
154 Missile launch rail
155 Fuselage stores pylon adaptor

# Vought F-8 Crusader (March 1955)

**Right:** Two F-8A Crusaders of US Navy Sqdn VF-211 home-based at NAS Moffett Field, California. VF-211 flew Crusaders from 1958 until it converted to the F-14A Tomcat in 1975, having recorded the most MiG "kills" of any US Navy Crusader squadron in the Vietnam conflict.

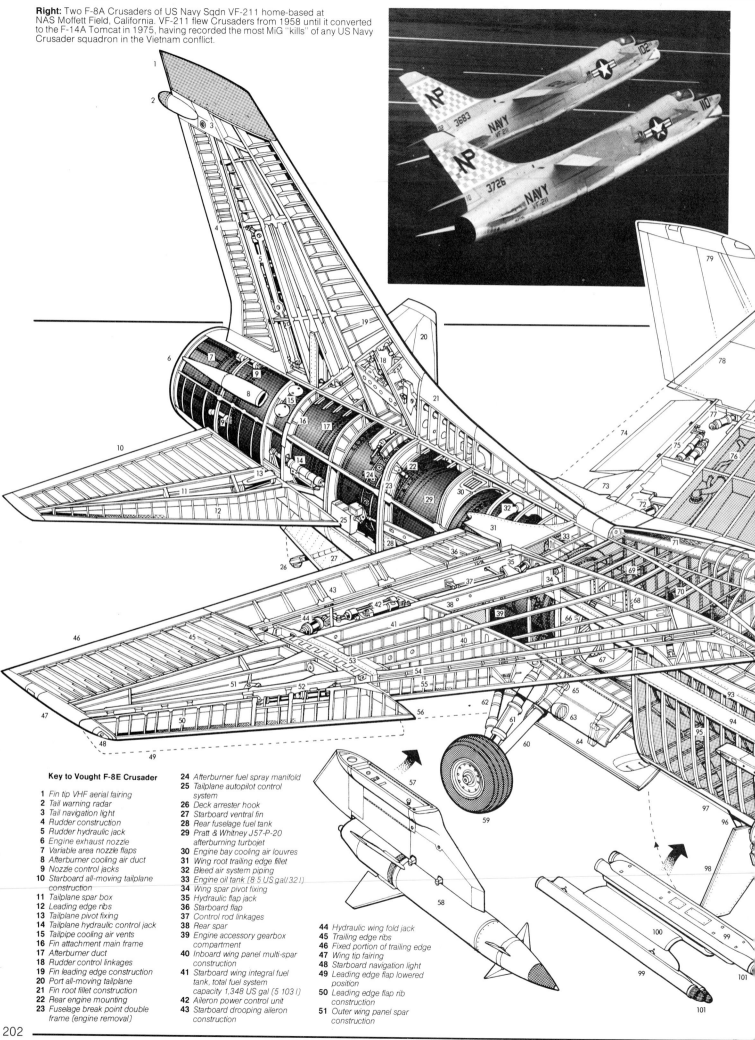

**Key to Vought F-8E Crusader**

1 Fin tip VHF aerial fairing
2 Tail warning radar
3 Tail navigation light
4 Rudder construction
5 Rudder hydraulic jack
6 Engine exhaust nozzle
7 Variable area nozzle flaps
8 Afterburner cooling air duct
9 Nozzle control jacks
10 Starboard all-moving tailplane construction
11 Tailplane spar box
12 Leading edge ribs
13 Tailplane pivot fixing
14 Tailplane hydraulic control jack
15 Tailpipe cooling air vents
16 Fin attachment main frame
17 Afterburner duct
18 Rudder control linkages
19 Fin leading edge construction
20 Port all-moving tailplane
21 Fin root fillet construction
22 Rear engine mounting
23 Fuselage break point double frame (engine removal)
24 Afterburner fuel spray manifold
25 Tailplane autopilot control system
26 Deck arrester hook
27 Starboard ventral fin
28 Rear fuselage fuel tank
29 Pratt & Whitney J57-P-20 afterburning turbojet
30 Engine bay cooling air louvres
31 Wing root trailing edge fillet
32 Bleed air system piping
33 Engine oil tank (8 5 US gal/32 l)
34 Wing spar pivot fixing
35 Hydraulic flap jack
36 Starboard flap
37 Control rod linkages
38 Rear spar
39 Engine accessory gearbox compartment
40 Inboard wing panel multi-spar construction
41 Starboard wing integral fuel tank, total fuel system capacity 1,348 US gal (5 103 l)
42 Aileron power control unit
43 Starboard drooping aileron construction
44 Hydraulic wing fold jack
45 Trailing edge ribs
46 Fixed portion of trailing edge
47 Wing tip fairing
48 Starboard navigation light
49 Leading edge flap lowered position
50 Leading edge flap rib construction
51 Outer wing panel spar construction

202

The first service shipboard fighter capable of genuine level flight supersonic performance, the F-8 Crusader was unique in utilising a two-position variable-incidence wing. Pivoted on the rear spar, this could be raised seven degrees to provide the optimum angle of attack for launching and approach without necessitating adoption of exaggerated nose-high attitudes, ensuring good pilot visibility at all times. Acceptable carrier operating speeds were achieved by combining hinged wing leading edges with inboard flaperons and conventional flaps which were lowered 25 deg in concert to increase effective camber.

The first prototype Crusader was flown (as the XF8U-1) on 25 March 1955, deliveries of the initial clear-weather day air superiority version (F-8A) commencing in March 1957. Successive improvements were introduced, the definitive production model being the limited all-weather F-8E, manufacture ending early 1965 with 1,261 Crusaders built. From 1966 through 1970, 551 Crusaders underwent re-manufacturing as F-8Hs (from F-8Ds), F-8Js (from F-8Es), F-8Ks (from F-8Cs) and F-8Ls (from F-8Bs), introducing boundary layer control and strengthened undercarriages.

### SPECIFICATION: F-8H Crusader

**Power Plant:** One Pratt & Whitney J57-P-420 turbojet rated at 12,400 lb (5 625 kg) dry thrust and 19,600 lb (8 890 kg) with afterburning. Internal fuel capacity, 1,122·5 Imp gal (5 103 l).

**Performance:** Max speed, 762 mph (1 227 km/h) or M=1·0 at sea level, 1,156 mph (1 860 km/h) or M=1·75 at 36,100 ft (11 005 m); initial climb, 23,300 ft/min (118,36 m/sec); combat ceiling 51,600 ft (15 730 m); combat range (cannon armament only), 1,427 mls (2 296 km) at 556 mph (895 km/h) at 33,815-40,985 ft (10 307-12 490 m).

**Weights:** Empty, 18,824 lb (8 538 kg); normal combat, 25,802 lb (11 704 kg), (with four Sidewinder AAMs), 27,124 lb (12 303 kg); max, 34,280 lb (15 549 kg).

**Dimensions:** Span, 35 ft 8 in (10,87 m); length, 54 ft 2¾ in (16,52 m); height, 15 ft 9 in (4,80 m); wing area, 375 sq ft (34,84 m²).

**Armament:** Four 20-mm MK-12 cannon with 125 rounds per gun, plus two or four Sidewinder air-to-air missiles, or up to 5,000 lb (2 268 kg) of external ordnance for close air support mission.

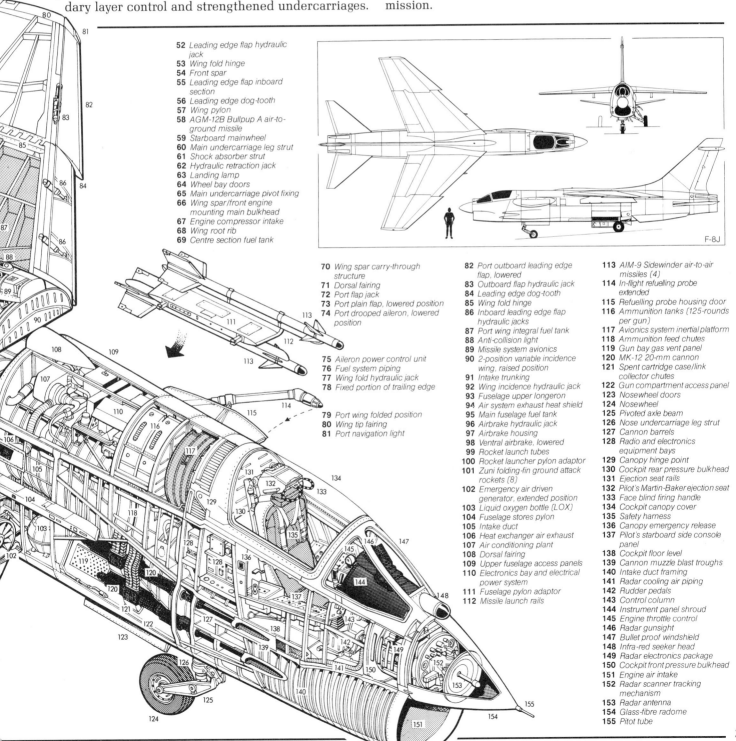

52 Leading edge flap hydraulic jack
53 Wing fold hinge
54 Front spar
55 Leading edge flap inboard section
56 Leading edge dog-tooth
57 Wing pylon
58 AGM-12B Bullpup A air-to-ground missile
59 Starboard mainwheel
60 Main undercarriage leg strut
61 Shock absorber strut
62 Hydraulic retraction jack
63 Landing lamp
64 Wheel bay doors
65 Main undercarriage pivot fixing
66 Wing spar/front engine mounting main bulkhead
67 Engine compressor intake
68 Wing root rib
69 Centre section fuel tank

70 Wing spar carry-through structure
71 Dorsal fairing
72 Port flap jack
73 Port plain flap, lowered position
74 Port drooped aileron, lowered position
75 Aileron power control unit
76 Fuel system piping
77 Wing fold hydraulic jack
78 Fixed portion of trailing edge
79 Port wing folded position
80 Wing tip fairing
81 Port navigation light

82 Port outboard leading edge flap, lowered
83 Outboard flap hydraulic jack
84 Leading edge dog-tooth
85 Wing fold hinge
86 Inboard leading edge flap hydraulic jacks
87 Port wing integral fuel tank
88 Anti-collision light
89 Missile system avionics
90 2-position variable incidence wing, raised position
91 Intake trunking
92 Wing incidence hydraulic jack
93 Fuselage upper longeron
94 Air system exhaust heat shield
95 Main fuselage fuel tank
96 Airbrake hydraulic jack
97 Airbrake housing
98 Ventral airbrake, lowered
99 Rocket launch tubes
100 Rocket launcher pylon adaptor
101 Zuni folding-fin ground attack rockets (8)
102 Emergency air driven generator, extended position
103 Liquid oxygen bottle (LOX)
104 Fuselage stores pylon
105 Intake duct
106 Heat exchanger air exhaust
107 Air conditioning plant
108 Dorsal fairing
109 Upper fuselage access panels
110 Electronics bay and electrical power system
111 Fuselage pylon adaptor
112 Missile launch rails

113 AIM-9 Sidewinder air-to-air missiles (4)
114 In-flight refuelling probe extended
115 Refuelling probe housing door
116 Ammunition tanks (125-rounds per gun)
117 Avionics system inertial platform
118 Ammunition feed chutes
119 Gun bay gas vent panel
120 MK-12 20-mm cannon
121 Spent cartridge case/link collector chutes
122 Gun compartment access panel
123 Nosewheel doors
124 Nosewheel
125 Pivoted axle beam
126 Nose undercarriage leg strut
127 Cannon barrels
128 Radio and electronics equipment bays
129 Canopy hinge point
130 Cockpit rear pressure bulkhead
131 Ejection seat rails
132 Pilot's Martin-Baker ejection seat
133 Face blind firing handle
134 Cockpit canopy cover
135 Safety harness
136 Canopy emergency release
137 Pilot's starboard side console panel
138 Cockpit floor level
139 Cannon muzzle blast troughs
140 Intake duct framing
141 Radar cooling air piping
142 Rudder pedals
143 Control column
144 Instrument panel shroud
145 Engine throttle control
146 Radar gunsight
147 Bullet proof windshield
148 Infra-red seeker head
149 Radar electronics package
150 Cockpit front pressure bulkhead
151 Engine air intake
152 Radar scanner tracking mechanism
153 Radar antenna
154 Glass-fibre radome
155 Pitot tube

F-8J

# Sukhoi Su-7 (mid 1955)

The trend initiated by such aircraft as the F-84F Thunderstreak (see pages 188-189) towards a category of fighters optimised for the strike and ground attack missions was taken a stage further in the Soviet Union, when, in 1959, the Su-7B entered service. A large, comparatively unsophisticated aeroplane powered by a massive turbojet, the Su-7B was the first dedicated ground attack fighter with supersonic capability to achieve service status, and one which was to be manufactured in vast numbers from the late 'fifties, through the 'sixties and into the 'seventies.

Created by the design bureau headed by Pavel O. Sukhoi, which flew an aerodynamic prototype as the S-1 mid-1955, the new ground attack fighter embodied several design innovations insofar as Soviet combat aircraft were concerned, such as a variable intake shock diffuser cone and a slab-type all-flying horizontal tail. A second prototype embodying some aerodynamic refinement, the S-2, was productionised as the S-22 and ordered into large-scale production in 1958 as the Su-7B. Progressive development resulted in the Su-7BM, with uprated engine and enhanced systems, and the Su-7BKL which introduced a unique "wheel-skid" (kolo lizhni) arrangement and a low-pressure nosewheel tyre. This overcame the inability of the aircraft to accept low-pressure mainwheel tyres and afforded a measure of rough-field capability. Equivalent tandem two-seat conversion trainer versions were the Su-7U and Su-7UMK, the definitive production single-seat model being the upgraded Su-7BMK.

The use by the Su-7 of a 60 deg swept wing resulted in embarrassingly limited external stores flexibility; the radius of action with a worthwhile ordnance load was overly modest, and with full afterburning the endurance on internal fuel was limited to barely more than eight minutes. However, the Sukhoi ground attack fighter possessed good low-level gust resistance, pleasant handling characteristics, and maintenance simplicity and a high standard of reliability under operational conditions.

## SPECIFICATION: Su-7BMK

**Power Plant:** One Lyulka AL-7F-1 turbojet rated at 15,740 lb (7 140 kg) dry thrust and 21,825 lb (9 900 kg) thrust with afterburning. Internal fuel capacity, 910 Imp gal (4 140 l),

### Key to Sukhoi Su-7MBK Fitter-A

1. Pitot tube
2. Pitch vanes
3. Yaw vanes
4. Engine air intake
5. Fixed intake centre-body
6. Radome
7. Ranging radar scanner
8. ILS aerial
9. Radar controller
10. Weapon release ballistic computer
11. Retractable taxying lamp
12. SRO-2M 'Odd-rods' IFF aerials
13. Intake suction relief doors
14. Intake duct divider
15. Instrument access panel
16. Su-U 'Moujik' two-seat operational training variant
17. Armoured glass windscreen
18. Reflector sight
19. Instrument panel shroud
20. Control column
21. Rudder pedals
22. Control linkages
23. Nose undercarriage wheel well
24. Nosewheel doors
25. Torque scissor links
26. Steerable nosewheel
27. Low pressure 'rough-field' tyre
28. Hydraulic retraction jack
29. Cockpit pressure floor
30. Engine throttle
31. Pilot's side console panel
32. Ejection seat
33. Canopy release handle
34. Parachute pack headrest
35. Rear view mirror
36. Sliding cockpit canopy cover
37. Instrument venturi
38. Radio and electronics equipment bay
39. Intake ducting
40. Air conditioning plant
41. Electrical and pneumatic systems ground connections
42. Cannon muzzle
43. Skin doubler/blast shield
44. Fuel system components access
45. Main fuel pumps
46. Fuel system accumulator
47. Filler cap
48. External piping ducts
49. Starboard main undercarriage leg pivot fixing
50. Shock absorber pressurization charging valve
51. Gun camera
52. Starboard wing integral fuel tank
53. Starboard wing fence
54. Outer wing panel dry bay
55. Wing tip fence
56. Static discharger
57. Starboard aileron
58. Flap guide rail
59. Starboard fowler flap
60. Flap jack
61. Fuselage skin plating
62. Fuselage fuel tank
63. Wing/fuselage attachment double frame
64. Engine compressor face
65. Ram air intake
66. Engine oil tank
67. Bleed air system 'blow-off' valve
68. Fuselage break point, engine removal
69. Lyulka AL-7F-1 turbojet
70. Afterburner duct
71. Fin root fillet
72. Autopilot controller
73. Starboard upper airbrake, open
74. Rudder power control unit
75. Artificial feel unit
76. Tailfin construction
77. VHF/UHF aerial fairing
78. RSIU (very short wave fighter radio) aerial
79. Tail navigation light
80. Sirena-3 tail warning radar
81. Rudder
82. Brake parachute release link
83. Brake parachute housing
84. Parachute doors
85. Engine exhaust nozzle
86. Port all-moving tailplane
87. Static discharger
88. Tailplane anti-flutter weight
89. Tailplane construction
90. Pivot mounting
91. Tailplane limit stops
92. Variable area exhaust nozzle flaps
93. Nozzle control jacks
94. Fin/tailplane attachment fuselage frame
95. Afterburner cooling air intake
96. Rear fuselage frame and stringer construction
97. Insulated tailpipe
98. Airbrake housing
99. Hydraulic jack
100. Tailplane power control unit
101. 'Odd-rods' IFF aerials
102. Port lower airbrake, open
103. Engine accessories
104. Jettisonable JATO bottle
105. Port fowler flap
106. Port wing integral fuel tanks
107. Aileron control rod
108. Port aileron construction
109. Static discharger
110. Wing tip fairing
111. Port navigation light
112. Wing tip fence
113. Pitot tube
114. Wing rib and stringer construction

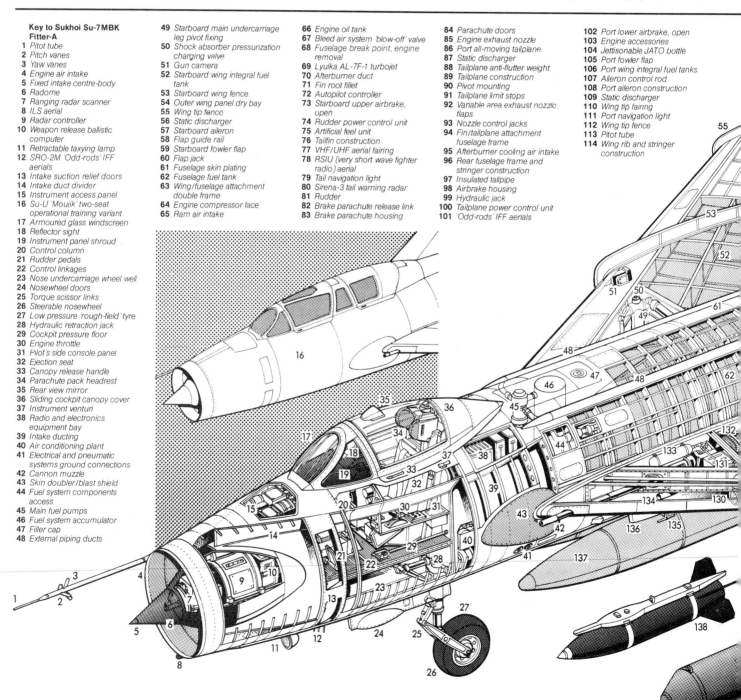

with provision for two 132 Imp gal (600 l) drop tanks.

**Performance:** Max speed without external stores, (max dry thrust), 540 mph (870 km/h) or M=0·72 at 1,000 ft (305 m), (max afterburning), 720 mph (1 160 km/h) or M=0·95 at 1,000 ft (305 m), 1,055 mph (1 700 km/h) or M=1·6 at 36,090 ft (11 000 m), (high-drag configuration), 790 mph or M=1·2 at 36,090 ft (11 000 m); max climb, 30,000 ft/min (152,4 m/sec); tactical radius (HI-LO-LO-HI profile), 285 mls (460 km); max range, 900 mls (1 450 km).

**Weights:** Empty equipped, 19,000 lb (8 620 kg); normal loaded, 26,455 lb (12 000 kg); max take-off, 29,750 lb (13 500 kg).

**Dimensions:** Span, 28 ft 9¼ in (8,77 m); length (including probe), 55 ft 1½ in (16,80 m); height 15 ft 0 in (4,57 m).

**Armament:** Two 30-mm Nudelman-Rikhter NR-30 cannon with 70 rpg. Four underwing stores stations for two 1,102-lb (500-kg) and two 1,653-lb (750-kg) bombs or equivalent loads of rocket pods and other ordnance.

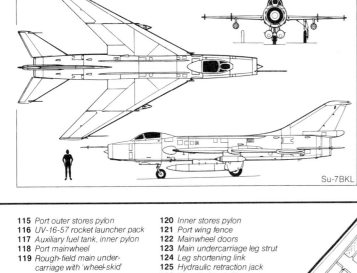

Su-7BKL

115 Port outer stores pylon
116 UV-16-57 rocket launcher pack
117 Auxiliary fuel tank, inner pylon
118 Port mainwheel
119 Rough-field main under-carriage with 'wheel-skid'
120 Inner stores pylon
121 Port wing fence
122 Mainwheel doors
123 Main undercarriage leg strut
124 Leg shortening link
125 Hydraulic retraction jack
126 Wing fuel tank filler cap
127 Port mainwheel bay
128 Main undercarriage up-lock
129 Aileron power control unit
130 Retractable landing lamp
131 Ammunition tank (70 rounds per gun)
132 30-mm NR-30 cannon
133 Cannon pressurization bottle
134 Ventral gun gas venting intake
135 Radar altimeter
136 Fuselage pylon, port and starboard
137 Twin fuselage mounted auxiliary fuel tanks
138 551-lb (250 kg) concrete piercing bomb
139 1,102-lb (500 kg) HE bomb

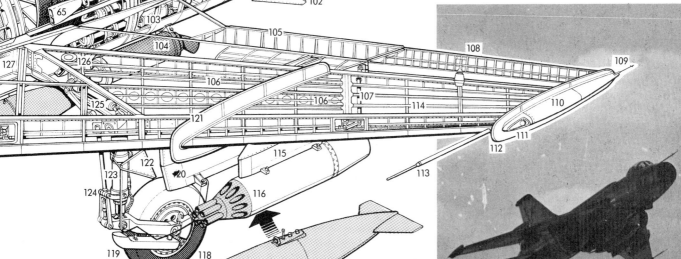

**Below:** An Su-7BKL of a Soviet support fighter regiment seen shortly after take-off. Note twin fuel tanks beneath fuselage and small wing rocket pods.

# Republic F-105 Thunderchief (October 1955)

**Above:** F-105B-15 Thunderchiefs of the 355th Tactical Fighter Squadron, 4th Tactical Fighter Wing, operating from Seymour Johnson AFB in 1959. The 335th was the first Thunderchief user from May 1958.

Signifying departure from the long-accepted philosophy of designing an interceptor fighter and subsequently adapting it for strike and close air support missions, the Thunderchief was optimised from the outset for the fighter-bomber role, albeit primarily for delivery of an internally-housed nuclear store in a *HI-LO-LO-HI* penetration sortie. Circumstances, however, were to dictate its employment with external conventional ordnance and the internal weapons bay occupied by a 325 Imp gal (1 477 l) fuel tank as an all-weather interdictor.

Flown (as the YF-105A) on 22 October 1955 as the largest and heaviest single-seat fighter conceived to that time, the Thunderchief first entered USAF service as the F-105B in 1958; the definitive single-seat model was the F-105D. Production (833 built) was completed in 1964.

**SPECIFICATION: F-105D-31 Thunderchief**
**Power Plant:** One Pratt & Whitney J75-P-19W turbojet rated at 16,100 lb (7 303 kg) dry thrust, 24,500 lb (11 113 kg) with afterburning and 26,500 lb (12 020 kg) for 2·5 min with afterburning and water injection. Internal fuel capacity,

## Key to Republic F-105D Thunderchief

1 Pitot tube
2 Radome
3 Radar scanner dish
4 Radar mounting and tracking mechanism
5 Forward electronic counter-measures (ECM) antenna
6 Aft-facing strike camera
7 Radome hinge
8 ADF sense aerial
9 Fire control radar transmitter/receiver
10 Cannon muzzle
11 Instrument electronics
12 In-flight refuelling position light
13 Air refuelling receptacle
14 Cannon ammunition drum (1,028 rounds)
15 Liquid oxygen converter
16 Angle of attack transmitter
17 Cannon barrels
18 Nosewheel doors
19 M-61 20-mm six-barrel rotary cannon
20 Ammunition feed chute
21 Gun gas venting pipe
22 Air refuelling probe housing
23 Alternator and electrical bay
24 Air driven turbine
25 Air refuelling probe
26 Windshield rain dispersal duct
27 Bullet proof windscreen panels
28 Radar attack sight
29 Instrument panel shroud
30 Navigation radar display
31 Rudder pedals
32 Cockpit front pressure bulkhead
33 Cannon mounting
34 Nosewheel leg strut
35 ILS system radar reflector
36 Taxying lamps
37 Nosewheel
38 Torque scissor links
39 Hydraulic steering controls
40 Flight control system hydraulics bay
41 Electronics cooling air outlet
42 IFF aerial
43 UHF aerial
44 Underfloor radio and electronics bay
45 Cockpit pressure floor level
46 Pilot's side console panel
47 Engine throttle
48 Control column
49 Pilot's ejection seat
50 Seat back parachute pack
51 Headrest
52 Cockpit canopy cover
53 3,000-lb (1 360-kg) HE bomb (inboard pylon)
54 Starboard air intake
55 Cockpit canopy jack
56 Canopy hinge
57 Air conditioning pack
58 Cockpit rear pressure bulkhead

59 Secondary electronics bay
60 Air data computer
61 Port air intake
62 Bomb bay fuel tank, 325 Imp gal (1 477 l)
63 Boundary layer splitter plate
64 Intake duct variable area sliding ramp
65 Forward group of fuselage fuel tanks; total internal fuel capacity 966 Imp gal (4390 l)
66 Gyro compass platform
67 Bomb bay fuel tank fuel transfer lines
68 Fuselage/front spar main frame
69 Dorsal spine fairing
70 Starboard mainwheel, stowed position
71 375 Imp gal (1 705 l) external fuel tank
72 AIM-9 Sidewinder air-to-air missile
73 Missile launcher rail
74 Twin missile carrier (outboard pylon)
75 Starboard leading edge flap
76 Outboard pylon fixing/drop tank filler cap
77 Starboard navigation light
78 Static dischargers
79 Starboard aileron
80 Starboard fowler flap
81 Trim tab, starboard only
82 Flap guide rails
83 Roll control spoilers
84 Anti-collision light
85 Air intake ducting
86 Ground running secondary air intake
87 Wing spar attachment joint
88 Fuselage/rear spar main frame
89 Engine compressor face
90 Forward engine mounting frame
91 Rear fuselage group of fuel tanks
92 Fuel pipe ducting
93 Drop tank tail fins
94 Afterburner duct cooling ram air intake
95 Starboard all-moving tailplane
96 Tailfin construction
97 Fin tip ECM aerials
98 Tail position light
99 Static dischargers
100 Rudder mass balance
101 Rudder

102 Formation light
103 Water injection tank, 30 Imp gal (136-l) capacity
104 Rudder power control unit
105 Brake parachute housing
106 Parachute door
107 Petal-type airbrakes, open position
108 Republic convergent/divergent ram air ejector nozzle flaps
109 Airbrake/nozzle flap jacks
110 Internal variable area afterburner nozzle
111 Afterburner nozzle actuators
112 Afterburner ducting
113 Tailplane pivot fixing
114 Port all-moving tailplane construction
115 Tailplane titanium box spar
116 Leading edge nose ribs
117 Ventral fuel vent
118 All-moving tailplane control jack
119 Rear fuselage break point
120 Engine firewall
121 Rear engine mounting
122 Engine turbine section heat shroud
123 Engine bay venting ram air intake
124 Rear fuselage frame and stringer construction
125 Runway arrester hook
126 Ventral fin

127 Accessory cooling air duct
128 Cartridge starter
129 Fuselage top longeron
130 Engine driven accessory gearbox
131 Oil tank 3·7 Imp gal (17-l) capacity
132 Pratt & Whitney J75-P-19W turbojet
133 Port Fowler-type flap construction
134 Five section roll control spoilers

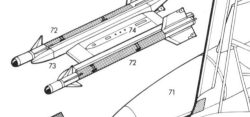

173

966 Imp gal (4 390 l), plus 325 Imp gal (1 477 l) weapons bay tank and provision for one centreline 541 Imp gal (2 460 l) or 375 Imp gal (1 705 l) and two underwing 375 Imp gal (1 705 l) drop tanks.

**Performance:** Max speed, 836 mph (1 345 km/h) or M=1·1 at sea level, 1,372 mph (2 208 km/h) or M=2·08 at 36,090 ft (11 000 m); max initial climb, 38,500 ft/min (195,58 m/sec); combat ceiling, 49,600 ft (15 120 m); combat radius (wing drop tanks and internal store), 778 mls (1 252 km) at 584 mph (940 km/h) at 30,000-39,450 ft (9 145-12 025 m); ferry range, 2,207 mls (3 552 km).

**Weights:** Empty, 26,855 lb (12 181 kg); normal combat, 35,637 lb (16 165 kg); max, 52,838 lb (23 967 kg).

**Dimensions:** Span, 34 ft 10¾ in (10,64 m); length, 64 ft 4¾ in (19,63 m); height, 19 ft 8½ in (6,00 m); wing area, 385 sq ft (35,77 m²).

**Armament:** One 20-mm M-61 rotary cannon with 1,028 rounds, and provision for up to 12,000 lb (5 443 kg) of external ordnance (eg, 16 x 750-lb/340-kg M 117 bombs).

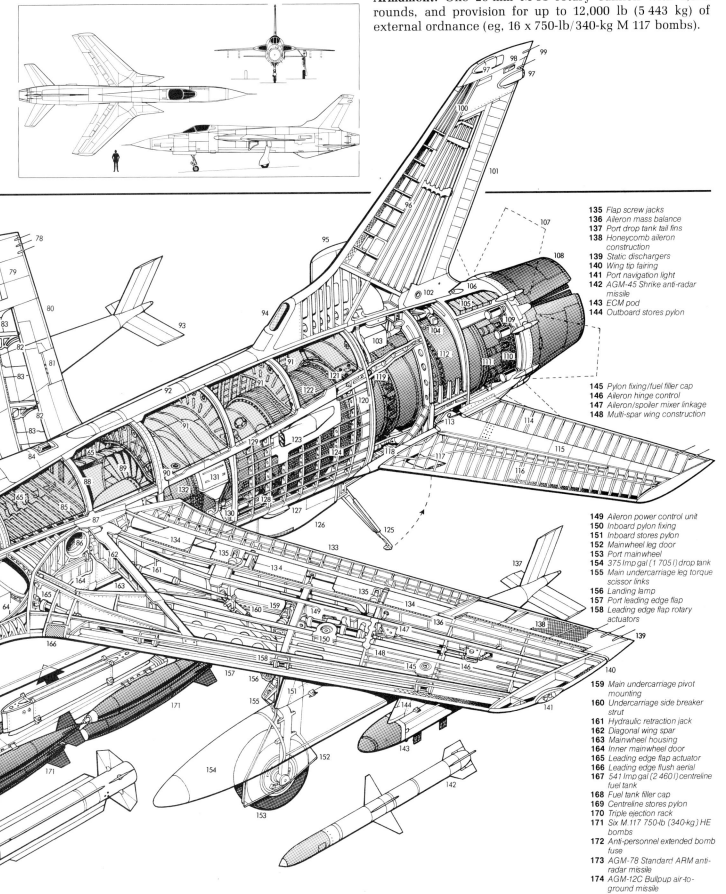

135 Flap screw jacks
136 Aileron mass balance
137 Port drop tank tail fins
138 Honeycomb aileron construction
139 Static dischargers
140 Wing tip fairing
141 Port navigation light
142 AGM-45 Shrike anti-radar missile
143 ECM pod
144 Outboard stores pylon

145 Pylon fixing/fuel filler cap
146 Aileron hinge control
147 Aileron/spoiler mixer linkage
148 Multi-spar wing construction

149 Aileron power control unit
150 Inboard pylon fixing
151 Inboard stores pylon
152 Mainwheel leg door
153 Port mainwheel
154 375 Imp gal (1 705 l) drop tank
155 Main undercarriage leg torque scissor links
156 Landing lamp
157 Port leading edge flap
158 Leading edge flap rotary actuators

159 Main undercarriage pivot mounting
160 Undercarriage side breaker strut
161 Hydraulic retraction jack
162 Diagonal wing spar
163 Mainwheel housing
164 Inner mainwheel door
165 Leading edge flap actuator
166 Leading edge flush aerial
167 541 Imp gal (2 460 l) centreline fuel tank
168 Fuel tank filler cap
169 Centreline stores pylon
170 Triple ejection rack
171 Six M.117 750-lb (340-kg) HE bombs
172 Anti-personnel extended bomb fuse
173 AGM-78 Standard ARM anti-radar missile
174 AGM-12C Bullpup air-to-ground missile

# Saab 35 Draken (October 1955)

Characterised by outstanding aerodynamic individuality, its double-delta configuration being unique at inception and remaining so to this day, the J 35 Draken (Dragon), designed under the leadership of Erik Bratt, was created to fulfil a specification almost as individualistic as the fighter in which it resulted. Formulated in 1949, this called for high supersonic speed, climb and altitude capabilities for the intercept mission, combining these attributes with exacting low-speed handling and field performance requirements to satisfy the needs of a newly-emerging Swedish quick-reaction and dispersal philosophy embracing operation from stretches of specially-prepared roadway.

The double-delta geometry arose from efforts to endow a dimensionally small airframe with the greatest possible volume; the sharply swept inner delta (80 deg) permitting sufficient depth to accommodate all fuel and the main undercarriage members, yet, in combination with the moderately swept (57 deg) outer delta, offering both favourable transonic and supersonic drag characteristics, and the loadings and lift necessary for the specified low-speed and field performance. Furthermore, it offered a more conventional relationship between centres of gravity and pressure than a normal delta wing.

The first Draken prototype was flown on 25 October 1955, the initial production model, the J 35A, entering service with Flygvapnet from March 1960. The J 35A (90 built), equipped for conventional lead pursuit attack, gave place to the J 35B (89 built) equipped for collision course attack, while the J 35D (92 built) and its tactical reconnaissance equivalent, the S 35E (60 built) replaced the RM 6B (Avon 200 Srs) turbojet with the uprated RM 6C (Avon 300 Srs). The definitive model, the J 35F (208 built), which began to enter service in 1965, featured a more potent missile armament and generally more sophisticated systems. Export versions of the J 35F were supplied to Denmark (40), together with (11) two-seater trainers, and Finland (15 ex-Swedish) where 12 were licence-assembled (J 35S).

**SPECIFICATION: Saab 35F-2 Draken**

**Power Plant:** One Volvo Flygmotor (Rolls-Royce) RM 6C (RB.146 Avon Mk 60) turbojet rated at 12,790 lb (5 800 kg) dry thrust and 17,635 lb (8 000 kg) with afterburning.

### Key to Saab 35F-2 Draken

1 Nose probe
2 Glass-fibre nose cone
3 Radar scanner
4 Scanner mounting frame
5 Radar pack
6 Saab S 7 collision-course fire control
7 L.M. Ericsson (Hughes licence) infra-red seeker
8 Electronics pack
9 Front pressure bulkhead
10 Data handling unit
11 Rudder pedal assembly
12 Port instrument console
13 Side panel
14 Instrument panel/radar scope shroud
15 Windscreen frame
16 Weapons sight
17 Windscreen
18 Starboard intake
19 Glass-fibre intake lip
20 Aft-hinged cockpit canopy
21 Cockpit sill
22 Starboard control panel
23 Control column
24 Throttle quadrant
25 Pilot's Saab RS 35 ejection seat
26 Canopy hinge mechanism
27 Seat support frame
28 Rear pressure bulkhead
29 Navigation computer
30 Forward avionics equipment bay
31 Gyro unit
32 TACAN transmitter-receiver
33 Auxiliary air intake
34 Starboard intake trunk
35 Starboard forward integral fuel tanks
36 Dorsal spine
37 Starboard forward bag-type fuel tank
38 30-mm Aden cannon
39 Ammunition magazine (100 rounds)
40 Dorsal antenna
41 Electrical wiring
42 Mid-fuselage production break line
43 Intake trunking
44 Oil cooler air intake
45 Volvo Flygmotor RM 6C (Rolls-Royce Avon 300 series) turbojet
46 Louvres
47 Access panels
48 Fuselage frames
49 Engine firewall
50 Cooling air inlet scoop
51 Fin root fairing
52 Fuel transfer
53 Starboard mainwheel door
54 Door actuating rod
55 Inner/outer wing joint strap
56 Starboard navigation light
57 Wing skinning
58 Starboard outer elevon
59 Hinge point
60 Actuating jack access
61 Control hinge
62 Access panels
63 Starboard aft integral fuel tank
64 Starboard aft bag-type fuel tanks (3)
65 Intake grille
66 Jet pipe
67 Engine aft mounting ring
68 Access
69 Tailfin main spar attachment
70 Control stick angle indicator unit
71 Computer amplifier
72 Synchronizer pack
73 Tailfin structure
74 Pitot tube
75 Rudder mass balance
76 Rudder structure
77 Rudder post
78 Tailfin rear spar
79 Rudder servo mechanism and actuator
80 Attachment point
81 Speed brake (4: 2 x upper, 2 x lower)
82 Fuselage structure
83 Detachable tail cone (engine removal)
84 Access
85 Brake parachute housing
86 Aft fairing
87 Afterburner assembly
88 Exhaust
89 Air intake (afterburner housing)
90 Control surface blunt trailing-edge
91 Port inner elevon
92 Hinge points
93 Elevon actuator
94 Rear spar
95 Twin (retractable) tailwheels
96 Port aft integral fuel tank
97 Inner/outer wing joint
98 Wing outer structure
99 Rib stations
100 Port outer elevon
101 Elevon actuator
102 Hinge points
103 Port wingtip
104 Anti-buffet underwing fences (6)
105 Stores pylons (9)
106 Nose ribs
107 Forward spar
108 Port mainwheel door
109 Port navigation light
110 Port mainwheel
111 Door inboard section
112 Port mainwheel well
113 Fuel transfer
114 Wing joint strap
115 Port aft bag-type fuel tanks (3)
116 Fuel collector tank
117 Mainwheel retraction mechanism
118 Mainwheel oleo leg mounting
119 Engine accessory gearbox
120 Port cannon ammunition magazine
121 Port 30-mm Aden cannon (Saab 35F has starboard gun only, earlier intercept and export Saab 35X versions retaining port gun as illustrated)
122 Port forward bag-type fuel tank
123 Port forward integral fuel tanks
124 Cannon muzzle port
125 Inner wing/fuselage integral structure
126 Angled frame member
127 Emergency ventral ram-air turbine
128 Trunking formers
129 Gyro amplifiers
130 Intake trunking
131 Nosewheel leg
132 Glass-fibre intake lip
133 Forward-retracting nosewheel
134 Steering mechanism
135 Possible stores (inc. jettisonable tanks)
136 Nineteen x 75-mm rocket pod
137 Rb 28 (Sidewinder) IR-homing missile
138 13,5-cm rocket
139 Rb 27 (Falcon) radar-homing missile
140 500-kg bomb

**Above left:** An RF 35 Draken tactical reconnaissance fighter of the Royal Danish Air Force's No 729 Eskadrille operating from Karup since 1970.

Internal capacity, 875 Imp gal (3 980 l), provision for two 280 Imp gal (1 275 l) and two 110 Imp gal (500 l) drop tanks.

**Performance:** Max speed, 1,320 mph (2 124 km/h) or M=2·0 at 36,090 ft (11 000 m), (with two Rb 27 and two Rb 28 AAMs), 924 mph (1 487 km/h) or M=1·4; initial climb, 34,450 ft/min (175 m/sec); time to 36,090 ft (11 000 m), 2·6 min, to 49,210 ft (15 000 m), 5·0 min; combat radius (internal fuel and *HI-LO-LO-HI* mission profile), 395 mls (635 km), (with two 280 Imp gal/1 275 l drop tanks and two 1,000-lb/453,6-kg bombs), 623 mls (1 003 km); ferry range, 2,020 mls (3 250 km).

**Weights:** Empty, 17,339 lb (7 865 kg); normal combat, 25,132 lb (11 400 kg); max, 35,273 lb (16 000 kg).

**Dimensions:** Span, 30 ft 10 in (9,40 m); length (including pitot), 50 ft 4in (15,35 m); height, 12 ft 9 in (3,89 m); wing area, 529·6 sq ft (49,20 m²).

**Armament:** One 30-mm Aden M/55 cannon with 100 rounds and (intercept mission) two radar-guided Rb 27 and two IR-guided Rb 28 (Falcon) missiles, or two or four Rb 24 (Sidewinder) missiles, or (attack mission) up to 9,000 lb (4 082 kg) of ordnance.

**Above:** A J 35F Draken of Flottilj 13 based at Norrkoping. Rb 27 and Rb 28 (Falcons) are seen respectively inboard and outboard.

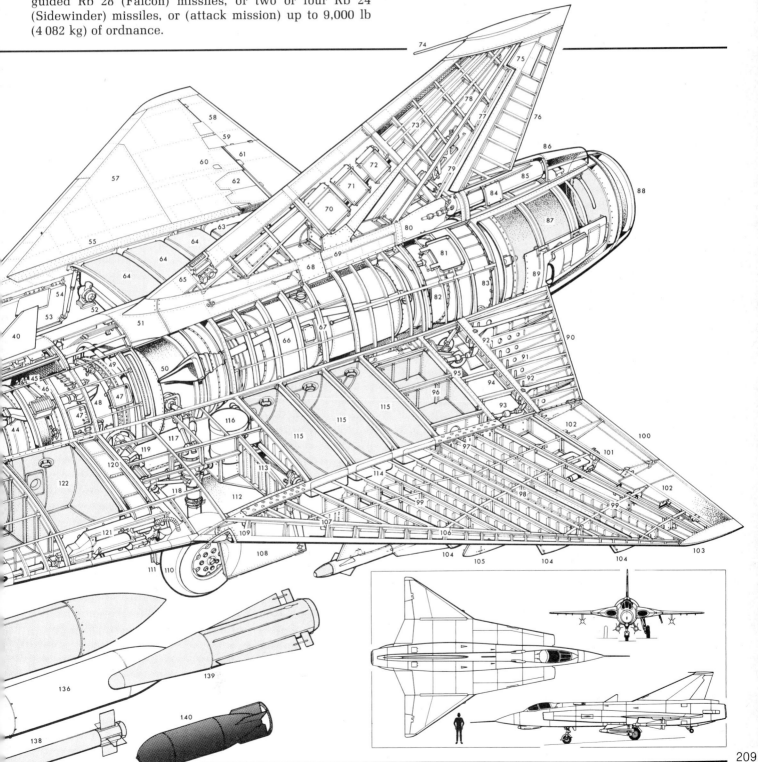

# Mikoyan-Gurevich MiG-21 (June 1956)

One of the generation of bi-sonic fighters following in the wake of the Korean conflict, the MiG-21, for long the subject of contention in the West, was, by the standards of its day, an outstanding warplane; but for certain fundamental shortcomings, it would have been a lightweight fighter *par excellence*. As it was, it possessed a better transonic capability, a smaller turning circle and markedly superior airfield performance than either of its western contemporaries, the Mirage and Starfighter.

The MiG-21 was, by any standard, a classic design; it exerted a profound influence on western fighter design thinking. Conceived as an unsophisticated day fighter, as which it entered service in 1959, it had evolved, by means of a complex genealogical process, as a limited all-weather dual-role fighter by the early 'seventies, retaining no more than a configurational similarity to the initial model. By the beginning of the 'eighties, it was finally outclassed in such vital dogfighting attributes as turn rate and radii, acceleration and sustained climb, yet although advanced in conceptual age, it remained in production (albeit for export) in 1981, by which time more than 6,000 had been manufactured.

The aerodynamic prototype of the MiG-21, the Ye-4 with an RD-9 engine, flew on 14 June 1956, being re-engined a year later with the more powerful R-11 as the Ye-5. Still further refined in 1958 as the Ye-6 with an R-11F-300 engine, it was productionised in the following year as the Ye-6T, entering large-scale production as the MiG-21F. What was to be a somewhat convoluted evolution of the basic design began in 1960, with the debut of the limited all-weather Ye-7 which was to be built in large numbers as the MiG-21PF and, subsequently, with flap-blowing (as the MiG-21PFS) and various equipment, armament and systems changes (as the MiG-21PFM and PFMA).

The lighter R-13 turbojet, affording 30 per cent greater dry thrust, resulted in a "second generation" (MiG-21MF and SMT) at the beginning of the 'seventies, which, in turn, gave place to the "third generation" MiG-21Mbis with an R-25 engine providing 13·6 per cent more afterburner power mated with upgraded avionics and improved structural standards.

The basic characteristics of the MiG-21 have remained virtually constant throughout. By the standards of its

**Key to Mikoyan-Guverich MiG-21MF**

1 Pitot-static boom
2 Pitch vanes
3 Yaw vanes
4 Conical three-position intake centrebody
5 "Spin Scan" search-and-track radar antenna
6 Boundary layer slot
7 Engine air intake
8 Radar ("Spin Scan")
9 Lower boundary layer exit
10 Antennae
11 Nosewheel doors
12 Nosewheel leg and shock absorbers
13 Castoring nosewheel
14 Anti-shimmy damper
15 Avionics bay access
16 Attitude sensor
17 Nosewheel well
18 Spill door
19 Nosewheel retraction pivot
20 Bifurcated intake trunking
21 Avionics bay
22 Electronics equipment
23 Intake trunking
24 Upper boundary layer exit
25 Dynamic pressure probe for q-feel
26 Semi-elliptical armour-glass windscreen
27 Gunsight mounting
28 Fixed quarterlight
29 Radar scope
30 Control column (with tailplane trim switch and two firing buttons)
31 Rudder pedals
32 Underfloor control runs
33 KM-1 two-position zero-level ejection seat
34 Port instrument console
35 Undercarriage handle
36 Seat harness
37 Canopy release/lock
38 Starboard wall switch panel
39 Rear-view mirror fairing
40 Starboard-hinged canopy
41 Ejection seat headrest
42 Avionics bay
43 Control rods
44 Air conditioning plant
45 Suction relief door
46 Intake trunking
47 Wingroot attachment fairing
48 Wing/fuselage spar-lug attachment points (four)
49 Fuselage ring frames
50 Intermediary frames
51 Main fuselage fuel tank
52 RSIU radio bay
53 Auxiliary intake
54 Leading-edge integral fuel tank
55 Starboard outer weapons pylon
56 Outboard wing construction
57 Starboard navigation light
58 Leading-edge suppressed aerial
59 Wing fence
60 Aileron control jack
61 Starboard aileron
62 Flap actuator fairing
63 Starboard blown flap – SPS (sduva pogranichnovo sloya)
64 Multi-spar wing structure
65 Main integral wing fuel tank
66 Undercarriage mounting/pivot point
67 Starboard mainwheel leg
68 Auxiliaries compartment
69 Fuselage fuel tanks Nos 2 and 3
70 Mainwheel well exernal fairing
71 Mainwheel (retracted)
72 Trunking contours
73 Control rods in dorsal spine
74 Compressor face
75 Oil tank
76 Avionics pack
77 Engine accessories
78 Tumansky R-13 turbojet (rated at 14,550 lb/6 600 kg with full reheat)
79 Fuselage break/transport joint
80 Intake
81 Tail surface control linkage
82 Artificial feel unit
83 Tailplane jack
84 Hydraulic accumulator
85 Tailplane trim motor
86 Tailfin spar attachment plate
87 Rudder jack
88 Rudder control linkage
89 Tailfin structure
90 Leading-edge panel
91 Radio cable access
92 Magnetic detector
93 Tailfin mainspar
94 RSIU (radio-stantsiya istrebitelnaya ultrakorotkykh vol'n – very-short-wave fighter radio) antenna plate
95 VHF/UHF aerials
96 IFF antenna
97 Formation light
98 Tail warning radar
99 Rear navigation light
100 Fuel vent
101 Rudder construction
102 Rudder hinge
103 Braking parachute hinged bullet fairing
104 Braking parachute stowage
105 Tailpipe (variable convergent nozzle)
106 Afterburner installation
107 Afterburner bay cooling intake
108 Tailplane linkage fairing
109 Nozzle actuating cylinders
110 Tailplane torque tube
111 All-moving tailplane
112 Anti-flutter weight
113 Intake
114 Afterburner mounting
115 Fixed tailplane root fairing
116 Longitudinal lap joint
117 External duct (nozzle hydraulics)
118 Ventral fin
119 Engine guide rail
120 JATO assembly canted nozzle
121 JATO assembly thrust plate forks (rear mounting)
122 JATO assembly pack
123 Ventral airbrake (retracted)

generation it is highly agile, but high turn rates are accompanied by steep drag rise and its radius of action is overly modest.

### SPECIFICATION: MiG-21MF

**Power Plant:** One Tumansky R-13-300 turbojet rated at 11,244 lb (5 100 kg) thrust dry and 14,550 lb (6 600 kg) thrust with afterburning. Internal fuel capacity, 572 Imp gal (2 600 l) and provision for three 108 Imp gal (490 l) drop tanks.

**Performance:** Max speed (clean), 808 mph (1 300 km/h) or M=1·06 at 1,000 ft (305 m), 1,386 mph (2 230 km/h) or M=2·1 above 36,090 ft (11 000 m); max range (internal fuel), 683 mls (1 100 km), (max external fuel), 1,118 mls (1 800 km).

**Weights:** Normal loaded (with four K-13A AAMs), 18,078 lb (8 200 kg), (two K-13As and two drop tanks), 19,731 lb (8 950 kg); max, 20,723 lb (9 400 kg).

**Dimensions:** Span, 23 ft 5½ in (7,15 m); length (without probe), 44 ft 2 in (13,46 m); wing area, 247·57 sq ft (23,00 m²).

**Armament:** One twin-barrel 23-mm GSh-23 cannon with 200 rounds and up to 3,307 lb (1 500 kg) of ordnance on four wing hardpoints.

124 Trestle point
125 JATO assembly release solenoid (front mounting)
126 Underwing landing light
127 Ventral stores pylon
128 Mainwheel inboard door
129 Splayed link chute
130 Twin 23-mm GSh-23 cannon installation
131 Cannon muzzle fairing
132 Debris deflector plate
133 Auxiliary ventral drop tank
134 Port forward air brake (extended)
135 Leading-edge integral fuel tank
136 Undercarriage retraction strut
137 Aileron control rods in leading-edge
138 Port inboard weapons pylon

139 UV-16-57 rocket pod
140 Port mainwheel
141 Mainwheel outboard door section
142 Mainwheel leg
143 Aileron control linkage
144 Mainwheel leg pivot point
145 Main integral wing fuel tank
146 Flap actuator fairing
147 Port aileron
148 Aileron control jack
149 Outboard wing construction
150 Port navigation light
151 Port outboard weapons pylon
152 "Advanced Atoll" infrared-guided AAM
153 Wing fence
154 Radio altimeter antenna

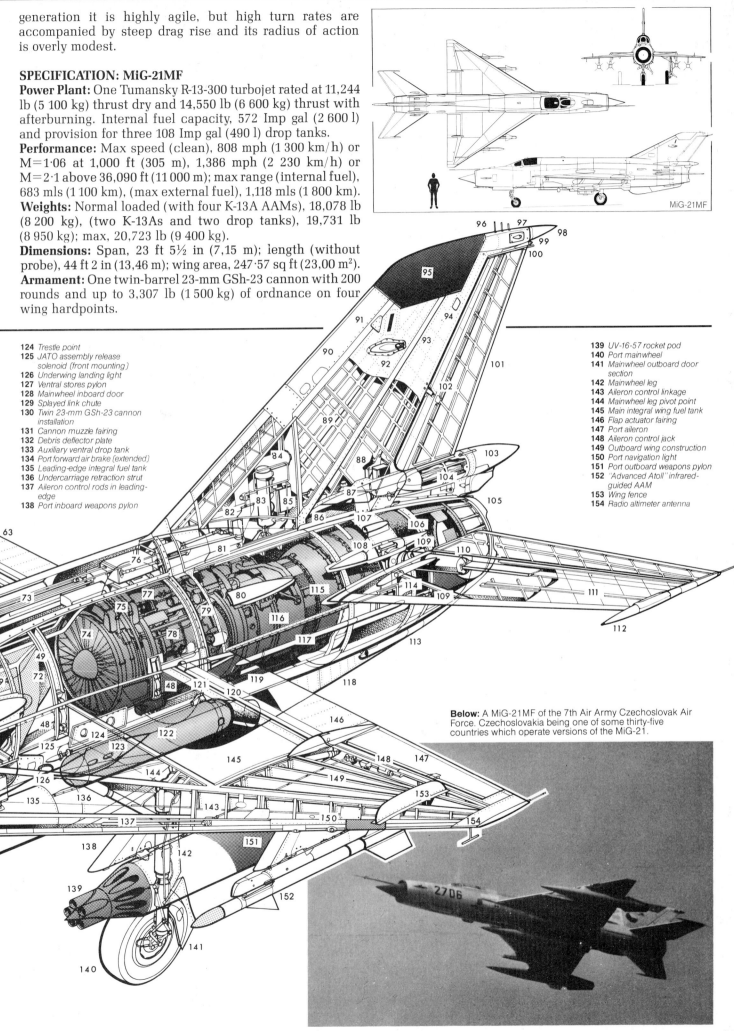

**Below:** A MiG-21MF of the 7th Air Army Czechoslovak Air Force. Czechoslovakia being one of some thirty-five countries which operate versions of the MiG-21.

# Dassault-Breguet Mirage III (November 1956)

**Above:** A Mirage 5V of the Escuadrón de Caza 36 of the Venezuelan Air Force. The Mirage 5 has a similar airframe to the Mirage IIIE.

From the late 'forties, many fighter designers were attracted to the simple tailless delta configuration offering low wave drag with excellent fuel volume and permitting traditional constructional methods. Few were to persist with the formula, however, for pure delta geometry invoked certain penalties. Having no horizontal tail, it could not be fitted with trailing-edge flaps and, in consequence, presented high approach speeds and poor landing performance. Its low aspect ratio resulted in high induced drag, penalising sustained turn, and manoeuvrability suffered further as a result of excessive trim drag.

Avions Marcel Dassault was one of only two manufacturers to retain interest in the tailless delta, and its Mirage III, first flown on 17 November 1956, was essentially an extrapolation of the MD 550 Mirage I lightweight mixed-power target-defence interceptor, but linearly some 20 per cent larger and about 30 per cent heavier. Intended primarily as a bomber interceptor, the restricted agility inherent in its configuration was of only limited significance, and the first series production model, the Mirage IIIC, flew on 9 October 1960.

**Key to Dassault-Breguet Mirage IIIE**
1 Glass-fibre fin tip aerial fairing
2 VHF aerial
3 Tail navigation and anti-collision lights
4 Tail radar warning antenna
5 Rudder construction
6 Fin main spar
7 Passive radar antenna
8 UHF aerial
9 Rudder hydraulic actuator
10 Magnetic detector
11 Parachute release link
12 Brake parachute housing
13 Parachute fairing
14 Exhaust nozzle shroud
15 Variable area exhaust nozzle flaps
16 Nozzle jacks
17 Cooling air louvres
18 Jet pipe
19 Rear fuselage frame and stringer construction

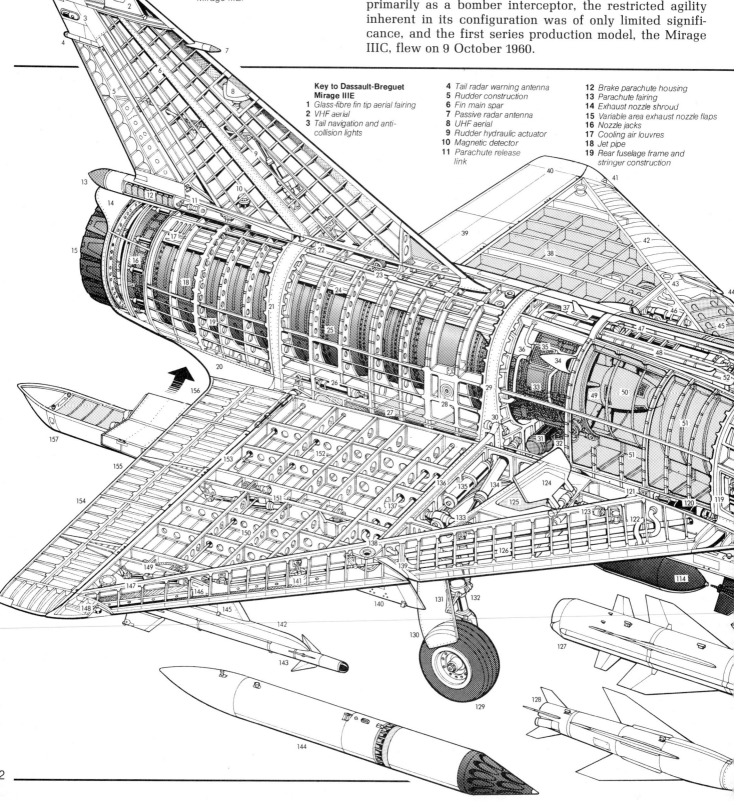

From this basic interceptor, an entire family of fundamentally similar aircraft was to evolve, commencing in 1961 with the dual-role Mirage IIIE and its recce equivalent, the IIIR; continuing in 1967 with the structurally similar but simpler Mirage 5; and reaching its apex in May 1979 with the more powerful Mirage 50. Production of all versions exceeds 1,400 and is expected to continue into 1983.

## SPECIFICATION: Mirage IIIE

**Power Plant:** One SNECMA Atar 9C turbojet rated at 9,436 lb (4 280 kg) dry thrust and 13,230 lb (6 000 kg) with afterburning. Internal fuel capacity, 733 Imp gal (3 330 l) with provision for two 137 Imp gal (625 l), 242 Imp gal (1 100 l), 285 Imp gal (1 300 l) or 374 Imp gal (1 700 l) drop tanks.
**Performance:** Max speed, 863 mph (1 390 km/h) or M = 1·13 at sea level, 1,460 mph (2 350 km/h) or M = 2·21 at 39,375 ft (12 000 m); cruise, 594 mph (956 km/h) or M = 0·9 at 36,090 ft (11 000 m); time to 49,210 ft (15 000 m), 6·83 min; service ceiling, 55,775 ft (17 000 m); combat radius (two 374 Imp gal/1 700 l drop tanks and *HI-LO-LO-HI*) 745 mls (1 200 km).
**Weights:** Empty, 15,540 lb (7 050 kg); normal loaded, 21,165 lb (9 600 kg); max, 30,200 lb (13 700 kg).
**Dimensions:** Span, 26 ft 11½ in (8,22 m); length (including pitot), 49 ft 3½ in (15,03 m); height, 14 ft 9 in (4,50 m); wing area, 375 sq ft (34,85 m²).
**Armament:** Two 30-mm DEFA cannon with 125 rpg and provision for up to 4,000 lb (1 814 kg) of external ordnance.

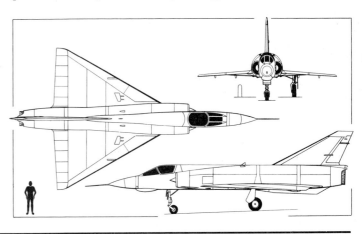

20 Wing root trailing edge fillet
21 Fin attachment main frame
22 Fin spar attachment joint
23 Control cable runs
24 Engine bay/jet pipe thermal lining
25 Afterburner duct
26 Elevon compensator hydraulic jack
27 Ventral fuel tank
28 Main engine mounting
29 Wing spar/fuselage main frame
30 Main spar joint
31 Engine gearbox driven generator
32 Engine accessory compartment
33 SNECMA Atar 9C afterburning turbojet
34 Cooling system air intakes
35 Heat exchanger
36 Engine oil tank
37 IFF aerial
38 Port wing integral fuel tank, total internal capacity 733 Imp gal (3 330 l)
39 Inboard elevon
40 Outboard elevon
41 Port navigation light
42 Cambered leading edge ribs
43 Port wing pylon fixing
44 Leading edge notch
45 Port leading edge fuel tank
46 Main undercarriage pivot fixing
47 Fuselage dorsal systems ducting
48 Air system piping
49 Turbojet intake
50 Engine starter housing
51 Fuselage fuel tanks
52 Equipment cooling system air filter
53 Computer system voltage regulator
54 Oxygen bottles
55 Inverted flight fuel system accumulator
56 Intake ducting
57 Matra 530 missile computor
58 VHF radio transmitter/receiver
59 Gyro platform multiplier
60 Doppler transceiver
61 Navigation system computor
62 Air data computor
63 Nord missile encoding supply
64 Radio altimeter transceiver
65 Heading and inertial correction computor
66 Armament junction box
67 Radar program controller
68 Canopy external release
69 Canopy hinge
70 Radio and electronics bay access fairing
71 Fuel tank stabilising fins
72 285 Imp gal (1300 l) auxiliary fuel tank (374 Imp gal/1 700 l alternative)
73 137 Imp gal (625 l) drop tank
74 Cockpit canopy cover
75 Canopy hydraulic jack
76 Ejection seat headrest
77 Face blind firing handle
78 Martin-Baker (Hispano licence) RM.4 ejection seat
79 Port side console panel
80 Canopy framing
81 Pilot's head-up display
82 Windscreen panels
83 Instrument panel shroud
84 Instrument pressure sensors
85 Thomson CSF Cyrano II fire control radar
86 Radar scanner dish
87 Glass-fibre radome
88 Pitot tube
89 Matra 530 air-to-air missile
90 Doppler radar fairing
91 Thomson CSF doppler navigation radar antenna
92 Cockpit front pressure bulkhead
93 Rudder pedals
94 Radar scope (head-down display)
95 Control column
96 Cockpit floor level
97 Starboard side console panel
98 Nosewheel leg doors
99 Nose undercarriage leg strut
100 Landing/taxying lamps
101 Levered suspension axle unit
102 Nosewheel
103 Shimmy damper
104 Hydraulic retraction strut
105 Cockpit rear pressure bulkhead
106 Air conditioning ram air intake
107 Moveable intake half-cone centre-body
108 Starboard air intake
109 Nosewheel well door (open position)
110 Intake centre-body screw jack
111 Air conditioning plant
112 Boundary layer bleed air duct
113 Centre fuselage bomb rack
114 882-lb (400-kg) HE bombs
115 Cannon barrels
116 30-mm DEFA cannon (2) 250-rounds per gun
117 Ventral gun pack
118 Auxiliary air intake door
119 Electrical system servicing panel
120 Starboard 30-mm DEFA cannon
121 Front spar attachment joint
122 Fuel system piping
123 Airbrake hydraulic jack
124 Starboard airbrake, upper and lower surfaces (open position)
125 Airbrake housing
126 Starboard leading edge fuel tank
127 AS.37 Martel, radar guided air-to-ground missile
128 Nord AS.30 air-to-air missile
129 Starboard mainwheel
130 Mainwheel leg door
131 Torque scissor links
132 Shock absorber leg strut
133 Starboard main undercarriage pivot fixing
134 Hydraulic retraction jack
135 Main undercarriage hydraulic accumulator
136 Wing main spar
137 Fuel system piping
138 Inboard pylon fixing
139 Leading edge notch
140 Starboard inner stores pylon
141 Control rod runs
142 Missile launch rail
143 AIM-9 Sidewinder air-to-air missile
144 JL-100 fuel and rocket pack, 55 Imp gal (250 l) of fuel plus 18 × 68-mm unguided rockets
145 Outboard wing pylon
146 Outboard pylon fixing
147 Front spar
148 Starboard navigation light
149 Outboard elevon hydraulic jack
150 Starboard wing integral fuel tank
151 Inboard elevon hydraulic actuator
152 Wing multi-spar and rib construction
153 Rear spar
154 Outboard elevon construction
155 Inboard elevon construction
156 Elevon compensator
157 110 Imp gal (500 l) auxiliary ventral fuel tank

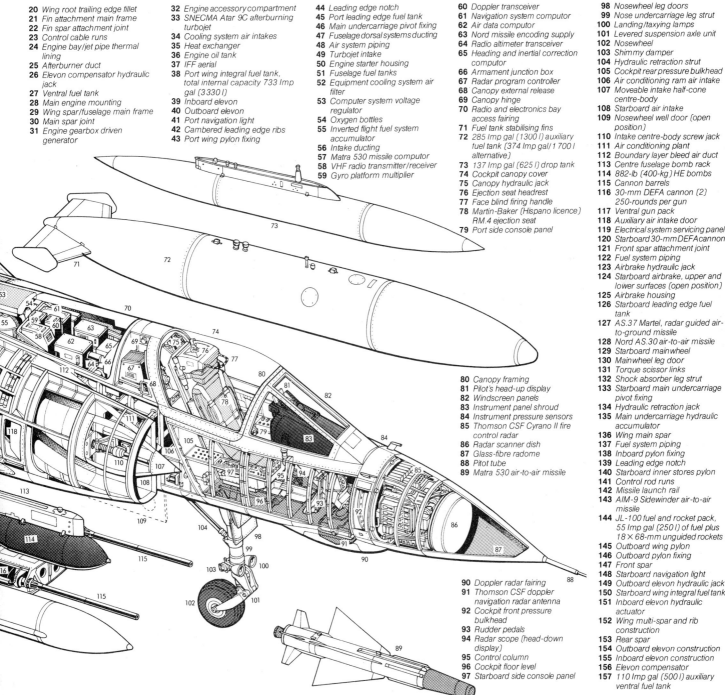

# BAC Lightning (April 1957)

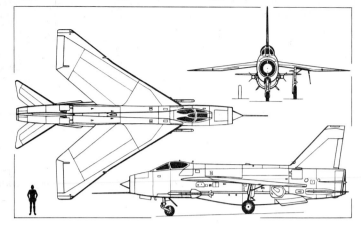

A highly novel approach to the problem of minimising the drag of a dual engine installation—and one that was to remain unique—was proffered by W.E.W. Petter in designing the Lightning interceptor. Minimal frontal area was achieved by staggering the two turbojets vertically, effectively tucking them behind the cockpit, and feeding them by means of a simple centre body external compression intake in the nose. Drag was further minimised by adoption of the maximum feasible sweepback of 60 deg at the leading edge, which, rivalled only by the somewhat earlier Su-7 (see pages 204-205), permitted a relatively deep wing with useful fuel volume. An unusual feature of this wing was the alignment of the wing-tips with the longitudinal axis which placed the ailerons on the torsional axis of the wing.

The first prototype Lightning, the P.1B, was flown on 4 April 1957, deliveries of the initial production version, the F Mk 1, commencing in June 1960. Developed specifically as a home defence interceptor, the formula produced an aeroplane strictly limited in operational flexibility, the initial version having a combat radius of only some 150 miles (240 km), but the Lightning offered superb handling, outstanding rates of climb and acceleration, and was one of the very few fighters capable of supersonic flight *without* recourse to afterburning.

Progressively developed, the Lightning remained in production until September 1972, 332 being built.

**Key to BAC Lightning F Mk 6**

1 Pitot head boom
2 Intake bullet fairing
3 Ferranti Airpass radar antenna/scanner
4 Engine air intake lip
5 Hot-air de-icing
6 Bullet lower spacer
7 G 90 camera
8 Radar pack
9 Bullet upper spacer (electrical leads)
10 Forward equipment bay
11 Forward fuse box
12 Capacitor box
13 Lox container
14 Light fighter sight control unit
15 De-icing/de-mister air
16 Radar ground cooling air coupling
17 Nosewheel door mechanism torque shaft and operating rods
18 Nosewheel bay
19 Nosewheel doors
20 Nosewheel strut
21 Roller guide bracket
22 Forward-retracting nosewheel
23 Caster auto-disconnect
24 Shimmy damper and centring unit
25 Aft door (linked to leg)
26 Flight refuelling probe (detachable)
27 Nosewheel strut pivot pin
28 Heat exchanger
29 Nosewheel hydraulic jack
30 Intake ducting
31 Cockpit canted floor
32 Engine power control panel
33 Control column
34 Instrument panel shroud
35 Rudder pedal assembly
36 Canopy forward frames
37 Rain dispersal duct
38 Windscreen (Electro-thermo)
39 CRT display unit (starboard)
40 Airpass (light fighter) attack sight
41 Standby magnetic compass
42 Canopy top panel de-misting ducts
43 Magnesium-forged canopy top frame
44 IFF aerial
45 Chemical air driers
46 Starboard (armaments) console
47 Ejection seat face-blind/firing-handle
48 Air-conditioning duct
49 Rear pressure bulkhead
50 Martin-Baker ejection seat
51 Port instrument panels
52 Cockpit ladder attachment
53 Cockpit emergency ram-air intake
54 Lower (No 1) engine intake duct frames
55 Firestreak weapons pack

56 Launch sequence units
57 Control units
58 Port missile pylon
59 Firestreak missile
60 Fuse 'windows'
61 Armament safety break panel
62 Aileron accumulator pressure gauges
63 Accumulator group bay
64 Plessey LTSA starter in lower (No 1) engine nose cone
65 Lower (No 1) engine intake
66 Wingroot inboard fairing
67 Main equipment bay
68 Selector address unit
69 Electronic unit
70 Air data computer
71 Converter signal unit (data link)
72 Communications T/R (2)
73 Canopy hinge
74 Dorsal spine bays
75 AC fuse and relay box (cold-air unit and water boiler to starboard)
76 28V battery
77 Upper (No 2) engine intake duct
78 Fuselage frames
79 Water heater tank and extractor
80 Wing/fuselage main attachment point
81 Aileron idler lever
82 Aileron control push-pull tubes
83 Tube attachment brackets
84 Fuselage multi-bolt forward/centre section join
85 Aden gun muzzle
86 Leading-edge integral fuel
87 Muzzle blast tube
88 Aileron tube triple-roller guides
89 Access
90 Fuel lines
91 Non-return valve
92 Detachable leading-edge sections
93 Shuttle valve
94 Undercarriage strut fixed fairing
95 Shock-absorber strut
96 Port mainwheel
97 Brake unit
98 Tubeless tyre
99 Torque links
100 Red Top missile

101 Aft fairing flap
102 Undercarriage pivot
103 Radius rod (inward-breaking)
104 Undercarriage retraction jack
105 Door jack sequence valve
106 Door master locking mechanism
107 Collector tank and booster pumps (2)
108 Aerodynamic leading-edge slot
109 Tank pressurizing intake/vent (in slot)
110 Mainwheel door
111 Undercarriage jack sequence valve
112 Door latch linkage
113 Port mainwheel well
114 Aileron control push-pull tubes
115 Aileron movement restrictor
116 Aileron autostabilizer actuator
117 Aileron control linkage
118 Aileron hydraulic runs
119 Cambered leading-edge extension
120 Localiser aerial
121 Port navigation light
122 Port wingtip
123 Port aileron
124 Aileron powered flying-control units
125 Control linkage
126 Wing outer structure
127 Aileron mass balance
128 Wing outer fixed section
129 Flap outer actuator jack
130 Flap sections
131 Flap integral tank
132 Angled aft spar
133 Undercarriage attachment
134 Refuelling/defuelling valve
135 Flap inner actuator jack
136 3-way cock (manual)

137 DC transfer pump
138 Gate valves
139 Wing/fuselage rear main attachment point
140 Lower (No 1) engine intermediate jet pipe forward face
141 Wing inboard structure
142 Wing integral fuel
143 Intermediate spar booms (T-section)
144 Port Aden cannon (forward ventral pack)
145 Wing rib stations
146 Fuel vent pipe
147 Multi-bolt wing attachment plate
148 Access panels
149 Upper (No 2) engine duct frames
150 Fuselage break frame
151 Voltage regulators
152 Start tank
153 Engine pump units
154 Solenoid valves
155 Communications antenna
156 Starter control unit
157 HF igniter units
158 Fuselage frame
159 Main wing box upper skin
160 Forged centre rib (multi-bolt attachment)
161 Starter exhaust
162 Upper (No 2) engine nose cone
163 Generator cooling ram-air intake
164 Stand-by generator
165 Anti-icing bleed air
166 Upper (No 2) Avon 301 turbojet engine and reheat units

167 Airpass recorder unit
168 Engine front mounting point
169 Engine accessories
170 No 2 engine bleed-air turbopump (reheat fuel)
171 Engine bay firewalls
172 Integral pumps (2)
173 HE ignition units
174 Voltage regulator
175 Current sensing unit
176 Rudder spring feel mechanism
177 Auxiliary intake
178 Main mounting trunnion
179 Aft (port) equipment bays
180 Electronic unit
181 IFF coder
182 Tailplane controls
183 Tailplane trim actuator and feel unit
184 Ventral fuel tank (aft section)
185 Fin
186 Reheat cooling lower intake
187 Tailplane autostabilizer actuator
188 Gearbox oil filler
189 AC generator
190 Glide-path receiver
191 IFF T/R unit
192 Outlet
193 No 2 engine intermediate jet pipe
194 Refrasil heat shrouds
195 Stress-bearing upper (No 2) engine hatch

## SPECIFICATION: Lightning F Mk 6

**Power Plant:** Two Rolls-Royce Avon 301 turbojets each rated at 11,100 lb (5 035 kg) dry thrust, 16,300 lb (7,394 kg) with afterburning. Internal capacity, 735 Imp gal (3 341 l), provision for non-jettisonable 535 Imp gal (2 432 l) ventral and (ferry) two 260 Imp gal (1 182 l) overwing tanks.

**Performance:** Max speed, 808 mph (1 300 km/h) or M=1·06 at sea level, 1,386 mph (2 230 km/h) or M=2·1 at 36,000 ft (10 975 m); initial climb, 50,000 ft/min (254 m/sec); time to 65,000 ft (19 810 m) and M=2·0, 5·0 min; max altitude, 77,000 ft (23 470 m); max sustained altitude, 57,000 ft (17 375 m); combat radius with ventral fuel pack (HI-LO), 489 mls (787 km); max combat radius, 604 mls (972 km); ferry range, 1,554 mls (2 500 km).

**Weights:** Empty, 25,820 lb (11 712 kg); combat loaded, 39,940 lb (18 117 kg); max, 41,700 lb (18 915 kg).

**Dimensions:** Span, 34 ft 10 in (10,61 m); length (including pitot), 55 ft 3 in (16,84 m); height, 19 ft 7 in (5,97 m); wing area, 474·5 sq ft (44,08 m²).

**Armament:** Two 30-mm Aden cannon with 130 rpg and two Firestreak AAMs.

**Above:** A Lightning F Mk 6 of No 11 Sqdn based at Binbrook, Lincs, and photographed in July 1980. The Mk 6 was the definitive production model of the Lightning for the RAF.

196 Port airbrake
197 Airbrake hydraulic actuator jack
198 DC generator
199 Main-accessory-drive unit
200 Airbrake lower frame
201 Turbine exhaust (from 199)
202 Tailplane accumulator and nitrogen bottle
203 Reheat 'hotshot' igniter box
204 Tailplane drive triangular unit
205 Tailplane powered flying-control unit
206 Tailplane spigot
207 Pivot spar
208 All-moving tailplane

209 Light-alloy honeycomb structure
210 Braking parachute box internally-retracting doors
211 Cable operating assembly
212 Fuselage aft frame
213 Lower (No 1) engine reheat jet pipe
214 Trunnion access panel
215 AMCU air pipes

216 Reheat cooling upper intake
217 Rudder feel unit
218 Rudder trim actuator
219 Rudder autostabilizer actuator
220 Rudder linkage
221 Fin spar/fuselage bolts
222 Fuselage frame formers
223 Rudder powered flying-control unit
224 Reheat jet pipe mounting rail
225 Upper (No 2) engine reheat jet pipe

233 Flutter damper
234 Communications antenna
235 Dielectric tip
236 Compass unit
237 Angled aft spars
238 Main fin structure
239 Fin leading-edge panels
240 Accessory drive cooling air
241 Starboard aileron
242 Aileron powered flying-control units
243 Control linkage
244 Starboard flap outer actuator jack
245 Starboard flap
246 Wing panels

226 Rear rollers
227 Air-driven nozzle actuator
228 Jet pipe trunnion access panel
229 Variable propelling nozzles
230 Streamer cable around rear lip (spring-clipped)

231 Parachute streaming anchor and jettison unit
232 Rudder light-alloy honeycomb structure

247 Wing skinning
248 Wing integral fuel
249 Aileron control push-pull tubes
250 Aileron movement restrictor
251 Aileron autostabilizer actuator
252 Starboard navigation light
253 Glide-slope aerial

# McDonnell Douglas F-4 Phantom II (May 1958)

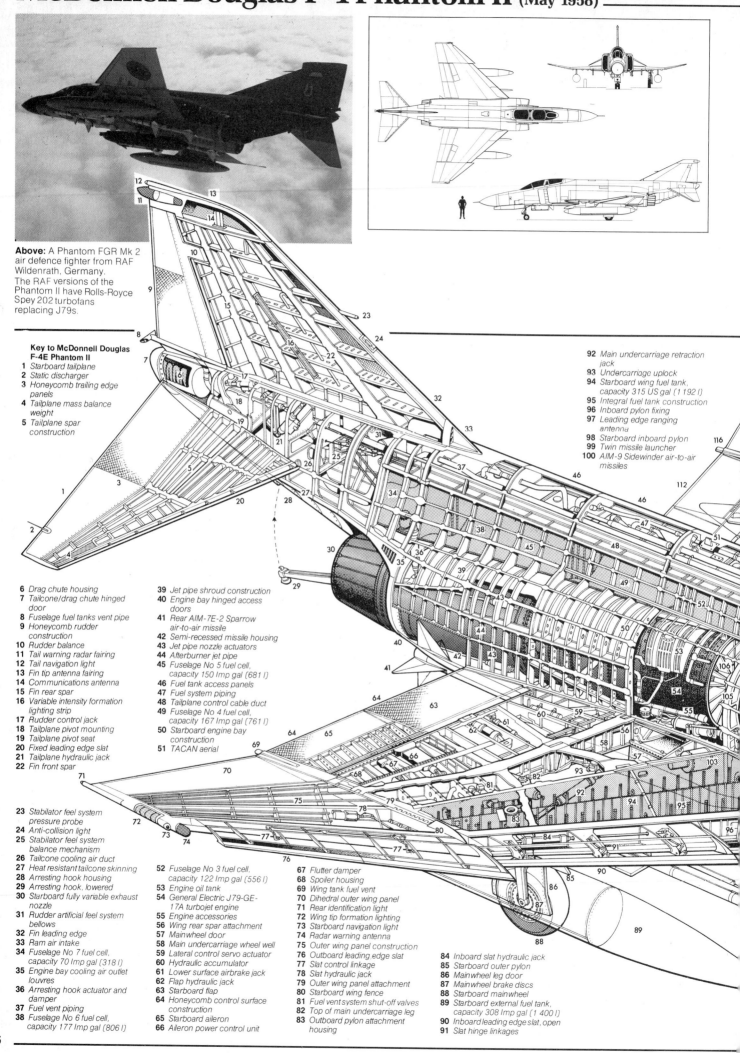

**Above:** A Phantom FGR Mk 2 air defence fighter from RAF Wildenrath, Germany. The RAF versions of the Phantom II have Rolls-Royce Spey 202 turbofans replacing J79s.

**Key to McDonnell Douglas F-4E Phantom II**

1 Starboard tailplane
2 Static discharger
3 Honeycomb trailing edge panels
4 Tailplane mass balance weight
5 Tailplane spar construction
6 Drag chute housing
7 Tailcone/drag chute hinged door
8 Fuselage fuel tanks vent pipe
9 Honeycomb rudder construction
10 Rudder balance
11 Tail warning radar fairing
12 Tail navigation light
13 Fin tip antenna fairing
14 Communications antenna
15 Fin rear spar
16 Variable intensity formation lighting strip
17 Rudder control jack
18 Tailplane pivot mounting
19 Tailplane pivot seat
20 Fixed leading edge slat
21 Tailplane hydraulic jack
22 Fin front spar
23 Stabilator feel system pressure probe
24 Anti-collision light
25 Stabilator feel system balance mechanism
26 Tailcone cooling air duct
27 Heat resistant tailcone skinning
28 Arresting hook housing
29 Arresting hook, lowered
30 Starboard fully variable exhaust nozzle
31 Rudder artificial feel system bellows
32 Fin leading edge
33 Ram air intake
34 Fuselage No 7 fuel cell, capacity 70 Imp gal (318 l)
35 Engine bay cooling air outlet louvres
36 Arresting hook actuator and damper
37 Fuel vent piping
38 Fuselage No 6 fuel cell, capacity 177 Imp gal (806 l)

39 Jet pipe shroud construction
40 Engine bay hinged access doors
41 Rear AIM-7E-2 Sparrow air-to-air missile
42 Semi-recessed missile housing
43 Jet pipe nozzle actuators
44 Afterburner jet pipe
45 Fuselage No 5 fuel cell, capacity 150 Imp gal (681 l)
46 Fuel tank access panels
47 Fuel system piping
48 Tailplane control cable duct
49 Fuselage No 4 fuel cell, capacity 167 Imp gal (761 l)
50 Starboard engine bay construction
51 TACAN aerial
52 Fuselage No 3 fuel cell, capacity 122 Imp gal (556 l)
53 Engine oil tank
54 General Electric J79-GE-17A turbojet engine
55 Engine accessories
56 Wing rear spar attachment
57 Mainwheel door
58 Main undercarriage wheel well
59 Lateral control servo actuator
60 Hydraulic accumulator
61 Lower surface airbrake jack
62 Flap hydraulic jack
63 Starboard flap
64 Honeycomb control surface construction
65 Starboard aileron
66 Aileron power control unit

67 Flutter damper
68 Spoiler housing
69 Wing tank fuel vent
70 Dihedral outer wing panel
71 Rear identification light
72 Wing tip formation light
73 Starboard navigation light
74 Radar warning antenna
75 Outer wing panel construction
76 Outboard leading edge slat
77 Slat control linkage
78 Slat hydraulic jack
79 Outer wing panel attachment
80 Starboard wing fence
81 Fuel vent system shut-off valves
82 Top of main undercarriage leg
83 Outboard pylon attachment housing

84 Inboard slat hydraulic jack
85 Starboard outer pylon
86 Mainwheel leg door
87 Mainwheel brake discs
88 Starboard mainwheel
89 Starboard external fuel tank, capacity 308 Imp gal (1 400 l)
90 Inboard leading edge slat, open
91 Slat hinge linkages
92 Main undercarriage retraction jack
93 Undercarriage uplock
94 Starboard wing fuel tank, capacity 315 US gal (1 192 l)
95 Integral fuel tank construction
96 Inboard pylon fixing
97 Leading edge ranging antenna
98 Starboard inboard pylon
99 Twin missile launcher
100 AIM-9 Sidewinder air-to-air missiles

Unquestionably the most significant and successful jet fighter of the 'sixties in the western hemisphere, the Phantom II was to claim uniquity in its conception solely as a shipboard warplane yet far wider usage as a non-naval shore-based multi-role fighter. Characterised by upward canted outer wing panels and downward canted tailplane, features adopted to enhance directional stability, the Phantom II first flew (as the YF4H-1) on 27 May 1958, entering US Navy service (F4H-1F) late in 1960.

The US Navy was to receive 1,218 Phantom IIs (the USMC receiving a further 46), deliveries terminating in December 1965. The Phantom II had meanwhile been adopted by the USAF with which it entered service in 1963, a total of 2,640 being procured. Eight countries were to adopt standard USAF models, and special versions were to be produced for the RAF and the Luftwaffe, a total of 5,211 Phantom IIs being built, 138 of them in Japan, the last in May 1981.

**SPECIFICATION: F-4E Phantom II**

**Power Plant:** Two General Electric J79-GE-17 turbojets each rated at 11,110 lb (5 040 kg) dry thrust and 17,900 lb (8 120 kg) with afterburning. Internal fuel capacity, 1,545 Imp gal (7 022 l) and up to 1,116 Imp gal (5 073 l) in three drop tanks.

**Performance:** Max speed, 1,006 mph (1 619 km/h) or M=1·32 at sea level, 1,434 mph (2 307 km/h) or M=2·17 at 40,000 ft (12 190 m); initial climb, 49,800 ft/min (253 m/sec); service ceiling, 58,400 ft (17 800 m); combat radius (*HI-LO-HI* mission profile with 2,000-lb/907-kg store and four AIM-7E AAMs), 423 mls (680 km) at average speed of 583 mph (938 km/h) at 32,950-39,400 ft (10 045-12 010 m); ferry range (with one 500 Imp gal/2 273 l and two 308 Imp gal/1 400 l drop tanks), 1,613 mls (2 596 km).

**Weights:** Empty, 30,328 lb (13 757 kg); combat, 41,487 lb (18 818 kg); max, 61,795 lb (28 030 kg).

**Dimensions:** Span, 38 ft 4 in (11,68 m); length, 63 ft 0 in (19,20 m); height, 16 ft 5 in (5,05 m); wing area, 530 sq ft (49,24 m²).

**Armament:** One 20-mm General Electric M61A1 multi-barrel rotary cannon and (intercept mission) four AIM-7E-2 Sparrow AAMs, or up to 16,000 lb (7 258 kg) of external ordnance in various combinations.

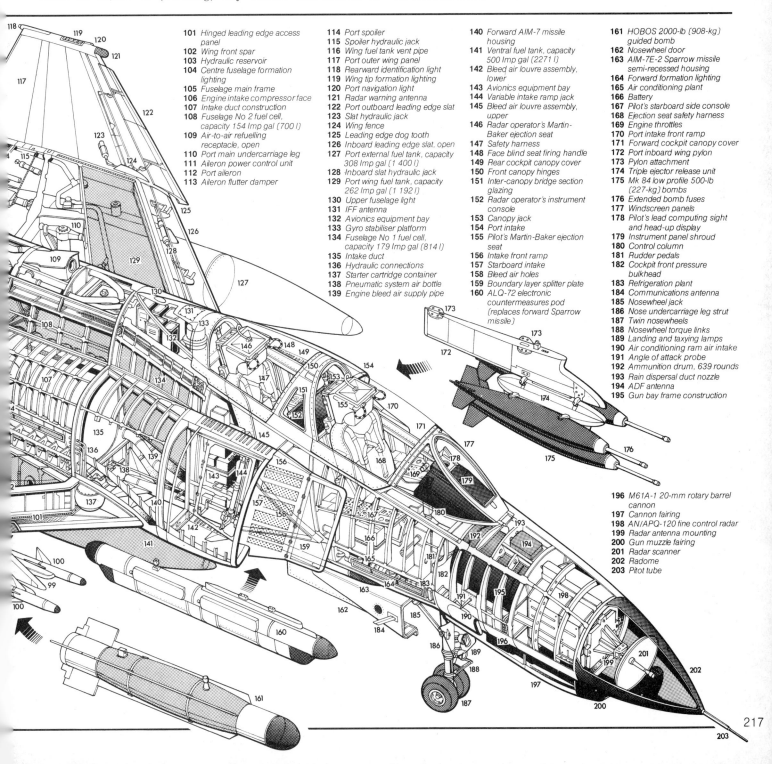

101 Hinged leading edge access panel
102 Wing front spar
103 Hydraulic reservoir
104 Centre fuselage formation lighting
105 Fuselage main frame
106 Engine intake compressor face
107 Intake duct construction
108 Fuselage No 2 fuel cell, capacity 154 Imp gal (700 l)
109 Air-to-air refuelling receptacle, open
110 Port main undercarriage leg
111 Aileron power control unit
112 Port aileron
113 Aileron flutter damper
114 Port spoiler
115 Spoiler hydraulic jack
116 Wing fuel tank vent pipe
117 Port outer wing panel
118 Rearward identification light
119 Wing tip formation lighting
120 Port navigation light
121 Radar warning antenna
122 Port outboard leading edge slat
123 Slat hydraulic jack
124 Wing fence
125 Leading edge dog tooth
126 Inboard leading edge slat, open
127 Port external fuel tank, capacity 308 Imp gal (1 400 l)
128 Inboard slat hydraulic jack
129 Port wing fuel tank, capacity 262 Imp gal (1 192 l)
130 Upper fuselage light
131 IFF antenna
132 Avionics equipment bay
133 Gyro stabiliser platform
134 Fuselage No 1 fuel cell, capacity 179 Imp gal (814 l)
135 Intake duct
136 Hydraulic connections
137 Starter cartridge container
138 Pneumatic system air bottle
139 Engine bleed air supply pipe
140 Forward AIM-7 missile housing
141 Ventral fuel tank, capacity 500 Imp gal (2271 l)
142 Bleed air louvre assembly, lower
143 Avionics equipment bay
144 Variable intake ramp jack
145 Bleed air louvre assembly, upper
146 Radar operator's Martin-Baker ejection seat
147 Safety harness
148 Face blind seat firing handle
149 Rear cockpit canopy cover
150 Front canopy hinges
151 Inter-canopy bridge section glazing
152 Radar operator's instrument console
153 Canopy jack
154 Port intake
155 Pilot's Martin-Baker ejection seat
156 Intake front ramp
157 Starboard intake
158 Bleed air holes
159 Boundary layer splitter plate
160 ALQ-72 electronic countermeasures pod (replaces forward Sparrow missile)
161 HOBOS 2000-lb (908-kg) guided bomb
162 Nosewheel door
163 AIM-7E-2 Sparrow missile semi-recessed housing
164 Forward formation lighting
165 Air conditioning plant
166 Battery
167 Pilot's starboard side console
168 Ejection seat safety harness
169 Engine throttles
170 Port intake front ramp
171 Forward cockpit canopy cover
172 Port inboard wing pylon
173 Pylon attachment
174 Triple ejector release unit
175 Mk 84 low profile 500-lb (227-kg) bombs
176 Extended bomb fuses
177 Windscreen panels
178 Pilot's lead computing sight and head-up display
179 Instrument panel shroud
180 Control column
181 Rudder pedals
182 Cockpit front pressure bulkhead
183 Refrigeration plant
184 Communications antenna
185 Nosewheel jack
186 Nose undercarriage leg strut
187 Twin nosewheels
188 Nosewheel torque links
189 Landing and taxiing lamps
190 Air conditioning ram air intake
191 Angle of attack probe
192 Ammunition drum, 639 rounds
193 Rain dispersal duct nozzle
194 ADF antenna
195 Gun bay frame construction

196 M61A-1 20-mm rotary barrel cannon
197 Cannon fairing
198 AN/APQ-120 fine control radar
199 Radar antenna mounting
200 Gun muzzle fairing
201 Radar scanner
202 Radome
203 Pitot tube

# Northrop F-5 (July 1959)

**Above:** Two F-5E Tiger IIs of the US Naval Fighter Weapons 'Top Gun' School at Miramar Naval Air Station, California, where these fighters are employed to provide dissimilar combat training.

From the late 'forties through the 'fifties, the term *fighter* became ever more a term of expedience in the traditional sense; as a warplane category it had undergone gradual metamorphosis. Its repertoire had expanded from interception and air superiority to take in close air support, interdiction and reconnaissance; the clear-weather diurnal aeroplane had taken on round-the-clock all-weather faculties. Increasing range and payload demands had paralleled this growing sophistication, and the upward size-weight-complexity-cost spiral was accelerating.

This rising helix was viewed with consternation by many, and several attempts were to be made at least to arrest if not reverse the trend; to translate the *traditional* fighter into modern terms and evolve, by the standards of the day, a relatively simple, comparatively low-cost clear weather fighter. The most successful of these attempts was to be the F-5 designed by Welko Gasich. Conceived as a pure air superiority fighter, the first prototype was flown on 30 July 1959. Ironically, the F-5 was selected for the *counterair* role for MAP supply to favoured nations, dictating a switch in emphasis from air-air to air-ground capability.

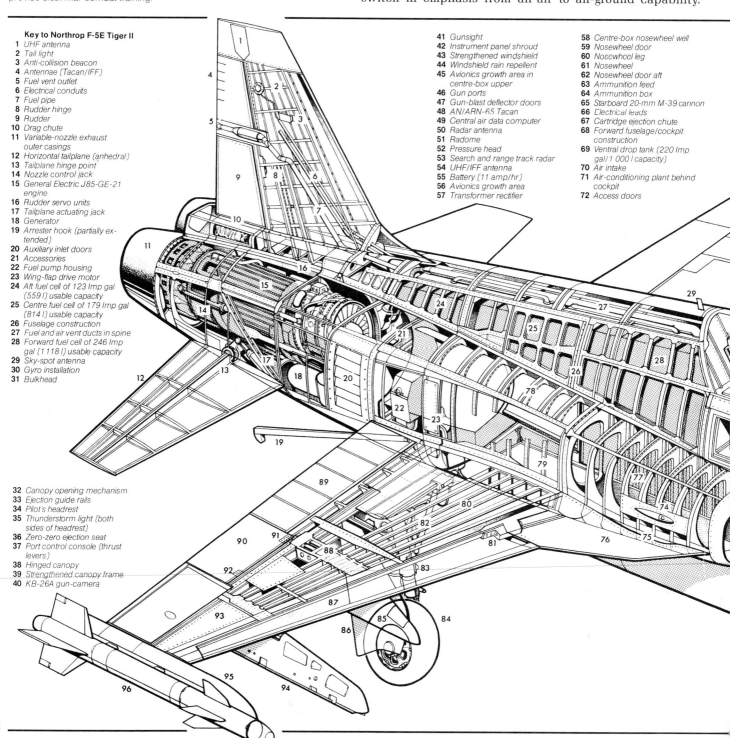

**Key to Northrop F-5E Tiger II**
1 UHF antenna
2 Tail light
3 Anti-collision beacon
4 Antennae (Tacan/IFF)
5 Fuel vent outlet
6 Electrical conduits
7 Fuel pipe
8 Rudder hinge
9 Rudder
10 Drag chute
11 Variable-nozzle exhaust outer casings
12 Horizontal tailplane (anhedral)
13 Tailplane hinge point
14 Nozzle control jack
15 General Electric J85-GE-21 engine
16 Rudder servo units
17 Tailplane actuating jack
18 Generator
19 Arrester hook (partially extended)
20 Auxiliary inlet doors
21 Accessories
22 Fuel pump housing
23 Wing-flap drive motor
24 Aft fuel cell of 123 Imp gal (559 l) usable capacity
25 Centre fuel cell of 179 Imp gal (814 l) usable capacity
26 Fuselage construction
27 Fuel and air vent ducts in spine
28 Forward fuel cell of 246 Imp gal (1 118 l) usable capacity
29 Sky-spot antenna
30 Gyro installation
31 Bulkhead

32 Canopy opening mechanism
33 Ejection guide rails
34 Pilot's headrest
35 Thunderstorm light (both sides of headrest)
36 Zero-zero ejection seat
37 Port control console (thrust levers)
38 Hinged canopy
39 Strengthened canopy frame
40 KB-26A gun-camera

41 Gunsight
42 Instrument panel shroud
43 Strengthened windshield
44 Windshield rain repellent
45 Avionics growth area in centre-box upper
46 Gun ports
47 Gun-blast deflector doors
48 AN/ARN-65 Tacan
49 Central air data computer
50 Radar antenna
51 Radome
52 Pressure head
53 Search and range track radar
54 UHF/IFF antenna
55 Battery (11 amp/hr)
56 Avionics growth area
57 Transformer rectifier

58 Centre-box nosewheel well
59 Nosewheel door
60 Nosewheel leg
61 Nosewheel
62 Nosewheel door aft
63 Ammunition feed
64 Ammunition box
65 Starboard 20-mm M-39 cannon
66 Electrical leads
67 Cartridge ejection chute
68 Forward fuselage/cockpit construction
69 Ventral drop tank (220 Imp gal/1 000 l capacity)
70 Air intake
71 Air-conditioning plant behind cockpit
72 Access doors

Designated F-5A in single-seat and F-5B in two-seat forms, the fighter attained service status early in 1965, 1,044 being produced, including 220 in Canada (as CF-5 and NF-5) and 69 in Spain (as SF-5). In 1970, an upgraded second-generation version, the F-5E Tiger II, was selected to fulfil the new International Fighter Aircraft (IFA) requirement, this variant being optimised for the air superiority mission. The F-5E flew on 11 August 1972, and, with its two-seat equivalent, the F-5F, more than 1,000 had been delivered to 16 customers by the end of 1981, when a third-generation development, the F-5G Tigershark, was under construction.

The F-5G, scheduled to fly September 1982, will be powered by a single General Electric F404-GE-F1G1 turbofan rated at 10,600 lb (4 810 kg) dry and 16,000 lb (7 260 kg) with afterburning. It will offer 48 per cent better acceleration, 32 per cent higher climb rate, a Mach=2·0 speed capability and nine per cent lower fuel consumption.

**SPECIFICATION: F-5E Tiger II**
**Power Plant:** Two General Electric J85-GE-21 turbojets each rated at 3,500 lb (1 588 kg) dry thrust and 5,000 lb (2 268 kg) with afterburning. Internal fuel capacity, 559 Imp gal (2 540 l), with provision for one 220 Imp gal (1 000 l) centreline drop tank.
**Performance:** Max speed (50% internal fuel and two AIM-9J AAMs), 843 mph (1 357 km/h) or M=1·17 at sea level, 997 mph (1 605 km/h) or M=1·51 at 36,090 ft (11 000 m); initial climb, 28,536 ft/min (145 m/sec); service ceiling, 53,800 ft (16 400 m); combat radius (subsonic intercept with internal fuel only and two AIM-9Js), 317 mls (510 km) at (average) 548 mph (882 km/h) at 36,090-43,470 ft (11 000-13 250 m); (CAS mission, *HI-LO-LO-HI* profile with drop tank, two AIM-9Js and four 500-lb/226,8-kg MK 82 bombs), 294 mls (472 km); ferry range, 1,353 mls (2 177 km).
**Weights:** Empty, 9,588 lb (4 349 kg); combat, 14,558 lb (6 603 kg); max, 24,676 lb (11 193 kg).
**Dimensions:** Span, 26 ft 8 in (8,13 m); length (including probe), 48 ft 2 in (14,68 m); height, 13 ft 4 in (4,06 m); wing area, 186 sq ft (17,30 m²).
**Armament:** Two 20-mm M-39 cannon with 280 rpg and (intercept) two AIM-9J Sidewinder AAMs, or up to 7,000 lb (3 175 kg) of external ordnance.

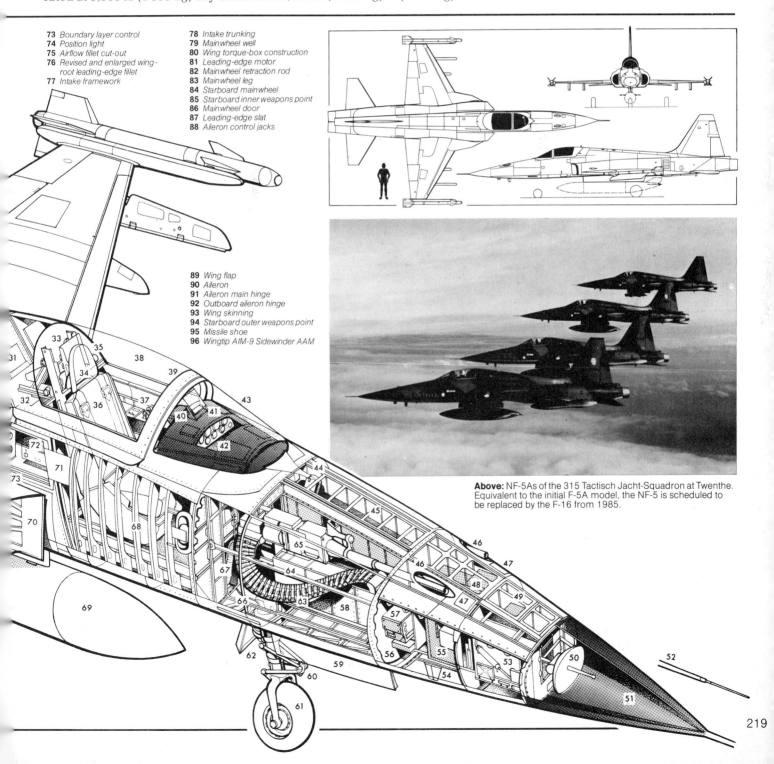

73 Boundary layer control
74 Position light
75 Airflow fillet cut-out
76 Revised and enlarged wing-root leading-edge fillet
77 Intake framework
78 Intake trunking
79 Mainwheel well
80 Wing torque-box construction
81 Leading-edge motor
82 Mainwheel retraction rod
83 Mainwheel leg
84 Starboard mainwheel
85 Starboard inner weapons point
86 Mainwheel door
87 Leading-edge slat
88 Aileron control jacks

89 Wing flap
90 Aileron
91 Aileron main hinge
92 Outboard aileron hinge
93 Wing skinning
94 Starboard outer weapons point
95 Missile shoe
96 Wingtip AIM-9 Sidewinder AAM

**Above:** NF-5As of the 315 Tactisch Jacht-Squadron at Twenthe. Equivalent to the initial F-5A model, the NF-5 is scheduled to be replaced by the F-16 from 1985.

# British Aerospace Harrier (October 1960)

The increase in the generic usage of *fighter* as a classification and the parallel broadening of the fighter spectrum was to be reflected by two aircraft providing the first practical applications of the most dramatic innovations since the advent of the turbojet: vertical and short take-off and landing (V/STOL) and variable wing geometry. These, the Harrier and F-111 (see pages 222-223) respectively, were antithetical in concept and intended mission: one subsonic and optimised for the short-action-radius ground attack task; the other, possessing twice the power and four times the laden weight, bisonic and suited for deep penetration counterair and interdiction missions. Yet both, by the terminology of the 'sixties, were *fighters*.

The Harrier was effectively an extrapolation of the P.1127, the first aircraft to offer VTOL by means of thrust vectoring. Radical yet brilliantly simple conceptually, the P.1127 rose vertically on the vectored thrust of an 11,300 lb (5 126 kg) Pegasus initially on 21 October 1960. Nine pre-series aircraft (then known as Kestrel FGA Mk 1s) followed the six prototypes, and although re-engineered to cater for more power and fuel, the production standard P.1127(RAF), named Harrier, embodied no fundamental design changes. The first of six development Harriers flew on 31 August 1966, 77 production Harrier GR Mk 1s being built as ground attack fighters. Capable of taking-off vertically at light weights, these early Harriers were, for operational pur-

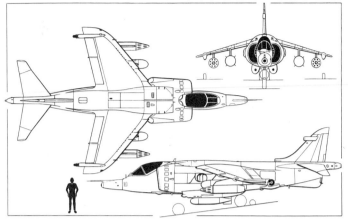

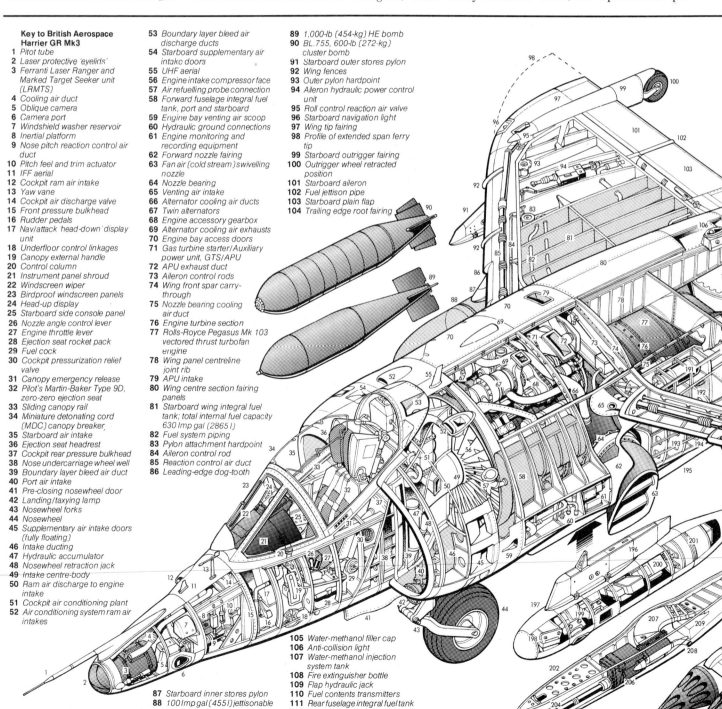

**Key to British Aerospace Harrier GR Mk3**
1 Pitot tube
2 Laser protective 'eyelids'
3 Ferranti Laser Ranger and Marked Target Seeker unit (LRMTS)
4 Cooling air duct
5 Oblique camera
6 Camera port
7 Windshield washer reservoir
8 Inertial platform
9 Nose pitch reaction control air duct
10 Pitch feel and trim actuator
11 IFF aerial
12 Cockpit ram air intake
13 Yaw vane
14 Cockpit air discharge valve
15 Front pressure bulkhead
16 Rudder pedals
17 Nav/attack 'head-down' display unit
18 Underfloor control linkages
19 Canopy external handle
20 Control column
21 Instrument panel shroud
22 Windscreen wiper
23 Birdproof windscreen panels
24 Head-up display
25 Starboard side console panel
26 Nozzle angle control lever
27 Engine throttle lever
28 Ejection seat rocket pack
29 Fuel cock
30 Cockpit pressurization relief valve
31 Canopy emergency release
32 Pilot's Martin-Baker Type 9D, zero-zero ejection seat
33 Sliding canopy rail
34 Miniature detonating cord (MDC) canopy breaker
35 Starboard air intake
36 Ejection seat headrest
37 Cockpit rear pressure bulkhead
38 Nose undercarriage wheel well
39 Boundary layer bleed air duct
40 Port air intake
41 Pre-closing nosewheel door
42 Landing/taxying lamp
43 Nosewheel forks
44 Nosewheel
45 Supplementary air intake doors (fully floating)
46 Intake ducting
47 Hydraulic accumulator
48 Nosewheel retraction jack
49 Intake centre-body
50 Ram air discharge to engine intake
51 Cockpit air conditioning plant
52 Air conditioning system ram air intakes

53 Boundary layer bleed air discharge ducts
54 Starboard supplementary air intake doors
55 UHF aerial
56 Engine intake compressor face
57 Air refuelling probe connection
58 Forward fuselage integral fuel tank, port and starboard
59 Engine bay venting air scoop
60 Hydraulic ground connections
61 Engine monitoring and recording equipment
62 Forward nozzle fairing
63 Fan air (cold stream) swivelling nozzle
64 Nozzle bearing
65 Venting air intake
66 Alternator cooling air ducts
67 Twin alternators
68 Engine accessory gearbox
69 Alternator cooling air exhausts
70 Engine bay access doors
71 Gas turbine starter/Auxiliary power unit, GTS/APU
72 APU exhaust duct
73 Aileron control rods
74 Wing front spar carry-through
75 Nozzle bearing cooling air duct
76 Engine turbine section
77 Rolls-Royce Pegasus Mk 103 vectored thrust turbofan engine
78 Wing panel centreline joint rib
79 APU intake
80 Wing centre section fairing panels
81 Starboard wing integral fuel tank; total internal fuel capacity 630 Imp gal (2865 l)
82 Fuel system piping
83 Pylon attachment hardpoint
84 Aileron control rod
85 Reaction control air duct
86 Leading-edge dog-tooth

89 1,000-lb (454-kg) HE bomb
90 BL.755, 600-lb (272-kg) cluster bomb
91 Starboard outer stores pylon
92 Wing fences
93 Outer pylon hardpoint
94 Aileron hydraulic power control unit
95 Roll control reaction air valve
96 Starboard navigation light
97 Wing tip fairing
98 Profile of extended span ferry tip
99 Starboard outrigger fairing
100 Outrigger wheel retracted position
101 Starboard aileron
102 Fuel jettison pipe
103 Starboard plain flap
104 Trailing edge root fairing

87 Starboard inner stores pylon
88 100 Imp gal (455 l) jettisonable combat fuel tank

105 Water-methanol filler cap
106 Anti-collision light
107 Water-methanol injection system tank
108 Fire extinguisher bottle
109 Flap hydraulic jack
110 Fuel contents transmitters
111 Rear fuselage integral fuel tank
112 Ram air turbine housing

poses, more realistically classed as short take-off and vertical landing (STOVL) aircraft.

The GR Mk 1s with 19,000 lb (8 618 kg) Pegasus 101 engines were progressively upgraded to GR Mk 2 (Pegasus 102) and then GR Mk 3 standards, a further 37 GR Mk 3s being built for the RAF and 102 similar aircraft as AV-8 As for the US Marine Corps, plus 11 for the Spanish Navy. A navalised derivative, the Sea Harrier, is being built for the Royal Navy and Indian Navy, and a progressive development is being developed jointly by BAe and McDonnell Douglas as the Harrier GR Mk 5 for the RAF and AV-8B for the USMC, the first full-scale development (AV-8B) aircraft having flown in late 1981.

### SPECIFICATION: Harrier GR Mk 3

**Power Plant:** One Rolls-Royce Pegasus 103 vectored-thrust turbofan rated at 21,500 lb (9 752 kg) dry thrust. Internal fuel capacity, 630 Imp gal (2,685 l), with provision for two 100 Imp gal (445 l) or (ferry) 330 Imp gal (1 500 l) drop tanks.

**Performance:** Max speed, 720 mph (1 160 km/h) or M=0·95 at 1,000 ft (305 m), 607 mph (977 km/h) or M=0·92 at 36,000 ft (10 970 m), (with typical external ordnance, 598 mph (962 km/h) or M=0·83 at sea level; tactical radius (rolling take-off, *LO-LO-LO* mission profile with 3,000 lb/1 361 kg external ordnance), 175 mls (282 km), (with two 100 Imp gal/455 l drop tanks and 1,500 lb/680 kg external ordnance), 230 mls (370 km), (*HI-LO-HI*), 460 mls (740 km); ferry range, 2,070 mls (3 330 km); time to 40,000 ft (12 190 m) VTO, 2·38 min; service ceiling, 48,000 ft (14 630 m).

**Weights:** Empty, 12,140 lb (5 507 kg); max (VTO), 18,000 lb (8 165 kg), (STO), 26,000 lb (11 794 kg).

**Dimensions:** Span, 25 ft 3 in (7,70 m); length, 45 ft 7¾ in, (13,91 m); height, 11 ft 4 in (3,45 m); wing area, 201.1 sq ft (18,68 m²).

**Armament:** Provision for two 30-mm Aden cannon with 130 rpg (supplemented late 1981 by two AIM-9 Sidewinder AAMs), and up to 5,000 lb (2 268 kg) of external ordnance.

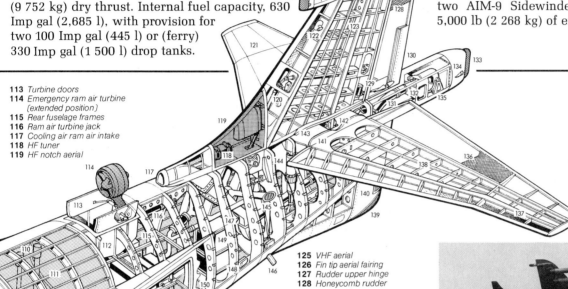

113 Turbine doors
114 Emergency ram air turbine (extended position)
115 Rear fuselage frames
116 Ram air turbine jack
117 Cooling air ram air intake
118 HF tuner
119 HF notch aerial

125 VHF aerial
126 Fin tip aerial fairing
127 Rudder upper hinge
128 Honeycomb rudder construction
129 Rudder trim jack
130 Rudder tab
131 Tail reaction control air ducting
132 Yaw control port
133 Aft radar warning receiver
134 Rear position light
135 Pitch reaction control valve
136 Tailplane honeycomb trailing edge
137 Extended tailplane tip
138 Tailplane construction
139 Tail bumper
140 IFF notch aerial
141 Tailplane sealing plate
142 Fin spar attachment
143 Tailplane centre section carry-through
144 All-moving tailplane control jack

185 Port inner stores pylon
186 Fuel and air connections to pylon
187 Inboard pylon hardpoint
188 Port wing fuel tank end rib
189 Pressure refuelling connection
190 Wing bottom skin panel/ fuselage attachment joint
191 No 1 hydraulic system reservoir (No 2 to starboard)
192 Centre fuselage integral fuel tank, port and starboard

**Above:** Harrier GR Mk 3 ground attack fighters of No 1 Sqdn operating from RAF Wittering. Note the Matra 155 rocket launchers (19 x 68-mm) on the wing pylons.

145 Ram air exhaust duct
146 UHF standby aerial
147 Equipment air conditioning plant
148 Ground power supply socket
149 Twin batteries
150 Ventral equipment bay access door
151 Radio and electronics equipment racks
152 Electronics bay access door
153 Ventral airbrake
154 Airbrake hydraulic jack
155 Nitrogen pressurising bottles for hydraulic system
156 Flap drive torque shaft
157 Rear spar/fuselage attachment joint
158 Nozzle blast shield
159 Rear (hot stream) swivelling exhaust nozzle

160 Wing rear spar
161 Port flap honeycomb construction
162 Fuel jettison valve
163 Fuel jettison pipe
164 Aileron honeycomb construction
165 Outrigger wheel fairing
166 Wing tip fairing
167 Profile of extended fuel-carrying ferry tip
168 Hydraulic retraction jack
169 Shock absorber leg strut
170 Port outrigger wheel
171 Torque scissor links
172 Outrigger wheel leg fairings
173 Port navigation light
174 Roll control reaction valve
175 Wing rib construction
176 Outer pylon hardpoint
177 Machined wing skin/stringer panel
178 Aileron power control unit
179 Front spar
180 Leading edge nose ribs
181 Reaction control air ducting
182 Port outer stores pylon
183 Leading edge fences
184 Twin mainwheels

193 Nozzle fairing construction
194 Leading-edge dog-tooth
195 Cushion augmentation strake (fitted in place of gun pod)
196 Centreline stores pylon
197 Reconnaissance pod
198 Forward F.135 camera
199 Port F.95 Mk7 oblique cameras
200 Starboard F.95 Mk7 oblique cameras
201 Signal data converter (SDC) unit
202 Cannon pod
203 Frangible nose cap
204 Cannon barrel
205 Blast suppression ports
206 Aden 30-mm revolver-type cannon
207 Ammunition feed chute
208 Link ejector chute
209 Ammunition box, 100 rounds
210 ML twin stores carrier
211 Matra 155 rocket launchers, 19 x 68-mm rockets
212 Matra 116M rocket launcher, 19 x 68-mm rockets
213 LEPUS flare
214 Twin light stores carrier
215 28-lb (13-kg) practice bombs

120 Rudder control rod linkages
121 Starboard all-moving tailplane
122 Temperature sensor
123 Tailfin construction
124 Forward radar warning receiver

# General Dynamics F-111 (December 1964)

The fixed-geometry wing has always been at best a compromise, and, before the fighter as a category had seen the end of its first decade, means were being sought of changing its wing geometry in flight. However, such polymorphs as *did* materialise were viewed as caprices of aeronautical design, with little practical application, and, in truth, they made no meaningful contribution to the variable-geometry (VG) wing as defined from the late 'forties, VG having become synonymous with variable sweep.

In highly-swept, low aspect ratio configuration, the VG wing promised low wave drag and a smooth ride in turbulence, with incidental benefits to structural fatigue life, and, at the opposite end of its sweep range, low unstick and touchdown speeds, plus efficient subsonic cruise and loiter. The key to VG's practical application was provided by the NASA-conceived outboard hinge introduced by the F-111, this enabling the wing to translate through a full range of movement (ie, 16 to 72·5 deg) without affecting the aerodynamic centre and thus avoiding dangerous instability.

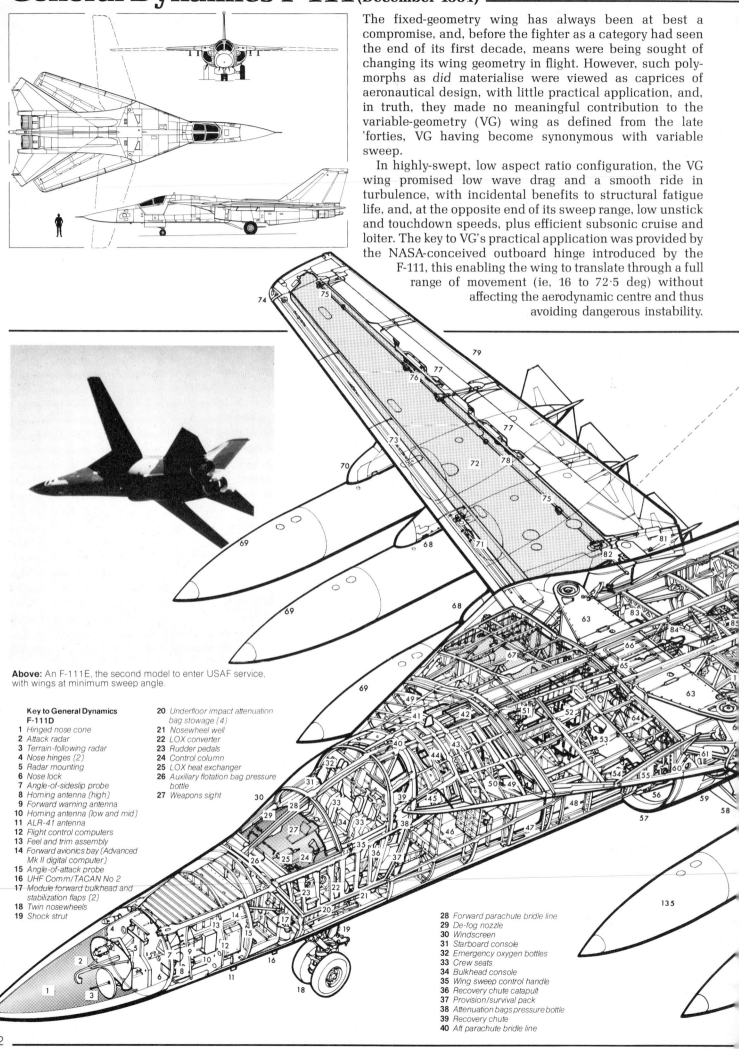

**Above:** An F-111E, the second model to enter USAF service, with wings at minimum sweep angle.

**Key to General Dynamics F-111D**

1 Hinged nose cone
2 Attack radar
3 Terrain-following radar
4 Nose hinges (2)
5 Radar mounting
6 Nose lock
7 Angle-of-sideslip probe
8 Homing antenna (high)
9 Forward warning antenna
10 Homing antenna (low and mid)
11 ALR-41 antenna
12 Flight control computers
13 Feel and trim assembly
14 Forward avionics bay (Advanced Mk II digital computer)
15 Angle-of-attack probe
16 UHF Comm/TACAN No 2
17 Module forward bulkhead and stabilization flaps (2)
18 Twin nosewheels
19 Shock strut
20 Underfloor impact attenuation bag stowage (4)
21 Nosewheel well
22 LOX converter
23 Rudder pedals
24 Control column
25 LOX heat exchanger
26 Auxiliary flotation bag pressure bottle
27 Weapons sight
28 Forward parachute bridle line
29 De-fog nozzle
30 Windscreen
31 Starboard console
32 Emergency oxygen bottles
33 Crew seats
34 Bulkhead console
35 Wing sweep control handle
36 Recovery chute catapult
37 Provision/survival pack
38 Attenuation bags pressure bottle
39 Recovery chute
40 Aft parachute bridle line

When the F-111A first flew, on 21 December 1964, VG was still a dubious novelty and the most controversial issue in the field of high-speed aviation. Embodying such ingenious features as a crew escape module and swivelling stores pylons, the F-111 was not the *first* VG fighter, but it was the first to demonstrate the practicability of this radical development, and the first VG fighter to attain production and service. Subjected to fierce political and technical controversy, the F-111 was to recover from its vicissitudes, but production was to end late 1973 with only 470 built (plus 76 of the FB-111A strategic bombing derivative), rather than the massive run of 1,700 plus originally envisaged.

## SPECIFICATION: F-111D

**Power Plant:** Two Pratt & Whitney TF30-P-9 turbofans each rated at 12,430 lb (5 638 kg) dry thrust and 20,840 lb (9 453 kg) with afterburning. Internal fuel capacity, 4,199 Imp gal (19 090 l) with provision for four 500 Imp gal (2 273 l) drop tanks.

**Performance:** Max speed, 914 mph (1 471 km/h) or M=1·2 at sea level, 1,453 mph (2 338 km/h) or M=2·2 at 50,100 ft (15 270 m); max climb, 25,800 ft/min (131 m/sec); service ceiling, 53,400 ft (16 276 m); combat radius (*HI-LO-HI* mission profile on internal fuel with one 2,000-lb/907-kg bomb internally), 1,233 mls (1 985 km) at (average) 500 mph (805 km/h) at 32,400-35,700 ft (9 875-10 880 m), (*LO-LO-HI* with two drop tanks), 921 mls (1 482 km); ferry range (internal fuel), 2,739 mls (4 408 km), (with two drop tanks), 3,298 mls (5 307 km).

**Weights:** Empty, 46,631 lb (21 152 kg); combat, 61,930 lb (28 091 kg); max, 100,000 lb (45 360 kg).

**Dimensions:** Span (wings extended) 63 ft 0 in (19,20 m), (max sweep), 31 ft 11¾ in (9,75 m); height 17 ft 0½ in (5,19 m); wing area, 525 sq ft (48,77 m²).

**Armament:** Provision for one 20-mm M61A1 rotary cannon with 2,050 rounds in starboard weapons bay. Up to two 2,000-lb (907-kg) stores in weapons bays, or up to 25,000 lb (11 340 kg) external ordnance.

41 UHF data link/AGIFF No 1 (see 123)
42 Stabilization-brake chute
43 Self-righting bag
44 UHF recovery
45 ECM antennae (port and starboard)
46 Forward fuselage fuel bay
47 Ground re-fuelling receptacle
48 Weapons bay
49 Module pitch flaps (port and starboard)
50 Aft flotation bag stowage
51 Aerial re-fuelling receptacle
52 Primary heat-exchanger (air-to-water)
53 Ram air inlet
54 Rate gyros
55 Rotating glove
56 Inlet variable spike
57 Port intake
58 Air brake/undercarriage door
59 Auxiliary inlet blow-in doors
60 Rotating glove pivot point
61 Inlet vortex generators
62 Wing sweep pivot
63 Wing centre-box assembly
64 Wing sweep actuator
65 Wing sweep feedback
66 Control runs
67 Rotating glove drive set
68 Inboard pivot pylons (2)
69 Auxiliary drop tanks 500 Imp gal/2 273 l)
70 Outboard fixed pylon(s); subsonic/jettisonable
71 Slat drive set
72 Wing fuel tank (324 Imp gal/1 473 l)
73 Leading-edge slat
74 Starboard navigation light
75 Flap drive set
76 Outboard spoiler actuator
77 Starboard spoilers
78 Inboard spoiler actuator
79 Flaps
80 Wing swept position
81 Auxiliary flap
82 Auxiliary flap actuator
83 Nuclear weapons and weapons control equipment package
84 Wing sweep/Hi Lift control box
85 Flap, slat and glove drive mechanism
86 Starboard engine bay
87 Yaw feel spring
88 Roll feel spring
89 Yaw trim actuator
90 Yaw damper servo
91 Roll stick position transducer
92 Pitch trim actuator (manual)
93 Roll damper servo
94 Pitch trim actuator (series)
95 Pitch feel spring
96 Pitch-roll mixer
97 Pitch damper servo
98 Pitch stick position transducer
99 Aft fuselage frames
100 Aft fuselage fuel bays
101 Horizontal stabilizer servo actuator
102 Starboard horizontal stabilizer
103 Aft warning antennae
104 HF antenna
105 Detector scanner
106 X-Band radar
107 Rudder
108 Integral vent tank
109 Fin aft spar
110 Fin structure
111 Fin/fuselage attachment
112 Rudder servo actuator
113 Variable nozzle
114 Tailfeathers
115 ECM antenna
116 ALR-41 antenna
117 Horizontal stabilizer structure
118 Horizontal stabilizer pivot point
119 Free floating blow-in doors
120 Afterburner section
121 Horizontal stabilizer servo actuator
122 Wing swept position
123 UHF data link/AG IFF No 2
124 Ventral fin
125 Fire detection sensing element loops
126 Cross frame
127 Engine access hatches
128 Engine accessories
129 Pratt and Whitney TF 30 turbofan
130 Three-stage fan
131 Intake duct
132 Fire extinguishing agent container and nozzles
133 Wing box skinning
134 Port mainwheel
135 Auxiliary drop tanks (500 Imp gal/2 273 l)
136 Pivot pylon
137 Pivot point
138 Pivot actuator
139 Flap tracks
140 Fixed pylon strong point
141 Outboard fixed jettisonable pylon
142 Wing integral fuel
143 Wing box structure
144 Port navigation light

# Dassault-Breguet Mirage F1 (December 1966)

As a result of parametric studies conducted in the early 'sixties and embracing all possible fighter configurations, Avions Marcel Dassault relinquished the tailless delta formula when choosing the form to be taken by the follow-on to the Mirage III (see pages 212-213). Electing to revert to a more conventional arrangement of swept wing trimmed by a horizontal tail, Dassault retained the appellation of "Mirage" for the new warplane despite lack of relationship to its delta-winged predecessors other than a common design origin.

Designated Mirage F1 and flown as a prototype on 23 December 1966, the new fighter was similar in size to the Mirage III, but its thin swept wing afforded only some 72 per cent of the area of the latter's delta and had almost double the loading. Nevertheless, with the aid of leading- and trailing-edge flaps, approach speed and landing run were reduced some 20 and 35 per cent respectively in comparison with the delta-winged fighter, and agility at both subsonic and supersonic speeds was greatly enhanced. These improvements were achieved at some expense to wave drag and wing volume, but the loss in

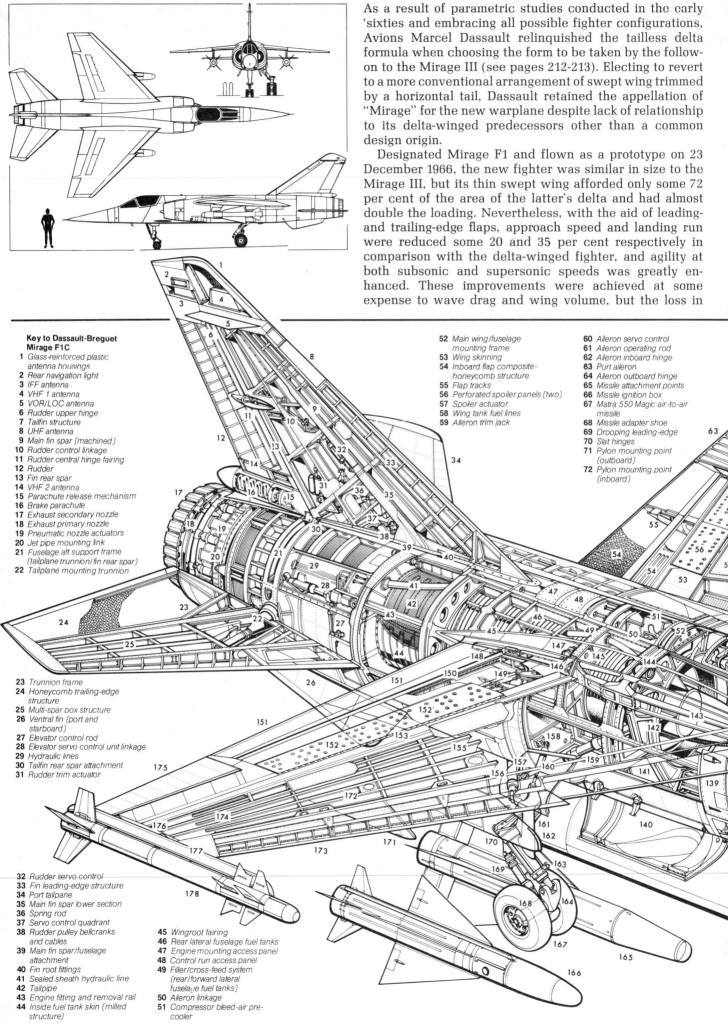

**Key to Dassault-Breguet Mirage F1C**

1 Glass-reinforced plastic antenna housings
2 Rear navigation light
3 IFF antenna
4 VHF 1 antenna
5 VOR/LOC antenna
6 Rudder upper hinge
7 Tailfin structure
8 UHF antenna
9 Main fin spar (machined)
10 Rudder control linkage
11 Rudder central hinge fairing
12 Rudder
13 Fin rear spar
14 VHF 2 antenna
15 Parachute release mechanism
16 Brake parachute
17 Exhaust secondary nozzle
18 Exhaust primary nozzle
19 Pneumatic nozzle actuators
20 Jet pipe mounting link
21 Fuselage aft support frame (tailplane trunnion/fin rear spar)
22 Tailplane mounting trunnion

23 Trunnion frame
24 Honeycomb trailing-edge structure
25 Multi-spar box structure
26 Ventral fin (port and starboard)
27 Elevator control rod
28 Elevator servo control unit linkage
29 Hydraulic lines
30 Tailfin rear spar attachment
31 Rudder trim actuator

32 Rudder servo control
33 Fin leading-edge structure
34 Port tailplane
35 Main fin spar lower section
36 Spring rod
37 Servo control quadrant
38 Rudder pulley bellcranks and cables
39 Main fin spar/fuselage attachment
40 Fin root fittings
41 Sealed sheath hydraulic line
42 Tailpipe
43 Engine fitting and removal rail
44 Inside fuel tank skin (milled structure)

45 Wingroot fairing
46 Rear lateral fuselage fuel tanks
47 Engine mounting access panel
48 Control run access panel
49 Filler/cross-feed system (rear/forward lateral fuselage fuel tanks)
50 Aileron linkage
51 Compressor bleed-air pre-cooler

52 Main wing/fuselage mounting frame
53 Wing skinning
54 Inboard flap composite-honeycomb structure
55 Flap tracks
56 Perforated spoiler panels (two)
57 Spoiler actuator
58 Wing tank fuel lines
59 Aileron trim jack

60 Aileron servo control
61 Aileron operating rod
62 Aileron inboard hinge
63 Port aileron
64 Aileron outboard hinge
65 Missile attachment points
66 Missile ignition box
67 Matra 550 Magic air-to-air missile
68 Missile adapter shoe
69 Drooping leading-edge
70 Slat hinges
71 Pylon mounting point (outboard)
72 Pylon mounting point (inboard)

wing fuel capacity was more than compensated for by use of integral stowage rather than bag tanks; internal fuel capacity was actually increased by some 30 per cent as a result of this measure and the outcome was a very much more flexible fighter than before.

The initial production version ordered for the Armée de l'Air, the Mirage F1C flown on 15 February 1973, was optimised for air defence and air superiority missions, with secondary ground attack capability. Maintaining the philosophy applied to the delta-winged Mirage of evolving a simplified export model (Mirage 5), the Mirage F1A was developed for VFR operations only in the ground attack role. In 1979, the Mirage F1C-200 began to enter French service, this being endowed with long-range reinforcement capability by means of a permanent flight refuelling probe; the Mirage F1CR tactical recce variant is to enter service in 1983. A total of 235 Mirage F1s in its various versions has been ordered for the Armée de l'Air, and more than 400 had been ordered by 10 export customers by the beginning of 1982, with production of the aircraft thus being assured until the end of 1984.

## SPECIFICATION: Mirage F1C

**Power Plant:** One SNECMA Atar 9K50 turbojet rated at 11,023 lb (5 000 kg) dry thrust and 15,873 lb (7 200 kg) with afterburning. Internal capacity, 940 Imp gal (4 260 l), with provision for up to three 264 Imp gal (1 200 l) drop tanks.

**Performance:** Max speed, 914 mph (1 471 km/h) or M=1·2 at sea level, 1,450 mph (2 335 km/h) or M=2·2 at 39,370 ft (12 000 m); cruise, 550 mph (885 km/h) at 29,530 ft (9 000 m); initial climb, 41,930 ft/min (213 m/sec); service ceiling, 65,600 ft (20 000 m); combat radius (max external ordnance and *HI-LO-LO-HI* profile), 260 mls (418 km), (with two drop tanks and 4,410-lb/2 000-kg bomb load), 670 mls (1 078 km); ferry range, 2,050 mls (3 300 km).

**Weights:** Empty, 16,314 lb (7 400 kg); normal loaded, 24,030 lb (10 900 kg); max, 32,850 lb (14 900 kg).

**Dimensions:** Span, 27 ft 6¾ in (8,40 m); length, 49 ft 2½ in (15,00 m); height, 14 ft 9 in (4,50 m); wing area, 269·1 sq ft.

**Armament:** Two 30-mm DEFA 553 cannon with 125 rpg and (intercept mission) one-three Matra 550 Magic plus two AIM-9 Sidewinder AAMs, or (ground attack) up to 8,818 lb (4 000 kg) of external ordnance.

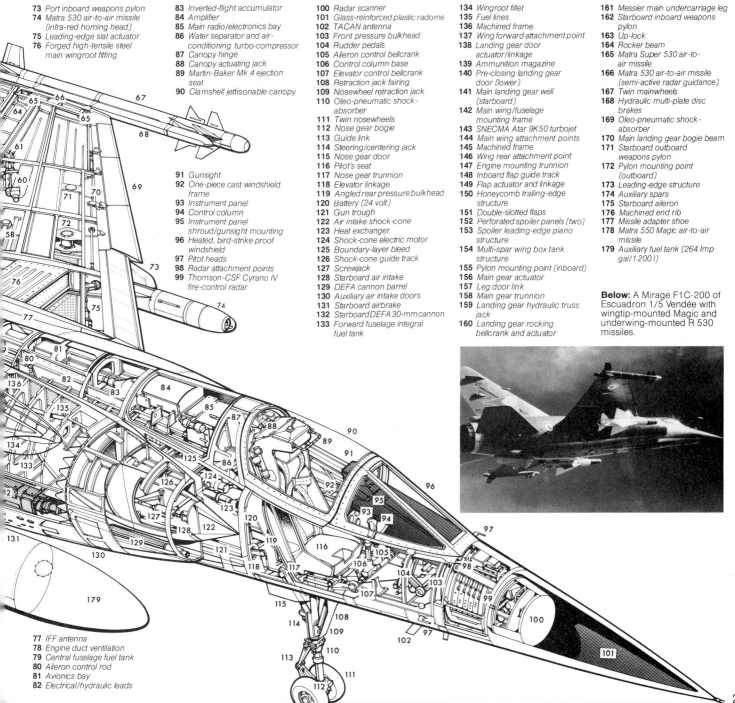

73 Port inboard weapons pylon
74 Matra 530 air-to-air missile (infra-red homing head)
75 Leading-edge slat actuator
76 Forged high-tensile steel main wingroot fitting
77 IFF antenna
78 Engine duct ventilation
79 Central fuselage fuel tank
80 Aileron control rod
81 Avionics bay
82 Electrical/hydraulic leads
83 Inverted-flight accumulator
84 Amplifier
85 Main radio/electronics bay
86 Water separator and air-conditioning turbo-compressor
87 Canopy hinge
88 Canopy actuating jack
89 Martin-Baker Mk 4 ejection seat
90 Clamshell jettisonable canopy
91 Gunsight
92 One-piece cast windshield frame
93 Instrument panel
94 Control column
95 Instrument panel shroud/gunsight mounting
96 Heated, bird-strike proof windshield
97 Pitot heads
98 Radar attachment points
99 Thomson-CSF Cyrano IV fire-control radar
100 Radar scanner
101 Glass-reinforced plastic radome
102 TACAN antenna
103 Front pressure bulkhead
104 Rudder pedals
105 Aileron control bellcrank
106 Control column base
107 Elevator control bellcrank
108 Retraction jack fairing
109 Nosewheel retraction jack
110 Oleo-pneumatic shock-absorber
111 Twin nosewheels
112 Nose gear bogie
113 Guide link
114 Steering/centering jack
115 Nose gear door
116 Pilot's seat
117 Nose gear trunnion
118 Elevator linkage
119 Angled rear pressure bulkhead
120 Battery (24 volt)
121 Gun trough
122 Air intake shock-cone
123 Heat exchanger
124 Shock-cone electric motor
125 Boundary-layer bleed
126 Shock-cone guide track
127 Screwjack
128 Starboard air intake
129 DEFA cannon barrel
130 Auxiliary air intake doors
131 Starboard airbrake
132 Starboard DEFA 30-mm cannon
133 Forward fuselage integral fuel tank
134 Wingroot fillet
135 Fuel lines
136 Machined frame
137 Wing forward attachment point
138 Landing gear door actuator/linkage
139 Ammunition magazine
140 Pre-closing landing gear door (lower)
141 Main landing gear well (starboard)
142 Main wing/fuselage mounting frame
143 SNECMA Atar 9K50 turbojet
144 Main wing attachment points
145 Machined frame
146 Wing rear attachment point
147 Engine mounting trunnion
148 Inboard flap guide track
149 Flap actuator and linkage
150 Honeycomb trailing-edge structure
151 Double-slotted flaps
152 Perforated spoiler panels (two)
153 Spoiler leading-edge piano structure
154 Multi-spar wing box tank structure
155 Pylon mounting point (inboard)
156 Main gear actuator
157 Leg door link
158 Main gear trunnion
159 Landing gear hydraulic truss jack
160 Landing gear rocking bellcrank and actuator
161 Messier main undercarriage leg
162 Starboard inboard weapons pylon
163 Up-lock
164 Rocker beam
165 Matra Super 530 air-to-air missile
166 Matra 530 air-to-air missile (semi-active radar guidance)
167 Twin mainwheels
168 Hydraulic multi-plate disc brakes
169 Oleo-pneumatic shock-absorber
170 Main landing gear bogie beam
171 Starboard outboard weapons pylon
172 Pylon mounting point (outboard)
173 Leading-edge structure
174 Auxiliary spars
175 Starboard aileron
176 Machined end rib
177 Missile adapter shoe
178 Matra 550 Magic air-to-air missile
179 Auxiliary fuel tank (264 Imp gal/1 200 l)

**Below:** A Mirage F1C-200 of Escuadron 1/5 Vendée with wingtip-mounted Magic and underwing-mounted R 530 missiles.

# Saab 37 Viggen (February 1967)

The Swedish aerospace industry has displayed something of a predilection for the exotic in fighter configuration, following the unique double-delta Draken (see pages 208-209) with the equally unconventional close-coupled canard delta Viggen (Thunderbolt). Design of the Viggen, which first flew on 8 February 1967, was heavily influenced by the demands of the Swedish quick-reaction and dispersal philosophy dictating emphasis on short-field characteristics. The canard delta arrangement was considered to offer the best combination achievable with a fixed-geometry wing of high and low speed characteristics, low turbulence sensitivity, and efficient subsonic cruise and loiter capabilities. By selecting optimum location for the canard, or foreplane, which affords nose-up control and lift in its own right, the most favourable interaction with the mainplane was achieved. The powerful vortex from the canard surfaces generated a high speed airflow over the principal surfaces at low speeds, thus enhancing lift and permitting adoption of higher incidence angles.

The Viggen adhered to the "standardised platform" concept; a basic design more or less readily adaptable to fulfil the four primary roles of attack, interception, reconnaissance and training, each mission-optimised version having a secondary role. The initial model, the AJ 37, was intended primarily for the attack mission, but possessing a secondary intercept capability, the first of 110 production examples flying on 23 February 1971. Seventy similarly-powered SF 37 and SH 37 reconnaissance aircraft and two-seat SK 37 trainers preceded the extensively re-engineered "second generation" JA 37 optimised for the air-air mission with secondary air-ground capability.

Featuring a more powerful engine, and new systems and weaponry, the production JA 37 flew on 4 November 1977, following six R&D models, and entering Flygvapen service mid-1980. Orders for 149 JA 37s have been placed with completion scheduled for 1985.

## SPECIFICATION: JA 37 Viggen

**Power Plant:** One Volvo Flygmotor RM 8B turbofan rated at 16,200 lb (7 350 kg) dry thrust and 28,110 lb (12 750 kg) with afterburning.

**Performance:** Max speed (with paired Rb 24 and Rb 71

**Left:** A JA 37 Viggen of the Bråvalla Flygflottilj (F 13) based at Norrköping and seen with a full complement of Sidewinder and Sky Flash missiles.

75 Tailfin forward spar
76 Fin spar/fuselage pick-up
77 Fuel lines
78 Gearbox pre-cooler installation
79 Wing root fairing
80 Wing main spar/fuselage attachment
81 Airbrake actuating ram
82 Fuselage port airbrake
83 Engine pipe
84 Afterburner assembly
85 Thrust-reverser aperture
86 Reverser lids
87 Lid actuating ram
88 Aft fuselage frame
89 Linkage
90 Tailfin aft attachment
91 Rudder operating ram
92 Rudder post
93 Tailfin leading edge

94 Tip extension
95 VHF antenna
96 Honeycomb rudder structure
97 Rudder
98 Rudder operating ram fairing
99 Blade antenna
100 Tail fairing
101 Tail fairing formers
102 Tail navigation light
103 Fuselage aft fairing
104 Tailplane exhaust
105 Inner elevon actuator fairings
106 Honeycomb elevon (inner)
107 Elevon outer fairing
108 Honeycomb elevon (outer)
109 Inner structure
110 Outboard leading-edge extension
111 Port outer weapons pylon
112 Port ECM bullet
113 Wing structure

## Key to Saab JA 37 Viggen

1 Dielectric nose cone
2 Radar scanner
3 PS-46/A radar pack
4 Avionics equipment
5 Forward pressure bulkhead
6 Avionics/electronics bay
7 Screen forward fairing
8 Canopy frame windscreen de-icing
9 One-piece windscreen assembly
10 Weapons sight
11 Fixed frame
12 Pilot's control column
13 Rudder pedal assembly
14 Control linkage
15 Fuselage skin panels
16 Nosewheel bay door
17 Twin nosewheels (forward-retracting)
18 Nosewheel leg assembly
19 Nosewheel retraction strut linkage
20 Nosewheel bay
21 Nosewheel leg pivot
22 Control links/pulleys
23 Pilot's seat frame support
24 Pilot's ejection seat
25 Starboard intake lip
26 Hinged canopy

34 Port intake
35 Intake duct frames
36 Low-vision light panels
37 Forward wing structure
38 Forward wing main spar
39 Fuselage/forward wing main attachment point
40 Engine oil coolers
41 Air conditioning bay
42 Radio equipment
43 Starboard forward wing
44 Flap hinge fairing
45 Honeycomb flap structure
46 Dorsal identification/recognition light
47 Cooling equipment bay
48 Cabin air outlet scoop
49 Cooling pipes
50 Coolers/blowers
51 Fuselage saddle fuel tanks

60 Fuselage upper main longeron
61 Fabricated fuselage frames
62 Volvo Flygmotor RM 8B turbofan
63 Skin panels
64 Dorsal auxiliary intake/outlet panel
65 Forged/machined main fuselage/wing frame member
66 Starboard wing skinning

27 Headrest
28 Ejection seat guiderails/mechanism
29 Cockpit canopy hinges
30 Main fuselage fuel tank bay
31 Fuselage frame structures
32 Intake separator
33 Forward wing root fairing

52 Forward wing aft attachment
53 Avionics bay
54 Ram-air turbine
55 Forward wing flap hinge fairing
56 Honeycomb flap structure
57 Hydraulic pump
58 Low-vision light panels (2)
59 Engine intake face

67 Starboard wing fuel bay
68 Starboard ECM bullet
69 Leading-edge extension
70 Starboard outer elevon hinge
71 Starboard elevon
72 Pitot tube
73 Fin leading-edge extension
74 Tailfin structure

AAMS), 838 mph (1 350 km/h) or M= 1·1 at sea level, 1,225-1,365 mph (2 020-2 195 km/h) or M=1·9-2·1 at 36,090 ft (11 000 m); time (from brakes off) to 32,810 ft (10 000 m), 1·4 min; tactical radius (M=2·0 intercept mission), 250 mls (400 km), (counterair mission *HI-LO-HI* profile with centre-line drop tank and 3,000 lb/1 360 kg external ordnance), 650 mls (1 046 km), (*LO-LO-LO* with same external load), 300 mls (480 km).

**Weights:** Empty (approx), 26,895 lb (12 200 kg); combat (cannon armament and half fuel), 33,070 lb (15 000 kg), (with four AAMs), 37,040 lb (16 800 kg); max, 49,600 lb (22 500 kg).

**Dimensions:** Span, 34 ft 9¼ in (10,60 m); length (excluding probe), 50 ft 8¼ in (15,45 m); height, 19 ft 4¼ in (5,90 m); total wing area (including foreplanes), 561·88 sq ft (52,20 m²).

**Armament:** One 30-mm Oerlikon KCA cannon with 150 rounds and (intercept) two Rb 71 Sky Flash and two or four Rb 24 Sidewinder air-to-air missiles, or (interdiction) 13,227 lb (6 000 kg) of ordnance mounted externally.

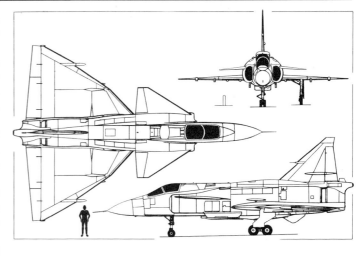

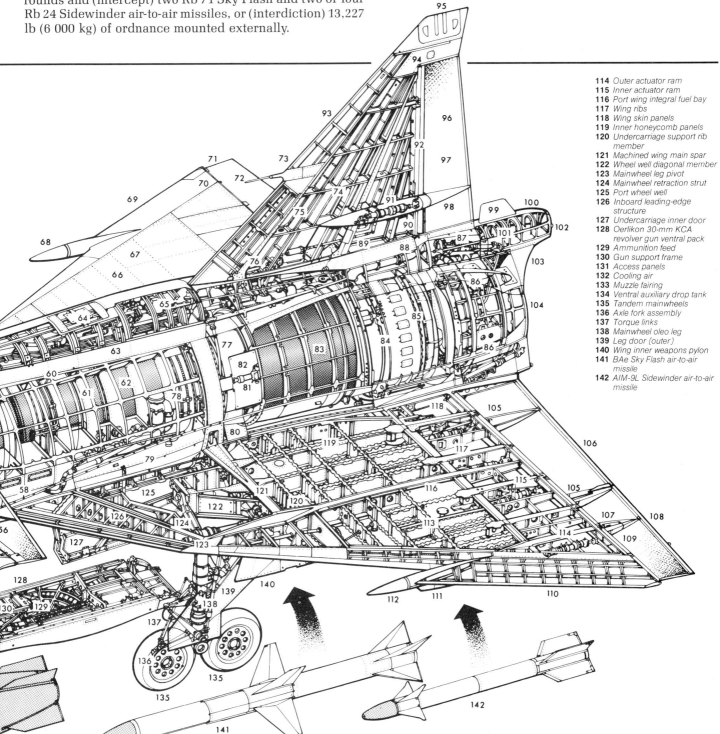

114 Outer actuator ram
115 Inner actuator ram
116 Port wing integral fuel bay
117 Wing ribs
118 Wing skin panels
119 Inner honeycomb panels
120 Undercarriage support rib member
121 Machined wing main spar
122 Wheel well diagonal member
123 Mainwheel leg pivot
124 Mainwheel retraction strut
125 Port wheel well
126 Inboard leading-edge structure
127 Undercarriage inner door
128 Oerlikon 30-mm KCA revolver gun ventral pack
129 Ammunition feed
130 Gun support frame
131 Access panels
132 Cooling air
133 Muzzle fairing
134 Ventral auxiliary drop tank
135 Tandem mainwheels
136 Axle fork assembly
137 Torque links
138 Mainwheel oleo leg
139 Leg door (outer)
140 Wing inner weapons pylon
141 BAe Sky Flash air-to-air missile
142 AIM-9L Sidewinder air-to-air missile

# Grumman F-14 Tomcat (December 1970)

Calling for a quantum advance in shipboard fighter capability, the US Navy's late 'sixties VFX requirement inevitably resulted in a variable-geometry aircraft. No fixed-geometry configuration could fulfil the exacting speed, endurance and load-carrying capabilities called for *and* meet deck-landing performance and shipboard stowage stipulations.

Equally inevitably, VFX was to be a formidably large and heavy fighter, and, indeed, the F-14A in which the requirement resulted was to be the largest and heaviest aircraft in its category when it achieved service status in the second half of 1974.

First flown on 21 December 1970, the F-14A offered a capability that was undoubtedly nonpareil. It was the first—and so far the only—fighter with completely automatic sweep angle (20-68 deg) variation and possessed a unique multiple-target engagement faculty. Some 350 F-14As were in US Navy service in late 1981, when development included the enhanced TF30-PW-414A-engined F-14C for 1983 delivery (with the existing F-14A fleet being modified to similar standards from the following year), and the General Electric F101-powered F-14D, introduction of which is called for in US Navy advanced planning after delivery of 605 Tomcats against a proposed total of 845.

**Above:** An F-14A Tomcat of US Navy VF-1, one of the first two operational squadrons to equip with this advanced fighter in 1974.

## SPECIFICATION: F-14A Tomcat
**Power Plant:** Two Pratt & Whitney TF30-P-412A turbofans each rated at 12,500 lb (5 670 kg) dry thrust and 20,900 lb

### Key to Grumman F-14A Tomcat

1 Pitot tube
2 Radar target horn
3 Glass-fibre radome
4 IFF aerial array
5 Hughes AWG-9 flat plate radar scanner
6 Scanner tracking mechanism
7 Ventral ALQ-100 antenna
8 Gun muzzle blast trough
9 Radar electronics equipment bay
10 AN/ASN-92 inertial navigation unit
11 Radome hinge
12 In-flight refuelling probe (extended)
13 ADF aerial
14 Windscreen rain removal air duct
15 Temperature probe
16 Cockpit front pressure bulkhead
17 Angle of attack transmitter
18 Formation lighting strip
19 Cannon barrels
20 Nosewheel doors
21 Gun gas vents
22 Rudder pedals
23 Cockpit pressurization valve
24 Navigation radar display
25 Control column
26 Instrument panel shroud
27 Kaiser AN/ANG-12 head-up-display
28 Windscreen panels
29 Cockpit canopy cover
30 Face blind seat firing handle
31 Ejection seat headrest
32 Pilot's Martin-Baker GRU-7A ejection seat
33 Starboard side console panel
34 Engine throttle levers
35 Port side console panel
36 Pitot static head
37 Canopy emergency release handle
38 Fold out step
39 M-61-A1 Vulcan 20-mm six-barrel rotary cannon
40 Nose undercarriage leg strut
41 Catapult strop link
42 Catapult strop, launch position
43 Twin nosewheels
44 Folding boarding ladder
45 Hughes AIM-54A Phoenix air-to-air missile (6)
46 Fuselage missile pallet
47 Cannon ammunition drum 675 rounds)
48 Rear boarding step
49 Ammunition feed chute
50 Armament control panels
51 Kick-in step
52 Tactical information display hand controller
53 Naval Flight Officer's instrument console
54 NFO's ejection seat
55 Starboard intake lip
56 Ejection seat launch rails
57 Cockpit aft decking
58 Electrical system controller
59 Rear radio and electronics equipment bay

60 Boundary layer bleed air duct
61 Port engine intake lip
62 Electrical system relay controls
63 Glove vane pivot
64 Port air intake
65 Glove vane housing
66 Navigation light
67 Variable area intake ramp doors
68 Cooling system boundary layer duct ram air intake
69 Intake ramp door hydraulic jacks
70 Air system piping
71 Air data computer
72 Heat exchanger
73 Heat exchanger exhaust duct
74 Forward fuselage fuel tanks
75 Canopy hinge point
76 Electrical and control system ducting
77 Control rod runs
78 UHF/TACAN aerial
79 Glove vane hydraulic jack
80 Starboard glove vane, extended
81 Honeycomb panel construction
82 Navigation light
83 Main undercarriage wheel bay
84 Starboard intake duct spill door
85 Wing slat/flap flexible drive shaft
86 Dorsal spine fairing
87 Fuselage top longeron
88 Central flap/slat drive motor
89 Emergency hydraulic generator
90 Bypass door hydraulic jack
91 Intake bypass door
92 Port intake ducting
93 Wing glove sealing horn
94 Flap/slat telescopic drive shaft
95 Port wing pivot bearing
96 Wing pivot carry through (electron beam welded titanium box construction)
97 Wing pivot box integral fuel tank
98 Fuselage longeron/pivot box attachment joint
99 UHF data link/IFF aerial
100 Honeycomb skin panelling
101 Wing glove stiffeners/dorsal fences

102 Starboard wing pivot bearing
103 Slat/flap drive shaft gearbox
104 Starboard wing integral fuel tank (total internal fuel capacity 1,969 lmp gal (8 951 l)
105 Leading edge slat drive shaft
106 Slat guide rails
107 Starboard leading edge slat segments (open)
108 Starboard navigation light
109 Low-voltage formation lighting
110 Wing tip fairing
111 Outboard manoeuvre flap segments (down position)

112 Port roll control spoilers
113 Spoiler hydraulic jacks
114 Inboard, high lift flap (down position)
115 Inboard flap hydraulic jack
116 Manoeuvre flap drive shaft
117 Variable wing sweep screw jack
118 Starboard undercarriage pivot fixing
119 Starboard engine compressor face
120 Wing glove sealing plates
121 Pratt & Whitney TF30-P-412A afterburning turbofan
122 Rear fuselage fuel tanks
123 Fuselage longeron joint
124 Control system artificial feel units
125 Tailplane control rods
126 Starboard engine bay
127 Wing glove pneumatic seal
128 Fin root fairing
129 Fin spar attachment joints
130 Starboard fin leading edge
131 Starboard all-moving tailplane
132 Starboard wing (fully swept position)
133 AN-ALR-45 tail warning radar antenna
134 Fin aluminium honeycomb skin panel construction
135 Fin-tip aerial fairing
136 Tail navigation light
137 Electronic countermeasures antenna (ECM)
138 Rudder honeycomb construction
139 Rudder hydraulic jack
140 Afterburner ducting
141 Variable area nozzle control jack

142 Airbrake (upper and lower surfaces)
143 Airbrake hydraulic jack
144 Starboard engine exhaust nozzle
145 Anti-collision light
146 Tail formation light
147 ECM aerial
148 Port rudder
149 Beaver tail fairing
150 Fuel jettison pipe
151 ECM antenna
152 Deck arrester hook (stowed position)

153 AN/ALE-29A chaff and flare dispensers
154 Nozzle shroud sealing flaps
155 Port convergent/divergent afterburner exhaust nozzle
156 Tailplane honeycomb construction
157 AN-ALR-45(V) tail warning radar antenna
158 Tailplane boron fibre skin panels
159 Port wing (fully swept position)
160 All-moving-tailplane construction
161 Tailplane pivot fixing
162 Jet pipe mounting
163 Fin/tailplane attachment mainframe
164 Cooling air louvres
165 Tailplane hydraulic jack
166 Hydraulic system equipment pack
167 Formation lighting strip
168 Oil cooler air intake
169 Port ventral fin
170 Engine accessory compartment
171 Ventral engine access doors
172 Hydraulic reservoir
173 Bleed air ducting
174 Port engine bay
175 Intake compressor face
176 Wing variable sweep screw jack

186 Wing tip fairing construction
187 Low-voltage formation lighting
188 Port navigation light
189 Wing rib construction
190 Port wing integral fuel tank
191 Front spar
192 Leading edge rib construction
193 Slat guide rails
194 Port leading edge slat segments, open
195 Slat honeycomb construction
196 Port mainwheel
197 Torque scissor links
198 Main undercarriage front bracing strut
199 Mainwheel door
200 Ventral pylon attachment
201 External fuel tank (222 lmp gal/ 8 951 l capacity)

177 Main undercarriage leg strut
178 Hydraulic retraction jack
179 Wing skin panel
180 Fuel system piping
181 Rear spar
182 Flap hinge brackets
183 Port roll control spoilers
184 Flap leading edge eyebrow seal fairing
185 Port manoeuvre flap honeycomb construction

202 Sparrow missile launch adaptor
203 AIM-7F Sparrow, air-to-air missile
204 Wing glove pylon attachment
205 Cranked wing glove pylon
206 Sidewinder missile launch rail
207 AIM-9C Sidewinder air-to-air missile
208 Phoenix launch pallet
209 AIM-54A Phoenix air-to-air missile

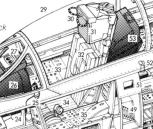

(9 480 kg) with afterburning. Internal fuel capacity, 1,969 Imp gal (8 951 l), with provision for two 222 Imp gal (1 009 l) drop tanks.

**Performance:** Max speed (with four semi-recessed AIM-7 AAMs), 913 mph (1 470 km/h) or M=1·2 at sea level, 1,584 mph (2 549 km/h) or M=2·4 at 49,000 ft (14 935 m); time to 60,000 ft (18 290 m) at 55,000 lb (24 948 kg), 2·1 min; tactical radius (interdiction mission HI-LO-LO-HI profile with drop tanks and 14 MK 82 bombs), 725 mls (1 167 km), (combat air patrol, internal fuel, six AIM-7 and four AIM-9 AAMs), 765 mls (1 232 km).

**Weights:** Empty, 39,930 lb (18 112 kg); loaded (intercept with four AIM-7s), 58,904 lb (26 718 kg), (with six AIM-54s), 69,790 lb (31 656 kg); combat air patrol, 70,345 lb (31 908 kg); max, 74,348 lb (33 724 kg).

**Dimensions:** Span (wings extended), 64 ft 1½ in (19,55 m), (max sweep), 37 ft 7 in (11,45 m), (oversweep on deck), 33 ft 3½ in (10,15 m); length, 61 ft 11⅞ in (18,90 m); height, 16 ft 0 in (4,88 m); wing area, 565 sq ft (52,48 m²).

**Armament:** One 20-mm M-61A1 rotary cannon with 675 rounds and (intercept) six AIM-7E/F Sparrow and four AIM-9G/H Sidewinder AAMs, or six AIM-54A Phoenix and two AIM-9G/H AAMs, or (attack) various combinations of missiles and bombs up to 14,500 lb (6 577 kg).

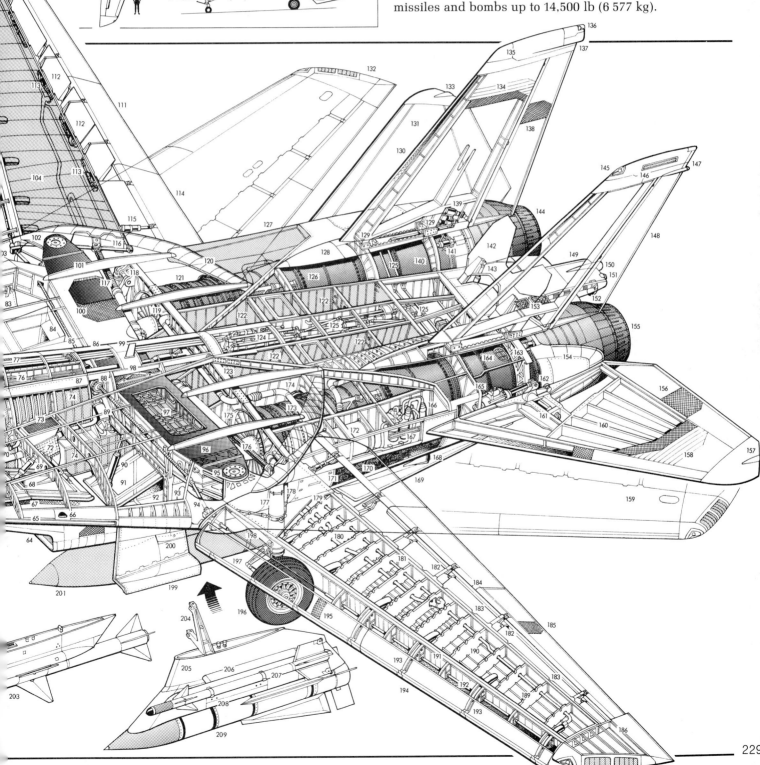

# McDonnell Douglas F-15 Eagle (July 1972)

Intimating re-emergence in the West of the optimised *dogfighter* after a lapse of many years, the Eagle, first flown on 27 July 1972, was essentially a fallout of Vietnam experience. The USAF had suffered an embarrassing inventory gap during that conflict which prompted the FX programme for a long-range air superiority fighter—a modern equivalent of the P-51 Mustang of WWII—and the Eagle was its end product. Featuring a very large, comparatively lightly loaded and essentially simple wing, which was to endow it with outstanding manoeuvrability, and a thrust-to-weight ratio at combat loadings well in excess of unity, the Eagle proffered such a performance advance that, today, it remains unrivalled in its class.

The first production F-15A flew on 25 December 1974, the USAF attaining initial operational capability with the new fighter in July 1975. The F-15A and its two-seat equivalent, the F-15B were supplanted in production from mid-1980 (with 383 and 60 built respectively) by the F-15C and two-seat F-15D with increased internal fuel, provision for conformal tanks and enhanced avionics, these being the current models, with exports to Israel (75), Saudi Arabia

**Above:** An F-15A Eagle of the 36th Tactical Fighter Wing, USAF, based at Bitburg, Germany, the first overseas-based Eagle-equipped Wing.

**Key to McDonnell Douglas F-15C Eagle**

1. Tailplane honeycomb construction
2. Boron fibre skin panel
3. Tailplane spars
4. All-moving tailplane pivot fixing
5. Leading edge dog-tooth
6. Low-voltage formation lighting strip
7. Fin root attachment frames
8. Rudder hydraulic rotary actuator
9. Rudder honeycomb construction
10. Fin spar construction
11. Boron fibre skin panel
12. Anti-collision light
13. Electronic countermeasures aerials (ECM)
14. Variable area afterburner exhaust nozzles
15. Nozzle sealing flaps
16. Fueldraulic nozzle actuators
17. Afterburner duct
18. Engine bay titanium ring frames
19. Rear engine mounting frame
20. Engine bay titanium frame and stringer construction
21. Titanium skin panelling
22. Port tailplane hydraulic actuator
23. Tailplane hinge arm
24. Port rudder
25. Tailboom fairing
26. ECM aerial
27. Port tailplane
28. Tail navigation light
29. ECM aerial
30. Radar warning aerials
31. Boron fibre skin panelling
32. Fin leading edge
33. Port air system equipment bay
34. Forward engine mounting
35. Engine mounting frame,
36. Bleed air system ducting
37. Engine support link
38. Engine bay fireproof bulkhead
39. Pratt & Whitney F100-PW-100 afterburning turbofan
40. Starboard air system equipment bay
41. Engine bleed air primary heat exchanger
42. Heat exchanger ventral exhaust duct
43. Retractable runway arrester hook
44. Wing trailing edge fuel tank
45. Flap hydraulic jack
46. Starboard plain flap
47. Flap and aileron honeycomb panel construction
48. Starboard aileron
49. Aileron hydraulic actuator
50. Fuel jettison pipe
51. Aluminium honeycomb wing tip fairing
52. Low-voltage formation lighting
53. Starboard navigation light
54. ECM aerial
55. Westinghouse ECM equipment pod
56. Outboard wing stores pylon
57. Pylon attachment spigot
58. Cambered leading edge ribs
59. Front spar
60. Machined wing skin/stringer panels
61. Outboard pylon fixing
62. HF flush aerial
63. Leading edge fuel tank
64. Inboard pylon fixing
65. Wing rib construction
66. Starboard wing integral fuel tank, total internal fuel load 1,724 Imp gal (7 837 l)
67. Wing root rib support struts
68. Titanium wing spars
69. Wing spar/fuselage attachment pin joints
70. Machine fuselage main bulkheads
71. Wing/fuselage fuel tank interconnections
72. Airframe mounted engine accessory gearbox
73. Standby hydraulic generator
74. Jet fuel starter (JFS)/auxiliary power unit (APU)
75. Engine intake compressor face
76. Cooling system intake bleed air spill duct
77. Port wing trailing edge fuel tank
78. Port plain flap
79. Flap hydraulic jack
80. Aileron control rod
81. Aileron hydraulic actuator
82. Port aileron
83. Fuel jettison pipe
84. Wing tip fairing
85. Low-voltage formation lighting
86. Port navigation light
87. ECM aerial
88. Cambered leading edge
89. Outboard pylon fixing
90. Port wing internal fuel tank
91. Fuel system piping
92. Inboard pylon fixing
93. Leading edge fuel tank
94. Anti-collision light
95. Boom-type air refuelling receptacle
96. Bleed air duct to air conditioning plant
97. Control rod runs
98. Dorsal airbrake (open)
99. Airbrake glass-fibre honeycomb construction
100. Airbrake hydraulic jack
101. Centre fuselage fuel tanks
102. Intake ducting
103. Ammunition feed chute
104. M61A-1 Vulcan 20-mm cannon
105. Hydraulic rotary cannon drive unit
106. Starboard anti-collision light
107. Ventral main undercarriage wheel bay
108. Main undercarriage leg strut
109. Starboard mainwheel
110. Inboard stores pylon
111. Air-to-air missile adapter
112. Bomb rack
113. Mk 82 500-lb (227-kg) low drag HE bombs
114. Bomb triple ejector rack
115. Missile launch rail
116. AIM-9L Sidewinder air-to-air missile
117. AIM-7F Sparrow air-to-air missile
118. Sparrow missile launcher unit
119. Cannon muzzle aperture
120. Cannon barrels
121. Central ammunition drum (950 rounds)
122. Airbrake hinges
123. Forward fuselage fuel tanks
124. UHF aerial
125. Intake duct bleed air louvres
126. Intake by-pass spill duct
127. Variable area intake ramp hydraulic actuator
128. Air conditioning system cooling air exhaust duct
129. Canopy hinge point
130. Air conditioning plant
131. Intake incidence control jack
132. Intake duct variable area ramp doors
133. Intake pivot fixing
134. Starboard engine air intake
135. Nosewheel leg door

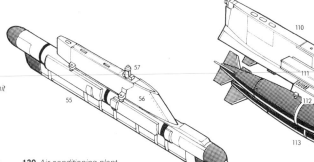

(62) and Japan (14 plus 86 licence manufactured). However, the design offers a flexible basis for development of versions for alternative roles, one such being the F-15E for long-range interdiction and counterair missions.

### SPECIFICATION: F-15C Eagle

**Power Plant:** Two Pratt & Whitney F100-PW-100 turbofans each rated at 14,780 lb (6 705 kg) dry thrust and 23,904 lb

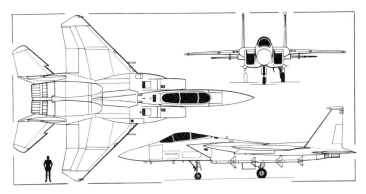

(10 843 kg) with afterburning. Internal fuel capacity, 1,724 Imp gal (7 837 l), with provision for two 710 Imp gal (3 228 l) in each of two conformal fuel pallets or three 500 Imp gal (2 273 l) drop tanks.

**Performance:** Max speed (short-endurance dash), 1,676 mph (2 697 km/h) or M=2·54, (sustained), 1,518 mph (2 443 km/h) or M=2·3 at 40,000 ft (12 192 m), 922 mph (1 484 km/h) or M=1·21 at sea level; max endurance (internal fuel), 2·9 hours (with conformal pallets), 5·25 hrs; ferry range (internal fuel), 1,950 mls (3 138 km), (with conformal pallets), 3,570 mls (5 745 km); ceiling, 63,000 ft (19,200 m).

**Weights:** Basic, 28,700 lb (13 018 kg); loaded (full internal fuel and four AIM-7 AAMs), 44,500 lb (20 185 kg), (plus three drop tanks), 57,400 lb (26 036 kg); max, 68,000 lb.

**Dimensions:** Span, 42 ft 9¾ in (13,05 m); length, 63 ft 9 in (19,43 m); height, 18 ft 5½ in (5,63 m); wing area, 608 sq ft (56,48 m²).

**Armament:** One 20-mm M-61A1 rotary cannon with 950 rounds and four AIM-7F Sparrow and four AIM-9L Sidewinder AAMs, or (secondary attack mission) up to 16,000 lb (7 258 kg) of external ordnance.

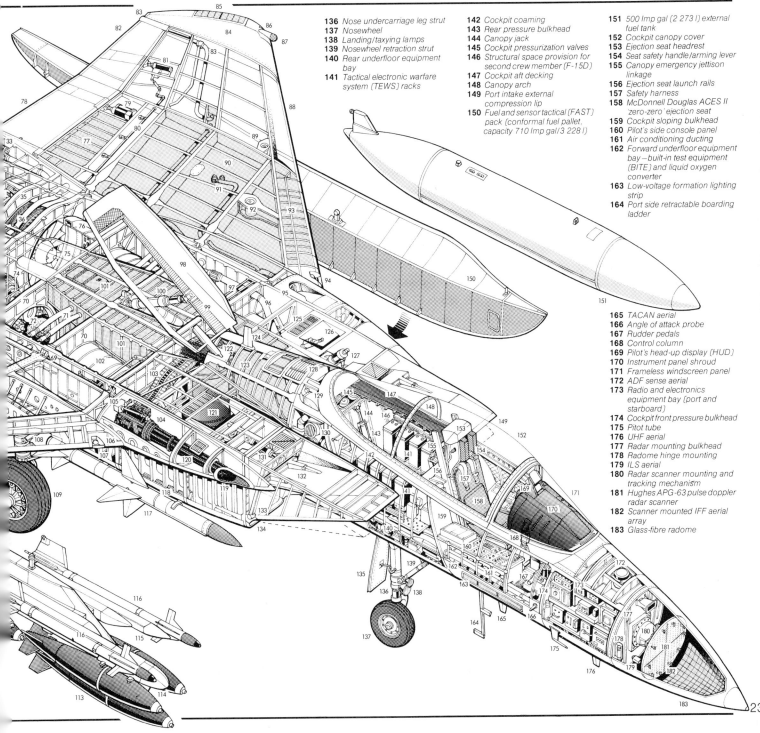

136 Nose undercarriage leg strut
137 Nosewheel
138 Landing/taxiing lamps
139 Nosewheel retraction strut
140 Rear underfloor equipment bay
141 Tactical electronic warfare system (TEWS) racks
142 Cockpit coaming
143 Rear pressure bulkhead
144 Canopy jack
145 Cockpit pressurization valves
146 Structural space provision for second crew member (F-15D)
147 Cockpit aft decking
148 Canopy arch
149 Port intake external compression lip
150 Fuel and sensor tactical (FAST) pack (conformal fuel pallet, capacity 710 Imp gal/3 228 l)

151 500 Imp gal (2 273 l) external fuel tank
152 Cockpit canopy cover
153 Ejection seat headrest
154 Seat safety handle/arming lever
155 Canopy emergency jettison linkage
156 Ejection seat launch rails
157 Safety harness
158 McDonnell Douglas ACES II 'zero-zero' ejection seat
159 Cockpit sloping bulkhead
160 Pilot's side console panel
161 Air conditioning ducting
162 Forward underfloor equipment bay — built-in test equipment (BITE) and liquid oxygen converter
163 Low-voltage formation lighting strip
164 Port side retractable boarding ladder

165 TACAN aerial
166 Angle of attack probe
167 Rudder pedals
168 Control column
169 Pilot's head-up display (HUD)
170 Instrument panel shroud
171 Frameless windscreen panel
172 ADF sense aerial
173 Radio and electronics equipment bay (port and starboard)
174 Cockpit front pressure bulkhead
175 Pitot tube
176 UHF aerial
177 Radar mounting bulkhead
178 Radome hinge mounting
179 ILS aerial
180 Radar scanner mounting and tracking mechanism
181 Hughes APG-63 pulse doppler radar scanner
182 Scanner mounted IFF aerial array
183 Glass-fibre radome

# General Dynamics F-16 Fighting Falcon (January 1974)

Claimed with some justification to be the first in a new generation of advanced-technology fighters, the F-16 is the first production aeroplane with full-time fly-by-wire (electrically-signalled) controls; it embodies automatically variable wing camber and some degree of artificial stability, and it features a blended-body fuselage design affording increased lift and internal volume. Reflecting a completely different design philosophy to that of the F-15 (see pages 230-231), the F-16 was nevertheless similarly conceived as essentially a dog fighter, stemming from the USAF's LWF (Lightweight Fighter) programme. However, steady weight growth accompanying evolution from solely air-air to full multi-role capability has gone some way towards invalidating the original *lightweight* concept.

Flown as an aerodynamic prototype (YF-16) on 20 January 1974, it entered service with the USAF in its initial F-16A version in January 1979, and is the subject of a multinational manufacturing programme, with final assembly lines in Belgium and the Netherlands. Illustrated by the accompanying drawings is the enlarged tailplane (to relax aft *CG* limits, increase the manoeuvre envelope with certain loads, and reduce take-off speeds and abort distances) introduced from November 1981.

**Above:** An F-16A of the Belgian Air Force's 349ᵉ escadrille which achieved operational status early in 1981 at Beauvechain.

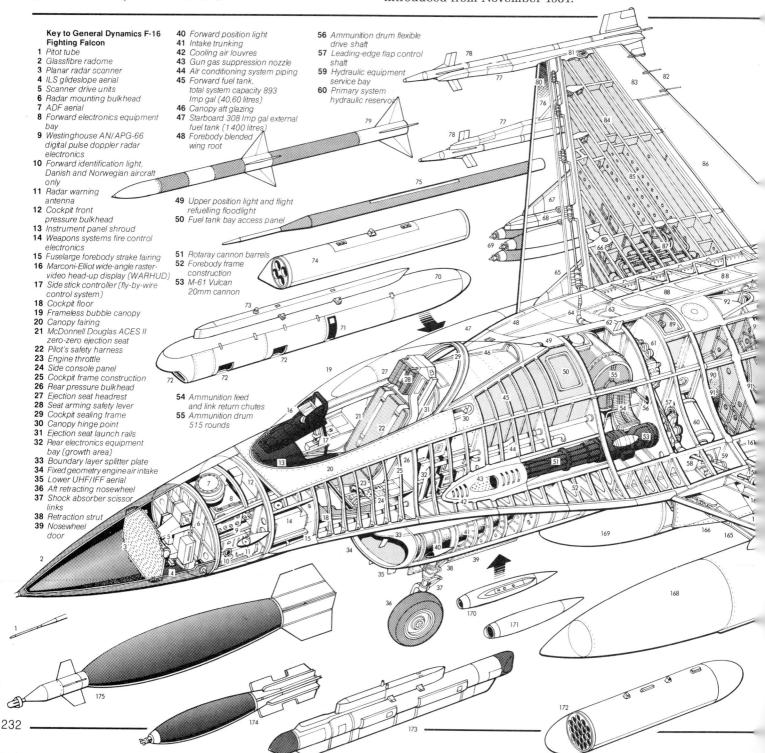

**Key to General Dynamics F-16 Fighting Falcon**
1 Pitot tube
2 Glassfibre radome
3 Planar radar scanner
4 ILS glideslope aerial
5 Scanner drive units
6 Radar mounting bulkhead
7 ADF aerial
8 Forward electronics equipment bay
9 Westinghouse AN/APG-66 digital pulse doppler radar electronics
10 Forward identification light, Danish and Norwegian aircraft only
11 Radar warning antenna
12 Cockpit front pressure bulkhead
13 Instrument panel shroud
14 Weapons systems fire control electronics
15 Fuselarge forebody strake fairing
16 Marconi-Elliot wide-angle raster-video head-up display (WARHUD)
17 Side stick controller (fly-by-wire control system)
18 Cockpit floor
19 Frameless bubble canopy
20 Canopy fairing
21 McDonnell Douglas ACES II zero-zero ejection seat
22 Pilot's safety harness
23 Engine throttle
24 Side console panel
25 Cockpit frame construction
26 Rear pressure bulkhead
27 Ejection seat headrest
28 Seat arming safety lever
29 Cockpit sealing frame
30 Canopy hinge point
31 Ejection seat launch rails
32 Rear electronics equipment bay (growth area)
33 Boundary layer splitter plate
34 Fixed geometry engine air intake
35 Lower UHF/IFF aerial
36 Aft retracting nosewheel
37 Shock absorber scissor links
38 Retraction strut
39 Nosewheel door

40 Forward position light
41 Intake trunking
42 Cooling air louvres
43 Gun gas suppression nozzle
44 Air conditioning system piping
45 Forward fuel tank, total system capacity 893 Imp gal (40,60 litres)
46 Canopy aft glazing
47 Starboard 308 Imp gal external fuel tank (1 400 litres)
48 Forebody blended wing root

49 Upper position light and flight refuelling floodlight
50 Fuel tank bay access panel

51 Rotaray cannon barrels
52 Forebody frame construction
53 M-61 Vulcan 20mm cannon

54 Ammunition feed and link return chutes
55 Ammunition drum 515 rounds

56 Ammunition drum flexible drive shaft
57 Leading-edge flap control shaft
59 Hydraulic equipment service bay
60 Primary system hydraulic reservoir

**SPECIFICATION: F-16A Fighting Falcon**

**Power Plant:** One Pratt & Whitney F100-PW-200 turbofan rated at 14,800 lb (6 713 kg) dry thrust and 23,830 lb (10 809 kg) with afterburning. Internal fuel capacity, 893 Imp gal (4 060 l), with provision for one 250 Imp gal (1 136 l) centreline and two 308 Imp gal (1 400 l) wing drop tanks.

**Performance:** Max speed (short endurance dash), 1,333 mph (2 145 km/h) or M=2·02, (sustained), 1,247 mph (2 007 km/h) or M=1·89 at 40,000 ft (12 190 m); tactical radius (*HI-LO-HI* interdiction with 4,000-lb/1 814-kg bombload, internal fuel and 7-min allowance for combat), 360 mls (580 km); range (similar ordnance load and internal fuel), 1,200 mls (1 930 km) at (average) 575 mph (925 km/h); ferry range (wing drop tanks), 2,535 mls (4 080 km).

**Weights:** Operational empty, 14,567 lb (6 608 kg); loaded (air-air mission with two AAMs), 23,357 lb (10 595 kg); max, 34,500 lb (15 649 kg).

**Dimensions:** Span, 31 ft 0 in (9,45 m), (over AAMs), 32 ft 10 in (10,01 m); length (excluding probe), 47 ft 7¾ in (14,52 m); height, 16 ft 5½ in (5,01 m); wing area, 300 sq ft (27,87 m²).

**Armament:** One 20-mm M-61A1 rotary cannon with 515 rounds and two-six AIM-9L/M Sidewinder AAMs. Provision for up to 12,000 lb (5 443 kg) ordnance.

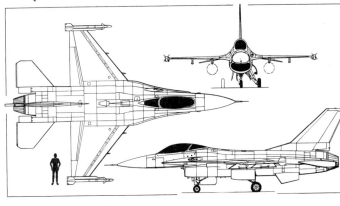

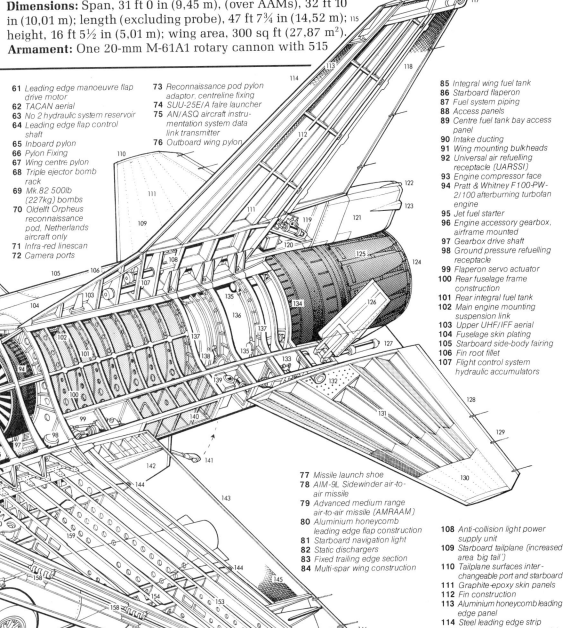

61 Leading edge manoeuvre flap drive motor
62 TACAN aerial
63 No 2 hydraulic system reservoir
64 Leading edge flap control shaft
65 Inboard pylon
66 Pylon Fixing
67 Wing centre pylon
68 Triple ejector bomb rack
69 Mk.82 500lb (227kg) bombs
70 Oldelft Orpheus reconnaissance pod, Netherlands aircraft only
71 Infra-red linescan
72 Camera ports
73 Reconnaissance pod pylon adaptor, centreline fixing
74 SUU-25E/A falre launcher
75 AN/ASQ aircraft instrumentation system data link transmitter
76 Outboard wing pylon
77 Missile launch shoe
78 AIM-9L Sidewinder air-to-air missile
79 Advanced medium range air-to-air missile (AMRAAM)
80 Aluminium honeycomb leading edge flap construction
81 Starboard navigation light
82 Static dischargers
83 Fixed trailing edge section
84 Multi-spar wing construction
85 Integral wing fuel tank
86 Starboard flaperon
87 Fuel system piping
88 Access panels
89 Centre fuel tank bay access panel
90 Intake ducting
91 Wing mounting bulkheads
92 Universal air refuelling receptacle (UARSSI)
93 Engine compressor face
94 Pratt & Whitney F100-PW-2/100 afterburning turbofan engine
95 Jet fuel starter
96 Engine accessory gearbox, airframe mounted
97 Gearbox drive shaft
98 Ground pressure refuelling receptacle
99 Flaperon servo actuator
100 Rear fuselage frame construction
101 Rear integral fuel tank
102 Main engine mounting suspension link
103 Upper UHF/IFF aerial
104 Fuselage skin plating
105 Starboard side-body fairing
106 Fin root fillet
107 Flight control system hydraulic accumulators
108 Anti-collision light power supply unit
109 Starboard tailplane (increased area 'big tail')
110 Tailplane surfaces interchangeable port and starboard
111 Graphite-epoxy skin panels
112 Fin construction
113 Aluminium honeycomb leading edge panel
114 Steel leading edge strip
115 VHF communications aerial
116 Anti-collision light
117 Tail radar warning antennae
118 Aluminium honeycomb rudder construction
119 Rudder servo actuator
120 Radar warning power supply
121 Brake parachute housing, Norwegian aircraft only
122 Tail navigation light
123 Electronic countermeasures aerials, port and starboard (ECM)
124 Fully variable exhaust nozzle
125 Nozzle flaps
126 Split trailing edge airbrake, upper and lower surfaces
127 Airbrake hydraulic jack
128 Port tailplane (increased area 'big tail')
129 Static dischargers
130 Graphite-epoxy tailplane skin panels
131 Corrugated aluminium sub-structure
132 Tailplane pivot fixing
133 Tailplane servo actuator
134 Nozzle sealing fairing
135 Fueldraulic nozzle actuators
136 Afterburner tailpipe
137 Rear fuselage bulkheads
138 Rear engine mounting
139 Aft position light
140 Port side-body fairing
141 Runway arrestor hook
142 Ventral fin, port and starboard
143 Port flaperon
144 Flaperon hinges
145 Aluminium honeycomb flaperon construction
146 Static dischargers
147 Fixed trailing edge section
148 Port AIM-9L Sidewinder air-to-air missiles
149 Missile launcher shoe
150 Wing tip launcher fixing
151 Port navigation light
152 Outboard pylon fixing rib
153 Multi-spar wing construction
154 Centre pylon attachment rib
155 Wing centre pylon
156 Mk 84 2000-lb (908-kg) low-drag bomb
157 Leading edge manoeuvre flap
158 Leading edge flap rotary actuators
159 Integral wing fuel tank
160 Inboard pylon fixing
161 Wing attachment fishplates
162 Landing/taxiing lamp
163 Main undercarriage shock absorber strut
164 Mainwheel leg strut
165 Retraction strut
166 Mainwheel door
167 Forward retracting mainwheel
168 Port underwing fuel tank, 308 Imp gal (1 400 litres)
169 Centreline external fuel tank, 308 Imp gal (1 400 litres)
170 Electro-optical forward looking infra-red pod (EO-FLIR)
171 Laser target designator pod (LAST)
172 LAU-3/A rocket launcher, 19 x 2.75in (6,98cm) ground attack rockets
173 Westinghouse AN/ALQ119-1 electronic suppression system radar jamming pod (ESM)
174 Snakeye, 500-lb (227-kg) retarded bomb
175 GBU-10C/B 2000-lb (908-kg) laser guided bomb

# Panavia Tornado (August 1974)

The Tornado originated in a late 'sixties UK-German-Italian government agreement on joint development of a warplane. then known as Multi-role Combat Aircraft (MRCA). The programme established final assembly lines in each country without component manufacture duplication.

The basic Tornado for tri-national use was optimised for interdiction and strike (IDS), the first prototype flying on 14 August 1974, with production aircraft delivered to the Tri-national Tornado Training Establishment at RAF Cottesmore in 1980. Planned deliveries to the RAF (200-220),

Luftwaffe (212), Marineflieger (112) and Aeronautica Militare (100) are scheduled to be completed in 1986-87.

In addition to the IDS Tornado GR Mk 1, the RAF has a requirement for an air defence fighter version (ADV), the first prototype flying on 27 October 1979. This, the Tornado F Mk 2 (165-185 to be procured), emphasizes range and endurance for combat air patrols far from Britain's coasts where fighter opposition is unlikely; thus, dogfight capability, tending to degrade performance as a bomber-destroyer, need not be considered.

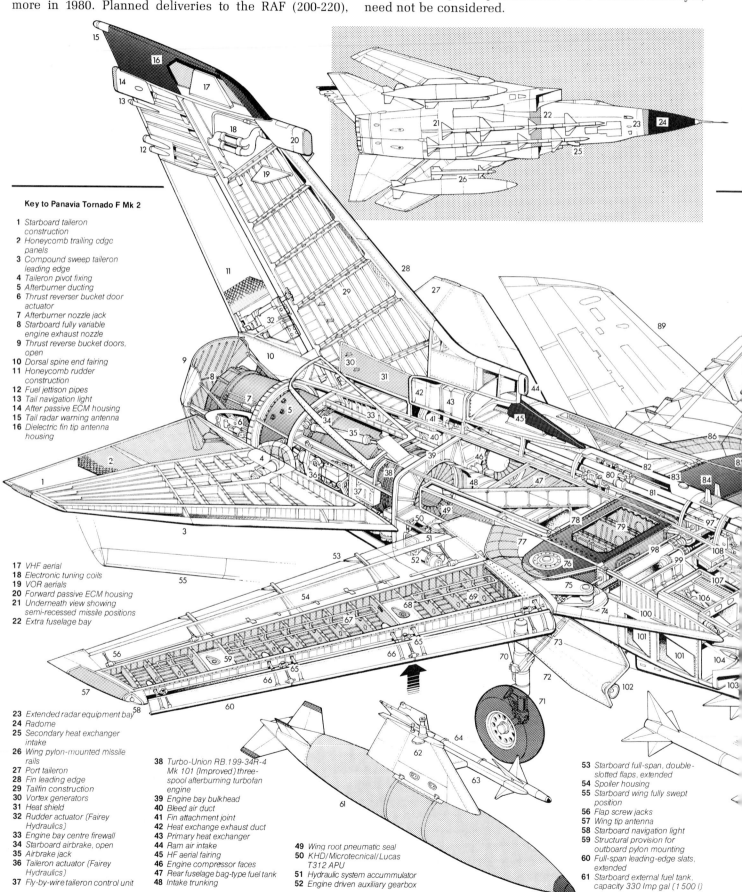

**Key to Panavia Tornado F Mk 2**

1 Starboard taileron construction
2 Honeycomb trailing edge panels
3 Compound sweep taileron leading edge
4 Taileron pivot fixing
5 Afterburner ducting
6 Thrust reverser bucket door actuator
7 Afterburner nozzle jack
8 Starboard fully variable engine exhaust nozzle
9 Thrust reverse bucket doors, open
10 Dorsal spine end fairing
11 Honeycomb rudder construction
12 Fuel jettison pipes
13 Tail navigation light
14 After passive ECM housing
15 Tail radar warning antenna
16 Dielectric fin tip antenna housing
17 VHF aerial
18 Electronic tuning coils
19 VOR aerials
20 Forward passive ECM housing
21 Underneath view showing semi-recessed missile positions
22 Extra fuselage bay
23 Extended radar equipment bay
24 Radome
25 Secondary heat exchanger intake
26 Wing pylon-mounted missile rails
27 Port taileron
28 Fin leading edge
29 Tailfin construction
30 Vortex generators
31 Heat shield
32 Rudder actuator (Fairey Hydraulics)
33 Engine bay centre firewall
34 Starboard airbrake, open
35 Airbrake jack
36 Taileron actuator (Fairey Hydraulics)
37 Fly-by-wire taileron control unit
38 Turbo-Union RB.199-34R-4 Mk 101 (Improved) three-spool afterburning turbofan engine
39 Engine bay bulkhead
40 Bleed air duct
41 Fin attachment joint
42 Heat exchange exhaust duct
43 Primary heat exchanger
44 Ram air intake
45 HF aerial fairing
46 Engine compressor faces
47 Rear fuselage bag-type fuel tank
48 Intake trunking
49 Wing root pneumatic seal
50 KHD/Microtecnical/Lucas T312 APU
51 Hydraulic system accummulator
52 Engine driven auxiliary gearbox
53 Starboard full-span, double-slotted flaps, extended
54 Spoiler housing
55 Starboard wing fully swept position
56 Flap screw jacks
57 Wing tip antenna
58 Starboard navigation light
59 Structural provision for outboard pylon mounting
60 Full-span leading-edge slats, extended
61 Starboard external fuel tank, capacity 330 Imp gal (1 500 l)

Retaining 80 per cent commonality with the GR Mk 1, the F Mk 2 features a redesigned nose for the intercept radar and a longer fuselage providing a 200 Imp gal (910 l) internal fuel increase and permitting mounting of four Sky Flash missiles. Increased fuselage fineness ratio results in some gain in supersonic efficiency and extension of the fixed wing glove to compensate for the CG change produces a modest drag reduction. Deliveries will commence in 1983, with initial operational capability being achieved in 1984.

### SPECIFICATION: Tornado F Mk 2

**Power Plant:** Two Turbo-Union RB.199-34R-04 Mk 101 (Improved) turbofans each rated at (approx) 9,000 lb (4 082 kg) dry thrust and (approx) 16,000 lb (7 258 kg) with afterburning. Internal fuel capacity (approx), 1,600 Imp gal (7 274 l), with provision for two 330 Imp gal (1 500 l) drop tanks.

**Performance:** Max speed, 920 mph (1 480 km/h) or M=1·2 at sea level, 1,450 mph (2 333 km/h) or M=2·2 at 40,000 ft (12 190 m); time to 30,000 ft (9 145 m) from brakes release, 1·7 min; radius of action (combat air patrol with drop tanks and allowance for 2 hrs plus loiter and 10 min combat), 350-450 mls (560-725 km); ferry range, 2,650 mls (4 265 km).

**Weights:** Empty equipped (approx), 25,000 lb (11 340 kg); max (max external fuel and six AAMs), 52,000 lb (23 587 kg).

**Dimensions:** Span (wings extended), 45 ft 7¼ in (13,90 m), (max sweep), 28 ft 2½ in (8,59 m); length, 59 ft 3 in (18,06 m); height, 18 ft 8½ in (5,70 m); wing area, 322·9 sq ft (30,00 m²).

**Armament:** One 27-mm IWKA-Mauser cannon, and two AIM-9L Sidewinder and four BAe Sky Flash AAMs.

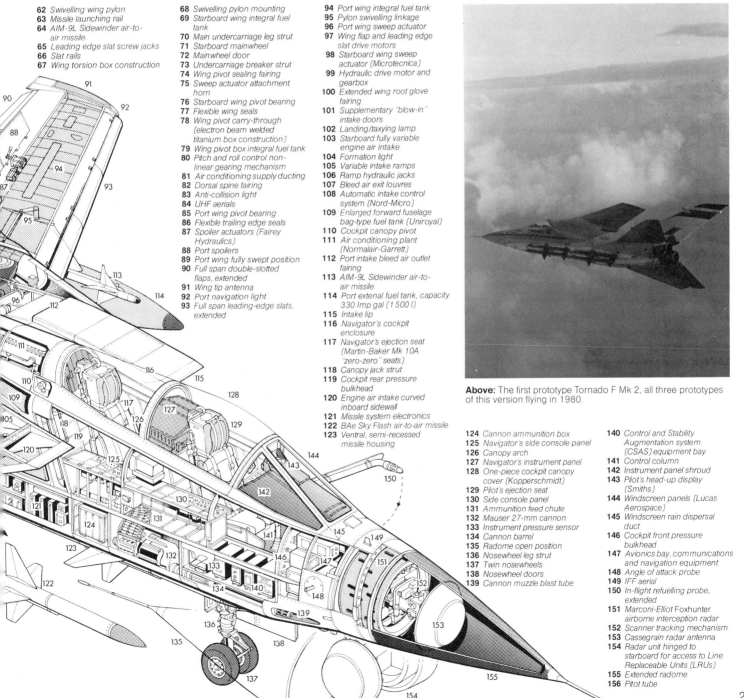

62 Swivelling wing pylon
63 Missile launching rail
64 AIM-9L Sidewinder air-to-air missile
65 Leading edge slat screw jacks
66 Slat rails
67 Wing torsion box construction
68 Swivelling pylon mounting
69 Starboard wing integral fuel tank
70 Main undercarriage leg strut
71 Starboard mainwheel
72 Mainwheel door
73 Undercarriage breaker strut
74 Wing pivot sealing fairing
75 Sweep actuator attachment horn
76 Starboard wing pivot bearing
77 Flexible wing seals
78 Wing pivot carry-through (electron beam welded titanium box construction)
79 Wing pivot box integral fuel tank
80 Pitch and roll control non-linear gearing mechanism
81 Air conditioning supply ducting
82 Dorsal spine fairing
83 Anti-collision light
84 UHF aerials
85 Port wing pivot bearing
86 Flexible trailing edge seals
87 Spoiler actuators (Fairey Hydraulics)
88 Port spoilers
89 Port wing fully swept position
90 Full span double-slotted flaps, extended
91 Wing tip antenna
92 Port navigation light
93 Full span leading-edge slats, extended
94 Port wing integral fuel tank
95 Pylon swivelling linkage
96 Port wing sweep actuator
97 Wing flap and leading edge slat drive motors
98 Starboard wing sweep actuator (Microtecnica)
99 Hydraulic drive motor and gearbox
100 Extended wing root glove fairing
101 Supplementary "blow-in" intake doors
102 Landing/taxiying lamp
103 Starboard fully variable engine air intake
104 Formation light
105 Variable intake ramps
106 Ramp hydraulic jacks
107 Bleed air exit louvres
108 Automatic intake control system (Nord-Micro)
109 Enlarged forward fuselage bag-type fuel tank (Uniroyal)
110 Cockpit canopy pivot
111 Air conditioning plant (Normalair-Garrett)
112 Port intake bleed air outlet fairing
113 AIM-9L Sidewinder air-to-air missile
114 Port extenal fuel tank, capacity 330 Imp gal (1 500 l)
115 Intake lip
116 Navigator's cockpit enclosure
117 Navigator's ejection seat (Martin-Baker Mk 10A "zero-zero" seats)
118 Canopy jack strut
119 Cockpit rear pressure bulkhead
120 Engine air intake curved inboard sidewall
121 Missile system electronics
122 BAe Sky Flash air-to-air missile
123 Ventral, semi-recessed missile housing

124 Cannon ammunition box
125 Navigator's side console panel
126 Canopy arch
127 Navigator's instrument panel
128 One-piece cockpit canopy cover (Kopperschmidt)
129 Pilot's ejection seat
130 Side console panel
131 Ammunition feed chute
132 Mauser 27-mm cannon
133 Instrument pressure sensor
134 Cannon barrel
135 Radome open position
136 Nosewheel leg strut
137 Twin nosewheels
138 Nosewheel doors
139 Cannon muzzle blast tube
140 Control and Stability Augmentation system (CSAS) equipment bay
141 Control column
142 Instrument panel shroud
143 Pilot's head-up display (Smiths)
144 Windscreen panels (Lucas Aerospace)
145 Windscreen rain dispersal duct
146 Cockpit front pressure bulkhead
147 Avionics bay, communications and navigation equipment
148 Angle of attack probe
149 IFF aerial
150 In-flight refuelling probe, extended
151 Marconi-Elliot Foxhunter airborne interception radar
152 Scanner tracking mechanism
153 Cassegrain radar antenna
154 Radar unit hinged to starboard for access to Line Replaceable Units (LRUs)
155 Extended radome
156 Pitot tube

**Above:** The first prototype Tornado F Mk 2, all three prototypes of this version flying in 1980.

# Dassault-Breguet Mirage 2000 (March 1978)

Although it was widely believed that the delta had provided merely an interim solution to the problems of building a supersonic wing and was passé by the mid 'sixties, Dassault-Breguet was induced by advances in control technology to revert to this formula for its third-generation Mirage. This, the Mirage 2000, first flew on 10 March 1978, and was configurationally similar to the first-generation Mirage III (see pages 212-213), but it exploited *negative* longitudinal stability and thus removed the principal shortcomings previously inherent in the tailless delta.

Traditionally, the maximum lift coefficient of the conventional stable delta is small and its trim drag high. If the centre of gravity (CG) is moved aft of the aerodynamic centre (AC), the delta becomes longitudinally unstable, but at high angles of attack, as in manoeuvring flight or landing, an aerodynamic upload on the elevons improves both trimmed lift coefficient and trim drag. The advent of electrically-signalled (fly-by-wire) controls in combination with an advanced automatic flight control system had rendered such highly unstable aircraft flyable.

Refined by computer-aided design to give a highly optimised shape, the Mirage 2000 could be flown with substantial instability, the lift gain being as much as 25 per cent over the conventional stable delta, automatic leading-edge flaps permitting safe operation up to high angles of attack. With an internal fuel capacity representing approximately 30 per cent of the clean take-off weight—a percentage previously attained only by certain US Navy fighters—and a highly effective nav-attack system with a radar range more than twice that of the Mirage F1, the Mirage 2000 will represent a quantum capability advance when it enters Armée de l'Air service in its initial single-seat air superiority version in 1984.

Single-seat attack and two-seat low-level penetration versions are also under development, prototypes of the latter, the Mirage 2000N (Nucléaire), being scheduled for flight test in 1983. From 1985 onwards, the M53-5 turbofan is to give place to the M53-P with military and afterburning ratings of 14,330 lb (6 500 kg) and 21,385 lb (9 700 kg).

**SPECIFICATION: Mirage 2000**
**Power Plant:** One SNECMA M53-5 turbofan rated at 12,345

**Key to Dassault-Breguet Mirage 2000**
1 Pitot tube
2 Glass-fibre radome
3 Flat-plate radar scanner
4 Thomson-CSF RDM multi-rôle radar unit (initial production aircraft)
5 Cassegrain monopulse planar antenna
6 Thomson-CSF RDI pulse doppler radar unit (later production aircraft)
7 Radar altimeter aerial
8 Angle of attack probe
9 Front pressure bulkhead
10 Instrument pitot heads
11 Temperature probe
12 Fixed in-flight refuelling probe
13 Frameless windscreen panel
14 Instrument panel shroud
15 Static ports
16 Rudder pedals
17 Low voltage formation light strip
18 VHF aerial
19 Nosewheel jack door
20 Hydraulic retraction jack
21 Nose undercarriage leg strut
22 Twin nosewheels
23 Towing bracket
24 Torque scissor links
25 Landing/taxiing lamps
26 Nosewheel steering jacks
27 Nose undercarriage leg doors
28 Cockpit flooring
29 Centre instrument console
30 Control column
31 Pilot's head-up display (HUD)
32 Canopy arch
33 Cockpit canopy cover
34 Starboard air intake
35 Ejection seat headrest
36 Safety harness
37 Martin-Baker MK 10 zero-zero ejection seat
38 Engine throttle control and airbrake switch
39 Port side console panel
40 Nosewheel bay
41 Cannon muzzle blast trough
42 Electrical equipment bay
43 Port air intake
44 Intake half-cone centre body
45 Air conditioning system ram air intake
46 Cockpit rear pressure bulkhead
47 Canopy emergency release handle

48 Hydraulic canopy jack
49 Canopy hinge point
50 Starboard intake strake
51 IFF aerial
52 Radio and electronics bay
53 Boundary layer bleed air duct
54 Air conditioning plant
55 Intake centre-body screw jack
56 Cannon muzzle
57 Pressure refuelling connection
58 Port intake strake
59 Intake suction relief doors (above and below)
60 DEFA 554 30-mm cannon
61 Cannon ammunition box
62 Forward fuselage integral fuel tanks
63 Radio and electronics equipment
64 Fuel system equipment
65 Anti-collision light
66 Air system pre-cooler
67 Air exit louvres
68 Starboard wing integral fuel tank (total internal fuel capacity 835 Imp gal (3 800 l)
69 Wing pylon attachment hardpoints
70 Leading-edge slat hydraulic drive motor and control shaft
71 Slat screw jacks
72 Slat guide rails
73 Starboard wing automatic leading-edge slats
74 Matra 550 Magic "dogfight" AAM
75 Missile launch rail
76 Outboard wing pylon
77 Radar warning antenna
78 Starboard navigation light
79 Outboard elevon
80 Elevon ventral hinge fairings
81 Flight control system access panels
82 Elevon hydraulic jacks

83 Engine intake by-pass air spill duct
84 Engine compressor face
85 Hydraulic accumulator
86 Microturbo auxiliary power unit
87 Main undercarriage wheel bay
88 Hydraulic pump
89 Alternator, port and starboard
90 Accessory gearbox
91 Engine transmission unit and drive shaft
92 Machined fuselage main frames
93 SNECMA M53-5 afterburning turbofan
94 Engine igniter unit
95 Electronic engine control unit
96 Bleed air ducting
97 Engine bleed air blow-off valve spill duct

98 Fin root fillet construction
99 Leading edge ribs
100 Boron/epoxy/carbon honeycomb sandwich fin skin panels
101 Tail low voltage formation light strip
102 ECM aerial fairing
103 VOR aerial
104 Di-electric fin tip fairing
105 VHF aerial

106 Tail navigation light
107 Tail radar warning antenna
108 Honeycomb rudder construction
109 Rudder hinge
110 Fin spar attachment joints
111 Rudder bay thermal jack
112 Engine bay thermal lining

113 ECM equipment housing
114 Variable area afterburner exhaust nozzle
115 Tailpipe sealing flaps
116 Fueldraulic nozzle control jacks
117 Afterburner tailpipe
118 Engine withdrawal rail

lb (5 600 kg) dry thrust and 19,840 lb (9 000 kg) with afterburning. Internal fuel capacity, 835 Imp gal (3 800 l), with provision for one 264 Imp gal (1 200 l) centreline and two 374 Imp gal (1 700 l) underwing drop tanks.

**Performance:** Max speed, 915 mph (1 472 km/h) or M=1·2 at sea level, 1,550 mph (2 495 km/h) or M=2·35 above 36,090 ft (11 000 m); max climb rate, 49,000 ft/min (249 m/sec); service ceiling, 65,000 ft (19 800 m); time to 49,200 ft (15 000 m) and M=2·0, 4·0 min; combat radius (intercept mission with two 374 Imp gal/1 700 l drop tanks and four AAMs), 435 mls (700 km); ferry range, 2,420 mls (3 900 km).

**Weights:** Combat loaded, 19,840 lb (9 000 kg); max, 33,070 lb (15 000 kg).

**Dimensions:** Span, 29 ft 6⅓ in (9,00 m); length 50 ft 3½ in (15,33 m); wing area, 441·3 sq ft (41,00 m²).

**Armament:** Two 30-mm DEFA 554 cannon and (air superiority mission) two Matra 550 Magic and two Matra Super 530D air-to-air missiles, or (for strike mission) up to 13,227 lb (6 000 kg) of ordnance carried externally.

**Above:** The first of five prototypes of the Mirage 2000, the fifth being a two-seat Mirage 2000B. Two Mirage 2000N prototypes will follow.

119 Wing root extended trailing edge fillet
120 Ventral brake parachute housing
121 Rear engine mounting main frame
122 Runway emergency arrestor hook

123 Port inboard elevon
124 Elevon honeycomb construction
125 Carbon fibre skin panels
126 Elevon hydraulic control jacks
127 Fly-by-wire electronic system command units
128 Outboard elevon
129 Elevon tip construction
130 Port navigation light
131 Radar warning antenna
132 Outboard automatic leading edge slat
133 Outboard wing pylon attachment hardpoints

134 Machined upper and lower wing skin/stringer panels
135 Port wing integral fuel tank
136 Wing rib construction
137 Rear fuselage/wing root
138 Wing spar attachment joints
139 Main spars
140 Undercarriage hydraulic retraction jack
141 Main undercarriage leg pivot fixing
142 Inboard pylon attachment hardpoints
143 Port airbrakes (open) above and beneath wing
144 Airbrake hydraulic jack
145 Main undercarriage leg strut
146 Leading edge slat hydraulic drive motor
147 Mainwheel leg door
148 Port mainwheel
149 Slat guide rails
150 Screw jacks
151 Auxiliary spar
152 Wing front spar
153 Front spar attachment joint
154 Inboard automatic leading-edge slat rib construction
155 374 Imp gal (1 700 l) auxiliary fuel tank (fuselage centreline or wing inboard stations)
156 Matra "Super 530" medium-range AAM
157 Missile launch rail
158 Inboard wing pylon

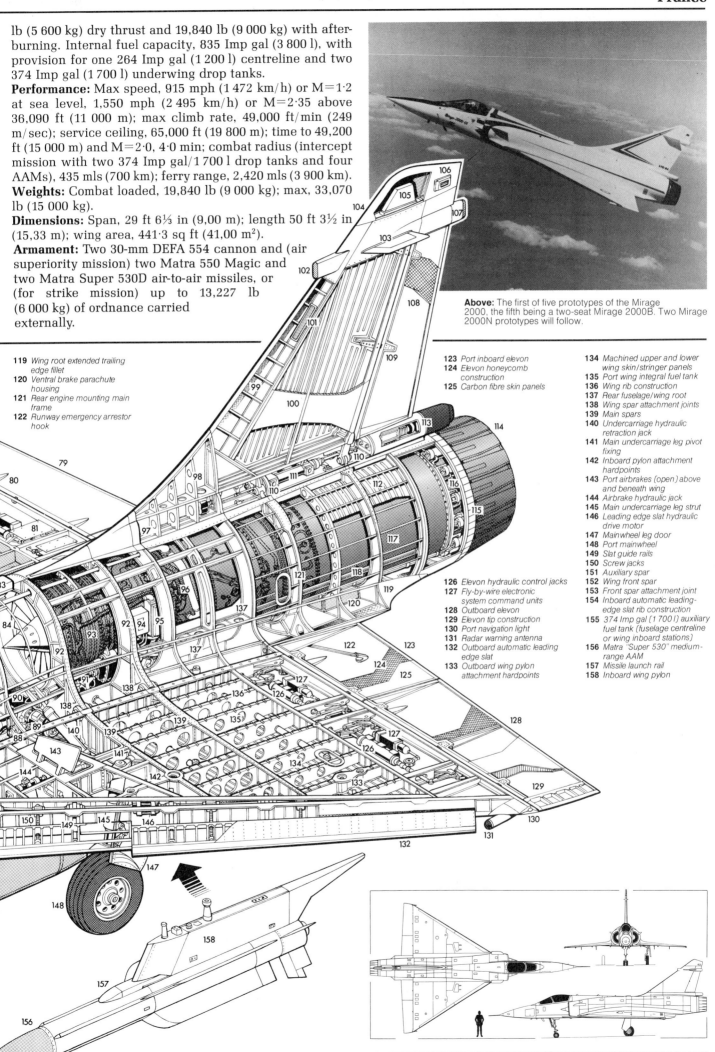

# McDonnell Douglas F-18 Hornet (November 1978)

**Above:** Four F-18A Hornets of the US Navy's Air Test and Development Squadron VX-4 at Point Mugu which has responsibility for the initial service trials of this new multi-role fighter.

Intended to integrate air superiority and attack functions within a common and comparatively inexpensive airframe, the F-18 Hornet shipboard fighter is derived from the Northrop YF-17 technology demonstrator lightweight fighter. Like the YF-17, the F-18 features a so-called hybrid wing with leading edge extensions increasing maximum lift by some 50 per cent, and reducing both lift-attributable drag and, by acting as a compression wedge, the Mach number at the engine intake face.

Retaining little more than the basic aerodynamic form of its progenitor, the F-18 is some 12 per cent larger overall, primarily to cater for a 70 per cent increase in internal fuel, and has been re-engineered throughout. Possessing automatic leading and trailing edge manoeuvring flaps, the F-18 is the first production aircraft with a digital (as opposed to analogue) fly-by-wire control system backed up by mechanical reversion on the taileron controls.

Two essentially similar but optimised versions are planned for air superiority (F-18) and attack (A-18), but full-scale production of only the former has so far been authorised, the US Navy having requested approval for procurement of

**Key to McDonnell Douglas F-18 Hornet**

1 Radome
2 Radar scanner (see item 9)
3 Scanner drive mechanism
4 Gun muzzle
5 Gun gas vents
6 Cannon barrels
7 Radar package sliding rails
8 Low voltage formation lighting
9 Hughes AN/APG-65 multi-mode radar package
10 Infra-red sensor housing
11 Ammunition drum (400 rounds)
12 Angle of attack probe
13 Gun mounting
14 Flight refuelling probe, extended
15 Refuelling probe hydraulic jack
16 M-61 20-mm rotary cannon
17 Ammunition feed track
18 Communications antenna
19 Cockpit front bulkhead
20 Pressurization valve
21 Frameless windshield panel
22 instrument panel shroud
23 Pilot's sight and Kaiser head-up display
24 Control column
25 Rudder pedals
26 Wing leading-edge extension (LEX)
27 Nosewheel bay
28 Nosewheel doors
29 Catapult strop link, landing position
30 Strop link launch position
31 Twin nosewheels
32 Boarding ladder extended from LEX
33 Catapult launch signal lights
34 Landing lamp
35 Cleveland nose undercarriage leg strut
36 Avionics bay
37 Control runs
38 Engine throttle controls
39 Pilot's port side console
40 Cockpit rear bulkhead
41 Martin-Baker SJU-5A ejection seat
42 Starboard side console
43 Ejection seat firing handle
44 Cockpit canopy cover
45 Canopy open position
46 Canopy jack
47 2nd seat structural space provision (TF-18)
48 Forward fuselage fuel tank (deleted for TF-18)
49 Honeycomb panel construction

50 Liquid oxygen converter
51 Nose undercarriage retraction strut
52 Centreline drop tank (capacity 262 Imp gal/1 192 l)
53 Avionics bay
54 LEX frame construction
55 Port navigation light
56 Air conditioning ducting
57 Intake splitter plate
58 Air conditioning intake
59 Bleed air noises
60 Fuselage/LEX longeron
61 Main fuel tanks (1,390 Imp gal/6 319 l internal fuel load)
62 Tacan aerial
63 Intake bleed air exit duct
64 Starboard leading edge extension
65 External fuel tank (capacity 508 Imp gal/2 309 l)
66 Laser spot tracker pod (LST), starboard fuselage station
67 Starboard inboard wing pylon
68 Pylon fixing
69 Mk 83 low-drag general-purpose (LDGP) bombs (A-18)
70 Bomb ejector rack
71 Starboard outer wing pylon
72 Pylon fixing
73 Wing fold break point
74 Upper skin panel hinge
75 Droop leading edge rotary actuator
76 Drooping leading edge
77 Starboard wing tip missile launcher rail
78 AIM-9L Sidewinder air-to-air missile
79 Outer wing panel folded position
80 Starboard drooping aileron
81 Starboard double slotted flap
82 Flap guides
83 Wing integral fuel tank
84 Hydraulic flap jacks
85 Graphite/epoxy dorsal fairing panels
86 UHF/IFF aerial
87 Fuel delivery piping
88 Fuselage longeron

89 Port intake bleed air exit duct
90 Port engine air intake
91 Intake ducting
92 Air conditioning plant
93 Leading edge flap hydraulic jack
94 Manoeuvre flap sequencing control unit
95 Control cable runs
96 Wing attachment pin joints
97 Rear fuselage fuel tank
98 APU exhaust duct
99 Starboard engine bay
100 Fin attachment fixing
101 Fin construction
102 Fuel jettison pipe
103 Graphite/epoxy skin
104 Anti-collision light
105 Steel leading edge strip
106 Honeycomb panel
107 Aerial tuners
108 Electronic countermeasures aerials (ECM)
109 Fin tip antenna housing
110 Communications aerial
111 Radar warning receiver
112 Tail navigation light
113 Fuel jettison
114 Low voltage formation lighting
115 Honeycomb rudder construction
116 Rudder hydraulic jacks
117 Airbrake open position
118 Starboard tailplane
119 Port fin tip antenna housing

120 Low voltage formation lighting
121 Airbrake housing
122 Airbrake hydraulic jack
123 Starboard engine tailpipe
124 Exhaust nozzle shroud
125 Variable area exhaust nozzle
126 Nozzle actuators
127 Afterburner duct
128 Port tailplane
129 Graphite/epoxy skin panels
130 Steel leading edge strip

131 Deck arresting hook
132 Tailplane pivot
133 Tailplane hinge lever
134 Hydraulic servo actuator
135 Port engine bay

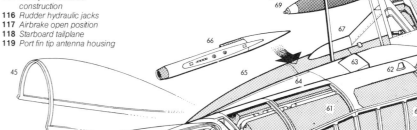

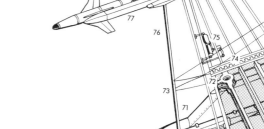
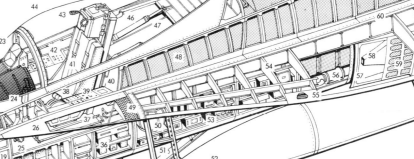

667 F-18As and two-seat TF-18As during 1981-86. A shore-based version of the F-18A has been ordered by Canada which is to receive 113 single- (CF-18A) and 24 two-seat (CF-18B) Hornets from late 1982.

**SPECIFICATION: F-18A Hornet**

**Power Plant:** Two General Electric F404-GE-400 turbofans each rated at (approx) 10,600 lb (4 810 kg) dry thrust and 15,800 lb (7 167 kg) with afterburning. Internal fuel capacity, 1,390 Imp gal (6 319 l) and provision for three 262 Imp gal (1 192 l) drop tanks.

**Performance:** Max speed, 915 mph (1 472 km/h) or M=1·2 at sea level, 1,190 mph (1 915 km/h) or M=1·8 at 40,000 ft (12 192 m); initial climb (half fuel and two AIM-9 AAMs), 60,000 ft/min (304,8 m/sec); acceleration from M=0·8 to M=1·6 at 35,000 ft (10 670 m), 1·8 min; radius (combat air patrol mission on internal fuel), 480 mls (770 km), (with three drop tanks), 740 mls (1 190 km); ferry range, 2,875 mls (4 627 km).

**Weights:** Empty equipped, 28,000 lb (12 700 kg); loaded (air superiority mission with half fuel and four AAMs), 35,800 lb (16,240 kg), (attack mission with full internal fuel and 7,500 lb/3 400 kg ordnance), 47,000 lb (21 315 kg); max, 56,000 lb (25 400 kg).

**Dimensions:** Span, 37 ft 6 in (11,43 m); length 56 ft 0 in (17,07 m); height, 15 ft 4 in (4,67 m); wing area, 396 sq ft. (36,79 m²).

**Armament:** One 20-mm M-61A1 rotary cannon with 570 rounds and (air-air) two AIM-7E/F and two AIM-9G/H AAMs.

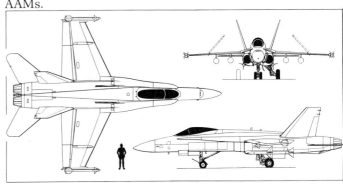

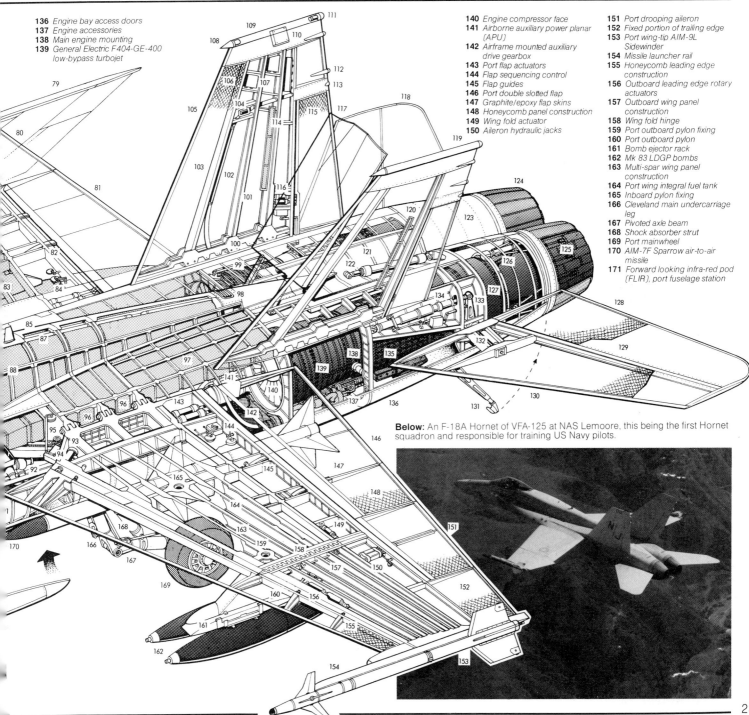

136 Engine bay access doors
137 Engine accessories
138 Main engine mounting
139 General Electric F404-GE-400 low-bypass turbojet
140 Engine compressor face
141 Airborne auxiliary power planar (APU)
142 Airframe mounted auxiliary drive gearbox
143 Port flap actuators
144 Flap sequencing control
145 Flap guides
146 Port double slotted flap
147 Graphite/epoxy flap skins
148 Honeycomb panel construction
149 Wing fold actuator
150 Aileron hydraulic jacks
151 Port drooping aileron
152 Fixed portion of trailing edge
153 Port wing-tip AIM-9L Sidewinder
154 Missile launcher rail
155 Honeycomb leading edge construction
156 Outboard leading edge rotary actuators
157 Outboard wing panel construction
158 Wing fold hinge
159 Port outboard pylon fixing
160 Port outboard pylon
161 Bomb ejector rack
162 Mk 83 LDGP bombs
163 Multi-spar wing panel construction
164 Port wing integral fuel tank
165 Inboard pylon fixing
166 Cleveland main undercarriage leg
167 Pivoted axle beam
168 Shock absorber strut
169 Port mainwheel
170 AIM-7F Sparrow air-to-air missile
171 Forward looking infra-red pod (FLIR), port fuselage station

**Below:** An F-18A Hornet of VFA-125 at NAS Lemoore, this being the first Hornet squadron and responsible for training US Navy pilots.

# Index of Aircraft Types

# Picture Credits

All the photographs in this book were supplied by Pilot Press Ltd. Cutaway drawings by:

John Weal: 38-9; 44-5; 50-51; 54-5; 58-79; 82-97; 100-105; 108-131; 134-137; 140-149; 152-167; 176-7; 194-5; 208-211; 214-5; 218-227.

Michael A. Badrocke: 34-37; 40-43; 46-49; 52-3; 56-7; 80-1; 98-9; 106-7; 132-3; 138-9; 150-1; 168-175; 178-193; 196-207; 212-3; 216-7; 228-239.